W9-APO-342

SPORTS IN NORTH AMERICA

IN MEMORY OF

ANNE RIZACK KIRSCH

SPORTS
IN

NORTH AMERICA

A DOCUMENTARY HISTORY

EDITED BY
GEORGE B. KIRSCH

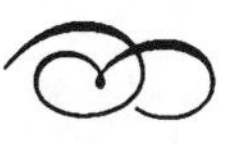

VOLUME 4

SPORTS IN WAR, REVIVAL AND EXPANSION

1860–1880

Academic International Press

1995

SPORTS IN NORTH AMERICA. A DOCUMENTARY HISTORY
VOLUME 4. SPORTS IN WAR, REVIVAL AND EXPANSION, 1860–1880
Edited by George B. Kirsch

ISBN: 0-87569-135-8

Composition by Janice Frye

Printed in the United States of America

By direct subscription with the publisher

A list of Academic International Press publications is found at the end of this volume

ACADEMIC INTERNATIONAL PRESS
POB 1111 • Gulf Breeze FL 32562–1111 • USA

CONTENTS

PREFACE

The purpose of this volume is to present a comprehensive collection of the most important primary source documents pertaining to the development of sports in North America between 1861 and 1880. These materials include rules and regulations, constitutions, and by-laws for clubs and associations, personal accounts of significant developments and events, newspaper editorials and reports of contests, essays, and other contemporary descriptions of athletics. The selections are reprinted here as they originally appeared, without any changes in form or spelling except for deleted sections. Illegible words and misspellings are indicated in the annotation in the text.

The Introduction provides an overview of the major themes and issues in North American sports during this era. It treats the effects of the American Civil War on athletics and it reviews the influence of British sportsmen and traditions, industrialization and the changing patterns of work and leisure, transportation and communication trends, and urbanization. It considers the impact of commercialism and professionalism and also the issues of ethnicity, social class, gender, and race. Chapter 1 addresses several ideological questions, including religious values and "muscular Christianity," the proper role of girls and women in athletics, and the definition of amateurism.

The remaining chapters reprint a variety of documents that chronicle the diversity of the North American sporting experience during this era. My decisions concerning which pastimes to include in this anthology have been governed by my definition of a sport as a competitive game that involves some significant degree of physical activity by the participants. I cover equestrianism because of the strength and skill required of the riders of the horses. The animal blood sports are borderline cases, but I have included them because of the efforts of the trainers and their importance for the sporting fraternity of the times. The chapter on gymnastics includes documents describing both its noncompetitive and competitive forms. I exclude such recreational activities as fishing, hunting, horseback riding, sleigh-riding, and other such pastimes. I have given more space to the major sports of the period, which include aquatics, baseball, boxing, cricket, equestrianism, football, and track and field.

Sporting clubs and governing bodies proliferated during these years, and they generated an increasing volume of records, letters, pamphlets, and other original source materials. Unfortunately, much of this material has been lost to the ravages of time. However, some of these documents were printed in national sporting periodicals or local newspapers. That explains my heavy reliance on the Spirit of the Times, the New York Clipper, and the daily press of New York City, which was then the publishing and sporting capital of North America. For Canada's sporting experience I have relied heavily on materials and newspapers from Montreal.

I have made every effort to find sources that describe the athletic experience of peoples from all regions of North America and from all social classes, racial and ethnic groups, and both sexes. However, this anthology does reflect the athletic dominance of white upper and middle class males from certain Canadian and United States cities, especially Montreal, Toronto, Boston, New York, and Philadelphia. However, this volume does include several pieces that describe the sporting experience of people from the American South and West, Canada, immigrants, native North American Indians, African-Americans, and women. Sources written by members of the latter three groups are scarce for this period, but the narratives by white males do reveal important characteristics of the sporting experiences of racial minorities and females.

Finally, I would like to thank the wonderful librarians at the following institutions who helped me track down these sources: the New York Public Library, the Columbia University Library, the Yale University Library, the Harvard University Library, the Rutgers University Library, the Municipal Library of the City of Montreal, the National Library and the National Archives of Canada, and the German Society of Pennsylvania. Special thanks go to Claire E. Nolte for translating a document on German gymnastics, and to Morris Mott and Nancy Bouchier for sending me materials. I am also grateful to Catherine Shanley, Maire Duchon, Dominick Caldiero, and Br. Thomas O'Connor of the Cardinal Hayes Library at Manhattan College. Gerard J. Belliveau and Todd Thompson of the Racquet and Tennis Club library were also extremely helpful. For their patience and diligence I owe a great deal to my student assistants, Angela Sweeny and Joseph Quinn.

Once again I express my love and appreciation to my wife, Susan Lavitt Kirsch, and my son Adam for their understanding and support over the past few years. This book is dedicated to the memory of my mother, Anne Rizack Kirsch. She was a talented, energetic, and devoted teacher who had a passion for prose and poetry. She loved her family and students very much. I thank her for the greatest gift she gave me—the example of the excitement of a life spent reading, thinking, writing, teaching.

George B. Kirsch

Manhattan College

INTRODUCTION

The years between 1861 and 1880 brought vast changes to the sporting experiences of North Americans. The period began with four years of devastating civil war in the United States which also had consequences for Canada. The renewal of peace and union in the United States in 1865 and Canada's attainment of Dominion status in 1867 had profound consequences for the development of competitive athletics in both nations. The forces of nationalism combined with modernizing tendencies to generate both a proliferation of sporting activities and a major transformation in their basic characteristics. British influences had a powerful impact throughout the continent, as did the effects of the industrial revolution, innovations in transportation and communication, and new patterns of urbanization. During this period religion became more favorably disposed toward physical training and competition as "muscular Christianity" gained adherents across North America. Amateurism flourished in private clubs and intercollegiate athletics, while professionalism and commercialism reached unprecedented levels of public acceptance. Men of all social classes, ethnic groups, and races joined in the athletic movements of these years either as active participants or spectators. Women also increased their involvement significantly in selective activities and sports as clergymen, editorialists, and other writers actively encouraged females to join the movement for health and recreation through sports.

In the United States the war which began at Fort Sumter, South Carolina in April 1865 had a dual effect on the development of American sports. Firstly, it disrupted the growth of both individual and team competition which had surged during the late 1850s. In particular, the hostilities curtailed (but did not terminate) the mania for the New York City version of baseball which was beginning to make inroads into such northeastern cities as Boston and Philadelphia. The conflict had a far more damaging impact on American cricket than it did on baseball, mainly because cricket was simply not as popular as its rival, especially among players who were too young to serve in the military. The war also dampened interest in other popular amusements such as rowing, yachting, horse racing, and pedestrianism as men left their home cities to serve as officers and soldiers in either the Union or Confederate armies.

In army camps athletic competitions took on new meanings as the men sought recreation as they prepared for mortal combat. Observers of American sporting life stressed the analogy between sports (especially baseball and cricket) and battle, urging the former as training for the latter. Thousands of players enlisted in regiments and competed on camp playgrounds as they awaited battle. Soldiers frequently arranged their own contests, while on a few occasions officers organized special sport festivals which attracted huge crowds. They did so because they believed that sports would lift morale and alleviate despondency, doubt, and homesickness. To counter the boredom that soldiers experienced during long intervals between battles they organized baseball, cricket, and football games, wrestling, boxing, and sharpshooting matches, running, leaping, and obstacle-course challenges, and even horse races and cockfights.

Canadian sportsmen also felt the effects of the American civil war in a number of ways. The conflict limited or halted sporting exchanges with clubs and selected all-star teams from the United States, especially in cricket and rowing. The fear that English recognition of the Confederacy might provoke a Union invasion of Canada (and perhaps even another attempt at annexation) heightened concern for military preparedness. As a result many men suspended their membership in sporting clubs and joined rifle companies. But the war also heightened interest in certain sports (such as snowshoeing) which seemed to foster physical training.

After the war ended in the spring of 1865 North America witnessed an explosion of interest in athletics. Sportsmen celebrated the return of peace in the United States with a renewed enthusiasm for a wide variety of premodern and modern pastimes. During these years certain traditional recreations maintained their popularity with relatively little change, while other amusements experienced dramatic transformations. In addition there were a few brand new sports (both indigenous and imported from Great Britain) that began to gain public favor by 1880. In the first category were such time-honored activities as cockfighting, rowing, skating, snowshoeing, swimming, boxing, bowling, quoits, and pedestrianism. In the second class were baseball, cricket, horse racing, football, and lacrosse. The last group included ice hockey (native to Canada) and badminton, croquet, and tennis (introduced from Great Britain.)

The process of modernization influenced the development of most of these sports to a greater or lesser degree. Democratization, rationalization, bureaucratization, specialization, regional, national, and international competition, extensive media coverage, and fascination with numbers all characterized the new style of athletics. Trends in each of these areas which had become manifest during the 1840s and 1850s now accelerated between 1865 and 1880. Social class distinctions were still important factors in determining club formation and choice of sporting activities, but now there were clearly greater opportunities for mass participation in all but the most expensive and restricted recreations. There were now thousands of clubs organized in dozens of sports which drew up detailed constitutions and by-laws. State, regional, and national associations revised their codes of laws governing competition. Players honed their skills and created new strategies and tactics to apply against their opponents; they traveled hundreds and sometimes thousands of miles on railroads and steamships for feature matches. Nationally distributed sporting periodicals reported on the whole range of athletics, while big-city and small town daily and weekly newspapers gave increased space to sports stories and statistics.

Several critical social and cultural factors spurred the proliferation and the modernization of sports in North America. The most significant were the sporting culture of Great Britain and the combined effects of changing patterns of industrialization, transportation, communication, and urbanization. The transformation of religious values also shaped the nature of sport during these years, as "muscular Christianity" gained wider acceptance in both the United States and Canada.

British sporting practices and traditions had exerted a profound impact on North American sports since the earliest days of settlement, and they continued to do so during the 1860s and 1870s. The English, Scottish, and Irish influences were stronger in Canada than in the United States because of the former nation's connection with the British Empire both before and after the new Confederation system established in 1867. The popularity of cricket, curling, and Highlander track and field games attested to the strength of these ethnic ties to the home isles, as did the importation of such new pastimes as croquet, golf, and tennis. To a lesser degree these sports were also enjoyed by British and other European immigrants in the United States, where some native born sportsmen also took up the newcomers' recreations. Moreover, an intensification of nationalism in both North American nations led directly to a series of international sporting excursions and challenges among individuals and teams from the United States, Canada, and England in rowing, yachting, baseball, cricket, lacrosse, and shooting. In Canada these athletic exchanges strengthened both feelings of loyalty to the Dominion and also pride in British imperialism. In the United States the contests promoted American nationalism as the players tried to defeat the former mother country.

After 1861 the industrial revolution continued to transform the lives of all North Americans, especially those who lived in cities and towns. The fabulous wealth earned by a few captains of industry enabled them to spend more time and money on such elite sports as horse racing and yachting. Many prosperous merchants, lawyers, and other businessmen and professionals patronized such sports as rowing, baseball, cricket, curling, lacrosse, and track and field. Middle class city dwellers felt the pressures of the new work discipline; small merchants, grocers, clerks, and bookkeepers were sedentary workers who naturally sought relief from their toil. They flocked to ball fields during early morning hours, after work, or on summer Saturday afternoons when many employers closed their shops, stores, and businesses. Many artisans experienced deteriorating conditions as they performed repetitious tasks in tight quarters with infrequent breaks in their monotonous routines. Some of the more fortunate skilled workers found relief through sports and pastimes before or after work or during weekends. Semiskilled and unskilled factor workers suffered more than the shop artisans and independent mechanics from the effects of industrialization. Most of them were too preoccupied with the struggle for survival and too poor to participate in the athletic boom of this period, except perhaps as occasional spectators.

Mass production and improvements in transportation and communication facilitated modern forms of athletics. Factories manufactured large quantities of bats, balls, bases, uniforms, and other sporting goods at a range of prices, thus providing a reasonable quality and selection of supplies that most players could afford. The railroad and steamboat made intercity and interstate competition possible, permitting traditional urban, state, and regional groups to play out their rivalries through athletics. Transatlantic competition between North American and British contestants was now feasible because of the oceanic steamships. The telegraph and high-speed printing presses allowed daily and weekly newspapers to recount the excitement of major matches while they were still fresh in people's minds.

Urbanization was also a critical factor in the development of North American sport during this era. The astounding growth and proliferation of cities brought major consequences for North American sport in many ways. Firstly, The deteriorating physical environment bred sickness and psychological stress that endangered the people's corporal and mental health. Huge population increases, higher density, and inadequate housing created staggering disease problems. The public health crisis led many civic leaders to lobby for more healthful recreation for the masses. Secondly, as expanding cities encroached upon traditional recreational areas, residents had to organize formal associations to acquire and maintain playing grounds—whether they be public parks or private club facilities. In certain cases practical conditions which restricted the amount of space available for a sporting activity led directly to a transformation in its rules. Hockey provides an example of this process. Traditionally it was played on any open frozen surface on bays, rivers, lakes, ponds, or fields. But its adaptation in an urban environment required new spatial boundaries and new rules and skills. Thirdly, as native and Europe migrants arrived in record numbers the metropolitan centers grew more diverse in race, ethnicity, religion, and social class. Communities grew more fragmented as social and class relations were strained. Many urbanites sought a sense of identity and fellowship in voluntary associations for political, religious, cultural, or sporting purposes. Sportsmen who banded together to acquire some playing space for themselves were also trying to preserve and strengthen their social identities in an increasingly impersonal environment. Fourthly, the population explosion and the accompanying pluralism also contributed to the expansion of modern forms of leisure and especially to their commercialization. The new urban masses sought diversion through whatever activities the new urban life could provide. Their sizable numbers filled the rosters of many clubs and also supplied the audiences for all types of entertainment.

Finally, urban symbolism was a powerful force as communities searched for identities that would distinguish them from their neighboring and distant rivals. Upstart towns competed for political and economic supremacy; local boosters puffed up their settlements and denigrated competitors. Modern sport both reflected and intensified boosterism and intercity rivalry, whether it be Philadelphia versus New York City in cricket, Cincinnati versus Chicago in baseball, or Montreal versus Toronto in lacrosse.

The twin trends of urban imperialism and interdependence are linked to the rise of modern sport in North America. Cities tried to extend their political, economic, and cultural influence over as wide an area as possible. Through this process of urban imperialism each sought to retain and expand its hinterland. But while each metropolis and town vied with its rivals, each also depended on them as well. The cities were part of a dynamic, complex system that exchanged people, produce, and finished products and shared information, expertise, and political power. In the United States and Canada this system of cities promoted sport in many ways, with New York City and Montreal leading the way in their respective countries. They fostered standardized rules as well as the formation of regional and national associations and leagues. Urban interdependence facilitated player and club mobility as well as communication about sport. Thus, in both the internal development of cities and their mutual interdependence, urbanization and the modernization of athletics were closely related.

The rage for athletics of this era swept through North American colleges, as young men sought relief from the regimentation of academic life through a variety of sports. The earliest athletic clubs were part of the new extracurriculum which also included fraternities and student societies in literature, politics, music, religion, and philosophy. Students took the initiative in organizing sports clubs for intramural and interclass competition. The first intercollegiate contests occurred during the 1850s in crew and baseball, while the next two decades brought competition in cricket, football, track and field, rifle shooting, lacrosse, and bicycling. Although these scholar-athletes were all technically amateurs, a few of the most talented received some support in the form of financial aid.

Amateur athletes and clubs dominated the North American sporting scene during these years, but there were also major developments in professionalism and commercialism in both individual and team sports. Skilled rowers and runners from the United States and Canada continued to compete for prize money and side bets in both North America and Great Britain. Bare-knuckle prize fights were still illegal in most regions but professional pugilists could earn large purses and wagers in feature bouts. The most polished billiard and quoit players could also pocket sizable sums through their artistry. Professional baseball gained wide public acceptance during the early 1870s and became the most popular team sport in the United States, while cricket and lacrosse held true to the amateur tradition.

The commercialization of both amateur and professional sports accelerated throughout North America during this period, as both private clubs and entrepreneurs began to profit from staging athletic contests. Amateur organizations (including some colleges) were compelled to charge "gate money" to defray the costs of maintaining grounds and fielding teams. A few businessmen, who also realized that sporting spectacles held great potential as marketable commodities, constructed facilities and charged admission to spectators. In the largest American cities the first baseball parks appeared, while promoters of horse racing constructed elaborate fancy new facilities for both thoroughbred and trotting events. During the late 1870s football elevens from Harvard, Yale, and Princeton played in front of thousands of spectators who paid to see the college boys compete on the gridiron. In Montreal, Canada the leading private cricket and lacrosse clubs rented their grounds for sporting activities, while some of the most prominent social and business leaders opened the Victoria Skating Rink in 1862 for skating parties, masquerades, tournaments, snowshoe races, and even lacrosse on ice. That arena was also the site of the first ice hockey matches during the late 1870s.

During this period sports both reflected and reinforced the structure of American and Canadian society. Class, ethnicity, race, and gender were all significant factors in shaping the athletic experience of all North Americans. (See chapter 1 for a discussion of the role of women in North American sports.) Class distinctions were apparent in the preferred pastimes of the wealthy, the middling ranks, and the poorer groups. The elite (especially the new rich) used sports as a means of separating themselves from the masses below them on the social scale. Thus they patronized such expensive amusements as thoroughbred horse racing, polo, yachting, tennis, and golf. Among ball games they played cricket rather than baseball. Their recreation tended to require considerable time, costly facilities, fancy equipment, and often extensive travel to distant sites for competition. When they formed clubs in sports favored by the middle and lower orders (such as rowing, lacrosse, and track and field) they created distinctions between "gentlemen" amateurs and professionals. By banning working class players from their competitions they heightened their own status through their exclusive communities.

In a similar fashion ethnic groups used their traditional games and amusements to preserve and strengthen their ties to the heritage of their respective homelands. In many ways sports reflected the process of acculturation of newcomers to both the United States and Canada. This was especially true of the Scots, who imported their beloved Highland costumes, track and field games, and curling into both countries. Up until the mid-1870s the Scottish clubs were the most important promoters of track and field in North America, both among themselves and native athletes. Although curling did not match track and field in popularity among outsiders, Scottish people enjoyed the "roaring game" in many Canadian towns and in a few cities in the northeastern part of the United States. English immigrants of all social classes brought with them their love of cricket. In Montreal, Toronto, Newark, N.J., Boston, Philadelphia, and other communities they taught natives the intricacies of their national game. From central Europe came thousands of Germans, who founded Turner societies to foster a love of their fatherland and to promote the practice of gymnastics.

Finally, race also played a prominent role in North American sports. White citizens of both nations borrowed from the sporting practices of native Indians, especially in running, lacrosse, and snowshoeing. Generally they adapted and modernized traditional Indian amusements and they welcomed competition with members of local tribes. Yet they never viewed Indians as their equals, and they excluded them from membership in their clubs. African-Americans in the United States were also active in several sports, especially in the northern and middle Atlantic states. They founded dozens of baseball clubs, and they also became prominent billiard players, pedestrians, and jockeys. During the period of Reconstruction after the Civil War whites occasionally competed against blacks, but they also barred them from regular membership in their clubs and national sporting associations.

Chapter 1

CULTURAL ISSUES

During the 1860s and 1870s physical training and competitive athletics gained greater public acceptance throughout North America. The ideological justification for fitness and sports gradually overcame traditional religious and social objections in both the United States and Canada. During this period clergymen, journalists, educators, professionals, and other molders of public sentiment addressed three major questions concerning the role of sports in American and Canadian society. The first involved the problem of reconciling Christianity (especially Protestantism) with the development of the body and the pursuit of athletics. The second was the proper role of girls and women in physical fitness and sports. The third issue concerned the attempt to distinguish between amateur and professional athletes.

This period witnessed the ascendancy of a new philosophy of "muscular Christianity" which superseded previous Protestant views of athletics. Prior to the mid-nineteenth century most ministers, writers, teachers, and businessmen had discouraged exercise and sports on the grounds that they were immoral, useless, and socially improper. But now propagandists for fitness and sports stressed that exercise promoted good physical, mental, and spiritual health, fostered proper moral and social conduct, and drew young men away from more sordid amusements. They also insisted that physical activity instilled character traits, strengthened the bonds of society, and helped to preserve order and advance the future prosperity of a rapidly changing society.

One of the central institutions which propounded the doctrine of muscular Christianity in North America was the Young Men's Christian Association (YMCA). Founded by laymen in England in 1844, it took root in North America in 1851 with organizations established in Montreal and Boston. Its original mission was to provide spiritual guidance and practical assistance to the young men who were pouring into the commercial and industrial nineteenth century cities. After the Civil War the YMCA expanded its services to include education and wholesome recreation, including gymnastics. It aimed to help bookkeepers, clerks, salesmen, skilled workers, and other boys and young males who sought support and assistance in the new urban world they inhabited. Its benefactors donated generously to support the construction of new facilities for the YMCA. The first document in this chapter is a newspaper editorial which comments on the proposed activities for a newly erected YMCA in Manhattan.

The question of female participation in physical training and sports also generated much interest in North America during this era in two ways. Firstly, their patronage through their attendance at major events was vital to the public acceptance of athletics for upper and middle class society. This was especially true of aquatics, horse racing, baseball, cricket, football, and track and field. On the other hand, blood (animal) sports and boxing remained male preserves. Secondly, many writers now argued that women should not confine themselves to being spectators, but rather should become more directly involved as active players. They were sharply critical of Victorian views of the ideal woman as a frail vessel or an invalid. They now championed the cause of better health for girls and ladies through moderate exercise and athletics. But they did have reservations about very strenuous activities and competition among women, and thus they stopped short of advocating full scale female participation in sports. Instead they recommended recreation which featured active but gentle exertion and graceful motion, especially through gymnastics, archery, croquet, badminton, tennis, horseback riding, and skating. Although no one advocated equality of competition among the sexes, the surge of enthusiasm for healthier girls and ladies marked a key transitional phase in the development of Canadian and American women's athletics. Moses Coit Tyler's satirical piece, "Deacon Snipp's Last Kick," is an amusing rebuttal to the old fashioned view which excluded women from physical training.

North American schools, colleges, and country clubs gradually expanded their athletic programs for girls and young women. In the United States Vassar College pioneered with required calisthenics and also the sports of archery, baseball, rowing, tennis, and track. Smith and Wellesley followed suit shortly thereafter. A few upper class women also founded athletic clubs during the late 1870s, including the Ladies Club for Outdoor Sports in Staten Island, New York, and the Crescent City Archery Club in New Orleans. The editorial "Athletic Sports" reprinted in this chapter comments approvingly on the women's club formed in Staten Island.

The period between 1861 and 1880 was also a transitional time in North American sports for the development of a philosophy of athletics which distinguished between amateur and professional players. The issue had troubled baseball and cricket clubs and conventions during the 1850s, and in the following decades it was a major item on the agendas of gatherings of sportsmen in those sports, lacrosse, and especially aquatics and track and field. During their formative years the most prominent rowing and athletic associations had permitted competition for wagers or prize money, and they had opened their regattas and meets to all contestants. But by the early 1870s the leading metropolitan clubs in both the United States and Canada had begun to exclude from their competitions all those whom they considered to be socially inferior. They did so by defining an amateur as anyone who had never competed for money or prizes or who did not earn a living through participation or instruction in athletics. The main motivation behind this trend was the desire by elite and upper-middle class associations to separate themselves from working class, ethnic, and black players.

Although American and Canadian sportsmen indirectly drew upon British traditions which distinguished between amateur "gentlemen" players and professionals, the English system was never truly relevant or applicable to the North American scene. Old World aristocratic manners held little meaning in the New World urban settings. North American officials drew up amateur codes to keep "undesirables" out of club and championship events, but in reality there were always exceptions which permitted a few talented "outsiders" the chance to compete in the major matches. This chapter concludes with a Montreal newspaper editorial which addresses the difficult problem of defining precisely the meaning of amateurism and professionalism.

MUSCULAR CHRISTIANITY

In 1869 the Young Men's Christian Association completed an impressive new building at the corner of Twenty-third Street and Fourth Avenue in New York City. William E. Dodge, Jr. took chief responsibility for the fund raising campaign, which recruited seventy-two donors who gave an average subscription of $3,000. The purpose of the institution was to promote Christian values among the clerks and other males who were expected to be its prime patrons. The new facilities included a gymnasium, public lecture hall, reading room and library. The following excerpt from a newspaper editorial stresses the connection between Christianity and wholesome recreation. It is reprinted from The New York Times, 18 July 1869.

THE YOUNG MEN'S CHRISTIAN ASSOCIATION ...SHALL IT BE A CLUB? ABOUT AMUSEMENTS

The theory of what the Association should be has received the most careful consideration of its managers, who are gentlemen of wisdom and experience in affairs. How far the new building shall partake of the character of a club is a question to which they have given grave study. The object, however, will in any event be to provide a place which shall present real attractions for young men, and do away with the idea any of them may have that the religious character of the Association must necessarily make it a sombre and forbidding place for the gay spirits of youth. There have been some among the friends of the institution who have gone so far as to advise the most radical concessions to the dominant love of amusement in young men. They have advised the introduction of chess, draughts, billiards and bowling, contending that the devil should not have all the amusements; that these games are not in themselves injurious to morals, but that it is the customary surroundings of bars and profanity which give them an immoral influence. They say, with a good deal of force, that hundreds of strict and exemplary Church members have put up billiard tables in their houses during the last few years, and have discovered that the amusement is one of the most delightful and healthful in the whole range of games. Clergymen, too, think nothing of publicly bowling at Saratoga; indeed, it is a favorite clerical amusement. They say, too, that it is of the utmost importance that every legitimate attraction should be utilized to gain the end desired, and that then the young men will soon learn that at the Young Men's Christian Association they can pursue their favorite amusements with pleasanter surroundings than in the public places they now frequent, so often to the great injury of their morals, and that here, in this magnificent building, they will have unequaled opportunities for that social enjoyment and good-fellowship which is a necessity to their happiness. The subject is an exceedingly important one, but it naturally encounters the strong prejudices of many of the friends of the Association, in its discussion, and one may hardly hope to see, therefore, the most liberal features of the proposed plan carried out, at least for several years to come.

It has also been advised that a partial restaurant be one of the features of the Association. The idea would be to provide at least tea and coffee to order, with perhaps a few more substantial eatable things. This would give the institution something of the complexion of a club, about the advantage of which there is certainly room for differences of opinion. It is said by the members that nothing has been more successful than the series of "tea parties," somewhat after the English fashion, and that of the delightful meetings of the Historical Society, which has been given during the last few years. Such parties have evoked good feeling, fellowship, acquaintance, and all the social graces and pleasures.

A CHRISTIAN GYMNASIUM

But what the Association *certainly* will have is a splendid gymnasium—a gymnasium which in size and appointments will be unequaled in the City. This concession to the muscular Christianity of the time has been made, we are glad to hear, almost without dissent, nor can any one who appreciates the moral force of the *sana mens in sano corpore* find fault with the athletic character it is proposed to give the young Christians of New-York. If the Association succeed in drawing to its gymnasium a large number of the young men of the City, and in giving them sound bodies and muscles of iron, as well as healthy religious principles and moral characters more enduring than steel, it will deserve and receive a double commendation. We may then hope for a next generation of New-Yorkers fully equal to the occasions of an advancing civilization....

THE BRAWNVILLE PAPERS

Moses Coit Tyler was a graduate of Yale University and Andover Theological Seminary who was a professor of English Literature at the University of Michigan (1867-81). When he accepted a post at Cornell in 1881 he became the first professor of American history in the United States. While teaching at Michigan he penned a fictional account of an athletic club. In the section excerpted here he pokes fun at those "old fogies" who resisted the idea of female athletics. This selection is from *The Brawnville Papers: Being Memorials of the Brawnville Athletic Club* (Boston, 1869), pp. 180-195.

DEACON SNIPP'S LAST KICK

Brawnville, September 4, 1867

This night has brought with it a vast surprise.

Ever since our great meeting early in the summer for the inauguration of the Club House, we had heard nothing from the redoubtable Deacon Snipp. On that occasion he stood forth valiantly, and fought a heroic fight against the world, the flesh, the Devil, and the gymnasium: but borne down by the torrent of superior numbers, he turned up his eyes, turned down the corners of his mouth, and beat an orderly retreat. Week after week, since then, had passed peacefully over our heads, and never one movement, one word, one groan, even, from this eminent sentinel in Zion. We began to suppose that the good Deacon had come to the stern resolution of making no further resistance to the inrushing of the dark flood against which opposition seemed so unavailing. Ah! we did pleasure to ourselves, but injustice to Deacon Snipp. Little did we know of the bottomless resource and the pertinacy of that excellent person. We considered our own convenience: we considered good sense, and liberal feeling, and courtesy; alas! we considered not the nature of Deacons. Grievously had we ignored the truthful aphorism of Mr. Spurgen: "Resist the Devil and he will flee from you; resist the Deacon and he will flee at you." During this interval of silence our inexhaustible antagonist had nursed, not buried, his wrath. The truce had been most faithfully kept in fabricating a weapon with which to renew the war. His next beginning was to be our ending. The long silence, had we but properly understood it, was only the hush of Titanic forces, in their awful recoil, before breaking forth anew in final and comprehensive havoc.

Silence!

'Tis but the note of wrath the while a-nursing,
The still precursor of the furious cursing.

With a tremulous hand, just after the awful shock, have I taken up my pen in the hope of giving some faint narrative of this supreme and most terrific explosion of our village volcano.

It was something thus:

We were pleasantly seated this evening around the long table in the Library of the Club House, and were discussing, with as much tranquillity as such a theme would permit, the subject of "Gymnastics for Woman." In the midst of this serene state of things, suddenly we heard a heavy step on the stairs, immediately followed by the abrupt and noisy opening of the Library door. Every one turned to behold the author of this rude intrusion, and every one, with the mixture of amazement and amusement, beheld the august form of Deacon Snipp, as he paused in the doorway in a kind of spasm of excitement—indignation already flaming in his eye, and the hue of New England rum blazing upon the end of his nose. The good man had evidently prepared himself for this crushing interview by an unusual amount of attention to his toilet. He had on a ruffled shirt, and an old-fashioned dress coat, with slender tails descending to his very heels. I do not mean to insinuate that these articles were all that this excellent person had on; for, I may add, that beside carrying under his arm a green cotton umbrella, he carried upon his legs a pair of venerable trousers, which had withered and shrunk with increasing age, and now descended upon his nether limbs no further than to the top of his ankles. Moreover, his manly bosom—a term which, when applied to Deacon Snipp, must always be understood to include his stomach—was covered by a voluminous though rather bilious buff vest. No one could fail to perceive that the Deacon was a very consistant man, and carried his general principals even into the matter of his wardrobe. Obviously, he was as decidedly opposed to novelties in wearing apparel as he was to novelties in theology, politics, or social science. Standing thus before us, arrayed in all the splender of his great-grandfather's old clothes, he seemed, indeed, a sort of monumental effigy of Conservatism—his ideas and his breeches being alike contracted and worn out.

For at least two minutes we sat gazing at Deacon Snipp in the doorway; and for at least two minutes Deacon Snipp in the doorway stood gazing at us.

"Will you walk in?" at last spoke Judge Fairplay.

"I will!" screamed the Deacon, in such high scolding accents as denoted that he was resolved to walk in anyway, whether invited or not. And upon this, advancing up the room with a defiant air, and drawing a letter from his breast pocket, he added in the same yelling tones : "And I've brought a doc-u-ment, the production of my daughter Jerushy which I demand to have read here, and which ought to convince you, if any thing can, of the scandals and unscriptural nature of your proceedings in this institution." By the time he had gasped his way to the end of the table where sat the Judge; and hurling the letter upon the table, he suddenly wheeled round and strode down the room, and out of it, with such speed as considerably elevated his coat tails in his rear, and caused them to flutter and flap in the air like a pair of sable streamers. "He hangs out the black flag," whispered the Parson, as the last flap of the Deacon's coat-tails faded from view; "he evidently means to take no prisoners."

The whole affair had occurred so suddenly that we did not at once comprehend its import; but when the apparition had departed, the ludicrous aspects of the scene broke simultaneously upon us all, and the whole company exploded into one long, loud roar of laughter—a laughter dropped, and taken up again, and again, for several minutes.

All this time, while we were giving ourselves up to the transports of mirth excited by the preposterous event which had just happened, the terrible "doc-u-ment" from "my daughter Jerushy" lay unopened upon the table, on the very spot to which it had been hurled by the indignant Deacon; the Judge gazing upon it with an admirably feigned alarm, as upon a bombshell which might at any moment explode.

And here let me pause to record one word of description concerning that utterly indescribable personage—"my daughter Jerushy." Be it known, then, that "my daughter Jerushy" is a worthy maiden of whom it becomes me to speak with all the respect due, not only to the gentle sex, but to antiquity. She is the only heir to her father's name—an honor so great as to explain the fact of her never having been induced to exchange that euphonious name for any appellation less worthy. Her many graces of soul appear to have had an uncommonly fine effect upon the growth of her body; for she is, indeed, enormously tall. To say that she is also lank, angular, and sour-visaged, might be accurate, but it would not be polite; while it would be equally a conformity to truth, and a deviation from propriety, to apply to her the last line of Chaucer's couplet descriptive of the Carpenter's Wife:

"Wincing she was as is a jolly colt;
Long as a mast, and upright as a bolt."

It is possible that miss Jerushy was once young, but if so, it was at a period anterior to any embraced in the memory of our oldest inhabitant. And, although to the eye of the moderns she has always presented the same appearance of egregious maturity, and of stern dislike to the follies of her sex, there are some dim traditions afloat that she once had a sort of love affair herself—a love affair which one fine day burst into a thousand pieces, and left her the tart, sanctified, withered, and uncompromising spinster who is known to us as "my daughter Jerushy."

Her letter ran as follows:

"Tuesday Afternoon.

"To the Members of the Athletic Club:

"Misguided Mortals—Dwelling as I do in the atmosphere of piety with which my father's home is always pervaded, and separated as I am from the vanities of this wicked world, it is not often that I receive explicit tiding from the valley of worldliness which stretches out far below me.

"But I have been made acquainted with that zeal for a fleshly gospel, and for a merely muscular and carnal grace, which has unhappily broken out in our once religious village.

"It was a sufficiently mournful token of the decay of Zion that so many professors fell from their allegiance and built that temple to Baal, which, I think, you call a Club House—an edifice erected to frivolity, and unconsecrated by one prayer or psalm.

"But my cup of spiritual grief was filled, when I learned that even the handmaidens of our village are also bowing down to this Pagan Fashion, and are learning the unscriptural practise of gymnastics; and having heard that you are this night to discuss formally the subject of woman's part in your gymnasium, I write unto you this letter of counsel, warning, and reproof.

"Where in the Bible can you find the least authority for gymnastics?

"Echo answers, Where!

"That Pagan name does not occur anywhere in the sacred volume, from Genesis to Revelation.

"But while gymnastics are not mentioned by name, they are referred to, and that with the severest censure. The Apostle Paul (I Tim. iv. 7, 8,) says to Timothy: 'Exercise thyself rather unto godliness. For bodily exercise profiteth little; but godliness is profitable unto all things.'

"Also, is it not a great shame and a scandal, that young ladies should be so negligent of propriety as to take part in diversions which must cause an unseemly exposure of their feet, and even their ankles?

"The Apostle Paul would not allow women to appear in public assemblies with the head uncovered. What would he have said to you who are willing to show not only your heads, but your ——. I am too much shocked to finish the sentence!

"The Scripture also teaches that woman was intended to be weak.

"But your gymnastics oppose the will of Providence, and the words of scripture, by making woman strong.

"It is the duty of woman to stay at home and comfort her husband {here there were smiles and profuse whispering among the ladies} and take care of his house. But how can she properly discharge this duty, if she goes to the gymnasium?

"We are also told in Scripture that it is the will of God that the great duty of woman should be attended with suffering: 'In sorrow thou shalt bring forth children.' But so profane has the world grown, that you gymnastic people openly boast that woman can be so strengthened as to bear children without great pain, and thus thwart the righteous will of Heaven.

"Need I say any more to prove to you the wickedness of your present course?

"I pray that you may soon see the error of your way, and turn your unscriptual Club House into a temple of the living God.

Yours, sorrowfully,
"JERUSHA SNIPP."

As the Judge finished reading this overwhelming "doc-u-ment," and laid it upon the table before him, he said: "Well, I have only one remark to make. As Mr. Squeers exclaimed, when contemplating the nice mixture of milk and water with which he fed the boys at his school, 'Here's richness!'" The Judge then added, in low tone, to those of us who sat nearest: "When young William Pitt made his first speech in the House of Commons, Edmund Burke, in great delight, declared, 'He is not only a chip off the old block, but the old block itself.'"

At this point, Mr. Leonidas Climax rose. It was his first appearance at the Club since the accident at the parallel bar, and his rising to speak was greeted with general applause, in which the ironical element was much less obvious than usual. His broken arm was still supported in a sling; but with the other arm he reached across the table, and, drawing the water pitcher to him, he proceeded to take a long draught. After this preparation he made a speech, which, for a wonder and for once, was both sensible and brief.

"Mr. Chairman—I confess I am a little disturbed by one quotation from Scripture given by Miss Snipp. I do not see how we can regard that verse of St. Paul's—'bodily exercise profiteth little'—in any other light than as a censure upon gymnastics. I had never before thought of the verse in this connection. Will you favor us with an explanation?"

"I will refer your question," replied the Judge, "to our reverend friend, Mr. Bland. His answer will be worth more than mine; for as he is what Leigh Hunt calls 'an official heaven expounder,' you perceive that what he says upon the subject will have a sort of official authority."

"Well," said the Parson, smiling, "while I disclaim the rather dubious compliment implied in the expression of Leigh Hunt, and while I desire for my words no other authority of sound learning and common sense, I will tell you all I know about the verse—be that of much worth or of none.

"Everything turns upon the meaning of the original phrase, which our translators have rendered 'bodily exercise.' Does that mean gymnastic bodily exercise? Not necessarily. If you will refer to Dr. Robinson's Lexicon of the New Testament, you will find that he translates the phrase 'ascetic training.' That is undoubtedly what the Apostle meant—that ascetic bodily discipline was not good for much. Turn to our honest, sensible American commentator, Albert Barnes, and see what he says. In his note on this passage he uses these words: 'Bodily exercise here refers, doubtless, to the mortification of the body by abstinence and penance which the ancient devotees, and particularly the Essenes, made so important, as a part of their religion.' You see, therefore, that the verse has nothing more to do with gymnastics than it has with sawing wood, hoeing corn, or splitting rails.

"Let us go on with the discussion of the question before us: "Is it desirable that women should practise gymnastics?"

This was the voice of our Chairman; and so the discussion went on for an hour or two, almost every man and woman in the room, taking some part in it.

At last the Judge closed the evening's debate with the following judicial charge to the jury - a jury not limited to one sex, or to any particular number of persons. He said:

"A vast amount of the present talk of the world is about woman. In fact, woman always has been the subject of plentiful talk; but it has been talk in the form of flattery, or talk in the form of ridicule. A new department has been added to the world's talk about woman-talk in the form of argument.

"This is a hopeful sign.

When any subject reaches the argumentative stage, depend upon it that the subject is approaching its solution. Schoolboys sometimes give up a problem—the world never does. It clings to its problem and works at it until it works daylight into it, and out of it, too. Furthermore, every question has its pivot. The pivot on which the woman question turns is: What do you consider woman to be? Is she a human being, or is she only a goose?

"You must determine this question before you can determine those other and minor questions which are covered by it; such as, 'Should woman vote? Should woman have a university education? Should woman enter the learned professions? Should woman practise gymnastics?

"Don't you see that if woman be considered a complete human being, it can not be said that she 'goes out of her sphere,' as the idiotic phrase is, when she merely goes into those affairs which belong to human beings?

"But, of course, if woman be only a goose—a very pretty one, perhaps, very fascinating, and all that, but still only a goose—a brainless, silly, cackling goose, why, the case is wholly altered, and she is certainly 'going out of her sphere' when she presumes to engage in activities which are the exclusive possession of human beings.

"I can not deny that up to latest dates, the goose theory of woman is by far the most popular one. Most men think all women geese. Of course, they have a multitude of equivalents for it. Thus, when a man calls a woman an angel, he really means a goose; and so on through the whole list of sugared evasions of the real world. Dryden illustrates the whole thing in four lines:

"'For true it is as *in principio*,
Mulier est hominis confusio.
Madam, the meaning of this Latin is,
That woman is to man his sovereign bliss.'

"It is sorrowful to add—for it almost proves the goose theory—that nearly all women likewise hold that theory about sex. Whenever a fine lady begins to cant to you about woman 'going out of their sphere,' set her down at once as an advocate of the goose theory: and in fact, so far as the lady is herself concerned, you will be quite safe in accepting that theory as the true one.

"A great deal of the shilly-shally, pretty Frenchy gallantry of society is the utterance of the goose theory; it means: 'Oh, adorable damsel, your worshipper believes that all you are good for is, just as the lady-adoring Parisians so sweetly express it, *habille, babille, dishabille!*'

"Let us come, now, to the precise question before us tonight: 'Is it desirable that woman should practise gymnastics?'

"But, in the jargon of Congress, 'I move the previous question!'

"Do you hold the goose theory of woman? Yes? Then pass on! I've nothing to say to you. We differ on fundamentals, and all argument between us is waste of temper.

"Or do you hold the human theory of woman? Very well. Then we have some common ground to stand upon, and we can talk with a prospect of benefit.

"Why should woman not practise gymnastics?

"Do you say that she is of a weaker sex? All the more need of becoming strong!

"Do you say that she is delicate? That is a sufficient argument for trying to become robust.

"At exactly this point we are confronted by a very prevalent, and a very silly sentiment—hatched from the egg of the goose theory. It is a sentiment so pernicious that we ought to knock it on the head at sight. On this occasion we will use a club furnished us by Herbert Spenser. In one of his masterful tracts on Education, he has said something which I must read to you. I've brought the book with me for purpose. Here it is:

"'Perhaps, however, we mistake the aim of those who train the gentler sex. We have a vague suspicion that to produce a robust physique is thought undesirable; that rude health and abundant vigor are considered somewhat plebeian; that a certain delicacy, a strength not competent to more than a mile or two's walk, an appetite fastidious and easily satisfied, joined with that timidity which commonly accompanies feebleness, are held more lady-like. We do not expect that any one would distinctly avow this; but we fancy that the governess mind is haunted by an ideal young lady bearing not a little resemblance to this type. If so, it must be admitted that the established system is admirably calculated to realize this ideal.'

"And if this portrait of the 'ideal young lady,' with which 'the governess mind' is haunted, be not sufficiently clear, you have but to turn to the witty Wendell Holmes, and you will find in his delineation of 'My Aunt' some of the lines drawn more sharply:

"'He sent her to a stylish school-
'T was in her thirteenth June;
And with her, as rules required,
Two towels and a spoon.

"'They braced my Aunt against a board,
To make her straight and tall;
They laced her up, they starved her down,
To make her light and small;

They pinched her feet, they singed her hair,
They screwed it up with pins;
Oh! never mortal suffered more
In penance for her sins!'

"Why should not women practice gymnastics? Will it be said that American women already get exercise enough? Then next to none is enough! No, no, no! Catherine Beecher says that in all her acquaintance (and you know the Beechers are acquainted with every body) there are not a dozen healthy women.

"Let us not flatter ourselves that this is a Yankee notion—this idea of having the ladies practice gymnastics. Three thousand years ago, Grecian women danced and ran races, and, in later times, took part in the public games with men. Some of you have read the great work of Mr. Grote, the 'History of Greece.' Perhaps you will remember a passage in his second volume, where he says: 'The Spartan damsels underwent a bodily training, analogous to that of the Spartan youth—being formally exercised, and contending with each other in running, wrestling, and boxing, agreeably to the forms of the Grecian agones. They seem to have worn a light tunic, cut open at the skirts, so as to leave the limbs both free and exposed to view. Now, ladies, do you want to know what was one charming result of all this gymnastic exercise? The answer is furnished by Mr. Grote, a page or two further on: 'The beauty of the Lacedemanian women was notorious throughout Greece.' There, ladies! the finest cosmetics are those with which Nature beautifies her faithful followers. There is nothing like a gymnasium, to give us a race of pretty girls!

"But, in justice to my fair countrywomen, I must declare, that if they were as strong as they are beautiful, if they were as vigorous as they are lovely, why—I don't know what would happen! They would have things all their own way, for they would be omnipotent. Alas, there is no lack of beauty among us, and a plentiful lack of strength! Did you ever hear the story of the Castle of Weinsberg? I'm sure you never did, so I'll tell it. It was in the terrible old wars between the Guelphs and the Ghibellines that Conrad III beseiged the Castle of Weinsberg. But Conrad could not carry it as easily as he had expected. So he swore, in his wrath, that when he should take the castle he would put every man to the sword; but, being a very polite ruffian he promised that the women of the garrison should be allowed to depart in peace, with whatever they chose to carry on their backs. So, when the castle surrendered and the gates were opened, every woman sallied forth with a man on her back; and luckily there were enough women to carry of the whole garrison. Now, ladies and gentlemen, the point in this story which excites my concern is this: Suppose those women had been our dainty, lovely, delicate, feeble American women, how many of that garrison would have escaped their bloody doom? Perhaps one; but I doubt it!"

WOMEN AND ATHLETICS

New York Daily Graphic, 16 June 1877.

ATHLETIC SPORTS

The *Graphic* to-day holds the mirror up to the face of the social world, and shows the new forms of recreation and enjoyment just coming into fashion. A quarter of a century ago gymnasiums for men were hardly thought of, and no such thing as a college gymnasium existed. Boat clubs, ball clubs and cricket clubs were rare, and these invigorating and exciting sports were looked upon with suspicion. There was no interest to speak of in athletic sports of any kind. But the movement had then begun, and has rapidly gained strength ever since, till every college in the country has not only its gymnasium, but its boat and other clubs, and athletic sports of all kinds are not only viewed with favor, but practiced with enthusiasm. Nor is the practice confined to young men. A few years ago the delightful game of croquet was welcomed by ladies, and soon became the fashion. It led the way to other out-of-door sports for ladies, and last week we reported the formation of an athletic club for the practice of archery and other field sports by ladies on Staten Island. The tendency is a good one, and ought to be heartily encouraged. These out-of-door exercises are as invigorating as they are enjoyable, and should be cultivated quite as much for physical development as for pleasure. Our people are fast relearning some of the old and forgotten truths of the Greeks and Romans and other ancient peoples. The care and culture of the body are essential to the full and free use of the mind and enjoyment of life, and there can never be a hardy and perfect race of men till women are properly developed and nurtured and trained. The physical side of life for women as well as for men, is beginning to receive the attention which is its due. A great deal has been written and said about physical exercise within twenty-five years, and heroic efforts have been made to get debilitated people to practice in gymnasiums. But it has been found that people will not take exercise alone if they can help it, any more than they will eat alone. The play of social instincts and affections adds as much to the benefit as it does to the pleasure of a dinner. Solitary eating is the next remove from fasting. To make physical exercise popular it must become a pastime. And athletic sports will become fashionable for ladies as well as for men in proportion as they are made sports, and ladies find pleasure in them. The sexes naturally go together, in joy as well as sorrow, in recreation as well as in toil, in play as well as in study and prayer. And the forms of exercise suited for both sexes will come into vogue, and many sports which a few years ago were considered unwomanly, will doubtless be fashionable. The coming woman is evidently determined not only to have culture and accomplishments, but a vigorous and healthy physical life. And athletic sports are the surest and pleasantest way of gaining this desirable result.

DEFINING AN AMATEUR ATHLETE

The following newspaper editorial suggests that the problem of defining the meaning of amateurism and professionalism troubled sporting clubs and governing bodies on both sides of the Atlantic. It also reveals that Americans in general and New Yorkers in particular strongly influenced Canadian views on this subject. This piece first appeared in The Gazette (Montreal), 30 August 1876.

AMATEUR VS. PROFESSIONAL

This troublesome question has of late caused discussion on more than one racing track or athletic field, and judges meet in the various protests placed in their hands some knotty points pro and con. English and French (and until recently the New York Athletic Club) rules class a professional as one who contests for money, who earns his livelihood by athletics or in training others for athletic sports, who runs in a race open to every one, who runs for money or is a *mechanic* or *laborer*. An amateur is held by these clubs to be one who indulges in athletic sports from the love of the exercise, a desire to emulate his fellows or to win a prize, provided money is not the stake. The New York Athletic Club has stricken out that part of the ruling which taboos the mechanic and laborer, and gives us the following as its law and opinion of what constitutes an amateur:—"An amateur is one who has never taught, professed or assisted in the pursuit of athletic exercises as a means of earning his livelihood; who has not, subsequent to June 1, 1874, entered in a competition open to all comers, or for public or admission money, or against a professional for a prize." Little need be said as to the English and French *caste* iron rule. The American rule is the one taken to govern all athletic clubs in our vicinity, and lays down the version, according to the expression of the majority at a convention held in New York. By it an amateur cannot be longer considered in that light after he may have competed for and won a dollar bill or fifty cents or $100 put up for public competition; he cannot be considered an amateur if a prize is put up in his vicinity for open competition—a stranger may come in and carry it off, though there should be fifty members of a local athletic club looking on. If any of the fifty has pluck enough to go, and does go in to win, for the honor of his city or club, whether he loses or wins, he is ever afterwards under the ban as a professional. If this were law it would prevent competition altogether. These rules should not be and are not held to govern all meetings, however, and unless the regulations under which the meeting is to run are openly stipulated before hand on the printed programme, the best guide to the judges are common sense and a standard English dictionary, the latter giving the literal definition of the words amateur and professional. Worcester's dictionary says an amateur is "One versed in or a lover of any particular pursuit, art, or science, but not engaged in it professionally." He styles professional, "pertaining to or employed in a profession or calling." Then again calling is "Vocation, trade, occupation, business, employment." Therefore a man is not a professional runner unless he adopts that branch of athletics as a means of earning his livelihoood—that is, becomes a teacher or trainer of running men, runs at races to earn his bread, makes matches for money, &c. A Thames waterman would be reckoned a professional in rowing, but strictly speaking might be an amateur at other sports. In the same manner a fencing or dancing master would be professional in their own lines, and amateurs in rowing or cricket. A cricketer engaged as care taker or coacher by a cricket club cannot be held to be a professional boxer, runner or athlete of any other kind unless he teaches these branches or indulges in them for gain. Weston is a professional pedestrian, O'Leary and others of that ilk in a like manner. Renforth, Kelly, Saddler and others of that ilk are professionals. To says that the Paris crew are profesionals because after rowing in the amateur races at Paris they pulled in the professional races and beat all comers, would be absurd. And yet that is the ruling of the Paris and London clubs. It is perfectly competent for the Montreal, New York, or London athletic or rowing clubs to adopt as law whatever, in their opinion, constitutes an amateur or professional contestant. But, as we have said, unless the judges and competitors are previously notified as to the code governing the races to be run, they can use their own judgment in estimating what are the qualifications necessary to constitute either amateur or professional.

Chapter 2

AQUATICS

Aquatic sports thrived during the 1860s and 1870s throughout North America, as rowing and yachting experienced new phases of growth and development into modern forms. Swimming remained popular as a recreational activity, but a few early challenges demonstrated its potential as a competitive sport for both men and women. The great enthusiasm for rowing matches in both Canada and the United States led to its commercialization in featured regattas among college, amateur and professional oarsmen who competed in both individual and crew events. In the elite world of yachting, this period witnessed the early challenges for the America's Cup. Indeed, a spirited international competition among sportsmen from Canada, the United States, and Great Britain was a major element in all three aquatic sports during these decades.

Prior to the Civil War Harvard and Yale had pioneered intercollegiate rowing in the United States, and after that conflict those two institutions kept their sport alive through an annual race. By far the most celebrated event of this period occurred on August 27, 1869 on the Thames River in London, when a Harvard crew of four men with coxswain lost to Oxford. This chapter includes a narrative of that event from a Harvard alumni publication, along with a newspaper editorial which suggests the great excitement and patriotic feelings this challenge stimulated among the general public in the United States.

The Harvard-Oxford race spurred a renewal of interest in rowing at several eastern colleges, and a dispute over an incident in the 1870 Harvard-Yale race led to the formation of a new intercollegiate rowing association. Bad feeling between the Harvard and Yale men over Harvard's claim of a foul by Yale in their 1870 contest resulted in Harvard's call for a convention of college rowing clubs. Although the Harvard club certainly did not intend to democratize their sport, its action wound up having that result later in the decade. In 1871 Harvard invited Yale, Massachusetts Agricultural College (later the University of Massachusetts), Brown, and Bowdoin to send representatives to a meeting at Springfield, Massachusetts. Yale "unofficially" was present as the other institutions' delegates met in April and founded the Rowing Association of American Colleges. In July the "Farmer Boys" from Massachusetts Agricultural College shocked favored Harvard and Brown with a stunning upset victory over a course near Springfield. The success of a small upstart school encouraged Amherst, Bowdoin, and Williams to enter crews in the 1872 regatta. Yale also competed in that race, which was won by Amherst. Crews from Columbia, Cornell, Dartmouth, Trinity, and Wesleyan helped to swell the field to eleven in the 1873 event, which ended with a Yale victory over Harvard which was controversial because of an incorrectly placed finish line.

In 1874 the Rowing Association agreed to move its featured regatta to Saratoga Lake in upstate New York. That popular upper class summer resort, developed by John

Morrissey and his partners, featured horse racing, gambling, and mineral springs. Although the lake offered an ideal location for the intercollegiate regattas, some of college delegations voiced strong reservations about choosing a site which they considered to be tainted with morally objectionable activities. Nine colleges entered the race in that year, which was won by Columbia after the Yale crew apparently fouled Harvard. The next year a record number of thirteen colleges vied for championship honors, with substantial subsidies for expenses, prizes, and entertainment provided by the sponsoring Saratoga Rowing Association. Included below is an account of that 1875 regatta, in which Cornell crews won both the freshmen and varsity races. The victory of the Ithacans marked yet another triumph for a newly founded college over the older and more prestigious institutions. Cornell President Andrew D. White recognized the importance of the college's victory when he declared that one hundred thousand dollars could not have purchased the amount of publicity gained by the Cornell triumph.

The 1875 spectacle at Saratoga turned out to be the high point of this era of intercollegiate regattas. Disgusted with losing to schools they viewed as inferior, Harvard and Yale decided to drop out of the Rowing Association and chose to concentrate on competing against each other. Clearly, their decision to pull out of the intercollegiate competition and schedule only dual meets was an expression of elitist sentiment and a setback for the principle of egalitarianism in college sport. Their defection led directly to the demise of the Saratoga regattas after another Cornell triumph in 1876. In later years both Cornell and Columbia were snubbed when they challenged Harvard and Yale. In 1878 Columbia became the first foreign crew to win a trophy in the Henly Regatta in England as it triumphed in the Visitor's Challenge Cup over three Oxford and Cambridge crews.

During these years club competition constituted a second branch of amateur rowing in both the United States and Canada. Although the professionals had dominated both individual and crew matches in prior decades, the period between 1865 and 1880 witnessed the rise of an amateur organization which would soon take control of the sport. In 1866 elite gentlemen representing eleven clubs from New York City and its vicinity founded the Hudson Amateur Rowing Association. Only Philadelphia approached the New York City region in the number of oarsmen and associations, but after the Civil War rowing clubs were established in every major city with access to a body of water. By 1870 there were at least 200 in the United States, with dozens more in Canada.

The proliferation of rowing clubs and disagreements over an acceptable definition of amateurism prompted a movement to create a new national organization. On August 28, 1872 delegates from twenty-seven clubs (including eleven from New York City and its environs) met in Manhattan and founded the National Association of Amateur Oarsmen. This chapter includes samples of some of its early codes of rules and several versions of its definition of an amateur oarsman. Its officers followed the example of their English counterparts and became the first Americans to distinguish amateurs from professionals in an individual sport. Many journalists criticized their terms, which they viewed as discriminatory against working class contestants. Eleven clubs which attended the inaugural meeting refused to join the National Association, but over the next few decades the wealthy and powerful New York City and Philadelphia organizations gradually increased the Association's control of the sport.

In Canada the great popularity of professional rowing and the rapid growth of amateur clubs led to the formation of another organization and a new code of amateurism. Upon its founding in 1880 the Canadian Association of Amateur Oarsmen defined an amateur as "one who has never assisted in the pursuit of athletic exercises as a means of livelihood, who rows for pleasure or recreation only and during his leisure hours, and does not abandon or neglect his usual business or occupation for the purpose of training more than two weeks during the season." This constituted the first attempt by Canadians to separate amateurs from professionals, and it became the basis for all future definitions in that country. It presented a negative interpretation of what an amateur was not, but it did not clearly define what constituted an amateur oarsman.

This period marked the high point of popularity for the greatest professional rowers of both the United States and Canada. In the former nation the most prominent were James Hamill of Pittsburgh, Joshua Ward and Walter Brown of Newburgh, and Charles Courtney of upstate New York. During the 1860s Hamill and Ward had a spirited competition, with each winning feature matches. In 1866 Hamill also distinguished himself in two races rowed on the Tyne in Newcastle, England, which he lost to the British champion, Henry Kelley. Brown gained fame in 1866 when he defeated Ward in a singles match at a regatta at Worcester; the same day he helped row the four-oared *Frank Queen* of New York to victory. Brown also won an international match over William Sadler of Putney at Newcastle on the Tyne in England.

In Canada the most prominent professional oarsmen were the Paris Crew of St. John, New Brunswick, and the country's greatest sports hero of his day, Edward "Ned" Hanlan. The Paris Crew from St. John earned their name and fame in 1867 when they startled the aquatic world with their surprising victory over British and French crews at an international exposition in Paris. The outcome was a surprise because the Canadian visitors were an unknown working-class crew composed of a lighthouse keeper and three fishermen. Subsidized with funds provided by the people of their city and province, these rowing upstarts defeated some of the elite clubs of Europe, including Oxford University, the London Rowing Club, and the Leanders of London. Three years later the Tyne Crew of Newcastle, England earned some revenge for Europe with a victory over the Paris Crew at Lachine, near Montreal, Canada. An account of that challenge appears below.

During the late 1870s "Ned" Hanlan became Canada's first internationally known sporting figure through a series of brilliant sculling victories. His first significant triumph came in the United States at the centennial sculls held in Philadelphia in 1876. Over the next eight years he won championships of his native country, the United States, England, and the World. His flair for showmanship and his theatrics during his races entertained crowds and gave him a kind of superhuman quality. Between 1877 and 1884 he became a national hero for all Canadians throughout all of its provinces. He symbolized his nation's quest to gain an identity independent of both Britain and the United States. The section on rowing concludes with a description of one of Hanlan's most memorable matches—his defeat of the American Charles Courtney at Lachine in October, 1878.

During these decades swimming remained primarily a premodern recreational activity for many North Americans who lived near a bay, lake, pond, river, or stream. But there were matches held at the local, state, provincial, and even international levels for both male and female contestants. This chapter includes an example of a women's race held in New York City, followed by an international challenge between an Englishman and an American. Both matches reveal an early degree of modernization, and both also show the model provided by rowing events.

The revival of yachting after the Civil War witnessed a series of international challenges involving affluent gentlemen from the United States, England, and Canada. The New York Yacht Club, custodian of the America's Cup, retained its status as the premier sailing organization in North America. The leading events of these years were contests for possession of the prized trophy captured by John C. Stevens and his partners off the coast of Great Britain in 1851. Unfortunately, the competition generated a prolonged and complicated controversy and much ill will because of disputes over the terms and conditions of the races.

The trouble resulted from the ambiguity of several of the clauses of the original deed which Stevens and his associates had drafted when they gave the America's Cup to the New York Yacht Club. The document clearly indicated their intention to offer the trophy as a prize for international competition. It also stipulated that arrangements should be made by the contending parties by "mutual consent," but if agreement could not be reached then the race would be sailed "over the usual course of the Annual Regatta of the Yacht Club in possession of the Cup, and subject to its Rules of Sailing Regulations." That section gave an enormous advantage to the New York Yacht Club in its negotiations with its challengers. Secondly, the deed did not clearly define the meaning of a "match" race. Initially the club insisted that an opponent was required to sail against its entire fleet, rather than a single yacht. Although that position seemed to be unfair, unsportsmanlike, and in conflict with the spirit of the deed, the American press and the public generally supported the members. After all, they argued, Stevens and his partners had defeated an entire squadron of vessels back in 1851. Shouldn't any rival yacht pass that same test to win the Cup?

A renewal of interest in sailing during the 1860s led directly to the first challenge for the America's Cup. In 1866 George A. Osgood, Pierre Lorillard, Jr., and James Gordon Bennett, Jr. each put up $30,000 for a trans-Atlantic race of schooners. Foolishly, the three vessels set off in December. Bennett's boat, the *Henrietta,* arrived off the coast of England first, but the contest took the lives of six sailors, who were washed overboard at night from one of the other yachts. In 1868 the Poillon brothers, Brooklyn shipwrights, built the *Sappho* to challenge English yachts for prize money. But when this American schooner finished behind four English yachts in a challenge race, it appeared likely that a British vessel could easily regain the coveted America's Cup.

James Ashbury's *Cambria* had defeated the *Sappho* in that contest, and the Englishman now dedicated himself to winning the trophy held by the New York Yacht Club. In his letter of October 1868 he fired off his first challenge by listing his terms. The club's officers replied that only yacht clubs, and not individuals, could compete for the cup. Ashbury then agreed to represent the Royal Thames Yacht Club. He also asked permission to sail against the club's champion schooner. He was told that he would have to race against the club's whole fleet. As these negotiations dragged on until 1870, Ashbury persuaded Bennett to sail his schooner, the *Dauntless,* against the *Cambria* in a trans-Atlantic race from England to New York. In July New York sportsmen were shocked when the *Cambria* came rolling in first. That victory raised Ashbury's spirits, and he reluctantly accepted the New York Yacht Club's conditions that he must race against its entire fleet for possession of the America's Cup.

The date set for this first challenge was August 8, 1870. The excitement in New York City was intense as twenty-three schooners (including the refurbished *America*) started the race. Although by courtesy the *Cambria* was given a favored position at the windward end of the line, the race went very badly for Ashbury. A shift in wind, a tactical error, and a possible foul by one of the other vessels brought the *Cambria* to the finish in eighth place out of the fifteen yachts that covered the course.

Disappointed but undaunted, Ashbury became even more determined to regain the prize for his home country. Back in England he ordered his shipbuilder to construct a new yacht for him, the *Livonia*. He then started a new round of correspondence with the New Yorkers in which he stated that his legal counsel had interpreted the word "match" in the deed to mean a race between a challenger and a single defender. He suggested that if the club did not agree with his conclusion he would sail the course alone and take or claim the trophy. In April 1871 the Spirit of the Times published a long letter from George Schuyler, who was the only surviving member of the group which donated the America's Cup to the New York Yacht Club in 1857. Schuyler's letter supported Ashbury's position. Although his view was not binding on the club, its officers finally consented to race a single defender against the *Livonia*. In June Ashbury further complicated the situation when he insisted that he had the right to represent twelve different yacht clubs, all members of the Royal Yacht Squadron. He demanded twelve races—one for each club—with seven victories required to win the Cup. After much wrangling Ashbury and the officers of the club finally agreed on a series of seven races over alternate courses. But the New Yorkers had a big advantage because they retained the right to choose one of four vessels for each of the contests.

The series began on October 16, 1871 with an easy victory by the *Columbia*. The second race, also won by the *Columbia*, created a controversy. Ashbury claimed that the course was only thirty miles and not forty, as agreed. He also had other objections, and he demanded the race be rerun or awarded to his yacht. After his protest was rejected the *Livonia* was able to win the third race, also against the *Columbia*. The New Yorkers then switched to the *Sappho*, which triumphed in the next two contests. The club thus had four victories and a successful defense of the Cup. Ashbury disagreed however, as he claimed victory in the second race. He insisted on competing in two more races. When he was ignored by the New Yorkers, he claimed the prize anyway by default before he stormed back to England in a huff. Over the next two years yachtsmen and sporting periodicals on both sides of the Atlantic sniped at each other over the fairness of this second challenge for the America's Cup.

The third challenge came from an unlikely source in 1876, the Centennial year of American independence. Major Charles Gifford, vice-commodore of the Royal Canadian Yacht Club of Toronto, acted in behalf of Captain Alexander Cuthbert of Cobourg, Ontario. Cuthbert was the designer and builder of the schooner, *Countess of Dufferin*. The members of the New York Yacht Club were pleased at this Canadian overture, because the organization had suffered from the banking and business depression caused by the Panic of 1873. The challenge generated a boost in membership and gave the club a much needed lift. At a meeting two-thirds of the members voted to defend the

Cup with a single yacht, the *Madeleine*. The contest was set for a best two-out-of-three series. The *Madeleine* easily outdistanced her Canadian rival in the two races held on August 11-12. The critics were harsh on the *Countess*, which they ridiculed as unattractive and overmatched. These were the final races between schooners in Cup matches. Soon afterward American designers switched to the sloop and the cutter for sailing races.

ROWING

HARVARD-OXFORD RACE, 1869

During the late 1860s Harvard's rowing club decided to challenge the winner of the annual Oxford-Cambridge race. The arrangements for this match required some compromises on both sides, because the two English institutions rowed with eight oarsmen and a coxswain, while Harvard's Varsity used six men with steering from the bow. In 1869 Oxford agreed to a contest with four men and a coxswain. On July 10th four Harvard rowers sailed from New York to England, leaving six of their teammates behind to compete against Yale in their annual match. After Harvard's victory over its arch rival, the stroke and another oarsman of the winning crew departed for England and later replaced two of their colleagues who had already arrived in London. The race was set for the same course used for the annual Oxford-Cambridge event, four-and-a-quarter miles from Putney to Mortlake on the Thames. This account of the match is reprinted from F.B. Vaille and H.A. Clark, eds., *The Harvard Book*, Vol. II (Cambridge, Mass, 1875), pp. 222-226.

ENGLISH RACE.

A.P. LORING, *stroke*,	'69, 153 lbs.	F.O. LYMAN,	'71, 158 lbs.
W.H. SIMMONS,	'69, 171 "	J.S. FAY, Jr., bow,	'69, 161 "

ARTHUR BURNHAM, *coxswain*,, '70, 107 lbs.

After the informal correspondence, in 1868, with Oxford, relative to a matchrace between the two universities, which came to naught at the time, the whole matter was supposed to be at an end. But in the early spring of 1869 it was suddenly announced that a match had been arranged, and a meeting of students was called April 28, to decide what to do further in the matter. At first the opinion of the meeting was adverse to the enterprise, because it was thought that the match had been originated and promoted by individuals not authorized to act. On further discussion, opinions changed, and it was finally voted to ratify what had been done, and to raise a crew to meet Oxford. Here at the outset it may be well to enumerate some of the objections which presented themselves for consideration, not here pleaded by way of extenuation, but to show rather the nature of the contest. Numerically the number of students in Harvard is very much smaller than in either of the English universities, and therefore there are fewer oarsmen from whom to select a crew. In America, rowing among college men is an art learned, for the most part, during an academic course of four years: while in England considerable perfection in the art is reached in the preparatory colleges before entering the higher universities. Again, the English crews row in eights, and carry coxswains, neither of which customs are in vogue in this country, it being difficult to obtain so many as eight good men for a crew from a comparatively small college, and a coxswain being regarded as too much of an impediment to speed. Many inquiries were also instituted at this time as to a course upon which it would be possible to row such a race. All that resulted was the ascertainment of two facts, namely, that there were but few, if any, good courses in England, and that the English crews would not consent to row anything but a four-oared match with coxswains, and that over their regular course on the Thames, from Putney, to Mortlake. All these points were yielded by Harvard, who thus met the Englishmen literally upon their own terms, as was perhaps proper enough for a new aspirant to coveted honors.

Now came the important question of the crew. At this time there was but one old University oarsman practising or intending to row that year, and two of the most promising of those working for places on the University crew had known but one year's rowing. The crew as first announced at the meeting was: Simmons (stroke), Bass, Rice; the bow not chosen, but Blaikie, '66, suggested. After some discussion, Loring was induced to row. Simmons, chosen in February captain of the University crew, resigned in Loring's favor, and the crew was organized. Practise now began at once: but here new obstacles were encountered, and especially in the matter of boats. A four-oared boat was a new thing at Harvard. Nobody knew how such a boat should be built, but one was at once ordered. The coxswain was the greatest difficulty. This officer had been something unknown in the College for many years, and after the merits of all the light weights had been canvassed, one was finally chosen. The crew rowed first in a six-oared shell, placing the coxswain in stroke's place, and balancing his weight with sand-bags placed in the bow. When the four-oared boat arranged for coxswain arrived, she proved a failure, being altogether too long, buckling badly, and her outriggers springing, on account of their length; but the crew used her for practise, and in races near Boston.

The fact hardly deserves mention, but there was also another abortive attempt to build a suitable boat, by a builder who claimed to have practise in England, but his production subsequently proved hardly worth putting into the water.

This latter boat, however, having been tried once or twice, was really taken to England with the idea that she would serve to practise in, but was never even uncovered there. The coxswain Harvard had chosen was not accustomed to boating or rowing of any sort, and of course could not be relied upon materially to assist the crew by advise. It is but just to say, however, that he did as well in his place as could have been expected under the circumstances. In England a coxswain is of use. Possibly one might have assisted the Harvard crew in their practise abroad, but the crew did not know how to use him, nor he how to help the crew.

Only two of the crew were old University oars, and the two new men had to be taught the stroke. Mr. Loring then, as captain, took his place in the bow, whence he could the better criticise and teach the crew, and Mr. Simmons rowed stroke. Thus organized, they worked hard and faithfully, and rowed in the three races before mentioned. They sailed for Europe, July 10, from New York, arrived in Liverpool in ten days in good condition (except Mr. Simmons, who suffered much from sea-sickness), and went immediately to Putney, where they were almost at once lodged in the White House (a detached villa on the riverbank), in excellent quarters. There was now a period of nearly five weeks before the day appointed for the race. Immediately on their arrival they were called upon by the London Rowing Club, who kindly placed boats and oars at their disposal, and gave them the exclusive use of one of their boat-houses, and who during their entire stay showed them every civility, making them Honorary Members of the club. Practise on the river commenced at once, and the coxswain, under the guidance of different watermen, went frequently on the river and studied all the peculiarities of this most intricate course as well as was possible.

Towards the latter part of the time, a small screw pleasure-boat was kindly furnished by an English gentleman, through the influence of some friend, and the coxswain thus had a opportunity of going over the course an additional number of times without requiring a crew to row him.

The boat they took with them being useless, they at once ordered new ones from no less than three of the most noted English boat-builders. These three boats were finished two weeks before the race; they were tried, and one selected and used in practise until within two or three days of the race, at which time the American boat-builder, Elliott, who had brought over the knees and draughts of a new boat, completed one which the crew preferred to any other, and therefore this boat was used.

The course was four and a quarter miles, and was rowed up stream with the tide, which runs about four miles per hour. The river is here very crooked, and the course is shaped something like the letter S, full of eddies, shoal in places, in places obstructed by piles, and crossed by three arched bridges. This course had been the scene of no less than twenty contests between Oxford and Cambridge, and was perfectly familiar to the English crew.

The Harvards as originally organized rowed every day back and forth over this course, not without eliciting sharp and generally adverse criticism from the English papers, which took an unusual interest in the coming race. After three weeks' practice it became evident that the crew could not approximate their styles so as to row well together, and it was decided to place on the crew the two substitutes who had just arrived, instead of the two middle men, then in the boat. A new crew was therefore made up, and the positions of the original bow and stroke oarsmen changed, thus rowing as they had been accustomed in previous years; i.e. the bow in stroke's place, and the former stroke directly behind him. The two substitutes filled the forward places. The crew as thus made up formed the crew which rowed in the race. This was about two weeks before the race, and at this time the Oxford crew appeared on the river. Their stroke was noticeably slower than that of the American crew, who, although they rowed more slowly than was their custom, still inclined to the more gliding and quicker stroke, which the mile and half turn races at home called for. It is said that a residence on the river-banks is not good for a crew, and that in England no crew ever stays there longer than two weeks. The Oxford crew, under their admirable organization, are not left to their own devices, nor worried by the management of their own affairs. All is left to others, who watch them carefully all the time in training as well as in their practice. They never row a stroke but under the eye of their "coach," who, following their boat in a small steamer, or on horseback along the river-back, continually criticises, and calls out to the individuals to mend this or that fault. The result of this is a most admirable machine. The total absence from all the cares of management keeps the minds of the men composing the crew free from all anxiety and worry. The management of all things pertaining to field sports is reduced by the English to a science. In this match with Harvard, everything, from the receipt of the first letter, was conducted on their part with the most business-like shrewdness. Nothing was yielded and nothing omitted which could in the least degree contribute to their chances of success. The Oxford crew was composed of veterans at the oar, and was considered the finest four-oared crew that ever rowed on the Thames. Its members were

S.D. DARBISHIRE, *stroke,*	160 lbs.	A.C. YARBOROUGH,	170 lbs.
J.C. TINNE,	190 "	F. WILLAN,	164 "

J.H. HALL, *coxswain,* 100 lbs.

Every man came to the line in perfect condition. The Harvard crew continued their practice and hard work to the very day of the race, though the two oldest and strongest men in the boat were overworked and stale several days before that event. This was noticed and quite generally commented on at the time. It had become gradually more and more apparent to the crew that they had undertaken a desperate contest under the greatest disadvantages, but they appeared, on the day of the race, determined, and eager to do their best.

On the 27th of August the day was fine and the water favorable. Immense crowds, estimated at hundreds of thousands, began to gather early in the day, and by the time of the race covered the banks of the river, swarming like bees on all the trees and houses, and especially on the bridges under which the boats must pass. The river itself was kept quite clear of boats, under the admirable management of the Thames Conservancy Board,—a feat never before accomplished in a boat-race there. At a little after five o'clock in the afternoon the two boats appeared. Harvard won the toss for position, and selected the Middlesex side. The rudder of each boat was held by a man in a boat. "Are you ready?" from the starter was answered "No!" by the Oxfords. "When will you be ready?" "Directly." Again the question from the starter, and the boats are off, Harvard rowing 46, Oxford 40 strokes. Harvard gained at once, and got clear at about one third of a mile. At Hammersmith Bridge, two miles away, this lead was increased to four lengths. But Harvard had rowed an uneven stroke, and too quick to last, and after passing the bridge Oxford began to draw up. Shortly after, as the bend in the river at Chiswick was approached, Oxford put on a spurt. This is the point in the course where, in the English University races between Oxford and Cambridge, the great struggle always occurs, and here, true to custom, the Oxford crew made their fight for the lead. They came up rapidly and headed over towards Harvard, calling out to Burnham to keep off. Seeing a foul imminent, he turned away. By doing so he got the boat into an eddy, the boat rocked, and all at once the crew lost their form, and looked like going to pieces. Oxford gained an immense advantage, and, in what seemed a moment, was past Harvard and leading by two lengths. They immediately afterwards increased this lead still more. From this point the Oxford crew showed more reserved power than the Harvard; for at the end of the third mile, during which the course lay tolerably straight away, the latter were three lengths astern. The rowing of Harvard now improved, and they regained part of the distance lost. Oxford rowed steadily on, and crossed the line 6 seconds ahead of Harvard. It was a hard race and a fair beat. When Oxford got ahead of Harvard, she took her water and gave her the back wash, which impeded the boat not a little. In the early part of the race Harvard might have done the same by the Oxford boat, but did not, with the mistaken idea that Oxford would not do it to them. Though beaten, the Harvard crew were not disgraced, and received almost as much praise for their great courage and determination as did the victors. After the race the crew were entertained at a few dinners given to them and the Oxfords; but they separated in a week, some to come home and some to travel in Europe.

EDITORIAL

The Harvard-Oxford boat race generated an enormous amount of excitement in the United States. Many journalists viewed the Harvard crew as representatives of America's sporting tradition and honor. Although the outcome disappointed those who anticipated another American victory over the English, native writers took pride in Harvard's good showing on foreign waters. Between 1820 and 1870 this match received more press coverage on any one day than any other athletic contest. The following editorial presents one critic's interpretation of the possible cultural meaning of the great international intercollegiate boat race. It first appeared in The New York Times, 28 August 1869, p. 4.

THE BOAT RACE

The two greatest commercial nations of the world were engaged yesterday, not in the usual pursuit of gain, but in watching an extraordinary trial of strength between eight young men. There is no race but the Anglo-Saxon with whom such a competition would have been possible. We may, without boasting, add that only Americans would have traveled three thousand miles from home in order to challenge the strongest crew ever seen upon foreign waters, under circumstances unavoidably adverse to themselves. It was impossible from the first that the conditions could be made quite equal on both sides. The Oxonians are at home on the Thames, and every man in their boat had already taken part in one or more successful struggles with a crew only second to their own. They were animated with all the confidence and buoyancy which a recent victory naturally inspires. They had nothing to learn about the river, and no changes to make in regard to the construction of their boat. Moreover, they had the sympathy of nine-tenths of the spectators with them, and in a trial which imposes the severest strain on all the powers this is an advantage difficult to overestimate. If we reverse the conditions, and suppose the Oxonians to have rowed on the Charles River, there is no one who will not readily admit that the chances at the start would have been against them. When we add to these considerations the additional facts, that the American crew had little more than three weeks active training, that they have been obliged to change their boat twice or thrice, and to recast the crew more than once, and that on the all-important day of the struggle the most powerful man of their number was in ill-health, it becomes evident that defeat never went so near to victory as when the Harvard men came in only a few seconds behind the Oxonians.

There are, perhaps, a few aberrant philosophers in existence who will look down from their serene eminence on this memorable contest, and smile at what they regard as the folly and vanity of mankind. But philosophers never rule the world, and seldom comprehend even the motive-power by which it is governed. If we carefully weighed the conclusions to be drawn from history, we should find that it has been superiority of physical strength quite as much as any moral qualities which has given the Anglo-Saxon race a noble supremacy in the world. A people which looks upon an athlete as a useless incumbrance upon the face of the earth, or as a paradox in nature, is not likely to hold its own for centuries together. It is often alleged that in this country we are too apt to neglect a purely physical training—the systematic and careful development of strength and muscle—in the education of our youth. If that charge were well-founded, nothing could so quickly remove all occasion for repeating it as a contest like that of yesterday. We undertake to say that boat-racing will henceforth be more popular than ever among us. Young men now beginning their college studies will be stimulated to earn the distinction which the Harvard crew so brilliantly won for themselves yesterday in the old and the new world. Emulation of this kind is of the greatest value to a people in an age when the young are thrust into the battle of life before there has been time for a full expansion of their powers. A weak, sickly, flabby race may be a pleasing spectacle to theorists who live chiefly in the clouds, but for the destiny yet lying before us we cannot have too many of the attributes which are popularly included in the word "manliness." There are situations in which "mind" can do nothing, and we are forced to base our hopes upon "matter." An international boat race between nations like the American and the English cannot, therefore, be regarded as a trivial incident. We are unable, indeed, to regard a single trial of the kind as a decisive test of the superiority either of a race and breed, or of a system of rowing. But it challenges the world to admire physical pluck, endurance, hardiness, a sound constitution, and other gifts which we were intended to cultivate and rejoice in no less than in the pretentious intellectual forces. How many men are there on either side of the Atlantic whose nerves would have enabled them even to begin the task which these young men from Harvard nearly carried to a successful issue yesterday? . . .

. . . Let us, then, have another race on the Charles River, or some other suitable water. Two such crews ought not to be broken up without one more trial of strength. We honor the Harvard men for persevering against all difficulties in one of the most gallant contests ever recorded, and we hope that we shall some day have the opportunity of congratulating the Oxonians on a similar exhibition of mettle. Let them return with their American competitors. We engage that they will never repent of the journey.

ROWING ASSOCIATION OF AMERICAN COLLEGES: REGATTA, 1875

The regatta held at Saratoga in July, 1875 was a spectacular social and sporting event which heralded the arrival of Cornell University as a major power among intercollegiate crews. Rowing at Cornell began during the late 1860s, and a visit by the prominent Englishman Thomas Hughes in 1870 provided the key stimulus for greater enthusiasm for the sport. President Andrew D. White supported the college's club with a gift of a new six-oared cedar shell, and he hired Henry Coulter, a former single scull champion of the United States, as the crew's first coach. During the early 1870s Cornell entered the Rowing Association's summer regattas. After the Association banned professional coaches, Jack Olson (a member of the crew) took over responsibility for training the oarsmen. In the winter of 1874-75 he installed the college's first rowing machines. His regimen for his men contributed greatly to Cornell's victories in both the freshmen and Varsity six-oared events at Saratoga. Its successes gave the new college extensive publicity and a brand new cheer for its athletic teams. This description of the social scene at Saratoga and the races is reprinted from The Spirit of the Times, 17 July 1875, pp. 600-601.

THE INTER-COLLEGIATE REGATTA.

SARATOGA, July 13.—It would really seem that some influential personage—probably an astronomer—connected with one of the various Universities here represented, is on excellent terms with that notorious old sinner, the clerk of the weather office, and had induced him to treat us in the finest possible manner. Nothing could be imagined better than the weather this morning. It is just perfect, neither hot nor cold, but a pleasing medium, like the temperature of Mark Anthony, according to Cleopatra. Never, say the oldest inhabitants of Saratoga, has the place been so crowded as at present. Each train, as it arrives from Albany, brings us a multitude so vast, that it really is fast becoming a problem how all the people are lodged. I see as I cross the porticoes and piazzas of these caravansari hotels, which are the cause of surprise and wonderment to all Europeans, faces well-known to me in New York, faces of fashionable, artistic, and sporting people of note. But to me, by far the most interesting portion of the crowd, is that formed by the College boys and their enthusiastic admirers of the fair sex, who evidently are, as a rule, more nearly connected to them, than by the ties of sweetheartdom. They are very enthusiastic, very gushing, and, above all, very natural, these young ladies. And there is not one of them who does not predict the immediate and most decided victory of her favorite brother, cousin, or lover's college. The four colleges Yale, Harvard, Columbia, and Amherst are so abundantly represented that the entire "village" seem to be laboring under an epidemic of ribbons of their colors. Every man and woman, boy and girl in Saratoga has at least one bit of ribbon of some vivid hue or other attached to his or her person, in some conspicuous place. The "boys" enjoy themselves "first rate, and are having a fine time." Last night all the colleges received a hundred tickets, which were distributed by the commodores to their friends. It is somewhat comical to consider the slightly doleful expression of countenance, which naturally settles at times on the faces of the young students from distant colleges, who seem somewhat lonely and friendless, not but they are most heartily welcomed by the men of the more popular Universities, but then the bright eyes of the fair maidens from their own States will not witness, from the grand stand, their feats of bravery. It will be to them like what a tournament, without a queen of beauty, would have been to knights of the middle ages. Last night we talked rowing and regattas till the small hours, on the piazzas, whilst Bernstein's band discoursed lively dance music, and a thousand feet pattered to its strains. Today, now all is over for the hour, we are talking of nothing but the result of Freshmen's race, and of the prospects for to-morrow.

It was past ten this morning when I got into a friend's drag, and was driven down to the lake. You cannot imagine what a struggle and rush there was for a vehicle! It seemed as if very life depended on the possession of a seat at any price, and I actually saw a man receive $2 a piece from four gentlemen for a place in a superannuated wagon, drawn by two skeletons of horses, which, before the journey was half over, broke down, and deposited a party of eight on the high road, to the infinite amusement of the passers-by....

The crowd, at the grand stand, by the half-past ten, was dense enough, about ten thousand persons being present. When the race began there was a good deal of cheering. The course was fully three miles straight ahead, and cut up into lanes for to-morrow's race, each of about one hundred feet wide. The boats started very evenly, and moved for some time in unbroken columns until broken into by Harvard on the right. She kept up for some time in this advanced position until Princeton made a hard sheer to starboard, but she got into the right course after the first mile flag was reached, and thenceforward the freshmen kept in famously. Towards the end of the said first mile Harvard crept to front with Brown, Cornell, and Princeton, but so closely that there was not ten feet between the boats. The Harvard boat kept ahead nicely, but Brown presently fell out of the line. During the second mile Princeton made an effort to get in advance, and breasted Cornell, which was now third. Brown made a fine spurt to make head of her, but suddenly the boat dipped and her progress was considerably checked. Harvard held out and finished the second mile in 11:31. Then the Cornelians suddenly showed forth their spirit, and displayed like a dart. For a time Harvard, Brown, and Cornell were abreast, but Cornell soon advanced quickly and, as is now known half over the world, won the victory.

To describe the cheering on shore would be a difficult task; suffice to say that it was as hearty as hearty could be. If it "awoke not the echoes of the surrounding valleys," as would say our erudite contemporary of the lofty tower, it did its best to do so. As the Cornellians, with very little on them worth speaking about, and that little wet through with perspiration and water, were carried round in triumph on their admirers' shoulders, such was the enthusiasm of the fair sex that they forgot to be shocked, and waved handkerchiefs, and "hurrahed" in the sweetest of trebles in such a manner, that the said Cornellians ought to have felt marvelously gratified, especially if any of them had chanced to hear the exclamation of an elderly spinster lady in cork-screw curls, and a spencer of very antique date, whom I overheard cry out, "Oh, my Maria! what noble-looking animals men are!" The rumor is that the fact of the Cornellians' boat being made of paper, was the chief cause of their victory, but the difference of the weight between it and the cedar is very slight, and if you could see the fellows, you would be inclined to think with me, that they owe much to their music. Besides that, people ought to reflect, that the Cornell boys have immediately opposite their college Lake Cayuga to practice in, and if they did not avail themselves thereof, it would be undoubtedly somewhat singular. The oarsmen of Connecticut and Massachusetts, will have to work hard next year, or the men of Cayuga and Harlem will wear the wreath again. Hamilton and Union, they say, will be amongst the last to-morrow. Yale is in high favor, and so is Cornell since the victory. I forgot to tell you that, during the first part of the race, there was a slight breeze, and the water was somewhat ruffled, but at the close of the match a dead calm set in. Clouds at [sic] been gathering all the morning, and we had to get home to Saratoga as fast as ever we could, for I told you, we were scarcely within the mammoth village gates, ere down came a tremendous hailstorm, accompanied by lightning and thunder, which lasted the whole of the afternoon. The talk during the rest of the day and evening, was, of course, about to-morrow's race, and some rumors are afloat that young Murphy's (of Columbia) hand being severely hurt. He has a boil on the back of it, and young Mr. Palmly, of Princeton, is also reportedly not over well. He has a felon on his finger, and has not slept for two nights. May be a night's rest will do them and us all good....

SUMMARY.

SARATOGA, July 13.—Freshmen race; three miles straightaway.
Cornell—Lynde Palmer (bow), J.L. Camp, V.L. Grave, A.W. Smith, H.J. Carpenter, J. Lewis (stroke). Time 17:32 1/4.
Harvard—B.W. Morgan (bow), W.A. Bancroft, W.M. Lemoyne, P. Van Renselaer, L.N. Littaner, A.P. Loring (stroke). Time, 17:37 1/4.
Brown—J.O. Winslow (bow), R. Case, A.N. Fairbank, F.T. Whitman, G. Goodwin, J.B. Parrott (stroke). Time, 17:39 1/4.
Princeton—J.C. Thurston (bow), J.H. Hess, J. McFarland, E.J. Van Lenness, R.F. Karge, H.L. Stevenson (stroke). Time, 17:49 1/4.

THE UNIVERSITY RACE.
SECOND DAY.

SARATOGA, July 14.—If ever there was a crowd in one little spot of the earth which is far too big for it to contain that little spot is Saratoga, and the time the present. This morning's trains are bringing in a population fit for a capital, and every cart and wagon in the country for miles around is being put into requisition. Broadway is as crowded as Broadway, New York, in the "down town" regions at noon, as it is a peril and a danger to cross the street, and a matter of time and serious calculation. Laduas, barouches, fours-in-hand, donkey-carts, omnibuses, tandems, gigs, nondescript, wagons, wagonettes, and, in a word in all matter of conveyances that go on wheels throng the thoroughfares, and the prices paid for a ride down to the Lake are, to use the word of a venerable lady, who sat next to me at breakfast, "fit to frighten a body."

The day has been lovely throughout, finer even than yesterday, about cloudlessly serene and yet not too hot, owing to the fine, light breeze which tempered the air, but which did not even ruffle the surface of the water. Yesterday's irruption of ribbons was as infant rash to scarletina compared with what it is to-day. Why, sir, the very chambermaids and the colored waters are bedecked with streamers of every rainbow hue. Families, as in the days of the Capulets and Montagues of old, are divided against themselves, and I know of a patriarchal home of eleven members, in which the ladies wear the crimson of Harvard, whereas the gentlemen are bedecked, out of pure spirit of opposition, with Columbian blue. The odd numbered member No. 2 is "baby," and dons both Universities colors at once. The toilettes of the ladies are remarkable for the wonderful ingenuity with which they contrive to weave in and about them the colors of one or the other of the crews.

But let's hasten—not to the wedding—but to the Regatta. By eleven the grand stand was densely packed. For certain there must have been at the very least 20,000 persons present, some say 30,000. The grand stand here is very long, at least a third of a mile's stretch from end to end, and in front of it, out in the blazing sun, were rows of seats which were soon taken and filled. On the grand stand I saw no end of big wigs, the Van Rennselears, the Cuttings, Mrs. Lorimer Graham, Miss Granger, Mrs. Pennyman, August Belmont and Mrs. B., Galusha Grow, and ex-Speaker of the House; Judge Willoughby, ex-Gov. Hoffman and Henry Wilson. The college boys filled the seat in sectional streaks, and made the stand lively with their colors. Columbia was uncommonly cheerful and demonstrative; so too was Harvard, the rich colors of which was a particular favorite amongst the ladies, who wore conspicuously in their dresses. It's so becoming you know! Poor Yale! she too was well represented, and it seems too bad the day was not for her, after all the fuss that has been made about her. *Mais que voulez vous*—the gods and little fishes decreed otherwise.

There was a man in the Boyton costume of waterproof-armor, who paddled about in the water, smoking cigars, much to the delight of the crowd, and evidently not a little to his own satisfaction. I saw a fellow, who had been up to the start point, and he told me the excitement up by Snake's Hill was pretty lively. The Cornell, Harvard, and Columbia boys are on excellent terms. All the boats were thoroughly inspected before the start, and nothing was left unattended to. At ten o'clock the first gun was fired, and indicated that the final preparations were being touched off. My informant told me Cook looked ill at ease and nervous. Out by Snake Hill the water was so rough that it was at one time feared the race would have to be postponed, but presently this difficulty disappeared, and the wind blew toward the stand, a decided advantage. Meantime down by the grand stand anxiety and impatience joined hands, and the buzz of conversation and the shouts of "When do they start?" "Not off yet!" "They are off!" "No, they ain't" and "Yes, they are!" were becoming Babel like and confusion. The Madge, with Mr. Watson, the referee, aboard, kept somewhat back. The heat was not unbearable, although there were one or two cases of sun-stroke, and one very beautiful girl had a fainting fit, and was gallantly assisted by a number of the Harvard boys, who had to carry her away into the shade between them, which they did with enviable good grace.

The start was somewhat prolonged beyond the appointed hour, and some grumblers began to accuse the Saratoga hotel keepers of a plot to swindle them. But suddenly up went the little white flag, and in an instant everybody flew to their feet, whereupon everybody was as promptly ordered to be seated again, which order everybody, for a wonder, obeyed with surprising docility. Right opposite the grand stand was a machine, not unlike a gallows, upon which were fixed the numbers of the boats, attached to each of which was a string, so that as the boats advanced in the distance, we could follow their movements by simply watching the machine in question. Up went a figure; it was to indicate the first half mile, and underneath it presently appeared figures 12 and 2. "Harvard," shouted some; "Cornell!" others, Then up went number 9, and folks roared out, "Dartmouth!" In a little time, as the boats approached the excitement was so intense that the order to keep seated was utterly set aside, and people springing to their feet shouting and crying out in the most frantic manner. "I'll bet you, Alice, my gold bracelets, Columbia will win," cried out a young lady. "Very well, dear-agreed!" "Against your lace parasol, in case Cornell gets in first, " answered another belle. The Cornell boys, with their red and white hat-bands, were in a rare state of excitement, and when they saw their beloved boat come in so splendidly, with such a commanding and graceful lead, they could scarcely control themselves. Columbia began the last quarter well, but Harvard fell off. As the boats neared the shore the shouts increased and became positively frantic. At last they came closer and closer yet. Like arrows shot from some mighty bow, nearer and nearer yet they came, and the shouts grew more and more deafening. "Cornell! Cornell! Columbia! Columbia! Cornell!" cries the multitude, and the college boys leave their seats and rush like mad towards the press-gang. The Cornell boys shouted their new war cry, I am assured, for the first time on this occasion. It is as follows: "Cornell, yell, yell, yell Cornell," and in an instant the six brave victors were in their arms and on the shoulders of their brother students, and being carried round in triumph amidst tremendous hurrahing. And the girls, the lovely girls, beat their pretty hands together, and cried out, in ringing tones, "Well done, Cornell! Columbia! Cornell!" "They look like lovely gladiators, don't they, papa!" said a grand-looking girl nineteen, who stood close by me, and who, I'll wager, has Roman blood in the veins. As the men passed her by she clapped her jeweled hands together in an ecstasy, just as Julia or Dometia must have done, in days gone by, when they saw the triumphant gladiators carried around the Colosseum.

I am sorry to say that what had been predicted of Mr. Palmly came to pass. The poor young gentlemen was taken ill in the Princeton boat, fainted, and had to be landed. He is a magnificent-looking youth, and a brave fellow, who bore up like a young lion to keep a stiff upper lip under excruciating pain. He had not slept for three nights from the agony he suffered from a nasty felon. It would have been wiser to have given up at the beginning, still I admired, and I think everybody else did, his almost Spartan pluck. Dartmouth had a fine crew, and got along nicely, and was one of the surprises of the race, and kept ahead of the more scientific Yale—poor Yale, we all pitied her—but it seems decreed that pride must have a fall sometimes. Columbia captured "a crab" within five lengths of the line, but Prof. Van Amrige told me, later in the day, he was delighted with his boys, and well he may be, and proud of them too. The Professor was radiant, and the Columbia boys determined to entertain the Cornellians right royally in the evening....

The return home was not unlike the coming out, attended by much inconvenience in the way of getting vehicles. An almost interminable line of carriages of every description wound down the hill and up the next, towards Saratoga.

During the evening the "boys" got up a kind of procession, into which they pressed the services of a brass band, and which Columbia led off with her well-known shout of C-o-l-u-m-b-i-a, Harvard answering with her nine short barks of Rah-rah-rah-rah-rah etc., and Cornell joining in with Cornell-ell-yell-yell-Cornell! Of course, the Cornell boys are the lions of the hour. Everybody wants to see and shake hands with them. Saratoga is so crowded to-night you can scarcely move in the streets, and there is a perfect "carnival" of gay ribbons and streamers abroad. As I close this letter the sounds of the music of the various bands at the hotel, "grand hops" invite us forth to enjoy a scene of rare beauty. The moon shines down gloriously, riding through the serenest and bluest heavens. A thousand Chinese lamps deck the hotel fronts. Congress is a blaze of lights, and the porticoes of all the other hotels are filled to very suffocation with gorgeously-dressed women, and with men in evening dress. Jewels flash, bright eyes glance, light forms tread the mazes of the waltz, and the bands play vigorously their liveliest tunes. For an hour or so even the saddest hearts in all this great glittering crowd, which is here, will bury their griefs and troubles deep down and forget them, and some 30,000 people will for once seem happy and merry as a cloud of gay butterflies. It will be the very smallest hours before we shall have any sleep here....

OFFICIAL PLACE AND TIME OF THE RACE

Place.	Time.	Place.	Time.
1. Cornell	16:53 1/4	8. Brown	17:33 3/4
2. Columbia	17:04 1/4	9. Williams	17:43 3/4
3. Harvard	17:05 3/4	10. Bowdoin	17:50 1/2
4. Dartmouth	17:10 3/4	11. Hamilton	Not taken
5. Wesleyan	17:14 3/4	12. Union	Not taken
6. Yale	17:14 3/4	13. Princeton	Not taken
7. Amherst	17:29 3/4		

TYNE CREW OF NEWCASTLE, ENGLAND VS. PARIS CREW OF ST. JOHN, N.B. 1870

Professional rowing for both individuals and crews was extremely popular in both North America and England during these decades. In 1870 Robert Fulton of the Paris Crew of St. John, New Brunswick, Canada accepted a challenge for a four-oared race from the English champions, James Renforth and his teammates of the Tyne Crew of Newcastle, England. This description of this challenge is reprinted from The New York Clipper, 24 September 1870, pp. 193-94.

GREAT FOUR-OARED RACE

ARTICLES OF AGREEMENT between James Renforth and three others, forming the "Tyne Crew," of Newcastle-upon-Tyne, Eng., and Robert Fulton and three others, forming the "Paris Crew," of St. John, N.B., for a four-oared boat race at Lachine, near Montreal, Canada, in Sept. 1870.

It is mutually understood and agreed between the two crews and Lachine Boating Club, Montreal, as follows:—

1. That they shall row a four-oared race in the best boats each crew can get, on the St. Lawrence river, at Lachine, near Montreal, Canada, on the first day of Sept., 1870, the distance to be six miles (three up the river from Lachine and back again), for the sum of £500 and the championship. The St. John Paris Crew to row without a coxswain, and the Tyne Crew to have the right of rowing with or without one, as they may see fit.

2. The boats to start from points, buoys, or line, such point, buoys or distances on line to be not less than 30 yards apart, and to row a distance of three miles up river, where there shall be two stake-boats, and turn each boat its own stake-boat, being the one on its own side of starting, the turn to be made from left to right and back to the line of starting, such turning stake-boats to be 150 yards apart.

3. The race to be rowed as above stated, on the 1st day of Sept., 1870, at the hour of 3 o'clock P.M., if the water is smooth, the umpires to be the judges of the fitness of the water. If the state of the water is, in the opinion of the umpires, unfit for rowing a satisfactory race, the umpires shall be empowered to postpone the race from day to day until the state of the river is favorable.

4. One-half of the stakes to be deposited by each party in the hands of Mr. Henry Hogan, proprietor of the St. Lawrence Hall, Montreal, or at the Bank of Montreal, on the signing of these articles, and the remaining half to be so deposited not later than the 1st day of August, 1870. Either party failing to make such latter deposit within ten days of the specified time to forfeit the amount previously deposited.

5. The Tyne crew hereby nominate ________________ and the Paris crew nominate ________________ as their respective umpires for the race in question. A referee to be decided upon the day before the race by the respective crews; failing to agree upon a referee, the president of the Lachine Boating Club, Montreal, is hereby vested with the right of appointing said referee.

6. In consideration of the race herein provided for being rowed under the auspices of the Lachine Boating Club, the same club hereby promises and agrees to pay to the stakeholder, immediately after the final deposit by the Tyne crew is made, the sum of two hundred pounds sterling, on account of the expenses incurred by that crew by reason of their rowing at Lachine as aforesaid; the said sum to be paid to the Tyne crew on their arrival at Lachine.

7. The rules of rowing and other details of the race to be left in the hands of the Lachine Boating Club, who hereby undertake to arrange and carry out the same with perfect impartiality, and as efficiently as possible.

8. The referee, when appointed, will be fully empowered to settle all and every matter of dispute which may arise.

9. The two crews hereby bind themselves that whatever may be their present or future interests, neither crew will, prior to the first of September, 1870, consent to row a race during their absence from home in any point in the States or Canada (Lachine excepted) unless with the knowledge and approval of the Lachine Boating Club.

These articles were received about the middle of April, but were objectionable to the Englishmen in the matter of date of rowing, manner of turning the stake-boats and duties of the referee; consequently they were returned unsigned, accompanied by a note stating their objections and wishes. Fresh articles were then drawn up, the date being altered to Sept. 15th; the referee empowered, in case of disagreement between the umpires as to the state of the weather, to postpone the race until the first favorable day thereafter; the manager of the Ontario Bank, Montreal, made final stakeholder and the date of the second deposit fixed as Sept. 1st; a clause was likewise added, whereby the Lachine Club agreed to have the stake-boats moored, and the course staked out, fourteen days before the race....

The Course.

A better course could not have been found anywhere in Canada. The starting point was about one hundred yards distant from and on a line with the railway pier at Lachine, the boats to proceed up stream on a straight line along the north side of Lake St. Louis three miles to two stake-boats, moored one hundred and fifty yards apart, each crew to turn a separate stake-boat and return to place of starting. The main objection to this course lies in the fact that it is too much exposed, and as a consequence the water is frequently rendered too lumpy for racing in shell boats. The banks are low, the highway runs along the shore and the course is fringed with pretty little cottages. That disputes might be avoided in regard to the actual distance rowed, the course was carefully surveyed and a map of it made by Mr. A.J. Pell, of Montreal; the correctness of the measure can be vouched for. In order to prevent small craft from intruding upon the course and interfering with the boats, booms were stretched along either side of the course for the space of a mile or more, while the shallowness of the stream for the greater part of the track precluded the possibility of steamboats retarding the contestants. A great number of booths had been erected along the shore by persons having an eye to business, from which were dispensed edibles and drinkables, each and all driving a brisk trade during the festivities.

Special Rules.

On the evening of the 10th inst. a meeting of the Lachine Club was held, at which, with a view to ensure the utmost fair dealing, the following special rules for the government of the race were adopted, to be taken in connection with and form part of the agreement for the race in question:—

Rule No. 1. The racing boats shall start from anchored boats, the bows of such racing boats being in line—the stem of each boat to be held by parties duly appointed by each crew. The boats to be started at the word "go," being given after the regular and proper caution.

2. No fouling whatever shall be allowed. It shall be considered a foul when, after the race has commenced, either of the crews in any way whatever, either by oar, boat or person, comes in contact with oar, boat or any of the persons forming the other crew.

3. A boat shall be held to have a clean lead of another boat when the stern is clearly past the stern of that other boat.

4. It shall be held that a boat's own water is the straight or true course from the station assigned to it at starting to its own buoy; but if two boats are racing, and one fairly takes the other's water by a clear lead, it shall be entitled to keep the water so taken to the end of the course; and if the boats afterwards come in contact while the leading boat remains in the water so taken, the boat whose water has been so taken shall be deemed to have committed a foul; but if they come into contact by the leading boat departing from the water so taken, the leading boat shall be deemed to have committed a foul.

5. Judges to be appointed by the club to decide the finish of the race....

At the Course.

At an early hour in the morning the city of Montreal was astir, indicating that something more than usual was agitating its inhabitants. Colors were hoisted at various points, handbills and posters announced railroad and steamboat excursions to the grand regatta, and in many shop windows appeared photographs of the St. John and Tyne crews, taken in various ways, in their boats, grouped together, in-doors and out-doors, in racing costume and in citizens' dress. In addition the boys were offering them for sale at all the principal hotels and thoroughfares, until one was fairly surfeited with the cry "Tyne crew" and "Paris crew." The hotels had been filled for days previous, and the hospitality and good nature of the citizens of Montreal were taxed to its utmost to provide for the hundreds who were temporarily houseless and in want of shelter. The business men made a half holiday of the occasion, fully one-third of them closing their establishments, so that "all hands" could see the sport. The Grand Trunk Railway ran trains every hour from 8 A.M. to Lachine. Each train had two locomotives and temporary wooden cars, open and made from rough, unplaned wood, [illegible] and all alike, similar to the cars extemporized in England to carry their thousands to an international yacht, [illegible] or prize encounter. The road from the city to Lachine, one of the driest, dustiest and on this day one of the "hardest" we ever had the misfortune to travel, was one continuing stream of carriages, wagons and every style of vehicle, or rather, more truthfully speaking, it was a double—yes, a treble—stream. From 1 to 3 P.M., this movement continued, and upon arriving at Lachine, as there was only about three miles of a road from which the race could be seen, they were obliged to range themselves four and five deep. Between them and in front of them the spectators stood in a solid mass, and the gaily decorated stands were resplendent with "youth and beauty," the ladies being in the ascendant. From the Lachine dock a line of twelve or thirteen excursion steamboats were moored, including the Star, which was the judges' boat. All of these steamboats were filled to a degree looking dangerous. From two or three of them music was heard, and all of them contained masses of the lovers of boat racing. The number in attendance was variously estimated by different judges, but we think forty thousand a truthful estimate....

The Race.

A more anxious period than that which intervened between the drawing into line for this race and the dip of each crew's oars has never been experienced in the annals of boating in North American waters. There they sat, side by side, eight stalwart men, inviting and challenging the criticisms of the connoisseurs of grand physique and muscular development in man. If the St. John crew acted a little anxious and nervous, it may certainly be pardonable; and if the Tyne crew were the most collected, it must be remembered that they have participated in regattas and match races, in a country where they are of frequent occurrence, from their boyhood. Renforth answered the referee in regard to the turn, etc., with a ringing voice easily heard on the judges' boat. Fulton, for his crew, also answered distinctly. As Mr. Brady, the starter, uttered the word "Go!" the St. John men caught the water first, and for six or seven stokes their bow showed fifteen or twenty feet ahead. As soon, however, as the Tyne crew had applied their full power to their boat, she crawled up instantly upon the St. Johns; in a few seconds they were level, and quicker than we can write it they were leading their opponents. Every stroke now showed the advantage and superiority of their matchless and perfect oarsmanship. A quarter of a mile away the Tyne had the race by more than two lengths, and at a mile by four, and the race was virtually over. The three mile buoy was turned in 23:40 by the Newcastle crew and 24:20 by the St. John. On the home pull the Tyne crew rowed easily, dropping down to 35 or 36 a minute, while they started with 40. The Tyne crew came in winners in 40:59 3/4, without being pressed; the St. John followed in 41:30, being defeated by 30 1/4 seconds. The St. John men started with 45, afterwards came down to 40, and at one time in race rowed but 38. As the Tyne crew spurted splendidly past the judges' steamer, rowing at 42 to the minute, and their shell gliding on the water at a greater pace than it had been pulled at any time in the six miles, one prolonged cheer and ovation greeted them from every spectator on land and shore, and it is safe to say that they never experienced a more enthusiastic demonstration even in their own waters. The "Paris Crew" was also received with every demonstration of pride and sympathy, as, although defeated, they were far from being disgraced, having done all that men could do—their level best. As they finished, a very interesting incident of the race made its beautiful finale. The Tyne men backed water until they were side by side with the St. John men. Each drew their oars in and Renforth grasped Fulton's hand, each of the two crews followed his example, and they thus joined hands fraternally, proving that no animosity or prejudice had entered into the contest. Renforth then proposed three cheers for the St. John crew, and Fulton's crew responded with three hearty ones for the Tynesiders. The cheers which greeted this act showed how truly the thousands appreciated it. Soon after Renforth came on board the Star, and, with cap in hand, solicited a "trifle for the losers," saying he hoped no one would be offended for his introducing an "old country custom of always remembering the stern boat." In a few moments he collected nearly two hundred dollars. While engaged in this a gentleman expressed his wonder to Renforth at the easy defeat of the St. John men, especially as the latter were so confident. Renforth answered, saying, "Sir, without both sides were confident there never would be any test."

Remarks.

This race may be considered to have settled definitely the superiority of the long, sweeping stroke so much in vogue in England, both on the Tyne and Thames, and also popular in this country over the less graceful, less powerful and more exhaustive short stroke. The Tyne men recover quickly, reaching well forward and going far back; and throw the whole strength of arms, body and legs, making energetic use of the toe straps, into the long sweep of the oar through the water. It is not only a graceful and beautiful way of rowing, but its superiority was practically illustrated in the race, as it has been in many a contest before, and will be again, until the straight back, or arm stroke, is done away with forever. The friends of the St. John stroke have always claimed it to be better and more effective than the long stroke, relying principally for its effect by the help of the arms and body, with the latter almost perpendicular, when the stroke is suddenly finished to begin another. They rely upon the beginning of the stroke for its greatest work, and think that when the body is brought to an upright position the rower gives a more effective application of strength in commencing another, rather than throw the body back to a position where it has less power.... The contest, in the opinion of capable judges, demonstrated beyond doubt the superiority of the English crew, and convinced them that they can beat the St. John crew in any kind of water, or any other four on the continent. This is a humiliating confession to make in regard to a country so large as ours, and where such excellent facilities are offered for the development of skilful oarsmanship and the formation of first-class crews, but to the lack of interest manifested by those who have the means, and their reluctance to furnish the Sinews of war, is alone atributable the fact that the states are without a crew to represent them in a race with the champions of England. We have the material amongst us, if those who can would but take proper measures to organize a crew to uphold the honor of the Stars and Stripes. To the victors all credit is due for the brilliant triumph which they have gained, and which constituted them CHAMPIONS OF THE WORLD, while the vanquished deserve equal praise for the determined effort they made to avert disaster, and their magnificent struggle with the best crew which Old England ever produced....

NATIONAL ASSOCIATION OF AMATEUR OARSMEN, 1872

The formal movement to create a national organization for amateur rowing in the United States began in 1872, when William B. Curtis of the Chicago Athletic Club and James Watson of the Atalanta Boat Club of New York City published several pamphlets which addressed the issue of distinguishing between amateurs and professionals in athletics in general and rowing in particular. The printing of these pamphlets led to a call for a convention of oarsmen to discuss the question of amateurism, to elect a judiciary committee to decide disputed cases, to establish a national regatta, and to revise the laws of boat racing. On August 28, 1872 the delegates met in New York City and drafted the following definition of an amateur oarsman and code of boat racing laws. It is reprinted from The New York Clipper, 7 September 1872, p. 181.

DEFINITION OF AN AMATEUR OARSMAN.

We define an amateur oarsman to be—one who does not enter in an open competition, or for either a stake, public or admission money, or entrance fees, or competes with or against a professional for any prize, or who has never taught, pursued or assisted in the pursuit of athletic exercises as a means of livelihood, or has not been employed in or about boats, or in manual labor on the water.

CODE OF BOAT RACING LAWS.

1. All boat races shall be started in the following manner:—The starter, on being satisfied that the competitors are ready, shall give the signal to start.

2. If the starter considers the start false he shall at once recall the boats to their stations, and any boat refusing to start again shall be disqualified.

3. Any boat not at its post at the time specified shall be liable to be disqualified by the umpire.

4. The umpire may act as starter as he thinks fit. When he does not act the starter shall be subject to his control.

5. Each boat shall keep its own water throughout the race, and any boat departing from its own water will do so at its peril.

6. A boat's own water is its straight-course, parallel with those of the other competing boats from the station assigned to it at starting to the finish.

7. The umpire shall be sole judge of a boat's own water and proper course during the race.

8, No fouling whatever shall be allowed; the boat committing a foul shall be disqualified.

9. It shall be considered a foul when, after the race has commenced, any competitor by his oar, boat or person, comes into contact with the oar, boat or person of another competitor, unless in the opinion of the umpire such contact is so slight as not to influence the race.

10. The umpire may, during a race, caution any competitor when in danger of committing a foul.

11. The umpire, when appealed to, shall decide all questions as to a foul.

12. A claim of foul must be made to the judge or the umpire by the competitor himself before getting out of his boat.

13. In case of a foul the umpire shall have the power; first, to place the boats, except the boat committing the foul, which is disqualified, in the order in which they come in; second, to order the boats engaged in the race, other than the boat committing the foul, to row over again on the same or another day; third, to restart the qualified boats from the place where the foul was committed.

14. Every boat shall abide by its accidents.

15. No boats shall be allowed to accompany a competitor for the purpose of directing his course or affording him other assistance. The boat receiving such direction or assistance shall be disqualified at the discretion of the umpire.

16. The jurisdiction of the umpire extends over the race and all matters connected with it from the time the race is specified to start until its final termination, and his decision in all cases shall be final and without appeal.

17. Any competitor refusing to abide by the decision or to follow the direction of the umpire shall be disqualified.

18. The umpire, if he thinks proper, may reserve his decision, provided that in every case such decision be given on the day of the race.

19. Boats shall be started by their sterns, and shall have completed their course when the bows reach the finish.

20. In turning races each competitor shall have a separate turning stake and shall turn from port to starboard. Any competitor may turn any stake other than his own, but does so at his peril.

RULES AND REGULATIONS FOR NATIONAL AMATEUR REGATTA, 1873

The first regatta of the National Association of Amateur Oarsmen was held on the Schuylkill River, Philadelphia, in October, 1873. Races included singles, doubles, and four-oared shells. The following code of rules for those matches is taken from The New York Clipper, 19 April 1873, p. 18.

1. No clubs but those which have subscribed to the rules of boat racing and the definition of an amateur oarsman adopted by the National Convention, and have agreed to recognize the decisions of the judiciary committee thereon, shall be entitled to compete. Entries of individuals will not be received.

2. No club shall be allowed to enter any person who has not been a member of that club for at least three months preceding the regatta.

3. Any club intending to compete for any of the prizes must give due notice to the secretary of the regatta on or before the appointed day for closing the entries. Entries shall close two weeks before the date of the regatta.

In all cases of entries for four-oared races a list of not more than eight names, and in all cases of entries for pair-oared or double-scull races a list of not more than four names, shall be sent to the secretary, and from these names the actual crew shall be selected.

The name of the captain and secretary of each crew or club entering for any race shall be sent at the time of entrance to the secretary.

A copy of the entrance list shall be forwarded by the secretary to the captain and secretary of each crew or club so duly entered.

4. No assumed names shall be given to the secretary.

5. No one shall be allowed to be entered twice for the same race.

6. The Secretary of the regatta shall not be permitted to declare any entry nor to report the state of the entrance list until such list shall be closed.

7. Objections to any entry shall be made in writing to the secretary within seven days from the declaration of the entries, when the committee shall investigate the grounds of objection and decide thereon forthwith.

8. Entrance money for each boat shall be paid to the secretary at the time of entering, as follows: Four oars, $15; pair oars, $10; double sculls, $10; single sculls, $5.

9. All races shall be mile and half heats, straightaway.

10. A meeting of the committee shall be held immediately preceding the regatta, at which the captain or secretary of each crew or club entered shall deliver to the secretary of the regatta a list containing the names of the actual crew appointed to contend in the ensuing races, to which list the name of one other member may be added, who may be substituted for any one of the crew in the event of illness or accident, subject to rule 11.

11. No member of a club shall be allowed to be substituted for another who has already rowed in a heat, nor shall any member of a club be allowed to row with more than one crew in any of the heats for the same prize.

12. In the event of a dead heat taking place, the same crews shall contend again, after such interval as the committee may appoint, or the crew refusing shall be adjudged to have lost the heat.

13. In the event of there being but one boat entered for any prize, or if more than one enter and all withdraw but one, the crew of the remaining boat must row over the course to be entitled to such prize.

14. Heats and stations shall be drawn for by the committee in the presence of such competitors or their representatives as may attend, after due notice having been given of a meeting of the committee for that purpose.

15. An umpire shall be chosen by the committee, and his decision shall be final.

16. The judge at the winning post shall be appointed by the umpire, and his decision shall be final.

17. The laws of boat-racing established by the National Convention of amateur oarsmen shall be observed at this regatta, and the definition of an amateur oarsman established by said convention shall govern the qualifications of each competitor.

18. The prizes shall be delivered at the conclusion of the regatta to their respective winners, who, in case of a challenge prize shall receipt for the same as may be required by the committee.

19. All questions of eligibility, qualification, or interpretation of the rules shall be referred to the committee, and their decision shall be final.

SPECIAL CONVENTION OF THE NATIONAL ASSOCIATION OF AMATEUR OARSMEN 1876

The thorny question of what exactly constituted a proper definition of an amateur oarsman continued to occupy the officers and members of the National Association throughout the 1870s. In January, 1876 Col. A.F. Dexter offered the following definition and interpretation, which was unanimously adopted by the special meeting called to consider amendments to the constitution and by-laws of the Association. It is reprinted from The New York Clipper, 29 January 1876, p. 346.

An amateur oarsman is one who does not enter in an open competition; or for either a stake, public or admission money, or entrance fee; or competes with or against a professional for any prize; has never taught, pursued or assisted in the pursuit of athletic exercises as a means of livelihood, and whose membership of any rowing or other athletic club was not brought about, or does not continue, because of any mutual agreement or understanding, express or implied, whereby his becoming or continuing a member of such club would be of any pecuniary benefit to him whatever, direct or indirect; who has never been employed in any occupation involving any use of the oar or paddle....

The construction to be put upon this clause may be arrived at by supposing a case brought before the Executive Committee as follows: A suspected man is summoned to qualify himself as an amateur. He is asked: "Was the business position you occupy given you on condition of your joining that club and rowing in its crew?" "Will you probably lose that position of profit if you leave your club or refuse to row in its crew?" If he answers "Yes" to either question, he is self-convicted. If he answers "No" to both, and the committee cannot contradict his testimony, he is a genuine amateur. However, always supposing that the position of profit that the man occupies is one in which he gives honest work as full return for his salary. Outside of these requirements, clubs or individual members may render any acts of kindly service to their members.

EDWARD HANLAN VS. CHARLES COURTNEY, 1878

The contest between Edward Hanlan of Canada and Charles Courtney of the United States in October of 1878 excited sports enthusiasts in both nations. Hanlan, born in Toronto on July 12, 1855, was raised in an Irish household of moderate means. He first gained fame by winning at the Centennial regatta in Philadelphia in 1876. Courtney was born in Union Springs, New York in 1849. When he challenged Hanlan he was six years older, more experienced, and considerably heavier than his opponent. The following articles of agreement for the match are taken from The New York Clipper, 12 October 1878, p. 229.

ARTICLES OF AGREEMENT

Articles of agreement made this fifth day of September, A.D. 1878, between Mr. Edward Hanlan of Toronto, Canada, and Mr. Charles E. Courtney of Union Springs, State of New York, U.S.

1. The parties hereby mutually agree to row a five mile race, two and a half miles and return, in best and best boats, over a course to be mutually agreed upon at Lachine, province of Quebec, Canada, Oct. 2, 1878.

2. The race to be for $2,500 a side, $500 forfeit, to be posted with Gen. J.N. Knapp of Auburn, N.Y., as stakeholder, on the signing of these articles, and the balance of $2,000 a side to be posted with said J.N. Knapp on or before the day immediately preceding the day above mentioned; each party paying his own expenses; the first $500 posted to be forfeited in case the second deposit of $2,000 is not promptly made.

3. The stakes to be paid over to the winning party on the written order of the referee.

4. The referee, after preliminary warning, shall start the race by the word "Go," the boats to be held by their sterns, and started from boats anchored 50 yards apart.

5. The race to be rowed on smooth water, the referee to be judge of the same, between the hours of 3 and 6 o'clock P.M., and the referee may postpone the same from day to day, between the same hours, if the water is not in suitable condition to start the race.

6. The race to occur in accordance with the rules adopted by the National Association of Amateur Oarsmen, subject, however, to the conditions of these articles.

7. The referee in case of outside interference—if it affects the result of the race—shall order the men to row over the course on the first favorable day under the original conditions.

8. No boat or boats in the interest of either contestant shall accompany them on the course.

9. The referee to be James A. Harding, Esq. of St. John, N.B., and his expenses to be paid by the contestants in equal shares.

10. Paragraph 2 of Art. 19 of the said laws of boat-racing is suspended, and each competitor is to turn his own stakeboat.

11. This race is not to be rowed for, and is not to involve or affect, the championship of either the United States or the Dominion of Canada, now held by said Edward Hanlan.

12. It is hereby further and mutually agreed that the said Edward Hanlan or his representatives do hereby guarantee the sum of $5,000 in the form of a purse, and as much more as may be raised, for the purposes of said match. (Signed)

EDWARD HANLAN.
CHARLES E. COURTNEY.

J. MAUGHAN, JR.,
J.H. BREWSTER, witnesses...

[additional agreement, the closing clause in the above article canceled.]

This memorandum of agreement, executed in duplicate, between the Hanlan Boating Club of Toronto, now represented by the vice-president and secretary of said club, and certain members of the Lachine Boating Club, represented by the signatures of said members hereto, and certain citizens of the city of Montreal, herein represented by the undersigned citizens of Montreal, forming a committee of a large body of citizens, and herein acting also in their own behalf; Witnesseth—That said Hanlan Boating Club, in consideration of the sum of $1, receipt whereof is acknowledged, do hereby guarantee to the said Lachine Boating Club and the said citizens that a boat-race shall take place at Lachine, between Edward Hanlan of Toronto and C.E. Courtney of New York State, on or about the 2d day of October next, upon the following conditions: To be a five-mile race, for the championship of America. That the Lachine Boating Club and the citizens of Montreal to guarantee and they do hereby guarantee, unto the said Hanlan Boating Club the sum of $6,000, said sum to be delivered in a chartered bank in the said city of Montreal ten days before the said race shall take place, and to be payable to the order of the vice president and secretary of the Hanlan Boating Club, after the said race shall have taken place; and should the said race not take place within the first ten days of the said month of October, weather permitting, the money to be forfeited and to be refunded to the original subscribers thereof. It is hereby understood and agreed that the Hanlan Boating Club shall not enter into any arrangement with the said Charles E. Courtney for any subsequent race between the said Edward Hanlan and the said Charles E. Courtney until the present race is pulled.

Entered in duplicate by the said Lachine Boating Club and the undersigned members of the said committee of citizens at Montreal, this 10th day of September, in the year of our Lord one thousand eight hundred and seventy-eight.

J. MAUGHAN, JR., Secretary and Treasurer Hanlan Boat Club.
A. MCGIBBON, Chairman of Committee.
ARTHUR ROSS, Secretary of Committee.
R.H. SOUTHGATE
SAMUEL COULTON,
C.P. DAVIDSON.

A CANADIAN ACCOUNT OF THE RACE

The great race between Hanlan and Courtney was originally scheduled for October 2, 1878, but bad weather and rough water forced a postponement until the following day. The delay disappointed a large crowd which had gathered at Lachine on October 2, and the expectation of another postponement produced a smaller turnout of spectators on October 3. Hanlan's narrow victory in a controversial finish led to speculation in the American sporting press that the contest may have been fixed. But Courtney's managers and the Canadian press angrily denounced those allegations. This report of the race is reprinted from The Gazette (Montreal), 4 October 1878.

CALLING OUT THE CONTESTANTS

By this time, the wind had gone down, and the water was apparently smooth, quite smooth enough, thought Sheriff Harding, for the race. Five whistles followed sharply by five others were the signal for the oarsmen to come down. A tremendous cheer along the shore announced the satisfaction of the crowd, and after a time it was observed that Hanlan was in his boat just rounding Miller's Point, and paddling towards the starting buoy. He had arrived nearly opposite Courtney's quarters when the American sculler was observed stepping into his boat, and a few minutes later than Hanlan, he came paddling leisurely down the course. The appearance of the men was a signal for a burst of cheering, loud, long and continued, all along both sides of the course. At length the men reached the places assigned them.

THE CONTRAST

afforded as the two men sat side by side was widely commented upon. One a giant in frame and muscle—a hearty, generously-looking giant though, his muscles standing out like ropes; the other, small, lithe but sinewy, with a good-natured smile upon his face. Clearly it was to be a trial of skill and style as against muscle and weight, backed, too, by a fair style. Hanlan's colors were blue and red—a red band bound about his head and blue trunks and shirt. Courtney wore a white shirt, with a blue star on the breast, and white trunks.

THE RACE.

The men having paddled into their positions, Courtney's boat on the inside of the course was held by Mr. Bryster, Dave Ward, of Toronto, performing a like service for Hanlan at the latter's starting buoy. The referee, Sheriff Harding, in a loud voice, gave to the oarsmen the necessary instructions; then followed the caution, "Make your men ready, gentlemen," and almost immediately after came the warning, "Are you ready?" A slight hissing of steam, which for some reason could not be stopped, prevented the referee from giving, the next instant, the last command. The hissing was stopped for a second or two, however, and in this interval was heard the stirring tones of Sheriff Harding saying, "Go." The men took water at the same instant, and quick as thought the boats started on their journey. Courtney lead by a few feet, having obtained a trifling advantage by his strong stroke of thirty-five to the minute. Hanlan had not got off quite so well; his boat rocked a little, and once or twice, in the recover, he sent the spray flying in a manner that looked nervous. He soon steadied down to his work, however, rowing up to 31, while the strong stroke of Courtney sent a wash from each oar that exhibited its strength very forcibly. Hanlan, in the meantime, pulling a fine stroke alongside of his giant rival, apparently took matters very easily. A quarter of a mile from the start Courtney had a lead of five or six feet, but Hanlan had steadied down to this work, and not withstanding the power of Courtney's tremendous sweeping stokes, came on even terms with him, just off Whiskey Point. At the half mile he had collared him and was leading several feet, the signal flag announcing the fact from the boat stationed at the half mile. On they flew, each man apparently doing his level best, and the cheering which had started at the grand stand, and from the barges and other craft on the outside of the booms, deepened into a roar, as it was noticed that Hanlan was forging his boat ahead. Up to this time the course of both men had been directed in a straight line for the turning buoys, but, at this moment, the wind had freshened, and its effect on both boats was visible, driving them shoreward. For a time it seemed as if wild steering was to be the order of things, but Hanlan was alive to the emergency, and soon it could be seen that his oar was taking an outward course. He was now pulling 29 stokes to the minute, and as he passed Miller's Point, was leading by over half a length. Just here, the current, is, perhaps, stronger than at any other point on the course, and its effect was observable, checking, as it did, the speed of the boats to some extent. Passing Courtney's quarters, Hanlan had increased his lead to three-quarters of a length, and here a burst of cheering from Courtney's friends called upon the latter for a spurt. He responded admirably, going up from 32 to 35 strokes to the minute, and before two hundred yards were passed, he had cut down half a length of Hanlan's lead, while his strong stroke looked dangerous. The boats, by this time, had reached a point nearly opposite Hanlan's quarters, and in response to the shouts of his friends on shore, he hit her up to 31 strokes per minute. The Elliot shell responded to the stroke, and with surprising velocity Hanlan again shot to the front, so that before Courtney was aware of it, his rival had placed clear water between them. Turning quickly, Courtney again spurted, his stroke of 35 having meantime fallen to 31. He reached 34 strokes to the minute, but Hanlan held him pretty well in hand, and a quarter of mile was covered, ere they were again upon even terms. Meanwhile the men had entered the current immediately below Dixie Island, and the wind had freshened so that the water was very lumpy. Altering his course, Hanlan turned southward to take advantage of the lee shore of the island, tactics which had no sooner been inaugurated than they were observed and followed by Courtney. Dixie Island having been reached, to all appearance Courtney had a lead of half a length over his rival, and the shout went up from the press boat on all sides, "Courtney has got him," while shouts of 100 to 50 on Hanlan, 200 to 50 on Hanlan rent the air. The excitement was intense, as there could be little doubt that the American sculler had again attained a lead. It was not for a long time, however; Hanlan, looking over his left shoulder and seeing the position of affairs, spurted to thirty strokes per minute, the result of which was to bring him again upon even terms with the American. So they went neck-and-neck, along the lee of Bushy Island, along in the shadow of Dorval; but here though it could hardly be determined from the press boat how the men stood, it was observed that Hanlan at the two miles was leading—at least the signal at the two mile boat showed it. Now the men straightened away for the stake boats. Both had hugged the lee shore of the Island very closely, in order to take advantage of the eddy, and avoid the strong current which sweeps around the upper end of Dorval; the stake boats were in mid-stream, and each had caught the current in shooting out from the Island, both losing considerable ground in the operation. Away they went, the Americans on board the press boat shouting their jubilee, because Hanlan was apparently behind their man. Courtney had furthest to go to his stake, and he seemed to know this. A length and a half, at least, was what he lost by keeping under cover of the island, and it is hard to say whether the assistance of the lee shore made up for his divergence from the course. He had, however, evidently made up his mind to follow Hanlan, and he did. As the stake-boat was reached Hanlan went straight up a good length past it to avoid the current, and he turned, the crowd on the Gatineau cheering their delight. His boat was broadside before Courtney had commenced to turn, and six splendid strokes were all that were required for him to get around. He was fairly past his buoy and straightened away for home when Courtney's boat was seen broadside to the turning buoy. Cheer upon cheer greeted this; but it was not for very long. Courtney straightened away and a splendid stroke of thirty-five to the minute placed him again on even terms with his flying rival. Away they came, and when the press boat was reached—which had turned and was waiting for them—the pair were even, and they were cheered to the echo. The reason why Hanlan was so easily caught was not hard to discern. He had dropped his stroke to a leisurely twenty-five to the minute, and as we looked upon him going backward and forward in his sliding seat we well knew he was rowing a waiting race—that he had been quietly holding his man in hand all over the course. They sped on and the Gatineau followed. The three mile signal boat was reached, and when the men passed there, Courtney was pulling thirty-three strong strokes to Hanlan's twenty-seven and twenty-eight alternately, as the case required. So far as any fear of Hanlan losing the race now was concerned, it was looked upon by us as a certainty for him. Without apparent effort he dashed along, and Courtney ploughed away with his quick, strong stroke, but without doing more than keeping up with his antagonist. The pair came flying along, and had reached the three and a half mile point with precisely the same result as has been noted all along. On nearing the close of the fourth mile, and just off Courtney's quarters, a cheer from the friends of the latter called for more work from the American sculler, and he rose to thirty-six strokes to the minute. To those who had not watched Hanlan closely the stroke looked very dangerous. We had no fear of it, however. Courtney drew up even with Hanlan and they were so close upon one another at the end of the four miles that it was impossible to say who was ahead. Hanlan on reaching the boat, however, shot his shell a trifle in advance, and in a second or two the red flag of Hanlan was floating in token of his premier position. Cheer upon cheer burst from the shore, was caught up on the grand stand and re-echoed from the long line of barges and steamers. Courtney was working away, and a look through the glass showed that he was still possessed of tremendous power. Whether it was through wind and weather, through water, or through some other mysterious agency, he could not get a better place than second. So this terribly fast pace continued up the course to the finish. Now they were reaching the last stage of the race. Who was going to pass the four a half mile signal post first? Courtney appeared to have a slight lead just before reaching it, and we were prepared to see the colors of Courtney this time. But no. There it flies again. "Hanlan's colors for ever," as some one shouts close to our ear. But the men are out of their course. Where are they going to? "Steer in shore, Hanlan," "You are out of your course, sir," is shouted from all around, and the cheering is tumultuous. The men have no time to listen to anyone now. They are upon the last stage of the race. Courtney is aware that his chance is now or never, and he shows that there is some stuff left in him yet, and from thirty-two he pushes up to thirty-five to the minute—the last time he reaches it. He has not shot his bolt, but sticks to Hanlan, and so closely that the latter is forced out of his course. Should he keep on he will run into some of the vessels which line the outside of the course. No sort of shouting will make the men see their error, and we just look to see Hanlan's boat get stove, when he looks over his shoulder, sees his error and pulls with a dozen powerful stokes to the front. Then he crosses the bow of his rival, who seems dazed by the cheers which are ringing around him. Hanlan still steers across the bow of Courtney's boat, and speaks to him. Will Courtney keep on and foul him? There is some fear of that. But no. Courtney just in time sees the error of his course and slows up to avoid running into the Toronto sculler, who pulls in a winner of a very close sculling race. Time, 36:22. Courtney paddles over to Hanlan and shakes hands with him. Then the crowd cheer themselves hoarse, and Hanlan is carried away by his friends, while Courtney paddles back to his quarters.

SWIMMING

WOMEN AND SWIMMING

Proponents of physical fitness had long argued for female participation in such athletic activities as calesthenics, horseback riding, and archery. The following editorial, which makes the case for women's participation in swimming, is reprinted from ***Beadle's*** *Dime Guide to Swimming* (N.Y., 1869), p. 27.

A CHAPTER FOR THE LADIES.

Shall females, old and young, learn to Swim? is a question which it is time was put to every person who has a sister, wife, or daughter. It has so long been the prevailing idea that woman is a helpless thing, fit only to ***depend*** upon the "stronger sex," that he has been characterized a petticoat prophet who claims the ***right*** of woman taking care of herself. At the risk of being called such a prophet we not only claim, but ***demand*** her right to learn how to preserve her own life and the lives of others. It is not only an act of humanity, but of solemn duty for woman to learn how to sustain herself in the water; while it is simply her right to enjoy the daily swim, the dive, the "spree in the water," with as much freedom as the male. It should be thought right and proper for females to practice swimming in any fit place; and he who denies them this right is simply arrogating to himself more of the prerogative of a censor than it is his right to exercise. Let any female who desires to learn (and we hope the day is not distant when every female in the land will be expected to learn the humane and diverting art), seek every opportunity to try the water of creek, river, lake, or pond—in company with others of her sex, or with some male friend who has the right to exercise a care over her. The dress, we have suggested to be adopted...will render it no breach of propriety or decorum, will not cause a start to the most modest, to appear in it before males; but even that suggested may be modified to suit the tastes of all. Equipped in the dress there is *no exposure* of person; and no female should hesitate to resort freely to bathing and swimming grounds.

FEMALE COMPETITION IN NEW YORK CITY, 1870

The following piece shows clearly that in New York City there were several skilled female swimmers who did not shy away from strenuous competition in front of a mixed audience. It is taken from The New York Clipper, 1 October 1870, p. 203.

SWIMMING RACES BY WOMEN.—The Public Free Bath, at the foot of Charles street, North River, N.Y., was quite the centre of attraction on the afternoon of the 21st of Sept., as it was generally known that there would be several contests between some of the female swimmists for prizes given by the lady superintendent, in a public exhibition in which both ladies and gentlemen would be present. The first race was for a silver caster, for which there were two contestants, namely:—Miss Mary Hane Hill and Susan Waters; both looked to be about 30 years of age, good looking, and very muscular in appearance. Miss Hill got a good start, and rapidly drew ahead of Miss Waters, who, however, soon overtook her opponent, and a neck and neck race took place to the stake ladder, which Miss Hill was the first to turn; the race back to the starting place was still more exciting, both the ladies being exceedingly close together until the end of the bath was almost reached, when Miss Hill made a spurt and won by a length. The second race was for a set of jewelry, for which there were five contestants. The race was very exciting, and furnished much amusement. Anna Price, Lucy Fisher and Catherine Underwood being the chief contestants; each one displayed much skill and knowledge of the art, and, after a close contest, Miss Price was declared the winner. Next followed several short races between the younger swimmers, and diving from elevated positions, some of the young ladies jumping from the roof of the bath—a distance of twenty feet—in fine style. At the close the prizes were distributed by the lady superintendent, the fortunate winners returning thanks to her for her courtesy and kindness to all who frequented the bath.

INTERNATIONAL SWIMMING MATCH, 1875

Given the precedents in cricket, horse racing, boxing, and boat racing, it was only natural to expect that Americans and Englishmen would also compete against each other in international swimming challenges. In 1875 J.B. Johnson of England, recognized as champion of the world, journeyed to Philadelphia to race against a local hero, Thomas Coyle of Chester, Pennsylvania. This account of the triumph of the visitor is reproduced from The New York Herald, 23 July 1875, p. 3.

THE GREAT SWIMMING MATCH

PHILADELPHIA, July 22, 1875

The great swimming match between J.B. Johnson, champion of the world, and Thomas Coyle of Chester, thirteen miles straight away for $1,000 a side, took place this afternoon at Gloucester Point. Fully 10,000 people lined the shores in hopes of witnessing the finish. At Chester, where the start was made, at least 5,000 people watched the contest. The river during the whole contest was covered with boats of all sizes and kinds, from the large barge to the smallest skiff, decked with flags, presenting a beautiful scene of brilliant color and animation, but also threatening to interfere with the race by crossing the course of the contestants. Nothing occurred to mar the race, however, and although the representative of America was naturally the favorite, the Englishman received the fairest of fair play.

After a long delay both men were seen undressed, except as to swimming drawers, on board the steamtug Amanda Powell, lying at the wharf at Chester. The crowd hooted and cheered, the tugs blew their whistles and crowded about the pier at which the Powell stood, and swarms of small craft were in everybody's way. There was some dispute between the men as to which boat the start should be made from, and Johnson objected to what Coyle wore on his leg as a preventive of cramps. This proved to be a piece of oiled silk tied with eel skin, and Johnson repeated his objections, and the wrapping was removed. At about half-past one, after a prolonged shouting and giving of orders by all sorts of authorized and unauthorized persons, the tugs and small boats were finally sufficiently cleared out of the way to permit of a reasonably good start. Johnson's judges were Dr. Thomas Steinagel, of New York, and James Gadsby, of Philadelphia. They were to follow Coyle in a small boat. Coyle's judges, Dr. J.L.M. Forward and Mr. Thomas Berry, were in a small boat, the Hannah Moulder, with the referee, Mr. Edward McGettigan, of Philadelphia, and they were to keep up with Johnson, to see all fair. Two steamboats, dozens of tugboats and smaller craft were on hand containing thousands of people. Many well known sporting men were among the gathering, among them Billy Edwards, Arthur Chambers, O'Baldwin, the Irish giant; Harry Hicken, Frank Gormley and others. A new agreement had been drawn up between the men by which the termination of the race was fixed at Gloucester Point instead of Philadelphia. It was also agreed, on Coyle's earnest protest, that the private boat to follow each man, containing the judges, should not approach nearer than five yards; that it should never lead him, but always follow, and that no other boat should come nearer than fifteen yards. Coyle did not insist on his original demand that each man should exhibit his hands and feet every twenty minutes to guard against the use of swimming stockings or other propelling contrivances.

THE START.

The two men plunged into the water at 1:45, Arthur Chambers and Frank Gormley acting as starters. A fair start was had, and both touched the water at the same instant. Johnson immediately went to the front, keeping to the left or Pennsylvania shore. Coyle took a course toward the easterly side or Jersey shore. He struck out with a strong stroke, and in three minutes was ahead of his adversary, swimming thirty-five to the minute. Johnson headed for the western channel, with a steady stroke of twenty-five to the minute, Coyle making for the outside or eastern channel. Johnson followed from the first what is called the inside channel, between Chester Island and Tinicum Island and Lazaretto. This is shallow water and said to be full of whirls and eddies. Boatmen say that the water here is very bad, and that the tide turns an hour sooner than in the main channel or that followed by Coyle. Johnson swam almost continuously on his right side, turning occasionally to this left. He was followed closely by a small boat containing the trainer, a pilot and a man pulling the boat. As the start was made the British ensign was hoisted astern, but was hauled in again as Coyle forged ahead, and was seen in the lead later in the race. Coyle was piloted by Captain Rudder, a Chester man, who is said to have a better knowledge of the river and its tides than almost any other waterman. About fifteen minutes after the start the men lost sight of each other around the point of Tinicum Island, Coyle, apparently, twenty yards ahead. Johnson kept close in toward the Pennsylvania shore. Three-quarters of an hour after the start Johnson was opposite the Lazaretto pier, four miles from Chester. At four o'clock he had gained the lighthouse, nine miles from Chester. He changed his course to the northeasterward, having passed Chester Island, Tinicum Island and the Two Sisters; and, having clear water to Gloucester Point, Coyle was then about a half mile ahead; and Johnson, upon learning this, quickened his stroke.

COYLE WEAKENS.

Meantime Coyle, although ahead, had gradually slacked his pace and began showing the signs of distress. When asked how he felt he replied, "Badly," and his boat kept close alongside. A steamer came by him and some excursionists began cheering. This gave him momentary encouragement and strength, but he was plainly fogged out. His face was whitish-blue and he looked pale and tired. At fifteen minutes past four he showed such manifest exhaustion that he was dragged on board the boat with his pilot. At this time he was opposite Red Bank, ten miles from Chester, having swum this distance in two hours and a half. Coyle had refused to take anything to drink but water up to within a few minutes before he gave out. Johnson had been drinking a small glass of whiskey at intervals of about ten or fifteen minutes during the race.

COYLE'S FAILURE.

The news of Coyle's failure was brought to Johnson within a few minutes after its occurrence. The men were at this time half a mile apart, and owing to the swarms of crafts of all kinds with which the river was covered, it was impossible to see what had taken place. The news gave him great encouragement and, amid the cheers of the spectators, Johnson shot ahead with some wonderfully strong hand over hand strokes, which gave him such an impetus that he shot forward with an astounding spurt. By this time the tide had turned and was just beginning to run down stream. Gloucester was about three miles away. At 4:55 the referee deciding that

JOHNSON HAD WON

the race by distancing his competitor, he was taken on board his boat, the steam whistle screeching a salute and the crowd cheering. He did not seem, by outward signs, the least fatigued, and expressed himself as willing to continue the race if the referee desired. When he was taken on board he had swam about ten miles and a quarter in three hours and ten minutes.

A great deal of money changed hands on the result, Johnson being the favorite.

YACHTING

JAMES ASHBURY'S CHALLENGE FOR THE AMERICA'S CUP

In 1868 James Ashbury began an extended correspondence with the New York Yacht Club in which he tried to extract the best possible terms for his challenge for the America's Cup. The letters involved complex negotiations more appropriate for legal, diplomatic, or commercial affairs than for a sporting event. Ashbury was newly rich, the son of an inventor and manufacturer of railway carriages. Ambitious, aggressive, and filled with pride, he hoped that winning the America's Cup would earn him great fame and high social status among the British elite.

When Ashbury made his first challenge the New York Yacht Club had recovered from membership losses suffered during the Civil War. It also had new leadership by men of more recent wealth than the founding fathers of the antebellum era. Yachtsmen such as James Gordon Bennett, Jr. were more audacious and aggressive than their predecessors. They were more than a match for Ashbury as they parried his demands and schemed to force him to accept terms that would insure that the Cup remained in their possession. This letter from Ashbury, a member of the Royal Thames Yacht Club, to the President of the New York Yacht Club, October, 1868, is reprinted from Roland F. Coffin, *The America's Cup* (N.Y., 1885), pp. 25-28.

SIR:—As the owner of the English schooner-yacht *Cambria*, which some time ago won the race around the Isle of Wight against the American Schooner *Sappho* and three crack English vessels, I cannot but regret the accident to your representative vessel; and also my inability to have remained in England to again race her round the Wight or across to the coast of France. I am now on a cruise along the coasts of Portugal and Spain, etc., a journey which I postponed at great inconvenience in order to give me the pleasure of being courteous to the extent of allowing me to enter against so splendid a vessel as the *Sappho*, the property of American gentlemen; and I am in hopes this communication will show the owners of the *Sappho* that they may probably have an opportunity of again testing her qualities against the *Cambria*, and in American waters.

All Englishmen believe that, taken as a whole, the art of yacht building received a great stimulus by the acknowledged victories of the *America*, in 1851, and now equally hope and believe that the leading English yachts can hold their own against the world; but, America excepted, there are no yachts which we think stand any reasonable degree of success against our vessels of the last few years. All yachtsmen, as well as others, duly appreciate the compliments your New York Club have paid us, by, from time to time, sending vessels over to this country; and it is a source of much regret on this side the water that those compliments have not been reciprocated by any leading yacht club deputing [?] one or more of their crack vessels to go to New York waters for racing purposes.

So much do I feel on this subject, that I proposed to one of the leading clubs last winter to send to New York an invitation for two or three or more vessels to come over in time for the races at Cowes and Ryde this year, and then for several of our leading yachts to sail them back to New York; and, in order to tempt our friends over here, I proposed that special subscriptions should be solicited from each member of a yacht club, wherewith to form a large fund for giving splendid prizes, irrespective of what the clubs might give. At the meeting in question, I offered to subscribe any sum up to £500, and to enter the *Cambria* for the return race to New York. I mention this in no egotistical spirit, but simply to show that I desire to fairly test the merits of my vessel against those of America in rough as well as smooth waters. Unfortunately, this arrangement could not be carried out, as most of the owners generally leave off yachting after the Wight races for grouse and partridge shooting, or to go abroad.

Before my yachting time, your schooner *America*, in 1851, had the honor of winning the Cup presented by Her Majesty to the Royal Yacht Squadron, and I am led to believe that the New York Yacht Club (or the winner) have in the most friendly and courteous manner offered the Cup in question to be sailed for in New York waters, to any English yacht which will compete for it. It is an esteemed honor for any Englishman to win at any time "the Queen's Prize"; but I venture to think no one would be so much valued as the one so triumphantly taken away in '51 by the *America*; and subject to conditions which I hope will be deemed equitable and reasonable to all concerned, I now have the pleasure to ask you to kindly state to your committee that I am disposed to challenge all America for the possession of the Cup in question.

Firstly. I propose that during or before the season of 1869, the New York Yacht Club select their champion schooner, of a tonnage not to exceed 10 per cent. of the Thames measurement (188 tons) of the *Cambria.*

Secondly. The vessel referred to, I would desire to see arrive in England in ample time to take part in the matches of the Royal Yacht Squadron at Cowes, and the Royal Victoria Yacht Club at Ryde, for which races she would, doubtless, be permitted to enter. These races take place early in August, six to eight or nine in number, round the island (60 miles) the Victoria and Queen's courses (also about 60 miles), and probably a run to Cherbourg and back; the prizes would be the annual Queen's Cup presented to the R.Y.S., two cups of £100 each from the towns of Cowes and Ryde, and several cups of £100 and £50; and I may add, that if the yacht could arrive about a month earlier, she would be in time for some of the best ocean races of the Royal Thames Yacht Club.

At these races your representative would meet all the best and fastest English and Scottish yachts; among others, schooners, and would have a fair opportunity of testing her qualities during the height of the Isle of Wight yachting season, and with the temptation of many prizes, highly valued, and much sought after, but not for their mere intrinsic value.

Thirdly. On or about the 1st of September I would race your vessel from the Isle of Wight to New York, for a cup or service of silver, value L250, no time allowances, and no restriction as to canvas or number of hands.

Fourthly. I would at an early date race the said vessel round Long Island, on the R.T.Y.C. measurement and their time allowances; two races out of three over this course to decide as to the championship and the final possession of the *America's* Queen's Cup of 1851; if lost I would present the N.Y.Y.C., or the owner of the successful vessel, with a cup value 100 guineas, or, I would race any other schooner of about my tonnage over the same course on the said conditions; the competing vessel to have been previously pronounced by the N.Y.Y.C. as the fastest vessel in America of her size and class, and providing the said vessel had not been built since the date of this communication, and was in all respects a sea-going vessel, and not a *mere shell or racing machine*.

ANNOUNCEMENT OF THE FIRST AMERICA'S CUP CHALLENGE, 1870

The first challenge for the America's Cup matched Ashbury's *Cambria* against a fleet of vessels representing the New York Yacht Club. This selection is an announcement of the event which appeared in The New York Clipper, 13 August 1870, p. 146.

The contest for the "America" cup, now held by the New York Yacht Club, will come off on Monday, August 8th, at 10 o'clock, A.M. A flag-boat will be anchored abreast of the club house, Clinton, Staten Island, about mid-channel. The yachts will anchor on an east and west line, 500 yards to the northward and westward of the flag-boat, and about 50 yards apart. In taking position in line, each yacht may select its own in the order of its arrival at the anchorage, subject to any change that the Executive Committee may deem expedient. A steam-tug will be in attendance to enable the yachts to assume their proper positions in line. Main sails, foresails and gaff-topsails may be set before starting, unless otherwise ordered by the committee.

The signal for starting will be one gun from the committee's steamer to prepare, and a second to start. Yachts will proceed from west and south, and thence to the Light Ship, rounding it to the northward and eastward, and return over the same course, passing to the west of the flag-boat of the club house, going and returning. Going and returning, all the buoys on the west bank, viz:—Nos. 13, 11, and 9, are to be passed to the eastward. Entries will be received until Saturday, August 6th, closing at 10 A.M., precisely. They must be directed to the Secretary of the club, and delivered at his office, No. 46 Liberty street, New York.

W.H. MAJOR,		MOSES H. GRINNELL,	
SHEPPARD HOMANE	Ex. Com.	W.B. DUNCAN	Judges.
STUART M. TAYLOR		ALEX. HAMILTON, Jr.	

The committee feel themselves imperatively called upon to enjoin most emphatically upon all vessels present on the occasion, whether steam or canvas, most scrupulously to avoid any interference, either directly or remotely, with any of the vessels engaged in the race, giving to all a "clear field and a wide berth," and in view of our national instincts for "fair play," that the representative vessel of the Royal Thames Yacht Club, the Cambria, should have no cause whatever to complain of an unfairness, or unnautical interference in this respect.

H. Morton, Secretary

LETTER FROM JAMES ASHBURY TO THE NEW YORK CLIPPER, AUGUST 9, 1870

James Ashbury wrote this letter to the editor of the New York Clipper the day after the race. In it he offers an explanation for his defeat and he issues a new challenge to his American rivals. It is taken from the Clipper, 20 August 1870, p. 155.

In the first place I desire, through your medium, to express to Commodore Stebbins and the committee generally, my best thanks for the able and impartial manner in which they organized and arranged the race for so splendid a fleet, and at the same time to confess my surprise at the marked manner in which the steamers and cruisers kept clear of the competing yachts; not that I ever doubted their intention to do so, but with the best feeling for "fair play," so engrafted in Americans as a body, I could scarcely hope that the course would be so entirely free, bearing in mind the incredible number of craft conveying an excited and interested public naturally anxious to secure the best view.

I had the honor yesterday to officially represent the Royal Thames Yacht Club, and I much regret that there were no other English yacht owners engaged in the race, to witness the most remarkable sight in the annals of yachting, and such as no pen could describe or any painter portray. As you can well understand, I am deeply sensible of the splendid demonstrations, receptions and hospitality afforded to me as an English yacht owner. The honored compliments so bestowed will, I am sure, be accepted in England as an evidence of American good feeling to sportsmen and Englishmen in general, and the recollections of which no time can efface from a grateful memory.

It is not my intention or desire to say anything controversially, or which can in any degree detract from the great success of the Magic, Dauntless and other yachts; still I cannot admit that the New York Yacht Club course is one of the best suited to test the capabilities of sea going yachts, any more than I believe a race across the Atlantic will settle which is the fastest and most weatherly vessel. Thanks to the great courtesy of the committee, the Cambria had the choice of positions; but, nevertheless, she made a bad start to leeward, fouled two or three times, consequent on other vessels not giving way when on the wrong tack, carried away the foretopmast (by the breaking of the stay) at a critical time, &c. With a fair start, no fouls and no mishaps, I still consider the Magic would have been the winning vessel; the Cambria, however, would have been very near the next vessel in.

Either through your columns, or direct to the Commodore of the New York Yacht Club, I shall at my earliest convenience issue invitations for races twenty miles dead to windward and back, outside Sandy Hook lightship or other open courses, and I hope to see such challenges respectively accepted by all the yachts which came in yesterday before the Cambria, viz:—Magic, Dauntless, Idler, America, Phantom, Madgie and Sylvie, as also by the Fleetwing, Palmer, Alarm, Vesta, Sappho, Tidal Wave, Tarolinta, Josephine, Halcyon, Rambler and Widgeon. The conditions will, I think, be considered equitable, seeing I shall be prepared to race under the rules of any royal yacht club in Great Britain and Ireland, or those of the New York Yacht Club. The *resume* of such various races would, in my opinion, better settle the question of superiority of American *versus* English yachts than any number of races on the Thames, inside the Isle of Wight, the New York Yacht Club course or across the Atlantic.

In conclusion, permit me to say that I think the winner of so important a race should have some record or souvenir to show he was the victor in a magical manner, especially so seeing he cannot take the cup so ably won, and I would respectfully suggest to the committee that an entrance fee of five or ten pounds should be paid by the owner of each vessel which raced and, with the proceeds a cup could be presented by the club to the popular, spirited and fortunate owner of the Magic. Yours truly,

JAMES ASHBURY

GEORGE L. SCHUYLER'S INTERPRETATION OF THE ORIGINAL DEED

George L. Schuyler was one of the founding members of the New York Yacht Club in 1844. He played a key role in the arrangements for the construction of the yacht *America* in 1851. In 1852 he drafted a letter in which the syndicate which had won the trophy offered by the Royal Yacht Squadron in 1851 presented it to the New York Yacht Club. In 1871 he wrote the following letter to explain his interpretation of the meaning of critical phrases in the original deed of the America's Cup. It first appeared in The Spirit of the Times, 15 April 1871, pp. 130-131. In 1881 the New York Yacht Club returned the Cup to Schuyler and requested that he revise the original deed. The following year he returned both the Cup and the revised document which contained more explicit terms to govern the international competition for this special yachting trophy.

At the meeting of the New York Yacht Club, when the correspondence with Mr. Ashbury in regard to his challenge for the possession of the America's Cup was considered, I listened with some surprise to the construction placed upon the word "match" in the letter of the owners of the America presenting the Cup to the club, viz., that all the vessels belonging to the squadron had a right to start against the challenger in the race; and with still more to the conclusion arrived at, in declining to accept Mr. Ashbury's terms, not to make a counterproposal, and that he should be required to fall back upon his right "to sail over the usual course of the annual regatta of the yacht club in possession of the Cup."

I have frequently been urged, as the sole survivor of the five gentlemen who presented the Cup to the New York Yacht Club, to make some statement as to their understanding of the word "match" as used by them in the letter of presentation; but my notion of what is due to my club associates in regard to any matter settled by their proceedings at a full meeting has precluded me from doing so until now.

Some time in March the Treasurer of the club called my attention to a legal opinion he had procured from Mr. Peet, and which he had published in THE SPIRIT OF THE TIMES of March 18. As this proceeding by authority of an executive officer of the club opens the question again for discussion, not only by the club, but publicly, I feel at liberty to publish some statements in regard to this subject.

In the first place, it seems to me there is nothing in the letter itself which justifies the construction put upon its terms by the members of the club....

If, after the preamble, the first condition had been written thus: 'Any organized yacht club...may claim the right of sailing a match for this Cup *against any one yacht or vessel* with any yacht or other vessel of not less than thirty nor more than three hundred tons,' etc., there could, of course, be no question whatsoever as to the meaning; but I still think such additional words would have been unnecessary and superfluous.

When the word 'match' is used in horse-racing or kindred sports without any qualification, it means a contest between two parties—and two only. If A offers to run his horse against B's horse for $1,000, and this offer is accepted, it is a 'match'; but if C desires to participate by entering his horse and by putting up his thousand dollars, the match becomes a 'sweepstakes.'

The same rule applies to yachts. The *Vesta* and *Fleetwing* made a match for a large sum to sail across the Atlantic. When the *Henrietta* was admitted into the contest it became a 'sweepstakes.'

A match may be qualified in terms—as, for instance, A may match his horse or yacht to beat two of B's horses or yachts. A match between two cricket or baseball clubs means one side against the other side; but the cardinal principle is that, in the absence of all qualifying expressions, 'a match' means one party contending with another party upon equal terms as regards the task or feat to be accomplished.

This general definition of the word 'match' is confirmed in its applications to the tenure of the America's Cup by legal opinions and corroborating testimony of experts in sporting matters.

It is true that Mr. Peet, in his published opinion, says, in conclusion: "Therefore I express with confidence my opinion that Mr. Ashbury has no right to claim a match against a selected one of our fleet"; but his "therefore" follows from an argument based upon the facts that the words "with any yacht or other vessel" refer to the challenger, and not to the challenged—an assumption which, as far as I know, no one has ever denied or ever questioned. From these mistaken premises, however, Mr. Peet infers that the donors of the Cup certainly meant that "just as we with our yacht America sailed against a fleet, singlehanded, you must with one yacht sail against us single-handed"—and if that was not their meaning they are convicted of stupid blundering—*a reductio ad absurdum,* as he calls it, which ought somewhat to surprise those who were familiar with the keenness in sporting matters which characterized such men as John C. Stevens, Edwin A. Stevens, and Hamilton Wilkes.

It is also proper for me to state that opinions adverse to my view were procured from Mr. Belmont, and from the President of the Saratoga Racing Association, Mr. W.R. Travers. Neither of these gentlemen, however, answers the question (if it were put to them) as to the accepted meaning of the word "match." Mr. Belmont says that in his opinion the conditions "authorize the New York Yacht club to compel any vessel which wished to compete for that Cup either to sail against a champion yacht selected for that purpose by the club, or against the entire yacht squadron of the New York club." But if permitted to start their whole squadron in a race, it is difficult to see how the club would be justified in risking the event on the performance of a single vessel. Mr. Travers concludes by saying emphatically: "I am of opinion that every yacht in the squadron has a right to sail in the match."

On the other hand, Judge Blatchford, of the United States District Court, in his written opinion, sums up as follows: "It would be a departure from both *the letter* and *the spirit* of the deed of gift for such club to insist that the challenging party shall sail the match against more than a single yacht."

Mr. E.H. Stoughton, a lawyer of distinction in New York, has written an opinion in which he gives the same interpretation as Judge Blatchford to the meaning of the word "match" in this letter of presentation. His opinion is endorsed by Judge Comstock, late Chief Judge of the Court of Appeals in this State, and by Judge Edwards Pierrepont of New York city.

The NEW YORK SPIRIT OF THE TIMES, considered as perhaps the highest authority on sporting matters, in an editorial article on this same subject (April 1), in which the Editor comes to certain conclusions as to the *intentions* of the donors of the Cup (which, perhaps, may be modified when he reads what I have presently to say on that subject), defines the word "match" as follows: "The whole difficulty, it appears to us, has arisen from a failure to grasp the sense in which the deed uses, and properly uses, the word 'match.' In ordinary language, 'sailing a match' means sailing between two vessels only—as the ocean match the Cambria and Dauntless; and it would not be proper to say there was an ocean match between the Henrietta, the Fleetwing, and the Vesta. In the latter case yachtsmen such as the Messrs. Stevens were would say 'race,' not 'match;' so that if Mr. Ashbury is going to sail a '*match*' for this Cup he has a right to sail against a single vessel."

And this definition of the word "match" is sustained by all yachtsmen "such as the Messrs. Stevens were," as well as by turfmen of the same period with whom I have conversed on the subject.

I now pass to the intentions of the donors.

In reply to a note from Commodore Stebbins of March, 1870, I said; "I can state with certainty that all the signers of the letter to the New York Yacht Club presenting the Cup won by the America in 1851 considered the word 'match,' in connection with the conditions proposed by them, as meaning that but one vessel could start against the party challenging for the possession of it." Although I repeat this assertion without any qualification, yet so much has been said and written as to what our intentions were,—or rather, ought to have been,—that I feel desirous of placing upon record some matters connected with the America's cruise in 1851, which had much to do with the conditions upon which it was determined by us to offer the Cup to the New York Yacht Club as a challenge cup...

...the America went to England for the purpose of sailing a *match,* if one could be made on satisfactory terms after her arrival; and that at the time her keel was laid (I speak for myself positively, and with great confidence for my associate) we did not even know that a cup, to be sailed for at Cowes open to all nations, had been offered by the Royal Yacht Squadron....

[The next part of this letter describes the victory of the yacht *America* in the regatta sponsored by the Royal Yacht Squadron.]

I think any candid person will admit that when the owners of the *America* sat down to write their letter of gift to the New York Yacht Club, they could hardly be expected to dwell upon an elaborate definition of their interpretation of the word 'match,' as distinguished from a 'sweep-stakes' or a regatta; nor would he think it very likely that any contestant for the Cup, upon conditions named by them, should be subjected to a trial such as they themselves had considered unfair and unsportsmanlike.

In the numerous articles which have been published concerning this letter, great weight is given to the circumstance that its preamble sets forth the conditions under which the Cup was won by the America.

As an argument, either as to the intention of the donors or the terms of the gift expressed in the body of the letter, this preamble, or any other which might have been inserted, is entitled to no consideration....

It seems to me that the present ruling of the club renders the *America's* trophy useless as a 'Challenge Cup,' and that for all sporting purposes it might as well be laid aside as family plate. I cannot conceive of any yachtsman giving six months' notice that he will cross the ocean for the sole purpose of entering into an almost hopeless contest for this Cup, when a challenge for love or money to meet any one yacht of the New York Yacht Squadron in any fair race would give him as great a triumph, if successful, or if his challenge were not accepted, as his heart could desire. If the ownership of the *'America's* Cup' depended upon the result, it would add greatly to the interest of the match; but the absence of that inducement would scarcely compensate for the long odds of sailing against the whole fleet.

In making this statement I do not intend to controvert the right of the New York Yacht Club to determine what interpretation attaches to the conditions of their acceptance of the Cup. That question must be determined by the meaning of the instrument itself as it stands, and not by referring back to what was intended by the parties who signed it. Mr. Ashbury's intimation of a resort to legal rights in a matter of this kind can hardly be seriously entertained.

I have availed myself of the opportunity afforded by the authorized publication of Mr. Peet's legal opinion to dispel the idea that the conclusion now arrived at is at all in harmony with the intentions of the donors of the Cup. In doing so I have only discharged what I consider a duty to my associates and myself.

ASHBURY'S LETTERS TO THE MEMBERS OF THE NEW YORK YACHT CLUB, 1871

Mr. Ashbury's determination to force his case on the officers of the New York Yacht Club is clear from these excerpts from his letters written prior to his second unsuccessful challenge in 1871. They are reprinted from Roland F. Coffin, *The America's Cup* (N.Y., 1885), pp. 52-54, 48-49.

June 15, 1871
James Gordon Bennett, Jr., Esq.,
Commodore N.Y.Y.C.

DEAR SIR:—The stipulated notice having been waived, the several clubs will shortly send you the necessary certificates for the *Livonia's* match and some in October. Agreeably with the intimation contained in my telegram of the 16th June, I now beg to inform you that twelve royal or recognized yacht clubs have honored me with certificates of representation not in any degree as indicating that I am the owner of the champion schooner of England, but as a conveyance of one of the stipulations in the deed of gift....

Strictly by the deed of trust six months' notice is required, which I was not in a position to make until the *Livonia* had been in several races or trials, inorder that I might know if her sailing and weatherly qualities were at least equal to those of the *Cambria*. Having come to the conclusion that she might ultimately beat the *Cambria,* I decided to enter for the 1851 Cup; but inasmuch as six months' notice would bring me in January, when I knew American yachts would be laid up, I had no desire to appear asking anything unsportsmanlike, or that you should specially file out your representative, or, I may say, champion vessel. The club having elected to accept it in lieu of January, the *Livonia* will leave for New York September next, and on arrival she will forthwith be prepared for the races.

I propose leaving on or about the 23d of September, and shall lose no time in paying my respects to the commodore in order to discuss as to the course and days most convenient for the series of races under the rules of the New York Yacht Club.

I admit the right of the New York Yacht Club to send any yacht they please for any or all races; but inasmuch as centre-board yachts are not admissable in England, I am satisfied that a powerful centre-board yacht would generally be looked upon as not being a fair test against a sea-going keel yacht. The New York Yacht Club possesses many large racing keel yachts of about the same size or larger than the *Livonia.* I therefore suggest that the club fix on one as near as possible the same size as the *Livonia.* As regards the course for the series of twelve races, for which certificates are herewith inclosed, I must be allowed to object to the New York Yacht Club course as not, in my judgment, being a fair course for a foreign yacht, and I therefore propose that we sail from a mark-boat off Sandy Hook Point three times round the Sandy Hook Lightship and back, the club having the power to modify the course. I feel there will be no difficulty in confirming this suggestion or arranging one on my arrival to the satisfaction of all concerned. The committee to be informed by the club to fix beforehand the days on which the several races shall take place; and if the *Livonia* should win the majority of races, the Cup would then go to the Club under whose flag I sailed in the last and final race, and would be held by the commodore *ex-officio* until won by some other royal or recognized yacht club in England or elsewhere.

August 12, 1871

Mr. COMMODORE AND GENTLEMEN:—In August, 1870 I had the pleasure of competing for the Cup of 1851 in American waters under the Royal Thames Yacht Club flag, consequent on having been honored with their certificate of representation in conformity with your club requirements. On giving my formal challenge, I claimed that a champion or representative vessel should be sent against the Cambria as a true and sporting interpretation of what I believed the deed of trust justified. The New York Yacht Club, by a vote of 18 to 1, ruled that a fleet should compete, and not a single vessel. I entered the race for sport, and with faint hope of winning; but in the firm belief that the club desired to put a faithful interpretation on what may then have been looked upon as a vague and uncertain document, I did not deem it necessary or courteous to sail under protest, but I sailed with the fixed determination of again reopening the controversy after having discussed the matter with my yachting friends in this country and taken eminent opinions as to the legal view. It is not now necessary to trouble you with the such opinions, inasmuch as Mr. Schuyler's letter of the 15th April, in the New York Spirit of the Times, has already specified what he believed the intention of the donors to have been, and after such a statement it was no surprise to me to find the New York Yacht Club unanimously passing a resolution whereby the important question at issue is finally disposed of to my satisfaction and that of the yachting world generally. If, however, the former vote had been confirmed it was still my intention to have taken the Livonia to New York, but under no circumstances for a single race, which might have been won or lost by a fluke, but for as many as I might have certificates for, taking care to see that each club only gave the necessary six months' notice.

It was in view of having again a fleet to meet which caused me in a speech at the Harwich dinner to say that I claimed as many races as I might possess certificates....

Chapter 3

BASEBALL

During the 1860s and 1870s baseball became the national pastime of the United States, and it also established itself as one of the leading recreations of Canada. The New York City version of the game (invented by the Knickerbocker Base Ball Club in 1845) completed its rout of both townball and cricket to claim its privileged position as the most popular team sport in North America. The American Civil War retarded the sport's progress in North America, but after the return of peace in 1865 a baseball mania swept across the continent.

Baseball's phenomenal surge in popularity during the next half decade generated a host of problems. Its startling success forced clubs, state organizations, and the National Association of Base Ball Players to adjust to new conditions and face new issues. Feature contests for local, state, regional, and even national championships stimulated mass excitement but also brought increased commercialism, professionalism, gambling, and crowd disorders, along with frequent hints of corruption involving betting rings and the bribery of players. While many lamented the passing of the old (more innocent) order of the prewar years, others proposed a variety of reforms to cure the ills of baseball. Despite the efforts of those who wished to retain the simplicity and idealism of the amateur era, baseball's future clearly belonged to commercialism and professionalism. The new sport was fast becoming a big business, tied to the booming economies and political machines of urban America in the Gilded Age. The 1870s witnessed the first professional leagues: the National Association of Professional Base Ball Players (1871), and the National League of Professional Base Ball Clubs (1876). During this period Canadian enthusiasts organized numerous clubs and held championship competition. By 1880 baseball was flourishing on both sides of the border.

In the spring of 1861, baseball players in dozens of American cities and towns prepared their minds, bodies, and grounds for another brilliant season of play. But the news from Fort Sumter, South Carolina, sent shock waves throughout the sporting world. The beginning of four terrible years of hostilities had important short- and long-term repercussions for baseball. Thousands of northern club members volunteered for service in the Union army, while a few enlisted in the Confederate cause. The sportsmen who marched off to war took their love of play (and sometimes their bats and balls) with them. Military authorities permitted recreation for soldiers at appropriate times and places because it supplied diversion and proved useful. To enjoy their games, baseball players improvised makeshift grounds, constructed rudimentary equipment, and arranged contests both in camp and perilously close to enemy positions. Both the Massachusetts and New York versions of ball were played, and the men arranged pickup games within their own regiments or challenged rival units from their own or other states. Generally they competed within the relative security of their encampments, though sometimes they violated army regulations and played outside the fortifications and beyond the line of pickets.

While baseball enthusiasts enjoyed their favorite sport in army camps, the game suffered some understandable setbacks on the homefront. With so many sportsmen marching off to war, and with civilian anxieties focused on battlefield news, interest in playful contests waned. Proof of the disruptive effects of the war on baseball was evident in the disbanding of many clubs, the reduction in the number of first-nine contests, and the drop in attendance at the annual conventions of the National Association of Base Ball Players.

Baseball nonetheless persisted and even progressed under trying conditions. The New York style of play gained momentum in New England when a tour by the Brooklyn Excelsiors excited Boston's sporting fraternity. In Philadelphia baseball overtook cricket in popularity during the early 1860s. Near the end of the ordeal the nation's capital experienced a baseball revival, thanks in part to resident New Yorkers who worked in the Treasury Department and played for the National and Union clubs on the grounds at the rear of the White House. In the South the conquest of New Orleans brought baseball back deep into Dixie, while in the West a contingent of "Rocky Mountain Boys" played the "New York game" in Denver in 1862.

As before the war, the Middle Atlantic region was the center of baseball fever. New York, New Jersey, and Pennsylvania inaugurated the sport's first championship system as well as several intercity all-star contests and club tours. The early 1860s also ushered in an era of commercialism and professionalism, while the National Association of Base Ball Players (NABBP) continued to supervise interclub play and experiment with the rules of the sport. During the war the New York style of play continued to gain ground over its New England rival. The "Massachusetts game" still remained quite popular among army men, but on the homefront the NABBP rules predominated. New York-style baseball also increased its presence in Canada during these years. In 1864 the Young Canadians of Woodstock met the Brooklyn Atlantics for "the championship of the American continent," at the Rochester (N.Y.) State Fair. The Atlantics crushed the foreign challengers, yet the event sparked interest in Ontario.

After an initial setback baseball generated a surprising amount of enthusiasm during the war era. The main events of the 1861 season were the championship contests between the Brooklyn Atlantics and the New York Mutuals, as well as a "Silver Ball" all-star game between select nines from New York City and Brooklyn. The next year witnessed great excitement over a championship series between the Atlantics and the Eckfords, the net proceeds going to the Brooklyn Sanitary Commission, earmarked for sick and wounded soldiers. The most striking evidence of baseball's capacity to flourish amid the adversity of war occurred in Philadelphia. The first invasion of Philadelphia players into the New York vicinity took place in 1862, as a select nine competed before about 15,000 spectators in a series of games against teams from Newark, New York, and Brooklyn. Picked nines from Brooklyn and New York returned the visit later in the summer, generating excitement in their contests with the local Olympics, Adriatics, Athletics, and Keystones. By the end of the war, trips by Brooklyn, New York, and New Jersey clubs to the City of Brotherly Love were commonplace, with some benefit matches arranged for the United States Sanitary Commission. These tours succeeded despite the atmosphere of crisis that pervaded the entire region. In most cases the war did not detract from the excitement of the contests, and there is very little evidence that citizens disapproved of men who played ball rather than fought.

While baseball clubs kept the sport alive during the nation's ordeal, the NABBP struggled to survive and to govern the game's growth. The annual December conventions in New York City experienced a sharp drop in attendance as many clubs disbanded and others did not send delegates. Local clubs dominated these meetings, which accomplished little during the first two years of the conflict. But in 1863 and 1864 the conventions addressed a series of significant issues, acting on important rule changes and on the eligibility of players to compete in recognized interclub matches. These sessions demonstrated the continuing vitality of baseball in the New York area and suggested the spirit of experimentation and the fluidity in rules that characterized early American baseball.

The 1863 meeting approved changes in pitching regulations that were designed to shift the balance of play toward batting and fielding. The primitive style of underhand slow pitching prevalent in the 1850s had given the advantage to the batter, but during the early 1860s the hurlers became more expert in swift (and often wild) deliveries. The NABBP acted to "transfer the interest of the game from the pitcher to the fielders" with new regulations that confined the pitcher to a small space, forced him to deliver "fair balls" to the batter (with the umpire empowered to declare a walk after three called balls), and required him to release the ball with both feet on the ground. (Umpires already had the authority to call strikes on a batter who refused to swing at good pitches.) The new rules were passed to produce slower but more accurate pitching, and to promote more scoring, better fielding, and more enjoyable games. In 1863, after many years of debate and defeat, the fly rule was finally adopted, eliminating a putout from a ball caught on one bounce. This, too, was meant to encourage better fielding, but of course it also gave the offense added advantage.

The return of peace in the spring of 1865 ignited a new baseball boom, as the passion infected players of both sexes and all ages, races, and levels of skill. From the rocky coast of Maine to the golden Gate of California, a baseball mania swept the land. Yet few if any promoters of the national game could predict the fantastic success or the host of difficulties it would experience over the next half decade. The season of 1865 began a new chapter in the sport's history. The same forces that had fueled its prewar developments fed its expansion during the late 1860s. As before, personal contacts (now enriched through military service), the press, interclub competition, urban rivalries, regional tours, and state and national organizations all contributed in varying degrees to new rounds of baseball excitement.

Baseball historians have stressed the importance of the army experience in popularizing the sport after the Civil War, and it is true that the pastime remained a favorite recreation among soldiers stationed in the West and South after 1865. However, many players who enjoyed baseball before the war but never served in the military helped to promote the sport in the cities to which they relocated after the conflict.

National, regional, and local newspapers and magazines also gave an enormous boost to baseball, as publishers, editors, and reporters appreciated the intimate connection between the fortunes of the new sport and the prospects of their respective publications. Before the war, detailed coverage of the game appeared only in the New York City sporting weeklies, such as The New York Clipper and the various versions of the Spirit of the Times. The first document in this chapter is a description of an early system of scoring baseball games, which was devised by Henry Chadwick. Beginning in 1865, family publications such as Harper's Weekly and Frank Leslie's Illustrated devoted more space to feature matches and leading players. City dailies and Sunday papers began to expand their baseball reporting, as a few editors who were prominent officers of ball clubs used their positions to popularize both their teams and their papers. The reciprocal relationship between baseball and the media included the use of the telegraph as well as newsprint. With public excitement at fever pitch for major intercity contests, crowd besieged newspaper and telegraph offices for the latest results.

While participants and press sang its praises after 1865, intercity competition provided most of the excitement that fanned baseball fever. Traditions of local pride, urban rivalries, and city boosterism spurred hometown clubs and newspapers to seek glory for their nines and communities. Quaint country villages, modest settlements, burgeoning upstart towns, small cities, and giant metropolises all competed for unofficial championships at local, state, regional, and national levels. The New York City area still claimed to be the baseball capital of the United States, and its sporting journals boosted local teams even as they claimed to be impartial in their reporting. Winning nines could propel quiet country towns and sleepy villages into the limelight, especially if they defeated or fought a close battle with celebrated metropolitan teams. State fairs and groups of sporting entreprenuers organized many baseball tournaments during the late 1860s to capitalize on the new mania. Popular in the Midwest, they often brought together nines from small and large towns and cities, as well as some rural teams. A few offered prize money or gifts to entice crack clubs from the East to seek more fame and fortune further west.

Urban boosterism contributed to the baseball boom, especially in such midwestern cities as Chicago, Cincinnati, and St. Louis, where competition for railroads, commerce, and industry was mirrored by these cities' baseball teams. Chicagoans were obsessed with dominating local and distant rivals in baseball and everything else. When the Cincinnati Red Stockings swept eastern and western honors in 1869, the people of Chicago were distraught by the success of the club from "Porkopolis." Leading businessmen funded a new club, the White Stockings. The city's sporting community went wild with joy in September of 1870, when the home town team triumphed over their arch-rivals from Cincinnati.

While these regional rivalries popularized baseball, intersectional matches accelerated the national growth of the sport. Once the eastern clubs began a series of long-distance tours via railroads and steamships, western and southern nines followed suit. The Cincinnati Red Stockings' 1869 tour to California via the newly completed transcontinental railroad was the most ambitious and successful of all, as they capped an undefeated season with lopsided victories in the San Francisco region. Baseball competition also had an impact on North-South relations immediately after the Civil War. Some observers viewed the revival of baseball in the border and southern states as a positive force in reuniting the nation. Northern and southern journalists believed that the postwar tours of the Nationals of Washington, D.C. and the Athletics of Philadelphia would help to heal the bitter wounds of war.

As baseball enthusiasts, journalists, and touring nines spread the gospel of the new pastime across America, national, state, and local sports organizations attempted to guide the game's growth. The New York City-based NABBP acted in a number of ways to recognize and encourage regional and national expansion. It voted to rotate the annual meeting site among several cities, including Philadelphia (1867), Washington, D.C. (1868), and Boston (1869), making its conventions accessible to more players and clubs. It also elected officials from a variety of cities in a conscious attempt to broaden representation. In another move toward regional and national expansion, the NABBP shifted its system of representation from individual clubs to state associations, allowing one delegate for each ten clubs in the state bodies. It did permit a few individual clubs to send delegates if their states lacked a formal association.

At the regional and state levels, clubs joined together to standardize rules, regulate competition, sanction championships, debate issues, and instruct delegates to the national meetings. Advocates of the formation of state associations believed that they would serve many needs of ball players and clubs, especially in arranging games and resolving disputes. These associations struggled to establish themselves as thriving bodies, but most of them only enrolled a small fraction of all baseball clubs in their jurisdiction. Apathy plagued their efforts to organize, while their annual gatherings were increasingly marred by interclub disputes and dissatisfaction over professionalism, commercialism, and corruption.

The national and state asssociations tried to enlist large numbers of white clubs while excluding black nines that were eager to join. Although the latter often shared playing fields and enjoyed good relations with white teams, they were denied equal representation in baseball gatherings, as they were excluded from Reconstruction era politics in the North. The 1867 NABBP convention flatly refused to admit clubs with black delegates, and state meetings followed the same segregationist policy.

The growing enthusiasm for baseball in post-Civil War America was tempered by the problems of an evolving sport and a strong backlash from journalists, businessmen, professionals, and religious leaders. Parents worried about the influence of the new sport on their children. Many businessmen and journalists remained deeply suspicious of the compatibility of baseball and commercial, industrial or professional careers. Many men of influence supported baseball playing in moderation but warned against excessive involvement that could distract a person from the practical obligations of life. Several daily and weekly newspapers warned against "Base Ball dissipation," and Baltimore and New Haven passed ordinances restricting the sport.

Championship competition at many levels brought out both the best and the worst in postwar baseball. Club rivalries within cities, states, and regions certainly raised the standard of play and stimulated enthusiasm among players and spectators, but these special contests also produced much ill will and controversy, in part because of the unofficial nature of the titles. Custom dictated that whichever nine won two out of three games from all of its rivals earned a championship. In the absence of any strong governing body to regulate challenges, resolve disputes, and designate a winner, controversies multiplied. While a few state and regional associations did attempt to regulate championship play by establishing rules to govern competition, for the most part these efforts failed to reduce or eliminate the problems that plagued title matches.

Emotions intensified when clubs from rival cities played for the honor of being called the champion club of the United States. The most heated competition during the period from 1865 to 1870 involved the Brooklyn Atlantics, the Philadelphia Athletics, the New York Mutuals, the Morrisania (Bronx) Unions, the Cincinnati Red Stockings, the Troy (N.Y.) Haymakers, and the Chicago White Stockings. In 1868 Frank Queen of the New York Clipper offered a gold ball as a prize for the champion club of that year. But the competition for the Clipper trophy did not turn out as Queen expected because of the difficulties of designating a winner. Queen and many others concluded that the NABBP or the top clubs should adopt rules to govern championship matches, but the national conventions of these years refused to establish a system to determine a champion for the United States.

Championship matches attracted large crowds throughout the 1860s, and it is not surprising that spectators would pay to see their favorite nines compete. The commercialization of baseball followed naturally from the long-accepted practice of charging admission fees for popular amusements in general and sporting events (such as horse racing) in particular. During the 1860s there were several ways of establishing a baseball business. The first involved capitalists who enclosed and improved a ground, which they offered rent-free to clubs in exchange for the right to charge an admission fee.

William H. Cammeyer inaugurated this practice in 1862 when he drained his winter skating pond for summer baseball and opened the Union Grounds in Brooklyn's eastern district. His success prompted Messrs. Weed and Decker to follow his example. They converted their skating facility into the Capitoline Grounds in Brooklyn's western district in 1864. After the war a few entrepreneurs across the country organized all-star contests, charity events, or tournaments, offering prize money to the participating clubs and charging spectators to see the action. A few clubs, like the Athletics and Olympics of Philadelphia, tried a third method of commercializing baseball when they purchased their own field, built a fence, and set an admission fee for matches.

Proponents of commercialized baseball pointed to several advantages of enclosed fields and admission fees. Some were alarmed at the disappearance of suitable playgrounds in the cities as the postwar building boom gobbled up empty lots. They urged clubs to acquire a permanent ground and to collect gate receipts on match days to defray the expenses of purchasing and maintaining it. This new system increased the chances that feature contests would be played on a field clear of spectators, with fewer problems with crowd disturbances. It also raised the caliber of competition. Commercialism also facilitated charity and benefit contests, with all-star and feature club matches raising money for orphans, southern war refugees, victims of mining disasters, and other needy people. Charging an admission fee restricted attendance to those who could pay, although people from the poorer classes still came to the grounds and congregated outside the fences. Critics of rowdy spectators applauded that result of commercialism.

In addition to stabilizing club finances, raising the caliber of play, and reducing crowd disorders, commercialism in baseball also stimulated professionalism. Clubs that owned their own field spent a portion of their income to hire players, while others negotiated with park proprietors for a percentage of the gate receipts so they, too, could begin to pay players. (Clubs that collected gate receipts but refrained from paying participants still claimed to be amateur.) Regrettably, the attraction of admission fees offered a powerful incentive for a team to win the opener of a series and then lose the second game in order to increase excitement (and gate receipts) for the deciding third match. The tendency of commercialism to foster both professionalism and corruption was clear by the late 1860s, as the leading clubs sought to strengthen their first nines by recruiting—and paying—skilled players.

During the 1860s participants and journalists debated the merits of professionalism. Despite the NABBP's ban on payment to participants, before and during the Civil War such premier performers as James Creighton and Al Reach accepted some form of compensation, including gifts, jobs, or direct payments. Certain organizations also staged annual benefit contests, with the gate receipts distributed among the contestants. After the war the sporting weeklies and daily papers were reporting that several clubs were subsidizing a few players through one means or another. Defenders of the new system justified it on the grounds that ball playing was a legitimate occupation and workers deserved remuneration for their toil. They did not see anything wrong with businessmen or politicians trying to promote their favorite nine or town by retaining athletes. According to this way of thinking, as long as a player was loyal to his club and avoided gambling or taking bribes to lose a match, he should be free to receive both pay and respect.

But critics had grave doubts about the new trend. Some players and club officials initially opposed paying players because they feared that the wealthiest clubs would monopolize the best players and thereby destroy competitive balance. Moreover, most lovers of baseball still thought of the sport as primarily recreational. To them it was a means of escape from business worries, a healthful diversion from the business of life. But professional baseball required a scientific approach, much practice, and an emphasis on victory—all of which would transform baseball into a rigorous discipline and thereby render it unacceptable to those who, raised in a puritanical tradition, were deeply suspicious of turning play into serious work. There were also worries that professionalism would accelerate the disturbing trends toward gambling and corruption that had already appeared among the amateurs. Many observers believed that paid players would inevitably become the tools of gamblers.

The advent of professionalism accelerated the trend toward open recruitment of players, as clubs that aspired to championships tried to acquire the best talent. Although many frowned upon this practice, the flagrant raiding of lesser nines by the most powerful teams became commonplace during the late 1860s. An NABBP rule prohibited multiple club memberships and required that a man wait thirty days after he resigned from one club before joining another. While many honored this restriction, others resorted to subterfuge to circumvent it. Violations of the thirty-day rule became a heated issue by 1867, when several clubs acquired new men from other nines and played them immediately in contests that they declared were merely "social" or "exhibition" games as opposed to formal matches. Importing outsiders tended to reduce club loyalty as well as solidarity.

The practice of players jumping from one club to another, which was known as the "revolver" system, had other negative consequences. First, it diminished the opportunity for regular members to compete on their club's first nine. Second, the raiding of certain clubs knocked them out of the ranks of contending nines. The "revolver" system hurt teams that would not or could not spend the money to keep their best men.

By the spring of 1869 professional baseball had come of age, with at least ten clubs compensating part or all of their first nines through one means or another. In the New York area these clubs included the Mutuals, the Eckfords, the Atlantics, and the Unions; they were joined by the Philadelphia Athletics, the Unions of Lansingburg, New York, and the Baltimore Marylands in the East and by clubs in Chicago, Pittsburgh, Cincinnati, Fort Wayne, and Columbus, all of which experimented with hired players. Earnings from gate receipts and salary probably netted participants on the better nines anywhere from $600 to $1,500 a year.

The professional baseball fever took hold in Cincinnati during the late 1860s. In that city a local booster and a transplanted New Yorker combined to create the first all-salaried team with players under yearly contracts. The Cincinnati Red Stockings, reorganized in 1867 by Aaron B. Champion and group of lawyers and businessmen, shared a grounds lease with the city's Union Cricket Club and had a bitter rivalry with the local Buckeye nine. Determine to outshine his competitors, Champion raised $26,000 over two years to improve the grounds and sign players. Thanks to successful raids on several eastern clubs and the Buckeyes, the Red Stockings fielded a team in 1869 that featured many of the best players in the United States. Its manager, Harry Wright, trained the nine that would become baseball's first legendary team.

Champion's investments and Wright's recruitment and training of his players paid handsome dividends on the field and at the box office. During the 1869 season the Red Stockings demolished their eastern rivals and rolled up victory after victory on extended tours across the country. The final triumphant trip to California climaxed a summer and fall that featured fifty-seven victories, one disputed tie with the Troy (N.Y.) Haymakers, and no defeats. The Red Stockings traveled nearly eleven thousand miles by rail and steamboat and performed before nearly 180,000 spectators. The squad began the 1870 campaign with twenty-seven victories before losing an eleven-inning thriller to the Atlantics, 8-7.

Championship contests, hired players, "revolving," and professional nines aside, there was one unwelcome trend that threatened to destroy early baseball just as it was passing through its adolescence: gambling. Journalists, clergymen, and advocates of Victorian values condemned the widespread wagering on first-class matches, which both reflected and fed the baseball mania of the late 1860s. These critics believed that it was intrinsically immoral to bet on a ball game; that it corrupted an innocent amusement and was the major cause of crowd disorders and bad feeling among clubs. Editorials in dozens of daily and weekly periodicals warned that gambling was tarnishing baseball's reputation and dragging the sport down to the level of boxing, horse racing, or even blood sports such as cock-fighting.

For promoters of the national pastime, the greatest threat to the integrity of the sport was the fixing of matches by gamblers and bribed players. In 1865 a special investigating committee of New York's Mutual club accused William Wansley of splitting one hundred dollars with two teammates, Edward Duffy and Thomas Devyr. The three men were subsequently expelled from the club but all were reinstated over the next few years. While this incident remains the only documented example of a fixed contest during this period, there was much suspicion that many matches may have been lost intentionally. The sporting and daily newspapers of the late 1860s are filled with speculation that the Atlantics, Athletics, Mutuals, and other prominent teams sometimes dropped games to set up a third, deciding contest, which would bring higher gate receipts and more bets. Some people charged that these clubs sold games outright for the benefit of gamblers' rings. But since the outcome of these contests was so uncertain, and since it was so difficult to obtain proof of wrongdoing, the extent of corruption was never clear. Yet despite these reservations about the negative consequences of gambling, there were some commentators who downplayed its supposed ill effects. They argued that gambling on baseball added to the excitement of the competition and was no different than risking money on the stock market.

In 1869 and 1870 the increasing problems of the new system of commercial and professional baseball forced many sportsmen to reevaluate the latest developments. They expressed dissatisfaction with the escalating expense of player contracts and the growing evidence of "revolving," the specter of gambling and corruption, the loss of playing opportunities for regular club members, interclub ill will, and an emphasis on championship matches. Club officers and members had to decide whether the gate receipts and fame earned by a paid nine were worth the costs and the headaches, or whether their organization should return to the simpler recreation of early amateur baseball. Some organizations either resisted the temptations of commercialism and professionalism or briefly flirted with them before returning to the old ways. The

Brooklyn Excelsiors and the Philadelphia Olympics stopped paying players after the war and were satisfied with amateurism. The revolt against professionalism also reached Cincinnati, when the officers of the powerful Red Stocking club shocked the baseball world with their announcement that the team would not use hired players for the 1871 season.

With professional baseball's problems on the rise, and as more clubs stopped hiring players, the sporting fraternity attempted to define precisely the differences between professional and amateur ball playing. Delegates to state and national conventions debated the merits of formally separating the two. Those who supported the idea of paying players believed that if professionalism were openly endorsed, many of its abuses could be eliminated.

Tensions between proponents of professionalism and amateurism increased throughout the late 1860s and climaxed at the meeting of the NABBP in November of 1870. The delegates voted against a resolution that condemned professional baseball. That action prompted a withdrawal of the amateur contingent. The Brooklyn Excelsiors, the Knickerbockers, and over thirty other clubs from several eastern cities then convened in Brooklyn in March of 1871 to found a new amateur association. Delegates adopted the 1867 constitution and 1870 rules of the NABBP, endorsed dividing the baseball fraternity into two classes, and prohibited amateur clubs from playing against professionals. The one issue that threatened to divide the amateurs at the outset—gate money—was left unresolved. In the end, "tacit consent" was given to admission fees when a club was on tour or needed funds to pay for their grounds, although it was agreed that this money could never be used to compensate players "in any shape or form." A nostalgic reminiscence of early baseball by "Old Peto Brine" and a call for an amateur national association are reprinted below.

Although legitimate amateur nines (including college teams) numbered in the hundreds during the early 1870s, attendance was sparse at the next few conventions. It is not surprising that the amateur association lasted only until 1874 and that the players who followed its rules soon faced many of the problems confronted by professionals. Tensions remained over the question of gate money as well as the issues of whether or not to go on tour or to play against professionals. Some amateur nines practiced diligently, took their pastime as seriously as professional teams, and gained glory on the diamond. Others limped along and then disbanded. A few, like the Knickerbockers, stuck to the old ways. They practiced, played instrasquad games and matches against those clubs that shared their philosophy, and partied much as they had done before the Civil War.

The defection of the amateurs did not disturb the professionals, who simultaneously organized themselves into the National Association of Professional Base Ball Players (NAPBBP) in March of 1871. Agents from ten clubs arranged tours and adopted the NABBP constitution and bylaws, "so far as they [did] not conflict with the interests of the professional clubs." The "Proceedings of Convention" reproduced in this chapter set rules of championship competition, as the delegates began the task of rationalizing baseball into a business. Harry Wright and the other founders of this association believed that professional baseball could be profitable as it provided the public with exciting, wholesome, and honest entertainment. While their amateur counterparts experimented with a trip back in time, these modernizers launched what would become a major new amusement industry in the United States.

During its five seasons this first professional league elevated the sport's standard of play through better competition, but it experienced a series of problems which led to its demise after the 1875 season. The NAPBBP, like its predecessor, was designed to give the players central importance and influence. Its officers included prominent former athletes, and it allowed players to switch clubs after each season. As the new organization stressed the business aspects of baseball, it encouraged the development of the game as a science. With a renewed emphasis on efficiency, discipline, and teamwork, the managers and their men applied habits of the workplace to the ball fields. Thus the 1870s witnessed refinements in the rules for calling balls and strikes, and better techniques for fielding and throwing. There were also advances in pitching (including changing speeds and the curve ball), new strategies for positioning fielders, and experiments with rudimentary equipment (including the catcher's mask and the first skin-tight gloves).

Perhaps the most ambitious undertaking of the NAPBBP was a tour of England by two of its best teams during the summer of 1874. Harry Wright of the champion Boston Red Stockings organized this missionary expedition, bringing along players from the Philadelphia Athletics for the opposition. The Americans played a series of exhibition matches against each other and they also tried their collective hands at cricket against local teams. The contests attracted modest crowds and received respectful reviews in English periodicals, but overall the excursion did not achieve its goal of planting baseball in the soil of the former mother country. The British clearly much preferred their beloved national game of cricket to the new American pastime, which they dismissed as simply a modification of their familiar recreation of rounders.

Despite its numerous accomplishments, the first professional league suffered from a host of difficulties. Since there was no formal schedule of games, each club was responsible for arranging its series of matches with the other teams contesting for the championship. But weaker clubs frequently refused to make late-season long distance trips. The NAPBBP also lacked a proper balance of financially solvent and competitive clubs. The result was a high rate of turnover of teams. At least twenty-five were members between 1871 and 1875, but only three (the Philadelphia Athletics, Boston Red Stockings, and New York Mutuals) competed every year. In addition, retaining players was difficult, because of the "revolving" of the contestants. As the most talented men jumped to the strongest clubs, the gap widened between the best and worst teams. Gate receipts declined as spectators lost interest in one-sided contests. Charges of corruption and gambling also alienated many fans.

Disenchantment with this state of affairs led a number of men to hatch a plot to replace the NAPBBP with a new professional league. The chief conspirator was William A. Hulbert, a Chicago businessman and officer of his city's White Stockings. It is highly probable that he was the source of the call for reform of professional baseball which was published in the Chicago Tribune on October 24, 1875. Hulbert was thoroughly disgusted with the instability of the NAPBBP and the heavy losses which even winning teams incurred. In December he met secretly in Louisville with representatives of western clubs. In late January he sent a circular letter to the most powerful eastern clubs inviting them to attend a meeting in New York City on February 2nd. At that convention Hulbert persuaded the easterners to join his revolution. The sportsmen thus launched the National League of Professional Base Ball Clubs and ratified its constitution and rules. The call for reform, the circular letter, and the charter and playing regulations of this new professional league are included in this chapter.

Although Hulbert and his supporters professed idealistic motives for reforming professional baseball, it is clear that their main goals were to create a monopoly and increase profits for their clubs. While they claimed that they were trying to rescue baseball from corruption and disgrace, in fact the new constitution and league rules restricted competition among clubs and permitted their men very limited rights. For the first few years players were still allowed to switch clubs after the season ended, but in September of 1879 the owners decided to reserve five of their players for their own teams, and prohibit them from contracting with another club. In the next decade this practice evolved into the "reserve clause," which gave each club a lifetime option on its players.

Although in the long run the National League survived many challenges and troubles, it did struggle with a number of serious problems during its formative years. Like the now defunct NAPBBP, it experienced a high rate of club turnover as many teams folded for financial reasons and others were expelled for not completing their schedules. It also dealt with an early scandal over player dishonesty. In 1877 the Louisville Club expelled four of its players for throwing games. The National League upheld their dismissals, despite the petition of the ringleader that he be reinstated.

The 1870s also witnessed an acceleration of interest in baseball in Canada, especially in Ontario. International matches between nines from the Dominion and the States heightened interest, and by 1876 most of the leading Canadian teams had adopted the New York rules. The pioneer professional team in Canada was the Maple Leafs of Guelph. Founded by George Sleeman (a wealthy local brewer) in 1864, by 1870 they had earned the reputation of being the Dominion's best club. They dominated their Canadian rivals and held their own against powerful professional teams from the United States. In their homeland the Maple Leafs' most formidable rival was the Tecumsehs of London. In 1876 those two clubs joined with several others to form a Canadian National Association. The championship code of that organization concludes this chapter.

During its infancy the National League also faced a threat from those teams which it excluded from membership. A group of non-League professional clubs met in Pittsburgh in February of 1877 to form the International Association of Professional Base Ball Players. That league included the two premier Canadian teams, the Maple Leafs and the Tecumsehs, and the latter won the circuit's inaugural championship. The National League countered with its own plan to invite non-League clubs to join as affiliated members. It offered respect for all player contracts and a judiciary procedure to resolve disputes. In essence this plan created a second-class category of membership which denied outside clubs full membership or equal status in the National League. The International Association never seriously challenged the National League because its membership was too weak and scattered. It suffered from defections in both the United States and Canada and expired in 1880.

During the late 1870s the National League grappled with three key issues—admission prices, Sunday games, and the sale of liquor. By gentlemen's agreement fifty cents was the standard fee to see a game, despite protests by several clubs which wished to charge less. The policy of banning Sunday contests was also controversial, even though many cities had laws prohibiting them. The League officials wished to promote baseball as a respectable, moral pastime and did not want to anger strict Protestants by playing on the Sabbath. But critics pointed out that the six-day work week left most people with only Sunday as a day of recreation. The banning of beer and other liquor was extremely unpopular in Cincinnati and other western cities. There Germans and other European immigrants observed the Continental Sabbath, with its picnics, excursions, and beer-drinking. But after the 1880 season the League amended its constitution to outlaw both Sunday baseball and the sale of liquor in its parks.

By 1880 baseball had established itself as an integral part of culture in North America, becoming the national pastime of the United States and the most widely played team sport in Canada. In the economic arena, it flourished as owners schemed to turn it into a profitable business. While professionalism and commercialism swept through the nation's major and minor cities and towns, very few clubs made money. Entrepreneurs discovered that the expense of constructing new ball parks and paying player salaries was often greater than the income generated by admission fees. Retaining and disciplining recalcitrant or "revolving" athletes proved to be a major headache until the National League developed the structure of a loosely organized cartel which restricted competition among franchises and limited player mobility through the reserve clause. While baseball bosses struggled to show a profit, sporting goods magnates like Albert G. Spalding and Al Reach accumulated fortunes in the manufacture of balls, bases, uniforms, and other materials for a growing market of amateurs and professionals who were wild about playing ball. The sport also extended into the political world of the continent's burgeoning cities. The ties between baseball and urban political machines grew stronger as owners turned to politicians for favors such as choice sites for the location of ball parks, timely arrangements with the transit lines that brought customers to their gates, and police protection for crowd control. In all these ways, baseball established itself as a powerful force in the social, political, and cultural worlds of the people of the United States and Canada.

AN EARLY SYSTEM OF SCORING BASEBALL GAMES

An early indicator of the modernization of baseball was the appearance of box scores and statistics in sporting periodicals. The man who was most influential in the development of a system of scoring games and tabulating the results was Henry Chadwick. Later honored as the "father of baseball" for his tireless efforts to promote the sport, Chadwick was an English immigrant who became one of the most prominent sportswriters in Brooklyn and New York City during the second half of the nineteenth century. In formulating the first method of scoring baseball matches he drew heavily on his prior experiences as a cricket player and reporter. The following scheme and explanation first appeared in The New York Clipper, 23 March 1861, p. 388.

INSTRUCTIONS IN SCORING

In the game of Cricket, scoring the result of the various contests has been reduced to a regular and perfect system, and it is about time that something of the kind was adopted in Base Ball, whereby a true and correct record of the games may be had, not only for publication, but also for the purpose of taking an analysis of the play of each member of a club throughout the season. With this view we have prepared an article on the subject, from which those unacquainted with the details of scoring, in Base Ball matches, may be fully competent to discharge the duty. It is true that our clubs have a method of scoring that answers the purpose well enough to a certain extent, but all do not score alike, nor is there any regular system. We have been surprised that the "Committee on Rules and Regulations," in the National Association, have not taken the subject into consideration, for it is one bearing on the interest and welfare of the game. Every club should have a regularly-appointed scorer, and he should be one who fully understands every point of the game, practically and theoretically, and a person, too, of sufficient powers of observation to note down correctly the details of each innings, and it would be desirable if, at the same time, he possessed that peculiarity of disposition that leads a man to observe carefully, in his actions to those around him, the amenities of social life; or, in other words, he should be a thorough gentleman, for assuredly it needs one to occupy a scorer's seat at a first class match; for the annoyances, of one kind or another, that scorers are subjected to, is a pretty severe trial of patience, and an admirable test of the gentlemanly qualifications of the individual in question; for what with devoting his attention to every movement of the players, replying to the almost endless questions of incompetent reporters; and interested spectators, and in addition being obliged to restrain the crowd from encroaching on the space around him, he has enough to do to try the patience of Job himself. For the information of new clubs, and those at a distance from the city, we give below the printed form of a regular Base Ball Score Book, the size of the squares devoted to the record of the play in each innings being not less than half an inch.

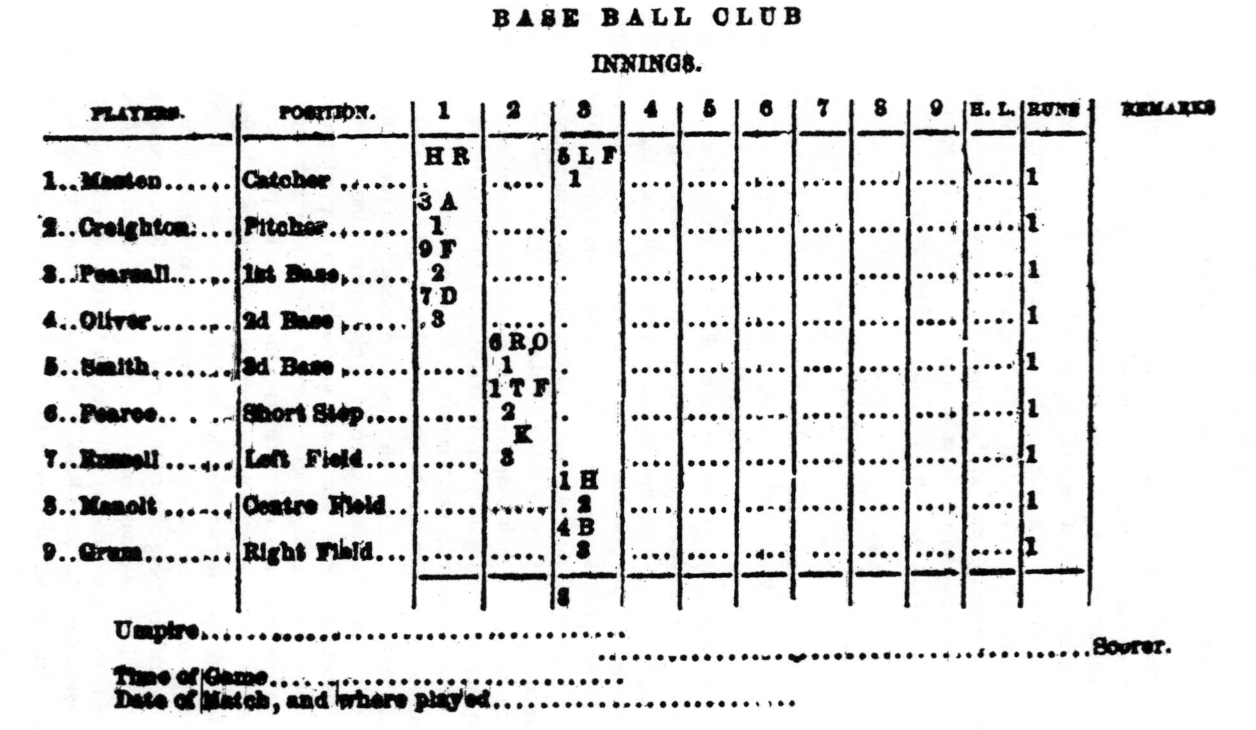

BASE BALL CLUB

INNINGS.

PLAYERS.	POSITION.	1	2	3	4	5	6	7	8	9	H. L.	RUNS	REMARKS
1..Masten......	Catcher	H R	......	5 L F 1	....	....	....	....	....	....	....	1	
2..Creighton....	Pitcher......	3 A 1	......	.	....	....	....	....	....	....	....	1	
3..Pearsall......	1st Base......	9 F 2	......	.	....	....	....	....	....	....	....	1	
4..Oliver......	2d Base	7 D 3	......	.	....	....	....	....	....	....	....	1	
5..Smith......	3d Base	......	6 R O 1	.	....	....	....	....	....	....	....	1	
6..Pearce......	Short Stop....	......	1 T F 2	.	....	....	....	....	....	....	....	1	
7..Russell......	Left Field....	......	K 3	.	....	....	....	....	....	....	....	1	
8..Manolt......	Centre Field..	......	......	1 H 2	....	....	....	....	....	....	....	1	
9..Grum......	Right Field...	......	......	4 B 3	....	....	....	....	....	....	....	1	
				3									

Umpire.......................................

....Scorer.

Time of Game.......................................
Date of Match, and where played.......................................

It will be observed that each player is numbered from one to nine, and his position on the score book remains the same throughout the game, no matter how often it may be changed on the field, such changes being recorded under the head of "remarks." We will now suppose a game to be commenced, and proceed to record it. Now suppose the first strike makes a run, we make a dot (.) in the corner of the square of the innings following his name, and also a mark (1) under the head of "Runs," thus locating the run made and checking it at the same time. Many only make the mark under the heading of "Runs," but the addition of the dot is advisable. The next striker is put out, and we place the figure one in the square of the innings following his name, and supposing the two following strikers to be put out in succession, we place first the figure 2 and then 3 in their respective squares, thus ending the innings. This is the simple record of the "hands lost" and "runs made" only, and gives no details of "how put out" or "by whom put out." In order to record these details effectively, we have to resort to a system of abbreviations, using certain letters and figures; and we now proceed to give the method we have adopted for years, and which we originated entirely. The names of each player being numbered, all we have to do is to use these numbers instead of writing their names; thus far we use figures. The letters we use as abbreviations of the various terms employed in the game, our alphabet being as follows:—

A for 1st Base.
B for 2d Base
C for 3d Base.
H for Home Base
K for Struck Out.
F for Catch on the Fly.
D for Catch on the Bound.
L for Foul Balls
T for Tips.
H R Home Runs.
R O for Run Out between Bases.
L F for Foul Ball on the Fly.
L D for Foul Ball on the Bound.
T F for Tip on the Fly.
T D for Tip on the Bound.

The above at first sight would appear to be a difficult alphabet to remember, but when the key is given it will at once be apparent that a boy could impress it indelibly on his memory in ten minutes. It is simply this. We take the first three letters of the alphabet to designate the first three bases, and we use the *first or last letter* of the word we wish to use afterwards; thus, H, for home, K, for struck; F, for fly, and D, for bound; T, for tip, and L, for foul; and then combine the letters, thus, T, F, stand for "tip on the fly," and L, D, for "foul on the bound." No one can glance over the above alphabet of abbreviations a dozen times without having it pretty well impressed on his memory. To illustrate the above method we will describe an imaginary game played by the nine whose names appear in the diagram of a score book, the opposing nine occupying the same relative positions. Masten, being the first striker, hit the ball to right field and made a home run, this we record by placing a dot in the left hand corner of the square, with the letters "h.r." over it, and at the same time making a mark under the head of run. Creighton, being the 2d striker, was put out at first base, and Pearsall, following, was caught out, at right field, on the fly, and Oliver, at left field, on the bound, thus ending the innings, one run only being scored. We thereupon place the figure one at the foot of the column of the 1st innings. Now, in recording how and by whom these players were put out, we use the alphabet as follows: Creighton, being put out at first base, we first place the figure, opposite the name of the first baseman, on the square of the innings, and then the letter A as shown in the diagram, and Pearsall, being put out on the fly by the right fielder, we record it with the letter F, and Oliver being put out on the bound, we simply use the letter D, prefixing, of course, in each case the figures indicating the name of the fielder by whom he was put out. In the second innings, Smith being the first striker, was run out between the bases, in this case we record it by first placing the figure indicating the name of the fielder who touched him with the ball, and then adding the letters R O. Peace being next, and tipping out on the fly, we use the figure as before, adding the letters T.F.; and Russell—third striker—striking out, we simply write the letter K without any figure, the result of the 2d innings being nothing. In the third innings, Manolt and Grum each make runs, which we record by dots and marks; Masten is caught out by a foul ball on the fly, and then each player makes a run, until Manolt again takes the bat, and he goes out at home base, Grum following suit at 2d base, which we regard as per diagram, using the letter H in the former case, and B in the latter. Each player thus loses one hand and makes the run, the total runs in the 3d innings being 8, and the grand total the three innings 9. No further illustration is required, we think, to give any person a complete idea of this method of scoring the details of the game, and as our space is somewhat limited, we shall defer any further reference to the subject to some future period.

REMINISCENCE OF THE EARLY DAYS OF BASEBALL

The following essay is one of the earliest examples of baseball nostalgia—a genre which still holds a prominent place in the sport's tradition and literature. Its author was probably Peter O'Brien, one of the best players of the Brooklyn Atlantics during the 1850s and 1860s. He wrote it as a column for an early sporting periodical edited by Henry Chadwick. In this piece he laments the passing of the old era of amateur ball playing, but he also hints at its darker side, when bad feelings and crowd disorders threatened to mar feature matches with violence. O'Brien no doubt had a rather romantic and selective memory of his ball-playing past, yet he did express the common feeling that the coming of professionalism and commercialism undermined the innocence, honesty, sportsmanship, and club loyalty of antebellum baseball. This essay first appeared in The American Chronicle of Sports and Pastimes, 9 January 1868, p. 10.

BALL TALK.

By Old Peto Brine.

...I'm out of ball playing now, though I like the old sport as much as ever; but the game has got beyond me, though the time was—and I aint afraid to say it neither—when I was pretty hard to beat in the place I occupied in "our nine." I aint going to tell you what nine that was, but it was a team that has taken the rag off the bush of many a party of fellows who thought they could beat all creation before they met our party. Somehow or other, they don't play ball nowadays, as they used to some eight or ten years ago. I don't mean to say that they don't play it as well, for the fact is I never saw the game played in the splendid style it was last season. But I mean that they don't play with the same kind of feelings or for the same objects they used to. It appears to me that ball matches have come to be controlled by different parties and for different purposes than those which prevailed in 1858 or '59. Just look at last season's games if you want to understand what I'm driving at, and then think of the games which were played in Brooklyn and Hoboken ten years ago. Look at the class of men who now fix up your matches, and then think of the fair and square style of men who controlled your clubs in the good old times of base ball. Ah! it's a pity things are so, boys; but I tell you now, you've got to put a stop to this heavy betting business, and to get your clubs out of the hands of the politicians, or the first thing you'll know will be that every respectable man will be down upon your game like a thousand of brick. But it's no use talking like a father to you fellows; you're in for "biz" in playing your matches now, and have forgotten the time when your club's name stood higher as a fair and square club than it does now. When I say "your club," I mean that you can take the cap and put it on, and if it fits, keep it there.

Mr. Editor, I saw in THE CHRONICLE the other day some scores of old games, which put me in mind of some of the best sport I ever had on a ball field. You remember the time when the Mutuals came over to Bedford, on the old Atlantic Ground, to polish off the champions; they thought they could give them a close rub anyhow. I remember the day as if it was but last week. I never saw the Atlantics do such batting as they did that day, especially in one innings. Harris was pitching, and he tossed the balls in just where the boys wanted them, and away they went to the right and left fields, until the poor out-fielders were so plaguey tired that they could scarcely move. Ance Taylor was one of the fielders, and when the innings was finished, he came in red in the face, and blowing like a porpoise. I remember, also, that the *City News* had an account of the victory printed, and the paper sold among the spectators before the game was finished, the reporter feeling sure that the New Yorkers would be beat.

The next game the same clubs played together at Bedford was quite a different style of game. The Mutuals had a new pitcher, and so did the Atlantics. McKeever pitching for New York, and Al. Smith—Charley's brother, you know—for Brooklyn. Mac. would neither pitch balls a feller could hit, or hit at balls the pitcher sent fair to him, and the result was a kind of unpleasant feeling among the players, and it looked very much like a row at one time; but Charley Smith ended the game by playing square when some of his brother players didn't exactly, and the Mutuals went off satisfied with having captured a ball. Those were the days when what they called "waiting games" were played oftener than they ought to have been. How wrathy Billy McKeever made Dicky Pearce that afternoon. Billy was smiling and chaffing him all the time, and Dick had his hands tied, for he saw that Billy was armed, and Dick being some on "putting up" for the square thing with the mauleys, didn't care to go in on the Southern style of knives and pistols, and so had to take the chaff as quiet as he could. There was an ugly crowd from York over that day, too, and some bad work would have been done had any blows been struck. I never saw a man stick to his work as well as Johnny

Grum did that day. Every man knew he was as honest as a rock, so they let him have his say as umpire. But there were some there who could have chawed him up without salt if they could have got at him alone.

Many's the exciting game I've seen—and more than seen, too—on that same old ground. In them days the Atlantics used to have out sometimes over fifty ladies, and you ought to have seen how old Cale Sniffen used to get seats for 'em, and get the crowd back so they could see all the fun. Nowadays the club can't muster a dozen of the fair sex; more shame for them. The fact is, it aint the club it was, although they play a heap better now than they did then. But somehow or other, there's a difference in the club, and I'm sorry to see that nearly all the old and best men of the Atlantics are losing interest in the club, and no wonder, when they see men having influence it who only care for it to get money out of it. We used to play matches for the honor of the thing in my young ball days; now clubs play for gate money and the betting rings. One man, I see, boasts that he can "buy up any club he likes;" so a fellow remarked on a ball ground last Fall when a match was named to be played that wasn't played. Old Stevens, at Hoboken, is as much to blame for helping this gate money business that is running the game into the ground, as any man, because if he hadn't drove the clubs out of Hoboken, there wouldn't have been so many York clubs playing for share of gate money.

I couldn't help laughing one day when I was over to the Union Grounds last Fall, where the Eckfords and Keystones, I think it was, were playing. The Eckfords were growling because they couldn't get their nine out as it was Saturday, and when some one asked them why they made up the match, they said, "Cammeyer made it up; he's boss of the clubs here:" and I guess they were right, too, for I saw that one of the Philadelphia papers said that even the Athletics couldn't make up a match without first asking Cammeyer. He's one of these shrewd fellows who knows how to manage ball clubs as well as skating ponds, and the way he made the clubs do as he said last year, was a caution to "independent" ball clubs. Cammeyer goes in to make money, and he's smart as a steel trap in doing it, too; I don't blame him, but how clubs can be made to knuckle under as they are, and used so, rather amazes me. The fact is, "there's money in it," and some fellows will sell their souls for dollars, even in the greenback form.

I see by the *Mercury* that some well known players have left their old clubs to join other nines. Now, if there is any one thing I'm down on, it is this "revolving" business. You may put it down as a pretty sure thing that any man that can be bought to leave his old club, is not to be trusted when a chance offers to sell the club he joins. Why, actually, it seems to me as if some men were in the market all the time. If a man don't get treated well after doing good service, and leaves his old club for one where he can find pleasanter companions and better treatment, it is excusable. But what I'm specially down upon is this putting one's self up to be knocked down at "so many dollars for my services." It is mean, that's where it is. But I've talked enough for once, so boys, here's to you till we meet again.

A CALL FOR AN AMATEUR NATIONAL ASSOCIATION

During the late 1860s and early 1870s officers of several New York and Brooklyn baseball clubs led a revolt against professionalism and commercialism in their favorite sport. After losing control of the National Association of Base Ball Players, these gentlemen founded an new organization of amateurs in the rooms of the Excelsior Base Ball Club in Brooklyn in March, 1871. The following address was written by Dr. J.B. Jones, Coroner of Brooklyn and a long-time official of the Excelsiors. His call for a new amateur association was also signed by men representing the Knickerbockers, Eagles, and Gothams of New York City, the Eurekas of Newark, and the Equities of Philadelphia. Jones's plea echoes many of the themes expressed by " Old Peto Brine." It presents an exaggerated, idyllic view of an amateur era marked by class harmony and ball playing for fun and recreation only. Jones's address may be interpreted in part as an expression of an upper-class refusal to accept the legitimacy of paid, skilled workers as ball players. It is more correct to state that Jones and his colleagues were traditionalists who wished to retain the best elements of early baseball while eliminating the worst. Many of them respected working-class ball players but hated the gamblers and others who corrupted their pastime. Their objections to professionalism lay not so much in the hiring of players as in the growth of commercialism, wagering, and the fixing of games. While there certainly was a class element in their hostility toward professionalism, it was not the most important factor. Jones's address is reprinted from The New York Clipper, 18 February 1871, p. 365.

AN ADDRESS TO AMATEUR CLUBS

The great want of physical out door culture in this country is so apparent that argument to establish the fact is rendered superfluous. While the vast majority of the thinking, intelligent public are in favor of the adoption of some means whereby our young men can avail themselves of a judicious physical training, they are decidedly adverse to sanction a course that, while it may to a certain degree improve and develop the physical man, establishes habits that are demoralizing. The playing of base ball affords one of the finest means of physical culture, and excels, if properly pursued, any other out door sport. As a recreative exercise, it brings into play every muscle of the system, expands the chest, improves the breathing capacity of the lungs, and thereby purifies the blood, strengthens the nervous system and exhilarates the mind, and secures to its devotees sound and refreshing sleep. A few years ago these facts became known, and were highly appreciated by the general community—all advocated and very large numbers participated in its practice and enjoyments; employers willingly and cheerfully gave their *employees* time to play base ball, and in may instances accompanied and participated in the pastime with them. All classes of society, the mechanic, the merchant, the professional classes, the school children, the collegiates, the aged and the young, the church member and minister, the public official, the private affluent member of society, all joined in the sport, either as a player or member of some base ball club, and hundreds upon hundreds of wives, mothers, sisters and daughters graced the ball field by their presence. Everything seemed to indicate that an American national out door pastime, fraught with influences the most beneficial and desirable, had been established, and so indeed it had; but the influences of the habits of the Old World soon manifested itself. England and other places had what they called professional cricket players, who made a living by playing cricket, a national sport of England. Why should not America have a professional class of ball players; there was money in it; why not secure it? the fiat went forth. The National Association was induced to hold its annual convention in other places besides the State of New York, and Philadelphia was the place first chosen. The annual convention of 1867 was held in the latter place, and at that convention the constitution under which our national game had attained its well earned popularity was ignored, and the foundation laid to bring the game into disrepute, by allowing the Association to be controlled by professionals. It stands in that position at the present time.

Friends of our national game, we appeal to you to aid us in our attempt to restore this pastime to its former high status; we desire, and will endeavor to carry that desire into effect, to eradicate the evils that have, by the machinations of the unprincipled, ambitious, or the money seeker, been fostered upon the game.

We, the undersigned, respectfully invite the Amateur Base Ball Clubs, to each appoint a delegate to attend a meeting to be held at the Excelsior Base Ball club Rooms, in Fulton street, Brooklyn, on Thursday, March 16th, for the purpose of organizing an Amateur Base Ball Association, that will discountenance the playing of the game for money, or as a business pursuit....

FORMATION OF THE FIRST PROFESSIONAL LEAGUE, 1871

The first professional baseball league in the United States was founded in New York City on March 17, 1871, when delegates from ten clubs created the National Association of Professional Base Ball Players. Participating organizations included the Athletics of Philadelphia, the Olympics of Washington, D.C., the Mutuals of New York City, the Unions of Troy, N.Y., the Forest Citys of Rockford, Illinois, the Forest Citys of Cleveland, Ohio, the White Stockings of Chicago, the Nationals of Washington, D.C., the Eckfords of Brooklyn, and the Red Stockings of Boston. The men who played prominent roles at this gathering of sportsmen were Harry Wright of the Red Stockings, James N. Kerns of the Athletics (the first President), and Nicholas E. Young of the Olympics (the first Secretary). The delegates approved arrangements for match tours and concluded with an agreement to convene again in Cleveland in March, 1872. The following resolutions on championship competition and player contracts are reprinted from the *Proceedings of Convention of the National Association of Professional Base Ball Players, Held in New York City, March 17, 1871* (Washington, D.C., 1871), pp. 6-10.

...*Resolved*, that inasmuch as the title of champions of the United States is a nominal one only, without any authority for, or rule to govern it, not being recognized by the National Association, therefore be it

Resolved, that this convention hereby authorizes a championship title to be contested for by the various professional clubs in the country, and decided as hereinafter set forth, and to be governed by the following rules:

1st. All clubs desiring to contest for the championship must make application in writing to the chairman of the championship committee, hereinafter mentioned, on or before May 1st, 1871; and no club to be admitted after that date, except in case of failure of application to reach him. Each application to be accompanied by a remittance of ($10) ten dollars. The Chairman to keep a record of the clubs so applying, and to announce the names of the clubs contesting for the title, by publication.

2d. The series for the championship to be best three in five games, each club to play best three in five games with every other contesting club, at such time and place as they may agree upon: the first games played to be the championship series, unless otherwise specified in writing, and all games to be played before November 1, 1871.

3d. The club winning the greatest number of games, in the championship series, with clubs entering for the championship during the season, shall be declared champions of the United States, and so certified to by a committee of three, who shall be appointed by the Chairman of this convention, and who shall be known as the Championship committee, and to the Chairman of which committee each club shall send its record on or before November 1st, 1871.

4th. In case of a tie between two or more contesting clubs, the committee shall examine the records of the club so tieing, and the one having the best average in championship contest, to be declared champions of the United States.

5th. A championship streamer shall be purchased by the said championship committee, with the funds accompanying the application of clubs, and present the same, on or before November 15th, 1871, to the club entitled to receive it.

6th. The club winning the championship at the end of the season shall be entitled to fly the streamer until the close of the following season, and then to be given to the club that the championship committee shall declare to be entitled to receive it.

The following resolution, as offered by Mr. Young and amended by Mr. Scofield, was unanimously agreed to:

Resolved, that the question of selecting an umpire between contending clubs be arranged by the visiting club presenting the names of five persons to the local club to select one of their number, and that sufficient time be given before the day of play to make such arrangements. The persons named for selection shall be known and acknowledged as competent men for the position, and shall be chosen from three or more clubs. In case the umpire selected should fail, from some unknown cause, to appear on the day of the game, then the umpire shall be selected by the two captains of the contesting nines.

Mr. Evans offered the following resolution which was carried:

Resolved, that any baseball player who is under an existing and valid contract to play ball with any club belonging to the Association shall not be eligible to play with any club in the match game, until each contract is honorably cancelled.

Mr. Thatcher offered the following, which was agreed to:

Resolved, that in case the services of a player are claimed by more than one club, each club so interested may select the President of another club, and those two a third, which three shall have power to send for persons and papers, and decide the question, and their action shall be binding.

Mr. Scofield offered the following resolution, which was carried:

That in case the club to which a player belongs does not live up to their agreement with the player, then the player, after a fair trial before the committee on championship, and the club found guilty of wrong, shall be declared freed from his contract.

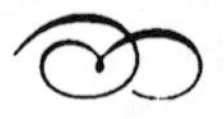

A CALL FOR REFORM OF PROFESSIONAL BASEBALL, 1875

The movement to reform and reorganize professional baseball originated in Chicago in the fall of 1875. William A. Hulbert, an officer of the White Stockings club, and Lewis Meacham, sports editor of the Chicago Tribune, prepared a critique of the National Association of Professional Base Ball Players and a proposal for changes. The following newspaper article was probably written by Meacham, but it highly likely that he was acting in large part as the spokesman for Hulbert. This piece first appeared in the Chicago Tribune, 24 October 1875, p. 12.

BASE BALL: A VITAL QUESTION FOR 1876

A glance over the ball-field for the season now nearly closed presents a problem for 1876 of more than ordinary importance to the game as an exhibition. At the beginning of this season thirteen clubs entered for the championship; three have disbanded, and three more—the Atlantic, New Haven, and St. Louis Reds—are out of the championship race by reason of not having played any return games. Of the last-named three, the Atlantics are

A SAMPLE OF TOO MANY PROFESSIONAL CLUBS;

they had never any organization, any association, any backing, or any elements of permanency or responsibility of any kind; they were simply a gang of amateurs and rejected professionals, who played such clubs as they could get to come to them, and shared the proceeds. They were not even a mob, for a mob must have a head. During the season so far they have played thirty-eight different men in their nine, and it has been too evident that whenever a game was to come off some one went out into the highways and byways and picked up almost the first nine he met. No one supposes that they ever intended to play any Western games; they simply entered the ring to force clubs to play as many games as possible with them, they taking two-thirds the receipts as on home ground. No large audiences have attended their games, because nobody felt any interest in the gang, and first-class visiting clubs under heavy expense have lost money every time they played with them, while the two-thirds which went to the gang was reason enough to induce them to get on as many games as they could.

A great part of the same description would apply to

THE ST. LOUIS REDS,

whose manager is said to have announced in March that he did not intend to go East at all. The club in question was formed by a man who thought he could make something out of a ball field on some ground controlled by him. In forming the club the manager calculated on nothing more than a few games on his own ground and then a country tour.

The case of the New Haven Club was somewhat different, and their fault appears to have been more that they went into the ball business without counting the cost than that they meant to deal unfairly with anybody. The town is too small to support a club, and yet the intense rivalty between it and Hartford led to the establishment of one which could not be sustained.

Now this same trick is to be attempted in 1876. Already announcements are made for the following

CLUBS FOR 1876,

eighteen in all:

Chicago,	Philadelphia,
St. Louis,	Americus,
Cincinnati,	New Haven,
Louisville,	Atlantic,
Mutual,	St. Louis Reds,
New York,	Buffalo,
Hartford,	Cleveland,
Boston,	Burlington,
Athletic,	Washington,

Some of these enterprises may be still-born, but others will spring up to take their places, and the Centennial year will be opened with not less than a dozen and half professional clubs. This may be fun to the little fellows, but it will be death to the first nine clubs named, who are really the only ones in the list who have much showing of permanency.

It may be asked why the advent of more clubs and a more general interest in the game will hurt it. The answer is

STATISTICAL;

the ball season in Chicago lasts about six months, or, in round numbers, 180 days. Deduct from this Sundays, rainy days, time used in traveling and in needed rest, and it will be seen that not more than ninety (or at the outside 100) games can be played. The total expense account of the Chicago Club for next year will approximate $28,000, and others in the ring will reach somewhat near the same figures. Thus it may be seen that every championship game played by the Chicago Club in 1876 will cost the management not far from $300. Nine clubs have been referred to above as on a solid basis; ten games all around, as this year, would give eighty games for each club and forty for each city which sustains a club, and this would give the nines some leeway, to be used in playing amateurs or exhibition games. On this plan every club of the nine first named could live respectably, pay good salaries, and perhaps a modest dividend, and put the exhibition on a sound basis.

ON THE OTHER HAND,

if the whole gang be let in, half of the games will not pay expenses. The best clubs in the country have played championship games for receipts of $10, $20, $36, when their opponents were the second class of clubs. Games of this class have been played this year with the St. Louis Reds, the Keokuks, the Washingtons, the Atlantics, and the New Havens. It doesn't require much figuring to see that this is a losing business where the game actually costs the first-class club from ten to twenty times what it takes in.

It may be noted that the Chicago Club played four games in Philadelphia on its present trip, and that their hotel bills in the city during their stay were more by $60 than their receipts from all the five games. This has a bearing on another point discussed further on.

The question which agitates the club management is,

"WHAT CAN WE DO ABOUT IT?"

They see the trouble ahead and are trying to work out their financial salvation. They know well enough that if eighteen clubs come into the ring next year, the poorest half of the list will utterly swamp the whole and destroy the prospects of the whole game. At the same time, the managers say they can hardly see how to keep the duffers out. It has been the custom to vote everybody in who applied, and unless some concerted action be at once taken the same thing will be done at the professional association this winter.

The remedy is not difficult, and it lies in the hands of a few men. When the Professional Association meets it should at once adopt the following

PRINCIPLES TO GOVERN THE CHAMPIONSHIP CONTESTS

for next year;

First—No club should be allowed to enter for the championship unless it be backed by a responsible association, financially capable of finishing a season when begun.

This, if adopted, would cut off the Atlantic club and other co-operative frauds.

Second—No club should be admitted from a city of less than 100,000 inhabitants,—excepting only Hartford.

This would cut off the New Havens and other clubs in places so small that, under the most favorable circumstances, a first-class club could never expect to get its expenses paid for going to them.

Third—No two clubs should be admitted from the same city.

The evil effects of having more than one club in a city have been shown in Philadelphia this year. First, the Centennials went under, and then the Philadelphias and

Athletics divided the interest, so that both of them have ended the season at a loss, poorer than poverty, and owing their players. One club can live in Philadelphia, but two must starve—not only themselves, but visiting clubs. This is shown in the statement of White Stocking receipts given above. And it is well known that the Athletic club owes $6,000 as its showing for the year, while the Philadelphias are not much better off—or would not be but for some peculiar practices.

Fourth—The faith of the management of a club should be shown by the deposit of $1,000, or perhaps 1,500, in the hands of the association before the season begins. This sum not to be played for, but returned to each club which carries out its agreements and plays its return games. If it refused to play all the games that it agrees to, let the sum be forfeited.

The adoption of these restrictions would limit the contestants next year to Chicago, Cincinnati, St. Louis, and Louisville in the West; Athletic, New York, and Mutual in the Middle States, and Hartford and Boston in the East; and with such an association the game would be prosperous, and the people who attended championship games would have a guarantee that they were to see the best clubs and the best games possible.

It may be doubted whether the Professional Association will be willing to vote the restrictions proposed, and, if they do not, it will be

THE PLAIN DUTY

of the nine clubs named to withdraw from the Association as it now stands, and form an organization of their own,—a close corporation, too. Every club which has a backing should discuss this matter before the meeting of Professional Association, and so instruct their representative that he will feel at liberty to take such action as may be for the best interests of the game.

CIRCULAR LETTER, 1876

In the fall of 1875 William Hulbert of Chicago's White Stockings traveled to St. Louis to confer with Charles Fowle, owner of that city's NAPBBP club. He and Fowle then arranged a secret conference in Louisville on December 17th, where they met with representatives of the Cincinnati and Louisville teams. The Louisville gathering then empowered Hulbert and Fowle to negotiate with eastern clubs concerning their reform proposals. Hulbert and Fowle decided to send the following circular letter to four clubs—the Red Stockings of Boston, the Hartfords, the Athletics of Philadelphia, and the Mutuals of New York. All of them accepted the invitation. This document is reprinted from *Spalding's Base Ball Guide, 1886* (N.Y., 1886), pp. 8-9.

Chicago, Jan. 23, 1876

The undersigned have been appointed by the Chicago, Cincinnati, Louisville and St. Louis clubs a committee to confer with you on matters of interest to the game at large, with special reference to the reformation of existing abuses, and the formation of a new association, and we are clothed with full authority in writing from the above named clubs to bind them to any arrangement we may make with you. We therefore invite your club to send a representative, clothed with like authority, to meet us at the Grand Central Hotel, in the city of New York, on Wednesday the 2d day of February next, at 12M. After careful consideration of the needs of the professional clubs, the organizations we represent are of the firm belief that existing circumstances demand prompt and vigorous action by those who are the natural sponsors of the game. It is the earnest recommendation of our constituents that all past troubles and differences be ignored and forgotten, and that the conference we propose shall be a calm, friendly and deliberate discussion, looking solely to the general good of the clubs who are calculated to give character and permanency to the game. We are confident that the propositions we have to submit will meet with your approval and support, and we shall be pleased to meet you at the time and place above mentioned.

Yours respectfully,
W.A. HULBERT.
CHAS. A. FOWLE.

CONSTITUTION AND RULES OF THE NATIONAL LEAGUE OF PROFESSIONAL BASE BALL CLUBS, 1876

Perhaps the single most important event in the history of professional baseball occurred in the Central Hotel in New York City on February 2, 1876. On that date William A. Hulbert and a group of delegates from eight eastern and western clubs conspired to defect from the National Association of Professional Base Ball Players and found a new organization that aimed to apply strict business principles to the professional game. According to the sport's folklore, Hulbert supposedly locked the eastern representatives in his hotel room and refused to let them go until he had obtained their agreement to support the new order. This story is probably fanciful; it seems more likely that Hulbert and his western colleagues were able to persuade the other gentlemen of the soundness of their plan. The new system reflected the trend toward monopoly in the Gilded Age. The change in name indicated that the clubs' interests would take precedence over the rights of the players. Each of the eight founding clubs was given exclusive "territorial rights" to its own city and the surrounding area within a radius of five miles. League clubs were barred from playing non-member teams in another League city, even with the consent of the local League club. New clubs had to represent cities with a population of at least 75,000. These and many other provisions listed in the following document suggests that the founders of the National

League were determined to turn baseball into a profitable business. This text is reprinted from the *Constitution and Playing Rules of the National League of Professional Base Ball Clubs* (Philadelphia, 1876), pp. 6-9, 11-22, 25-40.

CONSTITUTION.

ARTICLE I.
NAME.

This Association shall be called "The National League of Professional Base Ball Clubs."

ARTICLE II.
OBJECTS.

The objects of this League are:

1st. To encourage, foster, and elevate the game of base ball.

2nd. To enact and enforce proper rules for the exhibition and conduct of the game.

3rd. To make base ball playing respectable and honorable.

4th. To protect and promote the mutual interests of professional base ball clubs and professional base ball players; and

5th. To establish and regulate the base ball championship of the United States.

ARTICLE III.
MEMBERSHIP.

This League shall consist of the following named professional Base Ball Clubs, namely:

Athletic B. B. Club of Philadelphia, Pa.
Boston B. B. Club of Boston, Mass.
Chicago B. B. Club of Chicago, Ill.
Cincinnati B.B. Club of Cincinnati, O.
Hartford B. B. Club of Hartford, Conn.
Mutual B. B. Club of Brooklyn, N. Y.
Louisville B. B. Club of Louisville, Ky.
St. Louis B. B. Club of St. Louis, Mo.

And such other professional base ball clubs as may from time to time be elected to membership under the following rules, namely:

1. No club shall be admitted from either of the cities above named other than the clubs mentioned, except in the event that either of such clubs shall lose its membership, and in no event shall there be more than one club from any city.

2. No club shall be admitted from any city whose population is less than seventy-five thousand (75,000), except by unanimous vote of the League.

3. No club shall be admitted unless it shall first have delivered to the Secretary of the League, at least thirty days before the annual meeting, a written application for

membership, signed by its President and Secretary, accompanied by documents showing that such club bears the name of the city in which it is located, and that it is regularly organized and officered and (where the State law permits it) chartered, and accompanied also by a pledge that it will keep all its engagements with the clubs members of the League, and that it has not in its employ any player who has been dismissed or expelled by the League or any club member thereof.

4. The voting upon an application for membership shall be by white and black balls. Two black balls shall be sufficient to exclude the applicant, and no club shall be required, under any circumstances, to state how it voted upon such application.

ARTICLE IV.
OFFICERS.

SECTION 1. The affairs of this League shall be conducted and controlled by five Directors, who shall constitute "The Board," who shall hold their office for one year, and shall be chosen at the annual meeting in the following manner: The name of each club shall be plainly written upon a card—in full view of the delegates present—by the Secretary; the cards to be of the same size, shape, color, and material. The cards shall be placed in the same suitable receptacle and well shaken together; thereupon five of these cards shall be drawn successively and at random, and the delegates from the five clubs whose names are so drawn shall compose the Board.

SEC. 3. The Board shall also elect a gentleman of intelligence, honesty, and good repute, who is versed in base ball matters, but who is not, in any manner, connected with the press, and who is not a member of any professional base ball club either in or out of the League, to be the Secretary of the Board and of the League.

The Secretary shall be the Treasurer of the League, and as such shall be the custodian of all the funds of the League, receive all dues, fees, and assessments, pay out such sums as he may be directed to do by the Board or by vote of the League, and render annually a report of his accounts....

ARTICLE V.
CLUBS.

SECTION 1. Each club belonging to this League shall have the right to regulate its own affairs, to make its own contracts, to establish its own rules, and to discipline and punish its own players: *Provided*, That nothing shall be done in violation of, or contrary to, this Constitution or the Playing Rules.

No club shall employ as manager, scorer, or player any person who has wilfully violated any provision of this Constitution or of the Playing Rules, or who has been discharged, dismissed, or expelled from any club belonging to this League, or who shall be disqualified from playing with a club under any provision of this Constitution; and any club who shall employ or play in its nine a player disqualified by any provision of this Constitution, shall be at once considered as having forfeited its membership in the League, and all other League clubs must and shall, under penalty of the forfeiture of their membership in the League, abstain from playing any such club for the remainder of the season.

SEC. 2. Every club member of this League shall have exclusive control of the city in which it is located, and of the territory surrounding such city to the extent of five miles in every direction, and no visiting League club shall, under any circumstances—not even with the consent of the local League club—be allowed to play any club in such territory other than the League club therein located.

SEC. 3. The players and managers employed by the clubs belonging to this League shall be considered and treated as members hereof to the extent of being always amenable to the provisions of this Constitution, and entitled to all its privileges in matters of dispute, grievance, or discipline.

ARTICLE VI.
DUES AND ASSESSMENTS.

SECTION 1. Every club shall pay to the Secretary of the League, on or before the first day of January of each year, the sum of One Hundred Dollars as annual dues, and any club failing to pay said sum by such time shall be considered as having withdrawn from the League.

SEC. 2. In case of necessity thereof the Board may levy a pro rata assessment upon the clubs, to be paid as the Board may direct.

ARTICLE VII.
FORFEITING MEMBERSHIP.

The membership of any club belonging to this League shall be forfeited, if the League, by a two-thirds vote, shall so determine, under the following circumstances, namely:

1st. By disbanding, or by failing or refusing to keep its engagements in regard to games with other clubs.

2d. By failing or refusing to comply with any lawful requirement or order of the Board.

3d. By failing to keep its contracts with its players, either as to engagement or salary, where the player is not in fault.

4th. By wilfully violating any provision of this Constitution, or the Playing Rules adopted hereunder. And no club which has forfeited its membership shall be readmitted except by unanimous vote of the League.

ARTICLE VIII.
DISPUTES AND COMPLAINTS.

SECTION 1. Charges against clubs for conduct which, if proven, would render them liable to a forfeiture of membership under Article VII. of this Constitution, shall be preferred to the Board, who shall hear the evidence in the matter at their annual meeting, and certify their finding to the League at its first succeeding annual meeting, and the League shall, by vote, determine the question of forfeiture of membership: *Provided, however,* That nothing in this Section shall be construed as affecting the provisions of Article V., Section 1, of this Constitution during the playing season.

SEC. 2. The Board shall be the sole tribunal to determine disputes between two or more clubs which involve the interpretation or construction of this Constitution, or any of its Articles. When such a dispute arises, and either club shall signify to the other its desire for the Board to decide the matter, each club shall furnish to the Secretary as soon as possible a written statement of its side of the dispute, with the names of its witnesses, or an agreed statement of facts, if possible, which the Secretary shall docket in the order of its reception, and at the next annual meeting the clubs shall present themselves before the Board with their testimony, and the Board shall proceed to try the case impartially and render a true verdict. The Board shall have a right to put the witnesses under oath, and must do so if demanded thereto by either party. No director shall sit on the trial of a cause in which his club is interested, but must retire and permit the others alone to determine the matter. The finding of the Board, in such a case, shall be *final*, and under no circumstances shall be reconsidered, reopened, or inquired into, either by the League or any subsequent Board.

SEC. 3. The Board shall also be the sole tribunal for the hearing of an appeal made by any player who shall have been dismissed, expelled, or otherwise disciplined by his club. The matter shall be proceeded with in the following manner: The player shall file with the Secretary an affidavit signed by himself, in which he shall deny, under oath, that he is guilty of the offence for which he has been disciplined, accompanied by a request that an appeal be allowed by him. The Secretary shall notify the club of the affidavit and request for appeal, and at the next annual meeting the club and the player shall appear before the Board with their testimony. The Board shall impartially hear the matter and render their decision, which shall be *final* and forever binding on both club and player. In the event the club appealed from is represented in the Board, that representative shall be not be allowed to sit in the matter.

SEC. 4. All differences and disputes arising between clubs, in which the interpretation, construction, or violation of the Playing Rules is involved, shall be adjusted in the following manner: The complaining club shall file a written statement of its grievance, accompanied with the affidavits of its witnesses, with the Secretary, who (unless the other club has also filed its statement and affidavits, or an agreed case has been prepared) shall immediately notify the defendant club of the fact that a complaint—briefly stating the nature thereof—has been filed with him, and call for a counter statement with affidavits, which must be furnished to him within fifteen (15) days of the date of the notice. On receiving the counter statement, or agreed case, or in the event the defendant club does not comply with the call within fifteen (15) days, the Secretary shall notify the President of the matter, who shall appoint three disinterested persons, members of League clubs, as arbitrators, to the first of whom the Secretary shall transmit at once all the papers in the case, securely sealed, notifying him of the remaining arbitrators. Within three days such person shall attach his verdict in writing to the papers and transmit them to the second person, who shall within three days attach his written verdict and transmit them to the third, who, following the rule, shall finally return them to the Secretary, and he shall at once notify each club of the finding. A majority of the arbitrators shall determine the cause, and from their finding there shall be no appeal.

The expenses of all trials and arbitrations shall be equally borne by the parties litigant.

ARTICLE IX.
ANNUAL MEETING.

SECTION 1. The annual meeting of the League shall be held on the first Thursday after the first Monday of December of each year, at twelve o'clock, noon, and at such place as shall be determined by vote at the previous meeting. The annual meeting shall not be held in (nor within fifty miles of) any city where a club member of the League is located; but shall be held in some easily accessible place, and, as near as may be, equidistant from the several club members.

SEC. 2. At such meeting each club shall be entitled to two representatives, who shall present a certificate from the President or Secretary of their club, showing their authority to act; but no club shall have more than one vote.

A representation of a majority of clubs shall constitute a quorum for the transaction of business, but a less number may adjourn from time to time until a quorum is obtained.

ARTICLE X.
PLAYING RULES.

The league at its first meeting shall adopt a code of Playing Rules, which may be altered, amended, or abolished at any subsequent annual meeting.

ARTICLE XI.
CONTRACTS.

SECTION 1. Contracts hereafter made between the clubs, members of this League, and their players shall be made under and in view of the following provisions:

No club shall be prevented from contracting with a player for the reason that he is already under contract with another club: *Provided,* The service to be rendered under the second contract is not to begin until the expiration of the first contract.

No formal words of contract shall be required. It shall be sufficient if the contract be made in writing, be dated, specify the time, indicate the service, and be signed by the player and some officer or recognized agent of the club and one witness.

SEC. 2. It shall be the duty of a club, as soon as it shall have entered into a contract with a player, to file a notification of the same, signed by the club and the player, with the Secretary of the League, who shall endorse thereon the date of its reception, and forthwith notify every other League club of such contract.

SEC. 3. Whenever a club releases a player from his contract, that club shall at once notify the Secretary of the League in writing. In case the release shall have been granted for a cause that does not in any manner reflect upon the character of the player, there must be written upon the notice a statement to that effect, otherwise it shall be inferred from such notice that such player has been in fact dismissed, discharged, or expelled, and he shall not be eligible to make any contract for the remainder of the season with any League club.

A player who has been released from his contract without imputation may engage with any other club for twenty days thereafter; but such other club, before engaging him, shall satisfy itself by application to the Secretary, that such release has been given without imputation on the player's character.

No player who has been dismissed or expelled from a League club shall, at any time thereafter, be allowed to play with any League club (either the one expelling him or any other), unless, upon his appeal to the Board, such dismissal or expulsion shall have been set aside.

SEC. 4. A player whose contract has expired or become void by reason of his club's disbanding or withdrawing from the League, may engage for the remainder of the season with any other League club, provided such engagement shall not commence within twenty days of such disbanding or withdrawal.

ARTICLE XII.
CHAMPIONSHIP.

SECTION 1. The *Championship of the United States,* established by this League, shall be contended for under the following rules, namely:

No club shall be allowed to enter the lists for the championship until it has paid its annual dues.

The *championship season* shall extend from the 15th day of March to (and including) the 15th day of November, and no game shall count in the championship series unless played during the championship season.

No game played on Sunday shall count in the championship series.

Each club entering the lists shall play ten games with every other club so entering, and if any club shall, *of its own fault,* fail to finish its series with every other club, its games shall not be counted at the close of the season, and such club shall not be eligible to enter the championship lists the ensuing season.

SEC. 2. Each club shall be entitled to have five of its own games with every other club played on its own grounds; and when a club shall have first played one or more games, pursuant to agreement, upon it adversary's grounds, it may require its adversary to play an equal number upon its own ground in return within a reasonable time (not to exceed two months), under penalty of forfeiture of the number of games due: *Provided, however,* That if any game arranged according to the requirements of this rule be prevented by rain, or if a tie or drawn game be played, the visiting club shall not be required to extend its stay, or to again visit such city for the sole purpose of playing such tie or drawn game, or game prevented by rain.

SEC. 3. Clubs shall be entitled to forfeited games—to count in their series as games won by a score of nine runs to none—from other clubs in the following instances, namely:

Any club which has agreed to play with another club upon a day certain, and fails to meet its engagement, shall forfeit the game to the latter club, unless the failure is caused by an unavoidable accident in travelling, or the game is prevented by rain: *Provided, however,* That games shall be postponed upon the death of a player belonging to either of the contesting League clubs, at the request of either club.

Any club which shall appear on the field to play a game with another club and present in its nine a player who is, or has been within twenty days, a member of any other League club, or who has been dismissed or expelled from any League club, without having been reinstated by the Board, shall forfeit the game to the other club: *Provided,* The other club shall not be in the same fault; and should both clubs be in such fault, and play the game notwithstanding, such game shall not count in the championship series, and games shall further be forfeited as provided in Section 1 of this Article.

SEC. 4. Drawn, tie, and postponed games shall not count in the series in favor of either contestant, but may be played off if sufficient time exist before the close of the season.

The club which shall have won the greatest number of games in the championship series shall be declared the champion club of the United States for the season in which such games were played. In the event two or more clubs shall have won the same number of games, then the club which shall have lost the smallest number shall be declared the champion.

The emblem of the championship shall be a pennant (of the national colors), to cost not less than one hundred dollars ($100). It shall be inscribed with the motto, "Champion Base Ball Club of the United States," with the name of the club and the year in which the title was won; and the champion club shall be entitled to fly the pennant until the close of the ensuing season.

SEC. 5. The championship shall be decided in the following manner, namely:

Within twenty-four hours after every match game played for the championship, the home club shall prepare a statement, containing the *full score* of the game, the date, place where played, name of the clubs and of the umpire, and shall forward the same without delay to the Secretary of the League, who shall file the same carefully.

At the close of the season the Secretary shall prepare a tabular statement of the games won and lost by each club, according to the statements so sent him (which statements shall be the sole evidence in the matter), and submit the same, with the statements so sent him, to the Board, who shall make the award.

ARTICLE XIII.
FIELD RULES.

Every club in this League shall be bound by the following Field Rules, and must have the same conspicuously posted or placarded upon its grounds, namely: No club shall allow open betting or pool selling upon its grounds, nor in any building owned or occupied by it. No person shall be allowed upon any part of the field during the progress of a game, in addition to those playing and the umpire, except the managers, scorers, and necessary servants of the two clubs, and such officers of the law as may be present to preserve the peace.

Players in uniform shall not be permitted to seat themselves among the spectators.

The umpire is the sole judge of play, and is entitled to the respect of the spectators, and any person hissing or hooting at, or offering any insult or indignity to him, must be promptly ejected from the grounds.

Every club shall furnish sufficient police force upon its own grounds to preserve order, and in the event of a crowd entering the field during the progress of a game, and interfering with the play in any manner, the visiting club may refuse to play further until the field be cleared; and if the ground be not cleared within fifteen minutes thereafter, the visiting club may claim, and shall be entitled, to the game by a score of nine runs to none (no matter what number of innings have been played).

ARTICLE XIV.
AMENDMENTS.

This Constitution may be altered or amended by a two-thirds vote of the League at any annual meeting....

PLAYING RULES.

RULE I.—THE MATERIALS OF THE GAME.

SECTION 1. The ball must weigh not less than five, nor more than five and one-quarter ounces, avoirdupois. It must measure not less than nine, nor more than nine and one-quarter inches in circumference. It must be composed of woollen yarn, and shall not contain more than one ounce of vulcanized rubber in mould form, and shall be covered with leather.

SEC. 2. In all games the ball or balls played with shall be furnished by the home club, and shall become the property of the winning club.

SEC. 3. No ball shall be played with in any regular match game, unless it is of the regulation size, weight, and materials, and also have the name of its maker and figures indicating its weight and circumference plainly stamped on its cover. Should any ball used in a regular match game prove, on examination by the umpire, to be illegal in size, weight or materials, balls of the same manufacture shall not be used thereafter in regular match games.

SEC. 4. When the ball becomes out of shape, or cut or ripped so as to expose the yarn, or in any way so injured as to be unfit for use, a new ball shall be called for by the umpire at the end of an even innings, at the request of either captain. Should the ball be lost during a game, the umpire shall, at the expiration of five minutes, call for a new ball.

SEC. 5. The bat must be round, and must not exceed two and one-half inches in diameter in the thickest part. It must be made wholly of wood, and shall not exceed forty-two inches in length.

SEC. 6. The bases must be four in number, and they must be placed and securely fastened upon each corner of a square the sides of which are respectively thirty yards. The bases must be so constructed and placed as to be distinctly seen by the umpire, and must cover a space equal to one square foot of surface. The first, second, and third bases shall be canvas bags, painted white and filled with some soft material. The home base shall be of white marble or stone, so fixed in the ground as to be even with the surface, and with one corner facing the pitcher's position, said corner touching the intersection of the foul lines.

SEC. 7. The base from which the ball is struck shall be designated the home base, and must be directly opposite the second base. The first base must always be that upon the right hand, and the third base that upon the left hand side of the striker when occupying his position at the home base. In all match games lines connecting the home and first bases, and the home and third bases, and also the lines of the striker's and pitcher's positions, shall be marked by the use of chalk or other suitable material, so as to be distinctly seen by the umpire. The line of the home base shall extend four feet on each side of the base, and shall be drawn through its center and parallel with a line extending from first to third base.

RULE II.—THE GAME.

SECTION 1. The game shall consist of nine innings to each side, but should the score then be a tie, play shall be continued until a majority of runs for one side, upon an equal number of innings, shall be declared, when the game shall end. All innings shall be concluded when the third hand is put out.

SEC. 2. Positions of players and choice of first innings shall be determined by the two captains. The fielders of each club shall take any position in the field their captain may assign them, with the exception of pitcher, who must deliver the ball from his appointed position.

SEC. 3. No player taking part in a game shall be replaced by another after the commencement of the fourth innings, except as provided in Section 14 of Rule VI.

SEC. 4. No game shall be considered as played unless five innings on each side shall be completed. Should darkness or rain intervene before the third hand is put out in the closing part of the fifth innings of a game, the umpire shall declare "No game."

SEC. 5. Whenever a game of five or more innings is stopped by rain or darkness, and the score at the time is equal on the even innings played, the game shall be declared drawn, but, under no other circumstances shall a drawn game be declared.

SEC. 6. Should rain commence to fall during the progress of a match game, the umpire must note the time it began, and should it continue for five minutes, he shall, at the request of either captain, suspend play. Such suspended game shall not be resumed until, in the opinion of the umpire, the ground is in fit condition for fair fielding.

SEC. 7. When the umpire calls "play," the game must at once be proceeded with. Should either party fail to take their appointed positions in the game, or to commence play as requested, the umpire shall, at the expiration of five minutes, declare the game forfeited by the nine that refuses to play. When the umpire calls "play" again, and during the interim no player shall be put out, base be run or run be scored.

SEC. 8. The umpire, in any match game, shall determine when play shall be suspended, and, if the game cannot be fairly concluded, it shall be decided by the score of the last equal innings played, unless one nine shall have completed their innings, and the other nine shall have equalled or exceeded the score of their opponents in their incompleted innings, in which case the game shall be decided by the total score of the game.

SEC. 9. When the umpire calls a game it shall end, but when he merely suspends play for any stated period, it may be resumed at the point at which it was suspended; provided such suspension does not extend beyond the day of the match.

RULE III.—THE PLAYERS.

SECTION 1. Every player taking part in a regular match game, no matter what number of innings be played, shall be considered a member of the club with which he plays. All matches shall be considered regular in the meaning of this rule in which nines of two contesting clubs of this League take part.

SEC. 2. Any player who shall, in any way, be interested in any bet or wager on the game in which he takes part, either as umpire, player, or scorer, or who shall purchase or have purchased for him any "pool" or chance—sold or given away—on the game he plays in, shall be dishonorably expelled, both from the club of which he is a member and from the League.

A player who shall be similarly interested in any regular match game between two clubs of the League, shall be suspended from legal service as a member for the season during which he shall have violated this rule.

RULE IV.—PITCHING.

SECTION 1. The pitcher's position shall be within a space of ground six feet square, the front line of which shall be distant forty-five feet from the center of the home base, and the center of the square shall be equidistant from the first and the third bases. Each corner of the square shall be marked by a flat iron plate or stone six inches square fixed in the ground even with the surface.

SEC. 2. The player who delivers the ball to the bat must do so while within the lines of the pitcher's position. He must remain within them until the ball has left his hand, and he shall not make any motion to deliver the ball to the bat while any part of his person is outside the lines of the pitcher's position. The ball must be delivered to the bat with the arm swinging nearly perpendicular at the side of the body, and the hand in swinging forward must pass below the hip.

SEC. 3. Should the pitcher deliver the ball by an overhand throw, a "foul balk" shall be declared. Any outward swing of the arm, or any other swing save that of the perpendicular movement referred to in Section 2 of this rule, shall be considered an overhand throw.

SEC. 4. When a "foul balk" is called, the umpire shall warn the pitcher of the penalty incurred by such unfair delivery, and should such delivery be continued until *three foul balks* have been called in one innings, the umpire shall declare the game forfeited.

SEC. 5. Should the pitcher make any motion to deliver the ball to the bat and fail so to deliver it—except the ball be accidentally dropped—or should he unnecessarily delay the game by not delivering the ball to the bat, or should he, when in the act of delivering the ball, have any part of his person outside the lines of his position, the umpire shall call a "balk," and players occupying the bases shall take one base each.

SEC. 6. Every ball fairly delivered and sent in to the bat over the home base and at the height called for by the batsman, shall be considered a good ball.

SEC. 7. All balls delivered to the bat which are not sent in over the home base and at the height called for by the batsman, shall be considered unfair balls, and every third ball so delivered must be called. When "three balls" have been called, the striker shall take first base, and all players who are thereby forced to leave a base shall take one base. No "ball" shall be called until the ball has passed the home base.

SEC. 8. Should the batsman strike at a ball on which a "ball" has been called, such call shall be considered void, and the ball be regarded as fairly delivered.

SEC. 9. All balls delivered to the bat which shall touch the striker's bat without being struck at, or his (the batsman's) person while standing in his position, or which shall hit the person of the umpire—unless it be a passed ball—shall be considered *dead* balls and shall be so called by the umpire, and no players shall be put out, base be run, or run scored on any such ball.

RULE V.—BATTING DEPARTMENT.

SECTION 1. The batsman's or striker's position shall be within a space of ground located on either side of the home base, six feet long by three feet wide, extending two feet in front of and four feet behind the line of the home base, and with its nearest line distant one foot from the home base.

SEC. 2. The batsmen must take their positions in the order in which they are named on the score-book. After the first innings, the first striker in each innings shall be the batsman whose name follows that of the third man out in the preceding innings.

SEC. 3. Any batsman failing to take his position at the bat in his order of striking—unless by reason of illness or injury, or by consent of the captains of the contesting nines—shall be declared out, unless the error be discovered before a fair ball has been struck, or the striker put out.

SEC. 4. Any batsman failing to take his position at the bat within *three minutes* after the umpire has called for the striker, shall be declared out.

SEC. 5. The batsman, on taking his position, must call for either a "*high ball,*" a "*low ball,*" or a "*fair ball,*" and the umpire shall notify the pitcher to deliver the ball as required; such call shall not be changed after the first ball delivered.

SEC. 6. A "*high ball*" shall one be sent in above the waist of the batsman but not higher than his shoulder. A "*low ball*" shall be one sent in *not lower* than within *one foot* of the *ground,* but *not higher* than his *waist.* A "*fair ball*" shall be one between the range of *shoulder high* and *one foot* from the *ground.* All the above must be *over the home base,* and when fairly delivered, shall be considered good balls to the bat.

SEC. 7. Should the batsman fail to strike at a "good ball," or should he strike and fail to hit the ball, the umpire shall call "one strike," and "two strikes," should he again fail. When two strikes have been called, should the batsman not strike at the next "good ball" the umpire shall warn him by calling "good ball." But should he strike at and fail to hit the ball, or should he fail to strike at or to hit the next good ball, "three strikes" must be called, and the batsman must run to first base as in the case of hitting a fair ball.

SEC. 8. The batsman, when in the act of striking at the ball, must stand within the lines of his position.

SEC. 9. Should the batsman step outside the lines of his position when he strikes the ball, the umpire shall call "foul strike and out," and base-runners shall return to the bases they occupied when the ball was hit.

SEC. 10. The foul ball lines shall be unlimited in length, and shall run from the front corner of the home base through the center of first and third bases to the foul posts, which shall be located at the boundary of the field and within the range of home and first base, and home and third base. Said lines shall be marked, and on the inside, from base to base, with chalk, or some other white substance, so as to be plainly seen by the umpire.

SEC. 11. If the ball from a fair stroke of the bat first touches the ground, the person of a player, or any other object, either in front of, or on the foul ball lines, it shall be considered fair.

SEC. 12. If the ball from a fair stroke of the bat first touches the ground, the person of a player, or any other object, behind the foul ball lines, it shall be declared foul, and the ball so hit shall be called foul by the umpire even before touching the ground, if it be seen falling foul.

SEC. 13. Should the batsman strike at or hit any ball on which a "ball" has been called, the umpire shall disregard the call of such "ball," and render his decision simply on the strike or hit made.

SEC. 14. When the batsman has fairly struck a fair ball, he shall vacate his position, and he shall then be considered a base-runner until he is put out or scores his run.

SEC. 15. The batsman shall be declared out by the umpire as follows:

If a fair or foul ball be caught before touching the ground, provided it be not caught in a player's hat or cap.

If a foul ball be similarly held, or after touching the ground but once.

If a fair ball be securely held by a fielder while touching first base with any part of his person before the base-runner touches said base.

If after three strikes have been called, he fails to touch first base before the ball is legally held there.

If after three strikes have been called, the ball be caught before touching the ground or after touching the ground but once.

If he wilfully strikes at the ball to hinder the ball from being caught, or makes a "foul strike."

RULE VI.—RUNNING THE BASES.

SECTION 1. Players running bases must touch each base in regular order, viz.: first, second, third, and home base; and when obliged to return to bases they have occupied they must retouch them in reverse in order. No base shall be considered as having been occupied or held until it has been touched.

SEC. 2. No player running the bases shall be forced to vacate the base he occupies unless by the act of the batsman in striking a fair ball. Should the first base be occupied by a base-runner when a fair ball is struck, the base-runner shall cease to be entitled to hold said base until the player running to first base shall be put out. The same rule shall apply in the case of the occupancy of the other bases under similar circumstances. No base-runner shall be forced to vacate the base he occupies if the base-runner succeeding him is not thus obliged to vacate his base.

SEC. 3. Players forced to vacate their bases may be put out by any fielders in the same manner as when running to first base.

SEC. 4. The player running to first base shall be at liberty to overrun said base without his being put out for being off the base after first touching it, provided that in so overrunning the base he make no attempt to run to second base. In such case he must return at once and retouch first base, and after retouching said base he can be put out as any other base. If, in so overrunning first base, he also attempts to run to second base, he shall forfeit such exemption from being put out.

SEC. 5. Any player running a base who shall run beyond three feet from the line from base to base in order to avoid being touched by the ball in the hands of a fielder shall be declared out by the umpire with or without appeal.

SEC. 6. One run shall be scored every time a base-runner, after having regularly touched the first three bases, shall touch the home base before three hands are out. If the third hand out is forced out, or is put out before reaching first base, a run shall not be scored.

SEC. 7. When a "balk" is called by the umpire, every player running the bases shall take one base without being put out.

SEC. 8. When three "balls" have been called by the umpire, the batsman shall take one base without being put out, and should any base-runner be forced thereby to vacate his base, he also shall take one base. Each base-runner thus given a base shall be at liberty to run to other bases besides the base given, but only at the risk of being put out in so running.

SEC. 9. A player running bases shall be considered as holding a base, viz., entitled to occupy it, until he shall have regularly touched the next base in order.

SEC. 10. No base shall be run or run be scored when a fair or foul ball has been caught or momentarily held before touching the ground, unless the base held when the ball was hit is retouched by the base-runner after the ball has been so caught or held by the fielder.

SEC. 11. No run or base can be made upon a foul ball that shall touch the ground before being caught or held by a fielder, and any player running bases shall return, without being put out, to the base he occupied when the ball was struck, and remain on such base until the ball is held by the pitcher.

SEC. 12. Any player running the bases on fair or foul balls caught before touching the ground must return to the base he occupied when the ball was struck, and retouch such base before attempting to make another or score a run, and said player shall be liable to be put out in so returning, as in the case of running to first base when a fair ball is hit and not caught flying.

SEC. 13. If the player running the bases is prevented from making a base by the obstruction of an adversary, he shall be entitled to that base and shall not be put out.

SEC. 14. No player shall be allowed a substitute in running the bases, except for illness or injury, unless by special consent of the captain of the opposing nine; in such case the latter shall select the player to run as substitute. The substitute in question shall take his position so as to cross the batsman's position, and in front of the home base, and he shall not start to run until the ball is struck at or hit. The substitute shall be the player running the bases.

SEC. 15. Any player running the bases shall be declared out if, at any time, while the ball is in play, he be touched by a fielder, with the ball in hand, without some part of his person is touching a base. Should the said fielder, while in the act of touching the base-runner, have the ball knocked out of his hand, the player so touched shall be declared out.

If a ball be held by a fielder on the first base before the base-runner, after hitting a fair ball, touches the base, he shall be declared out.

Any base-runner who shall in any way interfere with or obstruct a fielder while attempting to catch a fair fly ball, or a foul ball, shall be declared out by the umpire with or without appeal. If he wilfully obstructs a fielder from fielding a ball, he shall be similarly declared out, and, if he intentionally kick, or let the ball strike him, he shall be declared out.

RULE VII.—THE UMPIRE AND HIS DUTIES.

SECTION 1. In selecting an umpire for a match game the visiting club shall submit the names of five persons, competent to act, who are not members of the visiting club. From this list the local club shall select two or more names, and answer not later than the following day. Should the visiting club be unable to secure the services of either of the two persons selected, then two more names shall be submitted to the local club to complete the list for them to select from. In case of the failure of the local club to select two of the names within forty-eight hours after said names have been telegraphed by the visiting club—if within five days of the day of the game—then the visiting club shall be at liberty to select one from the list of names sent, who shall act as umpire. All correspondence in relation to above shall be by telegraph.

SEC. 2. The umpire shall not be changed during the progress of a match game, except for reason of illness or injury, or by the consent of the captains of the two contesting nines, in case he shall have wilfully violated the rules of the game.

SEC. 3. Before the commencement of a match, the umpire shall see that the rules governing the materials of the game, and also those applicable to the positions of batsman and pitcher, are strictly observed. Also, that the fence in the rear of the catcher's position is distant not less than ninety feet from the home base, except it mark the boundary line of the field, in which case the umpire, for every ball passing the catcher and touching the fence, shall give each base-runner one base without his being put out.

Before calling "play" the umpire shall ask the captain of the players on whose ground the match is played, whether or not there are any special ground rules to be enforced, and if there are, he shall take note of such rules and see that they are duly enforced, provided they do not conflict with any rules of the game.

SEC. 4. No decision rendered by the umpire on any point of play in base-running shall be reversed upon the testimony of any of the players. But if it shall be shown by the two captains of the contesting clubs that the umpire has palpably misinterpreted the rules, or given an erroneous decision, he shall reverse said decision.

SEC. 5. Should the umpire be unable to see whether a catch has been fairly made or not, he shall be at liberty to appeal to the bystanders, and to render his decision according to the fairest testimony at command.

SEC. 6. No person, not engaged in the game, shall be permitted to occupy any position within the lines of the field of contest, or in any way interrupt the umpire during the progress of the game. No player shall be permitted to converse with the umpire during any part of the contest, except the two captains of the contesting nines, and then only as provided in Section 4 of this rule.

SEC. 7. The umpire shall render no decision in the game except when appealed to by a player, unless expressly required to do so by the rules of the game, as in calling "ball," etc.

SEC. 8. The umpire shall not enter the infield while the ball is in play, and he shall require the players on the batting side who are not at the bat or running the bases, to keep at a distance of not less than fifty feet from the line of home and first base and home and third base, or farther off if he decide. The captain and one assistant only shall be permitted to coach players running the bases, and they must not approach within fifteen feet of the foul lines.

SEC. 9. Should any fielder stop or catch the ball with his hat, cap, or any part of his dress the umpire should call "dead ball," and base-runners shall each be entitled to two bases for any fair hit ball so stopped or caught. Should the ball be wilfully stopped by any outside person not engaged in the game, the umpire must call "dead ball," and players running bases at the time shall be entitled to the bases they were running for, and the ball be regarded as dead until settled in the hands of the pitcher while standing within the lines of his position.

SEC. 10. Any match game in which the umpire shall declare any section of this code of rules to have been wilfully violated shall at once be declared by him to have been forfeited by the club at fault.

SEC. 11. No manager, captain, or player shall address the audience, except in case of necessary explanation; and any manager, captain or player who shall use abusive, threatening, or improper language to the audience, shall be punished by suspension from play for twenty days and forfeiture of his salary for such period.

SEC. 12. No Section of these Rules shall be construed as conflicting with or affecting any Article of the Constitution.

THE CANADIAN NATIONAL ASSOCIATION, 1876

During the late 1860s and early 1870s the American game of baseball gained enthusiasts in the midwestern regions of Canada. In 1876 sportsmen from the Maple Leaf Club of Guelph and other associations from London and Toronto founded the Canadian Association of Base Ball Players. Meeting in Toronto in early April, the delegates elected officers, adopted a constitution and by-laws, and passed a set of rules based on those of the amateur National Association of the United States. One of the main goals of the convention was to establish a competition for the championship of Canada. That code is reprinted here from *Bryce's Canadian Baseball Guide* (London, Canada, 1876) pp. 57-58.

CHAMPIONSHIP CODE.

SECTION 1.—All clubs, members of this Association, desiring to contest for the championship must make application in writing to the chairman of the Judiciary Committee on or before May 15th of each year, and no clubs shall be admitted as contestants after that date. Each application must be accompanied by a remittance of $10 (ten dollars.) The chairman shall keep a record of the clubs so applying and he shall announce the names of the clubs contesting for the title, by publication. Clubs shall be eligible to contest for the championship from the date of their *entree* as contestants.

2.—The series for the championship shall be four games, and each club shall play four games with every other contesting club at such time and place as they may mutually agree upon. All games must be played before October 1st of each year.

3. No game shall count in the series of contests for the championship in which the rules of this Association shall have been violated, and no games of clubs who have not played at least two games with each of the contending clubs shall count in the championship series.

4.—Should either of two clubs fail to meet a regular engagement to play, mutually agreed upon —except on account of the death or severe illness of one of its players, or on account of stormy weather —the club thus failing to play shall forfeit the game to the club having its men on the field ready to play at the time appointed; and such forfeited game shall count in the series of championship contests as a game won by a score of nine runs to none.

5.—In case of a tie game ending in a draw match in any series of championship contests between two clubs, said tie or draw game shall not count on the record of either club, if there be not due time to play such game over before the close of the season. And no tie or drawn game shall be played over again until after the full series of games have been played, including such drawn matches.

6.—The club winning the greatest number of games in the championship series, with clubs entering for the championship, during the season, shall be declared champions of Canada.

7.—In case of a tie in the total number of championship games played during the season between two or more contesting clubs, the championship committee shall examine the records of the clubs so tieing and the one having the greatest number of victories over the leading nines of the contesting clubs shall be declared champion.

8.—A championship streamer shall be purchased by the said championship committee with the funds accompanying the application of clubs, and they shall present the same on or before November 1st of each year to the club entitled to receive it.

9.—No contesting club in the championship arena shall play any "exhibition" or "tournament" games with any other contesting club until it has finished its regular series of championship games.

10.—Each club competing for the championship shall provide an enclosed ground of sufficient size, free from obstructions, for all championship matches to be played upon.

11.—The gate fee for all championship games shall be 25 cents to spectators, visiting clubs to be entitled to 40 per cent. of the cash receipts after expenses have been deducted.

Chapter 4

BICYCLING

THE AMERICAN BICYCLER

During the late 1860s a mania for a new machine called the "velocipede" swept across the United States. Manufacturers began producing the two wheeled vehicles in large quantities, as professionals, merchants, students, mechanics, and even a few ladies took lessons and practiced in rinks, halls, and riding schools. The craze soon passed, however, because the enthusiasts for the new pastime discovered that the new contraptions were dangerous and difficult to pedal on roads. Interest in the pastime was renewed in New England in 1877, when the firm of Cunningham and Company began to import and sell the latest models of English bicycles. In December of that year the first American bicycling journal began publication, and in February 1878 the Boston Bicycle Club became the pioneer organization in the United States. At that time the Pope Manufacturing company began importing and building bicycles, and by 1880 the pastime had gained greater acceptance in both the United States and Canada, with new associations founded in several towns in Massachusetts, Bangor, Maine, Buffalo, New York, Washington, D.C., Newark, New Jersey, San Francisco, California, and Montreal. In May of 1880 the first national organization of bicyclists, the League of American Wheelmen, convened in Newport, Rhode Island. Thirty clubs sent delegates to this gathering, which approved a constitution that stated that the organization's objects were "to promote the general interests of bicycling, to ascertain, defend and protect the rights of wheelmen, and to encourage and facilitate touring." At this time most bicyclists took up the pastime for recreational rides, but a few were serious competitors at races held in riding halls or on tracks as part of athletic meets.

The following document presents excerpts from a model constitution proposed by a leading authority on bicycling for adoption by new clubs. They are reprinted from Charles E. Pratt, *The American Bicycler: A Manual for the Observer, the Learner, and the Expert* (Boston, 1880), pp. 175-181.

ARTICLE XII.—*Bicycling Meetings, and Club Riding upon the Roads.*

At least once each year, there shall be an excursion or tour at a time to be appointed by the captain, in which all members of the club shall be expected to participate: the duration and distance of the tour to be decided upon and published not less than one month prior to the meet therefor; the absence from headquarters not to exceed two weeks; and each member participating, to remain with the club during the whole run, unless excused by the captain, or deterred by illness or accident.

The club may meet for runs in company at such times and places as shall be appointed; and, upon arriving at the outward terminal point of each run, those members who so desire shall be permitted by the captain to extend the run as far as they may wish. The captain, in such cases, if he does not accompany, to appoint some member to officiate in his stead. Upon all runs, tours, or excursions, the club will implicitly observe and obey the orders of the captain or his representative.

The position of the captain, while the club is in motion, is at the front; and, while the captain is in that position, no member shall be allowed to pass him without permission.

This rule, however, shall not operate to prevent the captain occupying any position along the line to which circumstances may call him.

When on a run, tour, or excursion, as a club, each member is requested to wear the club uniform.

On all club runs, tours, or excursions, it shall be governed by the following

ROAD RULES.

SECTION 1. The object of club excursions is not to ride against time, still less to encourage any competition between individual members attending them. Their intention is,—

(1) To provide an opportunity for members to get ordinary bicycle exercise in company, and

(2) To make them acquainted with the various roads suitable for bicycling, together with the objects of interest, &c., in the neighborhood.

SECT. 2. In the absence of any officer or member of committee, the senior member of the club (according to the date of his election) present should act as leader, and his directions should be implicitly obeyed. He should set a *moderate* pace, and bear well in mind the needs of the less experienced, not only as regards pace, but as to occasional halts, dismounting for hills, &c. These matters and many others must be left to his discretion, as the company and the occasion may suggest; but as a general rule it is not well to aim at more than ten miles to the hour, nor to keep with the company in the saddle for more than an hour at a stretch.

SECT. 3. For the better regulation of the pace, and to prevent straggling, one of the sub-captains should ride in the rear for the purpose of signalling whenever the tail of the company is getting out-distanced; and the leader should then slacken until he receives a second signal indicating that they have closed up. In case of accidents, &c., some special signal should be given, on hearing which the leader should dismount.

SECT. 4. In ordinary riding, on country roads, signals from the rear to the front of a company can be easily passed on by word of mouth. Whilst the wishes of the leader can as readily be ascertained by watching his movements (as regards a dismount or alteration of pace), a set of signals shall be used for the most obvious purposes:—

(1) For *extended* order (See Sect. 8), the *right* hand held *out*.

(2) For *closing* up again (See Sect. 8), the *left* hand held *out*.

(3) For slackening pace, whilst maintaining the same distance between each rider or pair, the *right* hand held *up*.

(4) For sudden halt, in case of danger, the *left* hand with a handkerchief in it to be held up.

Mere acceleration of pace gives its own signal; and for the formation of *single* and *double* file the leader has only to give the order to his own companion, and the rest of the company will naturally follow suit.

SECT. 5. But for cases of emergency, or where (as in towns) there is too much noise and interruption of view to admit of mere *verbal* or *manual* signalling, or whenever the captain may so elect, the orders shall be given by whistle or bugle.

The orders when given by bugle shall be as follows:—

REVEILLE (No 3, cavalry Tactics, United States Army) to be sounded first thing in the morning when the club is on a tour.

STABLE CALL (No. 14, Cavalry Tactics, United States Army), to be sounded twenty minutes after the "Reveille" to call club together to oil up, and put machines in order for the day's run; or may be sounded as an order to clean machines after the day's run.

MESS (No. 7, Cavalry Tactics, United States Army), to be sounded to summon to any meal.

ASSEMBLY (No. 2, Cavalry Tactics, United States Army), to be sounded to order to call club together, to fall in preparatory to mounting.

BOOTS AND SADDLES (No. 16, Cavalry Tactics, United States Army), at sound of which the club shall mount, always left in front.

GALLOP (No. 43, Cavalry Tactics, United States Army), to increase the pace.

WALK (No. 41, Cavalry Tactics, United States Army), at sound of which the club shall proceed more slowly.

HALT (No. 40, Cavalry Tactics, United States Army), at sound of which the club shall dismount and halt.

DISMOUNT (No. 38, cavalry Tactics, United States Army), at sound of which each man (commencing always from the rear) shall dismount, and walk by the left-hand side of his machine.

FORM TWOS (No. 42, Cavalry Tactics, United States Army), at sound of which the club will form twos; the even numbers always quickening, and taking their position as right-hand men.

QUICKSTEP (No. 33, Cavalry Tactics, United States Army) conveys no order to the club, but may be sounded by order of the captain, when passing through villages, or at the captain's discretion.

RIDE AT EASE (No. 15, Cavalry Tactics, United States Army), at sound of which each rider may choose his own companion.

RE-FORM, SINGLE FILE (No. 23, Cavalry Tactics, Unites States Army), at sound of which each rider shall resume his proper position in the column.

RETREAT (No. 4, Cavalry Tactics, United States Army) may be sounded if the captain so orders, to announce that the day's run is completed.

TATTOO (No. 5, Cavalry Tactics, United States Army) may be sounded if the captain so orders, as a suggestion to the club that it would be advisable to go to bed, and get ready for the exertions of the morrow.

In the absence of the bugler, and when the captain may elect to give the order by whistle, the following code shall be used:—

One long whistle—fall in.

One short whistle—mount.

Two short whistles—form twos.

Two long whistles—slacken speed.

Six short whistles—increase speed.

One short and one long whistle, repeated three times—dismount and walk.

Three short, well-separated whistles—dismount and halt.

One long, two short, and one long again, repeated three times—ride at ease.

No orders shall be given, or whistles or bugles sounded, except by the captain or his order.

SECT. 6. Where more than twenty riders attend a club meet, run or excursion, the captain shall divide them into companies not to exceed—if it can be avoided—sixteen members to each company; each division to be under order of a sub-captain, or officer specially appointed, and each division to preserve a distance of not less than two hundred yards between them.

SECT. 7. As a general rule, the company should ride *two* abreast; but in towns and villages, in passing and meeting vehicles, in riding up and down hills, and where the road is soft, rough, or stony, and requires picking, *single* file should invariably be adopted, the *left*-hand man always *quickening*, and the right-hand man dropping in behind him.

SECT. 8. When in *single* file, an interval of at least *ten* yards should be kept between each rider, and in *double* file *twenty* yards between each pair. These intervals should be doubled in hilly country. In approaching a hill, whether up or down, the leading files should quicken, and the rear files slacken, so as to allow of the company extending out to double distance; and on reaching the level they should slacken and quicken again respectively, till the original interval is attained.

SECT. 9. When rising in company down hill, the bicyclist, if the hill be a long one, should be careful to keep his machine well in hand, and not remove his feet from the treadles. It is very undesirable for a *company* to ride down a long hill if there is a curve obstructing the view to the bottom. It should not be forgotten that horses which will take one bicycle quietly may often turn restive when passed by several in succession; and, should any consequent complications arise toward the bottom of a long hill, it is very difficult to avoid disaster. In the case of winding hill, it is better that the leader should advance along till he sees that all is clear, and then whistle the company on. Much must be left to the discretion of the leader, whose own movements as regards dismounting, riding with the feet off, &c., must be taken as the rule for the rest.

SECT. 10. the ordinary rules of the road as regards passing vehicles, &c., should *be rigidly adhered to.*

a. A horse should *never* be passed *on both sides at once.*

b. A *led* horse should always be passed on the same side as the man who is leading it.

c. Before overtaking a vehicle or rider, it is well to give some sort of warning; not a shout, the intention of which may be misinterpreted and give offence. In company-riding, a word to your companion will suffice to attract the necessary attention. The mere sound of the human voice previously is often all that is wanted to prevent a horse from starting at the sudden passing of the noiseless machine.

d. The ground in front of a horse should never be taken till the bicyclist is at least ten yards ahead of him.

e. If a horse, on meeting a bicycle, show signs of restiveness, it is not always wise to dismount at once. To dismount *suddenly* is more likely to frighten a horse than to continue riding *slowly* by, *speaking to the horse* as you do so. But the leader should order a dismount at his discretion (even if he himself has passed the horse), and should *invariably* do so on any signal or request from the driver or horseman.

f. Foot-passengers on the roads should not be needlessly shouted at, but should always be given a *good side berth,* especially at crossings.

g. In company riding, the leader, on passing any one (whether riding, driving, or walking), should announce that *others* are following close after; and the rear man should in the same way signify that *all* have passed.

h. Inattention to these and other rules and courtesies of the road will cause annoyance to the public, and create prejudices against bicycling.

SECT. 11. Bicycling after dark is on all accounts most undesirable, but may be occasionally necessary. In company-riding, the leader and the rear man only should be provided with lights. A multiplication of lights is confusing to the bicyclist (owing to the attendant shadows, &c.) and very alarming to horses. Single file must be invariably adopted, and the leader and the rear man should always make the proper announcement (section 10g) in passing.

If the night be not over-dark, bells which can be rung or stopped at will may be substituted for lights. Bells should be always carried *in passing through towns and villages* after dark.

SECt. 12. A bicyclist, *when riding in company,* should never take a dog with him, however well he may have trained him to follow him when alone.

SECT. 13. The time named for a club-excursion is the exact time of *the start,* which will in all cases be punctually observed. Members are therefore requested to be at the spot named *at least ten minutes before,* that they may arrange themselves in order for the start, and receive the instructions of the leader as regards signals and any other directions that may be necessary.

SECT. 14. The leader may always alter the *direction* of the excursion at his discretion, to avoid a contrary wind or a bad road, &c.; but the *starting-place* named must be always adhered to.

SECT. 15. At all club-meets, the bugle will sound the "assembly" five minutes before the time appointed for the start. At this signal the club will form in line, left in front, the smaller wheels to the left. The company will then tell off by twos, and the *odd numbers will be the left-hand men.*

This order shall be preserved during the whole run, except the captain order the bugler to sound the "ride at ease," when each rider shall be at liberty to choose his own companion. In no case shall a member ride ahead of the captain; and, immediately the "Re-form single file" is sounded, he shall resume his proper place in the column.

Upon the bugle sounding "Boots and saddles," each man shall turn his machine to the left, and place his left foot upon the step, then each man shall mount; but he shall first be sure that the man immediately in front of him has mounted safely, and proceeded at least two revolutions, before doing so. As soon as the whole company has mounted, the distance of ten yards between each machine is to be kept.

Upon approaching a stopping-place, or the end of the run, the club will be brought into single file. The bugle will then sound the "Halt," when the dismounting will commence FROM THE REAR, each man passing the word forward as he gets off his machine.

ARTICLE XIII.—*ANNUAL RACE FOR CHAMPIONSHIP OF THE CLUB*

There shall be once in each year (preferably in the month of October), a race for the championship of the club. Each man shall ride a modern bicycle, without multiplying gear, and shall not employ any other means than pedal motion for covering the distance. The size of the wheel shall be at discretion of the rider.

The day and the course shall be left to the discretion of the committee, but the length of the championship race shall be not less than fifty miles.

The winner shall be the rider who covers the distance in the shortest time; and the prize shall be a silver trophy, which shall have the champion's name and the date of the race inscribed thereon, and shall be kept in the club headquarters until it is won by a competitor each year for three consecutive years, when it shall become his own private and personal property.

In addition to the above, each of the riders (up to ten) who covers the distance within five hours shall receive a silver medal suitably inscribed and commemorative of the event. This race shall be open to club-members only.

ARTICLE XIV.—*Club Racing.*

All club races shall be run subject to the following rules and conditions, together with such others as the judges may dictate.

RULE 1. None but members of the club, or invited members of other bicycle clubs, shall be allowed to compete.

RULE 2. All competitors shall wear the club colors, and a distinguishing number on the breast, during each race.

RULE 3. No attendants will be allowed to accompany a competitor.

RULE 4. Riders must pass each other on the outside, and be a clear length of the bicycle in front, before taking an inside position.

RULE 5. Competitors may stop or dismount during a race, but must not in any way obstruct the course.

RULE 6. The committee shall appoint the judges, who shall attend to all necessary duties, and whose decision shall be final.

RULE 7. No two machines shall touch each other while in motion, during a race.

RULE 8. Any violation of these rules must be reported to the judges immediately the race is concluded.

RULE 9. These rules shall operate equally in races on the road, cinder-paths, or other track.

Chapter 5

BLOOD (ANIMAL) SPORTS

Blood sports which pitted animals against each other remained a part of the lower class sporting scene in several North American cities during the 1860s and 1870s. Yet that era also brought a new movement for more humane treatment of animals, which included renewed efforts to enforce existing laws that prohibited these exhibitions.

In New York City cockfighting "mains" continued to draw crowds of lower and lower-middle class spectators, along with a few from the upper ranks of society. Kit Burns's Sportsman Hall was perhaps the town's most notorious animal pit. Located behind a bar at the end of a narrow corridor, it could hold up to 400 people. There members of the sporting fraternity could watch dogfighting and rat baiting along with the battles between roosters. Gambling was a vital feature of these contests, with tens of thousands of dollars changing hands at major spectacles.

Animal rights advocates had argued against these amusements for decades, but the crusade to ban blood sports gained new strength in 1866 when Henry Bergh founded the American Society for the Prevention of Cruelty to Animals (ASPCA). The son of a successful shipbuilder, Bergh modeled his new organization after England's Royal Society for the Prevention of Cruelty to Animals, which began operations in 1824. He dedicated his life to humanitarian treatment of animals, which included efforts to shelter homeless animals, to improve treatment of horses used for transportation in cities, to help farmers care for their livestock, and to encourage law enforcement officers to prosecute game law violators. (See chapter 9 for his criticism of pigeon shooting.) This chapter begins with an editorial and a story from The New York Times, which strongly supported Bergh and his Society in its campaign against cockfighting. It concludes with two pieces defending the sport from James Gordon Bennett's New York Herald. By 1880 the ASPCA, the clergy, and public opinion in general had finally gained the advantage over the proponents of blood sports, and by the end of the nineteenth century they had virtually disappeared from New York City's sporting scene, except for the occasional illicit, underground event.

COCKFIGHTING

EDITORIAL

This editorial reflects the view of New York City's Protestant establishment in its criticism of all kinds of blood sports. It suggests that the contests still fascinated some of the city's elite gentlemen. It first appeared in The New York Times, 22 March 1866, p. 4.

BRUTAL PASTIMES.—It seems strange that the exercise of brutality should be a pastime to any human being, yet so it is. We published a few days since an account of a cockfighting pandemonium in Brooklyn, at the "New Cockpit," at which many "business men and politicians" were present. There can be nothing more disgusting or more cruel. The days of bull-baiting, bear-baiting, and kindred sports, we thought had gone by. Dogfights, though still an amusement of the "fancy," are reprobated by decent people. But here is a number of moneyed men gathering together, with a secresy which marks their consciousness of guilt, though not of shame, glorying and betting over the combats of creatures whose torture and defeat is only accomplished by the death of one of the contestants. If this disgrace were confined to one instance there would be less occasion to speak of it; but we are assured that the practice of cock-fighting is privately carried on in many places in the City, and without any apparent effort to prevent it. In fact, this brutal work is organized as any other vile trade might be. There are no words to express the detestation in which men so engaged should be held. The only fit punishment for them, failing a residence at Sing Sing, is that they be set in pairs in an arena, with tied hands, and forced to kick and bite each other to the death of one of them, and then let the victor be escorted home in triumph.

A VISIT TO NEW JERSEY

This story suggests that the New York City sporting men who patronized animal fights could easily evade the local police by crossing the Hudson River, where they encountered little interference from New Jersey authorities. It is reproduced from The New York Times, 7 March 1867, p. 8.

A GATHERING OF THE FANCY AT UNION HILL, N.J.—FIGHTING A "MAIN" FOR $500 A SIDE—BRUTALITY OF THE UNFEATHERED BIPEDS—THE PLEASANT PASTIMES OF JERSEY "SPORTS."

Receiving a mysterious intimation that an affair of some importance in sporting circles was about to come off, yesterday afternoon, at an out-of-the-way place in the outskirts of Hoboken, we started in that direction, with the design of laying before our readers a full account of the occurrences which might take place.

It was said that careful and secret preparations had been made for the purpose of getting up an extraordinary exhibition of cock-fighting, a great "main" having been made for the occasion, which would call out a full representation of the "fancy" as well as the "roughs" of New-York. Not having a fancy for roughing it ourselves, we felt somewhat anxious to conceal our purposes in "mixing in" with such an affair; but owing to the lateness of the hour at which our information was received, we were obliged to set out in our usual costume, trusting to the universal adaptability of a newspaper man for the means of getting extricated from any difficulties which might arise in the course of our investigations.

Crossing the Barclay-street ferry, we entered the horse car for "Union Hill and Weehawken," together with about a dozen good-humored gentlemen, whose general appearance was suggestive of gin-cocktails and brandy-smashes, and after a ride of about three miles and a half, during which we strove to cultivate an intimate acquaintance with our fellow-travelers, and become possessed of some items of information respecting the object of our journey, we arrived at two big lager-beer breweries and a collection of houses, known as "Union Hill." Following in the wake of our companions, we presently appeared in the bar-room of MITCHELL'S Hotel, where twenty-five or thirty men were engaged in smoking, drinking and talking. It was quite evident that there was no particular desire to keep the affair secret, and, in fact, soon learned that in that part of the world cock fighting is regarded as an innocent and diverting pastime, combining pleasure with profit, patronized occasionally by the guardians of the public peace, and deserving of encouragement by every one interested in the improvement of Shanghais and [illegible] Chinas.

THE COCK-PIT

was discovered in a rickety frame building in the rear of the hotel, and consisted of a circular area about twelve feet in diameter, surrounded by a low railing and covered with a rag carpet, upon which were chalked in the centre of the ring, two lines about two feet apart, where the cocks were to be set up. An arrangement of seats of a primitive description environed the inclosure. One corner of the room was occupied by a red-hot stove, and another by a decrepit individual with a withered hand and a club foot, seated before a table improvised out of a couple of boards and spread with a "sweat-cloth" on which he invited the bystanders to engage in what he called his "little guess game."

At about 3 o'clock P.M. the votaries of the cock-pit began to enter the room, each paying the trifling sum of $3 to the little man in the bar-room outside who furnished the tickets—a price which it was supposed would secure a very select and reputable assemblage.

In conversing with several of the initiated we learned that these games, though prohibited by the State law, were regularly carried on there every week with little or no attempt at concealment. The business of rearing the cocks is largely engaged in by several persons, one man—DRAKE by name—being pointed out to us, who raises two or three hundred every year, putting them out among the farmers in the vicinity, so that each bird may become accustomed to "ruling the roost," and thus acquire confidence and pluck. They are subjected to a regular course of training for a few weeks before the fight, so that they may be in proper condition, and before being brought into the pit, are "heeled," or provided with steel spurs, which are formidable weapons, an inch and a quarter in length, firmly fastened over the natural spurs of the fowl.

A "main" is a certain number of matches or battles to be fought for a fixed wager, with a smaller sum depending on the issue of each match so as to insure fair play. In this instance, BRUMMEY "made" the main and DRAKE fought it for a wager of $500.

About a hundred men composed the crowd, made up of farmers from the vicinity and saloon keepers and sporting men from Hoboken and Jersey-City, with a considerable sprinkling from Gotham, and nearly all appeared to be well versed in the business. After some delay the first pair of "birds" was brought in and the sport began. Betting by the partisans of the respective sides was now the order. "I'll go eight to ten on Brummey." "Sixteen to Twenty." "I'll take that." "Who'll go twenty-five even?" and similar expressions, interlarded with oaths, formed the staple of the conversation.

There seemed to be two or three leading characters whose bets were generally successful. One fellow, with a cast in his eye, and who boasted that "he had always been on hand, ever since he was big enough, so that they'd let him into a cock-pit," had the shrewdness to win almost every time.

It was noticeable that the interest in the contest was entirely dependent on the sums at stake. The excitement was altogether mercenary. To a novice, the noble carriage of the game cocks, their courage and unwavering pluck, fighting bravely to the last until death closed the scene, was an exhibition of qualities which can never fail of exciting admiration, but among the *habitues* of the place the only question seemed to be which would win and whose were the stakes.

There could be no doubt of the brutalizing tendency of the whole affair. All the surroundings tended to immorality. The bar was well patronized during the intervals between the matches, and the "little guess game" in the corner received its share of attention.

After witnessing three battles, in each of which one of the brave combatants bit the dust, and learning that "they would keep it up" probably till 12 o'clock at night, we came away with the well-settled impression that of the two classes of bipeds engaged in the transaction the feathered ones were decidedly the most worthy of our respect and consideration.

GREAT COCKING CONTEST

This piece presents a more positive view of cockfighting. It is reprinted from The New York Herald, 27 January 1870.

MAIN OF GAME COCKS BETWEEN NEW JERSEY AND NEW YORK

New Jersey, all things considered, must be called the cock-pit of the United States, as within its limits some of the most desperate battles ever fought between game birds have been decided. Last evening another main came off there in a little village called Pamrapo, between New Jersey and New York, in which there was splendid fighting, and the Jersey boys achieved a decisive victory. Well informed persons are inclined to think that they will retain the belt to the end of the season. It could hardly be in better hands, for they are generally willing to accommodate anybody on fair terms. The main fought last night was made by a sagacious gentleman in the village referred to and parties in this city. The agreement was to show fifteen cocks a side, from four pounds four ounces to five pounds eight ounces, to fight all that fell in for $100 a battle and $1,000 the main. Thirteen couples fell in, and no better fighting has been seen this year than the birds afforded. The New Jersey fowls are mostly bred by a duck wing Sefton gray, lately accidentally killed, and a pony pyle, out of an Irish hen, while the New York cocks were from "up river"—Tarrytown and Albany—and from Uncle John Ludlow's, at Union Hill.

THE FIGHTING.

First fight.—The games began with the heavy weights, two five pound eight ounce birds, and Jersey was the favorite for the first battle and the main. The New York cock was from Troy, a red pyle, long legs, but well stationed. New Jersey showed a blue brass back, very handsome. They set to work in earnest. New Jersey got the worst of the first buckles, but soon turned the tables, and never stopped fighting until the pyle lay at his feet dying. Time, 3:13 1/2.

Second Fight.—The light weights, four pounds two ounces. The Yorkers had a black red, with white hackle, bred from a Derby cock and an Irish hen. New Jersey was a red pyle. The New Yorker was a rattler, and won the fight after a hard and obstinate struggle. Thrice did he take it from the foe, and only when both were blind and "cut to pieces" did the New Jersey bird succumb. Handfuls of money were lost on the fight. Time, 22:55 2/5.

Third Fight.—New York was again the favorite, twenty to eighteen. The Jerseyites showed a spangled muff from Staten Island. New York brought out another black red. The weights were four pounds fifteen ounces. The spangled had the best of it the first and second buckle, but then unfortunately fell and broke a wing, which crippled him badly. But even with this he knocked the black red "stiff, dumb and blind," and won a terrible "up hill fight" gallantly. Time, 15:17 1/5.

Fourth Fight.—The New York party sent in a black red and the Jerseyites a black red muff; weights, four pounds eleven ounces. The former was the favorite. It was a rattling, flap for flap fight, and Jersey was getting the best of it, when he got his throat cut and received a brain blow which used him up very quickly, the muff winning in style. Time, 2:45 3/4.

Fifth Fight.—The battles were now two and two and the excitement very great. New Jersey presented a blue red and their opponents a black gray from Brooklyn, weights, four pounds four ounces. The gray was the favorite. It was a desperate, scientific struggle and buckle for buckle, beak for beak were indulged in; but the gray soonest expended his powder, and New Jersey, never slacking up, won the battle. Both were true, fine fighters, and took a deal of cutting. Time, 9:23.

Sixth Fight.—New Jersey again the favorite for the fight and the main of two to one. They sent in a white pyle and the Yorkers a black red. Weight, four pounds, fourteen ounces. The Yorker was a "dancing master," but his terpsichorean feats were but few, as at the third buckle he got it in the neck and gave up instantly. His handler said that he was dead. Time, 5:02.

Seventh fight.—Great excitement among the betting fraternity, and from some supposed wrong committed by the Jerseyites considerable loud talking was indulged in. New York showed another black red and New Jersey a spangled muff. Weight, four pounds, eleven ounces. York the favorite. The red did all the fighting and was nicely winning the battle when the handler of Jersey picked up his bird while fighting, and the judge on appeal gave New York the battle, Time, 5:11.

Eighth Fight.—Weight, four pounds eight ounces. The Yorkers produced a black red, one of Ludlow's. New Jersey showed a brown red. The black was the favorite, 10 to 7. They set to work grandly, and, as the brown was a fine fighter, troubled his opponent greatly. The black got two or three painful pricks, when he down tan and ran away—a dunghill. Time, 7:16 1/5.

Ninth Fight.—New Jersey had but two more fights to win, and the main would be decided. It now stood five battles for New Jersey to the New Yorkers three. The latter sent in another black red, five pounds four ounces, and the Jerseyites produced a brown red, five pounds five ounces. Two better birds never entered a pit. The fighting was desperate, but at the outset the Jersey bird got a chance blow in the brain, which killed him instantly. Time: Fifty seconds.

Tenth Fight.—Weights, New York, four pounds ten ounces; New Jersey, four pounds nine ounces. The former was a brown red, white hackle; the latter a red pyle. It was ten to seven on the pyle, and he was a fighter, for in very quick order he cut the brown's throat and so demoralized him that he, "loafer like," cut sticks and tried to fly the pit. Time, 4:13 1/5.

Eleventh Fight.—This might decide the main. Amid an uproar almost ear splitting New Jersey produced a gray pyle, four pounds six ounces, and New York another black red, one ounce heavier. The black, although a hard, game looking bird, also showed the "white feather" after fighting but a little, and when he obtained a severe body blow quit badly. Time, 9:36.

New Jersey had won the main in gallant style, and her partisans much money.

The twelfth and thirteenth fights, two four pound five ounce and two four pound nine ounce birds, were also won by the Jerseyites.

THE ROOSTERS' ARENA

This editorial describes the state of cockfighting in the New York City vicinity in 1870 and also dismisses Henry Bergh's efforts to abolish the sport. It is reprinted from The New York Herald, 1 November 1870.

The present "cocking season," which will be formally ushered in on the night of November 24, promises to be quite as brilliant as any ever before known in this country. Already some half dozen single fights and one main of five fights have taken place in Brooklyn, Westchester and the vicinity of Jersey City, nearly all of which, however, were between cocks of last year's breeding, this year's stock being, as a general thing, still too young to wear the steel. The great impetus given to the sport during the last two or three years by the attendance at the pit of many persons of wealth and high standing in society has caused the old breeders in every part of the country, and New York and vicinity in particular, to enter, "soul and body," into the business, and the result is that as large and as fine a stock of the feathered gladiators has been produced as ever entered an arena. Many of the gentlemen who had good stock last year have continued to breed from the same this season, some have crossed a number of the most choice and favorite strains to be had, while others have imported foreign stock—principally English—which they have either bred with pure stock or crossed with well known domestic strains. Never before was there such universal interest taken in the sport. From the Rio Grande to the St. Lawrence the same great activity seems to prevail, and already several heavy mains are being negotiated between parties in different sections of the country. As far as preventing this sort of sport is concerned Mr. Bergh and his numerous corps of deputies may as well throw up the sponge first as last, for, beyond causing a little inconvenience and annoyance to those who frequent and participate in the enjoyment, they will never accomplish anything. Cock fighting never was carried on more extensively in and around New York city than since the creation of the very society of which these gentlemen are the representatives. It is a sport that always has and always will be indulged in, no matter what laws are enacted for its prevention; consequently the sooner Mr. Bergh ceases to trouble himself about it the more time he will have to prosecute those brutes in human form who are daily to be seen abusing and maltreating the frames of horses which are made to perambulate the streets of this and other cities of the States, dragging after them overloaded carts, drays and cars.

Chapter 6

BOXING

During the 1860s and 1870s boxing in North America passed through an era of transition that witnessed a significant decline in the sport's fortunes. The Civil War in the United States brought an end to the golden age of the antebellum era, which culminated with the great international contest between John C. Heenan and Tom Sayers in England in 1860. The war disrupted professional pugilism, but it also provided a new arena for fisticuffs within the armed forces of both the Union and the Confederacy. After the great intersectional struggle bare-knuckle prize fights found less favor among both the sporting fraternity and the general public because of problems with crowd control and corruption. A series of disorders, sham battles, and fixed matches brought boxing under a cloud of suspicion by the 1870s, just prior to the sport's revival during the 1880s with the rise of John L. Sullivan. Throughout this period amateur sparring matches continued to be popular among gentlemen in several cities in the United States and Canada.

Boxing gained in popularity during the American Civil War because of the connections between warfare and pugilism. Both activities involved violence coupled with destructive techniques of discipline and science. Skill, finesse, courage, toughness, and intelligence were central to both the art of war and the manly art of self-defense. Camp life also encouraged boxing because it brought large numbers of males together and put them through a demanding regimen that geared them to fight. It also facilitated sports because the officers permitted the men to use their leisure time for athletics to entertain themselves and to relieve boredom. Many soldiers organized team competitions in such new recreations as cricket and baseball, while others participated in sharpshooting, wrestling, obstacle course runs, and fighting. The trials of army life led to numerous personal quarrels which were resolved in fistfights conducted according to rules. These encounters became the equivalent of the more dangerous duels with weapons which officers had favored during earlier eras. In short, these army matches provided a ritual—a form of restrained violence that offered a symbolic and dramatic enactment of the more lethal combat of the field of battle.

Wartime experiences and the memories of the great fights of the preceding decade led to a flurry of interest in prize-fighting during the late 1860s. The west became a prime center of action, especially in mining towns of the Colorado and Nevada territories. There saloon keepers staged commercial bare-knuckle bouts, where men could settle their differences while avoiding more deadly combat with six-shooters. Celebrated law men such as Wyatt Earp of Dodge City fought grudge matches against cowboys. Earp's friend, Bat Masterson, attended these challenges armed, to make sure of a fair fight. Both Earp and Masterson later officiated at professional bouts, and Masterson wound up his career as a boxing reporter in New York City. The first selection in this chapter recounts an amateur contest in Denver, Colorado.

Back in the east and the south, professional prize fighting deteriorated in the United States during the late 1860s and 1870s. The sport's major problems included police interference, spectator violence, and dishonesty. After 1865 urban politicians in New York and other large cities were less dependent on the gangs and "roughs" who also patronized pugilism. Hence promoters of bouts could no longer be assured of the protection of local law enforcement officials. On several occasions police broke up bouts, and a few fighters spent time behind bars. In addition, boxing's outlaw status and the lack of any governing body created the potential for violent disorders in every match. On numerous occasions matches degenerated into brawls among spectators; the brandishing of knives and pistols intimidated participants, and stabbings and shootings caused fatalities and serious injuries. To a great extent these incidents resulted from a deeply held suspicion that the fights had been fixed. The idea of a fair fight to the finish had given way to a pattern of corruption with contestants and referees bought off by gamblers.

In England the new rules of the Marquis of Queensberry gained acceptance during the late 1860s, but that code was slow to win adherents in the United States. The bare-knuckle era would witness one more revival in the 1880s with the rise of John L. Sullivan before the final acceptance of padded gloves, three minute rounds, the ten second knockout, and other new reforms.

Although there were a few fine events during this era, the majority of the bouts were either broken up by the authorities or terminated in violence or an inconclusive result. The fight between Jem (or Jim) Mace and Tom Allen outside of New Orleans in 1870 featured excitement, action, and a clear cut winner. The report of that match reprinted below suggests that it was a fair bout contested in front of a well behaved crowd. Quite a different scenario unfolded one year later, when the champion Mace faced his challenger Joe Coburn just across the border in Canada. The third selection in this chapter presents the story of this fiasco, which featured no action before the sheriff and his militia arrived to send everyone home.

Finally, in both Canada and the United States sparring exhibitions (as opposed to prize fights) were legal and patronized by middle and upper class men. The last document suggests that these events were popular because of the wagering and the excitement of the combat. But they were more orderly and less intense than the professional bouts.

A BOXING MATCH IN THE WEST, 1869

Fighting naturally flourished in the wild west of the post Civil War era, as men flocked to mountain camps in search of gold and silver. This narrative of a minor match in Denver was written by an eastern journalist on a grand tour of the region. It is taken from A.K. McClure, *Three Thousand Miles Through the Rocky Mountains* (Philadelphia, 1869), pp. 422-425.

At last the team was brought up before the hall used by the House of Representatives. Colonel Beidler was sitting with the driver, and, with a merry twinkle of the eye, he said, "Fun ahead, boys: let's have a hand at it;" and he called our attention to a rude placard on the door, stating that a sparring-match would come off at about that time. "All hands come in," said the colonel; and he looked especially for the bishop. "Just a little fun in the manly art," he added; but the bishop pleaded an engagement, and, with a kind farewell and a pleasant bow he left us. The legislature had adjourned, and the hall of the House had been converted into a regular ring: the floor was covered with several inches of sawdust, a circle of rude board seats had been thrown around the ring, and what I supposed to be a sparring-match was to be exhibited at the moderate price of one dollar a head. "It's to be a square fight, and there will be fun," said Beidler; but still I did not comprehend the entertainment to which we were invited. After the Orem and Dwyer fight, the legislature had passed a law forbidding public exhibitions of the manly art, unless the contestants wore gloves,—intending, of course, that the heavily-padded boxing gloves should be used. Upon entering the hall, there was every indication of serious business on hand. A ring, some fifteen feet in diameter, was formed, and in it were four men. In one corner was Con. Orem, stripped to his under-shirt, with an assortment of bottles, sponges, etc.; and by his side was sitting a little, smooth-faced fellow, wrapped in a blanket, looking like anything else than a hero of the prize-ring. He answered to the euphonious title of "Teddy," although English-born, and weighed one hundred and twenty-four pounds. In the opposite corner was a sluggish-looking Hiberian, probably ten pounds heavier than "Teddy," but evidently lacking the action of his opponent. With him was also his second. He was placarded as "The Michigan-Chick;" and they had met to have a square set-to, according to the rules of the ring, for one hundred dollars a side. Both had thin, close-fitting buckskin gloves on; and they were to fight in that way, to bring themselves within the letter of the law. Packed in the hall were over one hundred of the "roughs" of the mines; and I confess that I did not feel comfortable as I surveyed the desperate countenances and the glistening revolvers with which I was surrounded. Regarding discretion as the better part of valor, I suggested to Colonel Beidler that we had better retire; but he would not entertain the proposition at all. "Stay close by me, and there's no danger," was his reply. I had seen almost every phase of mountain-life but a fight; and I concluded that I would see it out and take the chances of getting away alive. My old friend Con. Orem, who was to fight "Teddy," gave me a comfortable seat close by his corner, and reminded me that I was about to witness a most artistic exhibition of the manly art. "Is it to be a serious fight?" I asked. "You bet!" was Con.'s significant reply. A distinguished military gentleman was chosen umpire, and in a few minutes he called "time." Instantly "Teddy" and "Chick" flung off their blankets and stood up in the fighting-trim,—naked to the waist, and clad only in woolen drawers and light shoes. "Teddy" stripped as delicately as a woman. His skin was soft and fair, and his waist was exceedingly slender; but he had a full chest, and when he threw out his arms on guard he displayed a degree of muscle that indicated no easy victory for his opponent. "Chick" was leaner, but had superfluous flesh, and was evidently quite young, as was manifest when he put himself in position for action. He betrayed evident timidity, and was heavy in his movements; but he seemed to have the physical power to crush his foe with one stroke, if he could only get it fairly home upon him. They advanced to the centre when time was called, and shook hands with a grim smile that was mutual, and the fight commenced. Both fought shy for a considerable time, and "Teddy" soon gave evidence of superior tact and training generally. "If he only has the endurance to protract the fight, he will lam the 'Chick' certain, you *bet*," said Orem, while he was bathing his principal after the first harmless round. And he was right. Fifty rounds were fought, and fully an hour had been employed in mauling each other's mugs, when both showed evident symptoms of grief, and would have been glad to call it a draw; but considerable money was staked, and their reputations as professional pugilists was involved, and they had to go through until one or the other was vanquished. Soon after, the "Chick" got in a fearful blow on "Teddy," and, as he reeled to his corner, the crowd evidently believed the fight to be ended. The odds had been bet on "Teddy," and a rush was made into the ring to break up the fight in a general row, so that the bets might be "declared off;" and instantly fifty pistols clicked and were drawn, most of which seemed to be pointed directly at me. I could not get out, and could not dodge: so I had to nerve myself to face the consequences. Colonel Beidler at once sprang into the ring, drew his revolvers, and declared that he would kill the first man who attempted to interfere with the fight. All well understood that when Beidler's pistol was drawn it meant business; and the ring was almost instantly cleared, leaving him standing alone in the centre. "Boys," said he, "this must be a fair fight. Go on with the show!" and time was promptly called again. It was perhaps fortunate for "Teddy" that the interruption occurred; for it gave him considerable time to recover from the serious blow he had received, and he came up to the scratch smiling again, but fought thereafter with the greatest care, striking out only when he considered the blow certain to tell. I noticed that he struck the "Chick" seventeen times on the right eye in seven rounds, and it closed,—when he commenced pounding the left optic. "Chick" generally closed because of his superior strength, and took "Teddy" in chancery frequently, but often with more cost to his own ribs than to "Teddy's" mug. Finally, after a fight of one hour and forty-two minutes, embracing sixty-seven rounds, "Teddy" got in a terrible blow over "Chick's" heart, and sent him spinning to his corner like a top. The sponge was at once thrown up, and "Teddy" was victor. I went to "Chick's" corner, and found him in the most distressed condition. His face was battered almost into a jelly, one eye was entirely closed, and the other nearly shut. The gloves had prevented the skin from being cut, and he was forced to seek relief at once by the free use of the lance to get blood from his face. His nostrils were closed with clotted blood, and his mouth was full of dark, thick blood. "I am too young," he said. "I should have known better. But I will whip him yet," was his remark, as he was led away by his friends. The crowd at once dispersed peaceably, and that night "Teddy" was the lion of the theatre, and participated in numerous drinks in honor of himself, at the "Pony," between acts.

JIM MACE VS. TOM ALLEN, 1870

While some of England's leading boxers and gentlemen were lobbying for the adoption of the Marquis of Queensberry rules during the 1860s, several of that nation's most prominent pugilists migrated to the United States in search of fame and fortune in the ring. Two of these newcomers were Jim (also Jem) Mace and Tom Allen. Interestingly, one of Mace's backers was the Benecia Boy—John C. Heenan—who had fought a controversial bout with Tom Sayers in England in 1860 and who had then lost to Tom King in 1863. The following report shows how the promoters of this fight were able to avoid police interference and stage a match which was fairly contested and not marred by spectator violence. It is reprinted from The New York Clipper, 21 May 1870, pp. 50, 51.

MACE AND ALLEN.

In another part of this paper we give complete details of the contest between Mace and Allen for five thousand dollars and the championship of America, in which the former came off the winner. The affair, from the inception of the match until the sponge was elevated in token of Allen's defeat, has been conducted in a quiet and harmonious manner, neither man seeking nor asking for the slightest advantage over his adversary. There was none of that wrangling or bullying we too frequently witness in match making now-a-days, no trickery or intent to rob which have been manifest at many of these latter day ring matches; but both men showed from first to last that they meant to win or lose on their merits alone—that the prize was to be won *inside* the ropes, and not by hired bullies and other like roughs on the outside. The attendance was of a better class than has been seen at the ring side for some years, and quietness and good order prevailed; which was owing to the "little arrangement" by which the turbulent element was barred out, and which may serve as a guide for all future aspirants to pugilistic honors. That Allen did not make a more equal display with his leary adversary created some little disappointment, but it must be borne in mind that Mace has the reputation of being the cleverest boxer of the day; his movements are astonishingly quick, and his blows are not only delivered with rapidity and precision, but they cut terribly; though having the advantage of years and weight on his side, Allen lacks the skill necessary to successfully encounter such an out-and-outer as Mace—these advantages are more than overbalanced by the superior knowledge possessed by Mace of the science of the manual of self defence, and his ability to put that knowledge into execution. That it was a good, artistic fight, no one will deny after reading our description of it....

ARTICLES OF AGREEMENT entered into between Thomas Allen and James Mace, by which the said Thomas Allen and the said James Mace mutually agree to fight a fair stand up fight according to the new rules of the London prize ring. And they each do mutually agree to be bound that the fight shall take place on the tenth day of May, A.D. 1870, and within fifty (50) miles of New Orleans, state of Louisiana, the men to be in the ring between the hours of seven (7) o'clock, A.M. and twelve (12) o'clock, M., the man failing to be in the ring to forfeit all claim to the battle money up. The fight shall be for the sum of $2,500 a side, and the Championship of America.

The sum of $500 a side is now placed in the hands of FRANK QUEEN, who shall appoint the final stakeholder, if he will not act himself. The second deposit, of $1,000 a side, shall be made at the CLIPPER office on Tuesday, March the 22d, 1870; and the third and final deposit of $1,000 a side, shall be made at the CLIPPER office, April 22, 1870. And it is further agreed that all monies made by the excursion shall be equally divided, Allen naming one man on his part and Mace one man on his behalf to superintend all affairs pertaining to said excursion, the man not being in the ring to lose the money, no matter whether he is bound by magisterial interference to keep the peace or not-nor in what state; if he is not in the ring, he shall lose the money. And it is further agreed that each man shall send a man to New Orleans seven (7) days previous to the day named for the fight, to make arrangements for getting the conveyance to the fight, and that the reporter of the CLIPPER shall be present to see that there shall be no back out on either side; and that the referee shall be chosen on the ground. In pursuance of the foregoing articles, we hereunto place our names. Either party failing to make good the deposits at the time and place above mentioned to forfeit the monies deposited.

Witness—WM. CARROLL, THOMAS ALLEN,
FRED'K ABRAHAMS. JAMES MACE.
NEW YORK, Jan. 17, 1870....

THE BATTLE MORNING AND THE START.

Though the clouds hung heavy and grey and stars twinkled sleepily over their long watches, the morning of May 10th exhibited an activity which compared to the usual matutinal indifference, would have astonished the most unimpressive observer. The dull rumble of the market carts, plodding wearily under the bread and meat and esculents of a drowsy city, and the sharp clatter of homeward bound cabs freighted with their squads of shouting roysterers, far from monopolising the noise and confusion, found other vehicles dashing hither and thither, as though life depended on their speed, and hours before the time appointed for the start the thoroughfares resounded with the click of quick paced pedestrians. Far from presenting the usual knots of yawning loungers, all night saloons thronged with excited multitudes. Newspaper reporters in duck caps and brown linen dusters, sporting men, fishing warily for bets with the green ones, prominent merchants, who, deserting suburban residences, had descended to lodging homes for a few hours' sleep, men of nearly every degree and quality crowded the marble counters, each anxious for his say concerning the great event and his cup of fragrant java. A redness about the eyes, bedragglement in the hair, and a universal stretchiness faintly suggested an all night watch; while the loud and incoherent expressions of an unfortunate few rather hinted that the vigil had not passed without its entertainment, spiritual and otherwise. In a word, from appearances one would suppose upper-ten-dom had suddenly made up its mind to be as rough and uncouth as possible; and as sometimes happens on these occasions, the masquerade was not altogether a success. Notwithstanding the early hour (it was then about 4 A.M.) on reaching the Jackson depot we found the thoroughfares in the vicinity crowded with vehicles, and both reception rooms and platform thronged with representatives from nearly every profession in life. Prominent merchants jostled eminent physicians, heavy capitalists pushed clerks, theatrical managers, man about town, cotton brokers, circus men and a very few "roughs," mingled in indiscriminate disorder. Far from the least amusing features were the ideas of comfort manifested by the excursionists in their various packages. One decided himself fixed with a huge linen duster, an umbrella and a bottle of whiskey; others brought portable chairs and camp stools, nearly all carried baskets or satchels, and some struggled under packages of wine and provisions sufficient for a three weeks' siege. The train was reached without incident, about seventy policemen standing at the doors to preserve order; and after a brief delay for the examination of tickets, the pilgrimage was commenced, about 800 being on board. The train stopped at Carrollton Crossing, about five miles from the city, and preparations were commenced for pitching the ring; but a private conversation with a messenger from the Superintendent of Police changed the programme, and the cars moved eight miles further up.

The scene of the halt opened on broad, level fields, marked with the deep furrows of the sugar cane and seamed through their centres with broad draining ditches filled with early undergrowth. On one side of the track was a dense swamp, choked with bushes, water flags, and doubtless alive with countless serpents; on the other, perhaps a mile through the fields, the river, hidden from view by a long line of green levee. A yellow road at right angles from the rails ran through fields past a small village of whitewashed negro cabins and finally up a gentle slope to an immense brick sugar house, the green lawn of which was fixed upon as the scene of the encounter.

THE RING.

The ropes and stakes were taken from St. Louis by the Allen party, the ring being the same in which Tom had fought McCoole, Davis, and Gallagher. About one hour and a half was occupied in pitching it, during which the excursionists divided themselves between discussing the merits of the men and discussing their lunches. About half past eight o'clock, Heenan announced every thing in readiness, and proposed Rufus Hunt, for referee, who was accepted at once. (Mr. H., it will be recollected served in the same capacity in the McCoole-Jones fight at Cincinnati.) Heenan was selected as umpire for Mace, and Dad Ryan filled the same office for Allen. Al. Smith was appointed to the duties of "captain of the watch." Constables were then selected and armed with sticks, whose office proved a mere sinecure, and they soon melted away into the crowd of spectators. Mr. Hunt now made a short speech to the crowd, stating that New Orleans had been selected for the scene of this contest as the only place where a fair showing for both sides could be had. It was to be a fair stand-up fight, and no favor, and such a fight he was determined to have, he having sufficient force to back up this determination if attempted to be interfered with. He hoped the crowd present would show the champions that their confidence had not been misplaced, and join him in wishing "may the best man win."

Referee Hunt's speech being loudly applauded, the men were sent for, and at half past 8 o'clock Allen's bronzed face loomed above the crowd, as he flung his defiance into the lists. Mace's cap followed a few minutes later and both men stepped in and were conducted to the two shady corners. Joe Coburn and Sherman Thurston acted as esquires to Allen, Cusick and Jerry Donovan doing the same for Jim. Heenan winning the toss, sent Ryan's man to the sunny corner, and the champions commenced stripping for battle. An objection to Allen's spikes was quickly filed away, and without any further trouble or dispute the men sat ready for the contest, surrounded by an audience of quiet, orderly, gentlemanly spectators. Mace now went over to Allen with a $500 note which he offered to wager on the result. It was declined, however, as they eyed each other furtively, yet keenly, from their corners. It was plainly evident that Allen was somewhat discouraged, and Mace's face showed that he did not expect such an easy time of it as the result proved. As the principles and seconds stepped to the scratch for the hand shaking overture, the sun glared down wrathfully, and started the perspiration from the bared torsos of the fistic knights, who were speedily summoned to the scratch by the call of "time."

THE FIGHT.

Round 1. As they stood there on guard, erect and defiant, their dresses unsoiled, their flesh glowing in the warm sunlight like polished bronze, as yet unpolluted and undefiled, an almost unconscious murmur of admiration ran through the anxious waiting crowd. At the first glance it was evident that Mace had the advantage in condition, his flesh appearing hard and healthy, while that of his antagonist seemed a little too loose and flabby. Bets were now freely offered around the ring of a hundred and seventy on Mace, but no reply was elicited. Nevertheless Allen looked smiling and confident, and gave assurance of a determination to do all in his power to carry off the coveted honors. A look at the grinning but good humored frontispiece of Jim revealed nothing touching a sense of fear for the result. Jim and Tom both smiled beamingly on each other and then put themselves in position at the scratch. Mace's "walking beams" were in a constant state of terpsichorean movement, while his two formidable looking mawleys were most carelessly disposed. He fondled his chin, stroked his phiz, patted his "bellows" and conducted himself generally in such a mercurial sort of manner that to the unsophisticated observer gave no proof of the almost miraculous powers of the man. But his cunning was soon developed. Allen, as he stood like another Anak before his adversary, wary and watchful, looked the splendid athlete that he is. His feet were spread wide apart and his bunches of fives held artistically. They smiled and joked in an undertone as they walked around one another, with eyes firmly set on eyes and every movement sharply watched. The sparring, dodging and feinting lasted several minutes, each too cautious to do more than feel his man, Mace now and then dropping his guard and drawing Tom around after him. Then came few sharp passes, nearly stopped. Jim landed a pile-driver over Tom's left eye and danced back, avoiding the return. Again the scratch was toed, with another spell of cautious sparring, during which Allen shot a heavy one into the ribs, which sounded all over the ring. Both men warmed to more rapid and serious work, exhibiting pretty science during a bout which wound up with Allen receiving a heavy hit on the nose and countering lightly on Mace's forehead. At it they rushed again, Jim making an ugly threat with his right, which Tom avoided, planting another ugly thud on his opponent's blood pumps, at which Mace clinched—a quick tussle and both fell, with Allen the under dog in the fight. Time, 5:30.

2. Several minutes passed in sparring for an opening, Mace rubbing his hands, folding his arms and otherwise endeavoring to get Tom to lead off, followed by a few rapid feints, when, as quick as thought, Mace rushed in and delivered a poultice under the young 'uns right orb, raising an egg, and springing back in time to catch only lightly a rib pulverizer from his opponent's right. Jim grinned at his work, and now fully understood Tom's tactics. With hands down, but ever ready, he walked around him, inviting an offer, but prepared to take advantage of any essay. Allen grew serious; he seemed, for the first time, to properly appreciate his tasks and compressed his lips in a manner to show that he was determined to throw all his energies into the struggle and "die game," if necessary; he planted another crasher on the body, in return for a nasty one on the bad lamp, which now flickered, preparatory to being doused. Another long interval of cautious sparring ensued, during which both men blowed off steam, and contented themselves with watching for an opening; grinning at and joking with each other in undertones. Mace resumed hostilities with a shot at Allen's neck, but it glanced off, and he napped a return rather too close to the meat cellar to be pleasant. Claims of foul were made from the outside of the ring, but Mace gracefully disclaimed them and went in for the finish, giving Allen a smash on the proboscis, which drew *first blood for Mace*. Tom returned it by a couple of rib benders and clip on the jaw, but in return received a terrible sockdolager on the right eye, which sent him down, making a wild attempt to counter as he fell. Allen was now toted home by his carriers, Mace walking to his corner looking much pleased.

3. Bets were offered, without takers, of $100 to $30 on Mace. Allen came up dejectedly, with his right eye nearly closed, his left also showing an ugly cut. This Mace took advantage of by keeping the damaged observation well in the sun during the cautious, lazy sparring which opened the round. Allen now found that something had to be done to utilize the time fast slipping away, and essayed at the head, but the latter proved too quick, dodged and it passed over his shoulders. In the rally Mace slipped and stretched himself on terra firma. Allen again rode homeward; Mace footing it in the best of humor.

4. Allen looked worried and his face exhibited marks of severe punishment, bleeding profusely from a cut below the left optic, while his right look-out was rapidly being shut in by purple clouds. During the preliminary sparring Tom accidentally trod upon and spiked Jim's foot, but apologized, a courtesy which was loudly applauded. After rather an elaborate overture of feinting, guarding and dodging, Mace suddenly darted out his right and gave Allen a roaster on the damaged eye, distilling the ruby afresh and going down, partly from the recoil, just in time to escape a well intended receipt in full.

5. After the usual introductory, fiddling about, Mace let out with his left at the young 'uns neck, which the latter avoided, Mace going down from the force of his blow (cries of "foul," not allowed). He quickly recovered, however, and faced Tom, who sent his left on a voyage of discovery, landing on Jim's ribs, and napping a heavy counter on the dial from Mace's left, who followed it up with a rush, clinched and threw Allen very heavily, adding his weight to the fall. The seconds now rushed up and carried their men home amid intense excitement and enthusiasm.

6. The fight was now evidently all one way. Allen was game enough and glutton enough, but his inferiority to Mace in sparring and wrestling, was plainly, not to say

pitifully, apparent. $100 to $15 freely offered on him, without takers. Allen seemed freshening, while Mace was as smiling as a basket of chips. A few friendly passes preceded a clinch by the latter getting the young un in chancery, and fibbing sharply with his right. Jim hung on like death, but with one gigantic, almost superhuman effort, considering his great disadvantage, Allen turned the tide and went down heavily on top of Mace, amid great applause, in which even Mace's friends joined.

7. Time now told badly upon Tom's telescopes, the right being entirely darkened and the other gradually following suit. Mace's face, on the other hand, was unmarked. Neither appeared to have suffered either in temper or endurance. After another long spell of sparring, Mace invested on the breast, receiving the exchange on the ribs, and countered on the mouth with severity. Tom dashed in but Mace evaded his essay, clinched, and both went down in a close and loving embrace.

8. Allen was evidently tired and not at all hopeful, but desperate; Mace, lively as a cricket, danced about his man, who waited for an opportunity to drive a spike into Jim's boilers. He succeeded at last, and got in two crashers, but Mace squared accounts by hitting him heavily in the face thrice. They then rushed to the clinch and they went down with a light fall, Jim underneath.

9. Mace [illegible] and [illegible], Allen with a head on him like a wrecked capstan[illegible], but exhibiting a dogged and praiseworthy determination to see it out to the bitter end. That the game was well nigh up was apparent to all, and the only chance Tom now had was to plant a blow sufficiently forcible to knock sir James out of time. The prospects of this, however, were in nowise encouraging. Mace, seeing that he had everything safe, was contented to bide his time and not force matters, by doing which he might lay himself open to accident. He now went about his work like an artist. He visited Tom lightly on the face thrice, evidently picking out the soft spots with great delicacy and discrimination. Allen, in return, always [illegible] the ribs, but not heavily. Jim now gathered himself for a finisher and aimed for the throat, but Allen parried it beautifully, and catching the champion off his balance with a swinger under the right ear, sent him clean off his feet amid uproarious applause. *First knock-down for Allen.*

10 *and last*. Both men answered promptly and came up eager and determined. Allen, with the exception of a bad eye, actually looked better and more dangerous than at any time during the fight; but he still clung to the defensive policy, as he, indeed, did throughout the whole fight, not manifesting any desire to take the initiative. Both settled immediately to hard work, Allen following up Mace as the latter danced around him, putting cleverly aside several dangerous upper cuts, though he administered no punishment. Another by Jim at the head was neatly parried, and Tom dropped his right heavily just above the belt. Both again indulged in some terpischorean business, neither seeming in a hurry to resume serious work. They did get at it, however, and rattled away so fast that 'twas impossible to keep count of the blows. Mace had the best of it, punishing Tom badly about the eyes and escaping several vicious attempts. This could not and did not last long, and the men gradually edged away towards their respective corners, where they were refreshed outwardly and inwardly by their seconds. Mace had now gotten Allen's only useful eye in proper eclipsing condition, and it calmly awaited sunset. Allen, however, gamely marched up to the music, which opened

with sparring. Tom finally got home on the breast—a crack which made Jim wince and visit Tom's right lamp spitefully. The men now closed, and some terribly severe work at half arm distance was in order, Jim finally getting Tom's head in chancery and slashing away at it with serious effect. This was not relished by Allen, who, in order to stop it, clinched for the fall. The struggle was fearful. Like giants they swayed backward and forward, but Mace was too fine a wrestler for his game opponent. Holding Allen firmly in his vice like grasp, slowly but surely he bored his head down to the ground and threw him a complete somersault, alighting upon his right shoulder with great force, nearly dislocating it, Mace falling heavily on top of him. Tom gave an awful groan, and all around the ring rose to their feet, thinking his neck had been broken. Full of alarm the seconds of both sides rushed up to his assistance and carried him to his corner. The injury was not as great as feared, however, but was sufficient—the jig was up-and when "time" was again called, Coburn walked to the scratch and tossed up the sponge, thus giving the fight to Mace in 10 rounds lasting in all 44 minutes.

As soon as the referee had given his decision, Jim walked over and shook hands with his late opponent, and while Tom groaned in agony, patted him on the back, and said: "Tom, you are a game man, and I wish you well." Allen remained stretched out for some minutes, when a physician arrived, who examined him and pronounced him not seriously injured. Either from the effects of a blow or the fall, the muscles of his right shoulder were paralyzed and very painful to the touch. He soon recovered sufficiently to walk off, supported to his quarters, whence he emerged on the arrival of the train, in tolerable good condition. Mace quit without a scratch, except a slight abrasion on the forehead, and a few purple spots about the ribs. In the best of humor, he soon resumed his toggery, walked forth and took part in the fun that was going on, his friends crowding around him with congratulations.

He bore his honors meekly and received the attentions of his admirers in an easy, affable manner. In speaking of the fight, which he did in a very becoming and business like way, he marked that in the contest he never once used his right. He also referred in the highest terms to the pluck and metal of his late antagonist.

Although seemingly badly cut and bruised about the eyes and mouth, Allen did not pay much attention to it on the way home, saying that it would be "all right in a day or two." His defeat, he says, was owing to his condition, which he did not consider good, being somewhat too fat and heavy. He bore his defeat manfully, regarding it as only a vicissitude of fortune. He received many compliments for his prowess and gameness, all acknowledging that although he had lowered his colors to Mace, but few other men will be able to snatch them down in the future. A striking and solemn incident occurred at the first meeting of Mace and Heenan after the fight. The Benicia Boy grasped his friend by the hand with a congratulating gripe, and, drawing him aside, said:—"Jim you have won the fight, and now I claim your promise—raise your right hand:—'We solemnly swear, so help us God, never again to put up our hands in a prize ring, never! never! never!'" Mace bowed his head and repeated the oath. As illustrating the defence made by the devotees of the ring against the charge of brutality, it was estimated by experienced judges that the entire number of effective blows struck in the battle did not exceed thirty. In the second round Mace badly bruised or dislocated the little finger of his left hand. Throughout the entire fight he did not use his right hand otherwise than in guarding and feinting. It might be here stated that notwithstanding the great skill displayed by Mace, Allen, by his pluck and determination won the highest respect and sympathy and encouragement spoken to the defeated hero. It was apparent that no general losing a campaign could feel defeat more keenly than Tom his loss of laurels....

REMARKS.

...The superiority of Mace, in every respect, was so clearly manifest from the commencement, that the result was regarded by all as a foregone conclusion, and the only possibility of Allen's winning was by the occurrence of a "fluke," against which, however, Mace exercised every precaution. The latter's display fully equalled in brilliancy what had been anticipated from his record, but there can be no question that he had no occasion to call into action all his powers, and might have inflicted still greater punishment had he felt disposed. It proved conclusively that Allen's abilities had been over estimated by whose [sic] who were so enthusiastic in his support, and whose deductions were drawn from his performances upon McCoole, Davis and Gallagher, which were really no criterion at all. In gameness, endurance, and, perhaps, hitting powers, he is, doubtless, the equal of Mace, but in skill, quickness and wrestling ability he cannot compare with him. He struggled on gamely in the face of defeat, however, striving his utmost to turn the tide in his favor, but without avail, though had the accident above mentioned not occurred the battle would in all probability have lasted a considerable time longer. Allen is in nowise disgraced by the issue, for he had opposed to him a man who has for years been acknowledged the best boxer in the world, and had he gained the victory he would at once have been elevated to the topmost round of the pugilistic ladder. The bold, determined stand which he did make reflects great credit upon him as a game, resolute, and well-scienced pugilist, and renders him fully deserving of the respect and confidence which his backers entertain for and repose in him, and which is attested by their offer to stake their money upon him against any man in the country after the battle and the announced retirement of Mace from active participation in arenic displays. To all intents and purposes the victor becomes entitled to the position of "champion of the world," being the last man who actually fought for and won the champion belt of England, and his match with O'Baldwin having been the last save one (that between Joe Goss and Harry Allen) for that trophy.

JIM MACE VS. JOE COBURN, 1871

The two bouts between Mace and Joe Coburn in 1871 were more typical of boxing's problems than was the Mace-Allen affair. The matchup promised excitement, because Coburn was a naturalized American born in Ireland, who was squaring off against an

McCoole back in 1863. Those two had also spent forty days in jail in 1868 in an abortive attempt to settle the championship of America. The document below describes the first fight between Mace and Coburn in May in Canada. The rematch took place in Bay St. Louis, Mississippi. It also ended in a draw, when the referee stopped the fight after eleven uninspiring rounds. This report of the first contest is reprinted from The New York Clipper, 20 May 1871, p. 50.

THE FIGHT.

Every one gazed searchingly, first on one and then on the other, as the heroes of the day stood there in fighting attitude in the bright, warm sunlight, the eyes of each fixed intently and steadily upon those of the other. The men were well matched in height and weight, the slight elevation more than counterbalancing the trifling advantage in altitude possessed by Joe, who had lowered the scale on the day previous at 160 pounds exactly, while Mace was some three pounds the heavier. Coburn looked the bigger man of the two, however, as well as the most vigorous, his skin being ruddy with the hue imparted by perfect health and his body was devoid of all superfluous flesh, while the splendid development of muscle beneath evinced not only great strength but likewise endurance. His face was a trifle flushed, but this was occasioned, not, as some supposed, by fat, but by the improper manner in which a wash, used for hardening the flesh, had been applied. As is well known Joe's nose is his most prominent feature, forming a splendid target for an adversary's mawleys, but it takes a smart man to "get there," as he has a very sharp eye upon either side, and a pair of good hands with which to keep off intruders. His shoulders are wide and sloping, and behind them there loomed up under the skin great bunches of muscle to furnish propelling power to send his well-developed and long arm to the right spot with force. His chest was also finely developed, a strengthening plaster had been placed upon his loins, and he possessed a well-shaped, muscular pair of pins, upon which he knows as well how to get about as any man we ever saw, as he demonstrated on this occasion. That his appearance astonished the spectators, friends as well as foes, was evinced by the remarks we heard on all sides, for none had expected that he could possibly get into such condition, which assuredly left nothing wanting. Upon first sight, Mace appeared to be well, but a closer observation developed the fact that he was not in anything like as good fix as his opponent. He lacked that volume of muscle which was represented to have been so noticeable in him upon the occasion of previous fights, and his flesh was comparatively soft (that is, to what it should have been to stand the blows of a hard-hitting pugilist), while his face appeared anxious, and at times we thought we noticed a tremor of the lips, which betrayed a want of that confidence which we were led to expect he would show. His arms were more massive than those of Coburn, and as he worked them the muscles of the shoulders and back were plainly to be seen, but they had not attained the proper degree of hardness and elasticity. His shoulders are broader than Joe's, his chest deep, and his loins good; but his understandings were not as sturdy in appearance. In our opinion he had regarded Coburn too lightly as an opponent, and had not taken proper care to get himself in condition, and we think the anxious look he wore was due, in a measure, to the discovery he now made that he had made a mistake. He assumed a very artistic position, which betokened the masterly science for which he is famed; his hands were held well up, the left advanced slightly and the right placed so as to be ready for either offense or guard, nearly his entire weight resting upon his right leg and his body being almost erect. Joe's attitude also showed in itself that he was master of the art; his left was held higher than that of Mace, while the right was held across the body, ready to ward off any attack, as well as to return a hot shot for any that might be sent in. He stood very lightly upon his feet, but stooped somewhat, which detracted from the gracefulness of his position. They sparred cautiously for an opening, but for some time neither made an attempt to open the ball, each waiting for the other, until finally Jim baulked with the left, but Joe stepped back out of range. Mace would not follow, but, dropping his hands, rubbed the palms against his hips, transferring them thence to his breast, which he rubbed, and then nonchalantly folded his arms. Coburn also coolly lowered his dukes and stood "at rest," each eyeing the other for a few minutes, when a call of "time" from some impatient mortal (though for that matter all were impatient) brought Coburn to the mark again, and another bout of sparring, feinting and maneuvering ended, as before, in neither being hurt, Joe being plainly resolved to act solely on the defensive and wait for a chance to counter; but Jim was playing the same game, that being one of his old dodges, and wouldn't give Coburn the desired opportunity. Another spell of hand rubbing, &c., succeeded, until a quarter of an hour had passed, when Jim turned to go to his corner, saying "I'll drink with you, Joe," to which the latter responded "I'll take a drink with you, Jim," and took a few mouthfuls of water, while Jim had his with a "stick" in it. Being urged to commence, they moved up to the scratch again and it looked as though they were going to get to work in earnest, but it proved to be only another bout at sparring, feinting and breaking ground, Joe inviting Jim to his corner, but the latter manifesting no inclination to accept the invitation, though it had been expected that he would attempt to force the fighting, in consequence of the numerous bets to be decided by the time occupied. After looking at one another for a while, Mace stepped back to the middle stake nearest his corner, and stood there for full five minutes, resting one hand on his hip and the other on the top of the stake, while Coburn proceeded to do likewise. The importunities of the crowd finally caused them to step to the centre again, but after a brief period of rapid sparring, which once or twice looked likely to end in something being done, they parted again, Joe retreating to his corner, where Jim refused to go for the purpose of driving his opponent out, as some advised him to do. Chaffing was going on, meanwhile, at a rapid rate, the Maceites taunting Joe with cowardice in staying so close to his corner, while the Coburnites hurled back the base insinuation and asked why the "cleverest man in the world" didn't hit Joe or make him jump over the ropes. Offers to bet large and small amounts were plentiful, Al. Smith saying that he would stake $50 against $100 that Mace would win without a black eye, or $100 to $70 on the result of the battle as often as desired. Maguire was still ready to bet as much as $1,000 that Joe was not beaten in an hour's time, a like sum that Joe got first throw, $250 against $500 on the first blood, and $600 against $1,000 on the issue of the fight. It would be folly for us to go further into details of this shadow of a fight, as it was a repetition of the above from first to last. After they had been facing each other for a few minutes over the hour a cry was raised that the police were coming, which created considerable excitement and came near causing a stampede, but quiet was restored and then the men set to work as though they meant to do something before any interference could possibly occur, their lips being tightly compressed as they maneuvered rapidly for a chance; but it was just the same as before. So they continued until an hour and seventeen minutes had been consumed, when a sudden stop was put to the proceedings, by the appearance of two strangers within the enclosure, whose names, as we subsequently learned, were Judge Wilson and Edmund Deeds, High Sheriff of the county, the former of whom held up his hands and thusly spake:—

"The authorities have been made acquainted with this prize fight. It must not go on any farther. I have here the High Sheriff of Norfolk County, who will enforce the law, and after he has done this, should another blow be struck I have military enough to enforce it, and the blood that may be spilt be upon your own heads."

After which the sheriff, who was attired in a comical looking costume, his head being surmounted by a curious cocked hat, the appearance of which excited considerable laughter at his expense, even at such a time, read the following proclamation:—

"Our sovereign lady, the Queen, chargeth and commandeth all persons being assembled here to their habitations or to their lawful business, upon the pain contained in the act relating to high treason, to tumult and riotous assemblies, and to other offences. God save the Queen!"

While the officer was in the act of reading the above, some light-fingered chap, who had not the fear of the law before his eyes, relieved him of his gold repeater, valued at one hundred and seventy-five dollars, which must have given him an elevated opinion of the experiences of American professional pickpockets. We learn that the stolen property was subsequently restored to him, however. Nothing was left to be done but pull up stakes and depart, as the militia were drawn up in a line a short distance off, (though they were not very formidable in appearance) and so the principals donned their toggery and left with the disappointed spectators for the lake shore. The wind had arisen since noon and the water was now very rough, added to which the boats had moved further out from shore; so that the journey back was more difficult and tedious than that of the morning, as well as not without danger. Fortunately, however, all reached their respective vessels in safety, though not until several hours had been consumed in the operation and all had received a pretty good soaking....

REMARKS.

Though this meeting did not develop anything calculated to enable the observer to form a correct estimate of the relative abilities of the men, it demands a few remarks, in order that our readers may have a proper understanding of the motives which, in our opinion, induced them to pursue the course of tactics which they severally did, and that censure greater than deserved may not be uttered against either man, but simple justice be done to both, as the CLIPPER strives to be strictly impartial at all times. It must be remembered that Mace has all along been looked upon as by odds the cleverest man of his time, not only in his native land, where he made for himself a brilliant record by vanquishing the best men of his day, but in America, where he, in May of last year, defeated the then champion, Tom Allen, so signally. So great, indeed, was his reputation that people were disposed to laugh and look incredulous when the match between he and Coburn was announced, not believing that Joe could possibly have the slightest chance with him in a ring fight, adducing as reasons for entertaining this opinion his inferior ability and the utter impossibility of his getting into good milling condition. Extravagant offers were made and wagers laid that Mace would win in quick time, that he would not receive a black eye in the encounter, etc., all of which went to show how extremely confident were his backers. They expected to see him win in a canter—that he would, as some expressed it, "drive Coburn out of the ring." Under these circumstances it was to have been expected that he would have taken the offensive when they met, and done his utmost to win the money which had been bet upon him, as well as prove that the opinion entertained of him was correct in all respects. Instead of this, however, he pursued an opposite course, and was content to wait for his opponent, manifesting no disposition to force matters or to overstep the imaginary line in the centre of the ring known as the "scratch," although it was self-evident that if they were to come to blows he would have to be the first to offer, as Coburn had plainly made up his mind to act solely on the defensive. In explanation of this unlooked for action, and, with a view to justifying the same, it is asserted that Coburn would not come to the mark, and that Mace would not follow him into his corner because there was every likelihood of his being foully dealt with in case he did. When it is considered, however, that Jim had fully as many partisans on the ground as Coburn, and men, too, who would stand by him to the bitter end and see that he was fairly treated, it does not seem reasonable that he would allow such fears to deter him from doing that which his inclination prompted; besides, we do not honestly believe that there was any ground for the report that some persons in Coburn's corner intended to act unfairly in case opportunity offered—very few men care to take such chances, especially when the referee is not of their naming and will in all likelihood decide the fight against their favorite should such foul be committed. Most men, particularly if possessed of Mace's fine skill, artfulness and experience, would not have hesitated to have followed up and made an effort to compel Joe to leave his corner, and assuredly a man of such brilliant science as Jim should be able to work him out and away from personal danger, if he feared any. To sum it up, Mace did not do what his friends had confidently expected him to do, and we believe his reasons for so acting were as follows: he saw that in condition he was inferior to his antagonist, whose appearance evidently surprised him; second, a fear that he would receive personal violence if he attempted to force the fighting; third, the skill shown by Joe, his unexpected quickness in divining the intentions of his rival and in placing himself in position to return the expected compliment, together with his really formidable appearance generally. Whether these causes would have operated to produce such a result had he not been advised by those behind him to so conduct himself we are not prepared to say, but it was certainly only reasonable to expect that he would have made an earnest effort to open the ball, even though it became necessary to advance a few feet beyond the dividing line to do so. For the greater portion of the time Coburn kept his own corner, though they were frequently close enough to exchange blows, had either chosen to take the initiative. We have heard many censure Joe very severely for not moving away from his "home base." His instructions were to act strictly on the defensive, and, when we remember that he had opposed to him the smartest, most scientific professor of the art in the world, it is not be wondered at that he should conduct himself with extreme caution, but so long as he did nothing that was wrong, he is, in reality, no more to blame than is his antagonist, who made no more effort than he to open hostilities. Coburn was well aware of nist, who made no more effort than he to open hostilities. Coburn was well aware of the character of the man before him, and had sense enough to know that if he undertook to lead for Mace he would, in all probability, get the worst of it, for all know what Jim is capable of doing with a man who will lead for him. It was Coburn's idea to let Mace do the leading, while he held himself in readiness to counter and cross-counter, hoping to succeed in putting in such a blow as would prove effective enough to terminate the contest in his favor. Had he had a man in front of him of whose powers he did not entertain so high an opinion he would doubtless have acted differently, but he was resolved not to throw any chance away, and therefore awaited his opportunity, in doing which he considered himself justified, as he was rated a much inferior man, and considerable money was at stake, not only on the result of the battle itself, but upon the time of its duration.

AN EXHIBITION IN MONTREAL, 1877

Although Canada was sometimes the site of illicit prize fights staged by promoters of pugilists from the United States, that dominion also hosted legitimate amateur sparring matches. The following exhibition was typical of the entertainments staged for gentlemen of Montreal, as described in The Gazette (Montreal), 5 January 1877.

BOXING.

Professor Miller's glove contest with Mr. Laboissiere last evening excited considerable interest in sporting circles, and the Theatre Royal was well filled in anticipation of some excellent sport. For those who are fond of boxing—and there seemed to be many of that ilk—the sport was good. Mr. Miller had the call in betting and was expected to polish off his antagonist in short order. Laboissiere, however, did much better than was anticipated and the contest was prolonged. Seven rounds took place and some severe exchanges were recorded, while the hitting was often of the one-two-three order, and so close that the biceps were like a threshing machine at work. The utmost good humor prevailed, however, and after seven rounds had been fought Mr. Richardson, for Laboissiere, threw up the sponge. Mr. Miller was handled by Mr. Woods, of the Gymnasium, in whose hands he has been of late, while Professor Richardson engineered Mr. Laboissiere. Mr. Drenahan was referee and timer, and the time consumed in the contest was 35 minutes. Mr. Miller exhibited the most complete knowledge of the art of punishing anybody else, while his antagonist was slower, both in leading and countering. On the whole the contestants seemed satisfied, the audience evidently was pleased, and this performance concluded shortly after 10 o'clock.

Chapter 7

CRICKET

INTRODUCTION

North American cricket experienced hard times during the 1860s, but the next decade witnessed a revival of interest in the sport in both Canada and the United States. The Civil War sharply curtailed play in the United States and made intercity competition difficult and international challenges impossible. But after hostilities ceased, British and native born sportsmen revitalized clubs and renewed the rivalry among teams from England, Canada, and the United States. The leading clubs in Montreal, Toronto, Boston, New York, and Philadelphia arranged special events in 1868, 1872, and 1874. Once again elite Philadelphians showed the most enthusiasm and produced the best players in the United States. They took the lead in organizing a new cricket association and in resuming a regular series of contests between representative elevens from Canada and the United States. During the 1870s American and Canadian cricketers laid the foundation for the golden age of North American cricket, which lasted from the 1880s to World War I.

The Civil War had a far more damaging impact on American cricket than it did on baseball, mainly because cricket was simply not as popular as its rival, especially among players who were too young to serve in the military. Also, most of the Philadelphia leadership deserted the cricket fields for the battlegrounds, dealing a particularly severe blow to the fate of the English game in America. While cricket did not disappear completely from the sporting scene in the United States during the early 1860s, there were far fewer clubs, matches, and special all-star contests. To make matters worse, the annual cricket conventions commanded little respect and displayed much less vitality than the gatherings of the baseball crowd. The cricketers' version of a national organization deteriorated into confusion and inaction before passing into oblivion after 1862. At the war's end the sport revived quickly in Philadelphia and in several other cities, but the nation's troubles had seriously retarded cricket's prospects for future growth in the United States.

An early symbolic indication of the negative effects of the war on cricket in the New York City vicinity occurred in the spring of 1861, shortly after hostilities began at Fort Sumter. A large number of spectators appeared on the grounds of the East New York club, which was hosting the renowned Dragon Slayers of St. George. But they had not come to watch cricket. Instead, they had turned out to witness the drilling of regiments of cavalry and infantry camped at New York, which interfered with the cricketers' sport. Brooklyn and adjacent Long Island fielded eight teams in 1862, but by the following year there were only three. In 1864 New York City had just three active clubs, with Newark and other nearby New Jersey towns adding perhaps another half dozen.

The fate of American cricket did not rest with the sport's prospects in the New York City vicinity but rather with its fortunes in the City of Brotherly Love. There the news was discouraging. The Philadelphia Cricket Club's grounds committee report for 1861 complained that because of the outbreak of war it had been impossible to play any matches or even get the members out for practice. The officers had to wait until peace was restored to hire a professional. The club released its men from the payment of their annual dues during the time they were in the military. The war claimed the lives of several promising young players, including at least one star athlete, Walter Newhall. The Philadelphians, Young Americans, and a few lesser clubs played a reduced schedule during the war years, but clearly cricket in the city had suffered dramatically.

Outside of the Middle Atlantic region, cricket survived in curtailed form in Boston and neighboring Massachusetts factory towns, as well as in the South and West, especially New Orleans, Washington, D.C., Chicago, Cincinnati, Detroit, and San Francisco. While the war forced suspension of the annual international challenges with Canada, there were a few regional battles that kept interest alive in the Northeast. The two highlights of each of the wartime summers were the annual matches between the New York Cricket Club and an all-Massachusetts eleven and those between the St. George and Boston clubs. Each year a Massachusetts cricketers' convention chose participants for the contest against the New Yorkers, an event that stimulated the sport in such pockets of cricket as Boston, Lowell, Dorchester, Shelbourne Falls, Fall River, and Charleston.

Considering the unfavorable conditions that plagued American cricket during this period, it is not surprising that the New York City conventions failed to promote or regulate the sport in the United States. The 1861 session had been scheduled for Philadelphia for the first time, with high hopes for the inauguration of a new era. But these dreams were dashed by the news of the Confederate firing on Fort Sumter. Eleven clubs appeared to plan for special international and all-star matches that were never held. Their delegates also debated again the controversial proposal to bar players from competing for more than one organization. The measure was defeated in 1861, but the next year it passed amid considerable confusion and disorganization. Five clubs from New York City's Free Academy (later City College) attended the 1862 session and swung the balance toward prohibiting multiple memberships. But since the credentials of those clubs were questionable (they had no regular playing grounds), there was much dissatisfaction among the regulars. New York's prestigious St. George club did not bother to attend, and those clubs that did apparently did not take the proceedings very seriously. Most of the old clubs respected the English custom of permitting players to compete for several organizations, and therefore the ruling of the 1862 convention was moot. This abortive attempt to Americanize cricket ended the first effort to create a national association to govern the sport in the United States.

The coming of peace and spring in April 1865 encouraged American cricketers to return to their wickets and resume their favorite sport. Unfortunately, the prospects for cricket in the United States after the Civil War were not nearly as bright as those for baseball. Wartime disruptions had inflicted more damage on the English game, while America's national pastime had already surpassed cricket in popularity in all regions of the country. However, white-collar professionals and businessmen and blue-collar artisans and workers competed in cities and in factory towns in New England, the

Middle Atlantic region, the South, the Midwest, and along the Pacific coast. A proper understanding of postwar American cricket requires an analysis of the impact of personal mobility, the press, intercity competition, conventions, and special all-star and international matches. A review of each of these topics suggests both the difficulties faced by American cricket and its modest revival during the 1870s.

The continuing migration of British officials, businessmen, and skilled craftsmen to the United States after the war prevented cricket from dying out in areas where clubs had existed before 1861. Fresh blood from England reinvigorated both white-and blue-collar organizations. In San Francisco the California Cricket Club, founded in 1867, met in the same rooms as the British Benevolent Society, and its president was the British consul, William Lane Booker. In Trenton, New Jersey, potters from Staffordshire, England, were prominent in that city's industrial and recreational life. They formed lodges affiliated with the Sons of St. George and organized cricket clubs to secure and strengthen their ethnic identity, even as they also stimulated interest in cricket among the natives in New Jersey's capital throughout the 1860s and 1870s. Their promotion of the sport in Trenton repeated the earlier contribution of English craftsmen in Newark before the war.

The national sporting weeklies and the daily newspapers continued to editorialize on the virtues of cricket, but they decreased their coverage of contests as the game's popularity waned. Sportswriters such as Henry Chadwick and Frank Queen continued to admire cricket, but they also realized that it no longer merited feature stories in their publications. Both remained extremely critical of New York City's St. George Club for what they considered its abuse of the press. Club officials in Boston, Philadelphia, and other cities enjoyed better relations with journalists, but in general only the major intercity matches and especially the visits of English teams received much notice in the newspapers.

Intercity competition excited cricket followers after 1865, even though there was no official or even informal championship system comparable to that of baseball. While newspapers sometimes referred to Philadelphia's Young America club as the champions of the United States, no such title was actually recognized in cricket. Still, cricket fans eagerly awaited the contests between the Dragon Slayers of the St. George club and the leading elevens of Philadelphia. The Boston Cricket Club also toured the Middle Atlantic region and hosted sides from New York City and Philadelphia. The lesser-known clubs of the Midwest and the South also arranged contests with rivals from neighboring towns.

By the late 1860s many cricketers realized that their sport needed state, regional, or national associations that would institute reforms and promote the game across the United States. In 1867 Philadelphia's Olympic club issued a call and a plea for a gathering of delegates who would act to perpetuate a pastime that appeared to be in danger of extinction. The announcement proposed a rule for a forfeit if a side appeared late for a match and also suggested a curb on lavish entertainments. Delegates from at least ten clubs in Washington, D.C., New Jersey, and Pennsylvania met in Philadelphia to found the American Cricketers' Convention. They elected officers and drafted a constitution and bylaws but did not accomplish anything else. Small groups of sportsmen continued to meet periodically to select sides for special all-star and international matches. In 1872 a group of Philadelphia clubs convened to form a new organization which aimed to adapt cricket to American time constraints and business habits. In particular, it approved proposals to determine the winner of a match when two innings could not be completed and to impose penalties for lateness. That body also called for a United States general convention of cricketers, which finally occurred six years later.

American cricketers renewed international challenges after the war, hoping that matches between United States and Canadian or English elevens would prove as popular as they once were. In 1865 the United States versus Canada series resumed after a five year interruption. The American team (with only ten men) won that low-scoring encounter by one wicket. Unfortunately, cricketers on both sides of the border were unable to arrange another match until 1879, although it is not clear whether lack of interest or (more probably) differences over selection of sides led to the long interregnum. Notwithstanding this lack of formal North American competition, several groups of American and Canadian cricketers did arrange interclub games. In 1866 the Boston Cricket Club played five matches against teams in the British Maritime Provinces, while two years later a Canadian military eleven visited New York City. Out on the West Coast, in 1869, a California club split two matches with a select side from Victoria, British Columbia. In 1879 the series between the United States and Canada was renewed with both sides fielding elevens that lacked the strongest players of each nation. The United States won by five wickets on the grounds of the Ottawa club. The 1880 match ended in a draw (with the United States ahead) because of time lost due to rain on the first day.

Postwar cricket's major events were the visits by all-star squads from England. Canadian and American enthusiasts recalled the success of the 1859 all-England tour and arranged sporting excursions in 1868 and 1872. In the first series an English professional eleven played six matches against selected Canadian and United States teams, with a few exhibition baseball games added to increase excitement and income. The transatlantic cricket encounters stirred great interest in Philadelphia but got a mixed reaction in the New York City vicinity. In the former city, promoters tried to court the baseball fraternity when they advertised the international match at an Athletics-Atlantics game. But in the latter metropolis sentiment was divided because of the sport's lack of popularity, the press's dislike of the sponsoring Dragon Slayers, and doubts about the propriety of subsidizing a group of foreign professional athletes.

The Englishmen opened their North American tour in September with a 175-149 one-innings rout of twenty-two English residents of the New York, Willow, and St. George clubs at Hudson City, New Jersey. Crowds ranged from about 1,500 on the first and third days to around 3,000 on the second. While the size of the audiences was impressive by the standards of American cricket, the numbers fell far short of the average for feature baseball games. More important, the turnout was significantly below that for the 1859 international match at Hoboken. The English eleven next traveled to Montreal, where their match against twenty-two Canadians was called by rain with the English leading 310-28. The visitors continued their march of conquest in Boston with an easy 180-76 victory. As might be expected, the Philadelphians gave the British their greatest test, as twenty-two amateurs (all natives except one) lost by only two wickets in a very close, exciting contest. In a game held in Germantown, a combined amateur and professional twenty-two (including five men born in England) lost to the Englishmen, 181-109. The professionals ended their journey in North America at

Hudson City in mid-October with a 143-138 one-innings triumph over a side of twenty-two players selected by the St. George club. In their five victories and one draw they had outscored their opponents 1,113-623.

Since the sponsors of this international series anticipated that many people would be eager to see the English guests try the American national pastime, they scheduled baseball games to follow the cricket contests. Although the British players had no knowledge of or training at baseball, they agreed to play seven matches against American teams. At most of these games natives skilled at the sport joined the English side, but at least two contests matched nine English cricketers against nine American baseball players. The British defeated a group of cricketers from the St. George club who were even more inept at baseball than they were, but they lost to the Unions of Morrisania, the Athletics, and a composite team from the Lowell, Tri-Mountain, and Harvard clubs of Boston. Their experiences apparently taught the English something about the sport, while their efforts may have aided the cause of baseball among American cricketers. However, it is doubtful whether any of these games had any positive impact upon the fortunes of cricket in the United States.

Four years later another elite group of cricketers from England journeyed across the Atlantic to challenge Canadian and United States sides of twenty-two. This time the team consisted of twelve amateur gentlemen. They began their itinerary with five victories in Canada. They then journeyed down the Hudson River to play in Hoboken against a twenty-two picked by the St. George club. The English cricketers easily routed the New Yorkers. The first selection below is a report on this trip written by the English team's captain.

In 1872, as in 1868, the invading cricketers met their toughest test in the City of Brotherly Love. The Englishmen downed twenty-two determined natives by three wickets in a match that remained exciting to the conclusion. The visitors wound up their trip with a draw played on a miserably wet field in Boston. Their hosts actually held the lead as dusk fell on a match limited to one day's play.

An evaluation of the significance of the 1868 and 1872 British sporting adventures suggests mixed results for both the cause of American cricket and the future of international athletics. In Hoboken and Philadelphia the matches attracted sizable crowds and turned respectable profits. The contests greatly encouraged the leading cricketers in the East, both natives and resident Englishmen, strengthening their resolve to keep cricket alive in America. Unfortunately the two series did little if anything to popularize cricket among baseball players or the American masses. In truth, even in Philadelphia the excitement of the British visit did not generate much interest in regular interclub competition.

The English visits did lay the groundwork for the more frequent cricket contests between United States, Canadian, and English teams during the remaining years of the 1870s and the late nineteenth and early twentieth centuries. In the long run these early international matches promoted closer cultural ties and more harmony between at least some of the people of the two nations, which would soon become the chief justifications for international sport.

The 1870s brought three major developments for American cricket, especially for the Philadelphians. These were the successful participation of a Philadelphia Twelve in 1874 in an international tournament in Halifax, Nova Scotia; the appearance in 1877 of a new sporting periodical, The American Cricketer, and the founding in 1878 of a new organization, "The Cricketers' Association of the United States." This chapter concludes with an account of the triumphant sporting excursion to Nova Scotia, followed by the Constitution and Rules of the new governing body of American cricket.

An overview of the status of American cricket between 1865 and 1880 shows some life in each region of the United States but real vitality only in the Philadelphia vicinity. In New England the Massachusetts Cricket Association listed six clubs from Boston, Salem, Chelsea, Needham, and Waltham. A scattering of elevens remained in the factory towns and smaller cities of Maine, New Hampshire, and Connecticut. In the New York City area, only the Dragon Slayers of St. George were in a sound condition, although even that organization experienced sparse attendance on practice days and was forced to relocate several times. The New York Cricket Club struggled through the 1860s before it finally expired in 1871, and only a few more Manhattan and Brooklyn outfits survived. Across the Hudson, New Jersey cricket did not display the enthusiasm of the prewar period, but there were a few clubs that played in Newark, Paterson, Trenton, Jersey City, Belleville, Lambertville, and Orange.

The English national game prospered in Philadelphia after the war, especially among the city's elite, who patronized the four major associations—the Philadelphia, Young America, Germantown, and Merion clubs. The sport also retained some following among the region's English factory workers as well as students at a few schools and colleges, especially Haverford and the University of Pennsylvania. However, the rise of baseball diminished cricket's appeal among the Philadelphia masses, and the number of minor elevens dropped well below the prewar level. The chief concerns among the elite associations involved increasing membership and maintaining proper grounds. The Philadelphia Cricket Club experienced more difficulty than its rivals in both areas, and in 1872 it finally abandoned its field in Camden and agreed to share time and expenses at the Germantown club ground at Nicetown. The Young America club continued to restrict its rolls to natives and to prohibit outsiders from competing on its first eleven, which was dominated by the Newhall family. Its pitch was at Turnpike Bridge during the war, and later it also shared the facilities at Nicetown.

During these years Charles Cadwalader launched a reorganization of the Germantown club, which moved to the estate of Henry Pratt McKean. West Philadelphians founded the Merion Cricket Club in the fall of 1865, and the following April a majority of members defeated a move by one faction to switch to baseball. The cricketers opened play near the Wynne Wood station on the Pennsylvania Central Railroad, on a typical pitch where "Proper" Philadelphians could emulate the English.

While baseball was invading practically every corner of America during the late 1860s, there were pockets of support for cricket in the South, Midwest, and Far West. Below the Mason-Dixon line the English game survived in Baltimore, Washington, D.C., New Orleans, and St. Louis. Cricketers pitched wickets in Chicago, Detroit, Cincinnati, Cleveland, Indianapolis, Louisville, and as far west as the San Francisco Bay area. British residents and American enthusiasts were not always able to maintain prewar levels of interest, but they did prevent cricket from being wiped out completely by the tidal wave of baseball.

In Canada, as in the United States, the popularity of cricket during the 1860s and 1870s depended greatly on English immigration and the support of native born elites. The sport was played throughout the Dominion, with one or more active clubs in Victoria, Winnipeg, Montreal, the Eastern Townships, Quebec City, Toronto, and Halifax. Several towns in the Maritime provinces and southwestern Ontario also fielded elevens. But despite the pervasiveness of the pastime across the country, cricket did not experience any significant growth spurt during these decades. Not surprisingly, the cities were able to produce several teams, but the smaller communities generally only had one club. In urban centers the upper classes dominated the sport, while in the more rural towns and villages cricketers came from a wider social spectrum.

While the British influence and the patronage of social elites were key factors in club formation throughout Canada, local circumstances dictated the particular composition of organizations. In Toronto college men founded several clubs, while in Halifax and Victoria military garrisons organized several teams. In Montreal a variety of upper class officials, professionals, and businessmen predominated. In these cities cricket clubs often lasted decades, but in smaller towns teams were more short-lived and depended greatly on the influx of English newcomers to sustain their vitality.

During this era of Canadian cricket there were no leagues or formal championships, but there were a series of special international matches. A few of the leading clubs of Toronto, Montreal, and Halifax dominated interprovincial and international competition. The feature events included the visits by teams of English professionals and amateur gentlemen in 1868 and 1872, an Australian eleven in 1878, and another English squad and an Irish contingent in 1879, along with the games played against United States teams. Enthusiasts for Canadian cricket hoped that the imperial challenges would stimulate greater interest for the British national game in the Dominion. Unfortunately, the outcome proved to be discouraging, because during the 1870s Canadian teams compiled a record of no wins, fourteen losses, and two ties against sides from the mother country, Australia, and Ireland. Apologists for the Canadians tried to explain these setbacks by stressing the select talent of the opposition and the practical difficulties of climate, the lack of leisure time, and a shortage of funds. They also noted that there were few schools which developed skilled players, and that long distances between clubs made regular competition difficult. But they also admired the greatness of such luminaries as W.G. Grace and Frederick Spofforth and they viewed the sport of cricket as an important bond of the British empire.

By 1880 distinct patterns had become clear for North American cricket. In the United States the English sport was still strong in Philadelphia and to a lesser extent in New York City, Boston, and a few other smaller towns scattered across the nation. In Canada the game was widely played in urban areas, but its fate was uncertain in rural regions where American baseball was gaining ground. On both sides of the border cricket's future depended on support by native elites and continuing English immigration.

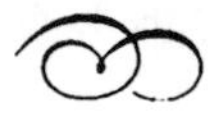

THE TOUR OF TWELVE GENTLEMEN OF ENGLAND, 1872

The select English amateur team that toured North America in the fall of 1872 included twelve highly skilled gentlemen. Captained by Robert A. Fitzgerald, the squad's star was the famed W.G. Grace. Although it was not made up of professionals, the twelve received $600 in gold for each match. The men began their trip with five victories in Canada. On September 18, 1872 they arrived in Hoboken, New Jersey to play a New York City twenty-two selected by the St. George club. The English amateurs repeated the one-innings massacre that the 1868 professionals had inflicted on the New Yorkers, winning 249-110. The team then traveled down to Philadelphia, where their game against twenty-two natives was much more closely contested. This narrative by Fitzgerald recounts his team's easy victory in New York and their exciting triumph by three wickets in the City of Brotherly Love. It is reprinted from Robert A. Fitzgerald, *Wickets in the West: Or the Twelve in America* (London, 1873), pp. 209-210, 220-221; and *Official Report of the International Cricket Fetes at Philadelphia in 1868 and 1872* (Philadelphia, 1873), pp. 10-11, 13-14, 16-23 (an edited version of *Wickets in the West*, pp. 236-279).

NEW YORK

Sept. 18. The Hoboken ground. The cricketer of New York must be an enthusiast, for to indulge in his favourite pastime he must submit to great inconvenience. To say nothing of finding your way to the Ferry, tramway cars, trucks of every kind obstructing the road, the route on the other side of the river in the State of New Jersey, would take an ordinary New York life to remember. The Twelve were invited to breakfast on board the Baltic, one of the magnificent steam vessels of the "White Star Line." Mr. Sparkes, the president of the St. George's Cricket Club, was the host. The internal accommodations of this fine ship are most striking. A most sumptuous meal, at which we were first introduced to "Reed Birds," prepared us for the rough ride to the ground.

The Hoboken ground is situated, we cannot quite say where, but it is "out of humanity's reach," approached by unfinished streets, and surrounded by "carcasses" of houses in an advanced stage of non-completion.

Quite a number of people were flocking to it, and at 12 noon, a good ring was formed. The wickets had been well prepared by Stubberfield, whom we regretted to see in bad health. The Captain lost his first toss. The ground played dead—one glance sufficed us to prognosticate a few visits to the adjoining gardens. It could be got "out of" on every side...

This match was not of an International character—*pur et simple*. Cricket is not a popular game at New York. It has a struggle for existence, and is indebted for life to a few determined Englishmen. The sporting portion of Americans, with whom we came in contact, took very little interest in the proceedings, at the same time the greatest courtesy was shown by them, and the Twelve are much indebted to several influential members for an introduction to two of the leading clubs in New York—the Union and the Travellers'.

PHILADELPHIA

The Twelve had not been many hours in Canada before they were met by a deputation from Philadelphia. At Montreal the first arrangements were made, and to the attention and kindness of Messrs. Patterson, Cadwalader, Outerbridge, and F. C. Newhall of the Committee, is eminently due the satisfactory result afterwards obtained.

In the first place, an International match was agreed upon. The Twenty-two of Philadelphia were to be selected from the local clubs, and to consist of Americans. The programme originally fixed was to include various kinds of amusement. The Philadelphians required a week, and it was with great regret that the Captain felt obliged to curtail the arrangements. An influential deputation had also met him from Boston, and it was found impracticable to arrange a longer stay at Philadelphia, and at the same time to do justice to the good folks of Massachusetts. The Twelve left New York for Philadelphia on Friday evening, September 20, and found excellent accommodations provided for them at the Continental Hotel. The papers were full of the coming contest.

Saturday, September 21.—There could be no doubt about the interest taken in the match. Immense crowds set towards the ground,—the road might have been to the Epsom Downs on the morning of the Derby. The railroad was a continuous train. On arriving at the scene of action, one glance was sufficient to tell that great attention had been paid to the ground, which is situated in a private demesne. It had been inclosed by high palings, and ropes and stakes marked the outer ring. By 11:30 every bough had a boy on it, every hayrick a tenant. The band piled up its music on the roof of the pavilion, and the grand-stand was rapidly filling with the fair daughters of Penn....

The attendance during the afternoon steadily increased. There was not a spare seat in the grand-stand. Upwards of seven thousand spectators were present. An honest English clique occupied one corner, and a gentle interchange of chaff with our American cousins was indulged in. The utmost good humour prevailed, and the first experience of a genuine American match was very gratifying. The day had been hot, but tempered by a breeze; the night was cool, almost to frosty. The Twelve were entertained in the evening by Mr. Fisher, at his residence in the country, a few miles from Germantown, where a large party had been invited to meet them. The cheer was of the best and the most; the house was replete with comfort and elegance. A well-stored library, and walls hung with old family pictures, speak of years that have rolled over successive generations under the same roof. Some fine pieces of modern sculpture speak to the cultivated taste, and to the traveled experience, which is an eminent characteristic of the wealthy Philadelphian. The long drive (in the course of which we lost our way) was well rewarded. The Twelve were introduced to the *elite* of the neighborhood; and, if no other reminiscence was due to the evening than that of a pleasant supper, it would still claim the honor and the charm of our first introduction to General Meade.

Sunday was intended as a day of rest. Practically it was not. Some of us did, indeed, go to church, and some, under the influence of the powerful sun, did obtain a few moments' repose. A drive to Fairmont Park occupied the afternoon. Philadelphia and its wife spends its Sundays in the Park....

The second innings [of the Philadelphians] resulted in 74. This left 33 runs for the Twelve to get on Tuesday. Speculation was rife, and the following curious coincidence was published in the papers: "In the match in 1868, between the All England Eleven and the Philadelphians, the Englishmen had 33 to win in the second innings, yet the Eleven only won by two wickets."

After the stumps were drawn, the crowd collected around the club-house, called loudly for Grace, Ottaway, Hornby, and others of the Twelve. Cheer after cheer was given when Grace appeared, and nothing would quiet the crowd but the appearance of all the players on the balcony. Mr. Fitz-Gerald, Captain of the Twelve, was then introduced, and made a neat little speech, when quiet was restored. Great excitement prevailed in the English section of the crowd at this exciting phase of the game, and many were the exhortations to the Twelve "not to be beaten." The day had been superb, and the attendance remarkable of all classes of the citizens.

Tuesday, September 24.—Another brilliant summer's day. Play commenced at a quarter-past twelve; the grand-stand was again filled, and the ring around the ground unbroken. Thirty-three runs did not look like a match, but never was the old adage, that a match is not lost till it is won, better exemplified. The Twenty-two meant mischief; there was no mistaking the keen look, the business-like attitude of the field. A glance at the wickets made Gilbert remark that the few runs would take some getting; it had worn tolerably well, but the intense heat, and the ordeal it had gone through, had taken the color out of it, and put a rough edge on it, which was much in favor of fast bowling.

Gilbert and Ottaway soon appeared. A general rustle of fans in the grand-stand proved the smothered excitement of the fair occupants. Gilbert scored one run off Newhall's third ball, and the fourth found its way unchecked to Ottaway's middle stump. Roars of applause greeted the event; one for 1. Hornby quickly filled the gap; made one good hit for 3 to leg, when another roar announced his capture at short-leg; two for 8. Alfred Lubbock filled the vacant throne; runs were stolen rather than made; over after over was bowled without the batsmen leaving their wickets.

The moments were worth pounds in a cricketer's life. Alfred had made 3, and Gilbert at last landed a 3 to leg; 15 runs had been obtained in three-quarters of an hour. Newhall's bowling rose dangerously high, and it was difficult to avoid his rib-roasters. Meade hammered away brilliantly dead on the spot. Alfred Lubbock was then caught and bowled; three for 15. Hadow approached amid general acclamations. He at once opened an account, scoring three in his first over. Gilbert meanwhile had been "in luck." There was a case for the umpire, which was awarded in his favor, and he narrowly missed capture among the slips. He displayed great caution, but it was not destined for him to land the Twelve in triumph.

A roar that might have made William Penn turn in his grave suddenly told that the Leviathan was out. The flutter among the ladies was now as great as if they were sitting under a wasps'-nest. The great man strode home; his seven had taken him nearly an hour; four for 18. Harris came in with a jaunty air, and with Hadow restored the aspect of the game, from the English point of view. The field was slightly shaken, hits at last penetrated the phalanx, and the return was less direct to the wicket, though no less sharp. The throwing in, was, however, as a rule, remarkably good in a match. The score had reached 29 and danger seemed to be averted,—when Harris became too impatient, and was caught off a mounter of Newhall's, at cover-point, for a most valuable 9; five for 29. Hadow soon followed him, bowled by Meade for 6; six for 29. The remaining four runs were fought out inch by inch., Francis went in "to do or die." He didn't,—he died; seven for 29. There seemed a chance for the Quakers yet. Nobody could sit still in the grand-stand. It was agony to answer a question. It was almost insulting to human nature to demand a light for a cigar. Appleby, the Unassuming, walked leisurely in; on him the Captain relied, and not in vain. Edgar Lubbock had filled Francesco's cell, and (to quote a local), "as he stood in his peculiar attitude, it seemed as if he must be bowled out by Newhall before he was on his legs; but the said legs stood him in good stead, for a leg bye off one of them was worth a pocketful of greenbacks, and 30 runs were up." It must be mentioned that *nearly half an hour had elapsed without a run being obtained*. If the Captain had given orders to prolong the excitement to the utmost limits, he could not have been better obeyed.

The end was now near. The Unaffected let out an over pitched ball of Newhall's to the off, four to the ropes was scored, and the battle was won. The pent-up excitement now broke loose. Shouts of "well bowled," "well fielded," were met by English counter-cheers of "well played." It was indeed a match that was worth the winning, and it reflected little disgrace on the defeated. If any mistake can be said to have been made by the Captain of the Twenty-Two, it was in bringing in all his men to save ones or twos; he should have saved all chances of fours, and he might thus have prolonged the game. It was scarcely possible that the Twelve would be beaten, although Fortune hung an unconscionable time upon her scales. Thirteen maiden overs were bowled at one time, in succession.

Great trouble had been taken in the selection of the Twenty-two. They were drafted from the leading clubs of Philadelphia. The proportion of work done or omitted by the various representatives was critically reckoned by the local press. Among other things, we read that the best bowling was done by Charles A. Newhall, of the Young America Club. We differ from this, as, to our mind, Meade is by far the best bowler, and on a good wicket we do not think Newhall can hold a rush-light to him. There is doubtless great praise due to both the bowlers, who, though aided by the ground and a smart field, contributed immensely to the exciting close. Newhall and Meade well deserve all that was printed of them by an admiring reporter. Hargreaves, "Joe," as wicket-keeper, once removed, did good service. Prizes were distributed to Newhall and Meade for bowling, to Large for batting, and to Joe Hargreaves for fielding. (An additional prize was afterward awarded to John Hargreaves for good all-round play, he having fielded excellently well, and having obtained the second highest score in the match.) F. Norley, who is in charge of the ground, deserves great credit for the pains that he had taken.

The account of this great match cannot be complete without congratulation to the committee in charge of the arrangements for their zeal in promoting the comfort of the spectators, as well as that of their visitors and all who were present.

The protracted struggle was so far unfortunate, that it led to a hurried departure of the Twelve from the scene of their hardly-earned victory, in order to catch a train for Boston. The train was not caught, and the press was rather severe on the apparent discourtesy of the Twelve in not remaining to acknowledge the last greetings of their antagonists. It was, however, solely and strictly in performance of their agreement with the cricketers of Boston that the Twelve reluctantly left Philadelphia. Saturday was the day fixed for sailing home from Quebec. It was necessary to rob Peter to pay Paul. Philadelphia must be curtailed of some of her attractions, New York must abandon some of her many temptations, or Boston will not be satisfied. It was sad indeed to slip away from Philadelphia, but not, as was ungenerously said in some quarters, in any want of grateful sentiment towards our entertainers there. It was strictly in accordance with our original plan,—to see as much of America and the Americans as we possibly could in the time.

It is possible that the Twelve may have committed many little social errors. Rumours have reached our ears of acts of apparent want of civility on our part,—for these we most humbly ask pardon. Our mistakes do admit of excuse; we had more to do in the time than we could do properly, and omissions must not be regarded in the same light as commissions.

The following paragraph appeared in a leading paper on the occasion of our leaving Philadelphia. "Thus ended the first visit of the gentlemen of England to Germantown; and, in closing this brief chronicle, it behooves us, and is a pleasing duty, to express their sincere appreciation of the cordiality and kindness with which they were everywhere welcomed, of the great hospitality which they experienced in the city of Philadelphia, and the good fellowship which was accorded to them; to tender their thanks for the same to the clubs with whom they were engaged, and to give vent to the hope that their first visit to Germantown may not be their last."

We were anxious to do justice to our gallant antagonists; we were not prepared for the interest taken in the match by the spectators, nor were we aware of the hold that cricket has taken upon the youth of Philadelphia. It was an agreeable surprise.

From the cricket-field to the cupboard was the regular course, and the evening spent at the Union League Club was one of the most memorable during the tour. Upwards of two hundred guests had been invited; the handsome rooms were well lighted, and an interesting series of portraits introduced the Twelve to many heroes of the late war. There was plenty of speechifying to a late hour. The evening was cheerful, the most distinguished of the citizens were present. Toasts of the most genial character set in, and the Captain was called upon to reply to, or to propose, at least a score. He could not miss such an opportunity of expressing the pleasure of his companions at making the personal acquaintance of American cricketers; he alluded gratefully to the services of the Philadelphia Committee, which had been so instrumental in securing a happy result; he trusted that this visit would lead to many others; and he augured, from the good cricket already exhibited, that a love for the game would long be cherished, and that it would take root in the *schools* of the State, and bear its fruit upward ere many years be past, in an even-handed struggle with the best proficients of England.

A melancholy interest is attached to this evening, full as it is of pleasant memories. General Meade, who presided, is now no more; his son had taken a great part in the match. The general had won all hearts by his kind demeanor; his manly form and eagle eye distinguished him outwardly among his fellow-men. It was our privilege to make his acquaintance, and to hear from his lips, as we walked together through the national gallery of the Union League Club, many anecdotes of the war, which came home to us with greater force in the martial worlds of the hero of Gettysburg....

Our last words are, that we received a hearty welcome, and we played a hearty match. Long may cricket continue to be played in the spirit which animated our kind friends at Germantown! But one feeling pervaded the whole cricket community,—to show the Englishmen that a love of the game does exist in America, and that its preservation and advancement would be secured by periodical visits of this nature from our side of the Atlantic. We can, in conclusion, only express a hope that many years will not elapse ere the expedition be repeated. We feel certain that the cricketers to come will re-echo the sentiment of the Captain and his companions,—that from Quebec to Philadelphia they passed as strangers but to part as friends.

SCORE.

PHILADELPHIA.

First Innings.		*Second Innings.*	
F. Brewster, b Appleby	4	c Rose, b Grace	0
H.I. Newhall, b Appleby	0	c Fitz-Gerald, b Grace	0
W. Welsh, b. Appleby	0	b Appleby	1
R.S. Newhall, b Appleby	4	c Hornby, b Appleby	0
John Large, hit wicket, b Grace.	13	c Appleby, b Grace	7
Cadwalader, hit wicket, b Rose.	2	b Grace	0
L. Baird, c Harris, b Rose	0	l b wicket, b Appleby	6
Geo. M. Newhall, b Appleby	0	b Appleby	9
Joe Hargreaves, b Appleby	2	b Grace	4
W. Morgan, c Ottaway, b Grace.	7	c Hadow, b Grace	1
Dan S. Newhall, b. Grace	0	at Ottaway, b Grace	15
S. Law, c Rose, b Grace	2	not out	2
Chas. A. Newhall, Appleby	3	l b wicket, by Appleby	0
S. Meade, c E. Lubbock, b Grace.	0	b Appleby	2
R. Pease hit wicket, b Grace.	0	hit wicket, b Appleby	0
C. Baird, run out	3	b Grace	1
T. Hargreaves c Ottaway b Grace.	0	st Ottaway, b Grace	3
R.W. Clay, b Grace	4	c Hadow, b Grace	11
John Hargreaves, run out	11	c and b Grace	7
G. Sanderson, b Appleby	0	b Grace	0
H. Magee, c Ottaway, b Grace.	3	b Appleby	1
S. Welsh, not out	3	run out	0
Byes	1		4
Leg bye	1		0
Total	63		74

ENGLAND.

First Innings.		*Second Innings.*	
Grace, b C. Newhall	14	c J. Hargreaves, b C. Newhall.	7
Ottaway, run out	10	b C. Newhall	0

Hornby, b Meade	9	c R. Newhall, b Meade	4
A. Lubbock	9	c and b C. Newhall	3
Hadow, c J. Hargreaves, b C.	6	Newhall	29
b Meade	6	Harris, c D. Newhall,	
b. C. Newhall	3	c J. Hargreaves, b Meade	8
Francis, b Meade	5	b C. Newhall	0
Appleby, c Magee, b Meade	2	not out	4
E. Lubbock, c J. Hargreaves, b			
C. Newhall	0	not out	0
Rose, c J. Hargreaves, b C.			
Newhall	0		
Pickering, b C. Newhall	7		
Fitz-Gerald, not out	1		
Byes	4		1
Leg Byes	7		1
Wides	5		
Total	105		34

ANALYSIS OF THE BOWLING.

ENGLAND.

First Innings.

	BALLS.	RUNS.	MAIDENS.	WICKETS.	WIDES.
Rose	64	16	6	2	0
Appleby	145	23	25	8	0
Grace	84	22	11	9	0
			Second Innings.		
Appleby	142	25	27	7	0
Grace	141	45	13	13	0

PHILADELPHIA.

First Innings.

	BALLS.	RUNS.	MAIDENS.	WICKETS.	WIDES.
C.A. Newhall	212	45	26	6	0
Meade	200	44	28	3	5
			Second Innings.		
C.A. Newhall	73	24	8	4	0
Meade	72	8	13	3	0

THE HALIFAX CRICKET TOURNAMENT, 1874

One of the greatest achievements in the history of Philadelphia cricket was the victory of a team of twelve players in an international tournament held in Halifax, Nova Scotia during the summer of 1874. The trophy that these gentlemen brought back to their native city was soon named the "Halifax Cup." Beginning in 1880 its owners offered it as a prize for the annual competition among the leading Philadelphia clubs. The following excerpts from a narrative of the Halifax tournament was written by A.A. Outerbridge and is reprinted from *The Halifax Tournament. An Account of the Visit of the American Twelve of Philadelphia to Halifax, in August, 1874* (Philadelphia, 1874), pp. 3-5,11-12,17,19-22,38-42,47-49.

In the spring of the present year (1874) Captain N.W. Wallace, of the 60th Royal Rifles, stationed at Halifax, N.S., wrote to many prominent cricketers in the United States and Canada, inviting their co-operation in a grand cricket tournament to be held at Halifax in the following August. It was known to us in Philadelphia that the Halifax garrison contained among its officers many first-class cricketers—English gentlemen who had played, as boys, on the celebrated English school elevens, and who had regularly kept up their favorite sport after entering the British army. It was also known that the Dominion of Canada could muster a very strong combined eleven, and the question here was, whether a United States eleven could be organized capable of holding their own against such strong teams.

The matches proposed were,—

America *vs.* Canada, England *vs.* Canada,

America *vs.* England, Halifax *vs.* All Comers.

A handsome silver cup was to be the prize for the champion team, and other valuable prizes were offered for individual excellence in batting and bowling.

The invitation to United States cricketers was widely circulated, by means of notices in "Forest and Stream," and otherwise, and correspondence ensued between Philadelphia, New York, Boston, and St. Louis, with the view of organizing a representative United States team. Without going into details, suffice it to say that this endeavor failed, no clubs outside Philadelphia tendering a quota of players. The Philadelphians, on the other hand, entered into the project with *esprit*, and at a general meeting of cricketers held at the Germantown cricket-house on the 27th of June, the names of no less than twenty-two well-known cricketers were handed in as desirous of going. A modified invitation from Captain Wallace to a *Philadelphia* twelve was received, and accepted; and it was decided by the meeting, first, "that the twelve to represent America in the tournament shall consist wholly of Americans born who have acquired cricket in this country; and secondly, that in the absence of any participation by other clubs, the members of the four leading clubs of Philadelphia represented in the meeting (to wit, the Philadelphia, Germantown, Young America, and Merion Clubs) shall select a Philadelphia team to take part in the tournament at Halifax. Mr. Albert A. Outerbridge was chosen as manager to make all the arrangements for the trip, and a committee, consisting of one member from each of the above-named clubs, with Mr. Outerbridge, *ex officio*, was appointed to select the twelve from those candidates who had signified their willingness to go.

The selection originally made by this committee was afterwards slightly modified by reason of a few of those chosen being prevented from going, but their places were filled, and the following was the final selection: Mr. Daniel S. Newhall (captain), Messrs. Charles A. Newhall, Robert S. Newhall, R. Loper Baird, and John Large, of the Young America Cricket Club; Spencer Meade, Horace Magee, and Edward Hopkinson, of the Philadelphia Club; Francis E. Brewster and R. Nelson Caldwell, of the Germantown Club; George Ashbridge and Richard Ashbridge, of the Merion Club. Two substitutes, Messers. William Welsh, Jr., and William Hopkinson, of the Philadelphia Club, with Mr. Alexander J.D. Dixon as scorer, and Thomas Rhoads, the capable professional of the Germantown ground, as umpire, completed the selection; but a number of other gentlemen decided to accompany the party for the pleasure of the trip.

The "Halifax Twelve," as they were now called, utilized the interval before leaving by individual practice, and by playing three one-innings matches against strong picked teams of the "stay-at-home" cricketers. Of these, they lost once and won two, making in the three innings a total of 552 runs. Allowing for absentees, this gave an average of over 19 for each player in each inning, which promised well....

The Halifax people seemed excited about the tournament. An American could not enter a shop without being politely questioned as to the strength of his team. The hotel was besieged by strangers and sporting men, some of whom wanted to get "points" for their betting. Said one individual, "Is that little fellow one of the American twelve?? "Yes, that is young Caldwell." "And that one?" "Oh, yes, that is Bob Newhall." "And that one, too?" "Yes, that is the captain of the team, Dan Newhall." "Well," he replied, "a friend who saw them play base-ball in St. John wrote me to back the American team; but I am not going to stake my money on *boys* against those big Englishmen,—not until I see them play, at any rate." It is right to say, however, that there was very little betting on the matches. Whether this is accounted for by the fact that no bets could be got against the "boys" after the first day's play, when "young Caldwell" made 18, "Dan" 35, not out, and "Bob" 79, may be a question....

Prizes.

The following prizes will be offered for competition:

A Silver Challenge Cup (Value £20).—Presented by His Worship the Mayor of Halifax to the Champion Eleven in three first Matches.

A Silver Subscription Cup (Value £10).—Presented for the highest individual average in Batting during the Tournament.

A Silver Cup (Value £5).—Presented for the best average in Bowling during the Tournament.

Prize Bats and Balls will also be offered for every 50 runs obtained in a single inning, and for superior bowling.

Rules and Conditions.

1. The conditions of the above Prizes will be made known on the Ground.
2. All matches to be played out or considered drawn.
3. No two Prize Cups to fall to the same individual.
4. All decisions of the Committee of Management to be considered final.

5. The players of both representative Elevens to be bona fide members of Clubs of the Dominion and the United States. Those of the English Eleven to be non-residents in the Dominion or United States. Those of the Halifax Eleven to include the Fleet and Garrison.

By kind permission the Bands of H.M.S. "Bellerophon" 60th Royal Rifles, and 87th Royal Irish Fusiliers, will play from 3:30 to 6:30 P.M., during the Tournament. Excursion trains and steamers will be run to Halifax during the Tournament at reduced rates.

Refreshments will be served on the ground.

The weather on Tuesday morning, the 18th, was very threatening. The harbor was draped in fog, and we found the cricket-ground enveloped in moist clouds. The field, which is about fifteen minutes drive from the hotel, is a large one, and its general appearance handsome. Being a new ground, the turfed platform in the centre is very limited in extent, but what there is of it is really first-class. It showed the result of great attention, and a better wicket could not have been desired. The general lay of the rest of the field is for the most part level, but taken in detail, the out-field is decidedly ridgy, and round work was predicted for the fielders, especially for long-stop. Tents large and small, flags, ropes, guidons, and a grand stand gave to the whole an attractive appearance, and as the ground on two sides was uninclosed by fences, a spacious effect was produced....

FIRST MATCH—AMERICA VS. CANADA, AUGUST 18, 19.

Visitors had been dropping in all the morning, and when play was resumed after lunch, the seats all round the ground were well filled, and between three and four o'clock carriages poured in almost in a continuous stream. It seemed as if everybody who is anybody in Halifax must keep a drag, or phaeton, or barouche, or tandem, or unicorn, or a carriage of some kind, and certainly the turn-out of stylish equipages which appeared daily on the cricket-field was unexpected to the Philadelphians. The ladies as a rule remained in their carriages, and received visits from the well-looking Englishmen, who to-day were off duty. Later on the Philadelphians and Canadians had ample opportunity of meeting the fair Haligonians. Some of the outsiders of our party who are connoisseurs in the matter of feminine beauty formed themselves into a committee of inspection and made the grand rounds; it required but a glance to decide that all the wealth and fashion of Halifax were represented on the grounds. Not a few horsemen and horsewomen, mounted on high-bred animals, made their occasional appearance during the tournament. The fine band of the 60th performed a select programme, and the soldiers, who took great interest in the cricket, furnished well in their scarlet uniform scattered in knots among the dark fringe of spectators. On the whole, it was a gay scene, and as it was repeated each afternoon, some idea can be formed of the general interest taken in the tournament....

The play of the Philadelphians in batting, bowling, and fielding was the subject of universal commendation, and the Canadians, Englishmen, and residents were alike generous in their congratulations. No attempt was made to detract from their fairly won victory; on the contrary, their laurels were ungrudgingly bestowed. The following excerpt from the "Evening Reporter and Times" is but a specimen of the tone of the general feeling which prevailed among the press and the people:

"We do congratulate most heartily the American team on their splendid victory and really fine playing; and we can cordially indorse what seems to be the general impression, that they are a fine, manly, honorable set of fellows; and we can only hope that we shall have the satisfaction of returning with interest the drubbing our cricketers have undergone. How dismally sounded the 'click' of the bails as they flew off the wicket as man after man succumbed yesterday to the excellent bowing of Meade and C. Newhall can more easily be felt than described."

Since the return of the Canadians, Rev. Mr. Phillips has taken the opportunity, in a most entertaining review of their tour, published in an Ottawa paper, to explain some of the causes of their defeat, while, at the same time, he accords the full meed of praise to their opponents; and we do both Canadians and Americans but justice in inserting his remarks, viz:

..."We were thus defeated in one innings with 31 runs to spare, a result which hardly gauges fairly the relative strength of the two parties. Tolerably familiar with Canadian cricket for nearly thirty years, and intimately acquainted with its present status, I have no hesitation in affirming that we can surpass the Americans in batting, and we can match their bowling; but their fielding is not only far superior to ours, but it is simply unapproachable. As it is not pretended we, the late team, fairly represented Canada, and as a demand may be made upon me for details in support of the sweeping assertions, I venture the statement that the Americans can be met on equal terms by a twelve selected from the following: Van Allen, Whelan, and Wright, of Chatham, Gillean, and Hyman, of London, Hope, and another man from Hamilton, Blake, Hempsted, and Spragge, of Toronto, three Ottawa men, and McLean and two others from Montreal. Of course other, perhaps better judges than myself, would vary this selection, but I mention some of these names to show how weak we really were, and how a consciousness of that weakness did not deter us from struggling manfully on behalf of the great country we were invited to represent. As to the Americans, I think it would be impossible to speak too highly of the favorable impression they made on the minds of all with whom they came in contact. There are times when defeat leaves a rankling, incurable fester; but with opponents such as those enthusiastic young Philadelphians, who made everything subservient for the time to the occupation on hand, one may look back to defeat almost with pleasure. Young Canada has many a lesson to learn from the late international contests; but the best of all will have been missed if we do not take the hint from young America, that whatever is worth doing at all is worth doing well."

The match being finished by half-past four, the remainder of the afternoon was occupied by a game of base-ball between a Halifax club and the same American nine that had distinguished themselves at St. John. The game was not understood by the spectators, and consequently excited little or no interest. It was not finished, nor was the score preserved....

SECOND MATCH—AMERICA VS. ENGLAND, AUGUST 20, 21.

It was evident that this was to be the great match of the tournament. The capabilities of the Englishmen were well known, and their truly brilliant batting was the pride of Halifax. Captain Wallace, the chief of the tournament and the captain of the English team, had recently scored 158 and 67 in practice matches, and Hon. Keith Turnour, Davies, and others, enjoyed home-earned reputations as batsmen. Lieutenants Reid and Mitchell, of the Engineers, had traveled by invitation from

"Where the remote Bermudas ride
In th' ocean's bosom unespied,"

expressly to play on this match, and the former was expected to play sad havoc among the American wickets by his destructive head-work bowling.

On the other hand, the Americans had made many friends, and not a few good judges of the game predicted close work. The feeling among the Philadelphians was that they would certainly have much harder work than had yet been met; but, encouraged by their own steady play in the Canada match, rather than elated by their easy victory, they were self-reliant and confident, and went into the game with a determination to win, no matter how well the Britishers might play. Among the English twelve, the feeling appeared to be, as far as one could judge, first, surprise that the Americans could play cricket as they did; and, secondly, that they themselves were, as a team, greatly stronger than the Canadians had shown themselves to be, and would fight a very different game, with a probability of winning, but a possibility of losing.

With the public the interest in this match was intensified, from the fact that if the Americans won it would decide the question of the Mayor's prize cup in their favor, as the champion team in two out of the three competitive matches....

[The Philadelphia team won this match by a score of 205 to 200, without batting in the second innings.]

The outsiders of the Philadelphia party hastened to congratulate their representatives on having won the coveted position of champion team, with its attendant trophy, the silver challenge cup, and the satisfaction which each of the party inwardly felt may be imagined. Congratulations also poured in from other friends, in which the Englishmen themselves joined. The victory was such a pronounced one, that it was admitted that while they would probably have saved the one innings defeat had it not been for the rain on the first day, yet the result of the game would not have been affected had the weather been fine....

On the afternoon of this day [August 25th] a particularly interesting ceremony took place on the cricket-ground. Between the innings of the Halifax *vs.* All Comers match all the cricketers and all the spectators including the ladies were invited to assemble at the grand stand to witness the presentation of the Mayor's challenge cup to the champion team. Mr. Outerbridge was called to the front, supported on either hand by the American Twelve, and Mayor Sinclair spoke as follows:

"Mr. Outerbridge and gentlemen of the American Team:—I have much pleasure in presenting to you the prize to which you have become so honorably entitled. The training and skill which you have exhibited in your play show to what perfection the noble game of cricket may be brought. The science displayed by you, so universally acknowledged by all who have witnessed the tournament, will, I have no doubt, have a most beneficial effect in stirring up the energies of those who have met you in the contest, and who may hereafter prove themselves to be more successful competitors for future prizes."

Mr. Outerbridge, having taken the cup, replied as follows: "In accepting this beautiful trophy on behalf of the American Twelve of Philadelphia, I cannot but avail myself of the opportunity to express, though inadequately, our deep sense of the kindness and hospitality with which we have been welcomed by the cricketers and citizens of Halifax. More than this, the distinguished gentlemen who fill with honor the highest official positions in the Province of Nova Scotia and the city of Halifax have indorsed the fine old English game of cricket, not only by the weight of their names as patrons of the cricket tournament, but by their presence at the matches, and by their hospitable entertainment of the visiting guests.

"To your Worship, Mr. Mayor, are due the thanks of one and all—English, Canadians, and Americans alike—for your practical enthusiasm in offering, as the highest prize, this exquisitely wrought silver cup, of great intrinsic value, but of far greater value in the associations and memories which will hereafter attach to it.

"Speaking for our young American cricketers, I must be permitted to say (although I shall say it as modestly as I can), that it is with great pleasure and pride that we have come out so successfully from the matches in which we have met such manly foemen.

"When Philadelphia accepted the invitation of Captain Wallace and the Tournament Committee to send a representative twelve, it was doubtful whether we should be able to furnish a team that would worthily represent the cricket strength of Philadelphia, and which would be competent to maintain the honor, which was thrust upon them, of playing for America as well as Philadelphia. That I was partly instrumental in organizing a team which has proved to be a strong one is the only merit which causes me to be the recipient of the honor of receiving the prize on their behalf, and of being their unworthy spokesman on this most pleasant occasion. We came determined to do our best, and success has crowned our efforts.

"The cricketers of America have spoken to those of Canada and of England, by their representatives, and their message is one of friendly rivalry as to our favorite sport, and of personal good friendship.

"I might speak of international amenities, and their tendency to bring about a practical realization of that mutual respect and regard which only a want of mutual acquaintance hinders; but I shall confine myself to a cricketer's legitimate theme, and I will only say that the result of our success in this very successful cricket tournament will be to draw general attention in the United States to the noble old English national game of cricket,—a game which stands pre-eminent in its attractions and advantages as a field sport, and which is not less pre-eminent by the absence of those demoralizing tendencies which, unfortunately, have attached themselves to some other manly sports. The fact that cricket is played by gentlemen, indorsed by dignitaries, and approved of and participated in by reverend clergymen (Hear, hear), who are not unmindful that youth must grow in stature as well as in grace, will go far towards elevating cricket, and extending it to schools and colleges of the United States.

"In receiving this cup, allow me again to endeavor to express for each and every man, not only of our playing Twelve, but for those of the somewhat numerous party of Philadelphians who accompanied them, our warm appreciation of the great hospitality and kindness which we have received on all hands, and to express the hope that at no distant day we shall have the pleasure of meeting as many of our hosts as possible at a Philadelphia cricket tournament, when we shall have an opportunity of reciprocating in kind the civilities which you have extended to us."

At the conclusion of his remarks Mr. Outerbridge proposed three cheers for the Mayor of Halifax and the Tournament Committee, which were given with a will by the Philadelphia party. Cheers were also given for Captain Wallace, Rev. Mr. Phillips, and the ladies,—this later sentiment being proposed by the American captain....

PRIZE LIST

Mayor's Champion Cup, awarded to American Twelve, of Philadelphia.

Cup for highest batting average, awarded to D.S. Newhall. Average 49.66.

Cup for highest bowling average, awarded to Charles A. Newhall. Runs per wicket, 6.88

Cup for highest aggregate score (extra prize), awarded to Rev. T.D. Phillips. Aggregate score, 197.

Prize bats for scores of 50, awarded to R.S. Newhall, score 79; Captain Wallace, score 68; Rev. T.D. Phillips, score 55; Hon. Keith Turnour, score 53; Lieutenant Mitchell, score 52 (not out); Rev. T.D. Phillips, 2d, score 52 (not out); D.S. Newhall, score 50.

Prize balls for superior bowling were awarded to Spencer Meade, runs per wicket, 7.93; Lieutenant Reid, runs per wicket, 12; B.B. Bullock, runs per wicket, 12.70; E. Kearney, runs per wicket, 16.

SCORES

FIRST MATCH—AMERICA VS. CANADA

Played Tuesday, August 18, and Wednesday, August 19.

CANADA.

First Innings.		Second Innings.	
Rev. T.D. Phillips, not out	52	c. Magee, b. C. Newhall	14
A.W. Powell, run out	0	b. C. Newhall	9
E. Kearney, c. and b. D.S. Newhall	9	b. Meade	8
J. Brunel, b. D.S. Newhall	1	c. and b. Meade	0
J. Gorham, c. Meade, b. C.A. Newhall.	2	b. Meade	2
J.H. Park, c. J. Large, b. D.S. Newhall.	0	not out	0
C.B. Brodie, c. C. Newhall, b. D. Newhall	2	run out	0
G. Brunel, l. b. w., b. C. Newhall	5	c. Hopkinson, b. C. Newhall.	0
M.C. Hebert, c. and b. C. Newhall	0	b. Meade	5
M.B. Daly, b. C. Newhall	1	b. C. Newhall	0
W. Snider, b. Meade	7	b. C. Newhall	11
W. Street, c. G. Ashbridge, b. C. Newhall	0	b. Meade	0

Byes 10, Leg bye 1, Wides 4	15	Byes 11, Leg byes 3, Wides 3.	17
	94		66

AMERICA—FIRST INNINGS.

John Large, c. Brodie, b. J. Brunel	9
F. E. Brewster, l. b. w., b. Kearney	2
R.S. Newhall, b. Kearney	79
C.A. Newhall, c. Hebert, b. Brodie	3
R.N. Caldwell, c. Street, b. Kearney	18
E. Hopkinson, c. J. Brunel, b. Kearney	0
D.S. Newhall, not out	35
R. L. Baird, l. b. w., b. Brodie	6
R. Ashbridge, b. Kearney	0
H. Magee, c. Phillips, b. Brodie	0
S. Meade, c. G. Brunel, b. Kearney	0
G. Ashbridge, run out	5
byes, 12, Leg byes 4, Wides 18	34
	191

Runs at fall of each Wicket

	1	2	3	4	5	6	7	8	9	10	11	Total.
America—1st.	4	41	50	91	91	147	170	181	182	183	191	191
Canada—1st.	2	27	31	51	52	60	73	75	79	91	94	
2nd.	1	8	14	16	16	40	40	58	61	65	66	
												160
America won in one innings and												31

Analysis of the Bowling.
AMERICA—FIRST INNINGS.

	Wides.	Total Balls.	Runs.	Maidens.	Wickets.
Meade,	2	116	14	22	1
C. Newhall,	2	167	19	27	5
Magee,	0	20	6	1	0
Brewster,	0	12	8	0	0
D.S. Newhall	0	60	32	3	4

SECOND INNINGS.

Meade,	3	120	24	18	5
C. Newhall,	0	120	24	20	5

CANADA—FIRST INNINGS.

Brodie,	2	192	56	20	3
Kearney,	8	205	75	21	6
J. Brunel,	4	20	10	1	1
Hebert,	1	20	10	0	0
G. Brunel,	3	8	6	0	0

SECOND MATCH—AMERICA VS. ENGLAND.
Played Thursday, August 20, Friday, 21st, and Saturday, 22d.

AMERICA—FIRST INNINGS.

F. E. Brewster, c. Gardiner, b. Taylor	29
C.A. Newhall, b. Reid	29
R.S. Newhall, c. Mitchell, b. Singleton	29
G. Ashbridge, b. Reid	18
J. Large, c. Davies, b. Singleton	7
E. Hopkinson, run out	4
D.S. Newhall, c. Stubbing, b. Reid	39
R.N. Caldwell, c. Stubbing, b. Carpenter	8
R.L. Baird, run out	3
H. Magee, c. Stubbing, b. Singeton	13
R. Ashbridge, l.b.w., b. Reid	0
S. Meade, not out	5
Byes 6, Leg byes 6, Wides 9	21
Total	205

ENGLAND.

First Innings.		Second Innings.	
Hon. Keith Turnour, c. Magee, b. Meade	46	c. Welsh (sub.), b. Magee. 12	
Lieut. Mitchell, b. Meade	3	c. Baird, b. Meade	21
Lieut., Davies, c. and b. Meade	5	b. Meade	14
Lieut. Barker, b. D.S. Newhall	7	c. Magee, b. C. Newhall. 1	
Lieut. Reid, b. C. Newhall	2	c. E. Hopkinson, b. C. Newhall	6
Capt. Wallace, c. D. Newhall, b. Meade.	3	c. E. Hopkinson, b. C. Newhall	1
Lieut. Gardiner, c.W. Hopkinson (sub.), b. Brewster	16	c.W. Hopkinson (sub.) b. C. Newhall	9
Mr. Stubbing, run out	2	b. Meade	4
Capt. Taylor, c. E. Hopkinson, b. Meade	5	b. Meade	1
Lieut. Carpenter, run out	1	not out	2
Lieut. Singleton, b. Meade	3	b. C. Newhall	2

Lieut. Farmer, not out	8	c. Brewster, b. C. Newhall.	1
Byes 8, Leg byes 2, Wides 5,			
No ball,	116	Byes 6, Leg byes 3	9
Total	117		83

Runs at fall of each Wicket.

	1	2	3	4	5	6	7	8	9	10	11	Total.
America—1st.	53	97	106		129		162	191	191	205		205
England—1st.	3	19	45	47	54	89	94	99	104	104	117	
2nd.	7	23	24	35	39	45	60	71	73	79	83	200

America won in one innings and 5

Analysis of the Bowling.

AMERICA—FIRST INNINGS.

	No Balls.	Wides.	Total Balls.	Runs.	Maidens.	Wickets.
C. Newhall	0	2	172	48	20	1
Meade,	1	3	157	29	22	6
D.S. Newhall	0	0	32	16	3	1
Brewster	0	0	20	8	1	1

SECOND INNNGS.

C. Newhall	0	0	139	36	16	6
Magee,	0	0	72	17	8	1
Meade,	0	0	64	22	5	4

ENGLAND—FIRST INNINGS.

Singleton,	0	3	137	44	15	3
Reid,	0	0	112	68	5	4
Taylor,	0	6	64	34	5	1
Carpenter,	0	0	52	28	6	1
Turnour,	0	0	20	10	1	0

CONSTITUTION OF THE CRICKETERS' ASSOCIATION OF THE UNITED STATES 1878

Although all previous attempts by American cricketers to found a national association for their favorite sport had failed, in 1878 several prominent Philadelphians tried again.

Delegates from Maryland, New York, and Pennsylvania representing thirteen clubs convened at the Penn Club in the City of Brotherly Love on April 17th. They launched the Cricketers' Association of the United States as they adopted the following constitution and rules. They set the annual assessment for each club at five dollars and elected officers. A.A. Outerbridge became the body's first President. The second rule, which barred a player from competing for more than one club, soon caused a serious controversy. At a meeting in mid-May four clubs—the St. George of New York City, Staten Island, Philadelphia, and Germantown—refused to ratify the new charter and regulations. They argued that the law banning multiple memberships interfered with the internal administration of their organizations. They pointed out that if enforced it would prevent one of the Philadelphia associations from playing any matches that season. Nine other clubs strenuously opposed the practice of "revolving," arguing that it deprived many of their men of the opportunity to compete in first eleven matches. They also stressed that it was impossible for a player to sustain a strong loyalty to more than one association, and that interclub contests lost most of their meaning through the practice of choosing teams that included men from different clubs. But to preserve harmony and save the fledgling association, the majority yielded and the prohibition was rescinded. This document is reprinted from The American Cricketer, 25 April 1878, pp. 98-99.

ARTICLE I.
NAME AND OBJECT.

The name of this organization shall be "The Cricketers' Association of the United States." Its object shall be the advancement of Cricket interests.

ARTICLE II.
MEMBERSHIP.

The Association shall consist of the several Cricket Clubs respectively represented by delegates at the first Annual Meeting, held at Philadelphia, April 17, 1878, and, subject to the approval of the Executive Committee of the Association, of such other regularly organized Cricket Clubs in the United States as shall make application for membership to the Secretary, and file with him a properly authenticated copy of a resolution of the applying Club, agreeing to comply with all the rules and regulations of the Association.

ARTICLE III.
OFFICERS.

SECTION 1. The officers shall consist of a President, A First and Second Vice-President, Secretary and Treasurer, and a Corresponding Secretary.

SEC. 2. The officers shall be elected at the Annual Meeting, to serve for one year, or until their successors shall be duly elected. Any vacancies occurring in the officers of the Association during the year, or in the Executive Committee, shall be filled by that Committee.

SEC. 3. It shall be the duty of the President to preside at all meetings, to direct the order of business, to appoint all committees not otherwise provided for, and generally to perform the duties relating to his office.

SEC. 4. The First Vice-President shall act as President in the absence or inability to act of the latter. The Second Vice-President shall act in the absence of the President and First Vice-President.

SEC. 5. The Secretary and Treasurer shall preserve a record and minutes of all meetings and transactions of the Association, and of the Executive Committee; shall give notices of meetings and other notices to the clubs constituting the Association, and generally perform the duties of Secretary. As Treasurer, he shall collect all assessments made by the Executive Committee, make all proper payments, and shall present his account and report at each annual meeting. The Corresponding Secretary shall conduct all correspondence of the Association.

SEC. 6. There shall be an Executive Committee of five members elected at the annual meeting, of whom the President, or, in his absence, the First Vice-President (and, in his absence, the Second Vice-President), and the Secretary and Treasurer shall be *ex-officio* members. A majority of the Executive Committee shall constitute a quorum. It shall be the duty of the Executive to see that the general provisions of the Constitution and the Rules and Regulations of the Association are complied with by the clubs composing it; to hear and decide all questions that may be submitted by any of the associated clubs for decision, notice of the hearing being given to any other club which may be affected by the question; to construe and enforce all rules of the Association; to fix, at least one month prior to each annual meeting, such assessment upon the associated clubs as shall, in their judgment, be sufficient to cover the estimated cost of printing, postage, and other proper expenses of the Association for the ensuing year, including any past deficit. All assessments shall be payable at the annual meetings.

In case of a refusal or failure on the part of any club to comply with any of the Rules and Regulations of the Association, after two notices in writing, the last of which shall be at least one month before taking action thereon, the Executive Committee shall have power to suspend the club in default from all rights and privileges of the Association, and at the next annual or special meeting the Committee shall bring the matter up for such action as the Association shall see fit to take thereon. All decisions of *the Executive Committee shall be complied with* forthwith, but an appeal therefrom may be taken by any club to the Association at its next annual meeting.

The Executive Committee and the Secretary and Treasurer may cause official notices, decisions, and such other matter of information as they shall deem of interest to the Association, to be published in "The American Cricketer," which paper shall be the bulletin of the Association. All clubs are expected to take notice of official publications therein.

The Executive Committee shall have the arrangement and management of all matches in which teams representing the United States shall take part.

SEC. 7. In case of suspension by the Executive Committee no matches shall be played with the suspended club or clubs by any other member of the Association until said club is reinstated by the Executive Committee or the Association.

ARTICLE IV.
MEETINGS.

SEC. 1. There shall be a stated Annual Meeting, to be held on a date to be fixed by the Secretary, between the 1st and 15th of April in each year, at which a majority of the clubs composing the Association shall be a quorum. At each annual meeting the place shall be fixed at which the next annual meeting shall be held.

SEC. 2. Special Meetings may be called by order of the Executive Committee, at any time, under the same provision as to a quorum; and shall be called by the Committee at the request of the delegates from any five clubs, members of this Association; the place for holding special meetings to be fixed by the Executive Committee.

SEC. 3. At least ten days' notice shall be given of all meetings.

SEC. 4. Each club of the Association shall be entitled to one vote at all meetings, to be cast by its duly appointed delegate or delegates. A delegate must be a member of a club in good standing in the Association, and present credentials properly certified to by the Secretary of the club he represents. A delegate can only represent one club.

ARTICLE V.
ADOPTION AND AMENDMENTS.

SEC. 1. This Constitution, and the By-Laws, Rules and Regulations adopted in connection therewith, shall go into effect one month from this date (April 17, 1878), and shall be considered obligatory on all the clubs represented at this first meeting, unless official notice is sent to the Secretary of refusal to join the Association within that time.

SEC. 2. Amendments to this Constitution may be made at any annual meeting, by the vote of at least two-thirds of the members present.

SEC. 3. The By-Laws may be amended at any annual or special meeting by the vote of at least two-thirds of the members present.

The Committee on rules and suggestions then presented the following Report:

Your committee beg to report that they have considered the following questions presented to their consideration, with a view to the improvement of the game, and the shortening of the time allowed to play it:

1st. Whether a member shall be permitted to play in matches with more than one club.

2d. The regulation of the "Overs," and the enforcement of such changes as will save the time now wasted in the playing of the game.

They suggested the adoption of the following:

RULES.

First. That the laws of Cricket, as laid down by the Marylebone Cricket Club, shall govern this Association, except as they may hereinafter be modified.

Second. That no player be allowed to play in matches with more than one club in the Association, during the season, unless he shall actually have resigned from one club and joined another. But undergraduates of colleges may play with one other club besides their college club.

Third. The Time for commencing a match shall be settled in writing between the playing clubs, prior to the day of the match; and the club failing or refusing to play within half an hour of the time named shall lose the match.

Fourth. No practising [sic] shall be allowed on the ground, during a match, which will interfere with the strict enforcement of Law 38th of the Marylebone Club.

Fifth. Each playing eleven shall provide an umpire for each match, and no player taking part in the match shall officiate as umpire.

Sixth. Six balls shall constitute an "over," but by mutual agreement, eight balls may be allowed.

Seventh. When one side has had one full innings, and the other has not, but has exceeded its opponent's score, the side having an excess of runs shall be the winner of the match.

Eighth. All matches played by club members of the Association shall be played under the rules adopted by it.

Your committee also submit the following suggestions for the consideration of the members of the Association, and recommend a trial thereof by them during the coming season, in connection with the determination of matches on the *Average* System where the game is not fully played out, with a view to final action thereupon by the Association at another time.

SUGGESTIONS AS TO THE RULES TO GOVERN THE AVERAGE SYSTEM.

No match shall be decided on the average system unless each side have played one full innings, and ten wickets shall be counted in said innings, whether a full eleven plays or not.

In playing matches, clubs shall alternate in taking the bat and the field.

1. To get the average, the total score of the play of each side shall be divided by the total number of batsmen less one. Thus, the score of two full innings will be divided by 21.

2. The striker carrying his bat out in the first innings shall go in first in the second innings.

3. The side going in second must play their full innings, unless when stumps are drawn their score shall exceed the score of their opponents; in that event they may win with wickets to spare.

4. Innings must be followed by a side according to the rule for a two days' match.

5. If a wicket be lost within two minutes of the time agreed upon to draw stumps, the captain of the batting side may send the next man in or not, as he chooses.

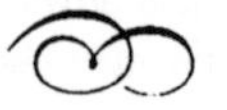

Chapter 8

CROQUET

RULES OF CROQUET, 1869

Croquet was a popular lawn game in England which gained favor among the middle and upper classes in North America during the 1860s. At that time it was undergoing a process of modernization which included the formation of clubs, codification of rules, development of strategy and tactics for "scientific play," and manufacture of equipment. Its supporters promoted it as a wholesome family pastime which was perfectly suited for female participation. Yet it was also adaptable to serious competition in which gamesmanship and aggressive play prevailed over sociability and polite etiquette.

Earlier versions of croquet were enjoyed by English and French gentlemen during the seventeenth and eighteenth centuries, but a new form of the sport was re-introduced into England from Ireland in 1852. A London manufacturer then promoted the game by producing mallets, hoops, and balls and by printing a brief pamphlet of instructions for play. The next few years brought several new rule and guide books, including a manual by a novelist, Captain Mayne Reid. An American edition of Reid's book, pirated from the London edition, appeared in Boston in 1863. Later in the decade Reid issued new editions of his work and became the leading advocate of the new recreation in the United States. Another key factor which aided the growth of the sport was the patenting and manufacture of croquet sets by the Milton Bradley company of Massachusetts, beginning in 1866. The introduction of inexpensive hand-propelled lawn mowing machines also facilitated croquet's rise as a popular amusement in the first suburban communities in the United States.

A croquet craze swept through American middle and upper class society because the game was well designed for country life and family entertainment. Although its equipment was moderately expensive, the sport could be played on modest sized grassy yards. A refreshing outdoor recreation which required several hours of leisurely play, it brought family members together for light-hearted fun. Its domestic and pastoral elements provided parents, children, and friends with a pleasurable escape from the troubles of the outside world. Like skating and archery, it was an ideal sport for women who were seeking a healthy amusement which was not too strenuous or serious. Reid and other advocates also argued that croquet also helped to cultivate a player's mental powers through its strategy and tactics. In short, the new pastime was morally uplifting, socially useful, and beneficial for mind and body.

Because of its inherent competitive qualities, croquet also had the potential to generate ill will and controversy. The lack of a national governing body in both England and the United States and the continued variation in rules produced confusion and dissension among its adherents. Proponents of the sport addressed this problem by distinguishing between serious matches (which featured captains, umpires, and a strict enforcement of rules) and playful domestic games. In the latter the participants were more forgiving and flexible in deciding questionable points, and they were more careful about social niceties. Contestants avoided over-aggressive play, gamesmanship, and the bending of the rules to gain an advantage. Sociability took precedence over winning at any cost. By 1880 croquet had attained a reputation of being a genteel domestic recreation that gentlemen could enjoy with their wives and children, but it did not qualify as a "manly" sport such as baseball, cricket, or football.

The following rules of croquet are reprinted from Captain Mayne Reid, *Croquet: A Treatise, with Notes and Commentaries* (New York, 1869), pp. 29-45.

THE START.

1. The chief, who has won the first choice of friends, has the right to lead off the play.

2. The enemy's chief plays the second ball.

3. When the chiefs have all played, the first chosen friend of the first chief plays next; then the first friend of the second chief, and so on in similar succession, until each player has had his "tour" of play.

4. Each ball at starting is played from the Spot.

5. The stroke given by the mallet may be either a *blow* or a *push*; and one or both hands may be used in giving it.

6. The blow is made, if the mallet move the ball—no matter how short the distance to which the latter may have been driven.

7. The blow may be given with the side of the mallet.

THE BRIDGES.

8. If a bridge chance to be obliqued, either to the line of the course or the plane of the horizon, any player has the right to restore it to the perpendicular.

9. No player may oblique a bridge already standing perpendicular; or change it from one oblique to another.

10. If a bridge get accidentally displaced by a stroke of the mallet, the foot of a player, or otherwise, it is to be restored to its proper position without any forfeit.

11. If a bridge get displaced by a "friend," while a ball is in the act of running it, the run will not hold good, even if evident that the ball would have passed between the piers, or, in other words, *run* the bridge, had the latter been in its place.

12. If the bridge be displaced by an "enemy," and it is evident that the ball would have run it, the run holds good.

13. A ball *runs* a bridge, when struck through it by a direct blow of the mallet.

14. A ball runs a bridge, if driven through by a roquet or blow from another ball.

15. A ball runs a bridge, driven through by ricochet.

16. A ball runs a bridge, when croque'd through it.

17. A ball runs a bridge, when sent through it by roquet-croquet.

18. A ball runs a bridge, if it pass through after rebounding from any fixed object, or from another ball.

19. A ball runs a bridge, if it pass through after rebounding from any fixed object, or from another ball.

20. A ball runs a bridge, if it pass through it after rebound from the person of an enemy.

21. If a ball pass through its proper bridge, after rebounding from the person of a friend, it does *not* run it.

22. If a ball after running a bridge strike an obstacle, and recoil back through the bridge, the run remains good, no matter what be the obstacle—whether uneven ground, a stake, a bridge, or the person of friend or enemy.

23. A ball passing through any other than its proper bridge makes no point in the play.

24. A ball passing through its proper bridge from the *reverse* side—that is, in the direction contrary to its course—makes no point in the play.

25. A ball may run two or more bridges by a direct blow of the mallet, or from a roquet, ricochet, croquet, concussion, or rebound.

26. A bridge is not run unless the ball has passed clear through, so that no part of it remains under the arch.

27. A ball resting under the arch of its proper bridge is *in position* to run it, if it have come there from the *front*, or in the direction of its course.

28. A ball resting under the arch of a bridge is *not in position* to run it, if it have come there from the *reverse* side, or contrary to the direction of its course.

29. If a ball be placed under the arch of its proper bridge by *hand*, for the purpose of making croquet on another ball which it has roque'd, it will *not* be in position for running that bridge.

30. If a ball lying upon the arena be sent through its proper bridge by any accident whatsoever, said accident being caused by the enemy—the bridge will be run.

31. If a ball, in executing the croquet, slip, or *flinch* from under the foot of the player after the blow is made, and pass through its proper bridge in the direction of the course, it does not run it.

32. A ball by striking, or being struck, against the piers of a bridge, makes no point in the game.

THE STAKES.

33. If a stake be oblique to the plane of the horizon, any player may require it to be sent vertically, or perpendicular.

34. No player may oblique a stake already standing perpendicular, or change it from one oblique to another.

35. A ball can *toll* the stake after making the *half round*, and only then.

36. A ball *tolls* the stake, by coming in contact with it.

37. A ball tolls the stake, by a direct blow by the mallet.

38. A ball tolls the stake, when roque'd or propelled against it by another ball.

39. A ball tolls the stake, when ricoche'd against it.

40. A ball tolls the stake, when croqu'ed against it.

41. A ball tolls the stake, when roquet-croqu'ed against it.

42. A ball tolls the stake, if sent against it by concussion.

43. A ball tolls the stake, if it touch it by rebound from any fixed object, or from another ball.

44. A ball touching the stake, by rebound from the person of an enemy, tolls it.

45. A ball touching the stake, by rebound from the person of a friend, does *not* toll it.

46. A ball touching the stake, through any accident or mischance caused by an enemy, tolls it.

47. A ball touching the stake, through any accident or mischance caused by a friend, does *not* toll it.

48. If a ball, in executing the croquet, flinch from under the foot of the player, and touch the stake, it does *not* toll it.

49. A ball can "strike out," or be struck out, against the starting-stake, after it has made the *grand round,* and only then.

50. The slightest touch, or contact, with the stake constitutes a striking out.

51. A ball can be struck out, by a direct blow of the mallet.

52. A ball, roque'd, or driven, against the stake by another ball, is struck out.

53. A ball, ricoche'd against the stake, is struck out.

54. A ball, croque'd against the stake, is struck out.

55. A ball, roquet-croque'd against the stake, is struck out.

56. A ball, driven against the stake, by concussion, is struck out.

57. A ball coming in contact with the stake, by rebound from a fixed object, or another ball, is struck out.

58. A ball coming in contact with the stake, by rebound from the person of a friend, is struck out, if the enemy so decide.

59. A ball coming in contact with the stake, by rebound from the person of an enemy, is struck out, if the friend so decide.

60. A ball driven against the stake through any accident or mischance caused by an enemy, is struck out, if the friend so decide; and if the accident be caused by a friend, the enemy has the right of deciding.

61. A ball coming in contact with the stake from a flinch in making the croquet, is struck out, if the enemy so decide.

62. A ball striking, or struck, against either of the stakes, at any other time than after making the half-round or the grand-round, makes no point in the game.

THE ROQUET.

63. A ball proceeding from a blow of the mallet, makes *roquet* upon another ball, when it touches or comes in contact with it.

64. A ball cannot roquet another, till it has run the first bridge—in other words, become a *bridged ball.*

65. A ball, whether bridged or not, cannot make roquet on an unbridged ball; that is, on a "booby."

66. If a ball proceeding from the mallet come in contact with another ball, by rebound from any fixed object, it makes roquet.

67. If a ball proceeding from the mallet come in contact with another ball, by rebound from the person of an enemy, it makes roquet.

68. If a ball proceeding from the mallet come in contact with another, by rebound from the person of a friend, it does *not* make roquet.

69. If a ball in executing the croquet flinch from under the foot of the player, and come in contact with another ball, it does not make roquet.

70. If a ball in executing the roquet-croquet do not displace the ball to be roquet-croque'd, and then come in contact with another, it makes no roquet on this other.

71. A roque'd ball remains in the place to which it may have been driven by the roquet, subject only to further displacement by the croquet, or roquet-croquet.

72. A ball cannot make roquet upon another ball twice during the same tour of play, unless in interval it have run a bridge, or tolled the stake.

THE RICOCHET.

73. A ball makes *ricochet* upon another, proceeding from the mallet, not direct, but after having roque'd or struck some other ball.

74. If a ball make ricochet upon another, it obtains all the advantages of a roquet, and is subject to like laws of forfeiture.

THE CONCUSSION.

75. A ball, displaced by concussion, remains in the spot to which it may have been driven.

THE CROQUET.

76. A ball can only *croquet* another, on which it has made roquet, or ricochet.

77. A ball having made roquet, or ricochet, may decline to take the croquet, and continue its play in any other way the player may deem preferable.

78. A ball declining the croquet, may play from the place into which it has rolled after making the roquet, or ricochet; or it may be played from the side of the roque'd, or ricoche'd, ball.

79. A ball having made ricochet on several others, may croquet any or all of them.

80. If the croquet be taken on a series of ricoche'd balls, it must be made upon them in the order in which they have been ricoche'd.

81. If the croquet be taken on only some of the ricoche'd balls, and declined on the others, it must be forfeited on those declined; and taken or forfeited on each, according to the order in which they have been ricoche'd.

82. If a ball after having made roquet, or ricochet, be taken up from the ground by its player, he must continue his play from the side of the roque'd or ricoche'd ball, whether he make croquet on them or not.

83. A ball can croquet every other ball in the game—whether friend or enemy—but only once between the running of two bridges—unless under the rule next following.

84. A ball can croquet every other ball in the game—whether friend or enemy—once, and only once, between the running of a bridge and the tolling of the stake, or *vice-versa.*

85. If a ball make roquet on another, and by the same blow afterward run a bridge, it may either decline the croquet, or go back and take it.

86. If a ball under the circumstances described in Rule 85 decline to take the croquet on the roque'd ball, it may roquet it again without any intervening play.

87. If a ball, under the circumstances described in Rule 85, go back and take the croquet on the roque'd ball, it forfeits the right to roquet or croquet it again during the same tour—unless after running another bridge, or tolling the stake.

88. If a ball make roquet upon another, and by the same blow afterward toll the stake, it may either decline the croquet, or take it.

89. If a ball, under the conditions as in Rule 88, take the croquet on the roque'd ball, it forfeits the right to roquet or croquet it again during the same tour, unless after running a bridge.

90. If a ball, under the conditions as in Rule 88, decline to take the croquet on the roque'd ball, it may roquet it again without any intervening play.

91. If a ball, after running a bridge, by the same blow make roquet upon another ball, it can take the croquet or decline it; but in either case it cannot roquet or croquet the same ball again, unless after running another bridge, or tolling stake.

92. If a ball, after tolling the stake, at the same blow make roquet on another ball, it can either take the croquet or decline it; but in either case it cannot roquet or croquet the same ball again, unless after running a bridge.

93. If the mallet in making the blow do not touch the croque'ing ball, the croquet is not complete, and the blow may be repeated.

94. If the mallet in making the blow come in contact with the croque'ing ball, the croquet is to be considered as complete, whether the ball to be croque'd move from its place or not.

THE ROQUET-CROQUET.

95. The *roquet-croquet* can only be executed by a ball that has made the grand round—in other words, by a "Rover."

96. Roquet-croquet can be made upon any ball that has been roque'd, or ricoche'd.

97. Roquet-croquet can be made upon any ball that has been roque'd or ricoche'd—but only once upon each during the same tour of play.

98. In executing the roquet-croquet, the ball upon which it is made must be displaced.

99. In executing the roquet-croquet, if the ball upon which it is being made be not displaced, it is not a roquet-croquet, and the blow does not make a point.

100. The roquet-croquet can be taken, or declined—just as with the croquet.

101. If a roquet or ricochet be made, whether the roquet-croquet be taken or declined, it cannot again be made upon the same ball or balls, during the same tour of play.

102. If ricochet be made, the rover making it may take the roquet-croquet or decline it on all, or may take it on some and decline upon others; but the acceptance or refusal must be made upon each according to the order in which they have been ricoche'd.

103. A ball that has not run the first bridge—in other words, a *booby*—cannot make roquet either upon another booby, or a bridged ball.

104. A booby cannot make ricochet on any other ball.

105. A booby cannot croquet any other ball.

106. A booby cannot be roque'd by a bridged ball.

107. A booby cannot be ricoche'd by a bridged ball.

108. A booby cannot be roquet-croque'd by a rover.

109. If a booby be driven through the first bridge by another ball, whether the latter be a booby or a bridged ball, and whether friend or enemy, it runs the bridge, and is thenceforth a bridged ball.

110. If a booby be driven through the first bridge, by any accident or mischance caused by the enemy, it runs it.

111. If a booby be driven through the first bridge by any accident or mischance caused by a friend, it does *not* run it.

112. If a booby drive another booby through the first bridge, and at the same blow run the bridge itself, it cannot croquet the other, without making roquet upon it.

113. If a booby strike a bridged ball, and afterward run the first bridge, it cannot croquet the ball, without again striking, or roque'ing it.

THE ROVER.

114. The *rover*, and he only, can execute the roquet-croquet.

115. The rover can either make croquet, or roquet-croquet, on a ball he has roque'd, or ricoche'd; but not both, on the same ball.

116. The rover cannot make croquet, or roquet-croquet, more than once on the same ball during a single tour of play.

117. The rover cannot make roquet or ricochet, more that once on the same ball, during the single tour of play.

118. If the rover made roquet or ricochet, he may decline to make croquet, or roquet-croquet, on either the roque'd or ricoche'd balls, or he may make croquet or roquet-croquet on one of them, and decline it on the others.

119. If the rover make roquet or ricochet, and decline to take the croquet or roquet-croquet, he may either continue his play from the spot in which he is lying, or from the side of the roque'd or ricoche'd ball.

120. If the rover make the ricochet on two or more balls, and desire to croquet or roquet-croquet them, he must do so in the order in which they have been ricoche'd.

121. If the rover, after making a roquet or ricochet take his ball up from the ground, he must then croquet or roquet-croquet, or else play from the side of the roque'd, or ricoche'd ball.

122. The rover can make roquet and ricochet on another rover, and of course also croquet and roquet-croquet.

123. If the rover make roquet or ricochet, and decline taking the croquet or roquet-croquet on the roque'd or ricoche'd ball, he cannot roquet or ricochet it again during the same tour of play.

124. A ball that has become a rover by a blow of the mallet must be taken up, placed upon the Spot, and thence continue its play.

125. A ball that has become a rover, otherwise than by a blow of the mallet, does not continue its play from the Spot.

126. If the rover run through a bridge, or strike the turning-stake, neither act makes any point in the game.

THE TOUR OF PLAY.

127. Each ball takes its tour of play, in the same order of succession as when first played from the Spot.

128. A ball continues its tour, so long as it make a successful play, or *point,* in the game.

129. A point is made by the running of a bridge.

130. A point is made by the tolling of the stake.

131. A point is made by a roquet, a ricochet, a croquet, and a roquet-croquet.

132. The tour terminates on the failure to make a point.

133. If a ball attempt to run a bridge, and either *rue* or *overrun* it, its tour terminates.

134. If a ball attempt to toll the stake and fail, it terminates its tour.

135. If a ball attempt to make roquet and fail, its tour terminates.

136. A ball striking a booby terminates its tour.

137. A ball striking any other ball, on which it has no right of roquet or ricochet, terminates its tour.

138. If a ball in making the croquet flinch from under the foot of the player, it terminates its tour.

139. If a ball in making the roquet-croquet fail to displace the ball played upon, it terminates its tour.

140. If a ball declining the croquet play from the side of the roque'd or ricoche'd ball, and displace the latter, it terminates its tour.

141. When the rover has made roquet, ricochet, croquet, or roquet-croquet on all the other balls, he has but one more blow before terminating his tour.

142. A booby terminates its tour by a single blow, unless by the same it may have succeeded in making itself a bridged ball.

143. A player can decline to take his tour of play, or at any time bring it to a termination.

144. The commencement of each new tour of play restores the playing ball to all the privileges of the game.

MISPLAY.

145. Playing a ball out of its proper time, or tour, constitutes a misplay.

146. If a player have two or more balls, playing any of them out of its proper tour constitutes a misplay.

147. If a player play upon a ball not his own—either that of friend or enemy—the act constitute a misplay.

148. If a ball be played out of its proper tour, it forfeits that tour when its time comes round.

149. If a ball be playing out of its proper tour, it can at any time be challenged and stopped, either by friend or enemy.

150. If a ball playing out of its proper tour be first challenged by a friend, its play, so far as it has gone, will hold good, though it shall forfeit the tour that would have been due to it, when its time came.

151. If a ball playing out of its proper tour be first challenged by the enemy, it is at the option of the enemy to annul the whole of its play so far as it has gone, or to let it hold good up to the point of stoppage—in addition to the loss of the tour that would have been accrued to it, in due place and time.

152. If a ball playing out of its proper tour shall have completed its play before being stopped, it may still be challenged by the enemy, and rendered subject to the same forfeits as when stopped during its progress of misplay.

153. If a ball, played out of its proper tour, and challenged by the enemy, be required to return to its place of starting, all and every act of its play must be annulled.

154. If a ball played out of its proper tour be permitted to complete its play, and not challenged until the next succeeding player shall have commenced his, every act of its play will hold good; but it still forfeits the tour that would otherwise have been due to it.

155. If a ball that has been played out of its proper tour, and not challenged, be followed by the ball next in succession of color, the latter will also be a misplayed ball, and therefore subject to all the penalties, as in the rules preceding.

156. If a player, having two or more balls, play any of them out of its proper tour, the forfeits will be the same as if the misplay were made by a friend.

157. If there be partners in the game, no player is permitted to play the ball of a friend, without consent of the enemy.

158. If a player, by mistake or otherwise, be playing the ball of a friend, he can be challenged and stopped by the enemy, who can annul every act of the play, so far as it has gone, or leave it to hold good—the ball at the same losing its tour.

159. If a player, by mistake or otherwise, playing upon a friend's ball, have succeeded in completing the play, he may still be challenged by the enemy, and subjected to forfeitures by the preceding rule.

160. If a player, by mistake or otherwise, be playing the ball of an enemy, the enemy may challenge and stop him at any time, and require the play to be annulled, or decide it to hold good, while the ball thus misplayed still retains the right to its tour.

161. If a player, by mistake or otherwise, have played the ball of an enemy to the end of its tour, he can still be challenged by the enemy, and subjected to the same damages as laid down in the preceding rule.

162. If a player, by mistake or otherwise, have played the ball of an enemy, and the play be not challenged until the player next in succession has commenced his tour, the misplay holds good.

163. If a ball make croquet upon another ball twice during the same tour of play, having neither run a bridge nor tolled the stake between the two croquets, it is an act of misplay.

164. If the second croquet spoken of in Rule 163 be made on the ball of a friend, the croque'd ball must be restored to its place, and that illegally making it go back to where it came from before making the roquet upon it—the roquet being also illegal.

165. If the second croquet, as above, be made on the ball of an enemy, the enemy will have the option to restore the croque'd ball to its place, or leave it where it has rolled, and also cause the croque'ing ball to go back to its original place, or leave it on the spot from which it has made the illegal croquet.

166. If a rover make croquet, or roquet-croquet, twice, or each of them once, on the same ball during the same tour of play, he is subject to the same forfeits as above; Rule 164 covering his case if it be the ball of a friend, and 165 if an enemy.

167. If a bridged ball make croquet on a booby, or the rover should croquet or roquet-croquet one, the forfeits would be as in the three preceding rules.

DOUBLE POINTS.

168. If a ball sent direct from the mallet run two bridges by the same blow, it obtains the right to take ground up to one mallet's length, in any direction from the spot where it has rested.

169. If a ball sent direct from the mallet run three bridges by the same below, it can take ground up to two mallet-lengths from the spot in which it has rested.

170. If a ball sent direct from the mallet run a bridge, and by the same blow toll the stake, or *vice versa*, it can take ground up to one length of the mallet.

171. If a ball sent direct form the mallet run two bridges, and by the same blow toll the stake, it can take ground up to two lengths of the mallet.

172. If a ball roquet another ball, and afterwards run a bridge at the same blow, it makes a double point, but one that gives no reward beyond the right to croquet and continue its tour.

173. If a ball run a bridge, and afterwards roquet another ball at the same blow, it makes a double point; but one that gives no reward beyond the right to croquet and continue its tour.

174. If a ball toll the stake, and by the same blow roquet another ball, either before or after, it makes a double point; but one giving no reward beyond the right of croquet and continuance of tour.

175. If a ball be accidentally on intentionally displaced by a friend, the enemy may require it to be restored to its place, or remain in that to which it has rolled.

176. If a ball be accidentally or intentionally displaced by an enemy, the friend can require it to be restored to its place, or remain in that which it has rolled.

177. If a ball, in its progress over the ground, be interrupted by coming in contact with the person of a friend, it may either remain where it has rested after the interruption, or be carried to any part of the arena, in the same line in which it was running—the option belonging to the enemy.

178. If a ball, in its progress over the ground, be interrupted by coming in contact with the person of an enemy, it may either remain in the place where it has rested after the interruption, or be carried to any part of the arena, in the same line in which it was running—the option belonging to the friend.

BARRIERS AND BOUNDARIES.

179. If a playing ball lie contiguous to a stake, or the piers of a bridge, so that it cannot be struck by the mallet, a blow given to the stake, or iron rod of the bridge, and driving the ball by concussion, will count as if the ball itself has received the blow direct from the mallet.

180. If a ball that is played at lie contiguous to the stake, or one of the piers of a bridge, and be displaced by a concussion from the stake or rod, caused by the playing ball, the displacement holds good; but the playing ball makes no point, unless it have at the same time touched the displaced ball, and so made roquet upon it.

181. A ball driven over the boundary of the arena, must be returned into it, in the shortest straight line from the point in which it has been found lying, and placed on this line, inside the arena, not more than twenty inches from its edge.

182. If a ball be driven over the boundary, it must be returned into the arena, and placed, before the play proceed.

183. A ball struck out against the stake, is proclaimed a "dead ball;" and should be at once removed from the arena.

STRIKING OUT.

184. Victory is obtained when all the friends of a side have struck out.

Chapter 9

EQUESTRIANISM

During the 1860s North American equestrianism passed through a key transition era which ushered in several decades of growth. In the United States the Civil War disrupted all forms of horse racing in all regions, but the return of peace in 1865 led to a revival of both thoroughbred and harness racing and the introduction of polo. In Canada trotting and pacing fared somewhat better than thoroughbred events during these years. New Yorkers inaugurated the new era by building tracks and sponsoring regular meetings and new stakes races at Saratoga and at the new Jerome Park just north of New York City. Southerners and Westerners responded by establishing jockey clubs, constructing new facilities, and holding premier contests in Maryland, Kentucky, California, and other states. As before, elites dominated the sport of kings, but now they experimented with new types of racing and new systems of gambling which would ultimately gain wide acceptance by the early twentieth century.

During these years prominent turfmen introduced a number of changes in racing which were designed to make the contests more competitive, fair, and attractive to spectators and gamblers. First, they instituted dash racing at fractional distances, which generally replaced the earlier custom of holding several heats at longer distances. Speed now took precedence over endurance. Secondly, they regularly scheduled handicap events, in which weights were assigned according to a horse's assessed ability, age, or gender. In addition, to promote larger fields and more betting many tracks held "selling races," after which the winner was sold at auction, with the listed price as the opening bid. The purpose of this system was to encourage owners to run their horses at their appropriate level of competition.

Owners of tracks also tried to encourage more popular patronage of their facilities by experimenting with different betting systems. Prior to 1860 the most common form of gambling had been the auction pool, in which each horse in a contest was "sold" to the highest bidder. The auctioneer paid the racing association a fee for the privilege of operating on its premises, and paid the winner all of the money collected minus a percentage as his fee. But after the Civil War bookmaking gained wide acceptance at racetracks. This new system gave gamblers of modest means a chance to join in the fun. The bookmaker would pay a flat fee (often about $100 a day) to metropolitan tracks, and would set odds in advance on each of the horses in a race. The New York Herald credited the Philadelphia firm of Sanford, Sykes, and Eaves with the introduction of bookmaking in the United States around 1866; the American Racing Manual gives the honor to James E. Kelley of New York, who set odds in advance on the 1871 Belmont Stakes.

In the long run the most significant development in racetrack betting was the introduction of the pari-mutuel system. Invented by a Frenchman, it was tried in various American cities during the 1870s and 1880s. A modification of the old auction pool, it permitted multiple bets on the same horse. The amount wagered on a particular horse would then determine the final odds and payoff to the winners. Although pari-mutuel gambling was well received at a tryout at Jerome Park in New York in 1872, several decades passed before it finally gained general acceptance across North America.

New Yorkers spearheaded the revival of northern racing in the United States during and after the Civil War. John Morrissey, John Hunter, and William R. Travers joined together in 1863 to found a racetrack at Saratoga Springs, which soon became a fashionable summer stop for elite followers of the turf. Morrissey was a celebrated bare-knuckle boxer of the 1850s, gambler and prominent politician. (He served a term in the U.S. House of Representatives.) The inaugural four day meeting began on August 3rd. It proved to be a smashing success for the upper classes, despite the wartime atmosphere and the tensions that persisted in the aftermath of the bloody draft riots of mid-July in New York City. "Saratoga Races" describes that first upstate New York race meeting, with its festive atmosphere and upper class crowds enjoying the scenic and refreshing setting for the sport.

The success of summer racing at Saratoga naturally encouraged the turfmen of New York City to renew their favorite pastime in their own region. The driving force behind the founding of the American Jockey Club and the creation of an elegant and extensive new racecourse was Leonard W. Jerome, a wealthy Wall Street financier and grandfather of Winston Churchill. His new association purchased the 230-acre Bathgate estate in Westchester County and modeled the new facility after the elaborate European racetracks. The club chose the site north of Manhattan because of widespread dissatisfaction with the previous Long Island courses. Jerome's chief partner was August Belmont, who soon became the dominant personality in the group. Jerome Park's opening day on September 25, 1866 was a gala celebration attended by General Ulysses S.

Grant and many of the local elite. The track quickly became known for the high quality of its racing and its fashionable and respectable following. Prominent New Yorkers also capitalized on improved economic conditions and the weakened state of the southern horsemen to build up their racing stables. By purchasing and breeding fine thoroughbreds Belmont and other local horsemen assumed a prominent role in North American racing. This chapter includes an account of opening day at Jerome Park by John B. Irving, Secretary of the American Jockey Club, followed by an editorial from the New York Clipper which criticized the club for its high admission fee.

New Jersey turfmen also played a leading role in the rebirth of thoroughbred racing in the North. In 1861 the Passaic County Agricultural Society constructed a race course outside Paterson, on the banks of the Passaic River. It held its inaugural meeting in June, 1863, in the midst of the Civil War. The turmoil in the border and southern states disrupted racing in those regions but aided the Paterson enterprise. Surprisingly, several Kentucky and other southern breeders sent horses to this small New Jersey city. The Passaic Society enlarged its plans for 1864, and for the next few years racing at Paterson flourished. Special events included the Jersey Derby, a sweepstakes for three-year-olds over a mile and a half, which was modeled after the famous Epsom Derby in England. Between eight and ten thousand spectators converged on Paterson on June 7, 1864, for the first derby held in the United States. They watched R.A. Alexander's Norfolk gallop to an easy victory. This feature attraction was the highlight of the Paterson races until the track closed in 1869. It shifted to the Monmouth course in 1871, where it was renamed the Lorillard Stakes in 1881. Unfortunately for the Passaic County group, the opening of Jerome Park in 1866 doomed the Paterson track. The American Jockey Club's new course was more convenient for horsemen and spectators, and its facilities and more fashionable ambiance made it far more attractive to New Yorkers.

New Jersey gained a more promising race course with the opening of Monmouth Park in 1870. At least as early as 1865, entrepreneurs at the shore resort of Long Branch planned a racetrack that would draw more people to that popular summer retreat. After several attempts fell through, two members of the American Jockey Club, John F. Chamberlain and John Hoey, joined with the President of the New Jersey Senate, Amos Robins, to construct a facility at Little Silver, three miles from Long Branch. Its gala inaugural meeting on July 30, 1870 was a stunning success, and Monmouth Park soon became the mecca for stakes races. During this period the track was the perennial leader in daily average purse distribution. It also had an unusually long meeting, which ran from July 4th to the end of August. In 1878 George Lorillard, David D. Withers, G. P. Wetmore and James Gordon Bennett purchased the course. It is significant and ironic that New Yorkers were responsible for the creation and development of Monmouth Park—New Jersey's new long term rival to New York City and Saratoga racing.

During the 1860s and 1870s southern racing lost the preeminent position it had enjoyed in the United States prior to the Civil War, but that region did witness a renewal in Maryland and Kentucky. The war devastated the stock of horses and forced breeders to send their best thoroughbreds to Saratoga, Paterson, and Jerome Park. A symbol of the decline of the turf in the South was the deterioration of the famed Metairie Course in New Orleans, which closed in 1872. Its grounds were turned into a cemetery.

In contrast, Maryland and Kentucky produced two jockey clubs and courses which launched two of the most prestigious stakes races in the United States. In Maryland Governor Oden Bowie was President and one of the founders of the Pimlico Race Course, which opened on October 25, 1870. On that day the feature event was the Dinner Party Stakes. The winner was Preakness, and later the Preakness Stakes became the premier contest of the spring meeting at Pimlico. "The Race Meeting at Baltimore" recounts the excitement of opening day at that historic course.

In Kentucky racing at Lexington had continued throughout the Civil War, while at Louisville the hostilities disrupted the meetings, which were resumed before the war ended. But peace brought a postwar depression as the Greenland and Woodlawn tracks closed in 1869 and 1870, respectively. Five years later Colonel M. Lewis Clark led a new group which founded the Louisville Jockey Club. It held its inaugural session at a course which would later be renamed Churchill Downs. One of its feature attractions that year was the Kentucky Derby, which soon became perhaps the most famous horse race in North America. This chapter contains descriptions of the first Kentucky Derby from the Spirit of the Times.

In the West there were brief meetings of thoroughbreds at a variety of tracks in Chicago, Cincinnati, and St. Louis, but more interest and activity in racing in San Francisco. In 1863 Senator George Hearst, father of William Randolph Hearst, built Bay View Park at a cost of more than $200,000. Two years later Theodore Winters, Nathan Coombs, and A.J. Bryant founded the Pacific Jockey Club, and constructed Ocean View Park. That course became the site of a major event in 1873, when the Pacific Jockey Club announced a race at four mile heats for a purse of $20,000 in gold. This chapter includes a description of that contest, won by Thad Stevens in four demanding heats. The next few years brought greater excitement and higher stakes to this northern California spectacle sponsored by the Pacific Jockey Club.

In Canada Ontario took the lead in thoroughbred horse racing. Queen Victoria offered a prize for what became the Queen's Plate contest, first held in Toronto in 1860. For its first fifteen years that race was held at various locations around Ontario. The leading tracks were at Toronto, Barrie, Kingston, and London. By 1880 the Woodbine course in Toronto had become one of the most important facilities in North America. The withdrawal of the British garrisons during the 1870s retarded the growth of the sport in that region, but that decade did witness the appearance of commercially operated racetracks. The increasing popularity of trotting and pacing helped to offset the declining interest in the thoroughbreds.

As was the case with thoroughbred racing, trotting in the United States during the 1860s and 1870s passed through an era of transition. The period began with the continuation of the antebellum pattern of drivers challenging their rivals to tests on city streets. It ended with the rationalization and commercialization of the sport through more scientific breeding, new formats for matches, new systems of classifying horses, a national organization to govern competition, and the appearance of a major racing circuit. During these years critics of trotting often accused owners, drivers, and gamblers with fixing races. To counter these charges and also to bring more order and efficiency to the sport, promoters and horsemen took a number of steps to modernize trotting. In particular, wealthy gentlemen took control and adopted measures which made trotting one of the nation's leading spectator sports.

A good example of both the persistence of earlier forms of trotting and the shift toward participation by more affluent classes was the rivalry between Cornelius Vanderbilt and Robert Bonner in New York City during the early 1860s. Prior to the Civil War middle class and elite owners had often competed on Third Avenue in Manhattan, but now the growth of the city forced them uptown to Harlem Lane. A new round of urban construction then led horsemen to form private associations which rented or purchased their own tracks. Vanderbilt was a steamship and railroad magnate who offered to race his team of horses in a match for $10,000 against any challenger. Bonner was the owner of the New York Ledger and a strict Presbyterian whose religious principles and aversion to gambling prevented him from entering public contests. "Rare Scene on 'The Fashion'" recounts how Bonner successfully responded to Vanderbilt's challenge in 1862. After the Civil War Bonner developed one of the largest and best stables of trotters in the country. Even more importantly, he did more than any other man to raise the sport to a position of greater respectability.

Trotting differed from other elite sports during this era in that it did not have a long upper-class tradition, nor did it require great wealth for participation. Bonner was representative of a new elite which patronized and eventually dominated trotting. They transformed it into an upper-class sport by purchasing the fastest horses and by developing a breeding industry in which large farms concentrated on producing exceptionally speedy racers.

The rationalization of this industry proceeded through four steps during the 1870s. First came the creation of the first turf register devoted exclusively to the trotting horse (1871). Next was the appearance in 1875 of Wallace's Monthly Magazine, the first periodical to specialize in trotting news. 1876 witnessed the formation of the National Association of Trotting Horse Breeders. Finally, 1879 brought the establishment of a standard breed of trotting horse. All of these measures furthered the rationalization of the breeding industry and widened the distance between the gentlemen who controlled trotting and the middle class tradesmen and businessmen who had pioneered the sport before the Civil War.

These years also brought innovations in the format of trotting races which were clear signs of modernization. Crowds grew bored with longer distance events of two, three, or four mile heats, and promoters switched to tests of speed by mile heats (usually best three of five). The lighter sulkies which replaced heavier wagons also contributed to faster, action packed races. Moreover, a new system of handicapping horses appeared which classified them according to their speed. Races among horses which had never beaten a fixed time created more competition for owners and drivers and more excitement for spectators. This new system thus spurred a new boom in commercial trotting and broke the monopoly of eastern tracks, as Buffalo, Cleveland, and other inland and midwestern cities staged major events.

Another manifestation of modernization was the formation of the National Trotting Association in 1870. Two major factors contributed to the founding of this new organization. The first was the long standing belief among the press and the general public that trotting was plagued by widespread corruption. The second and perhaps more important element was the need to establish a more efficient and standardized system for regulating competition throughout the nation. Horsemen needed a more uniform system of racing and a national code to replace the older way of adapting to the requirements and rules of local organizations and tracks. The "Rules and Regulations of the National Association for the Promotion of the Interests of the American Trotting Turf" reprinted here established uniform rules for all of the federated tracks. It provided that penalties imposed at any one of the member tracks would apply to all of them.

One of the main purposes of the new code was to elevate the power of the officials and reduce that of the drivers. In 1873 forty-four leading drivers organized "The Drivers' Protective Association," which was a union whose goal was to weaken the disciplinary power of track officials. But when the owners refused to yield to their demands, the drivers capitulated to the new order. The National Trotting Association did face numerous problems and scandals, but it elevated public trust in trotting as it also rationalized and regulated the sport.

Proof of the flourishing state of the new order was the development of a new racing circuit. The idea was first developed in Cleveland in 1871 and tried in 1873 when Cleveland, Buffalo, Utica, and Springfield formed "The Quadrilateral Trotting Combination." Two years later Rochester and Poughkeepsie joined the newly reconstituted "Central Trotting Circuit," which added Hartford in 1876. The success of this circuit broke what remained of the control of the big cities over trotting; it also stimulated the formation of numerous larger and smaller circuits, which became the dominant pattern of scheduling. The final selection in this chapter recounts an exciting race between two of the most celebrated trotters of this era, Goldsmith Maid and Smuggler. This gala event at Hartford's Charter Oak Park in 1876 was a showcase of the sport during a period when it was one of America's most popular entertainments.

In addition to these developments in thoroughbred and harness racing, this period also witnessed the introduction of the elite sport of polo into North America. The credit goes to James Gordon Bennett, publisher of the New York Herald, who became fascinated by the game which he observed at Hurlingham, England in 1876. He brought back a supply of polo balls and mallets to New York City, and later that year he sent a local riding master to Texas to purchase a carload of ponies. Over the winter of 1876-77 he and some friends tried out the sport at Dickel's Riding Academy on Fifth Ave. In the spring their polo club relocated to more spacious quarters at the Jerome Park Race Course, where the players organized the Westchester Polo Club. That association took the game to Newport, Rhode Island, where the fashionable crowd which gathered each summer enjoyed the horsemen's demonstration of their newest pastime. Challenge matches between the Westchester club and rival outfits from Buffalo and Queens County intensified interest in polo among the elite and the sporting fraternity of the northeastern United States.

THOROUGHBRED RACING

SARATOGA SPRINGS, 1863

Summer racing at Saratoga was the pet project of John Morrissey, the pugilist and politician who had earned a fortune as a casino operator. Although he aspired to join the elite of New York City, his humble origins and background as a prizefighter disqualified him. But he counted several prominent turfmen (including John R. Hunter and William R. Travers) among his associates. He persuaded these sportsmen and others to lend their names and respectability to his scheme. Although he put up most of the money, he refrained from adding his name to the list of socially prominent incorporators of the Saratoga Association for the Improvement of the Breed. Yet he held a majority of the stock in the company, and he prospered greatly as the track flourished. The first four day meeting was held on the Horse Haven track in the woods outside of town. Its success coupled with criticism of the location and layout of the course led the founders to build a new facility across the road. Racing at Saratoga Springs resumed there the following year, and it immediately gained the popularity which it has retained to the present day. This account is from The Spirit of the Times, 15 August 1863, p. 369.

SARATOGA RACES

The meeting at Saratoga Springs was a great success. We have always thought that it would be so since the publication in our columns of the well-considered and liberal programme for the races which have just been run. The sport was quite worthy of such meetings as we have had this year at Paterson, Philadelphia and Centerville, while remarkable incidents and surprises were more numerous at the late gathering than at either of the others. It must have laid the foundation for a great fashionable race meeting at the Springs, like that at Ascot in England, where the elegance and superb costumes of the ladies vie with the blood and beauty of the running horses, and the neat but splendid appointments of the various riders. It is now established, that of the many thousand of people to be found at Saratoga at this season of the year, there are but few who will not eagerly avail themselves of the opportunity for such amusement and interest as the sports of the turf afford. It is also made manifest that the people of New York will give such support to racing at Saratoga Springs as will add to the zest and flavor of the occasion. We are not among those who hold that you can have good racing without the speculation which naturally attends it. It is the fact, that at Baden and some other places on the continent of Europe, there is racing and very little betting, the latter being systematically discouraged. But what is the real truth? Why, the Grand Duke, having an interest in the gaming tables, wants all the money of the guests reserved for play upon them, and that is why there is no man like Jackson, shouting "four to one on the field," nor any man like Doctor Underwood, knocking down pools for a matter of ten dollars by which the lucky purchaser is finally entitled to the receipt of some seven or eight hundred. The kindness of his Royal Highness is a little too much like that of the savages, who treat their captives well and feed them daintily, with a view to a cannibal repast. When we see a fire that won't burn anybody, we expect to see first-rate horse racing without betting. Meantime, the ladies, who would bet if they could, and the gentlemen, who abstain from betting on the principle, know well enough that the race which does not command the attendance and fire up the speculative enterprise of betting men, is likely to be a very slow and dull affair. Therefore it was, that a lady of a good deal of penetration and uncommon fine sense remarked to us on the Francis Skiddy on Sunday evening, "I think the races will be very fine, sir, for I am informed that all the great betting men of New York are going up on the boat."

There was a very pretty party, and numerous. They did not then know the fate that was in store for them; for, with all their shrewdness, knowledge and aptitude for generalization, most of them lost money during the meeting. Fortune, indeed, dispensed her favors with a liberal hand, but, instead of rewarding the constant worshippers who knelt close to her golden altar, she flung her richest prizes afar among the crowd of outsiders, some of whose hands, "like the base Indian's threw a pearl away richer than all their tribe." The trip on the Francis Skiddy was pleasant, though she was crowded to her utmost capacity. Through the shining reaches of the glorious river, silvered by the beams of the full harvest-moon—winding in and out among the beautiful hills which border the Hudson, and from whose recesses one can almost fancy that he hears the rumble of the bowls played by old Hendrick and his quaint companions that gusty afternoon, for the relief and entertainment of honest Rip Van Winkle—on we went. There was choice anecdote, joyous joke and much hilarity. Hour after hour some fell away and sought their state-rooms, until, when the morn stood tip-toe on the mountain-tops, only a very few choice spirits remained on deck. Leaving the boat at Troy, we took the cars; and, after a small delay on the passage, caused by the chase and capture of a pickpocket, who had relieved a gentleman on the train of his watch and purse, we reached Saratoga. The main street of the place is a wide and handsome one. It is chiefly composed of hotels, which are very large, well adapted to the comfort of summer visitors, and no doubt well kept. A glance at these and at the crowds of people under the porches and piazzas with which they are fronted, gave some idea of the number of visitors there. It was immense. We soon learned that all the hotels were full, the United States alone having two thousand people staying at it. The race course is well situated, and quite near enough to the town. You can stand in the stable doors, and look over a rich, cultivated valley, many miles in width, to purple hills curtained with light summer haze far beyond. But the course itself is not well calculated for racing purposes. It is too narrow, and the turns are too sharp to be good for the horses. Then, again, it runs round a sandy knoll covered with a growth of small scrub pines, which obstruct the view of the spectator, besides which a barn, stables and other buildings shut out the last turn, and completely mask that part of the course. Everything had been done, however, which could be done, to remedy the present defects, and the track itself had been got in good order to run upon. It is to be hoped that other ground will be provided and suitable buildings erected another year. The want of a spacious and substantial stand for the ladies was very apparent. There was no accommodation for them if they had not carriages, and we imagine that there were not half enough vehicles in Saratoga to accommodate all the ladies who wished to attend. It was not to be expected that John Morrissey would go to the expense of purchasing and constructing a new course and erecting suitable buildings thereon. By giving a great deal of money in purses and additions to the stakes, he secured fine sport, and such an attendance as must have more than reimbursed him. With this example, the formation of a competent club, and further proceedings, would seem to be a matter of course. It is a short mile from the hotels to the track, and as the road lies by the famous Congress Spring, it afforded an opportunity to the *habitues* of the turf to do that which they protested they had come for—"drink the waters." On the whole, we believe they were much approved, although we heard one or two Western gentlemen declare that, for "steady drinking," there is nothing at Saratoga equal to the favorite, medicinal beverage of Bourbon County, Kentucky. Race horses were in attendance from the stables of Mr. Watson, Col. Murphy, Mr. Clay, Captain Moore, Dr. Weldon, Mr. Morris, Mr. Wilkes, Mr. Bush, Mr. Strong, etc. Besides which, the famous gray horse Thunder was on hand from Canada, in charge of his trainer, Mr. Reedy; and the equally famous horse, Jerome Edgar, formerly owned by John M. Clay, but now the property of John Morrissey, and renamed John B. Davidson, was also there. The attendance was large, and the number of ladies, graced with every charm of beauty and elegant attire, was extremely gratifying. Congratulations on that head were generally exchanged, mingled with regrets at the want of a grand stand. The truth is that the gentlemen of the turf like to run their horses in the presence of the ladies, and we have a theory that the racers like it too:

"Give me a glance of thine hazel eye,
  If I falter in my race—
Give me a breath of thine honey mouth
  Upon my heated face."

The number of gentlemen present was also very large, and the best of order was insured by the admirable arrangements made by the proprietor and Mr. Wheatly, of Kentucky, who managed the racing. The West was well represented by gentlemen who breed and run race-horses. Besides the Kentucky party, represented by John M. Clay, Colonel Murphy, Captain Moore, Mr. Fields, Mr. Vaughan, Mr. Mayfield, Mr. Bell, Dr. Underwood, etc., there were observed by us, General McIndoe, of Wisconsin, Mr. Leonard and Mr. Smith, of Ohio, Mr. Patrick and Mr. Sims, of Illinois, Mr. Chamberlain, of Missouri, and other gentlemen of prominence. Pool-selling had commenced with great briskness on the Saturday evening prior to the races, and no sooner had the gentleman reached the ground on Monday, than Dr. Underwood began to sell again. Indeed, all through the meeting, the doctor was mighty busy by night and day. Issuing from the crowd, almost always there was to be heard his clear, ringing voice, expatiating upon the merits of first choice, second choice, or outsider, as the case might be. Underwood is the prince of pool-sellers. It was said of a famous auctioneer that he elevated his business to a branch of the fine arts. We can imagine some other business rightfully elevated to a branch of another sort of tree, but let that pass.

"You've heard of George Robbins, of great London town,
The man who was famous for knocking things down!"

Underwood is only second to that bright genius in the auctioneer line, in general, and in pool-selling he is without a rival. At these races the amount invested in these sweeps was very large.

THE AMERICAN JOCKEY CLUB'S INAUGURATION MEETING, 1866

The American Jockey Club's 1300 members included many of the United States' most powerful and affluent gentlemen. Its headquarters was located in downtown Manhattan, but its new racecourse was in the Fordham section of Westchester County (now in the Bronx). Its special features included a luxurious clubhouse with spacious dining rooms and a ballroom. The grounds had facilities for sleighing, trap shooting, and skating; a polo field was added later. The first Belmont Stakes was run at Jerome Park in 1867. This selection is from John B. Irving, *The American Jockey Club: Official Summary of the Races at Jerome Park, Fall of 1866, with Reminiscences of the Inauguration Meeting* (New York, 1866), pp. 5-11, 16-17.

RACES AT JEROME PARK

After the Inauguration Meeting of the AMERICAN JOCKEY CLUB had been the absorbing topic of interest and conversation among Turfmen and every other class in the community for many weeks, the Races came off with a credit and renown alike gratifying to the Club and the public. Such a scene as was daily presented is without a parallel in the history of the American Turf, and reminded many of its old patrons and well wishers of those palmy days of the Northern Turf, when men like Stevens, Livingston, Stockton, met such kindred spirits from the South, in generous rivalry, as Col. Wm. R. Johnson, O.P. Hare and others.

From the convenient distance of the Course from the City of New York there was not a very early start for the scene of action, but as the time drew near for the Races to commence, the bustle on the several highways and by-ways for getting to it, by road, rail and water, became very lively. The "Jerome Park" became the *fashion* of the day, not altogether by those who live in fine houses and fare sumptuously every day, but with one consent, by all classes and conditions of men alike, *most orderly in their demeanor.*

Every description and variety of conveyance was seen upon the road. The elegant coupe, the light and highly finished wagon, driven by fast men, and pulled by fast horses, dashed along the different avenues to the Course; but "the drag" of Mr. Jerome, with six horses in hand, and he "handling the ribbons" with his well known skill, and Mr. Belmont's noble "turnout," with four magnificent horses, ridden artistically by positions, in his own attractive livery, seemed to rivet the gaze of the admiring crowd, and were truly "the observed of all observers."

Continuous streams of vehicles, all progressing towards the same centre, produced occasionally a slight degree of entanglement. All along the road, too, foot passengers trudged, kicking up an awful dust—so dense in a few spots that the mass seemed to go into it and out of it like a fog!

A denser crowd we never saw collected on any similar occasion in this country. We recollect "the big gathering" at the Union Course, when Eclipse and Henry ran their match, but *it* was only a *little family party* compared to this *great mass convention.* From every direction the excited populace came, gathering thicker and thicker....

As the gates of the enclosure round the Course were approached the animated throng increased. Everybody thought everybody else to blame for being in the way and occasioning delay. There is a transient pause in that dense mass—then there is a little move forward, but it is only a little—vehicles are wedged in for a moment, closer and closer together—there is not room even for the pedestrians to worm their way through—they make for the road-side, jump the fences, run helter-skelter, racing on in the adjacent fields. At last, after a great deal of trying to turn the horses in one direction, then another, in the hope of finding an opening to get by those who happened to be before, and were just as anxious to advance but could not, a slight delay, and the becoming exercise of a little patience, the gates are reached, and then the troubles of the day were over....

When all had assembled on the Course by the various routes, the spectacle presented was very brilliant and imposing. Every position from which the Races could be seen was crowded with carriages and pedestrians, whilst a magnificent assemblage of beauty and fashion graced the Grand Stand. From the general happiness and hilarity which prevailed around there was a good humor among that goodly company which augured well for a fair field; as if one and all had come out to have a good day's sport, and would neither do anything themselves, nor encourage others to do aught that might interrupt the promised enjoyment. The Course was, consequently, well kept; the crowd submitting with promptness to every restraint put upon it. I did not hear a single demurrer, when the command of those in authority was given, "Thus far shalt thou go and no farther."

The weather was propitious. Previous to the Race, and between the heats, a portion of the more aristocratic of the company promenaded about in the enclosure before the stands and recognized with hearty cheerfulness friends they had not met, perhaps, for years before, on a Race Ground.

From the Jockey Stand the scene was a very beautiful and animated one....

The gentleman "of elegant leisure"—the honest farmer—the upright, independent tiller of the soil, his face weather-beaten and tanned, with a rude intelligence, denoting a man living *manlike*—the scientific artisan and the industrious mechanic, stood side by side in friendly juxtaposition with him

"Born to hereditary wealth,

Heap'd copious by a wise forefather's care."

I have already hinted at the decorum that prevailed during the meeting at Jerome Park. I now desire to state *emphatically* that I have witnessed many a Race, on many a crowded Course, both in this country and in England, yet never saw I a more orderly assemblage than that to which I now proudly refer. Well may I claim, then, for "the Stewards of the meeting," as justly their due, that the business of the Club was by them well considered and conducted. What they deemed proper to be done for the comfort and benefit of all they carried out "wisely and well." Yes, the business of the Club was indeed well conducted.

What can the most rigid moralist desire more? No loud talking—no ungentlemanly slang—no coarse demeanor—no angry controversies—but all was quiet. Horses may have lost their races but their owners never lost their temper. If it should so have happened that they backed their horses with confidence, when their favorites failed to equal their expectations they showed no vexation, but paid their money cheerfully, manifesting in every respect as much good blood and training as the noble animals they bred. In the "sacred precincts" on the ground, the wise, the dignified, the best men of the land were seen mingling, walking familiarly arm in arm, comparing notes, and *exchanging opinions* of the pending events of the day.

...Part of the day passed in admiration of the fine horses, well-bred and beautiful; and part of the day in admiration of no less fine, well-bred, and beautiful specimens of womankind....

And, when the day's sport was over, no wild glee—no wilder despair from loss of fortune, marks the issue of the day—there was only the bustle inseparable from the simultaneous movement of a large body of people. The higher classes step into their carriages, the more independent into the innumerable vehicles, of all kinds and shapes, that make their appearance on such special occasions, and with one consent return to the places from whence they came, *as orderly as they arrived.* The hotels and clubs in the city were soon crowded with those who have been to the Races, talking over the events of the day, and preparing to refresh the inner man, whilst the more aristocratic householders have repaired to their respective homes, as courteous hosts, to do becoming honor to favored quests....

I will, in conclusion, merely add that the result of the Inauguration Meeting at Jerome Park guarantees the permanent establish of an institution that promises to be the pride and glory of the American Turf; and that "putting money in the pockets" of individuals is not to be "the end-all and the be-all" of this extensive and magnificent and patriotic enterprise—far from it—it will be made, by the high-minded and practical gentlemen who are in authority, conducive to the true interests and legitimate end of Horse Racing "itself alone."....

My views may be inferred from this simple remark, that they are to be considered *the true pillars of the Turf who breed fine colts and fillies, and keep up the strongest stables in their power, not only for their own amusement and fair remuneration, but with a view to improve the breed of the Race-horse and to contribute to the general social enjoyment.*

EDITORIAL

Jerome Park's high admission fee and its restrictions on access to the grandstand reflected the social exclusiveness of the American Jockey Club. The stiff price of admission raised revenues which helped the club meet its expenses, but it was also designed to discourage attendance by the lower classes. The rule which barred non-members from the choice sections of the grandstand drew criticism from a number of New York City newspapers and sporting periodicals. These journals charged the club's governing board with aristocratic, illiberal, and undemocratic practices which were inconsistent with American values and customs. Typical of the criticism is this selection, reprinted from The New York Clipper, 6 October 1866, p. 202.

JEROME PARK

This is the name of a new race track which was opened to the public for the first time on Tuesday, September 25th, under the auspices of an association called the American Jockey Club. The newspapers, for the past few weeks, have given us numerous articles laudatory of Mr. Leonard Jerome and the enterprise originated by him; we have been told that the object of the club is to improve the breed of the horse, to popularize the sport of horse racing, and all that sort of thing; we have also been informed that Mr. Jerome—who is a very wealthy gentleman—at his own expense and risk purchased the section of land on which the new course is located, constructed the track, and placed the project upon a sound basis before appealing to the patrons of the turf for co-operation in the enterprise, etc. Gentlemen of the highest social position, wealth, intelligence, and influence unhesitatingly became active participants in the movement, we have been given to understand. Hints were also thrown out some time ago that the public would be admitted to the course free of charge, in order that the sport should be made popular. Well, the opening of this new track took place, as we have said, on September 25th, under the most encouraging circumstances; the day was all that could be desired, being clear, cool and pleasant in every way. The attendance was very large, it being estimated that thirty thousand spectators were present, including between two and three hundred policemen, as well as many ladies. There were two races on the programme for the opening day—a dash of a mile and a quarter and a race of four-mile heats—both of which were witnessed with seeming interest by the large assemblage. And so ended the inaugural ceremonies at Jerome Park. We are willing to give due credit to the wealthy gentleman who set the ball in motion; to the influential citizens who have co-operated with him in the enterprise, and to the stewards of the meeting for the races they prepared for the entertainment of their patrons; but we are not willing to let the opportunity pass without entering our protest against certain practices which will *not* have a tendency to popularise the sport of racing as conducted by the American Jockey Club and the wealthy founder of Jerome Park. We have frequently exposed frauds practiced on the Long Island tracks, race courses which were *not* founded by Mr. Jerome, nor managed by wealthy citizens; and we shall not be backward in exposing the shortcomings of this rich combination at Fordham. In the first place, the public were led to believe, until the day before the opening ceremonies, that Asteroid, the great Western turf representative, would take part in the four mile race, and contend with Kentucky for the victory; we should not like to believe that it was known some time previous that Asteroid had gone amiss, and would not start for the prize. With Asteroid out of the race, the event was divested of all interest, for it was well known that none of the others could compete with Kentucky with the slightest chance of success. Yet his was the grand event that the masses went to see, and which attracted so many strangers to the city. To say that the disappointment was great at the non-appearance of Asteroid is to put it in a mild form. But what the public most object to is the somewhat exalted scale of prices of admission to the track and stands. Instead of the public being admitted free, a high tariff was imposed upon all who sought to enter the gates of Jerome Park. At the first gate one dollar was demanded of each person; this did not give the privilege of going upon the track; to do this, and to gain admission to the public stand, another dollar must be paid; and to pass on to the quarter stretch, five dollars is the toll. So the reader will see that, and notwithstanding the high social position of the gentlemen composing the club, the almighty dollar has not been lost sight of by Mr. Jerome and his co-operators.

To make racing popular, in this country, the public should be permitted to enjoy the privileges of our race tracks at a small charge for admission, say fifty cents. When two and five dollars are charged, very few except the wealthy classes can afford to indulge in "the luxury of horse racing." To make the track accessible to the masses, and thus popularise sports of the turf, we were given to understand, was one of the objects in forming the American Jockey Club and locating the new track. That such was not really the intention of those gentlemen is now quite evident, for the enterprise looks more like a money making speculation than a public spirited endeavor to provide amusement for the people at reasonable prices. The press has not had a word to say upon this subject; yet this is not to be wondered at when the wealth of the Jockey Club is taken into consideration. For our part, we can see no difference between Jerome Park and the race tracks on Long Island. Money is the great object of all alike, and the idea of elevating and popularising the sports of the turf is entirely lost sight of in the eager greed for gain. The new track savors of Wall Street, and its projector doubtless figured up the chances of making the concern pay a heavy per centage on the original investment when he purchased the ground and erected the buildings for Jerome Park.

INAUGURATION MEETING AT PIMLICO RACE COURSE, 1870

The feature stakes race on opening day at the Pimlico course was the Dinner Party Stakes, run for three-year olds over two miles. The idea for this contest originated at an evening entertainment at Saratoga in 1868. There several sportsmen agreed to hold a sweepstakes in Baltimore two years later. Seven subscribers initially pledged to participate, but by the end of October of that year thirty gentlemen had filed nominations. The owner of the winner, Preakness, was M.H. Sanford, one of the original subscribers. This account is from The Spirit of the Times, 29 October 1870, pp. 164-65.

THE RACE MEETING AT BALTIMORE

The Maryland Jockey Club and its able and courteous officers, from Governor Bowie to the youngest subscriber and last ardent recruit upon the swelling lists of the turf, have reason to be proud of the first fruits which have followed their praiseworthy exertions. They must have felt honored, as the followers of racing from other States did, by that vast and magnificent gathering of the people which put the seal of approbation upon their enterprise and so greatly enjoyed the useful and exciting sports of the turf. On Tuesday the streets of the beautiful city of Baltimore were full of handsome equipages, and the sidewalks were lined with eager groups. All the hotels were filled, and we were glad that New York was so fully and so ably represented. At early dawn there had been fresh arrivals, and when the sun rose over the nearest hills and the fresh breeze from the adjacent ranges swept away the mists of the morning, we saw with uncommon interest and pleasure the beauty and convenience of the place, the air of prosperity and intelligence which pervaded the people. Baltimore is not built upon a plain, but upon a rolling surface, and standing upon some of the undulations one can see through the long vistas of the handsome streets the slopes and swells of the ground on which the city stands. Happily, the great geniuses who delight in uniform grades, and cut down here and fill up there until they have reduced everything to one monotonous flat, had not obtained the control of affairs when Baltimore was built. Consequently, the owners of the soil and the architects of her handsome buildings were not humbled in their designs and crippled in their resources by the vicious artificial levels of the pancake plan which has prevailed in some other places. The result is excellent in more points than one. The street views, so pleasantly diversified, are full of interest. The nobler edifices, occupying commanding sites, stand out and worthily challenge the admiration of the spectator. In our opinion, too, the preservation of the natural drainage, in its main features, has made the city much more clean and healthy than otherwise it might have been. As we drove toward Druid Hill Park on our way to the race-course, we greatly admired the wide paved streets and handsome houses. The latter are mostly of fine brick, with steps, lintels, window-sills, etc., of marble white....

Handsome ladies, fair young girls, and joyous children stood upon the stoops and gazed from the windows. These are the happy homes! Neither the pinchings of poverty nor the cumberings of excessive wealth and obtrusive grandeur. Their inhabitants have reason to rejoice in their surroundings, more especially in their close proximity to Druid Hill Park. In this extensive, diversified and romantic domain, the ground was ready moulded and it has been mostly let alone. Nature! so buxom and so beautiful!... The beauties of the place we saw, and we dare say we did not see a tithe of them, are too many for more than mere mention here. The drive through it, preceded by long lines of vehicles and horsemen and followed by other cavalcades, was one of the enjoyments of the day. The race-course lies some distance beyond it. The site is excellent and the course well-laid out. By-and-by it will be one of the finest race-courses in the country. A spacious and convenient stand, calculated to seat 6,000 people, has been erected, and opposite to it, on the far side of the course, a club-house is to be built. On this opening day the grand stand was not large enough to accommodate all who wished to have seats in it. The crowd was vast in every quarter, and we think nearly 20,000 people were present. The scene was magnificent. The stately dignity of the handsome matrons, the loveliness of maidens fresh and fair, and the glorious beauty of the little girls, 'twas a joy to see. The family groups plainly predominated, and the presence of so many beautiful children was a capital sign. The interest the ladies took was marvelous. They laughed, they clapped their graceful hands, and with their golden voices they applauded. They rejoiced with the winners, and sympathized with the losers. A more enthusiastic and impressible gathering of the best kind of people we never saw, and we have attended races in various countries and seen the racehorses of many distant lands. Such assemblages of the people do honor to the turf, and tend to exalt the character of the turfmen. Many able and distinguished gentlemen were present—too many for a particular list to be given. From first to last there was nothing to interfere with the pleasures of the day, and delight universally prevailed. Even the backers of the favorites, three times ground between the upper and the nether millstones of adverse fortune, had fortitude enough to grin and bear it....

THE DINNER PARTY STAKES

It is almost unnecessary for us to repeat facts familiar as household words concerning this stake. It took its name from having been proposed at a dinner party during the Saratoga meeting of 1868. It was a sweepstakes of $1,000 each, half forfeit, two miles, for three-year-olds. There were thirty entries, and of these seven came to the post. Remorseless, the filly by Eclipse out of barbarity, winner of several stakes last year, of the Ladies' Stakes this year, and second to Foster in the Lambard Stakes at Jerome Park two weeks ago, was not present. Had she been at the post in good condition, the result of the race would probably have been different. We think she could have won it. She was kept away because of the defeat she received in the Lambard Stakes from Foster, it being considered by Mr. Morris that she could not be improved sufficiently to beat him. Foster, a son of Lexington and Verona, by Yorkshire, became favorite against the field for the Dinner Party Stakes as soon as he had won the Lambard. After his safe arrival at Baltimore with his stable companion, M'Closky, he was backed at strong odds, and finally, the night before the race, when it was known that six or seven would start, about three to one was laid upon him. We considered these odds much too large, and so stated in conversation many times. But they said, What is there to beat him? This question was put to us by two able trainers who had seen him in his work and in his race at Jerome Park. We were not altogether prepared to reply, but suggested Mr. Sanford's Preakness, as he came of a great running family, was known to be a fine colt, and had never run in public. To this they observed that he could not be in condition; that he had been stopped in his work at Saratoga, and was fat as an ox. In conversation it could be, and was made to appear, that barring accidents in running, Foster was nearly sure to win. Reasoning and reflections of this sort made nearly everybody anxious to get on him, and a kind of pity was expressed for those who bought the field in the pools, or purchased Preakness at the rate of about 40 to 1. Now, all such reasoning *assumes* the great premise upon which it ought to rest, and as the same fallacy pervades the vaticinations of nearly all the English turf writers, we shall point it out. It is, that the good condition of the horse backed is taken for granted. It seems never to have occurred to those who declared that Preakness could not be in condition, or to Mr. Morris, who kept Remorseless at home, that Foster himself might be remiss. Yet the result showed that, in spite of all the care of his owner and trainer, Captain Moore, one of the ablest and most experienced men in this profession, he was nothing like as good a horse as he had been at Jerome Park.... Preakness is a very powerful bay colt by Lexington, out of Bayleaf, by Yorkshire. Five of his family have distinguished themselves, and the last and greatest was Bayonet.... At the finish the horses were all much tired. Main strength and the saving grace of Hayward's riding just enabled Preakness to beat Ecliptic, and dead gameness, in distress, under strong persuasion, brought Foster up so as to beat Susan Ann by a neck and get a place. [Time: 3:47 1/2]

THE FIRST KENTUCKY DERBY, 1875

The first Kentucky Derby was a race for three-year-olds at a mile and a half. About 10,000 persons attended the event, which was won by H. Price McGrath's Aristides. McGrath was a colorful Kentucky horseman who earned a fortune in gambling in New York City. He then returned to his native state and founded McGrathiana Stud Farm outside Lexington. Aristides won $2,850 in this race and a total of $15,700 as a three-year-old. These excerpts are reprinted from The Spirit of the Times, 15 and 22 May 1875, pp. 347, 371.

LOUISVILLE JOCKEY CLUB SPRING MEETING.—Monday next, the 17th of May, will be a day memorable in the turf annals of Kentucky, for it will witness the inauguratory meeting of the new racing organization, the Louisville Jockey Club. Commencing under the most favorable auspices, this association promises fair to make the beautiful Falls City a formidable rival to Lexington as the great racing centre of the Blue-grass Region. The executive of the new Jockey Club are gentlemen of high social position and acknowledged business qualifications, and they have provided a programme of racing sport distinguished for liberality and judgment. The inauguratory race of the day and meeting is a dash of one mile and a quarter for the association purse of $300, the entries for which are yet to be made. Then follows the great event of the meeting, the race for the Kentucky Derby, a sweepstakes for three-year-olds, $50 entrance, p.p. with $1,000 added. Like its prototype, the English Derby, the distance is one mile and a half, and no less than forty-two three-year-olds, the flower of the American thoroughbreds, have entered for this race. Among them we note the names of Aristides and Chesapeake, the fleet representatives of the famous McGrath stable; Steinbok, Verdigris, and Playmate, recently winners at Nashville; Bob Woolley and Ten Broeck, victorious at the Lexington meeting, now in progress; and the flying Alabama filly Ascension, the victress of the Fortuna Stakes at New Orleans. The interest attached to this race is very great among turfmen, for it is generally thought the result will throw considerable light on the subsequent great three-year-old races for the Withers, Belmont, Travers, and Kenner Stakes, at Jerome Park and Saratoga....

LOUISVILLE (KY.) JOCKEY CLUB INAUGURAL MEETING.

First Day, Monday, May 17.—The inaugural meeting of the newly-organized Louisville Jockey Club commenced on Monday, May 17 and continues over six says. A more brilliant opening was never witnessed, and the anticipations of the most sanguine and enthusiastic Kentuckian were more than realized. Fully ten thousand people witnessed the sport, and the spacious grand stand was crowded to its utmost capacity. Delightful weather favored the Jockey Club on its opening day, and the presence of a dazzling array of female loveliness, representative of Kentucky's proverbially beautiful daughters, enhanced the attractiveness of the occasion. The track was in superb order for fast running, and betokened the care and attention bestowed on its preparation this spring. The result of the first day of the meeting assures the future success of the Louisville Jockey Club, and it will now take its place as the great racing centre of a State so distinguished in the turf annals of America....

The Kentucky Derby, the great racing event of the meeting, and one which has created deep interest throughout the country, in view of its important bearing upon the prospects of future great events, was the next race. It was a sweepstakes of $50 each, p.p. with $1,000 added by the association, the second horse to have $200; one mile and a half. Of the forty entries to this stake, fifteen came to the post, viz.: H.P. McGrath's ch c Aristides, by Leamington, and b c Chesapeake, by Lexington; C. A. Lewis' ch c Verdigris, by Versailles; A. Buford's ch c McCreery, by Enquirer; Stringfield and Clay's gr c Enlister, by Enquirer; F.B. Harper's b c Ten Broeck, by Phaeton; S.J. Salyer's br c Bill Bruce, by Enquirer; J.A. Grinstead's ch f Gold Mine, by Australian; A. Bashford's br c. by Baywood out of Lute; Robinson, Morgan and Co.'s br c Bob Woolley, by Leamington; A.B. Lewis' b c Vagabond, by Vandal; G.H. Rice's b c Volcano, by Vandal, and W. Cottrill's ch f Ascension, by Australian. This was a magnificent field of three-year-olds, the majority of them having been winners. The betting showed McGrath's entries—Aristides and Chesapeake—to be the favorites in public estimation, for they brought $105 to Ascension's $55, Searcher $65, and the field $270. Chesapeake, from his successful running at Lexington, was generally thought to be the representative of the McGrath stable, especially as Aristides had cut up badly in the Phoenix Hotel Stakes at that meeting, owing to the fearfully heavy state of the course. The horses got off at the first attempt, Chesapeake being one of the last to get away. Volcano made the running, closely attended by Verdigris, Aristides, and McCreery, the rest well together, a length or two behind. They ran thus throughout the first half mile, 50 1/2 s., but the pace then began to tell on some of the rear division, and Enlister, Vagabond, and Chesapeake fell back. Aristides took second place as they ran along the backstretch, lapped Volcano as they reached the half-mile pole, the starting point (the mile being run in 1:43 1/4), and showed in front directly afterwards. The tremendous pace had already told a tale upon the field, which was now strung out a hundred yards behind, Chesapeake and Enlister being conspicuously in the rear. Aristides was steadily increasing his lead, Howard having taken a steadying pull on Volcano for a final effort. At the head of the stretch stood Mr. McGrath, who waved to Lewis, the rider of Aristides, to "go on," and he at once obeyed instructions by loosing his pull on his horse's bridle. Half way home, Volcano came with a determined rush, but Aristides stalled off the challenge in gallant style, and went over the score a winner of the first Kentucky Derby by a length from Volcano, with Verdigris third in 2:37 3/4, the fastest time ever made by a three-year-old at the distance. Bob Woolley was fourth and Ten Broeck fifth. Searcher, from whom so much was expected, never showed conspicuously in the race. Value of the stakes $3,100; of which $200 goes to the second horse.

RACING IN CALIFORNIA

During the 1870s the Pacific Jockey Club of California sponsored a series of high stakes races which attracted some of the leading thoroughbreds of the United States. The first of these challenges took place in San Francisco on November 15, 1873. The Pacific Jockey Club offered a purse of $20,000 in gold, with $13,000 to the winner, $5,000 to the second place horse, and $2,000 to the third finisher. The match was at four mile heats, with two victories required to claim the winner's prize. The favorite was George Treat's California-bred champion, Thad Stevens, who had a history of losing early heats before coming on strong to win the final races. His main competitors were two eastern horses: Colonel David McDaniel's Joe Daniels, and J.F. Chamberlain's True Blue. Joe Daniels had won the Belmont, Jerome, Travers, Annual, and Kenner Stakes, while True Blue had four recent wins including a record-setting time for a two mile race at Saratoga. The only other starter was a mare named Mamie Hall, who stood no chance against her rivals. This account is from The Turf, Field, and Farm, 21 November 1873, p. 324.

SAN FRANCISCO, Cal., Nov. 15, 1873

An immense assemblage, variously estimated at from ten to fifteen thousand persons, were present at the Ocean View Park Course to-day, to witness the great $20,000 four-mile heat contest. The occasion evoked the greatest enthusiasm, and it is estimated that previous to and during the race at least $100,000 changed hands. Never before was so much excitement evinced at a race meeting by all classes of people, even by the straight-laced, long-faced Jeremiahs, with whom nothing at the present is equal to what they had seen in the past. The managers were particularly favored by the fine weather, the day being one of the most delightful of the season. The turnout of aristocratic equipages was numerically larger than at any previous gathering in the State, while the number and styles of other vehicles were simply legion. Less pretentious pedestrians came in platoons from all quarters, and at 1 1/2 P.M. the scene and the countless objects that vivified it with bustling animation were strongly suggestive of Derby day at Epsom Downs.

The entries for this great event, which was a post stake for all ages, were five in all, viz: George Treat's ch g Thad Stevens, G. A. Johnson's ch c Joe Daniels, J.F. Chamberlin's b c True Blue, the bay mare Mamie Hall, and the chestnut colt Hubbard—the latter being drawn previous to the race, as he was not deemed in fit condition for the arduous work. It should be mentioned here that the sudden adoption of a new scale of weights by the Pacific Jockey Club, after the arrival of True Blue in California, was very detrimental to his chances for winning. Joe Daniels also suffered by the change, both being four-year-old colts not yet acclimated, and the former having much too short a time for preparation. According to the new scale of weights, five pounds each were added to the youngsters, and four pounds allowed the California horse Thad Stevens. This discrimination, I am constrained to say, at the particular time it was made, does not reflect any great credit upon the Pacific Jockey Club, and has not a parallel in the history of the American turf. Had the Club in their original advertisement announced the change, it is more than possible Mr. Chamberlin would not have entered True Blue. As it was the accident he met with in the third heat deprives his owner even of third money.

As the horses severally made their appearance on the track the enthusiasm of the crowd was worked up to fever heat. Thad Stevens was in tip-top condition, with muscles like bunches of steel wire and sinews like whipcord. He was set down by the knowing ones as a winner, unless distanced by one or the other of the youngsters in the first heat. Joe Daniels and True Blue made a fine appearance, but neither were in proper condition for the tremendous strain incident to a heat race of four miles, and it was rumoured that previous to his morning exercise there was a perceptible stiffness in the hind legs of the latter, which was not noticeable, however, during the race. Mamie Hall looked well; but no one ever dreamed of anything else but of seeing her left behind the distance flag in the first heat, an event which duly came to pass.

THE BETTING.

A large amount of money was invested in pools previous to the day of the race, Thad Stevens being largely the favorite in all the pools. To-day the sales on the course averaged as follows:

Thad Stevens	$260	$275	$325	$300	$325
True Blue	$165	$152	$165	$165	$155
Joe Daniels	$105	$100	$90	$8	$75
The Field	$10	$9	$8	$5	$5

THE RACE.

First Heat.—Promptly at the call Thad Stevens, Joe Daniels, True Blue and Mamie Hall went to the post, with Thad on the inside and Joe Daniels on the outside. At the signal Mamie Hall jumped off with the lead and held on for the first mile, with Thad Stevens running second, True Blue third, and Joe Daniels fourth. In the second mile True Blue took the lead and held it to the fourth mile, when Joe Daniels, who had been trailing, made play for the lead, and after a fine brush with True Blue, took it, winning the heat by two lengths in 7:45, True Blue second, Thad Stevens third, and Mamie Hall distanced.

The result of this heat was almost entirely unexpected, and gave a different turn to the betting. The excitement around the pool-sellers was tremendous, and high figures were the order. The friends of Thad Stevens rallied promptly to his support, and backed their opinion in the handsomest manner. In one of the first pools sold after the first heat, Thad Stevens was made first choice for $2,000, Joe Daniels bringing $1,500, and True Blue $800. Before the call for the second heat several large pools were sold, averaging in amount from $1,500 to $3,000.

Second heat.—The horses were called for the second heat at a quarter to four, and the preliminary rubbing down and saddling having been accomplished, at five minutes to four another excellent start was made, the three horses passing the score even. Before reaching the half mile Thad had pulled out ahead three lengths. True Blue following, and at the end of the first mile Thad crossed the score three lengths ahead, True Blue second and Daniels lagging five lengths. On the second mile the relative positions of the horses were about the same, Thad gaining a few yards, if anything. On the third mile all of the horses crossed the score in close company, Thad a neck ahead of True

Blue, with Daniels lapping on the flank. On the fourth mile Thad and True Blue began a neck-and-neck- struggle, with Joe Daniels close up. In the last half True Blue shoved ahead and opened a gap of five lengths, which he held in crossing the score. Thad Stevens being seven lengths behind Joe Daniels. Time, 8:03.

This result completely upset the calculations of the Thad Stevens' party and changed the betting. True Blue was now the favorite, the choice of second alternating between Thad Stevens and Joe Daniels, the betting being conducted on the hedging plan.

Third heat.—The horses were called for the third heat at half-past four, and got off in good style at twenty-five minutes to five. Thad took the lead again and pulled out handsomely a couple of lengths before reaching the first quarter, with True Blue second. Thad held his own through the first mile and crossed the score two lengths ahead, True Blue and Daniels running neck and neck. The second mile was a close run between the three. They crossed the score in almost precisely the same order as in the first mile. The third mile was a repetition of the first and second. They crossed the score as follows: Thad Stevens leading, Joe Daniels lapping him and True Blue a close third. At the first quarter of the fourth mile True Blue quit and fell behind, and was speedily lost in the distance. Thad Stevens pulled out at his best and parted company with Daniels, crossing the score nearly ten lengths ahead, in 7:57, with True Blue distanced.

The excitement was tremendous at this result. The cause of the quitting of True Blue was not definitely ascertained. It was at first rumoured that the horse broke down, but this was not the case. A little later it was said that in the first quarter of the fourth mile the horse fell and broke his leg. Another rumor followed that the horse got his foot into a gopher hole, all of which proved to be groundless. Barbee, the rider of True Blue, says his horse was cut down by Palmer, on Joe Daniels. There is no doubt an investigation will be called for. Meanwhile True Blue was declared distanced, leaving Thad Stevens and Joe Daniels to contest the finish, each having won a heat.

Fourth heat.—It was almost dark when the horses got the word for the fourth and deciding heat. They made a capital start, Thad Stevens at once taking the lead, and as they disappeared in the gloom the old horse was leading by fully five lengths, an advantage he held all through the heat, Joe never once being able to overtake him, the result being that Thad won the heat and race in 7:46, which is remarkable time, considering the distance he had run, the track being some seconds slower in a four-mile race than the Oakland Park track.

TROTTING

A TROTTING CHALLENGE, 1862

Although the emergency of the Civil War disrupted traditional recreations and pastimes in New York City, it did not abolish them entirely. Upper class gentlemen and ladies and many middle class enthusiasts still flocked to the race tracks to witness exciting trotting exhibitions. Once of the most noteworthy of these entertainments occurred in May of 1862, when Robert Bonner, editor of the New York Ledger, drove his famed team before an audience which included Commodore Cornelius Vanderbilt. George Wilkes wrote this account of that memorable day, which he published in his sporting journal, Wilkes' Spirit of the Times, 24 May 1862, pp. 188-89.

THE LEDGER MARES "IN FLIGHT."

Tuesday of last week, the day set down for the black mare Sunnyside, Gray Eddy and Native American, proved to be, up to its date, the very finest day of the season, and allured by the velvet puffs of the summer wind that came pelting our cheek through the slats of the bed-room blinds, we rather suddenly decided that the broad back seat of a coach, would, for a few hours, be an agreeable exchange for the arm-chair and darkened atmosphere of a sick chamber.

Presently, therefore and in accordance with this conclusion, we were sharing with a friend the comfortable locomotion of a steady four-wheeled vehicle, and in due time, after rejoicing through the five miles of verdue which unrolls itself on either side of the Queens County road toward the Fashion Pleasure Grounds, our team found itself standing up to its knees amid the thrifty crop of coming oats, that waved over the inner circle of the track. The attendance at the course was good. Invited by the beauty of the afternoon, the excellence of the roads, and the anticipation of a really fine race, the owners of the fast stock of New York, and particularly of that class of it which is known under the description of "double Teams," had come out in extraordinary force. Of this latter class of "flyers" the wondrous *Ledger* team, the famous span of Commodore Vanderbilt, and the black mares of Mr. Turnbull, elicited the largest observation, and little crowds followed these distinguished beauties as they severally turned slowly over the lawn, toward the shed, as if they were under the influence of an irresistible fascination. But the concentrated criticism of the "posted" portion of the audience was directed chiefly upon the team of Mr. Bonner (which, on this occasion, consisted of Lady Palmer and the Flatbush Maid), and upon that of Mr. Vanderbilt; which latter, from the reported statement of the Commodore that he always stood ready to match them against the *Ledger* team for $10,000, had come to be largely regarded as their proper rival. The judgment of the crowd, however, went in favor of the *Ledger* mares, and the reports of their having once, in private, made a mile together in 2:27! and more recently in 2:26! sent all the observers off with wonder in their minds.

"I'd sooner see it done than hear tell of it," said one.

"Why, that beats Lady Suffolk's best time under saddle?" exclaimed another.

"It beats everything!" said a third. "The fastest mile time, *double*, on the record is the 2:41 1/4 of Lantern and Don: and the fastest two-mile time ever made in public, was that of Lady Suffolk and Rifle, in 5:19!" and shaking his head, this gentleman closed with: "I don't see how these here mares of Mr. Bonner's can get away with a mile in 2:27; and to a road wagon, too, and he a drivin'!" and then he shook his head more doubtfully than ever.

"Pretty long striding watches them that timed the 2:26, I reckon!" said a forth, incredulously; and with these and similar expressions, all intermixed with strong regrets that Mr. Bonner was opposed to betting, and would not allow his mares to be used for racing purposes, the crowd, at the signal of the starters, turned to the course, and left the beautiful mares to enjoy the quiet of the shed by themselves....

Thus ended the great expectations which had been formed of sport of the opening days of the Fashion Association for 1862, and the audience were on the point of dispersing in dissatisfaction, when the buzz of a new and extraordinary entertainment arrested that intention.

During the heats between Sunnyside and Eddy, Mr. Bonner had met with a gentleman upon the course whom he had long desired to treat with an exhibition of his horses' mettle, and as so good an opportunity might not soon occur again, he promised to "speed" them for a mile around the track, as soon as the then pending race had closed. This matter got about, and the result was, that Mr. Bonner, who probably imagined the crowd would be reduced to a mere handful of lookers-on, found he would be obliged, if he desired to keep his word, to trot before the entire audience of the day. Being, however, a man of pluck, and never doubtful of his mares, he promptly accepted the alternative, and gathering up his reins with a "business" air, turned with them for a moment before the stand. There he requested several gentlemen by name, and among others Commodore Vanderbilt, to hold their watches and to mark his speed, and then pointing to the blackboard of the judges, which still bore the record of 2:31 1/4 for Sunnyside, he exclaimed, "I will beat that time!"

The former owner of Lantern who was in the ladies' balcony, not believing that the record of that horse and Don, could be beaten more than ten seconds by a pair of road mares to a road wagon, with an amateur owner driving, immediately wagered $250 with a bystander that the exploit would not be done. A few similar exchanges followed, and then amid the breathless silence of the crowds—a silence most unusual with the racing audience—Mr. Bonner and the "*Ledger* team" jogged off for a preliminary turn previous to coming up for a word.

It may appear singular to some that an audience so weary with a fruitless afternoon, and so accustomed to the more fierce rivalries of horse with horse, would have exhibited so deep an interest in the mere uncontested mile trial of a private team; but there are incidents connected with the *Ledger* mares which have created a special attraction, and which exact a commanding attention for them wherever they appear.

Taste in all things is progressive, and it always travels fastest with expense. But a few years ago the fancier of fast stock contented himself with the possession of a single trotter, and the highest ambitions of the road were reasonably gratified by the possession of a nag whose measure could be taken by five or six hundred dollars. As, however, emulation developed speed, and the increasing prosperity of the country encouraged outlay, the owners of the "singles" began to hunt up mates, and by great exhibitions of style and speed combined, the highest pretentions of the road were transferred to drivers of a pair. The lone "flyer," for a time, stubbornly contested the superiority and palm of fashion; but two or three "thundering doubles" having appeared in a single season to contest successfully with the old champions of the road, the new and more expensive fancy triumphed. The new result was, that with those who could spread to the extremes of art, double harness and a spanking span were all the go.

It was about the time when this taste had become established that Mr. Robert Bonner, who had been handling the *New York Ledger* (a most unpromising two-year-old when he got it) into vast renown and fortune, felt himself entitled to occasional relaxation with a horse of another color; so he bought a good, sound and rather fast road nag, and put it out at livery at a popular trotting stable. The intense fondness which he exhibited for horses, soon attracted the attention of the horse experts, and it being naturally supposed by those acute gentlemen that a man who had made his money fast would be willing to part with it easily, all sorts of "bargains," in the way of "ripping and tearing goore," were temptingly laid before him. Strange enough, however, Mr. Bonner, though a literary man, seemed to have as good an eye for a horse as the best of the dealers, and presently, when he discovered how the public taste had "set," he found, on his own judgement, a mate for his single horse, that enabled him to constitute a very excellent and rather rapid team.

His engagements in this way, brought him, of course, in contact with the leading owners of fast horses on the road, and among others with Commodore Vanderbilt; and it so happened that some badinage took place on one occasion between him and the Commodore, in relation to the merits of their respective teams, that resulted in a lasting rivalry. No bet resulted, because Mr. Bonner would not bet, but a duel of expense ensued to secure the best horses, that was very interesting to the outside world.

It was a fair contest. Commodore Vanderbilt was worth some eight or nine millions of dollars; while Bonner, who had raised the *Ledger* to the enormous circulation of nearly five hundred thousand copies per week, had an income of considerably more than a hundred thousand dollars a year. Every one, therefore, looked on with pleasure at the rivalry, and the efforts which each gentleman made to secure pre-eminence, made the contest conspicuous to all lookers on. As it fluctuated, now in favor of the Commodore on the purchase of some new horse, and now on the side of Bonner in consequence of some fresh accession to the *Ledger* stable, the alternations were duly chronicled in these columns, and the public, according to the changes of the game, awarded its applause.

By degrees, however, both gentlemen secured between them what certainly were the two best teams known in the United States, and whenever a whisper was heard, to the effect that this person or that had a better, the agent of Vanderbilt or Bonner were soon hunting after them with a *carte blanche*. At length Bonner spurred by a certain degree of uneasiness at some rumored recent addition to the stable of the Commodore, determined to take possession of the field, by a movement which could not be outflanked.

There is always a limit to even what is termed an unlimited margin, or *carte blanche*, and when the Commodore and Bonner had mentally agreed to stop at no expense to accomplish their desires, their respective judgements had, most probably, halted at a barrier of something like $5,000—inside of which they would seem to have an abundant range.

When a man gets his mind in this sort of fix, it requires a peculiar vigor to think beyond the mark. Both of the gentlemen we have before us, however, were capable of doing this; but Bonner was the first to jump the margin. He probably said to himself, "Well, what is any ordinary sum to me against triumph in this matter?" and having solved that part of the problem so handily, it is also quite likely that he went direct to Col. Joseph Hall, and opened vertures for the purchase of the famous trotter *Lantern*. That horse was acknowledged to be the fastest of all trotters to the pole and was the hero conjointly with Don, as has been already said, of the 2:41 1/4 in double harness, which, even to this day, stands as the best "recorded" double harness trotting time in mile heats. Now, *Lantern* was an especial pet of Col. Hall, and for a time, the transaction consequently was most difficult; but an offer by Bonner to plank down nine thousand dollars cash for Lantern, and a horse called *Light*, which had recently been trotting with him, decided the matter in the *Ledger's* favor, and *Lantern* passed into Mr. Bonner's hands. *Light*, however, was of but trifling value; but a purchase by Mr. Bonner, soon afterward, of the celebrated Lady Woodruff, for the sum of $4,200, gave the *Ledger* the supremacy it had so long desired. The fleet steamships of the Commodore were distanced by the double-cylinder rotary presses of the journalist, and the only solace which the partizans of the former had was the sneer of—"Well, now that he's got 'em, he don't know how to drive 'em!" We must do justice to the Commodore, however, by saying that *he* did not share in any such remark. The rivalry between him and Mr. Bonner had been in all respects a gentlemanly one, and, while admiring the *Ledger's* boldness, the Commodore was probably only cogitating some new combination to excel it. Indeed, he made several good efforts to that end, and Bonner, being cognizant of them, did not feel entirely safe until he had obtained possession, as a new mate for Lantern, of a mare called *The Flatbush Maid*.

This mare had never performed in public, but her owner showed Mr. Bonner such wondrous "time" in private, that he was glad to pay the round sum of $5,000 for her. The *Flatbush Maid*, in addition to her qualities of speed, had additional merit of being blazed down the face precisely like Lantern; but above that, and above all, her peculiar merit was a handy knack of traveling well in double harness, which probably made her as speedy to the pole, as if under saddle. Bonner now felt that he was really invincible, and feeling thus, there was nothing left to ruffle his complete satisfaction, but the continual assumption on the part of the wily Commodore, that he did not consider his teams inferior to anything belonging to the *Ledger*, and that he was always ready to try conclusions with any pair from that quarter for five or ten thousand dollars—*owners to drive*. It was probably this latter condition that nettled Bonners most; while as to the main intimidation, he was without an answer, as he did not bet.

As to the insinuation that he could not drive, *that* proceeded from the stable and hay-seed division, a class of gentry who deny even the most simple powers of intellect, to any person who was not born in a stall.

It may be said that, with the acquisition of the Flatbush Maid, anything like actual rivalry between the Commodore and Mr. Bonner ceased, and the latter, secure in his command, relinquished himself purely to the enjoyment of driving his unparalleled animals up on the road. Stimulated by his example, fine teams appeared in all parts of the country, and some of these were even bold enough to hope that they might eventually measure speed with him. The last of these that we have heard of, are a pair belonging to Mr. Reeside, of Cincinnati, known as the Alley colt and Joe Dimmick team, behind which we would have taken a ride in April last; but for the refusal of the weather. They doubtless rate next to the best team of Mr. Bonner.

With Mr. Bonner's purchase of the Flatbush Maid, however, his encouragement of fine stock was not done, and he soon after bought Lady Palmer for $5,500, and a gray mare unknown to fame, for the sum of $5,000. Lady Palmer has now taken the place of Lantern alongside the Flatbush Maid, and forms Mr. Bonner's favorite team; and the Gray Mare, who is said to have been timed privately in 2:20, is the trotting mate of the distinguished gelding. Mr. Bonner has, therefore, really two teams, with either of which he can beat anything else in the country; yet the willingness of the Commodore to trot him for ten thousand dollars a-side still obstinately stands.

All these things are known, to some extent, throughout the United States; and they were particularly current with the audience assembled on the Fashion Course on Tuesday week; and now that we have made this explanation, it probably will no longer appear singular that the audience at the Fashion paused with so deep an interest, on that occasion, when they saw Mr. Bonner virtually put a watch in Commodore Vanderbilt's hand, and requested him to take the time of the wondrous mares, whose superior fleetness he had so long disputed.

As the two splendid mares daintily stepped off with a light mincing gait, each now and then tossed her head gaily as if opening her throttle for the impending effort, it was plain to see that they were conscious of vast speed; and as Bonner sat admirably balanced in his wagon, with his reins well gathered, and his whip handsomely in hand, it was likewise plain that they would be managed with no ordinary skill. The whole team and its driver was a picture, and even taken in detail, would have borne in all parts, the closest criticism.

Those who studied it closely, saw that the Flatbush Maid exhibited most admirable points, and were prepared to expect wonders from her. The long fine shoulder, deep girth behind the elbows, powerful back and loins, and clean muscular legs, which she exhibited, arrested everyone's attention, and promised all in the way of speed and bottom that could be required of a trotter; while Lady Palmer, though eliciting an equal admiration, seemed at the same time to take everybody by surprise. Instead of the ordinary figure and lines of a trotting horse, they beheld what was at every point, from the muzzle to the heels, a pure, fine-drawn, high-mettled, thorough-bred mare. There was the long, lean head, fit model for the sculptor of a barb; the light, thin neck, composed entirely of cords and muscle; the vast throttle, broad nostril, deep chest, sloping shoulder, and faultless legs, with a length from hip to hock that could not be made greater without disproportion. The full, broad eye bespoke intelligence and courage, and it required no great strength of faith in the beholder to believe that her heart would be the last thing to yield, if she ever required to make a desperate and exhausting struggle. Lady Palmer obtains these qualities of blood legitimately, for she is of the lofty lineage of Glencoe, having been got by him, out of a thorough-bred mare in Kentucky, for running purposes. Having accidentally got in foal, however, when three-year-old, she was incapable of being trained, and, by a list of natural circumstances, became finally consigned to the destinies of harness.

Both of these mares are bay, the Lady being of the darkest shade, and both are about fifteen two. Each has had a colt, the thorough-bred foal being Chicago; and the trotter being in the possession of Mr. Hoagland, of Long Island, who very judiciously has named him the *New York Ledger*.

Slowly our magnificent pair moved round the first quarter of the oval, their owner talking to them affectionately as they went. Nearly the half mile pole, a slight increase of action was perceptible; and as they passed up toward the third quarter, it was plain to be seen that the forelegs of the now slightly animated beauties were reaching forward with a more nervous and broadening stride. As they passed by the third quarter, up toward the home stretch, their owner shook them loose, and at the same instant he burst forth with a long, ringing shout like a halloo, which might have been heard half to the Ferry, and which his mares appeared to clearly understand. Instantly they seemed to squat to the ground, and to tear forward with a vigor so intense, that it almost looked like rage at their previous restraint.

The First Mile.

Driver and team from that moment seemed to forget everything but each other, and the usually quiet unobtrusive gentleman who steadily and strongly held the reins, appeared lost in common frenzy with his steeds. At every stride of theirs he halloed, and in the prevailing stillness maintained by the profoundly interested audience, that solitary shout seemed to occupy the entire air for miles. As the rushing phantasm neared the stand, the crowd on the track flowed back, and when the word "go" was given, an irrepressible hurrah from the audience bespoke him good luck on his journey.

Instantly, however, it became profoundly still again, and while the multitude looked on with an almost breathless silence, the absorbed and excited driver made the air continue to ring with his incessant shouts. The mares took it as his challenge, and under its impulse they all the while gradually increased their speed. The first quarter was passed in 38 1/2 seconds, a rate (2:34) which though greater than any other trotting team has ever made, showed that these marvels of the equine race were not yet thoroughly "extended." From the first quarter, however, the pace was gradually improved, and it was the prevailing impression, as the team came tearing towards the home stretch, that the time indicated would be made. Mr. Bonner, however, though he had no watch to consult, and could receive no information of his rate of speed, felt that his mares had not gone through the first half of the mile anywhere near the mark; but perceiving now, that they were in full flight, he determined to make his mark in the second mile. The crowd flowed back again from the course as he approached the stand, and as he went by, a score of fingers fell upon their watches, marking 2:32 1/2, and a universal clapping of hands, in warm applause, rained from all portions of the course. The trial was thought by everybody to be over, but lo, instead of hauling up, the *Ledger* clarion was still heard sounding the charge, and a general exclamation broke fourth of: "He's going for the second mile!"

The Second Mile.

And in good earnest he did go for it, and with a terrible energy his gallant mares seconded his purpose.

"Look at that! look at that!" burst from hundreds of voices as they went into the first quarter, "There's speed for you!"

"And there's driving for you too!" exclaimed several with involuntary admiration at the masterly manner in which Bonner felt and humored every emotion of his steeds. It was now established by a vast concurrent observation, that his skill was of the highest order, and the absurd professional assumption, that there is anything so intricate in driving, that a man of good intellect, with his heart in the business, cannot acquire it in eight or ten years, was disposed of (at least so far as Bonner was concerned) forever. Indeed, we have no hesitation, on our part, in saying that we do not believe there is a driver in the country who can handle the *Ledger* mares better than can Mr. Bonner, and we very much doubt if there are many more accomplished drivers, even among the experts. The audience, at the Fashion, evidently took a great liking to him for the bold and free manner in which he poured his whole soul into his task, and their admiration was equally divided between his performance and the performance of the mares.

From the time the team had left the stand, in the second mile, and particularly after they bade good-bye to the first quarter, it was plain that the mares were continually increasing in their speed, and regrets were very numerous, in all quarters, that the watches had been stopped at the end of the first mile by most of those who had been timing. Everyone could see, however, that the rate of speed was much beyond that of the first experiment, and also see that the 2:31 1/2 would be freely beaten.

As the team passed up the back-stretch and into the third quarter, it seemed to be absolutely flying, or as if gliding swiftly, and without apparent effort, along a line of railway. Each stroke of both the grand animals fell together with the smoothness and exactitude of clock-work, and at every few yards Lady Palmer gave evidence of her enjoyment of the sport, by friskily flinging her broad tail in the air and over back. The little Flatbush Maid, however, laid down to her work without a wink or motion other than her trot; and as she went along, she was probably thinking of nothing else than how she could pass the clay-colored strip of earth under her feet, and get ahead of her driver's resounding voice. In this mad way the noble creatures came into the home-stretch and up towards the stand, and finally flew past it, without having made a skip or break, in the unparallelled time of *five minutes one second and a quarter* for two miles and marking but *two minutes twenty-eight seconds and three-quarters* for the second mile. Another universal clapping of hands followed this brilliant result; and Mr. Bonner, with remarkable skill and power of control, hauled up and stopped his mares within two hundred yards of their point of top speed.

We have no hesitation in saying that this was the finest exploit we ever saw performed upon a trotting track, and when we take into consideration that these mares were not in train, but in their usual stable trim, that they went to an ordinary road wagon which had been drawn by them from the City to the Course, and that an amateur owner drove, the performance seems almost marvellous. It was, however, publicly and bravely done, and it must now pass into the record, as an authentic and recognized portion of the trotting history of the United States.

Having seen this performance, no one can doubt that these mares can, under more favorable circumstances, trot in 2:27, or even in 2:26; nor can we prevent the question rising in our mind, whether either of them (or the best of the two), or the mysterious gray mare, is not fit to contend single against Patchen, or even Flora Temple herself? The speed shown by the Flatbush Maid and Palmer, in double harness represents, of course, only the merits of the slowest of the two; and while we admire Mr. Bonner's spirit liberality, we are forced to regret that they cannot get out of his stable long enough to collar other steeds of dreadful note. Mr. Bonner is, however, entitled to the thanks of all lovers of the horse, for the encouragement which his examples has given to the production of fine stock. Whatever makes a market for a high-priced article, induces extra efforts for its production, and until the horse is condemned as an animal unworthy of improvement, the approbation of society is due to every man, whose efforts tend to render this grandest friend of man popular with people.

There is but one feature of the above described exploit left for us to mention, which is, that when Mr. Bonner returned with his horses to the judges' stand to get the time of the race, he openly declared to all present on this track, "that while it was a rule with him never to make a bet, he would present ten thousand dollars *as a gift*, to any gentleman who owned a team, if he would drive them in the time just recorded by Lady Palmer and the Flatbush Maid."

As Commodore Vanderbilt was present, and as with peculiar shrewdness Mr. Bonner had got him into the stand with a watch in his hand, this latter incident may be regarded as a formal and official closing of the rivalry of the *Ledger* and the steamship stables, and a disposal of the Commodore's presumptive ten thousand dollars standing wager—*owners to drive!*

TROTTING RULES, 1870

Public dissatisfaction over abuses and the corruption of trotting races led to the formation of a new governing body which aimed to institute a series of reforms and to punish frauds in the sport. Amasa Sprague of Providence, Rhode Island took the initiative in calling for the creation of an organization which eventually became known as the National Trotting Association. Forty-eight trotting associations and track owners signed its initial articles. This code is reproduced from *Rules and Regulations to govern All Trials of Speed over the various courses associated under the name of the National Association for the Promotion of the Interests of the American Trotting Turf* (Providence, R.I., 1870), pp. 3-16.

RULES AND REGULATIONS OF THE NATIONAL ASSOCIATION FOR THE PROMOTION OF THE INTERESTS OF THE AMERICAN TROTTING TURF

ARTICLE 1. All trotting and pacing over the courses of this Association shall be governed by the following rules:

ARTICLE 2. *Entries*. All entries for premiums must be made under cover, enclosing the entrance money for purses and forfeits in sweepstakes, and then sealed and addressed to or deposited with the Secretary, or some person authorized to receive the same, at such time and place as the Associations may have prescribed. Notices of intention to enter will be received by telegraph up to the hour advertised for closing; and all such entries shall be eligible, provided the entrance fee specified shall be paid in due course by mail, or otherwise.

An accurate and satisfactory description of each entry will be required, and shall be in the following form, to wit:

1. *Color*. The color and marks shall be accurately given.

2. *Sex*. It shall be distinctly stated whether the entry be a stallion, mare or gelding.

3. *Name*. Every horse shall be named, and the name correctly and plainly written in the entry; and if the horse has ever trotted in a race under a different name within two years, such former name or names must be given. If a horse has trotted in any race,

without a name, mention must be made in the entry of a sufficient number of his or her most recent performances, to enable persons interested to identify the horse; provided that it shall not be necessary to furnish any one association or proprietor with the same record the second time.

It shall be the duty of the Secretary, or other persons authorized, to prepare the list of entries for publication, comprising all such information in a comprehensive manner, for the enlightenment of the general public and parties to the race; and all entries, as aforesaid, shall be opened and announced at a public meeting, of which reasonable notice by advertisement or otherwise, shall be given to the parties of interest.

A horse having once been named, shall not again start in a race on any course in the United States or Canada, without a name or under a different name, unless the foregoing provisions have been complied with.

4. *Name and Address.* The post office address in full of the person or persons in whose name an entry is made, and if he or they be not the owner, then that of the owner or owners also, must accompany each nomination.

5. *Double Teams.* In all double team races, the entry must contain the name and description of each horse, in the manner provided for entry of single horses.

CONDITIONS

1. A horse shall not be eligible to start in any race, that has beaten the time advertised, prior to the closing of the entries for the race in which he is entered.

Horses shall not be eligible if the time specified has been beaten by them at a greater distance; that is, a horse having made two miles in five minutes is eligible for a 2:30 race, but not eligible for a race slower than that time.

2. As many horses may be entered by one owner, or as many horses trained in the same stable as may be desired, but only one that has been owned in whole or in part by the same person or persons, or trained in the same stable within ten days previous to the race, can start in any race of heats.

3. In all purses, three or more entries are required, and two to start, unless otherwise specified.

4. No purse will be given for a "walk over," but in cases where only one of the horses entered for any premium shall appear on the course, he shall be entitled to his own entrance money and to one-half of the entrance money received from all horses entered for said premium.

5. Time made in single or double harness, at fairs, and on any track, whether short or not, shall constitute a record; but time made under the saddle, shall not be a record in harness or wagon races.

6. The entrance fee shall be ten per cent. of the purse, unless otherwise specified; and any person refusing to pay his entrance dues upon demand by the proper authority, shall, together with his horse or horses, be suspended until they are paid in full.

7. No person shall be permitted to draw his horse after said horse has appeared on the track, saddled or harnessed, after having been summoned to prepare for the race, or *during* a race, except by permission of the Judges, under penalty of being expelled.

ARTICLE 3. *In case of Death.* All engagements are void upon the decease of either party or horse, so far as they shall affect the deceased party or horse; but forfeits or matches made play or pay, shall not be affected by the death of a horse.

ARTICLE 4. *Fraudulent Entries, or Meddling with Horses.* Any person found guilty of dosing or tampering with any horse, or of making a fraudulent entry of any horse, or of disguising a horse with intent to conceal his identity, or being in any way concerned in such a transaction, shall be punished by the forfeiture of entrance money and expulsion; and any horse that shall have been painted or disguised, to represent another or a different horse, or shall have been entered in a purse in which he does not belong, shall be expelled.

ARTICLE 5. *Reward.* A reward of $50 will be paid to the person who shall first give information leading to the detection of any fraudulent entry and the parties thereto, to be paid out of the funds of the National Association for the Promotion of the Interests of the American Trotting Turf, by the Treasurer, upon recommendation of the officers of the course where such fraudulent entry was made, provided that this shall not be construed to extend to courses outside of this association.

ARTICLE 6. *Decorum.* If any owner, trainer, rider, driver or attendant of a horse, or any other person, use improper language to the officers of the course or the Judges in a race, or be guilty of any improper conduct, the person or persons so offending, shall be punished by a fine not exceeding $100, or by suspension or expulsion.

ARTICLE 7. *Selection of Judges.* There shall be chosen by the proper authority, three (3) competent Judges, for the day or race, who shall understand the rules of this Association, and shall be held accountable for their rigid enforcement, and all their decisions shall be in accordance therewith. Any person having a bet upon, or an interest, either direct or indirect, in any or either of the horses in a race, shall not be entitled to judge that race. In all match races these rules shall govern, unless the contrary be expressly stipulated and assented to by the club, association or proprietors of the course over which the race is to come off.

ARTICLE 8. *Power of Judges.* The Judges of the day or race shall have power to appoint distance and patrol Judges; they shall decide the questions and matters of dispute between parties to the race, that are not provided for in the Rules and Regulations, and shall have full power to inflict all fines and penalties provided by these rules.

They shall have entire control and authority over the horses about to start, and any such person refusing to obey their orders, shall be punished by a fine not exceeding $100, or by suspension or expulsion. No rider or driver shall cause unnecessary delay after the horses are called up, either by neglecting to prepare for the race in time, or by neglecting to come for the word, or otherwise, and when in scoring, the signal is not given, all the horses in the race shall immediately turn at the tap of the bell, or other signal given, and jog back for a fresh start. If this rule is not complied with on the part of any rider or driver, the Judges may give the word without regard to the offending party or parties, and they may be punished by a fine not exceeding $100, or by suspension not to exceed one year.

When any horse or horses keep so far ahead of others in scoring that the Judges cannot give a fair start, they shall give the offending party or parties notice of the penalties attached to such offensive conduct, and should they still persist, shall enforce said penalties. When the Judges are prevented from giving the word by a horse or horses being refractory, or from any other cause, they may, after a reasonable time, give the word without reference to the position of the refractory horse or horses, or may give them any position they think proper to facilitate the start. In all cases the word shall be given from the Judges' stand, and in no case shall a standing start be given. If the

Judges have reason to suppose that a horse is being or has been "pulled," to fraudulently prevent his winning, they shall have power to substitute a competent and reliable driver or rider for the remainder of the race, and if the result of the succeeding heat or heats shall confirm their suspicion, the rider or driver so removed shall be punished by suspension or expulsion. When disputes and contingencies arise, which are not provided for in the Rules, the Judges shall have power to decide in such cases; but in no case can there be compromise in the manner of punishment, where the Rules express or name what the penalty shall be, but the same shall be strictly enforced.

Judges may require riders and drivers to be properly dressed.

ARTICLE 9. *Judges' Duty.* The Judges shall be in the stand fifteen minutes before the time for starting; they shall weigh the riders or drivers, and determine the positions of the horses, and give each rider or driver his place before starting. They shall ring the bell or give other notice ten minutes previous to the time announced for the race to come off, which shall be notice to all parties to prepare for the race at the appointed time, when all the horses must be ready, and any party failing to comply with this rule, shall be punished by a fine not exceeding $100; or the horse may be ruled out by the Judges and considered drawn; but in all stakes and matches they shall be liable to forfeit. The Judges shall not notice or receive complaints of foul from any person or persons, except those appointed by the Judges for that purpose, and owners, riders or drivers in the race. The result of a heat shall not be announced until the Judges are satisfied as to the weights of the riders or drivers, and sufficient time has elapsed to receive the reports of the Distance and Patrol Judges. When the Judges are satisfied that a race is being or has been conducted improperly on any part of the rider or driver in a race, they shall punish the offender by suspension not to exceed one year, or by expulsion. If a horse is purposely pulled or broken, to allow another horse to win the heat, the horse so pulled or broken shall be distanced, unless such decision shall be deemed to favor a fraud, and the rider or driver shall be punished by suspension not to exceed one year, or by expulsion; but in case the Judges shall deem such decision as the above to favor a fraud, they shall declare that heat no heat, and shall substitute another driver or rider for the offending one.

The presiding Judge shall instruct the riders or drivers in relation to scoring and breaking, prior to the commencement of the race.

ARTICLE 10. *Distance and Patrol Judges.* In all races of heats there shall be a Distance Judge, appointed by the proper authority, who shall remain in the distance stand during the heats, and immediately after each heat shall repair to the Judges stand, and report to the Judges the horse or horses that are distanced, and any act of foul, if any has occurred under his observation.

The Patrol Judges shall repair in like manner to the Judges' stand, and report any act of foul, if any has occurred under their observation; the reports of the Distance and Patrol Judges shall be alone received.

ARTICLE 11. *Accidents.* In case of accidents, ten minutes shall be allowed, but the Judges may allow more time when deemed necessary and proper.

ARTICLE 12. *Judges' Stand.* None but the Judges of the race in process, and their assistants, shall be allowed in the Judges' Stand during the pendency of a heat, except members of the Board of Appeals.

ARTICLE 13. *Power of Postponement.* In case of unfavorable weather, or other unavoidable causes, each Association or proprietor shall have power to postpone to a future time all purses or sweepstakes or any race to which they have contributed money, upon giving notice thereof. No heat shall be trotted when it is so dark that the horses cannot be plainly seen by the Judges from the stand, but all such races shall be continued by the Judges to the next day, omitting Sunday, at such hour as they shall designate.

ARTICLE 14. *Starting and Keeping Positions*. The horse winning a heat shall take the pole the succeeding heat, and all others shall take their positions in the order in which they came home in the last heat. When two or more horses shall make a dead heat, the horses shall start for the succeeding heat in the same positions they occupied at the finish of the dead heat. In coming out in the home stretch, the foremost horse or horses shall keep the position they first selected, or be liable to be distanced; and the hindmost horse or horses, when there is sufficient room to pass on the inside or anywhere on the home stretch, without interfering with others, shall be allowed to do so, and any party interfering to prevent him or them shall be distanced. If a horse should at any time cross or swerve on the home stretch *so as to impede the progress of another horse*, he shall not be entitled to win that heat.

If a horse, rider or driver shall cross, jostle or strike another horse, rider or driver, or shall swerve, *or do anything that impedes the progress of another horse*, he shall not be entitled to win that heat; and if the impropriety was intentional on the part of the rider or driver, the horse that impedes the other shall be distanced, and the rider or driver shall be punished by suspension not to exceed one year, or by expulsion.

Although a leading horse is entitled to any part of the track, except after selecting his position on the home stretch, if he crosses from the right to the left, or from the inner to the outer side of the track, when a horse is so near him that in changing his position he compels the horse behind him to shorten his stride, or if he cause the rider or driver to pull him out of his stride, it is foul; and if, in passing a leading horse, the track is taken so soon after getting the lead as to cause the horse passed to shorten his stride, it is foul.

ARTICLE 15. *Loud Shouting*. Any rider or driver guilty of loud shouting or making other unnecessary noise, or of making improper use of his whip, during the pendency of a heat, shall be punished by a fine not to exceed $25 for the first offence, and for the second offence by suspension during a meeting.

ARTICLE 16. *Horses Breaking*. When any horse or horses break from their gait in trotting or pacing, their riders or drivers shall at once pull them to the gait in which they were to go the race, and any party refusing or neglecting to comply with this rule, shall lose the heat, and the next best horse shall win the heat; and all other horses shall be placed ahead in the heat, and the Judges shall have discretionary power to distance the offending horse or horses, and the rider or driver shall be punished by a fine not to exceed $100 dollars, or by suspension not exceeding one year. Should the rider or driver comply with this rule, and the horse should gain by a break, twice the distance so gained shall be taken from him at the coming out. In case of a horse repeatedly breaking, or running or pacing while another horse is trotting, the Judges shall punish the horse, so breaking, running or pacing, by placing him last in the heat, or by distancing him. A horse breaking at or near the score shall be subject to the same penalty as if he broke on any other part of the track.

All complaints of foul by riders or drivers must be made at the termination of the heat, and before the rider or driver dismounts or leaves his vehicle by order of the Judges.

ARTICLE 17. *Fraudulent Collisions or Interference.* In any case where a driver is run into and his wagon or sulky broken down without fault on his part, the heat shall be deemed no heat so far as the horses not in fault are concerned, but he who causes the breakdown, may be distanced; and if the Judges find that it was done wilfully, the driver in fault shall be forthwith suspended or expelled, and his horse shall distanced.

If by any outside interference or obstruction a vehicle is broken down and the horse prevented from winning a heat, that heat shall be deemed no heat.

ARTICLE 18. *Relative to Heats, and Horses eligible to start.* In heats, one, two, three, of four miles, a horse not winning one heat in three shall not start for a fourth unless such horse shall have made a dead heat. But where eight or more horses start in a race, every horse not distanced shall have the right to compete until the race is completed.

A dead heat shall be considered a heat as regards all excepting the horses making such dead heat, and those only shall start for the next heat that would have been entitled had the heat been won by either horse making the dead heat. A horse prevented from starting by this rule shall not be distanced but ruled out.

A horse must win a majority of the heats which are required by the conditions of the race, to be entitled to the purse or stakes, unless such horse shall have distanced all others in one heat, except when otherwise provided in the published conditions.

ARTICLE 19. *Placing Horses.* Horses distanced in the first heat of a race shall be equal, but horses that are distanced in any subsequent heat shall rank as to each other in the order of the positions to which they were entitled at the start of the heat in which they are distanced, and in deciding the result of any race between the horse contending in the last heat thereof, the relative position of each horse so contending shall be considered as to every heat in the race; that is, horses having won two heats better than those winning one; a horse that has won a heat better than a horse only making a dead heat; a horse winning one or two heats and making a dead heat, better than one winning an equal number of heats, but not making a dead heat; a horse winning a heat or making a dead heat and distanced in the race, better than a horse that has not won a heat or made a dead heat; a horse that has placed "second" twice, better than a horse that has been placed "second" only once, etc.

When two or more horses shall be equal in the race at the commencement of a final heat thereof, they shall rank as to each other as they are placed in the decision of such final heat.

In case these provisions shall not give a specific decision as to second and third money, &c., the Judges of the race are to make the awards according to their best judgement and in conformity with the principles of this rule.

ARTICLE 20. *Time between Heats.* The time between heats shall be twenty minutes for mile heats; and for mile heats, best 3 in 5, twenty-five minutes; and for two mile heats, thirty minutes; for three mile heats, thirty-five minutes; and should there be a race of four mile heats, the time shall be forty minutes.

After the first heat, the horses shall be called five minutes prior to the time of starting.

ARTICLE 21. *Heats in which the time is null and void.* If for any cause a heat shall be taken away from a horse that comes in ahead, the heat shall be awarded to the next best horse and no time shall be given out by the Judges, or recorded against either horse, and the Judges may waive the application of the rule in regard to distance in that heat, except for foul riding or driving.

ARICLE 22. *Weights and Weighing*. Every horse starting for purse, sweepstakes or match., in any trotting or pacing race, shall carry, if to wagon or sulky, 150 lbs., exclusive of harness; and if under the saddle, 145 lbs., the saddle and whip only to be weighed with the rider.

Riders and drivers shall weigh in the presence of one or more of the Judges previous to starting for any race, and after each heat, shall come to the starting stand and not dismount or leave their vehicle without permission of the Judges. Any party violating this rule may be distanced. But a rider or driver thrown or taken by force from his horse or vehicle, after having passed the winning post, shall not be considered as having dismounted without permission of the Judges; and if disabled may be carried to the Judges' stand to be weighed, and the Judges may take the circumstances into consideration and decide accordingly.

ARTICLE 23. *Handicaps and Miscellaneous Weights*. In matches or handicaps, where extra or lesser weights are to be carried, the Judges shall carefully examine and ascertain before starting, whether the riders, drivers or vehicles are of such weights as have been agreed upon or required by the match or handicap; and the riders or drivers who shall carry during the race and bring home with them the weights which have been announced correct and proper by the Judges, shall be subject to no penalty for light weight in that heat, provided the Judges are satisfied of their own mistake, and that there has been no deception on the part of the rider or driver who shall be deficient in weight; but for all parties thereafter shall carry the required weight.

ARTICLE 24. *Size of Whips*. Riders and drivers will be allowed whips of the following lengths: for saddle horses, 2 ft. 10 in.; sulkies, 4 ft. 8 in.; wagons, 5 ft. 10 in. Double teams, 6 ft. 6 in.; tandem teams and four-in-hand, unlimited.

ARTICLE 25. *Distances*. In heats of one mile, 80 yards shall be a distance. In heats of two miles, 150 yards shall be a distance. In heats of three miles, 220 yards shall be a distance. In heats of one mile, best 3 in 5, 100 yards shall be a distance. Except in heats where eight or more horses contend, then the distance shall be increased one-half.

All horses whose heads have not reached the distance stand as soon as the leading horse arrives at the winning post, shall be declared distanced, except in cases of unavoidable accidents, when it shall be left to the discretion of the Judges.

ARTICLE 26. *Purse or Stake Wrongfully Obtained*. A person obtaining a stake or purse through fraud, shall return it to the Treasurer on demand, or be punished as follows: He, together with all the parties interested, and the horse or horses, shall be expelled until such demand is complied with.

ARTICLE 27. *Protests*. Protests may be made verbally before or during a race, and shall be reduced to writing, and shall contain at least one specific charge and a statement of the evidence upon which it is based, and shall be filed with the Judges, Association or Proprietor before the close of the meeting. The Judges shall in every case of protest demand that the rider or driver and the owner or owners, if present shall immediately testify under oath in the manner hereinafter provided; and in case of their refusal to do so, the horse shall not be allowed thereupon to start in that race, or any heat thereof, but shall be considered and declared ruled out.

But if they do comply and take the oath, as herein required, then the Judges shall allow the horse to start, or continue in the race, and the premium, if any is won by that horse, shall be retained a sufficient length of time, (say three weeks), to allow the parties interested a chance to sustain their protest.

Associations or Proprietors shall be warranted in retaining the premium of any horse in the manner herein mentioned, if at any time before it is paid they shall receive information in their judgment tending to show fraud.

Any person found guilty of protesting a horse without cause, or with intent to embarrass a race, shall be punished by a fine not exceeding $100, or by suspension not to exceed one year, or by expulsion.

The required oath shall be in the following form, to wit:

I

of in the county of

State of

on oath depose and say,

that I am the of the

called the same entered in a purse for horses that have never trotted better than

minutes and seconds, to be trotted this day on this course, and the same that has been protested, and to which this affidavit is in answer, hereby declare and affirm that *to the best of my knowledge and belief,* said before-mentioned horse is eligible to start or compete in the race aforesaid, according to the Rules of this course; and that I fully believe all the provisions and conditions required in the rules and Regulations for the government of trials of speed over this course, were fully and honestly complied with in making the entry aforesaid.

Given under my hand, at

this day of

A.D. 187

Subscribed and sworn to before me,

this

day of

A.D. 187

Justice of the Peace.

ARTICLE 28. *A race "to go as they please."* When a race is made to go as they please, it shall be construed that the performance shall be in harness, to wagon or under the saddle; but after the race is commenced no change shall be made in the mode of going.

ARTICLE 29. *A race "in harness."* When a race is made to go in harness it shall be construed to mean that the performance shall be to a sulky.

ARTICLE 30. *Trotting Horse and Running Mate.* A race wherein a trotting horse goes with a running mate shall not create a record for time as a trotting performance.

ARTICLE 31. *A race made and no distance specified.* When a race is made and no distance specified, it shall be restricted to the following distances, viz.: one mile and repeat; mile heats, best 3 in 5; 2 miles and repeat; or 3 miles and repeat; and may be performed in harness, to wagon, or under the saddle.

ARTICLE 32. *Matches against Time.* When a horse is matched against time, it shall be proper to allow any other horse to accompany him in the performance, but not to be harnessed with, or in any way attached to him.

In matches made against time, the parties making the match shall be entitled to three trials, unless expressly stipulated to the contrary, which trials shall be had in the same day; the time between trials to be the same as the time between heats in similar distances.

ARTICLE 33. *When Matches become Play or Pay.* In all matches made to come off over any of these courses, the parties shall place the amount of the match in the hands of the stakeholder one day before the event (omitting Sunday) is to come off, at such time and place as the Club, Association or Proprietor, upon application may determine, and the race shall then become play or pay.

ARTICLE 34. *Age of Horses—how reckoned.* The age of a horse shall be reckoned from the first day of January preceding the period of foaling.

ARTICLE 35. *A Green Horse.* A green horse is one that has never trotted or paced for premiums or money, either double or single.

ARTICLE 36. *Horses sold with engagements.* The seller of a horse sold with his engagements has not the power of striking him out. In case of private sale, the written acknowledgment of the parties that the horse was sold with engagements is necessary to entitle the buyer to the benefit of this.

ARTICLE 37. *Suspension.* The words suspended or suspension wherever they occur in these rules, shall be construed to mean suspension from entering, riding, driving, training or assisting on the grounds of any course represented in this Association.

ARTICLE 38. *Expulsion.* The words expelled or expulsion wherever they occur in these rules, shall be construed to mean unconditional expulsion from all the courses represented in this Association.

ARTICLE 39. *Right of Appeal.* Any person who has been subjected to any of the penalties provided by these rules, can appeal from the decision of the Judges, to the Association or Proprietors, upon whose grounds the penalty was imposed, and from their decision can appeal to the Board of Appeals, provided they shall do so within one week from the announcement of such decisions, and provided also that where the penalty was a fine it shall have been previously paid.

ARTICLE 40. *Fines.* All persons who may have been fined under these rules, unless they pay them in full on the day of assessment shall be suspended until they are paid in full.

All fines shall be paid to the Association or Proprietor on whose grounds they were imposed, and by them shall be paid to the Treasurer of the National Association upon demand.

SMUGGLER VS. GOLDSMITH MAID, 1876

During the early 1870s a new system of organized trotting developed in the United States as several leading tracks joined forces to form a racing circuit. Cleveland, Buffalo, Utica, and Springfield founded the "Quadrilateral Trotting Combination" in 1875. The group added Rochester and Poughkeepsie in 1875 and changed its name to the "Central Trotting Circuit." Hartford, with its new Charter Oak track, was admitted in 1876. That summer witnessed a series of stirring races between a long-time star and champion mare, Goldsmith Maid, and an upstart stallion, Smuggler. In July in Cleveland Smuggler (driven by Marvin of Kansas) won a surprising victory in five grueling heats from Budd Doble's Goldsmith Maid. But at Hartford later that season the mare won a rematch in six heats, which was marred by controversy over both the start and finish of the third mile. This description of that exciting contest is from The Turf, Field, and Farm, 8 September 1876, p. 152.

GALA DAYS AT CHARTER OAK PARK

That for which we have waited and longed has come at last. There has been another great race among the free-for-all flyers. There are at least two red letter Thursdays in the Septilateral campaign. Those who in after years speak of Smuggler and Goldsmith Maid will link with the names of the horses Cleveland and Hartford. In the lake city of Ohio and the proud capital of Connecticut the two great equine battles of the year and of the world have been fought. There was an unusual buzz in the streets of Hartford before yesterday's sun was an hour high. The early risers drove out to Charter Oak Park to see the horses at work, and the early trains brought the holiday throng. From all parts of New England and New York the crowd gathered, and every one spoke of the coming conflict. A great many were of the opinion that the race was a sure thing for the Maid. The uncertainty of Smuggler was so well known as to make people backward in putting money on him. Lulu and Lucille Golddust were out, and Bodine and Judge Fullerton were expected to play only indifferent parts in the contest....

When I reached the track at 2 o'clock in the afternoon I found every available spot for sight-seeing occupied. Never before was the grand stand so crowded, and never before did so much of the fashion and beauty of Hartford pass through the gates of Charter Oak Park. The open stands, like the covered ones, presented a crush of people, while the field was full of carriages. At least twelve thousand persons had assembled to do honor to the kings and queens of the trotting turf. . . The public took but feeble interest in the 2:32 race as compared with that made manifest in the free for all. The magic names were Goldsmith Maid, Smuggler, Judge Fullerton and Bodine, and in the presence of these all others sunk into insignificance. Each of the flyers was received with cheers and the clapping of hands. Bodine had the pole, with Smuggler next to him, Judge Fullerton third and Goldsmith maid on the outside. As the Maid has spent so many years on the turf, and has been trained to get off quickly, she outscored her rivals. The wound which a blade of glass had made in Smuggler's foot the previous day had not rendered the stallion lame. He came down to the wire more steadily than is his custom, going into a break only once, and that in the second score. Judge Fullerton was the nervous horse of the party, and not until the eighth attempt was the word given. The Maid was in the lead, but Fullerton went by her like a flash, and reached the quarter pole in thirty-three seconds, closely pursued by the trim bay mare. Bodine was lapping her ladyship, and Smuggler was driving away in the rear. "He is safely around the turn," hoarsely whispered his friends, "and now look out for telling work." Just then Bodine went into the air, the pace being too hot for him, and Smuggler began to slowly close his gap. Fullerton led to the half, in 1:07, but the Maid was hard upon him, and she had the best of him at the third quarter. Will Smuggler try for the heat? was anxiously asked. None of us were long kept in suspense. When the brown stallion squared away at the head of the home-stretch those of us who had seen him on other fields knew that he meant business. His finishing stride is irresistible. Doble scented danger, and he urged the mare to her best efforts. All in vain. The brown stallion crept slowly, but surely and remorselessly, near him, while twelve thousand brave men and fair women strained their eyes and held their breath. Doble lifted the Maid by a skillful play upon the lines, but he could not keep the blaze of Smuggler from shining like the headlight of a locomotive just under the wire. The stallion won the heat by half a length, while the shouts of the multitude made the ground quake and the buildings tremble. The time was 2:15 1/4. "Is that not fast?" queried Gov. Jewell, his broad, manly face aglow with excitement. "Fast? Why, bless you, man, it is the greatest stallion performance known to the record! It is the fastest mile ever trotted by an stallion in the world." "And it is the fastest mile I ever saw in a race," exclaimed J. Elliott, the gray-bearded critic of the New York *Herald,* as he nervously wiped his glasses and noted the figures which stared from the blackboard. Smuggler was cheered to the echo when he returned to the judges' stand, and Marvin modestly, almost shyly, lifted his red cap in recognition of the ovation. Doble smiled grimly, as if he felt that his second day of judgment had come, and the Maid held her head unusually low as her attendants gathered around her and tenderly led her from the track. But little attention was paid to Judge Fullerton and Bodine, although the chestnut son of Edward Everett had made a splendid show in the race. Smuggler and Goldsmith Maid were the two central, overshadowing figures of the fight, and the public had eyes for them alone. The speculators, who had offered in the morning the most reckless odds on the Maid, now began to talk in a different strain. That struggle down the home-stretch had made it plain that the stallion had more speed than the mare, and, judged by the Cleveland performance, his sticking qualities were superior to hers. The hedging process made Smuggler an equal favorite with Goldsmith Maid.

Every one was on tiptoe when the horses came on the stretch for the second heat. The stallion seemed to have won the sympathy of the crowd, and he was the most warmly applauded. The word was not long delayed. It was given on the second score, with the favorites head and head, but with Fullerton a length behind. The mare made her first skip about sixty yards from the wire. She did not seem to relish the idea of the brown getting off on even terms with her. Smuggler led around the turn and was never headed, although the Maid and Fullerton were equal with him for a moment or two on the backstretch. The pace was not so hot, as the time at the half mile was 1:09, but the defeat in the first heat appeared to have a depressing effect upon the mare. She was easily shaken off by her great rival. She tried again to pass him on the upper turn, but failed. There was clear daylight between them at third quarter. Down the home-stretch Smuggler maintained his commanding position, and when Doble found that he could not get to the front, he eased his mare, and both came somewhat gently under the wire. The time of the heat was 2:17. The cheering was tremendous. The horses were cooled out under the trees, and admiring hundreds gathered around the stallion, while sympathizing knots looked sadly upon the Maid as she stood with quivering nostrils and trembling flanks. Every one deemed the race as good as over. It was dollars to cents that the brown would win. Nothing, it was said with emphasis, could defeat him but an accident. As the accidental element is a strong one in every race, and as your intense speculator will bet on anything, from the flip of a copper coin to the stomach capacity of an elephant, the pool-stand was not deserted. In the face of the forlorn hope men stood up and backed the Maid at short odds against Smuggler. It was the policy of all the other horses in the race to fight the stallion.

Doble was downcast when he appeared on the track behind the mare for the third heat. That floral collar which had been ostentatiously woven for the Maid, and which hung against the judges' stand where all could see and admire, was destined by the fortunes of war to adorn the neck of the great rival of the great mare. Twice had he tried his best to beat the brown when every advantage was on his side, and twice had he failed. No wonder that his heart pulsated faint and low. And no wonder that Marvin, securely seated behind the powerful stallion, was confident to the verge of recklessness. Once, twice, three times, the horses scored, Smuggler as steady as a clock, and well up, but no word. For the fourth time they came down to the wire, the maid was in the lead and the stallion behind. The people impatiently shook their heads, for they reasoned that under no circumstances whatever could it be a start. But while yet shaking their heads they were surprised to hear "Go!" shouted from the judges' stand. By this most unfair advantage Goldsmith Maid was given the position next to the rail which Smuggler had won, and the stallion, who was entitled by virtue of his two heats, to at least a moderately even send off, was forced to commence his fight three lengths behind all the others. Such a volume of hisses, such a storm of indignation as burst from the crowded grand and field stands, I never before heard and hope never to hear again. Angry shouts of "Call them back!" "Take them out," rose above the hisses and were continued until after Goldsmith Maid had passed the first quarter with Fullerton on her wheel, Bodine third and Smuggler seven lengths in the rear. Along the back-stretch the stallion began to close the fearful gap which the wretched start had opened, and at the half-mile he was a length behind Fullerton, who was three lengths behind the mare. Bodine got in a tangle at this point and dropped so far to the rear that it was thought that the distance flag would fall in his face. At the third quarter Smuggler had passed the Judge and was three lengths behind the Maid. The heat is lost to him, was the expression which the mind flashed from every eye, and the judges' stand was viewed with frowns of discontent. That gap is too great to be overcome by a mortal horse when Goldsmith Maid is in the lead. Some spirit steed, some ghostly form might reduce it to nothing, but not living flesh and blood. Remember, it is the Queen which Doble drives, a queen which was queen when the brown stallion felt the gall of servitude in a far Western State. But look at Smuggler now! He has squared away at the head of the home-stretch as if the fire of victory was rolling from his nostrils. And, by the soul of the prophet, he is gaining on the mare! Slowly, relentlessly, he creeps up to her. They are near the distance stand and he is hard on her wheel. Twelve thousand hearts beat in suspense, and twelve thousand tongues are palsied for the moment. "The finish will be close," I whispered to Chester," and we must keep sharp eyes to mark the winner, standing here as we do over the wire!" He nodded assent, and the next moment the bay and brown drew near the goal. They were head and head, and Smuggler moving with the greatest momentum. Our eyes are bent upon the wire, and all our faculties on the alert. Below the line I plainly saw the nose of the stallion in front of that of the mare. Without turning, I said to Chester, "Who wins?" His reply was brief but to the point, "Smuggler, by five inches." The vast audience, as soon as relieved from the spell which held them silent, joined in a deafening roar. Somebody shouted "Smuggler's heat," and the words were echoed all over the park. The judges pondered awhile, then hung out the time, 2:16 3/4, and then made the announcement that the heat was dead between the stallion and the mare. This decision did not give satisfaction. First, Goldsmith Maid was sent off three lengths ahead of Smuggler, because, as the judges say, Marvin nodded for the word. It is true that Marvin lost his head and nodded, but under the circumstances the judges should have paid no attention to it. Smuggler was scoring as steadily as any horse in the race, and there was no reason in the world why he should be placed at a disadvantage. The interests of the public, and genuine sport, must be consulted as well as some other things, and these interests require that when a horse wins the pole it shall not be taken from him and given to his most dangerous opponent, especially when he is on his good behavior. Secondly, although Smuggler was forced by the start given him to fight his way around Judge Fullerton and Bodine before he could take up the battle with the Maid, he trotted the entire mile without skip or break, while the mare indulged in two or three of her little running jumps by which she gained ground and rested herself at the same time. Had the two gone under the wire nose and nose, the heat, by every principle of equity, should have been awarded to the stallion. Thirdly, Smuggler, as noted by as sharp eyes as any in the judges' stand, actually crossed the score from four to six inches ahead of the mare. I do not write in this vein simply to make a show of critical knowledge, but to tell the truth as I understand it. The close of the third heat was rendered more exciting by a startling incident. Following the trotters there came flying down the homestretch a runaway horse. He was bridleless, and his eyes shone like two balls of fire. After him he dragged a top buggy in which was seated a gray-haired lady holding a child in her arms. Madly, furiously the horse galloped, and as the face went by us we saw settling down upon it an expression of despair. The drivers of the trotters heard the clatter behind them, and they rushed their horses to the first turn and pulled next to the outer rail in order to get out of the way. Around the turn went the runaway, and as he neared the quarter his stride began to shorten. He was a crazy-headed dunghill and soon pumped himself out. He would have stopped of his own accord had not some fool shied his hat at him. He swerved, and over went the buggy and its load. Fortunately neither the lady nor the child was hurt. The whole scene was highly dramatic. In cooling out for the fourth heat it was noticed that Smuggler manifested weariness in the legs. The great strain which he had undergone had left its marks. It was believed, however, that he would recover, and he remained the favorite at large odds. Col. Russell directed that his toe weights, three ounces each, should be taken off, as his road shoes weighed twenty-five ounces a piece, and, after all the work he had done, it was prudent to lighten him up.

There was a fair start for the fourth heat. At the quarter the Maid was two lengths ahead, and along the back-stretch she rested herself with a skip. Smuggler was moving with great precision, but Fullerton and Bodine were full of uncertainty. At the third quarter they were so far behind that it seemed to be out of the question for them to save their distance. When Smuggler settled down to actual work at the head of the home-stretch, every one expected to see him first under the wire. He was crawling up on the mare, when all at once he went to pieces, and it was plain that crown for which he had fought so hard, and which he had actually won, would go to another. Doble's face was now lighted up with triumph, and Marvin's was deeply clouded. The Maid crossed the score in 2:17 3/4, and Smuggler jogged home. Fuller got inside the flag, but Bodine was about as near outside as it was possible for a horse to be and not be distanced. Those who flocked to the little grove used as a cooling-out ground required but one glance to satisfy them as to what the result would be. While Goldsmith Maid breathed as if not distressed, Smuggler trembled on his legs and the fire was gone from his eyes. His terrific gait on a track which cupped more or less had done its business. He was unmistakably leg tired.

In scoring for the fifth heat he broke badly. On the second score the word was given. Goldsmith Maid went to the front and was never headed. Smuggler could not overhaul her down the home-stretch, and she won by two lengths in 2:18. Bodine and Judge Fullerton did not appear in the sixth heat, having been sent to the stable under the rule. Smuggler was used up. Three times he came down for the word and broke. Marvin stopped to re-arrange his boots and Doble petulantly objected. It was growing dark, and the partisans of the Maid wished to have the race trotted out that night. On the fifth score "go" was shouted. Smuggler struggled along behind until he reached the upper turn, when he gave it up. His heart failed him and he left his feet. Marvin had to pull him to a walk before he could get him to trot again. Doble looked behind him, and seeing his opportunity, uncharitably urged his mare forward to shut the stallion out. Marvin whipped his horse into a run and thus got inside the flag. Legally, Smuggler was distanced, but the judges decided otherwise, probably for the reason they wished to make amends for the errors committed in the third heat. The time of the sixth heat was 2:19 3/4. It was a great race, and in it Goldsmith Maid added to her laurels. Though beaten, Smuggler was not disgraced. He tired, but because he did so we must not stamp him as a coward. At Cleveland he trotted as game a race as mortal man ever saw. His condition may not have been the best at Hartford, and then the great strain forced upon him in the third heat robbed him of all surplus vitality. Those who witnessed the grand struggle which took place yesterday will remember it to their dying day. Look at the time of the heats, 2:15 1/4, 2:17, 2:16 3/4, 2:17 1/4, 2:18, 2:19 3/4. Who would have put faith in such a story a few years ago?

Chapter 10

FIELD SPORTS

North Americans enjoyed a variety of field recreations during the middle decades of the nineteenth century. In most cases the hunting, fishing, and other activities of sportsmen were noncompetitive amusements in the mountains, forests, and streams of the continent. But urban residents and country dwellers also organized clubs and arranged contests in archery and pigeon and target rifle shooting. Middle and upper class men dominated these sports, but several immigrant groups also participated, especially in riflery. Women were active in archery associations, and a few even joined shooting clubs. By the 1870s regional, national, and international tournaments heightened public interest in these field sports.

After the Civil War archery became a favorite pastime of the more privileged classes in the United States. Gentlemen and ladies founded dozens (perhaps even hundreds) of clubs. The names of these organizations reflected the prevailing view of the twin origins of the sport—English and native American Indian. Some associations honored the English heritage with names such as Robin Hood, Sherwood, Nottingham, and Toxophilites, while others paid homage to indigenous peoples with titles such as Tamenend, Pequosset, Oritani, and Analostan. Henry C. Carver and Albert G. Spalding of Chicago and several of their friends took the initiative in calling for a national governing body, the National Archery Association of the United States, which they founded in 1879. This chapter begins with the Constitution and Rules of that organization. Its first tournament (which featured a premier band and refreshments) was held on the baseball field of the Chicago White Stockings. The next year the event moved to the private estate of Franklin Sidway of Buffalo on an island in the Niagara River.

Women played an active role in archery clubs, and they were included in the championship competition of the National Archery Association. The new rules included a special "Columbia Round" for ladies which required that they shoot fewer arrows over shorter distances than the males, perhaps out of fear that the men's regulations would prove too tiring for females. They were also handicapped by their costumes, which included constricted corsets, skin-tight sleeves, and several layers of skirts supported by wires.

Pigeon shooting had long been a popular amusement among upper class gentlemen in North America, and after 1865 it experienced a new round of growth. The New York Sportsmen's Club had pioneered the modernization of this sport by drawing up a code of rules, which was widely adopted by other groups in the northeastern United States. This chapter includes a new set of regulations for trap shooting established by the Rhode Island Sportsman's Club. During these years pigeon shooting came under attack by activists fighting for animal rights. Henry Bergh, founder and president of the

American Society for the Prevention of Cruelty to Animals (ASPCA), launched a crusade against the sport in 1869. He invoked a state anticruelty law and a city ordinance to stop a match in New York City. Several sportsmen responded by arguing that they had done more than any other group to protect and preserve wild game. They also countered with threats to challenge Bergh in court if he persisted in his efforts to interfere with their pastime. Although apparently Bergh did moderate his efforts against pigeon shooting, his letter of 1875 to James Gordon Bennett of the New York Herald suggests that he continued to view the sport as inhumane.

Target rifle shooting was less costly, more humane, and more popular than pigeon shooting. The Civil War naturally intensified interest in riflery through men's service in militia companies and the army. After the war there were three types of rifle clubs in both the United States and Canada. The first was the private organization whose members shot on their own property. The second was the target company, which seems to have evolved from the tradition of military training days. Most prevalent in New York and New Jersey, it typically met only once a year, and its annual event combined marksmanship with socializing that featured marching bands and much food and drink. Promoted and financed by local political organizations, it usually recruited men from a broad spectrum of a city's social strata, with large numbers from the artisan and middle classes. Ethnic associations constituted the third category of shooting clubs. Swiss and especially German immigrants brought to North America a love of the sport, and during this period they founded numerous clubs and held annual festivals. German *Schutzen* organizations flourished wherever there were large concentrations of German newcomers, particularly in New York City, Newark, Buffalo, Cincinnati, Chicago, Milwaukee, St. Louis, and San Francisco. Most sponsored elaborate *Schutzenfestes*, which normally featured a parade, a dinner, displays of sharpshooting, special contests for women who shot lances swinging on wires, and songs, rides, and lottery booths for the entertainment of families.

1871 brought the first move towards national organization of riflery with the creation of the first version of the National Rifle Association. Colonel William Conant Church of the Army and Navy Journal and George Wood Wingate, a New York City lawyer, pioneered this body. Their founding of this society apparently stemmed from their concern over a bloody riot between Irish and Protestant paraders, which killed fifty people. Wingate played a major role in training National Guard officers and in supervising construction of the NRA's new range at Creedmoor, Long Island.

The 1870s also witnessed a series of major international shooting tournaments. New York's newly organized Amateur Rifle Club accepted a challenge from the Irish champions of a great match at Wimbledon, England. The final selection in this chapter presents Arthur B. Leech's account of the Irish riflemen's visit to North America, which ended with a dramatic victory by the New Yorkers. An American delegation won a return match in Ireland in 1875, and in the following year the Amateur Club and the National Rifle Association sponsored a Centennial tournament at Creedmoor. Once again the United States team prevailed, defeating squads from Ireland, Scotland, Australia, and Canada.

The success of the New Yorkers in these challenges did generate some ill will between easterners and their counterparts in the West and South. Journalists and sharpshooters from those regions were especially annoyed when eastern gentlemen claimed superiority. Hunters wrote semi-literate letters to the press in which they expressed their disdain for the Creedmoor crowd. A New Orleans team refused to give permission to its (and perhaps the South's) best long-range shot to participate in the Centennial match.

These special events helped to increase interest in shooting, and as of 1880 the sport had broadened its base of support beyond aristocrats and hunters. Many churches set up rifle ranges in their basements for use by both sexes. Ladies also shot at fairs, and several cities had all-women clubs. College students at Harvard, Yale, Columbia, and several other institutions founded rifle clubs and requested training from local militia officers. Riflery had attained a degree of respectability and popularity in all regions and among a wide range of social classes.

ARCHERY

CONSTITUTION AND RULES OF THE NATIONAL ARCHERY ASSOCIATION OF THE UNITED STATES OF AMERICA, 1879

At Crawfordsville, Illinois on 23 January 1879, eight clubs representing communities in Illinois, Indiana, Iowa, Pennsylvania, New York, and Wisconsin founded the National Archery Association of the United States. The following charter and rules of that organization are reprinted from Horsman dolls, inc., *Book of Instruction in Archery* (N.Y., 1879), pp. 23-30.

ARTCLE I.

Name.

The Association shall be called THE NATIONAL ARCHERY ASSOCIATION.

ARTICLE II.

Objects.

The objects of this association are:

To encourage, foster, and promote the practice of Archery in the United States of America.

To associate under one general management and head the various Archery societies of the United States, and encourage frequent competitions between them, and to enact and enforce proper rules governing their meetings.

To promote and facilitate acquaintance and social intercourse between lovers of this noble pastime, wherever resident.

To establish and regulate the "Archery Championship of the United States of America."

ARTICLE III.

Membership.

This Association shall be composed of the following Archery societies, viz:

The Wabash Merry Bowmen,	of Crawfordsville, Ind.
The Chicago Archery Association,	" Chicago, Ill.
The Kokomo Archers,	" Kokomo, Ind.
The Highland Park Archery Club,	" Highland Park, Ill.
The Toxophilites,	" Des Moines, Iowa.
The Nottingham Archers,	" Pittsburgh, Pa.
The Buffalo Toxophilites,	" Buffalo N. Y.
The Robin Hood Archery Club,	" De Pere, Wis.

and such other societies as may, from time to time, be elected to membership.

All societies formed for the purpose of practising Archery and acquiring proficiency in the use of the Long-Bow, regularly officered and located in the United States of America, shall be eligible to membership, which may be secured in the following manner to wit:

1st. By making application in writing to the Corresponding Secretary of this Association at least ten days before its annual business meeting.

The application must be signed by the President and Secretary of the society so applying, and state the name of the society, its location, date of organization and number of members, and must be accompanied by a pledge to abide by and be governed by the rules of the National Archery Association.

This application shall be voted upon at the annual business meeting by written ballots marked "For" or "Against." Two ballots "Against" shall be sufficient to exclude this applicant.

2d. Or by making written application, as above, at any time after the adjournment of the annual business meeting and before the first day of July, following, to the Corresponding Secretary of this Association, who shall at once communicate such application to all the societies composing this Association, each of which shall, within ten days from the date of the Secretary's letter, transmit to this Association one ballot "For" or "Against" the applicant; and if two ballots "Against" be not cast, the Secretary shall, upon receipt of the initiation fee, issue to such applicant a certificate of membership....

ARTICLE VIII.

Grand Annual Meeting.

A national meeting for competitive target practice with the long-bow, to be known as "The Grand Annual Meeting of The National Archery Association of the United States of America," shall be held each year, between the first day of July and the last day of August, and shall continue during three consecutive days.

The place where such a meeting shall be held shall be decided by ballot at the previous annual business meeting.

At the Grand Annual Meeting, in addition to the "National Medals," the Association shall offer suitable cash and other prizes, and any special prizes which may be contributed by members or others, to be competed for only by members of this Association, and in accordance with a programme to be arranged and issued by the Executive Committee on or before the first day of May.

The shooting shall be governed by the following rules, viz:

The President of the Association shall be the "Field Captain." He shall have entire control of the ranges, targets and order of shooting, and he shall appoint a "Target Captain" for each target, who shall direct the order of shooting at his target.

Each "Target Captain" shall appoint a "Scorer" and a "Herald" to act at his target. The "Scorer" shall keep a record of each arrow shot, upon blanks provided for the purpose by the Association. The "Herald" shall announce the result of each shot.

An arrow must remain in the target until the "hit" is recorded, otherwise the "hit" shall not be counted.

The targets shall be four feet in diameter, and placed on easels, the center of the "gold" being four feet from the ground.

The "gold" shall be 9 6-10 inches in diameter, and each ring shall be 4 8-10 inches in width.

The value of colors shall be: gold, 9; red, 7; blue, 5; black, 3; white, 1.

In case an arrow cuts two colors it shall count as having hit the inner one.

All disputes shall be referred for decision to the Captain of the target where they arise.

Every society, a member of this Association, shall adopt a "society color," and provide for its members a uniform badge, of a size not less than two inches in diameter, from which shall depend a ribbon of the color adopted, and no Archer shall be permitted to shoot, at any Grand Annual Meeting, unless he wear such badge upon his left breast.

Every Archer shall shoot with arrows bearing his distinctive mark, and every arrow leaving the bow shall be deemed as having been shot, unless the Archer can reach it with his bow while standing inside the line from which he is shooting.

No person, unless competing for prizes, shall be allowed within the bounds of the Archers' grounds during the progress of the shooting.

ARTICLE IX.

Rounds and Distances.

Matches between members of this Association shall not be considered as being shot, under the rules of The National Archery Association, unless they be shot at one of the following "rounds," each Archer shooting three arrows at an end:

The "York Round," consisting of-

72 arrows at 100 yards.
48 arrows at 80 yards.
24 " " 60 "
—
144 arrows.

The "American Round," consisting of-

30 arrows at 60 yards.
30 " " 50 "
30 " " 40 "
—
90 arrows.

The "Columbia Round" (for ladies), consisting of-

24 arrows at 50 yards.
24 " " 40 "
24 " " 30 "
—
72 arrows.

ARTICLE X.

Archery Championship.

This Association shall establish the "Archery Championship of the United States of America," which shall be represented by suitable champion and championess medals, to be contested for at each Grand Annual Meeting by members of this Association only, and under the following rules, viz:

The champion medal shall be awarded to the individual making the highest aggregate score at the "Double York Round," consisting of-

144 arrows at 100 yards.
96 " " 80 "
48 " " 60 "

Each Archer shooting three arrows at an end.

The championess medal shall be awarded to the individual lady member making the highest aggregate score at the "Double Columbia Round," consisting of-

48 arrows at 50 yards.
48 " " 40 "
48 " " 30 "

Each Archer shooting three arrows at an end.

The shooting for these medals shall commence on the opening day of each Grand Annual Meeting, and be concluded in its course, in accordance with the programme of the meeting.

The National Medals shall be presented to the winners by the President of the Association immediately after the official declaration of the completed scores and shall remain in their custody until fifteen days prior to the next Grand Annual Meeting, when they shall return them to the President of the Association to be competed for as before.

Should any person win the National Medal at each of two consecutive Grand Annual Meetings, the same shall become his (or her) property.

Winners of each day's prizes, in the competition for the National Medals, shall have the following percentages deducted from all scores made by them in shooting on the same day for any other money or special prizes, viz:

Winners of First Prizes,		30 per cent.
" Second	"	25 "
" Third	"	20 "
" Fourth	"	15 "
" Fifth	"	10 "
" Sixth	"	5 "

ARTICLE XI.

Amendment of Constitution and Rules.

This Constitution may be altered or amended only at the annual business meeting of the Association, and by two-thirds majority of the delegates present.

PIGEON SHOOTING

RULES OF THE RHODE ISLAND SPORTSMAN'S CLUB FOR TRAP SHOOTING 1872

In 1872 the American Pigeon Shooting Championship was determined by the new rules of the Rhode Island Sportsman's Club, in place of the old rules of trap shooting adopted by the New York Sportsman's Club. The winner was also honored by receiving a gold badge. By the regulations governing the championship, the holder of the badge was obliged to shoot any challenger for a sum not less than $500 a side, within four months from the date of the challenge, under penalty of forfeiting the badge. If the holder defended his title successfully for a period of two years he could keep the gold badge. These rules are reprinted from The New York Clipper, 30 April 1872, p. 30.

RULE 1. *Traps Rise and Bounds.*—All matches shall be shot from H and T ground traps, the choice of which the referee shall decide by toss.

The boundaries shall be eighty (80) yards for single birds, which, in single bird shooting, shall be measured from a point equi-distant from and in a direct line between the two traps, and in double bird shooting, from a point equi-distant from and in a direct line between the centre traps.

2. *Placing the Traps.*—In single bird shooting, the distance between the traps shall be four yards; in double bird shooting, as four traps are used, the H and T traps shall be set alternately, and two yards apart.

3. *Scoring.*—After the party is at the score and ready to shoot, he shall take the bird or birds, unless barred by the referee.

The party at the score must not leave it to shoot, and must hold the butt of his gun below his elbow until the bird or birds rise, and in case of infraction of this provision, the bird or birds shall be scored as missed.

4. *Rising of Birds.*—All birds must be on the wing when shot at; all contingencies of miss fire, non-explosion of caps, gun not cocked, etc., are at the risk of the party shooting.

5. *Recovering Birds.*—It shall be optional with the party shooting to recover his own birds, or appoint a person for that purpose.

In all cases the bird shall be gathered by hand, without the use of extraneous means, within three minutes from the time it alights, or be scored a miss. A bird once out of bounds shall be scored a miss.

6. *Loading.*—The charge of shot shall not exceed one ounce and a half (1 1/2oz). All guns shall be loaded from the same charger, except in case of breech loaders, when the referee may open one or more cartridges to ascertain if the charge of shot is correct. Any person infringing this rule shall lose the match.

7. *Ties.*—In case of a tie at single birds, the distance shall be increased five yards, and shall be shot off at five birds each. In case of a second tie, the distance shall again be increased five yards, and this distance shall be maintained until the match is decided. The ties in double bird shooting shall be shot off at twenty one yards without any increase, at five double rises.

8. *Judges and Referee.*—Two judges and a referee shall be appointed before the shooting commences. The referee's decision shall be final. He shall have power to call "No Bird," in case any birds fail to fly, and may allow a contestant another bird, in case the latter shall have been balked or interfered with, or may for any reason satisfactory to the referee be entitled to it.

In case of any unnecessary delay on the part of either of the contestants the referee shall order the party so delaying to the score, and in case of his failing to comply within five minutes said party shall lose the match.

If a bird shall fly towards parties within the bounds, in such a manner that to shoot at it would endanger any person, another bird will be allowed; and if any bird is shot at by any person beside the party at the score, the referee shall decide how it shall be scored, or whether a new bird shall be allowed.

LETTER PROTESTING PIGEON SHOOTING

In the following letter Henry Bergh, President of the American Society for the Prevention of Cruelty to Animals, expresses his objections to the sport of pigeon shooting. These words were addressed to James Gordon Bennett, affluent publisher of the New York Herald and one of the most prominent sportsmen in the United States. Bennett refused to print this piece, but in his reply to Bergh he did state that he would have published it if it had not contained personal references to himself. This letter first appeared in the ASPCA'S *Tenth Annual Report* (New York, 1876), pp. 10-12.

New York, September 30, 1875

James Gordon Bennett, Esq.:

Sir: The relation you bear to the public, as proprietor of a widely circulating journal, is the excuse I have for intruding myself on your notice. As such, I am sure that you will agree with me that your moral responsibility surpasses that of ordinary men. Through the columns of your paper, as well as by the personal example which you exhibit to the world as its representative, you largely influence public sentiment and shape the action, for good or evil, of old and young. Whether you do this in the interest of our country's moral and material progress, when you sanction and promote by your position, wealth and active participation, the useless slaughter and mutilation of innocent animals, is the purpose of this communication. I assume that you will not deny the postulate, that all living creatures are endowed with the right to live, so long as they do not, by reason of their acts or hurtful presence, forfeit that right. To do otherwise would be to question Divine wisdom and authority. Now let us suppose a case. It is that of a bird, which has already been captured by your artifice or skill. It is not only harmless, but by reason of its beauty, innocence and helplessness, appeals most touchingly to your pity, justice and humanity. You are a practical marksman, and you require, perhaps, recreation or demand relief from wasting *ennui*. The arms which minister to your passion for the chase, are of the richest and most approved quality; the day is fine, and the fields and groves are melodious with the songs of happy feathered creatures. Suddenly, you experience the strange desire to kill; to destroy the hapless being in your power, and disfigure the scene which lies like a dream of Paradise before you.

You are not alone—friends and admirers of your accuracy of aim are with you, and among them—horribly out of place—fair women are also seen! Your servants place the unresisting animal in a trap, and the life which God gave for the profit and support of our race, awaits its unrequited sacrifice.

Now let us imagine for a moment, that this unoffending little being is suddenly endowed with speech. Might not its language be somewhat like the following?

"I am wholly in your power; you will not pretend that I have ever harmed you, or that there exists any natural or legitimate reason for my destruction. The sphere in which I moved was assigned to me by the same Allwise Being who made you, and so bountifully endowed you with wealth, reason, and all the material possessions of this world. I was betrayed into captivity while seeking to provide nourishment for my little family, now dead of starvation.

"You are about to immolate me upon the blood-stained altar of inglorious rivalry, and what will you gain by the crashing of my delicate limbs, and ruptured arteries, that a senseless target would not afford you? If, however this little body, so cunningly and so mysteriously contrived by its Creator, be necessary to your reasonable benefit—if the brief existence which it inherits, be required for any purpose which religion and human policy condemn not—take it, it is yours; but offend not its author, nor insult the cultivated spirit of your generation, by a deed which your own conscience on reflection will characterize, but which I refrain from doing."

Thus, I say, might the unoffending little creature address you, and what answer could you make? None, absolutely none; nor could the combined intellect and learning of the world, controvert the argument of the tiny pleader awaiting your irresistible fiat.

If you have favored me with your attention thus far, permit me to claim you indulgence for a moment longer. Believing, perhaps, in the harmlessness of your views touching the subject, to which I have ventured to invite your consideration; I learn that you have drawn from your abundant resources, the tempting offer of $10,000, to him who will *kill* or disable the greatest number of pigeons on a certain day. To me there is always something indescribably sorrowful in the word "kill." I lay claim to no exceptional delicacy or humanity, but that little word seems to me, to embrace within its single syllable, a more startling and portentous meaning, than all the rest in our language. That the taking of life is a acquired necessity of our civilization, I regretfully admit; all I urge is, that it be rendered as just and merciful as it is necessary. In a recent narrative of a pigeon match, which appeared in the *Herald,* the word "kill" I found was repeated one hundred times! I beg that you will not regard me as either disrespectful or censorious, for I mean neither. I believe that patriotism, and morality, require of every citizen, the exercise of his powers to advance the general prosperity of his country; and to no other, in my opinion has been confided is so great a degree, the elements of so doing as to yourself. To the famous journal founded by the wisdom and sagacity of your late father millions of people look annually for precept, example and advice, and when they read in your fair columns, your sanction of betting, and unnecessary mutilation and killing of unoffending animals, can you consistently rebuke the demoralization of the age in which you live, and exercise so commanding an influence.

I am your obedient servant,
HENRY BERGH, President

RIFLE SHOOTING

INTERNATIONAL RIFLE MATCH: UNITED STATES VS. IRELAND, 1874

When the Amateur Rifle Club of New York accepted the challenge of the Irish champions for a match in 1874, the members agreed to shoot at distances far greater than their normal range. The contest required new weapons for the American side, which were provided by the Remington and Sharps arms companies. Those organizations also put up the five hundred dollar stake which had been promised by the Amateur Club. Thus the great international rifle challenge pitted not only America versus Ireland, but also the U.S. machine-made breechloader weapon against the handmade muzzleloader of Europe. This narrative is from Arthur B. Leech, *Irish Riflemen in America* (N.Y., 1875), pp. 47-49, 57-67.

THE CREEDMOOR CONTEST.

Plan showing the scene of the International Shooting Match between the Irish and American teams.

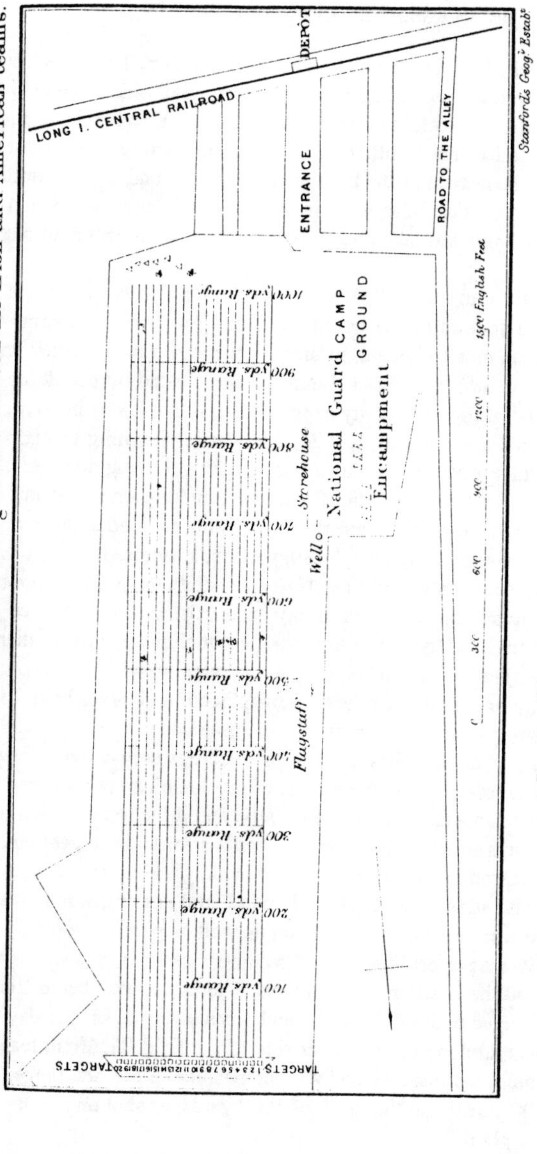

TARGETS 1 2 3 4 5 6 7 8 9 10 11 12 13 14 15 16 17 18 19 20 TARGETS
100 yds. Range
200 yds. Range
300 yds. Range
400 yds. Range
500 yds. Range
600 yds. Range
700 yds. Range
800 yds. Range
900 yds. Range
1000 yds. Range
Flagstaff
Well
Storehouse
National Guard Encampment
CAMP GROUND
ENTRANCE
DEPÔT
LONG I. CENTRAL RAILROAD
ROAD TO THE ALLEY
0 300 600 900 1200 1500 English Feet
Stanford's Geog.l Estab.t

London: Edward Stanford, 55. Charing Cross, S.W.

IRISH RIFLEMEN IN AMERICA

The great International Match itself now claims our attention. This match was at once the most novel as well as interesting meeting of the kind which had ever been proposed. It was a meeting between the champions of America and Ireland, the two countries which profess to like one another best; nor is this merely a profession, for not only does Ireland, as the nearest of the European countries, send a large contingent across the Atlantic, but other causes also have arisen, in consequence of which a large and flourishing Irish population has taken deep root, and become in fact naturalized in America.

I had heard much of the danger of allowing myself and my party to become associated with any political section of the community in New York; and some well-intentioned people gave me much advice as to the proper method of procedure and my choice of associates. I was informed that I should be surrounded by people desirous of making political capital of myself and my expedition, and that it was impossible for me to avoid being exposed to such danger. Well, this was all alarming enough, especially as I was engaged in a purely philanthropic undertaking, having no other objects to attain than success for my team, or rather for Ireland, and the improvement of the friendly relations already existing between the two countries. Under these circumstances, while willing to attend to any friendly suggestion, I ventured to think that the object which took me to America was not calculated to excite the political prejudices of any class, but rather to soothe asperities, if any such existed, and to induce good-will. Thus I relied upon my countrymen in America (although it was against them that I was particularly warned) to protect and support an undertaking which was conceived in the friendliest spirit. Nor was this confidence misplaced; and never have I felt so proud of being an Irishman as since my return from America.

In giving an account of the matches and the proceedings connected therewith, I shall quote somewhat extensively from the reports of my American press friends, who were so kind to the Irish team and to myself personally; and if the reproduction of their quaint and original remarks in my unpretending records affords these gentlemen any satisfaction, I shall be pleased indeed. From our first landing and up to the hour of our departure, our movements were indefatigably attended, and nothing was left undone to make us feel that we were for the time national as well as popular guests.

The annexed plan gives a perfect idea of the Creedmoor grounds, and shows clearly the number of ranges and the position of the targets. The targets numbered from 1 to 14, are employed for ranges under 600 yards, and were not used on the day of the match. The shooting was all done on the upper side of the field. The Irish team used targets 16 and 17, and the Americans, 19 and 20. The position of the first range, of 800 yards; the second, of 900 yards; and the third, of 1000 yards, as shot on the day of the match, are shown in the plan.

The first look at the Creedmoor Rifle Ranges, on the 18th of September, was by no means encouraging. The weather on that day reminded me so much of the damp days of our own dear "Green Isle," on many of which I had seen our Irish champions, undeterred by the elements, competing at the North Bull Ranges, that I almost wished the match had taken place there and then. I venture—not ill-naturedly, of course—to say that if this had been the case, the Irish team would have been "at home" and the Americans "at sea." The 'New York Sun' describes this first visit as a "thoroughly Hibernian feat." Starting, as they did, to see Creedmoor and not seeing it, "I guess" the Americans who went with them "were in the same boat," and as strongly objected to plod through "pulpy mud" as their Irish friends, while they were equally unable to see through blinding torrents of rain....

I now come to the description of the match itself, and as that has been so admirably described by the American Press, I prefer giving extracts from their reports to entering upon any labored disquisition of my own. But first of all I must bear my testimony to the excellence of the arrangements in every way to the attention and kindness shown to the visitors and to the abundant hospitality extended to us all.

In the words of the 'American Sportsman,' "the targets had been admirably arranged, Nos. 19 and 20 being grouped into one brace, and Nos. 16 and 17 into another. No. 18 being omitted, left a break which easily allowed the distinctness of targets to be observed. Colonel Wingate, the captain of the American team, took charge of the preliminary arrangements. Two gentlemen, one from each party, were sent down to the butts to sit there and see that the markers did their duty and at once decide upon any disputed shot; a pair sat at each target, and their weary duties were most admirably performed. Besides these a gentleman from each side was put at each target as a 'spotter.' Armed with a good glass, these kept a keen watch upon the target and decided whether the shots had been correctly signalled. Scorers were appointed, one from each side for each target, whereby duplicate sets of scores were received, which were compared at the close of the shooting. Major Leech, who had won the choice of target, chose Nos. 16 and 17, the Americans taking the right-hand group. On target 16, Messrs. Rigby, Walker, and Hamilton were stationed; on No. 17, Messrs. Millner, Wilson, and Johnson. The Americans were divided into Sharpe and Remington riflemen; the Sharpe men, Yale, Hepburn, Gildersleeve, and Dakin taking target No. 20; while Hepburn, Bodin, and Fulton took No. 19. This was the arrangement at the opening of the shooting. When the call was given to open, the wind was almost at a lull, and throughout the day, although the vane pointed at different hours in directly contrary directions, the wind was not strong enough to require any but the most delicate manipulation of the wind gauges.

"The light was excellent, and the targets scarcely looked half their distance away. The people were admirably behaved from the first to the last, and the services of the police, captain and officers, who had been brought up from New York to the range, were not once called into active play to regulate any boisterous or riotous demonstration. The shooting at the first range occupied over an hour and a half. The shooting went steadily on without a break or a flaw, a machine-like precision governed the raising and lowering of the marking discs, and without a grumble or hint of dissatisfaction the 800 yards range closed, and the footing up showed 326 for the Americans, and 317 for the Irish. Lunch was then the order of the hour, the crowd at large pouring away to the booths and refreshment stands, while the shooters, the ladies of the Irish and American parties, and prominent citizens and press-men, assembled in a large tent, where a fine collation had been provided.

"After lunch, a surprise was awaiting both teams in a courteous act of generosity by Major Leech, who, rising in his place, said that he had resolved to afford himself the opportunity of discharging a further duty, and it would have been particularly gratifying to him if the occasion had been more public. When the Irish team came to this great country they naturally expected that they would be received with a great deal of courtesy and kind attention, but he would say that if they had the one-twentieth part of the hospitality extended to them, it would have been far in excess of what they anticipated. On behalf of the Irish riflemen he would say that they were deeply sensible of and greatly impressed with the kindness and consideration shown them on the occasion of their visit to America. (Applause.) The result of the match—while both sides were of course anxious to win—he held to be of complete insignificance, as weighed with the circumstances of their visit in making acquaintances and meeting their countrymen on this side of the Atlantic. (Applause.) He would like under the circumstances to leave his friends in America a little souvenir of the visit of the Irish team, to be shot for on any terms that might be deemed advisable. (Here Major Leech uncovered a beautiful silver pitcher, exquisitely worked and surmounted by a little silver tower, representative of the famous old towers of Ireland.) He went on to say that it was made of Irish silver and wrought in Ireland. It was as Irish as the rifles they shot with and the hearts that beat in the bosoms of the marksmen. It was indeed racy of the soil. He begged the Amateur Rifle Club to accept it, with his goodwill, and he would take the liberty of reading the inscription: 'Presented for competition to the riflemen of America, by Arthur Blennerhassett Leech, Captain of the International Team of Riflemen, on the occasion of their visit to New York, 1874.' (Cheers.) The blank space remained for themselves to fill up, and he hoped that the best would win it. (Applause.) He trusted that in times to come they would have the opportunity of meeting frequently under the same happy circumstances as now marked the visit of the Irish riflemen. (Applause.)

"The Irish vase is a fine affair in hammered silver, the sides being covered with varied clusters of roses and shamrocks in bas-relief, the inscription above quoted being enclosed in a wreath of flowers; the whole height of the affair, with the stand, is about fifteen inches.

"Colonel Wingate responded in acknowledgment of the acceptance of this gift by the American riflemen. He said it gave him great pleasure, on behalf of the Amateur Rifle Club, to accept the very handsome present which had been so graciously tendered. He was not wholly unprepared for something of the kind, but he nevertheless found himself at a loss to give expression to his thanks in view of the beautiful souvenir which had just been tendered. When the match was first arranged, the American team had never calculated on anything more than a creditable display on their own part and such as would encourage future contests; but they were determined, even if they did not succeed, that Americans would not be surpassed in courtesy, hospitality, and kindness. (Applause.) He regretted to say that he now found himself making a speech, for he had two speeches ready—one to deliver in case the American riflemen won, and the other in case they lost (laughter)—and he was afraid if he proceeded much further he would spoil both of them. Whatever might be the result of the contest, he was certain it would establish more friendly relationship among the two teams. He concluded by assuring the party that when they left America their memories would be kept fresh and green in the hearts of their competitors. (Applause.)

"Colonel Wingate was then formally decorated by Major Leech with a personal medal, and amid cheers the party emerged into the open field."

The kindness that dictated this report speaks for itself, and requires no remarks from me.

I quote the description of the shooting at the 900 and 1000 yards ranges from the 'World,' Sept. 27:

"These little civilities were soon over, and with reciprocal cheers the riflemen again returned to the work before the targets at 900 yards. Here the two parties brought themselves down to work in dead earnest, the Irishmen to wipe out the balance of nine points against them, and the Americans to raise their advantage as high as their skill would permit. Here the Irishmen seemed to be the superior, and at the announcement of the result of the fifteen shots, it was seen that the Irish had made 312 points, while the Americans had scored but 310. Both sets of men had fallen away, but the visitors seemed best able to overcome the difficulties of this medium and awkward range. Their gain of two points still left them seven points behind at the aggregate score, but the 1000 yards range still remained, and at this distance the Irish were confessedly superior. The spirits of the Irish backers were raised, and at the same time the determination of the American riflemen to win, or die game. The Irish riflemen themselves, however, did not seem so sanguine. From the very start, or at least as soon as it was known that they were some points behind, they seemed to shoot with a sullen display of grit. They consulted one with another in whispers, and went to and from the firing-rug without a glance or outward notice of the immense throng present. Large beads of perspiration stood out upon their foreheads, and at every instant's grace from loading or firing they dodged under the umbrellas with which they were provided. With the prospect of a stern chase, and to them an uncomfortably hot day, they were under a load which even their superior science and long experience could not remove. The fight, however, was a desperate one. Slowly they stretched themselves along the ground, steadily they took aim, care and deliberation marked every step, and that they were doing their very best is evidenced in the fact that by their own admissions they had never surpassed their record of yesterday. The excellence of one team seemed to inoculate the other with the fever of luck and skill, and while the Americans forged ahead until at one stage in the match they were fourteen points ahead, the Irishmen closed the gap, and at their finish, which occurred several shots before their rivals, it was actually found that they were ahead. Then came the critical moment of the whole day's sport. The Irishmen had done their work—had placed themselves upon the record beyond possibility of change, and the Americans had yet several shots to make. Lieutenant Fulton asked to know the opposite score before firing his last shot, and as a consequence of his anxiety and worry made a center, leaving the Irishmen one point ahead. Only the few scorers and counters were aware of this. In the rapidity of the closing shots the crowd had lost track of the course of things, and it was not generally known that the Americans were behind. Had it been so it is not likely that the excitement would have run so high as to destroy the steadiness of the one American upon whom the national chances now depended. Colonel Bodine had not yet shot. If he missed this his last trial, the Americans lost the prize by but one point. If he made a 'bull's-eye' four would be added to their aggregate, and their opponents would be left three points in the rear. Knowing this, and with the blood running across his hand from a wound received from a broken ginger-ale bottle a few moments before, Colonel Bodine stretched himself carefully out, grasped his familiar weapon with a firm hand, and taking a long, steady aim, fired. The crowd stood, not one moved, several thousand pair of eyes fixed upon one little point a half mile off, looking for the metal disc which indicates the opening of the trap for the marking of a shot. 'There it is!' cried one; and in a second more the white bull's-eye disc came slowly up, as if from a weary marker's hand, and rested plainly before the bull's-eye, covering its blackness from the gladdened eyes of at least half the crowd. No sooner had the mere edge of the disc appeared than such a shout went up as notified to all those on the range that the match was over. No need of asking who had won—the character of the cry told it at once. Everybody looked upon Colonel Bodine as in some measure the saviour of the national honor, when in fact he had simply fired, by mere chance, the closing shot. Had it not been for the almost marvelously perfect score of the leading American shot, the Americans must have been beaten, not badly, but as well and as completely as they are now the vanquishers. One of the usual blunders, which accompany rifle shooting, attended General Akin, of the American side. In his fourth shot at 900 yards the cartridge happened to be defective from a hidden flaw in the composition of the bullet. The instant it left the rifle's mouth the fact was patent in the wabbling flight and different sound of the 'whistle' made by the missile in its passage through the air. The number of outers also points out the general degree of perfection attained by the contestants. The whole six Irishmen in a total of 270 shots made but five outers and six missed, while the Americans out of the same number of shots have recorded ten outers and six misses. The prediction of the 'World' that the Irishmen were the better marksmen at 1000 yards is verified in the result. Starting at that range with seven odds against them, they closed up and ran one ahead just before the close. It is fair to assume that those making the best score at 1000 yards are the superior riflemen, and are able to do equally good work at 800 and 900 yards. The Irish yesterday actually beat the American team at the most difficult range. They did not prove equally successful at the lesser distances. Had the day been a cool, cloudy day, with more wind, the victory would not have been so cheaply won. At one time, when for a few moments a cloud covered the targets, the shots made were a succession of bull's-eyes. Though the Americans are victorious on a show of totals, the Irish really accomplished the finest feats of marksmanship. As soon as the day's work was over a few moments' examination of the score tickets served to convince Major Leech that no error had been made in the computations. The winning team were then called together and addressed by Mr. Leech, in the presentation of novel badges. These were the emblems described in the 'World' some days ago as intended for the winning riflemen. In a few words the Lady Massereene was introduced, and by her hands were the several badges attached to the breasts of the several winners. Cheers for one and the other, cheers for the Irish and cheers for the home team with an extra round for General Shaler, who had filled the honorary office of umpire during the day, and a general rush was made for the homewardbound cars. Here a most unfortunate miscalculation had occurred, and a three hours' ride, at a snail's pace, in crowded, dark, and creaking cars over the thirteen miles between Creedmoor and the city, was the finish of an excellent afternoon's enjoyment. One man was seriously injured in grasping too eagerly and recklessly for a place on the cars. As showing the closeness of the two teams to each other, the following table, indicating their relative standing at the conclusion of each five shots, is given:

Yards.	Rounds.	Irish Total.	American Total.	Difference.
	5	100	106	6
800	10	206	215	9
	15	317	326	9
	20	413	427	14
900	25	527	535	8
	30	629	636	7
	35	732	734	2
1000	40	831	838	7
	45	931	934	3

Chapter 11

FOOTBALL

During the 1860s and 1870s several versions of football competed for supremacy among school boys, college men, and young adults in both Canada and the United States. Every fall some players enjoyed early forms of rugby and soccer imported from England, while others preferred a variety of traditional kicking games which had long been popular in a number of North American towns and cities. By 1880 no type had clearly emerged as the dominant game in Canada, but by that year a new code of rules drafted by the Intercollegiate Football Association had gained a decided advantage over rival versions in the United States. College matches featuring teams from Harvard, Yale, Princeton, and other prestigious eastern colleges became exciting spectacles for both students and the general public. During this period football joined baseball and crew as popular commercialized team sports.

During the early 1860s both the disruptions of the Civil War and the opposition of college administrations curtailed football playing in the United States. Although the war took young men away from their traditional pastimes, it could not entirely wipe out a sport whose combative characteristics were so well suited to the martial arts. The "Football Rules" of 1864 reprinted below describe an active, kicking game popular among young men in the New York city vicinity. But in the colleges the effects of the war and especially the prohibitions imposed by Harvard and other institutions halted the traditional spirited interclass matches.

In the United States college athletics in general and football in particular developed out of students' disenchantment with the rigid curriculum and the regimentation imposed by their institutions prior to the Civil War. Clergymen still dominated the administrations, and they strictly applied the policy of *in loco parentis*. College officers and professors banned drinking, smoking, dancing, card playing, and absence from the campus without permission. They also required students to attend chapel services and study halls.

Students reacted in both negative and positive ways. Rebellions ranged from stamping feet in recitation rooms to throwing rocks or sticks through windows to disrupting religious exercises. A few angry undergraduates even assaulted administrators or tried to burn down the college. But more constructive students created a variety of extracurricular activities, including fraternities, newspapers and magazines, literary, debating, and musical societies, and political, religious, and cultural clubs.

For those who were athletically inclined, sports provided an excellent outlet for the frustrations and tensions of college life. Interclass battles, played out as early forms of football, were extremely popular. College students tended to favor team sports like crew, cricket, baseball, and football over individual competitions because they better served their need for communal rituals. Shortly after the Civil War, group athletics began to dominate the extracurriculum and threatened to overshadow athletics.

Intercollegiate football began in the United States on November 6, 1869, when a contingent of Princeton players journeyed to New Brunswick to test their skill and strength against the Rutgers team. The Princeton captain, William S. Gummere, graciously agreed to virtually all of the rules proposed by the Rutgers captain, William Leggett. These regulations resembled the code for the game of association football, later known as soccer. The teams had twenty-five men on a side who could kick or bat the round, inflated ball with their hands or fists. The field's dimensions were 360 feet by 225 feet, with goals at each end eight paces wide. Tripping and holding were prohibited, and victory went to the first team to score six goals. Rutgers won this inaugural contest, 6-4. One week later the Rutgers players traveled to Princeton for the second contest. But this time Princeton's rules governed play, which allowed the "free kick." This meant that a player could catch the ball in the air or on the first bounce and kick it without interference by an opponent. The outcome was an easy win for the home team by a score of 8-0. The third and deciding match was never played, perhaps because of opposition by college authorities, but more likely because the contestants could not agree on a set of rules. This chapter includes several contemporary accounts of these first college games.

During the early 1870s several other eastern colleges followed the example of Rutgers and Princeton and organized teams. All except Harvard played by rules that resemble modern soccer. At Cornell Thomas Hughes, the English author of *Tom Brown's Schooldays,* played football with the students, who then organized the Cornell Football Association. In 1873 a western institution, The University of Michigan, first challenged an eastern school with a proposal to play a game against Cornell at Cleveland, mid-way between the two colleges. But Cornell's faculty opposed the game, and its President, Andrew D. White, replied to Michigan: "I will not permit 30 men to travel four hundred miles merely to agitate a bag of wind." During this period the University of Pennsylvania and Columbia University also founded teams, and football was also revived at Harvard and Yale.

Harvard played a critical role in the evolution of football, because its playing rules differed from those of the other colleges which pioneered the sport. The students who organized the Harvard University Foot Ball Club in December 1872 favored the "Boston game" which had long been popular among school boys in that city. The rules permitted any number to play on a side, although generally it was between ten and fifteen. To score a goal the football had to be kicked on a fly over the goal lines, which at first were simply on the ground at both ends of the field. After match games became common a rope was strung across supports about five feet off of the ground. The key difference between the Harvard regulations and those of the other colleges was that a player could pick up, carry, or throw the ball to a teammate, but only if he was being pursued by an opponent. He could also seize and hold or try to take the ball away from a rival contestant. But once an opponent ceased chasing the ball carrier, the latter was compelled to stop and either kick or throw the ball. Rough play (such as kicking the shins, striking, or tripping) was forbidden. Positions were "tenders" and "half tends" (for goalkeeper and defenders) and "rushers" or "forwards." The ball was round, air tight, but non-elastic. The game began with a kickoff from the center of the field. If the ball went over the sidelines the player who first got to it was entitled to a "fair-lick" (free or fair kick) from a spot in bounds anywhere on a line at right angles to the side-line and opposite to the spot where the ball went out of bounds.

While Harvard men institutionalized the beloved "Boston game" of their boyhoods, their counterparts at Yale called for a convention to meet in New York City in October 1873 to consider the formation of an intercollegiate football league and to draft a common set of rules. The Yale men sent invitations to Columbia, Harvard, Princeton, and Rutgers, but not Cornell or Michigan. Columbia chose not to attend, and Harvard declined to participate because its "Boston game" differed substantially from the rules preferred by the other colleges. As Harvard Captain Henry Grant explained in his reply to Yale: "We cannot but recognize in your game much but brute force, weight, and especially 'shin' element. Our game depends upon running, dodging, and position playing,—i.e., kicking across field into another's hands...we gave the matter a fair discussion last spring. We even went so far as to practice and try the Yale game. We gave it up at once as hopeless." In short, the Harvard men wished to keep their own sport and chose not to be in a minority position where they might be forced to accept another set of laws. With Harvard absent the delegates from Yale, Rutgers, and Princeton voted against establishing a formal league. They then adopted regulations modeled after the Yale game, an early version of soccer. Both the Harvard rules and the code adopted by the New York City intercollegiate convention are included in this chapter.

Harvard's refusal to participate in this meeting profoundly affected the development of college football in the United States. After the Cambridge men rejected the soccer rules favored by the other colleges, they experimented with the rules of rugby, which soon provided the foundation for a new version of the sport. The occasion was a series of matches in 1874 with McGill University of Montreal. McGill's captain, David Rodger, sent a challenge to Grant in which he proposed one contest to be played according to the rugby rules preferred by McGill, and another under Harvard's code. After considerable correspondence the games were scheduled for May 14th and 15th, with the first encounter to be played by Harvard's rules. About five hundred spectators appeared on Jarvis field for the first contest, which Harvard won easily, three goals to nothing. It was obvious that the McGill men had not bothered to practice the Harvard game; the rout lasted only about twenty-two minutes. The rugby match played the next day turned out to be a different story. Another large crowd witnessed a draw, as neither side was able to score either a goal or a touchdown in the three half-hour periods. The rugby regulations made a favorable impression on the Harvard players, and their good showing encouraged them to try another challenge against their Canadian rivals. In the fall they traveled to Montreal to play a return rugby match against

McGill. About 1500 fans watched the Harvard team defeat their hosts by a score of three touchdowns to none. The newspaper accounts of these games included in this chapter capture the excitement and the sportsmanship of these early international intercollegiate contests.

Harvard's successful experiment with the rules of rugby and its athletic rivalry with Yale led to efforts to bring the two colleges together on the football field in 1875. After losing to Tufts by a score of one goal to nothing in June in the first American intercollegiate rugby game, the Harvard team negotiated an agreement to play rugby against Yale. Under a set of "concessionary" rules, Yale agreed to fifteen players on a team, and Harvard gave up the right to try to kick a goal after scoring a touchdown. The clubs agreed to use a leather covered ball thirty inches in circumference and slightly pointed at the ends. In November the Cambridge students routed their rivals from New Haven, four goals and four touchdowns to nothing. Perhaps the most interested spectators who watched this first Harvard-Yale game were a number of Princeton players. Over the next year they weighed the merits of the rugby rules against their own soccer-style game.

In the fall of 1876 Princeton chose to follow the example of Harvard and Yale and to invite men from those colleges and Columbia to a convention which would adopt a standard set of rules and found a new association. Delegates from the four schools gathered in Springfield, Massachusetts in late November and agreed to play a modified version of rugby and to establish the Intercollegiate Football Association. The first constitution of this league, reprinted in this chapter, introduced the idea of an annual Thanksgiving Day game between the two leading teams of the previous year. Although Yale accepted the rugby game, it refused to join the new league because of objections over the number of players on a team and the scoring system. The rules of this new organization, reproduced in this chapter, include alterations made during the late 1870s.

A critical episode in the transformation of English rugby into American football occurred in the convention of October, 1880. At that gathering Yale's delegate, Walter Camp, proposed a radical change in the rules which allowed a team to retain possession of the ball after a player was tackled. Under the rugby regulation, when a player was downed the ball was then placed in a "scrummage." Both teams then attempted to kick the ball towards the opposition's goal. When the ball emerged from this mass of players one of them would then pick it up and run with it. Camp persuaded the other representatives to pass a rule which permitted a team to keep control of the ball after a player was tackled. According to the new regulation, there would then be a new type of "scrimmage" in which a center "snap-back" would push the ball with his foot back to a "quarterback." The new scrimmage thus replaced the chaotic scramble of the rugby "scrum," and it also made possible the development of strategy and tactical plays that became characteristic of American football within a few years. But the new rule also allowed one team to keep the ball indefinitely if it did not kick or fumble it away. The changes in rules enacted in 1880 thus mark an important transition point in the history of the sport.

This chapter ends with a report of the Thanksgiving Day game between Princeton and Yale in 1880. That document shows how far American football had progressed in a decade. It had become the premier intercollegiate sporting spectacle for college students, upper class enthusiasts, and the sporting crowd of the major eastern cities.

In Canada the development of football reflected the same theme of local variation of rules which characterized the growth of the sport in the United States. However, in the Dominion a few private clubs and military garrisons also played a prominent role, along with college squads from Montreal and Toronto. During the 1870s different forms of football appeared in Montreal, Toronto, Quebec City, Ottawa, and Halifax. The Montreal teams then took the lead in promoting a variant of rugby, which the McGill University men played in their tests against Harvard. The Montreal game gained adherents during the late 1870s in eastern Ontario, especially in Ottawa and Kingston. Meanwhile, in Toronto the struggle between supporters of soccer and rugby led to the adoption of a version of the latter game, modified through the incorporation of American elements. By 1880 in both Montreal and Toronto a distinctive brand of Canadian football had evolved with reflected both British and American influences. Throughout North America football was still in the early stages of its transition from a premodern to a modern sport.

FOOTBALL, 1864

This list of regulations defines a game which combines elements of kicking, catching, throwing, charging, holding, and tripping. The sporting press recommended it as a rough but exhilarating amusement which was well suited for the cold winter weather. This brief description, list of regulations, and definition of terms is from The New York Clipper, 3 December 1864, p. 266.

THE GAME OF FOOTBALL

The game of foot ball is not very generally played in this country, although more games have been played the past year or two than formerly. As it is now the season for this rollicking pastime it is proposed to organize two clubs, one in New York, the other in Brooklyn, so that matches can be played between them. We think well of the project and hope it may succeed. To further the same, we publish by request the revised RULES FOR FOOT BALL:

1. The maximum length of the ground shall be 200 yards, the maximum breadth shall be 100 yards, the length and breadth shall be marked off with flags, and the goal shall be defined by two upright posts, eight yards apart, without any tape or bar across them.

2. The game shall be commenced by a place kick from the centre of the ground by the side winning the toss, the other side shall not approach within 10 yards of the ball until it is kicked off. After a goal is won the losing side shall be entitled to kick off.

3. The two sides shall change goals after each goal is won.

4. A goal shall be won when the ball passes over the space between the goal posts (at whatever height), not being thrown, knocked on, or carried.

5. When the ball is in touch the first player who touches it shall kick or throw it from the point on the boundary line where it left the ground, in a direction at right angles with the boundary line.

6. A player shall be out of play immediately he is in front of the ball, and must return behind the ball as soon as possible. If the ball is kicked past a player by his own side, he shall not touch or kick it or advance until one of the other side has first kicked it or one of his own side on a level with or in front of him has been able to kick it.

7. In case the ball goes behind the goal line, if a player on the side to whom the goal belongs first touches the ball, one of his side shall be entitled to a free kick from the goal line at the point opposite the place where the ball shall be touched. If a player of the opposite side first touches the ball, one of his side shall be entitled to a free kick from a point 15 yards outside the goal line, opposite the place where the ball is touched.

8. If a player makes a fair catch he shall be entitled to a free kick, provided he claims it by making a mark with his heel at once; and in order to take such kick he may go as far back as he pleases, and no player on the opposite side shall advance beyond his mark until he has kicked.

9. A player shall be entitled to run with the ball towards his adversaries' goal if he makes a fair catch, or catches the ball on the first bound; but in the case of a fair catch, if he makes his mark, he shall not then run.

10. If any player shall run with the ball towards his adversaries' goal, any player on the opposite side shall be at liberty to charge, hold, trip, or hack him, or to wrest the ball from him; but no player shall be held and hacked at the same time.

11. Neither tripping nor backing shall be allowed, and no player shall use his hands or elbows to hold or push his adversary, except in the case provided by Law 10.

12. Any player shall be allowed to charge another, provided they are both in active play. A player shall be allowed to charge if even he is out of play.

13. A player shall be allowed to throw the ball or pass it to another if he make a fair catch, or catches the ball on the first bound.

14. No player shall be allowed to wear projecting nails, iron plates, or gutta percha on the soles or heels of his boots.

DEFINITION OF TERMS

A Place Kick is a kick at the ball while it is on the ground, in any position which the kicker may choose to place it.

A Free Kick is the privilege of kicking the ball, without obstruction, in such a manner as the kicker may see fit.

A Fair Catch is when the ball is caught, after it has touched the person of an adversary or has been kicked, knocked on, or thrown by an adversary, and before it has touched the ground or one of the side catching it; but if the ball is kicked from out of touch, or from behind goal line, a fair catch cannot be made.

Hacking is kicking an adversary on the front of the leg, below the knee.

Tripping is throwing an adversary by the use of the legs without the hands, and without hacking or charging.

Charging is attacking an adversary with the shoulder, chest, or body, without using the hands or legs.

Knocking On is when a player strikes or propels the ball with his hands, arms, or body, without kicking or throwing it.

Holding includes the obstruction of a player by the hand or any part of the arm below the elbow.

Touch is that part of the field, on either side of the ground, which is beyond the line of flags.

RUTGERS VS. PRINCETON, 1869

The following descriptions of the inaugural series between Rutgers and Princeton are from the Rutgers student newspaper, The Targum, November, 1869, p. 5.

THE FOOT-BALL MATCH.

On Saturday, November 6th, Princeton sent twenty-five picked men to play our twenty-five a match game of foot-ball. The strangers came up in the 10 o'clock train, and brought a good number of backers with them. After dinner, and a stroll around the town, during which stroll billiards received a good deal of attention, the crowds began to assemble at the ball ground, which, for the benefit of the ignorant, we would say, is a lot about a hundred yards wide, extending from College Avenue to Sicard-street. Previous to calling the game, the ground presented an animated picture. Grim-looking players were silently stripping, each one surrounded by sympathizing friends, while around each of the captains was a little crowd, intent upon giving advice, and saying as much as possible. The appearance of the Princeton men was very different from that of our own players. They were almost without exception tall and muscular, while the majority of our twenty-five are small and light, but possess the merit of being up to much more than they look.

Very few were the preliminaries, and they were quickly agreed upon. The Princeton captain, for some reason or other, gave up every point to our men without contesting one. The only material points were, that Princeton gave up "free kicks," whereby a player, when he catches the ball in the air is allowed to kick it without hindrance. On the other hand, our practice of "babying" the ball on the start was discarded, and the ball was mounted, in every instance, by a vigorous "long kick."

Princeton won the toss, and chose the first mount, rather oddly, since it had been agreed to start the ball against the wind. At 3 P.M., the game was called. The Princetonians suffered from making a very bad "mount," or "buck" as they call it; the effects of which were not remedied before the sides closed, and after a brief struggle, Rutgers drove it home, and won, amid great applause from the crowd. The sides were changed, Rutgers started the ball, and after a somewhat longer fight, Princeton made it a tie by a well directed kick, from a gentleman whose name we don't know, but who did the best kicking on the Princeton side.

To describe the varying fortunes of the match, game by game, would be a waste of labor, for every game was like the one before. There was the same headlong running, wild shouting, and frantic kicking. In every game the cool goaltenders saved the Rutgers goal half a dozen times; in every game the heavy charger of the Princeton side overthrew everything he came in contact with; and in every game, just when the interest in one of those delightful rushes at the fence was culminating, the persecuted ball would fly for refuge into the next lot, and produce a cessation of hostilities until, after the invariable "foul," it was put in straight.

Well, at last we won the match, having won the 1st, 3d, 5th, 6th, 9th, and 10th games; leaving Princeton the 2d, 4th, 7th, and 8th. The seventh game would probably have been added to our score, but for one of our players, who, in his ardor, forgot which way he was kicking, a mistake he fully atoned for afterward.

To sum up. Princeton had the most muscle, but didn't kick very well, and wanted organization. They evidently don't like to kick the ball on the ground. Our men, on the other hand, though comparatively weak, ran well, and kicked well throughout. But their great point was their organization, for which great praise is due to the Captain, Leggett, '72. The right men were always in the right place.

After the match, the players had an amicable "feed" together, and at 8 o'clock our guests went home, in high good spirits, but thirsting to beat us next time, if they can.

PRINCETON VS. RUTGERS.

The second of the three games of Foot Ball between Princeton and Rutgers was won by the former at their ball-grounds, on Saturday, the 13th inst. Eight out of fifteen was the game, but as Princeton won the first eight the other innings were not played. The style of playing differs, materially, in the two Colleges. A fly, or first bound catch, entitles to a "free kick," a la Princeton. We bat with hands, feet, head, sideways, backwards, any way to get the ball along. We must say that we think our style much more exciting, and more as Foot Ball should be. After the regular game two innings were played after our fashion, and we won them. It is but fair to our twenty-five to say that they never have practiced the "free-kick" system. At half-past six we sat down to a very fine supper, prepared for us by our hosts. Speeches and songs, accompanied, of course, by the study of practical gastronomy, passed the time pleasantly until the evening train bore us Brunswickwards. We hope soon to welcome Princeton to New-Brunswick for the third game, and beat them. Their cheer, sounding as if they meant to explode, but for a fortunate escape of air, followed by a grateful yell at the deliverance of such a catastrophe, still sounds in our ears as we thank them for their hospitality. If we must be beaten we are glad to have such conquerors.

OTHER VIEWS OF THE FIRST FOOTBALL GAMES

These two pieces are from the William E. Griffin Collection, Scrapbook of Clippings, Rutgers University Library. The first is from the New Brunswick Fredonian, 8 November 1869; the second seems to be from the Newark Journal, undated, but probably mid-November 1869.

RUTGERS VERSUS PRINCETON.—"Hurrah for the boys of good old Rutgers," who are waking up as was fully demonstrated last Saturday afternoon, in the lively, but rough game of football.

Our neighbor "Princeton" sent her chosen twenty four stalwart men, and one Goliath to combat our twenty-five striplings. There is not recorded in the history of the Olympic games a more interesting and decisive match, played in so short a time, by such a number of contestants, as this game was. Rutgers led off by winning the first inning amid the vociferous cheering of the bystanders. Princeton seemed to play a little wild at the beginning, but the second inning they recovered themselves, and came out the victors. So it continued, off and on, one gaining, then the other, until the ninth and tenth innings, when notwithstanding the desperate efforts of the Princeton giants, Rutgers quickly and boldly followed in successive victory, giving them six runs to four of Princeton—thereby coming off conquerors, which was hailed with exulting shouts of applause by the admirers of Rutgers. The victorious twenty-five then gave three rousing cheers and a "tiger," which was followed by the Princeton twenty-five cheering, and a something sounding very much like "Ou!" "Bum!" "haugh!!" The game thus ended in good feeling, although during the playing we observed some rather unnecessary sparring on the part of a few of the Princeton "Philistines." "All is well that ends well." Through the generous liberality of the students of Rutgers College, a bountiful entertainment was prepared for our Princeton friends, at the favorite resort in Church-street known as Northrop's, where "mine host" and his estimable lady know how to get up a good supper. May they live long to serve the students of Rutgers thus. How are you seventy-three? So ends a pleasant rivalry between sister Colleges, of which there are none more honorable in the land. Princeton did well, but Rutgers did better, and let it continue to be, not alone in athletic sports, but also in the more energetic struggle of the mind. SPECTATOR.

PRINCETON VS. RUTGERS.

A PRINCETON correspondent of the Newark *Journal* gives the following in reference to the recent game of football played by the students of Princeton and Rutgers. Speaking of the first game, he says:—

"As far as men were concerned we were about equal, or if in point of physical strength and endurance there was any superiority Rutgers had this advantage, since she has [missing] crew, and her men had many of them been under training, and consequently were more developed. Then we play a thoroughly English game in every particular, the same game that is played at Rugby, Oxford, and through the universities of Germany.

Our style of game is vigorous, exciting, interesting and manly, supported by the first-class colleges in the world, and thoroughly explained in Hughes' familiar book, "Tom Brown at Rugby." The principal points of the game we play—*i.e.*, the true English game—are these: A player catching the ball on the fly, or first bound, is allowed a free kick; that is he is entitled to a certain space, and can be as deliberate as he wishes. We never allow the ball to be thrown, it must be kicked.

Well, we went to Rutgers; we found an American style of game—a style, by the way, which we think was invented by Rutgers—and decided to play their style. They *never* allow a man a free kick; they never kick a ball when they can throw it; they never catch a ball on the fly; they will always trip an adversary when he attempts to kick a ball and always hold him when he attempts to run after it. In their game they use the hands entirely.

So you see we went on the field to follow a new system, whose rules we were ignorant of, and a system which we had never heard of, much less seen played; besides, six of our very best players, and players who did all the work in the last game, were absent from the game, while two players who had come to Brunswick, but owing to a misunderstanding were not at the place of contest, forced us to put eight substitutes on the field. As it was, although we were beaten, we have nothing to be ashamed of, since we only lost the game by two goals, while we played a new game.

Last Saturday Rutgers came to play the second game of the series of three. They came here with their twenty-five, and at a quarter before three the game began, Rutgers having the first "buck," or, in their dialect, the first "mount."

Never since we have been in Princeton have we seen such an immense crowd assembled to witness an athletic sport. The seats were all occupied, and all around the football ground, which was large and marked off by nine orange colored flags, the crowd formed a solid and compact square; the fences were filled as well. To enter upon a long description of the entire game by analysis would be dull to the reader and doubly dull to the writer. Suffice it to say that our system was played. Rutgers had practised our system two hours each day for a week, and so were "pulled" up on it. The score was to be the best eight goals out of fifteen. *We gained eight successive goals, while Rutgers did not gain a single one*. They were whitewashed. The game was exceedingly interesting. Our men kept the last game before their eyes, and played, run, caught and kicked like heroes. Every man had his place; there were men to guard both goals, men to remain in certain positions, men to run; it was reduced to a science, and a science that was vigorous and manly. The time of game 45 minutes; the score 8 to 0.

After the game the boys were shown around town, refreshed and "*smoked*," and at half-past six both sides, the players and umpires numbering in all about sixty persons [missing] to a fine supper that had been prepared [missing] Mansion House. The supper was a very fine one indeed. Speeches and toasts were given by Leggett, Stephens and Anderson, of Rutgers, and by Gummere, Brown, Michael and Field, of Princeton; after which both colleges joined in singing the glorious, ringing old college songs.

Soon after supper the Rutgers boys were escorted to the depot, and left town amid the cheers and hurrahing bums and rockets from the Princeton boys.

FOOTBALL AT HARVARD, 1873

In the autumn of 1871 a group of Harvard students gathered together on Cambridge Common to play a game which they had enjoyed as school boys. Called the "Boston game," it was popular in many preparatory schools throughout New England, including the Boston Latin School, Dixwell's, Andover, and Exeter. Well known for many years, it even antedated premodern baseball in several schools. This pastime was an open and entertaining sport which stressed individual initiative, agility, and kicking skill. It put a premium on speed, quickness, and the ability to dodge or catch opponents. These rules are reprinted from the Harvard Advocate, 31 October 1873, p. 53.

RULES OF THE HARVARD UNIVERSITY FOOT-BALL CLUB, 1873

1. The number of players on each side shall be not less than ten and not more than fifteen.

2. The grounds shall be not less than 350, nor more than 450 feet in length, and not less than 225, nor more than 325 in width.

3. There shall be two end boundaries and two side boundaries.

4. The two end boundaries shall form the goals. To win a game, the ball must strike the ground beyond either goal, passing over it on the fly; but no game can be won on a fair lick.

5. When the ball passes over either side boundary, it shall be considered dead; and the player first holding it shall be entitled to a fair lick, and shall carry the ball within the bounds at right angles to the boundary line at the spot where it first *struck.*

6. When the ball passes over either goal, in any manner other than to win a game, it shall be considered dead, as in No. 5, and may be placed anywhere within a line drawn parallel to the goal, and ten feet distant from it.

7. The winners of the toss shall have either the warning kick or the choice of goals. The warning kick shall be taken from a point half way between the two goals.

8. Any player is allowed to catch or pick up the ball. No player is allowed to run with or "baby" the ball, unless pursued by an opponent, and then only while so pursued.

9. No player is allowed to throw or pass the ball to another player, unless pursued by an opponent.

10. No lurking, striking, hacking, tripping, nor butting among the players is allowed.

11. Any player, when on the adversary's side of the ball, must *either walk toward the ball, or must walk toward his own goal, in a line at right angles with that goal.* Any player not complying with this law shall be considered as lurking, and shall not be allowed to touch the ball until he has reached a point on his own side of the ball.

12. A match shall consist of five games. The side winning three games out of the five shall be the winner of said match.

13. Each side shall appoint an umpire, who shall select in turn a referee.

14. It shall be the duty of the umpires to settle all disputes, see that the rules of the game are complied with, name the victors in all matches, and perform in short all the ordinary duties of an umpire.

15. The referee shall be applied to when the umpires disagree, and his decision shall be final.

THE FIRST INTERCOLLEGIATE FOOTBALL CONVENTION, 1873

Yale men took the initiative in calling for the first intercollegiate football conference. After Harvard declined their invitation it was easy for them to persuade the delegates from Princeton and Rutgers to approve their proposed rules, which closely resembled the regulations practiced by those two colleges. The result was a sport which featured kicking but not holding or throwing the ball. This code is reprinted from the Harvard Advocate, 31 October 1873, p. 52.

FOOTBALL RULES: YALE, PRINCETON, AND RUTGERS

1. The grounds shall be 400 feet long by 200 feet broad.
2. The distance between the posts of each goal shall be 25 feet.
3. The number for match games shall be twenty to a side.
4. To win a game, six goals are necessary, but that side shall be considered the victor which, when the game is called, shall have secured the greatest number of goals, provided that number be two or more. To secure a goal, the ball must pass between the posts.
5. No player shall throw or carry the ball. Any violation of this regulation shall constitute a foul, and the player so offending shall throw the ball perpendicularly into the air, to a height of at least twelve feet from the place where the foul occurred, and the ball shall not be in play until it has touched the ground.
6. When the ball passes out of bounds, it is a foul; and the player causing it shall advance, at right angles to the boundary line, fifteen paces from the point where the ball went out, and shall there proceed as in rule 5.
7. No tripping shall be allowed, nor shall any player use his hands to hold or push an adversary.
8. The winners of the toss shall have the choice of first goal, and the sides shall change goals at every successive inning. In starting the ball, it shall be fairly kicked, not babied, from a point 150 feet in front of the starters' goal.
9. Until the ball is kicked, no player on either side shall be in advance of a line parallel to the line of his goal, and distant from it 150 feet.
10. There shall be two judges, one from each of the contesting colleges, and one referee; all to be chosen by the captains.
11. No player shall wear spikes or iron plates on his shoes.
12. In all match games a No. 6 ball shall be used, furnished by the challenging side, and to become the property of the victors.

McGILL VS. HARVARD, MAY 15, 1874

The McGill-Harvard matches in the spring of 1874 were critically important in the evolution of college football in the United States because they provided the players with the opportunity to experiment with two very different sets of rules. In both games each side played with eleven men. The Cambridge men played in black trousers, white undershirts, and magenta handkerchiefs upon their heads. Their Canadian opponents sported a more handsome uniform of red and black striped shirts, caps and stockings, and white trousers. The ball used in the first contest played by the Harvard rules was round and made of a rubber fabric, while the one employed in the Rugby game was a leather covered oval. After the matches the Harvard hosts used the gate receipts to treat their guests to a banquet in Boston, where the champagne flowed freely. This story on the rugby match is reprinted from the Harvard Magenta, 22 May 1874, p. 93.

RUGBY GAME

The second game of foot-ball between the McGill and Harvard Tens last Friday was awaited with the greatest impatience, not to say anxiety, by every one in College. The game on Thursday had been a disappointment to all who saw it, for the Canadians, from ignorance of the Harvard rules, had failed utterly in resisting the Harvard Ten, who won the three goals so easily that the McGill players seemed standing in the field merely as spectators of their opponents' excellent kicking. But on Friday, when the game was to be played according to the McGill or rather Rugby rules, it was feared that the result would be quite different, that the Canadians would win the match with little difficulty.

After a half-hour past the time for the beginning of the game, the McGill men, dressed in the English foot-ball suit, straggled into the field, and, after a few minutes, were followed by a shabby looking set of men, who turned out to be the Harvard Ten. As it happened, the dilapidated appearance of the Harvard players was quite a boon to the lookers-on, for if they had been respectably clad in a uniform of some kind it might have been quite impossible to distinguish between the two sides, but, as it was, one merely had to notice whether or no a few rags were floating gracefully behind the player, to know on which side be belonged. Indeed, in the last half-hour, one of Harvard's players had excited the spectators to the utmost with the hope that he was about to gain a long wished for "touch down," when one of his pursuers bethought himself of stretching out his hand and seizing one of the many pennons that were waving behind him, with which he drew him skillfully to the ground, awakening in him the same sensation that a kite has when pulled to the ground by a little boy.

For the first half-hour the Harvard men had the wind in their favor. To the agreeable surprise of most of us, the Canadians did not kick the ball over the cross-bar in the first five minutes, and they seemed indeed hardly able to hold their own. The two first half-hours passed without either side winning even a touch down, although several times it was barely lost; but the last half-hour was the most exciting of all. Both sides were evidently doing their best, though several of the McGill men already showed signs of rough usage they had received in the first part of the game. The end of the half-hour came at last, and the game was drawn.

On the whole it was a very successful contest and it is to be hoped that next year several games may be played between the Tens of McGill and Harvard.

McGILL VS. HARVARD, OCTOBER 23, 1874

When Harvard played McGill in the return engagement in Montreal in the fall, each side fielded only nine men. Embarrassed by their ragged appearance in the spring contests, the Cambridge men purchased some magenta and white striped sweaters. Once again they wore magenta handkerchiefs on their heads. After their decisive victory in the rugby match the second game was called off. In the evening the McGill men entertained their guests with an elaborate dinner; the following morning they escorted them to a fox hunt and breakfast. These reports are from the Boston Advertiser, 24 October 1874, and The Gazette (Montreal), 24 October 1874.

RETURN MATCH AT RUGBY

Montreal, Oct. 23. The Harvard foot-ball eleven arrived here yesterday and at once took up their quarters at St. Lawrence Hall, where they met many of the McGill students. The committee presented the visiting eleven with appropriate badges and invitations and invited their attention to the sports which took place yesterday, on the McGill grounds.

The international foot-ball match, which has been so thoroughly advertised throughout this city, was played on the grounds of the Montreal Cricket Club this afternoon. The Harvards won the toss and took the side which had the wind, the McGills having the send-off. Every inch of ground was desperately fought for and the elevens seemed to be very evenly matched. At the beginning of the game things looked ominous for the Harvards, for two of their men, Cole [Cate] and Watson, were disabled yesterday in a practice game and did not play, and besides this their opponents were in all respects better acquainted with the wiles of their own game. The game began at half past three and finished at five, as at that time the Harvards had won three touchdowns, which is the equivalent of a goal. During the first half hour there were many good struggles and one touch-down was won by Wetherbee, who ran splendidly for it and who also secured a second in the next half hour. It was not until the middle of the game that the McGills got well down to work. This time they were kept well down to their own goal by the steady work and sharp play of the Harvards, the latter club securing their ground by sharp nursing and final rushes. As the McGills got the kickoff they had a slight advantage which was offset by the winning of the toss and wind by the visitors. Faucon got the touch-out [down] in the third half-hour, by quickly dodging his pursuers, and Willis came within two feet of getting a fourth. All this time the McGills had won no touches but in all their attempts they were met by the bone and muscle of the other side. Every man of the Harvard eleven worked as though life depended on the result and the manner in which they backed up the brilliant running of their men secured for them the game. The umpires were F.C. Henderson [Henshaw] and H. Williams of '75.

The attendance was very large and the excitement and enthusiasm great. Every good play on the part of the home club was loudly applauded and the men friends of the Harvards cheered their men in a like manner. The Victoria band was present and enlivened the scene by playing inspiring airs, which seemed to give the players extra nerve. The match was very exciting from beginning to end, and was pronounced to be the best ever played on the grounds. The McGills have invited the visitors to a supper given in their honor. No one was injured during the game although there were many hard falls. The club leaves for home tomorrow afternoon and expects to play a match according to their own rules in the morning....

The Grand International Foot Ball Match yesterday was played according to the Rugby Rules, which is a far more scientific mode of playing the game than that in vogue some years ago. Fully 1,500 spectators, a large number of whom were ladies, were present to witness the contest, and seemed well pleased with the game, if the frequent bursts of applause which greeted the players whenever a cleverly executed tumble was performed, was any criterion.

About three o'clock the game was commenced, the ball being kicked off by D. Rodger, Jr., the Captain of the McGill team, who sent it spinning through the air toward the Harvard goal only to be returned as swiftly from the energetic toe of a Harvardite. Now up and now down the field, backward and forward shot the ball, the Harvard men doing the most carrying, while the Montrealers showed an aptitude for kicking that would have made a New York interviewer or a sewing machine agent tremble. After some fifty minutes brisk playing the Harvards succeeded in scoring a "touch down," which was made by Faucon in splendid style. At the end of each half-hour the teams exchanged positions on the field, this being agreed to on the start. After a magnificent run and numerous hair breadth escapes, Wetherbee of the Harvards managed to secure a second touch down, but failed to make a "goal" in the free kick. During the third half-hour some vigorous play was exhibited, each side evidently determined to win at any cost, which the Harvards did. To be particular, the exact cost of that game to the Harvards was two shirts. What seemed to amuse the spectators were the scrimmages, which would have done credit to Rugby itself. A swaying of heads, legs, arms, and other anatomical specimens wriggling and knotting themselves up in a most extraordinary manner, while every now and then a smothered "Oh," led the bystanders to believe that someone had engaged in the game who was not prepared to be totally dismembered without some exclamation of remonstrance or surprise. The last "touch down" which was also secured by Wetherbee, decided the match, for, although the Harvards failed to make a goal by it, the three "touches" counted equal to a game. During the game the Victoria Cornet Band played some fine selections, concluding with "God Save the Queen" and "Yankee Doodle." Three cheers having been given for the Harvard team by the McGill boys, the Harvard team responding with their peculiar College cheer. We hope this will not be the last friendly contest between the two clubs, and that better fortune may attend the McGill boys in the future.

THE FIRST INTERCOLLEGIATE FOOTBALL LEAGUE, 1876

The following draft of the first college football association shows the early interest of the players in both the commercialization of their sport and championship competition.

It is reprinted from the Walter Camp Papers, Manuscripts and Archives, Yale University Library, with the permission of the Yale University Library.

ORIGINAL CONSTITUTION OF THE AMERICAN INTERCOLLEGIATE FOOTBALL ASSOCIATION

Art. I.

Sec. 1. The name of the association shall be the American Intercollegiate Football Association.

Art. II.

Sec. 1. The following colleges shall constitute the Association: Columbia, Harvard, Princeton, Yale.
Sec. 2. No colleges except those named shall be admitted to membership, except by the unanimous consent of the members of the association.

Art. III.

Sec. 1. The officers shall consist of a president, secretary and treasurer. The presidency shall be held by the college holding the championship. secretary and treasurer shall be elected.

Art. IV.

Sec. 1. The series of games shall consist of one with each college and shall be upon home grounds or grounds mutually agreed upon. The two leading clubs of previous year shall play in New York on Thanksgiving. The championship shall be decided by greatest number of games won. In case of a tie in games won the college losing the fewest games shall take the championship. In case of a tie the championship shall not hold over but to decide the teams for Thanksgiving the record shall hold over.

Art. V.

Sec. 1. Each club shall receive its entire home gate receipts and pay its own expenses.

Art. VI.

Sec. 1. Any club having agreed to play a championship game with another club on a certain day and refusing or failing to meet its engagement, shall, unless the failure be caused by an unavoidable accident in traveling or postponed with the consent in writing of the other club, forfeit the game. This club shall forfeit its membership. A certificate signed by three members of the faculty shall be considered sufficient excuse for failure to play.

Art. VII.

Sec. 1. The annual meeting of this association shall be held at New York within a week after Thanksgiving—each college to be represented by not more than three delegates. Any extra meeting may be called, at the request of two colleges, by the president.

Art. VIII.

Sec. 1. A majority vote shall be necessary to pass any measure, Each college having but one vote.

Art. IX.

Sec. 1. The home club shall choose a referee from four names presented by the visiting club which names must include the names of the captains of the remaining teams.

By-laws.

1. It shall be the duty of the president to preside at all meetings and to give information to the secretary when and where such meetings shall occur.
2. It shall be the duty of the secretary to keep records of the meetings and to inform the colleges of all meetings and to inform the colleges of all meetings.
3. Immediately on the completion of all games necessary to the award of the championship, the formal vote of each college signed by the captain and one of the delegates to the annual convention shall be forwarded to the secretary of the association.

INTERCOLLEGIATE FOOTBALL RULES, 1879

The football rules adopted in Springfield, Massachusetts in November 1876 effectively ended the possibility that the soccer-style version might become the dominant form of the sport in the United States. The men from Harvard, Yale, Princeton, and Columbia clearly preferred a game that combined kicking, holding, throwing and running with the ball, along with tackling their opponents. Although representatives from Yale took an active part in the deliberations of this meeting, in the end they refused to join the league. The men from New Haven favored eleven men on a side (instead of fifteen) and also insisted on a scoring system that counted only kicked goals, not touchdowns. The following code of rules, which includes changes made through the 1879 season, is from Henry Chadwick, *Handbook of Winter Sports, Embracing Skating, Rink-ball, Curling, Ice-boating, and American Football* (New York, 1879), pp. 51-59.

RULES OF THE RUGBY GAME OF FOOT-BALL. AS AMENDED BY THE INTER-COLLEGIATE ASSOCIATION NOV. 23D, 1876; OCT. 9TH, 1877; OCT. 4TH, 1879.

1. Grounds must be 330 feet in length and 160 feet in width.

2. Each Goal shall be composed of two upright posts exceeding 20 feet in height, and placed 18 feet and 6 inches apart, with cross-bar 10 feet from the ground.

3. Time of game is an hour and a half, each side playing forty-five minutes from each goal.

4. A match shall be decided by a majority of touchdowns. A goal shall be equal to four touch-downs. But in case of a tie, a goal kicked from a touch-down shall take precedence over touch-downs.

5. There shall be two judges and a referee in every match.

6. No one wearing projecting nails, iron plates, or gutta percha, on any part of his boots or shoes, shall be allowed to play in a match.

7. NO HACKING, or THROTTLING, BUCKING or tripping up, or tackling below the hips, shall be allowed under any circumstances.

8. A Drop Kick or Drop is made by letting the ball fall from the hands, and kicking it the *very instant* it rises.

9. A Place Kick or Place is made by kicking the ball after it has been placed in a nick made in the ground for the purpose of keeping it at rest.

10. A Punt is made by letting the ball fall from the hands and kicking it *before* it touches the ground.

11. The Captains of the respective sides shall toss up before commencement of the Match; the winner of the toss shall have the option of the choice of Goal, or of kick off.

12. A Kick off is a place *kick* from the centre of the field of play, and cannot count as a goal. The opposite side must stand at least *ten yards* in front of the ball until it has been kicked.

13. The ball shall be *kicked off* (i.) at the commencement of the game; (ii.) after a goal has been obtained.

14. A Goal may be obtained by any kind of a kick except a *punt*.

15. A Goal can be obtained by kicking the ball from the field of play direct (*i. e.*, without touching the ground, or the dress or person of any player of either side) over the cross-bar of the opponents' goal, but if it touch such cross-bar, or the posts, it is called a *poster*, and is not a goal.

16. Whenever a goal shall have been obtained, the side which has lost the goal shall then kick off.

17. Throwing Back. It is lawful for any player who has the ball, to throw it back towards his own goal, or to pass it back to any player of his own side who is at the time behind him.

18. Knocking on, *i. e.*, deliberately hitting the ball with the hand, and Throwing Forward, *i. e.*, throwing the ball in the direction of the opponents' goal line, are not lawful. If the ball be either *knocked on* or *thrown forward*, the Captain of the opposite side may (unless a fair catch has been made, as provided by the next Rule) require to have it brought back to the spot where it was *knocked* or *thrown on*, and there put down.

19. A Fair Catch is a catch made direct from a kick, or a *throw forward*, or a *knock on* by one of the opposite side, or from a *punt out* (See Rule 51) provided the catcher makes a mark with his heel at the spot where he has made the catch, and no other of his own side touch the ball (See Rules 20 and 21.)

20. A Player who has made and claimed a *fair catch* shall thereupon either take a *drop kick* or a *punt*, or *place* the ball for a place kick.

21. After a *fair catch* has been made, the opposite side may come up to the catcher's mark, and (except in cases under rule 54,) the catcher's side retiring, the ball shall be kicked from such mark, or from a spot any distance behind it.

22. A catch made when the ball is thrown out of touch is not a *fair catch*.

23. In cases of a *fair catch* the opposite side may come up to and charge from anywhere on or behind a line drawn through the mark made by the player who has made the catch, and parallel to their own goal line; but in the case of a *fair catch* from a *punt out* or a *punt on*, (See Rule 54,) they may not advance further in the direction of the touch line nearest to such mark than a line drawn through such mark to their goal line, and parallel to such touch line. In all cases (except a *punt out* and a *punt on*) the kicker's side must be behind the ball when it is kicked, but may not charge until it has been kicked.

24. The ball is *dead* when it rests absolutely motionless on the ground.

25. The ball is *dead* whenever a goal has been obtained; but if a *try at goal* be not successful, the kick shall be considered as only an ordinary kick in the course of the game.

26. It is not lawful to take up the ball when dead (except in order to bring it out after it has been touched down in touch or in goal) for any purpose whatever; whenever the ball shall have been so unlawfully taken up, it shall at once be brought back to where it was so taken up, and there put down.

27. A player may *take up* the ball wherever it is rolling or bounding, except in a scrimmage.

28. It is lawful for any player who has the ball to run with it, and if he does so it is called a *Run*. If a player runs with the ball until he gets behind his opponents' goal line, and there touches it down, it is called a *Run in*.

29. It is lawful to *run in* anywhere across the goal line.

30. A Tackle is when the holder of the ball is held by one or more players of the opposite side.

31. In the event of the any player holding or running with the ball being tackled, and the ball fairly held, he must at once cry *down*, and there put it down.

32. A Scrimmage takes place, when the holder of the ball being in the field of play, puts it down on the ground in front of him.

33. In a scrimmage it is not lawful for the man who has the ball, nor the man opposite and opposed to him, to pick out the ball with the hand under any circumstances whatever, but if the ball touch a third man, either may.

34. Every player is *on side*, but if put *off side* if he enters a scrimmage from his opponents' side, or being in a scrimmage, gets in front of the ball, or when the ball has been kicked, touched, or is being run with by any of his own side behind him, (*i. e.*, between himself and his goal line.) No player can be off side in his own goal.

35. Every player when *off side*, is out of the game, and shall not touch the ball in any case whatever, either in or out of touch or goal, or in any way interrupt or obstruct any player until he is again *on side*.

36. A player being *off side* is put *on side* when the ball has been kicked by or has touched the dress or person of any player of the opposite side, or when one of his own side has run in front of him, either with the ball or having kicked it when behind him.

37. Touch (bounds). If a ball goes into *touch*, any player on the side which touches it down must bring it to the spot where it crossed the touch line; or if a player, when running with the ball, cross or put any part of either foot across the touch line, he must return with the ball to the spot where the line was so crossed, and thence return into

the field of play in one of the modes provided by the following Rule. If the player only has his hand over the line it is not out of bounds.

38. He must then himself or by one of his own side, either (i.) *bound* the ball in the field of play at right angles to the touch line, and then run with it, kick it, of throw it back to this own side; or (ii.) throw it out at right angles to the touch line; or (iii.) walk out with it at right angles to the touch line, any distance not less than *five* nor more than fifteen yards, and there put it down, first declaring how far he intends to walk out. The man who throws the ball in must face the field or his opponents' goal.

39. If two or more players holding the ball are pushed into *touch,* the ball shall belong *in touch* to the player who first had hold of it in the field of play, and has not released his hold of it.

40. If the ball when thrown out of *touch* be not thrown out at right angles to the touch line, the Captain of either side may at once claim to have it thrown out again.

41. The goal line is in goal, and the touch line in touch.

42. Touch in goal. Immediately the ball, whether in the hands of a player (except for the purpose of a *punt out* (see Rule 50) or not, goes into touch in goal, it is at once *dead* and out of the game, and must be brought out as provided by Rules 57 and 58.

43. A Maul in Goal is when the holder of the ball is tackled inside the goal line, or being tackled immediately outside, is carried or pushed across it, and he, or the opposite side, or both, endeavor to touch the ball down. In all cases, when so touched down, the ball shall belong to the players of the side who first had possession of it before the maul commenced, unless the opposite side have gained complete possession of it.

44. In case of *maul in goal,* those players only, who are touching the ball with their hands, when it crosses the goal line, may continue the maul in goal, and when a player has once released his hold of the ball after it is inside the goal line, he may not again join in the maul, and if he attempts to do so, may be dragged out by the opposite side.

45. But, if a player when *running in* is tackled inside the goal line, then only the player who first tackled him, or if two or more tackle simultaneously, they only may join in the maul.

46. A Touch-Down is when a player, putting his hand upon the ball on the ground in goal, stops it so that it remains dead.

47. When the ball has been touched down in the opponents' goal, none of the side in whose goal it has been so touched down shall touch it, or in no way displace it, or interfere with the player of the other side who may be taking it up or out.

48. A side having touched the ball down in their opponents goal, shall *try at goal* either by a *place kick* or a *punt out*.

49. If a *try at goal* be made by a *place kick*, a player of the side which has touched the ball down shall bring it up to the goal line in a straight line from and opposite to the spot where the ball was touched down, and there make a mark on the goal line, and thence walk straight out with it at right angles to the goal line, to such distance as he thinks proper, and there place it for another of his side to kick. The kicker's side must be behind the ball when it is kicked, and the opposite side must remain behind their goal line until the ball has been placed on the ground. If the man does not make his mark, the opposite side may charge.

50. A Punt out is a *punt* made after a touch-down by a player from behind his opponents' goal line, and from touch in goal if necessary, towards another of his own side, who must stand *outside* the goal line and endeavor to make a fair catch, or get the ball and *run in* or *drop* a goal (see Rules 52, 53 and 54), but he cannot pass it.

51. A Punt on is a *punt* made in a manner similar to a *punt out,* and from touch if necessary, by a player who has made a fair catch from a *punt out* or another *punt on.*

52. If the *try at goal* be by a *punt out* (See Rule 50), a player of the side which has touched the ball down shall bring it straight up to the goal line opposite to the spot where it was touched down, and there make a mark on the goal line, and then *punt out* from touch in goal, if necessary, or from any part behind the goal line not nearer to the goal post than such mark, beyond which mark it is not lawful for the opposite side (who must keep behind their goal line) to pass until the ball has been kicked. (See Rules 59 and 61.) If punter does not make his mark he must *punt* over again.

53. When a player is about to *punt out,* neither side may stand nearer the touch line than a line drawn at right angles to the goal line and passing through the punter's mark. Punter himself being only exception.

54. If a *fair catch* be made from a *punt out* or a *punt on,* the catcher may either proceed as provided by Rules 21 and 52, or himself take a *punt on,* in which case the mark made on making the *fair catch* shall be regarded (for the purpose of determining as well the position of the player who makes the *punt on* as of the other players of both sides) as the mark made on the goal line in the case of a *punt out.*

55. A catch made in touch from a *punt out* or a *punt on* is not a fair catch; the ball must then be taken or thrown out of touch, as provided by Rule 37; but if the catch be made in touch in goal, the ball is at once dead, and must be *kicked out,* as provided by Rules 57 and 58.

56. A player may touch the ball down in his own goal at any time.

57. Kick out is a drop kick by one of the players of the side which has had to touch the ball down in their own goal, or into whose touch in goal the ball has gone (Rule 8), is the mode of bringing the ball again into play, and cannot count as goal.

58. Kick out must be a *drop kick,* and from not more than *twenty-five yards* outside the kicker's goal; if the ball, when kicked out, *pitch* in touch, it must be taken back and kicked out again. The kicker's side must be behind the ball when kicked out (*Pitch* means either on the fly-bound or roll.)

59. If a player having the ball, when about to *punt it out,* goes outside the goal line; or when about to *punt on,* advances nearer to his own goal line than his mark, made on making the *fair catch*; or a *fair catch* has been made, more than one player on the side which has so touched it down or made the fair catch, touch the ball before it is again kicked, the opposite side may *charge* at once.

60. Charging, *i. e.,* rushing forward to kick the ball, or tackle a player, is lawful for the opposite side in all cases of a *place kick* after a fair catch, or upon a *try at goal,* immediately the ball touches, or is placed on the ground; and in cases of a *drop kick* or *punt* after a *fair catch,* as soon as the player having the ball commences to run or

offers to kick, or the ball has touched the ground; but he may always draw back, and unless he has dropped the ball, or actually touched it with his foot, they must again retire to his mark. The opposite side in the case of a *punt out* or a *punt on,* and the kicker's side in *all* cases, may not *charge* until the ball has been kicked.

61. If a player purposefully foul an opponent in order to gain ground for his own side, the opponent's side may either have the ball *down* where the foul was made, or take a *free kick,* which free kick cannot possibly score a goal. The purpose of the foul must be decided by the referee.

62. No player shall intentionally lay hands upon or interfere with an opponent, unless he has the ball.

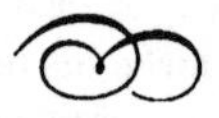

INTERCOLLEGIATE FOOTBALL ASSOCIATION: RULE CHANGES OF 1880

Walter Camp was the driving force behind the key changes in the rules of college football in 1880 and for many years thereafter. A prominent player for six years with the Yale club until he retired in 1882, he became Yale's unofficial coach and chief advisor and an enthusiastic promoter of American football for several decades. In 1880 Columbia was readmitted to the association after dropping out for a few years after the initial 1876 convention. However, Columbia was denied the right to vote in the case of a tie among the other schools, and it was subject to removal upon a majority vote. These amendments are reprinted from Parke Hill Davis, *Football, the Intercollegiate Game* (N.Y., 1911) pp. 468-469.

AMENDMENTS TO RULES

1. A scrimmage takes place when the holder of the ball, being in the field of play, puts it down on the ground in front of him and puts it into play while on side, first, by kicking the ball; second, by snapping it back with his foot. The man who first receives the ball from the snap-back shall be called the quarter-back, and shall not then rush forward with the ball under penalty of foul.

2. If the ball either fly, bound, or roll in touch from a kick-out, it must be brought back; but if it touch any player, it need not be brought back.

3. In case of a punt-out, the players of the side to which the ball is punted out must be at least 15 feet from the goal-line. The opposing side may line up anywhere in goal provided the punter has 5 feet clear extending from his scratch in the direction of touch. The punter out must not be interfered with in any way. A punt-out must be a kick from the toe.

4. If any player purposely foul an opponent when such opponent is about to try for a fair catch, the opponent's side may either have the ball down where the foul was made or take a free kick, which kick cannot score a goal.

5. The penalty for fouls when judged to be intentional by a referee, except as provided, shall be a down for the opposing side.

6. The game shall be played by eleven men on each side.

PRINCETON VS. YALE, 1880

Princeton and Yale dominated the early years of football in the United States, and their annual battles on Thanksgiving Day drew thousands to neutral sites, first at the grounds of the St. George Cricket Club in Hoboken, and later at the Polo Grounds in Manhattan. The following newspaper story shows the extent to which this game had become a major social event for New Yorkers. It is reprinted from The New York Daily Tribune, 26 November 1880, p. 8.

YALE AND PRINCETON AT FOOT-BALL.

Brains and not muscle, at the Polo Grounds, yesterday, enabled Princeton to come off with the title of "College Foot-ball Champion"—a somewhat empty honor, since Princeton was unable actually to defeat Yale in the match. Princeton legs being weaker than the Yale legs, shrewdness was made to take the place of strength. Princeton, by long continued delays and slow defensive playing, exhausted the allotted time and was thus enabled to leave the field nominally not beaten, and, for the third year, the champion. There was much disgust expressed that the game ended in a draw, and also that Princeton peremptorily refused Yale's challenge to another game. The distinguishing features of the closely contested struggle yesterday were the frequent disputes, and, appropriately enough, the large number of fouls. Despite the snow and clouds, an immense crowd assembled to witness the sport. The white mantle that early covered the field had been swept away, leaving a huge black rectangle for the players. But this, like the dark crowds which filled the stands, encircled the field and perched upon the tops of the coaches, soon became whitened by the fast-falling flakes.

On the north side of the field was a long line of hotel coaches and drags, which were filled with friends of the contesting teams, who maintained a spirited rivalry in cheering. They were distinguished by the flags and bunting with which their carriages were elaborately adorned, and also by their peculiar yells. One drag bore a large blue flag, on which was inscribed "Yale" in white letters. This was kept in continual motion. The Princeton coaches were draped with orange and black, and flags or ribbons of blue or orange were fluttering in every part of the field. Whenever an advantage was gained by either side, its sympathizers on the coaches led in the applause that followed, assisted occasionally by the notes of tin horns with which they were well supplied.

Men were engaged in clearing the field of its covering of snow when the crowd began to arrive. The opening of the game was thus delayed for half an hour, and during this time the men on the coaches sang college songs, and the field rang with the

"Rah! Rah! Rah!" of Yale and the "Boom-la!" of the Princeton men. Among sporting men bets were freely made, partisans of Yale offering odds of two to one, such was their confidence in their team.

At length the appearance of the Yale team immediately followed by Princeton was a signal for a storm of cheers which lasted for some moments. The Princeton eleven were dressed in orange and black striped jerseys; while the Yale team wore blue with canvas jackets. The men appeared to be almost equally matched in size and muscle, each team being remarkable for the size and weight of its men. The teams were made up as follows:

Princeton—Rushers: C.B. Bradford, '81; H. McDermott, '81; C.A. McKee, '81; E. Peace, '83; F. Loney, '81 (captain); J.P. Flint, '83. half backs: D.P. Morgan, '83; C. Winton, '81; J. Chetwood, '82. Backs: J. Harlan, '83; T.W. Cauldwell, '81.

Yale—Rushers: P.C. Fuller, '81; C.F. Beck, '83; F. Vernon, '81; J.S. Harding, L.S.; B.B. Lamb, '81; C.B. Storrs, '82; F.M. Adams, '82. Quarter back: W.J. Badger, '82. Half-backs: R.W. Watson, '81 (captain); W.C. Camp, M.S. Back: B.W. Bacon, '81.

Judges—For Princeton: H. McAlpine, '81. For Yale: Geo. H. Clark, '80.

Referee—W.H. Manning, '81, captain of the Harvard team.

Princeton won the lead, and chose the west goal with the wind in her favor, while the snow, which was now falling, thickly, blew directly into the faces of the Yale men. At 2:30 o'clock the ball was placed in the centre of the field, and Camp, of Yale, kicked it off. The ball was quickly recovered by Morgan, of Princeton, who lifted it high over Yale's rushers. Lamb muffed the ball, and in a twinkling the Princeton rushers were upon him. They captured the ball directly in front of Yale's goal. In the scrimmage that followed, Peace sent the ball over Yale's line, counselling her to touch down for safety, amid the cheers of Princeton, and the waving of orange ribbons. The ball was then kicked out by Camp, but was almost immediately afterward brought back to Yale's territory, where, after a short struggle, Yale was compelled to make another safety touch-down within five minutes from the beginning of the game. It seemed that Yale was being hard pushed, and the faces of her supporters began to lengthen. But after the second kick out a desperate rally was made, and a long run and kick by Camp carried the ball to the centre of the field. Hard fighting now followed, and after several scrimmages neither side seemed to have gained much advantage. When after a hard fight Yale gained the ball, the rushers ranged themselves in a double line, keenly watching each others' movements, and dodging backward and forward. Suddenly there was a confused rush. The ball had been tossed out toward the Yale goal and Watson, of Yale, seized it and started on a run. He had hardly gone fifteen feet before the Princeton rushers were upon him and he was thrown to the ground. In the scrimmage the ball was driven out of the field amid cries of "foul" and shouts from the excited crowd. Then came an angry argument. The ball was next kicked off by Harlan, and there was another claim of foul. A Yale rusher drove the ball over toward the Princeton goal, but Chetwood, of Princeton, batted it with his hand and foul was called again. But despite the wrangling the ball had been forced well up to Princeton's goal. There was a rush in which yellow, black and white flashed before the eye like the colors of a kaleidoscope—then the ball was forced outside the bounds. Just at this point had been heaped a large pile of snow. A Princeton rusher tripped and went into it head foremost. Three others met the same fate while the snow flew in clouds, almost concealing them from sight. But Princeton emerged, half smothered, with the ball. The others, covered with snow from head to foot, cleared their eyes and plunged into another scrimmage. A long kick by Princeton sent the ball sailing down the field, but it settled into Camp's outstretched hands. Like a flash he was off. For a few feet his way was clear. Then two Princeton rushers threw themselves in his way. He staggered, but kept on dodging past the hands that sought to grasp him, until after an exceptionally brilliant run, he was pulled to the earth just outside the boundary line. From one side to the other of the field rang out the "Rah! Rah!" of Yale. The ball was brought back, and Harding taking it, after several feints, passed it back. In the hurried scramble Badger failed to grasp the ball, already wet and slippery, and Watson securing it, sent it well into Princeton territory. Thereupon a long argument was held in the middle of the filed, while the spectators shivered and the grumbled. At last play was resumed, and an oblique kick drove the ball out into the crowd. It playfully caromed on the hat of a venerable policeman, then rolled among the spectators, who beat a hasty retreat over each other's feet in preference to being kicked out of the way by the "rushers." A Yale man kicked the ball when it was brought in, and Harlan missed it. The ball was slowly fought up toward the Princeton goal, and the "Boom-la" became refreshingly infrequent. At five minutes of 3 o'clock Princeton was forced to a safety touch-down. Yale reluctantly fell back and Princeton kicked out the ball. It was returned by Watson, of Yale, and caught by Winton. It was carefully placed in position and kicked toward the Yale goal, but it soon came flying back, and then formed the centre of a swaying group worrying the harmless leather globe as dog would worry a bone. At length the ball came into sight, quickly passed from hand to hand, until Harding, of Yale, sent it sailing toward the Princeton goal. The Yale rushers were up almost before it reached the ground, and in the scrimmage it was forced outside. Then a Princeton rusher obtained it. He braced himself for a run, but the instant's hesitation was fatal, and before he had decided what course he would take, he was quickly rolled over on the ground. Then Princeton saved herself by another safety touch-down. But the ball was no sooner kicked off from the goal than Watson sent it back, and the Yale men, excited by their nearness to victory, darted eagerly forward. Confusedly mingled, now clutching at each other, now rolling on the snowy ground, the yellow and the blue struggled until Harlan, after one or two vain attempts, grasped the ball, and Princeton again touched-down for safety.

In the kickoff one of the judges encountered the full force of the ball and immediately claimed a foul. When the ball was driven out into the field Watson was ready to kick it back. A Princeton rusher caught it and tried to run, but the canvas jackets were too near him. Brawny arms were thrown around his neck and waist, and he pitched headlong to the ground. Another safety touch-down for Princeton followed. Then a pretty bit of playing was witnessed. When the ball was kicked off, Watson, of Yale, caught it and made a short but brilliant dash. Finding his way blocked, by Princeton runners, he passed the ball to Lamb, who darted on until Princeton was dangerously near, when he tossed it over toward Camp. But Peace, of Princeton, was between, and leaping from the ground he caught the ball in mid air amid a roar of Princeton cheers, which silenced the exultant shouts of Yale. A hot rally by Princeton turned the tide in her favor and the ball crept steadily toward the Yale goal. Loney, the Princeton captain, tried to burst through the Yale rushers on his way to the desired haven, but he was incontinently topped over.

A desperate struggle followed. Faster and faster came the snow, almost hiding the writhing, swaying bodies of the players. Suddenly the dark ball rose in the air, hovering just over the Yale line, and the wearers of the blue were breathless with suspense as the Princeton rushers swept on toward the Yale goal. But Watson catching the ball effected a safety touch-down, and Princeton fell back. A long kick relieved Yale from immediate danger, and the savage way in which Lamb tackled a Princeton rusher showed that the Yale blood was up. Then the men formed in lines. Watson attempted to burst through the Princeton ranks, but came to grief, and soon Yale made another safety touch-down. Presently, Peace, of Princeton, getting the ball passed it to Bradford, who dodged, and doubled, and twisted, until his pursuers were fairly beside themselves. Winton seized the ball at last, and rolled over and over until he brought up in a snow-bank outside the line. The ball was brought back, and, as soon as the men had taken position, it was passed to Watson, who kicked it up the field. But McKee, of Princeton caught it, and Princeton was therefore entitled to a "place kick." The noisy cheers were hushed, for the distance to the Yale line seemed comparatively small. "Can he kick a goal?" was the universal thought as Winton of Princeton advanced. A moment's suspense—then the ball shot diagonally off to one side amid Yale cheers and Princeton groans. Beck, Camp and Watson struggled to better Yale's fortunes by spirited runs, but they were quickly tackled and thrown and half-time was called with the ball near the Yale line.

The dark lines of hats and coats filling the out-of-doors stand had became white with snow. The few umbrellas around the field had changed to rounded graceful domes. The snow drove down the field in the faces of the patient men, who swung their arms and stamped their feet to keep off the insidious chilliness of the air. Another means of keeping out the chill (still more popular) was sold at so much a glass in a tent at the end of the grand stand. A hollow thumping issued from the stand as impatient spectators danced upon the seats to gain a little warmth.

At about 3:30 the second half of the game was called. Yale took the west, or stable goal, favored by the wind, and Princeton the east. Winton, of Princeton, kicked off, greeted by thundering volleys of "Boom-las." Camp sent the ball back. It was fought outside the line, passed back, picked up by Harlan, and finally caught by Badger who then gained a "place" or "scratch" kick. This, however, proved of little value, and one struggle succeeded another, while Yale and Princeton rushers hurled each other down with a pleasing disregard of possible broken bones. The field, before white, now showed bare black patches where men had rolled over and over, or fallen on the ball in writhing heaps. Watson delivered a well-meant kick, but a Princeton rusher opposed his body and stopped the ball at the expense of a considerable personal discomfort. The ball approached the Yale line and a hard-fought tussle ended in a safety touch-down by Yale. Several betting men, who had invested heavily, had gained access within the lines, and shouted at the referee until they were gently but firmly ejected by a policeman.

A long kick by Yale was well caught by Princeton, and in an attempt to pass the ball a Yale rusher gained a round of applause by jumping into the air and catching it. A kick by Camp well followed up by the Yale rushers, brought Princeton into danger, and a safety touch-down was effected. The ball had become so slippery that it was almost universally fumbled. On both sides the fighting was desperate. Once, a Yale and Princeton rusher rolled over and over, clinching each other, under the ropes out into the crowd. Loney, of Princeton, and Bacon, of Yale, showed good play, and several others exhibited a commendable willingness to dive into the snow banks beyond the line. Chances for several kicks were offered, but failed to be particularly advantageous. A kick by Watson sent the ball near the Princeton goal, and a hot scrimmage took place well inside the twenty-five yard line. The wriggling mass of arms and legs seemed upon the very goal line. For an instant the crowd was silent, but Yale failed to secure the hoped-for touch-down. The ball was fought back. Watson kicked it; then, starting on a sharp run, was underneath it when it fell. Harding, of Yale, plunged across the field with two men hanging around his neck. There was a quick, breathless scurry—then Princeton protected herself by a safety touch-down. The battle continued close to the Princeton goal, the defenders of which were forced to save themselves by safety touch-downs. Both sides fought as if for very life. Once or twice the ball went over Princeton's line.

Hisses, cheers, and groans rose from the excited crowd at various decisions of the referee. For an instant the figures of the players were still; then a rush followed and a heap of four men was seen on the ground from which an arm waved and a voice called "foul." For the rest of the time Princeton simply fumbled the ball, acting on the defensive without trying to gain any advantage. The crowd grew restless as one Princeton man after another with monotonous regularity fell flat on the ball and very slowly picked himself up. Calls of "Why don't you play foot-ball?" from the crowd were mingled with hisses from Yale spectators as it was evident that Princeton was simply playing against time. The Princeton captain claimed that the time was up, but his claim was not allowed, and Yale doggedly kept on. Suddenly Loney, the Princeton captain, darted out from the contending group with the ball.

"The time's now up," he shrieked, waving his cap.

The game was drawn. At once a shrill yell rose from every Princeton throat. Yellow and black flags waved wildly, hats were tossed in the air and there was a rush into the field. Princeton had made twice as many safety touch-downs as Yale. As soon as the referee called "time," Watson, the Yale captain, challenged Princeton to play for another hour. This was refused. Princeton was then challenged to play Yale at any time or place, and this also was declined. Then the Princeton players were exultantly carried around the field on the shoulders of their comrades. The great crowd poured over the snow toward the gate. The drags wheeled into line, the men on top cheering defiantly for their respective colleges; and amid a deafening din of "Boom-las" and "Rah, Rahs," the football season of 1880 came to an end.

Chapter 12

GYMNASTICS

Two groups made major contributions to the development of gymnastics in North America during the years between 1860 and 1880. The first included native proponents of physical training who sharply criticized the poor health of the people, especially in the United States. The second was German immigrants who organized clubs (turnvereins) to promote their favorite activity along with their political and social philosophy. Both the domestic and foreign approaches focused primarily on improving personal fitness through exercise, but they also contributed to the beginnings of competitive gymnastics as a modern sport.

During the 1860s the growing interest in physical training, the new philosophy of "muscular Christianity" (discussed in Chapter 1), and the impact of the Civil War all boosted public support for gymnastics in both the United States and Canada. Many newspaper editors, educators, and clergymen preached the new gospel of fitness for both men and women. They condemned the males' obsession with work and their neglect of their bodies; they also argued that females should pay more attention to their health so that they could perform better as wives and mothers. Dio Lewis's *The New Gymnastics for Men, Women, and Children* presents a system which featured free exercises with light weights, performed with minimal apparatus, and accompanied by music. During the war years many schools and colleges instituted military drills for students. In the Morrill Act of 1862 the federal government required military training in state universities founded under its provision. Although some institutions substituted military exercise for physical education, in general the martial spirit did heighten public concern for health and personal conditioning.

The German Turner societies also grew substantially during this period, and they profoundly influenced the growth of gymnastics. During the war they contributed substantial numbers to the ranks of the Union army, with large numbers of recruits (and sometimes entire companies) enrolling in New York City, Newark, Philadelphia, Cincinnati, St. Louis, Chicago, Milwaukee, and Indianapolis. After peace returned associations of these societies (turnerbunds) launched new campaigns for gymnastics and also various political, social, and educational reforms. By 1867 the North American Turnerbund included eighteen districts, 148 clubs, and a total membership of 10,200. The Constitution and By-Laws of the Philadelphia Gymnastic Society reprinted in this chapter also includes the platform of the North American association. During the 1870s the Turners joined with officials from local gymnasiums and athletic clubs to sponsor tournaments in which participants displayed their skills and competed for prizes. The third document below is a narrative of a gymnastic and athletic meet held in New York City in 1873.

Finally, during this period a few colleges in the northeastern United States actively supported the new discipline of physical education. Amherst, Bowdoin, Yale, and

Harvard took the lead in requiring undergraduates to pursue training in gymnastic exercises. "The Gymnasium, and Gymnastics in Harvard College" describes the pioneering efforts of the instructors at that institution, while the final selection is an excerpt from the autobiography of one of the most influential proponents of physical fitness, Dudley A. Sargent.

DIO LEWIS AND THE NEW GYMNASTICS

Dioclesian Lewis (1823-1886), a native of Auburn, New York, dedicated his life to the causes of temperance reform and physical culture. After one year of training at Harvard Medical School (1845-46) he began a private practice, without a degree. During this period he devised a system of "free gymnastics," or exercises without fixed apparatus. In 1851 he received an honorary medical degree from a college in Cleveland, Ohio. In 1861 he incorporated the Boston Normal Institute for Physical Education. The following year he published his best known book, which went through many editions over the next few decades. These excerpts are reprinted from that work, *The New Gymnastics For Men, Women, and Children* (Boston, 1864), pp. 9-14,16-18, 59-69.

PHYSICAL EDUCATION

I have nothing to say of the importance of Physical Education.

He who has not seen in the imperfect growth, pale faces, distorted forms and painful nervousness of the American People, enough to justify any and all efforts to elevate our physical tone, would not be awakened by words, written or spoken. Presuming that all who read this work are fully cognizant of the imperative need which calls it forth, I shall enter at once upon my task.

My object is to present a new system of Gymnastics. Novel in philosophy, and practical details, its distinguishing peculiarity is a complete adaptation, alike, to the strongest man, the feeblest woman, and the frailest child. The athlete finds abundant opportunity for the greatest exertions, while the delicate child is never injured.

Dispensing with the cumbrous apparatus of the ordinary gymnasium, its implements are all calculated not only to impart strength of muscle, but to give flexibleness, agility and grace of movement.

None of the apparatus, (with one or two slight exceptions,) is fixed. Each and every piece is held in the hand, so that any hall or other room may be used for exercises.

PUBLIC INTEREST IN PHYSICAL EDUCATION.

The true educator sees in the present public interest in physical education, a hope and a promise.

And now he is only solicitous that the great movement so auspiciously inaugurated, may not degenerate into some unprofitable specialty.

One man strikes a blow equal to five hundred pounds; another lifts eleven hundred pounds; another bends his back so that his head rests against his heels; another walks a rope over the great cataract; another runs eleven miles an hour; another turns sixty somersets without resting.

We are greatly delighted with all these—pay our money to see them perform; but as neither one of these could do what either of the others does, so we all know that such feats, even if they were at all desirable, are not possible with one in a thousand. The question is not what shall be done for these few extraordinary persons. Each has instinctively sought and found his natural specialty.

But the question is, what shall be done for the millions of women, children and men, who are dying for physical training? My attempt to answer this momentous question will be found in this work.

DO CHILDREN REQUIRE SPECIAL GYMNASTIC TRAINING?

An eminent writer has recently declared his conviction that boys need no studied muscle culture. "Give them," he says, "the unrestrained use of the grove, the field, the yard, the street, with the various sorts of apparatus for boys' games and sports, and they can well dispense with the scientific gymnasium."

This is a misapprehension, as is easy to convince all, who are disposed to think!

With all our lectures, conversations, newspapers, and other similar means of mental culture, we are not willing to trust the intellect without scientific training. The poorest man in the State demands for his children the culture of the organized school; and he is right. An education left to chance and the street, would be but a disjointed product. To insure strength, patience and consistency, there must be methodical cultivation and symmetrical growth. But there is no need of argument on this point. In regard to mental training, there is, fortunately, among Americans, no difference of opinion. Discriminating, systematic, scientific culture, is our demand.

No man doubts that chess and the newspaper furnish exercise and growth; but we hold, and very justly too, that exercise and growth without qualification, are not our purpose. We require that the growth shall be of our purpose. We require that the growth shall be of a peculiar kind—what we call scientific and symmetrical. This is vital. The education of chance would prove unbalanced, morbid, profitless.

Is not this equally true of the body? Is the body one single organ, which, if exercised is sure to grow in the right way? On the contrary, is it not an exceedingly complicated machine, the symmetrical development of which requires discriminating, studied management? With the thoughtful mind, argument and illustration are scarcely necessary; but I may perhaps be excused by the intelligent reader for one simple illustration. A boy has round or stooping shoulders: hereby the organs of the chest and abdomen are all displaced. Give him the freedom of the yard and street—give him marbles, a ball, the skates! Does any body suppose he will become straight? Must he not, for this, and a hundred other defects have special, scientific training? There can be no doubt of it!

Before our system of education can claim an approach to perfection, we must have attached to each school a Professor, who thoroughly comprehends the wants of the body, and knows practically the means by which it may be made symmetrical, flexible, vigorous and enduring.

MILITARY DRILLS.

Since we have, unhappily, become a military people, the soldier's special training has been much considered as a means of general physical culture. Numberless schools, public and private, have already introduced the drill and make it a part of each day's exercises.

But this mode of exercise can never furnish the muscle culture which we Americans so much need. Nearly all our exercise is of the lower half of the body—we walk, we run up and down stairs, and thus cultivate hips and legs, which, as compared with the upper half of the body, are muscular. But our arms, shoulders, and chests are ill-formed and weak. Whatever artificial muscular training is employed, should be specially adapted to the development of the upper half of the body.

Need I say that the military drill fails to bring into varied and vigorous play the chest and shoulders? Indeed in almost the entire drill, are not these parts held immovably in one constrained position? In all but the cultivation of uprightness, the military drill is singularly deficient in the requisites of a system of muscle training, adapted to a weak-chested people.

The exercise employed to invigorate the body, should be such as are calculated to make the form erect, and the shoulders and chest, large and vigorous.

Dancing, to say nothing of its almost inevitably mischievous concomitants, brings into play chiefly that part of the body which is already in comparative vigor, and which, besides, has less to do directly, with the size, position and vigor of the vital organs.

Horse-back exercise is admirable, and has many peculiar advantages which can be claimed for no other training, but may it not be much indulged, while the chest and shoulders are left drooping and weak?

Skating is graceful and exhilarating, but to say nothing of the injury which not infrequently attends the sudden change from the stagnant heat of our furnaced dwellings to the bleak winds of the icy lake, is it not true that the chest muscles are so little moved, that the finest skating may be done with the arms folded?

I suggest these thoughts for the intelligent reader, and then take the liberty to request his careful examination of the "Ring" and other exercises which appear in this work. Are they not completely adapted to the obvious necessities of our bodies?

MUSIC WITH GYMNASTICS.

A party may dance without music. I have seen it done. But the exercise is a little dull.

Exercises with the upper extremities are as much improved by music as those with the lower extremities. Indeed with the former there is much more need of music, as the arms make no noise, such as might secure concert in exercises with the lower extremities.

A small drum, costing perhaps $5, which may be used as a bass drum, with the one beating stick, with which any one may keep time, is, I suppose, the sort of music most classes in gymnastics will use at first. And it has advantages. While it is less pleasing than some other instruments, it secures more perfect concert than any other.

The violin and piano are excellent, but on some accounts the hand-organ is the best of all.

Feeble and apathetic people, who have little courage to undertake gymnastic training, accomplish wonders under the inspiration of music. I believe five times as much muscle can be coaxed out, under this delightful stimulus, as without it.

THE GYMNASIUM.

The gymnasium must not be cold, but should be well ventilated. The best plan is to raise it to 65 or 68, and when the class begins, drop the upper sash of the windows, raising them again when the teacher announces a period of rest.

It is a common mistake to suppose that the gymnast should exercise in a cold room until he is warm. It is not difficult to accomplish this, but cold air is unfavorable to the development of muscle. My own rule is to make the hall as warm as for a lecture, and then open the windows freely during the exercise....

GYMNASTIC DRESS.

...The most essential feature of the dress is perfect liberty about the waist and shoulders. The female costume may be never so short, if the waist or shoulders be trammelled, the exertions will serve no good purpose. If the arms can be thrust perpendicularly upward without drawing a quarter of an ounce on the dress, the most vital point has been secured.

It is made very loose about the waist and shoulders worn without hoops, but with a thin skirt as near the color of the dress as possible, and only stiff enough to keep the outside skirt from hanging closely to the legs. This skirt should be fastened to the belt of the dress so that is will not hang below the dress when the arms are raised.

The present style of Garibaldi waist is very beautiful. It is particularly appropriate for gymnastics, as it allows the freest action of the arms and shoulders. But to permit this waist to fall over the belt, which is its peculiar feature, the belt is usually made tight enough to keep it in its position. This is wrong. Buttons should be placed on the inside of the belt, the same as on gentlemen's pants for suspenders, and the same kind of suspenders should be worn. In this way the belt may be very loose, and yet being supported over the shoulders, it will remain in its proper position.

...the gentlemen's dress has no belt. The jacket is buttoned to the pants, as is the fashion with small boys. The tailor will easily manage to conceal the buttons. The dress about the shoulders should be *very loose*. The pants must be loose, and may be fastened at the knee, as in the Zouave dress, or worn down to the ankle.

At all seasons of the year the material should be flannel.

The shoe I am in the habit of wearing is low quartered, fastened with a strong buckle, and the bottom is covered with a layer of rubber. In many of the difficult feats the foot is apt to slip, unless the rubber is added.

A majority of my pupils simply remove their coats and exercise in the street dress, but the garb I have described, has signal advantages....

DUMB BELL EXERCISES.

For more than two thousand years the dumb bell has been in use as a means of physical culture. It was highly prized by the Greeks. Many advantages are justly claimed in its behalf. If used in private, it occupies little space either at rest or in action. For the same reason it is excellent in the training of large classes. Although not to be compared with the New Gymnastic Ring, the Dumb Bell deserves its great popularity.

Among the Greeks it had a peculiar shape, and in this respect has undergone many changes, of which something will be said hereafter. Its present shape is well known. A practical suggestion upon this point may not be amiss. The handle should be at least half an inch longer than the width of the hand, of such size as can be easily grasped, with a slight swell in the middle. The manufacturer must not forget there is a wide difference between the hand of a little girl and that of a large man.

Heretofore dumb bells have been made of metals. The weight in this country has usually been considerable. The general policy at present is to employ those as heavy as the health seeker can put up. This is wrong. In the great German Gymnastic Institutes dumb bells were formerly employed weighing from one hundred pounds, but now, SCHREBER and other distinguished authors, condemn such weights and advocate those weighing from two to five pounds. I think those weighing two pounds are heavy enough for any man, and as it is important that they be of considerable size, I introduced some years ago, those made of wood. Every year my faith grows stronger in their superiority.

In my early experience as a teacher of Gymnastics I advocated heavy dumb bells, prescribing for those who could put up one hundred pounds, a bell of that weight. As my success had always been with heavy weights, pride led me to continue their use, long after I doubted the wisdom of such a course. For some years I have employed only those made of wood.

I know it will be said that dumb bells of two pounds weight will do for women and children, but can not answer the requirements of strong men.

The weight of the dumb bell turns entirely on the manner in which it is used. If only lifted over the head, one or two pounds would be absurdly light; but if used as we employ them, then one weighing ten pounds is beyond the strength of the strongest. No man can enter one of my classes of little girls even and go through the exercises with bells weighing ten pounds each.

We had a good opportunity to laugh at a class of young men last year, who, upon entering the gymnasium organized an insurrection against the wooden dumb bells, and through a committee asked me to procure iron ones; I ordered a quantity weighing three pounds each; they used them part of one evening, and when asked the following evening, which they would have, replied, "the wooden ones will do."

A just statement of the issue is this: if you only lift the dumb bell from the floor, put it up, and then put it down again, of course it should be heavy, or there is no exercise; but if you would use it in a great variety of ways, assuming a hundred graceful attitudes, and bringing the muscles into use in every direction, requiring skill and followed by a harmonious development, the bell must be light.

There need be no controversy between the light weight and the heavy weight party on this point. We of the light weight party agree that if the bell is to be used as the heavy weight party uses it, it must be heavy; but if we use it, then it must be light. If they of the heavy weight party think not, we only ask them to try it.

The only question remains is that which lies between all heavy and light gymnastics, viz: whether strength or flexibility is to be preferred. Without entering upon a discussion of the physiological principles which underlie this subject, I will simply say that I prefer the latter. The Hanlon brothers and Heenan are, physiologically considered, greatly superior to heavy lifters.

But there I ought to say that no man can be flexible without a good degree of strength. It is not however, the kind of strength involved in great lifting. Heenan is a very strong man, can strike a blow twice as hard as Windship, but cannot lift seven hundred pounds nor put up an eighty-pound dumb bell. Wm. Hanlon, who is probably the finest gymnast, with the exception of Blondin, ever seen on this continent, cannot lift six hundred pounds. Such men have a great fear of lifting. They know almost by instinct that it spoils their muscles.

One of the finest gymnasts in the country told me that in several attempts to lift five hundred pounds he failed, and that he should never try it again. This same gymnast owns a fine horse. Ask him to lend that horse to draw before a cart and he will refuse, because such labor would make the animal stiff, and unfit him for light, graceful movements before the carriage.

The same physiological law holds true of man; lifting great weights affects him as drawing heavy loads affects the horse. So far from man's body being an exception to this law, it bears with peculiar force upon him. Moving great weights through small spaces, produces a slow, inelastic, inflexible man. No matter how flexible a young man may be, let him join a circus company, and lift the cannon twice a day, for two or three years, and he will become as inflexible as a cart horse. No matter how elastic the colt is when first harnessed to the cart, he will soon become so inelastic that he is unfit to serve before the carriage.

Men, women and children should be strong, but it should be the strength of grace, flexibility, agility and endurance; it should not be the strength of a great lifter. I alluded to the gymnastics of the circus. Let all who are curious in regard to the point I am discussing, visit it. Permit me to call special attention to three features—to the man who lifts the cannon, to the india-rubber man, and to the general performer.

The lifter and the india-rubber man constitute the two mischievous extremes. It is impossible that in either there should be the highest physiological conditions; but in the persons of the Hanlon brothers, who are general performers is found the model gymnast. They can neither lift great weights nor tie themselves into knots, but they occupy a point between the these two extremes. They possess both strength and flexibility, and resemble fine, active, agile, vigorous carriage horses, which occupy a point between the slow cart horse and the long-legged, loose-jointed animal.

With heavy dumb bells the extent of motions is very slight, and of course the range and freedom of action will be correspondingly so. This is a point of great importance. The limbs, and indeed the entire body, should have the widest and freest range of motion. It is only thus that our performances in the business or pleasures of life become most effective. A complete, equable circulation of the blood is thereby most perfectly secured. And this, I may remark, is in one aspect the physiological purpose of all exercise. The race horse has a much more vigorous circulation than the cart horse. It is a fact not unfamiliar with horsemen, that when a horse is transferred from slow, heavy work to the carriage, the surface veins about the neck and legs begins at once to enlarge; when the change is made from the carriage to the cart, the reverse is the result.

And when we consider that the principal object of all physical training is an elastic, vigorous condition of the nervous system, the superiority of light gymnastics becomes still more obvious. The nervous system is the fundamental fact of our earthly life. All other parts of the organism exist and work for it. It controls all and is the seat of pain and pleasure.

The impressions upon the stomach, for example, resulting in a better or worse digestion, must be made through the nerves. This supreme control of the nervous system is forcibly illustrated in the change made by joyful or sad tidings.

The overdue ship is believed to have gone down with her valuable, uninsured cargo. Her owner paces the wharf, sallow and wan; appetite and digestion gone. She heaves in sight! She lies at the wharf! The happy man goes aboard, hears all is safe, and, taking the officers to a hotel, devours with them a dozen monstrous compounds, with the keenest appetite, and without a subsequent pang....

Could we have an unbroken succession of good news, we should all have good digestion without a gymnasium. But in a world of vexation and disappointment, we are driven to the necessity of muscle culture, and other hygienic expedients, to give the nervous system that support and vitality, which our fitful surroundings deny.

If we would make our muscle training contributive in the highest degree to the healthful elasticity of our nerves, the exercises must be such, as will bring into varied combinations and play all our muscles and nerves. Those exercises which require great accuracy, skill and dash, are just those which secure this happy and complete intermarriage of nerve and muscle. If any one doubts that boxing and small sword will do more to give elasticity and tone to the nervous system, than lifting kegs of nails, then I will give him over to the heavy lifters.

Another point I take the liberty to urge. Without *accuracy* in the performance of the feats, the interest must be transient. This principle is strikingly exemplified in military training. Those who have studied our infantry drill, have been struck with its simplicity and have wondered that men could go through with its details every day for years, without disgust. If the drill master permit carelessness, then, authority alone can force the men through the evolutions; but if he enforce the greatest precision, they return to their task every morning, for twenty years, with fresh and increasing interest.

What precision, permit me to ask, is possible in "putting up" a heavy dumb-bell? But in the new dumb bell exercises, there is opportunity and necessity for all the accuracy and skill which are found in the most elaborate military drills.

I have been a teacher of boxing and fencing, and I say with confidence, that in neither or both is there such a field for fine posturing, wide, graceful action, and studied accuracy, as is to be found in the new series of dumb bell exercises.

But, it is said, if you use bells weighing only two pounds, you must work an hour to reach the exercise which the heavy ones would furnish in five minutes. I need not inform those who have practiced the new series with the light bells, that this objection is made in ignorance. If you simply "put up" the light bell, it is true, but if you use it as herein described and illustrated, it is not true. On the contrary, in less than five minutes, legs, hip, back, arms, shoulders, neck, lungs and heart, will each and all make the most emphatic remonstrance against even a quarter of an hour's practice of such feats.

At this point it may be urged that those exercises which hasten the action of the thoracic vicera, to any considerable degree, are simply exhaustive. This is another blunder of the "big muscle" men. They seem to think you can determine every man's constitution and health, by the tape line; and that all exercises whose results are not determinable by measurement are worthless.

I need scarcely say, there are certain conditions of brain, muscle and of every other tissue, far more important in size; but what I desire to urge more particularly in this connection, is the importance, the great physiological advantages, of just those exercises in which the lungs and heart are brought into active play. These organs are no exceptions to the law that exercise is the principle condition of development.—Their vigorous training adds more to the stock of vitality, than that of other organs. A man may stand still and lift kegs of nails and heavy dumb bells until his shoulders and arms are Sampsonian, he will contribute far less to his health and longevity, than by a daily run of a mile or two.

Speaking in a general way, those exercises in which the lungs and heart are made to go at a vigorous pace, are to be ranked among the most useful. The "double-quick" of the soldier contributes more in five minutes to his digestion and endurance, than ordinary drill in two hours.

I have said an elastic tone of the nervous system is the physiological purpose of all physical training. If one may be allowed such analysis, I would add that we exercise our muscles to invigorate the thoracic and abdominal viscera. These in their turn support and invigorate the nervous system. All exercises which operate more directly upon these internal organs,—as for example, laughing, deep breathing and running, contribute most effectively to the stamina of the brain and nerves. It is only mania for monstrous arms and shoulders that could have misled the intelligent gymnast on this point.

But finally, it is said, you certainly cannot deny that rapid motions with great sweep, exhaust more than slow motions through limited spaces. A great lifter said to me the other day, "do you pretend to deny that a locomotive with a light train, flying at the rate of forty miles an hour, consumes more fuel than one with a heavy train, moving at the rate of five miles?" I did not attempt to deny it. "Well then," he added with an air of triumph, "what have you to say now about these great sweeping feats with your light dumb bells, as compared with the slow putting up of heavy ones?"

I replied by asking him another question. "Do you pretend to deny that when you drive your horse ten miles within an hour, before a light carriage, he is more exhausted than by drawing a load two miles an hour?" "That's my doctrine exactly," he said. Then I asked, "why don't you always drive two miles an hour?" "But my patients would all die," replied my friend. I did not say aloud what was passing in my mind—that the danger to his patients might be less than he imagined; but I suggested, that nearly every man as well as every horse, had duties in this life which involved the necessity of rapid and vigorous motions. That were this slow movement generally adopted, every phase of human life would be stripped of progress, success and glory.

As our artificial training is designed to fit us for the more successful performance of the business of life, I suggest that the training should be, in character, somewhat assimilated to those duties. If you would train a horse for the carriage, you would not prepare him by driving at a slow pace before a heavy load. If you did, the first fast drive would go hard with him.

Just so with a man. If he is to lift hogsheads of sugar, or kegs of nails, as a business, he may be trained by heavy lifting; but if his business requires the average velocity and free motions of human occupations, then upon the basis of his heavy, slow training, he will find himself in actual life, in the condition of the dray horse, who is pushed before the light carriage at high speed.

Perhaps it is not improper to add, that to me, all this talk about expenditure of vitality is full of sophistry. Teachers and writers speak of our stock of vitality, as if it were a vault of gold, upon which you cannot draw without lessening the quantity. Whereas it is rather like the mind or heart enlarging by action, gaining by expenditure.

When Daniel Boone was living alone in Kentucky, his intellectual exercises were doubtless of the quiet, slow, heavy character. Other white men joined him. Under the social stimulus, his thinking became more sprightly. Suppose that in time he had come to write vigorously, and to speak in the most eloquent brilliant manner, does any one imagine that he would have lost in mental vigor and dash by the process? Would not the brain, which had only slow exercise in his isolated life, become bold, brilliant and dashing, by bold, brilliant and dashing efforts.

A farm boy has slow, heavy muscles. He has been accustomed to heavy exercises. He is transferred to the circus, and performs, after a few years training, a hundred beautiful, splendid feats! He at length reaches the matchless Zampillaerstation of Wm. Hanlon. Does any one think that his body has lost power in this brilliant education?

Is it true in either intellectual or physical training, bold, brilliant efforts, under proper conditions and limitations, exhaust the powers of life? On the contrary, is it not true that we find vigorous, bold, dashing, brilliant efforts, the only source of vigorous, bold, dashing and brilliant powers?

In this discussion I have not considered the treatment of invalids. The principles presented are applicable to the training of the children and adults of average vitality.

In a work upon which I am now engaged, devoted to the "Movement Cure,".... I shall advocate, and for reasons which will appear in the work, an entirely different policy.

In the mean time I will rest upon the general statement, that all persons of both sexes, and of every age, who are possessed of average vitality, should, in the department of physical education, employ light apparatus, and execute a great variety of feats, which require skill, accuracy, courage, dash, presence of mind, quick eye and hand-in brief, which demand a vigorous and complete exercise of all the powers and faculties with which the Creator has endowed us.

While deformed and diseased persons should be treated in consonance with the philosophy of the *Swedish Movement Cure,* in which the movements are slow and limited.

THE PHILADELPHIA TURNVEREIN

The following excerpts from *The Constitution and By-Laws of the Philadelphia Gymnastic Club* (Philadelphia, 1872), pp. 3-4, 31-38 are reprinted with the permission of the German Society of Pennsylvania. These passages were translated by Claire E. Nolte.

PLATFORM OF THE NORTH AMERICAN GYMNASTIC UNION

The North American Gymnastic Union (Turnerbund) aspires to support, through the unification of all clubs supporting this platform, the efforts these clubs undertake to make their members men of strong bodies and free spirits. It is its special task to give its members, through the use of all the means at its disposal, a proper understanding of the efforts at radical reform in social, political, and religious arenas, to assist in their realization, as well as in the protection of the rights with which men were born.

This union shall be a nursery for all ideas, which arise from a natural, and therefore a rational, view of the world. The gymnasts will fight every effort to limit freedom of conscience, along with all efforts to abridge human rights, for these are not reconcilable with truly humane and democratic principles.

The gymnastic union sees in the manner in which public affairs are handled in most cases in this country a great danger to the development of true freedom; therefore it is the duty of individual clubs to undertake the education of their members about the outstanding political questions of the day, and to oppose political corruption as much as they can.

Further, it is the duty of this union to the best of its ability to support all efforts to expand adult education, and to promote as much as possible a free and ethical education for young people through founding and supporting good schools....

PART TWO

2. Rules of Gymnastics

1. The Gymnastic Director (Turnwart), along with the Club Trainers (Vorturner), will maintain the proper order on the training field, and each gymnast is obligated to follow their orders.

2. It is the duty of every gymnast, when not prevented by serious reasons, to appear regularly on the training ground. The reason for failure to appear must be given to the Gymnastic Director at the latest on the first evening of training following the missed session. Whoever misses three sessions in one month without good reasons will, in the first instance, be invited to appear before the club's Executive Council. In case of repetition of such behavior, he is to be barred from the club for a period of three months.

3. No one should execute without help any exercise which he has not properly learned, or with which he is not familiar. Also, no one should exercise on a horizontal bar whose crossbar he can not reach by standing or jumping.

4. The Gymnastic Director, as he wishes, must either take roll call himself and notify the missing gymnasts, or let the Club Trainers do so.

5. The Club Trainers and their assistants will train on a certain day of the week under the leadership of the Gymnastic Director.

6. No one is permitted in the exercise area during a training evening who is not taking part in the exercising, with the exception of those who can not participate because of illness, or passive members of the club. Guests may attend only if accompanied by a member; they must be introduced to the Gymnastic Director, who must show them seats where they will not disturb the gymnasts in their exercising.

7. The club will decide when to hold training sessions.

3. Rules of Gymnastic Squads

1. The gymnasts will be divided up into various squads by the Gymnastic Director, who will likewise select the Club Trainers to lead them.

2. It is the duty of the Trainers not to demonstrate any exercises which are beyond the ability of the group, and also to pay special attention to, and make them aware of, proper handgrips.

3. Each individual must copy, or attempt to copy, each exercise demonstrated by the Trainers.

4. Following the call to line up, each individual must take the place assigned him and proceed in order to the apparatus as indicated.

5. There will be no talking during squad training except that relevant to the issue at hand. No one may leave his squad without informing the Club Trainer.

6. The Gymnastic Director will give the signal for individual practice (Kurturnen), as well as for squad shifting and starting.

7. Each Trainer must see to it that the movable apparatus is returned to its assigned place.

8. Only one individual may train on one piece of apparatus. Each without exception must comply with the call "Make Way!"

4. Gymnastic School

Purpose

1. To prevent one-sided development, to give the body a calm and strong bearing and the upbringing an enduring foundation, a gymnastic school for children will be created as an opportunity to strengthen and perfect their young bodies through healthy training, as well as to familiarize them early with order and proper behavior.

Stipulations for Application and Acceptance

2. a] Only children older than six years will be accepted....

Leadership

4. The gymnastic school will be led by a gymnastic teacher chosen by the club and its executive council. Nominations for this position should be made in a regular club assembly, however other names may be added by the club on the day the vote is taken. The gymnastic teacher is chosen for a term of one year. The gymnastic teacher must, in regard to his students:

a] Pay attention to maintaining proper behavior and strict order.

b] Be intent on the harmonious development of the body through systematic gymnastic training.

c] Take special care to only use appropriate instructional methods.

d] Offer sessions at the time established by the club's Executive Council.

e] Select necessary assistants with the approval of the club's Executive Council.

f] Go to the club's Executive Council with any desires or complaints.

g] Have the right to expel from a session any student who, after three warnings, still does not maintain discipline; in case of repetition, to bar this student for eight days; and in case of a third offense, to bring this student's name to the club's Executive Council for exclusion from the list. The person who proposed the student for membership, or a member of the club, may appeal such an expulsion to the club's Executive Council.

The club's Executive Council must give a report to the club every three months about the status of the gymnastic school.

The club will appoint the Gymnastic Teacher along with a helper for every thirty students.

Gymnastic Rules

5. a] The Gymnastic Teacher will maintain the proper order on the training field, and each student is obligated to follow his orders.

b] Each student who is absent from the training field should bring an appropriate excuse from his parents or guardians to the following training session.

c] No student should execute any exercise which he has not properly learned, or with which he is not familiar, without help from the teacher. Also, no one should exercise on a horizontal bar whose crossbar he can not reach by standing or jumping.

d] The premises will not be opened before the time specified for instruction.

e] Entrance to the training area is closed to non-students.

f] Students must leave the premises in an orderly and quiet fashion after the end of sessions.

6. Gymnastic students have the right to free sketch classes.

5. Youth-Clubs

Purpose

1. The purpose of the Youth Clubs is to cultivate physically and morally strong youth, to familiarize them with proper gymnastic club life as well as with parliamentary procedures, and in them and through them to uphold and propagate a respectable lifestyle for German youth.

Organization and Administration

2. Youth between the ages of 16 and 21, who desire to attain the above-stated goal, will organize themselves as an autonomous entity, create a constitution, and attend to club business with the assistance of committee chosen by the men's club from among its members.

GYMNASTIC COMPETITION

The German Turners, the Scottish Caledonians, and native born athletes all contributed to the development of gymnastics in North America. On special occasions representatives from all three groups gathered to compete for prizes. This selection describes the action and results for a meet held in New York City in 1873 in which men competed in a variety of gymnastic and field events. The contestants included delegations from John Wood's Gymnasium, Manhattan, the New York Athletic Club, the New York Turnverein, the New York YMCA, the New York Caledonian Club, Princeton College, the Young Men's Christian Union, Boston, the Catholic Institute of Newark, N.J., the Yonkers (N.Y.) Lyceum, the Staten Island Turnverein, the Newark Caledonian Club, and the Chicago Caledonian Club. It is reprinted from The Turf, Field and Farm, 14 November 1873, p. 314.

AMATEUR GYMNASTIC AND ATHLETIC TOURNAMENT

...In addition to the official summary of the competitions we will give as general an account of the entire meeting as our space will allow, bearing in mind the great importance of this undertaking in view of its undeniable influence on the strength and habits of our young men and the thousand diverting benefits to be expected from an entertainment which will bring hundreds of recruits under the flag of health and morality—two things the need of which is more felt at the present time than at any previous period.

To begin at the beginning, it is necessary to state that the original object of this tournament was to give an impetus to athletic sports by an exhibition of the almost incredible skill and strength of representative amateur gymnasts and athletes from every section of the country. Shortly after the plans had matured, the yellow fever plague at Memphis pointed out a worthy charity upon which to bestow the proceeds, but all the wants of the stricken people being relieved, it was decided to devote whatever profit there might be to the poor of New York. Thirty solid gold medals were offered by the Association as first prizes in the various competitions, and handsome diplomas as second prizes. A number of special prizes were offered, of which more will follow—among them one by Mr. John Wood, who offered $100 as a prize for the best written essay on physical culture. As this competition was the first decided, we give the result in advance of the athletic trials. There were six essays, several of which were pronounced excellent, but there was no doubt that the award of the judges was as fair as it was well deserved—the victor being William Wood, Esq., whose great experience in and enthusiastic love for, the subject treated, combined with unusual literary ability and ripe discrimination, are fully united in this little work, the persual of which is no less a pleasure than the following of its excellent advice must prove a bane to ills, aches and doctors' bills.

The entertainment at the Academy commenced with an exhibition of a class from Burnham's Gymnasium, Brooklyn, in calisthenic exercises.

The numerous graceful and strength-giving movements were executed in a manner which reflected the utmost credit on the principal of that establishment. Prof. A.S.

Lewis, who conducted the exercises of the Burnham class by a piano accompaniment, also deserves a special word of favor.

Dumb-bell feats were next in order, and brought out an array of athletes, whose magnificent *contour* challenged the admiration of all. The central figure was Richard A. Pennell, whose matchless proportion and outline, grace and herculean strength became the subjects of conversation for the time being. There were other very elegant, massive forms there, but they were clad in ordinary apparel, and therefore unfortunately invisible. The contest in heavy bells was soon confined to a few, many who had done well in practice failing entirely. Pennell sent 120 lbs. up with a broad smile on his face, and afterwards put up 140 with the left hand, winning easily with 165, being far from the maximum of his strength. This bell also gave him the prize in proportion to weight. Ernest Bohlig labored hard with a 133 lbs. bell for second prize, which he got by main strength, having evidently no idea of the knack of elevating heavy single bells. Parmly, quite a young man, a student of Princeton college, made a creditable attempt with 133 lbs., and Stillwell, who had repeatedly put up 140 in the gymnasium, failed entirely. Sands, who is a little bit of a fellow, took second prize in proportion to lifter's weights; his extraordinary strength and skill displayed in this, as well as several other successful competitions, entitle him to more than passing notice, and the judges will no doubt have him in view among the few entitled to be considered as candidates for the enviable prize to be given to the best general gymnast.

The first prize in heavy double bells was taken with ease by Henry E. Buermeyer, Samuel Strasburger taking second prize, also apparently without any great effort. It is claimed that Richard del Prace, who was entered for this competition, did not hear his name called by the judges and was therefore left out. It is asserted that he afterwards raised 75 and 80 lb. double bells, which he claims, at his weight—132 lbs., entitled him to the prize in proportion. A special prize, given by Mr. Frank H. Lord, was presented to Mr. del Prado; but his was evidently entirely out of order, as he was entitled to no prize in the competitions under the auspices of the Association. The honors of the double-bell feat, in proportion to weight, were carried off by Samuel Strasburger and Fr. Steinbuch. Raising the 100 lb. bell the greatest number of times was mere child's play for Pennell, who raised his bell ten times with great rapidity. Bohlig made a good display of his recently-acquired strength by putting his bell up seven times; Steinbuch also sent his bell up seven times, but Bohlig was entitled to second prize in consideration of a prior trial. Van Wyck all but failed on the sixth time, and Flaherty succeeded in elevating it four times. Mr. P. Gilsey gave a special medal for this competition, of the award of which we have to learn. It came through Mr. Van Wyck, but at latest accounts he had not yet placed it at the disposal of the committee.

The single trapeze brought out three competitors, the first—Sharpe—giving a performance which fell far short of his ordinary practice. Newton came next, leading off with a perfect back and then front horizontal, following them up in rapid succession with many beautiful and difficult feats; but his brilliant performance was marred, in the judges' eyes at least, by a few slips occasioned by haste and lack of strength, owing to an injudicious expenditure of the same in the beginning of his act. Newton was awarded second prize, also a special medal given by Mr. Simmons.

Bennet Greig, the winner, led off with a perfect hand balance, and brought in a series of feats which were notable for difficulty, brilliancy of execution, strength and a remarkable balancing power. Greig is a very clever gymnast, and did remarkably well in everything in which he took part.

Hand-lifting was the next in order, starting at 600 lbs., Pennell, Parmly, Bohlig, Murray, Sands and Cain taking part. Sands quit after lifting 910 lbs., which gave him second prize in proportion to his weight, 118. Cain and Parmly went out on 1,010, Murray lifting 1,060, which not alone entitled him to first prize in proportion to his own weight (121 lbs.), but, we believe, to the distinction of having made the greatest hand-lift on record in proportion to lifter's weight. Mr. Murray, like nearly all the rest of the competitors, owes nothing to his business for strength, being a lawyer by profession; but he is a faithful ***habitue*** of the gymnasium. Bohlig followed our modern Hercules, Pennel, up to 1,100, and was feign to content himself with second prize, Pennell lifting 1,210, winning another medal.

The rope-climbing was among the least exciting, although it is among the most practical of our games....

The parallel bar performances were generally admitted as the most remarkable feature of the gymnastic portion of the entertainment. After the grasshopper jumps had been successfully (and otherwise) accomplished by a large number of contestants, the general performance on the bars came in order. In this particular exercise the members of the N.Y. Turnverein can hardly be excelled. Mr. Christ. Meller carried off the palm of this competition, with the unanimous verdict of the judges, competitors, audience and all. Among the several wonderful feats which entitled Mr. Meller to the first prize in his competition was the successful execution of the giant swing and a perfect and rapid backward roll. Kramer, who won the second prize on the bars, was more brilliant than Meller, and in rapid and graceful movements made an even more favorable impression on the majority of the audience. Kramer has also a very beautiful figure, a little less than the medium size, but showing a great combination of strength and agility in a fine development. His brilliant performance in numerous other competitions also entitle him to the consideration of the judges in the award of the prize for the best general gymnast. Quite a number of others gave very excellent exhibitions on the bars. Among them Stahl and Schiessel, also of the Turnverein, and Marquand, Sheldon and others.

For the club-swinging there were eight competitors, and none without merit, The first on the floor was Bennett Greig, who commenced with a very small pair of clubs, his forte apparently being the short back and front circles and moulinets. He wound up with a larger pair of clubs, giving a fair display of combinations of the longer and more graceful-looking outer and inner, front, side and back circles. Allan Marquand, who also figured, if not very successfully, yet with undeniable credit in the very numerous competitions in which he took part, came next. His motions were limited in variety, but executed with rapidity and precision, embracing also a few tricks, which rank more with juggling than club-swinging.

Frank Clifford was the third in order, and in the opinion of the large number present, who were thoroughly familiar with this exercise, among them the writer, he fully deserved the second prize in this competition, his motions being strictly confined to those described under club exercise, and barring jugglery, were more numerous and effective than all the rest, excepting Burnton's, of course. McCarthy gave a very fair exhibition with a heavier pair of clubs than those used who preceded him, which made the execution of the finer combinations, even had he known them, an impossibility. M.E. Burnton followed. This gentleman is renowned for his skill in the use of the clubs, and his performance with a pair of about six pounds in weight was truly beautiful, his great variety of brilliant combinations belonging strictly to the legitimate, although he did a little clever juggling just before ending, evidently to show that he was not unfamiliar therewith. His work was done with clock-like precision, showing long special training, the latter also being clearly visible in the disproportionate development of his body, the shoulders, arms and chest being very large in proportion to the stomach, hips and legs. S. Kimble commenced with swinging and juggling combined, finishing with a clever bit of legitimate club-swinging with a larger pair. Theo. Sheldon, who also deserves a good share of praise as a general gymnast, came next, and acquitted himself with honor, although his combinations were limited. W.H. Salt came last, making his appearance with a solid pair of genuine Kehoe maples, about twelve pounds in weight, and the derisive smile on his countenance showed his utter contempt of the little potato-mashers used by some of the others. Salt did very well; but failed to convince us, as well as the judges, of his superiority.

The next thing on the programme was "putting the shot," a ball of sixteen pounds weight, one of the favorite games of the Caledonians. John Anderson, a youthful Scot of elegant proportions and especially beautiful legs, hurled the ball nearly forty feet, distancing all competitors, F. Biddle coming second to him.

An exhibition of Calisthenic exercises by a class of the New York turnverein opened the second part of the programme with considerable effect.

Jumping came next, the high jump first. The competitors were very numerous, and some as agile and graceful as deer, but as the string went above four feet every inch reduced the number of contestants rapidly. Burris, a model for an Apollo, and the winner of many other medals in similar exercises, on this and previous occasions, found no difficulty in carrying off the first prize, although Marquand followed him to within an inch, taking second place. X.S. Lee, a lithe and pretty little form, continued well up with the leaders, but was disqualified because he had acquired the bad fault of taking a double start, which is not admissible in a standing jump. One other noteworthy fact in connection with this subject is the difference between the Americans, Scots and Germans, the former with a side jump, rather slinging their legs over parallel with the string, while the latter face their work squarely and consequently do not succeed in reaching so great an attitude. Burris also took the first prize in the standing broad jump, E.J. Mason being next best, and 6 1/2 inches behind at that. The running high jump was won by Edgar B. Clark, E.B. Foote jumping a half inch higher than the winner in jumping off a tie for second prize. Burris did not compete in the running high hump. The running broad jump proved another hollow victory for Burris, who laid out a bit of work for the others which enabled him to take quite a walk around with his coat on, until one of the bonny Scots had obliterated his mark and compelled him to make another which was not reached by 8 1/2 inches, Andrew Rennie making a beautiful leap for second place. The horizontal bar again brought the strength of the New York Turnverein to the front, the prize for general excellence being gallantly won by L. Kramer, whose matchless performance on the single bar was a fit companion piece to Meller's parallel, or to his own for that matter, there being but little difference in merit.

The second prize was awarded to young Sheldon. Raising the body with one arm, a feat belonging to the horizontal bar, was successfully won by Otto Schhiessel, also a Turner, who raised himself three times without apparent effort, his only other contestant, Dave Hageman, failing on the first time. Raising the body with both arms, proved the extraordinary endurance of the little pocket giant, Sands, who "chinned" the bar twenty-three times, J.H. Lionberger making a good show with twenty-one for second prize.

The vaulting brought out ten aspirants. Seven of them continued up to six feet: Foote, Steinbuch, Newton, Sheldon, Marquand, Kramer and Mason. The first five named continued together to 6 feet 4 inches; then Sheldon and Marquand went out, the contest being confined to Foote, Steinbuch and Newton. Foote won, at an altitude of 6 feet 6 inches. Steinbuch and Newton, a tie for second prize, vaulted very beautifully, Steinbuch finally winning second honors at the same height as the winner, 6 feet 6 inches, defeating Newton by 1 inch.

The pole-leaping proved quite interesting, and caused considerable merriment, as the gyrations of the leapers, when fairly upon their poles, were not always in accordance with their original intentions. George Brymer, who is the best acknowledged pole-leaper in this country, had but little difficulty in securing first prize at 8 feet 6 inches, which is about two feet less than his maximum. F. Duke, who took second prize, hardly looked as if he made an effort to leap, running scarcely half the distance of the others and rising very slowly and gracefully.

The performance on the suspended rings proved another victory for Kramer, who again astonished the critical assemblage with his great skill and strength. Among his very beautifully executed feats was a most perfect cross. The second prize was awarded to Theo. Sheldon, who did some very clever work on the rings, his cut-off and catch being superb. Many present, however, thought Bennett Greig more deserving, his performance being certainly much more effective to the common eye.

The batoutte leaping was very interesting, and finally became quite exciting. The little hero, Sands, made run after run, and alighted in all shapes and places imaginable, bounding like a rubber ball, raising his followers inch by inch until they were unable to keep up with him. Lionberger made a hard fight for it, but was compelled to succumb to Sands, and be content with second place. James Garrah, who was third, did some very excellent leaping, but subsequently forfeited the good opinion had in his favor by some very ungenerous and ungentlemanly remarks in regard to the decision of the judges.

The double trapeze brought two of the Princeton College boys—Lionberger and Sheldon—out to their best advantage. Their work was well concerted, clean, quick and moderately difficult, for which they received first prize. Two of the Turners, R. Kunze and C. Nen, did a greater variety of feats and some exceedingly difficult ones; but their continual explanatory dialogue and hesitation spoiled the entire effect of a performance, which had it been properly executed, would have entitled them to first prize. This completed the programme, and it is scarcely necessary to say anything in praise of the glorious revival of the Olympian games, especially to those who were present on the three evenings.

EARLY GYMNASTICS AT HARVARD

Harvard College was one of the first institutions of higher learning in the United States to provide facilities and instruction in physical training for its undergraduates. This account of early gymnastics at Harvard by Thomas Wentworth Higginson is reprinted from F.O. Vaille and H.A. Clark, eds., *The Harvard Book*, Vol. II (Cambridge, Mass., 1875), pp. 186, 189-190.

THE GYMNASIUM, AND GYMNASTICS IN HARVARD COLLEGE.

One of my most impressive early reminiscences is of a certain moment when I looked out timidly from my father's gateway, on what is now Kirkland Street, in Cambridge, and saw the forms of young men climbing, swinging, and twirling aloft in the open play-ground opposite. It was the triangular field then called the "Delta," where the great Memorial Hall now stands. The apparatus on which these youths were exercising was, to childish eyes, as inexplicable as if it had been a pillory or a gallows, which indeed it somewhat resembled. It consisted of high uprights and cross-bars, with ladders and swinging ropes, and complications of wood and cordage, whose details are vanished from my memory. Beneath some parts of the apparatus there were pits sunk in the earth, and so well constructed that they remained long after the woodwork had been removed. This early recollection must date as far back as 1830; and by 1840, I suspect, no trace of Dr. Follen's gymnasium remained above the level of the ground. It shared the fate of Voelcker's pioneer gymnasium in London, established about the same time; both having been hailed with enthusiasm at first, and soon abandoned. A full account of the London institution may be found in Hone's "Every Day Book." Dr. Edward Jarvis, in his "Practical Physiology," reports from personal recollection that the Harvard experiment ended in "general failure."...

The present Gymnasium was erected in 1860. The following extract is taken from the Report of Mr. Amos A. Lawrence, the College Treasurer, for the year 1859: "The want of a gymnasium has been supplied by the presentation of eight thousand dollars, through Rev. Dr. Huntington, by a gentleman who declines to be known, except as a 'Graduate' of the College. The building has been erected and furnished, at a cost of $9,488.05." The architect was Edward C. Cabot, of Boston. The building is of brick, octagonal in form, 74 feet in diameter and 40 feet high. It includes as great a variety of apparatus as is compatible with the size of the building; there are also two bowling-alleys, and there are dressing-rooms, but no bath-rooms. The building was supposed, when first erected, to be large enough for the needs of the College, but experience has proved it to be far too small; and it was proposed by the President of the College, in his last Annual Report, that a new Gymnasium should be erected, and the present building used for a swimming-bath. This would certainly be a most desirable improvement.

The first teacher of gymnastics in Harvard College was Abram Molineaux Hewlitt. He was a professional teacher of boxing, and had established a gymnasium of his own in Worcester, Mass., where he was highly esteemed. He was a mulatto, of very fine physique, and of respectable and estimable character. He was, moreover, a fair gymnast and a remarkably good teacher of boxing. In the first years of his term of service there was a good deal of activity in the Gymnasium, and regular class-exercises went on. After a few years the interest fell off in some degree, or concentrated itself chiefly on the "rowing-weights." Mr. Hewlitt died December 6, 1871, and the present teacher, Mr. Frederic William Lister, was appointed in 1872. Under his administration, the interest of the students in the Gymnasium has revived, the average daily attendance being reported as "about 200" in the winter of 1873-4 against 130 during the previous winter. The greatest number in attendance on any one day in 1873-4 was 370, and at any one time 80.

In the Harvard Gymnasium, as in all such institutions, the measurement of chest and arms has exhibited a marked increase of physical development as the result of gymnastics exercises. Since this is, however, difficult to distinguish from the natural expansion of the different parts of the body at the growing age, it is not worth while to dwell very closely on such statistics. Of the general benefit of gymnastics there can hardly be a doubt; and it is the opinion of many friends of Harvard University that the whole department of physical training merits a separate organization and a professorship of its own, as at Amherst College. An institution like Harvard University, which undertakes to provide board and lodging for its undergraduates, makes itself so far responsible for their bodily well-being that it should certainly have an educated Professor of Hygiene and Physical Education. It is a question whether the regular practise of "free gymnastics," at least, should not be made a required exercise, under the direction of such a Professor, at least as regards the Freshman class.

Borrowing this from Amherst College, Harvard would also do well to borrow from Princeton something of the variety of exercise which George Goldie there teaches so efficiently,—running, leaping, vaulting, throwing weights, and tossing the caber. These are often called among us "Scottish Games," but they now flourish chiefly in the universities, Scotch, English, and Irish. They are there sustained by athletic clubs composed partly of graduates; and such clubs could easily be formed among ourselves. The newly organized boat-clubs will supply, let us hope, better opportunities at the oar than have hitherto been open to Harvard undergraduates generally; but a sufficient variety of sports should be encouraged to call out the athletic activity of all. When at Cambridge in England, two years ago, I saw thirteen eight-oared crews—only half of the fleet belonging to that one university—pull in quick succession along the narrow stream, in one of the university races; and I felt ashamed to think that three or four six-oars at most were all that our Cambridge had yet to show. Yet at the English universities the boating constitutes but a part of the athletic interest; and no young man is so hard a student that he does not make physical exercise, in some form, an essential portion of his daily task. It should be so among us.

DUDLEY A. SARGENT

Dudley Sargent (1849-1924), a native of Belfast, Maine, was a prominent teacher who exerted a great influence on the development of physical education in American colleges and schools. An early passion for the circus first sparked his love of fitness and gymnastics. While director of Bowdoin College's gymnasium he began his academic studies, which ultimately earned him a bachelor's degree from Bowdoin and a medical degree from Yale. From 1879 until his retirement forty years later he served as professor and director of Harvard's Hemenway Gymnasium. He dedicated himself to the cause of proper physical training for the youth of America. He pioneered the science of statistical measurements of the human body and he authored several handbooks on exercises and anthropometric apparatus. These excerpts were compiled by his son and are reprinted from Ledyard W. Sargent, ed., *Dudley Allen Sargent, An Autobiography*, (Philadelphia, 1927), pp. 97-101, 104-108, 173-177, 180-181.

THE PROGRESS OF GYMNASTICS AT BOWDOIN.

...What did the public expect? What did our critics look for in a gymnasium? How did we decide upon a standard? A word in regard to the popular gymnastic concepts of 1870 may not be amiss at this point. The educational temperature of the State of Maine regulated itself almost entirely by the fevers or chills of Boston and New York, those great collecting and distributing news centers of the East. What New York and Boston decreed was law. And their absolute jurisdiction extended to all branches of education. Their theories on physical education were as definite as their theories on the more intellectual side of the program.

In Boston, Dr. Winship had established heavy-weight lifting as a satisfactory means of all round development. His convictions came from his own amusing training that began with his lifting a calf. He continued to lift and gain strength as the calf gained weight, until one day he was lifting a full grown ox. His feat, widely advertised, became proof of the efficacy of lifting weights. William B. Curtis, at one time called "The Father of Athletics in America," made a record by lifting 1323 pounds with a hand grip, and 3239 pounds when the harness was attached to his body. Like mushrooms after rain, lifting machines sprang up in parlors and offices and schools everywhere. The exercises for young and old were proclaimed widely. The converts hurled their slogan, "A maximum of exercise in a minimum of time," into the faces of all comers. They persuaded busy people, merchants, students, and professional men.

The reaction to this heavy-weight lifting system came in the introduction of new gymnastics by Dr. Dio Lewis. He substituted wooden for iron dumb-bells, used light Indian clubs, wooden wands, and bean-bags for his exercises. At first the public looked upon such exercise as fitting play for young ladies' seminaries; but little by little its worth was recognized, and the system was adopted in schools and colleges for boys. For example, the required gymnastics at Amherst were built up round the varied use of wooden dumb-bells.

Military drill was another form of exercise which had received impetus from the shocking unpreparedness of the Civil War, unpreparedness not so much military as physical. Furthermore Congress encouraged this undertaking by furnishing officers to give military instruction where it was required.

Finally, in addition to the heavy-weight lifting, the light dumb-bell work and military training, Dr. Follen and Dr. Beck had introduced a class of gymnastics which had been made famous by Jahn in Germany. In 1870, this work had developed into a series of high-class stunts performed by experts on various kinds of apparatus. George

Goldie... a professional acrobat, was teaching this work as Director of the Gymnasium at Princeton College. John Doldt was demonstrating it at the Tremont Street Gymnasium in Boston, and I hoped to introduce it at Bowdoin.

Little attention was given to wrestling; this sport was left to farmers at country fairs. We did find occasional interest in boxing fostered by athletic clubs and social organizations. And there was some spirited boxing at the colleges....

With all these various methods, and in the face of ardent partisanship, I had to make my choice at Bowdoin in 1870. Since I had found interest in heavy gymnastics and boxing established by my predecessor, and considerable proficiency developed among the upper-class men, I decided to extend the work along the same lines, and gradually introduce my own ideas; for I realized the wisdom of cherishing what was already there. Proficiency in gymnastics is not acquired in a few weeks. The existing talent made for our first exhibition a possibility.... I tried to increase the students' interest. Finally my endeavors were rewarded by a press notice in the "College Bulletin." "The gymnasium, under the charge of its new Director, a man of whom the college may justly be proud, has been repaired, and that the students enter into the enthusiasm of Mr. Sargent is evident from the unusual number that may be seen there every morning and noon. *We only wish it might become one of the regular college exercises.*"

I had been waiting for just such an expression of feeling, and recognized my opportunity to act. More equipment was indispensable for larger classes, and I saw a chance to introduce my own theories in the form of new apparatus. Consequently, I ordered two dozen pairs of Indian clubs and wooden dumb-bells, so that I might start work immediately with larger classes. The Indian clubs caused an amusing disturbance. They arrived with an escort, the sheriff. Mistaking my gymnasium paraphernalia for bludgeons, he came to arrest me for encouraging the strife that already existed between the town boys and the students. He fancied that I was arming the "gowns" for the annihilation of the "towns." To him, Indian clubs meant the large heavy variety used by my predecessor, and the only use that he could imagine for my apparatus was to clout and vanquish some hostile mob.

My first problem in the enlargement of my gymnastic classes was to persuade the small, unathletic men to take an interest. Up to this time only the strong and vigorous were able to compete in the exercises, and the very men who needed their strength developed by exercise came but to watch the prowess of their more robust friends, and to take their gymnastics by proxy. Such a situation was of course basically wrong. With the new light equipment, I intended to attract everyone, robust and delicate. The non-athletic men were, as usual, in the majority. In the colleges of those days, men who had mental ability, but who were physically weak, were in greater proportion than they are today. But these men, who were taking the academic side of college with profound seriousness, looked for all the edicts to come from the Faculty. Any precepts for physical preparedness must come from the same source if it was to carry weight with them. I began my fifty years' fight for the establishment of gymnastics as part of the college curriculum....

Bowdoin, I believe, was among the first of the American colleges to require attendance at the gymnasium five days a week for everyone, and to grade the work not only by classes but according to individual ability....

...the catalogue of 1874 continues in an explanatory method: "In order to secure proper attention to the physical culture, a gymnasium has been put into successful operation...The exercises constitute a systematic course based upon physiological and hygienic principles, and are under the immediate supervision of the Director, who will strictly prohibit any violent or injurious practice. The salutary effects of this exercise will be perceived not only in the general tone of health and strength among the students, but in the correction of physical defects and weaknesses, and even of incipient disease in individual cases. Each student, not for sufficient reasons excused by the Faculty, will be required to elect between the gymnastic and military exercises."

The significant and outstanding feature of these announcements is that the preceptors, sensitive to outside criticism, had softened their aggressive attitude, but they had, at the same time, left a definite gymnastic requirement. They might separate me from the Faculty as an undesirable member but I had won my point. Every student, non-athletic or athletic, had to exercise in some way, and develop his physical capacity as well as his mental. We established ourselves without doubt at Bowdoin, and we aimed definitely to develop our physical education without rousing the enmity of that public, that was always watching for a chance to condemn anything new. I will at this point enumerate some of the endeavors of the gymnasium at Bowdoin. I can think of no better way than to number them as so many separate objectives.

1. To meet the varied needs of all classes of students.

2. To allay the fears of anxious parents against the dangers of accidents in the gymnasium.

3. To gratify the pride of some parents in the improved bearing and personal appearance of their sons at college.

4. To meet the objectives of the school men as to the amount of time devoted to purely physical work, as they called it.

5. To meet the objectives of the "grinds" who were jealous of anything that took them from their strictly scholastic pursuits.

6. To cause the exercise of the gymnasium to be looked upon as play and a form of amusement and diversion from the more serious work of the college.

7. To serve as a means of bringing about a more hygienic method of living and to build up and strengthen the body as well as to fortify it against disease.

Can anyone argue that these aspirations did not aim at serious and helpful physical preparedness for every student in the college? The President and Faculty strove to perfect a natural, pleasant course of physical education that would make their graduates better men. To have been with them during this transition period was an excellent and interesting experience. What progress I made, and what concessions were made to me, were more gratifying than I can tell. It was like the working out a dream, not entirely complete in the fulfillment perhaps, according to the standards of today, but almost a miracle at that time. Bowdoin marks the first period of my work, a period of youthful aspiration and partial success, enough at any rate to spur me on in my work, and to whet my ambition. And each day, as I planned the next, new problems arose to baffle and perplex me.

GYMNASTICS AT MEMORIAL HALL.

From the beginning of my work at Bowdoin, the Faculty, with great understanding and infinite tact, led the horse, step by step, to water; it was up to me to make him drink. With the present attitude towards athletics, this task seems easy enough. In 1870, however, college athletics were unheard of; popular sentiment decreed that gymnastics were well enough for those who had time to waste. The attendance at the gymnasium during my first year exceeded all my expectations, and the exhibition which we held in March of that year showed remarkable results. The men who made this work seem so successful, and who constantly attended the classes at the gymnasium, were those interested in heavy apparatus work. They accomplished difficult feats, and might have ranked well among skilled professional gymnasts. Now this work showed off to excellent advantage, but it did not make for the greatest good of the college. The men who most needed exercise did not take part at all. Consequently the gymnasium was spending its energy developing the physiques of those students who were least in need of it, and missing the very men for whose well being it was intended.

We could not arouse a general love of competition with inter-class and intercollegiate contests; for such games did not exist. Football was an excuse for a scrimmage between freshman and sophomores several times each fall. The baseball and crew, for want of organization, attracted a deplorably small group of men. There was no feeling of obligation to do something in athletics for the college. Those men who played on a few teams that did exist, or rowed on the crews, did whatever they did for the love of the sport, and not many men were enthusiastic enough to follow these sketchy athletics systematically when there was no systematic organization. Athletics were in a scrub condition.

The under-classmen worked off some of their surplus energy in occasional tugs-of-war, but since they practiced no more for these events than they did for football games, the results were generally rough and tumble affairs ending in a "free-for-all." The game, peculiar to Bowdoin, called "Hold In," gave another opportunity for a friendly fight. After a college meeting, that called forth most of the two lower classes, a few sturdy sophomores would make a rush for the door, form a barricade round it, and shout "Hold In! Hold In!" Thereupon the freshmen rushed madly to force their way through, the sophomores inside the room held them back as best they could, and the scrimmage was on, until the barricade gave way, or the upper-classmen declared the freshman "Held In!"

Occasionally a boxing match would be arranged more or less secretly for the amusement of a small group. Here again, it was the sport-loving students who arranged these events, and the athletic value bore a doubtful relation to the pugnacious inspiration. All these games, if games they may be called, took on the nature of hazing and inter-class rushes, rather than beneficial athletics. They stirred up bad blood rather than wholesome rivalry.

Besides the need for organized games, Bowdoin suffered from a lack of facilities for natural outdoor sports. The skating and coasting were poor, and the seasons for swimming were so short during the college year that they were almost negligible. As a result, for six months of the year, the boys were driven to the gymnasium by sheer necessity, if they wanted exercise, or physical training. My heavy apparatus experts never failed me. But the men who came to watch them, and the many more who did not bother to come to all, both lacked the power to perform as did my skillful enthusiasts. These were the very men that needed gymnastics work, and whom I was trying to reach. They could not do even the simpler exercises on the heavy apparatus, and it was my task to bring them up to such a point. Naturally, unsuccessful attempts would not mean large classes of beginners. Some new preparatory apparatus was necessary....

MY FIRST SEASON AT HARVARD.

The equipment of the Hemenway Gymnasium was completed in December, 1879, and we opened the building to the students in January, 1880, just after the Christmas holidays. Since the attendance was entirely voluntary, my duties at first consisted of arranging the time for various sports, and posting a list of rules and regulations for the use of apparatus, and for the special rowing-,boxing-,and fencing-rooms, as well as for the locker-rooms and baths. I had special instructors for the boxing-and fencing-rooms, and a supervisor for the bowling alleys, while the captains of the other sports attended to their particular rooms. Owing to the great popularity of the bowling alley, we had to provide a general supervisor and boys to set up the pins and return the balls. I had no assistant in my gymnastic work except the janitor, but since that omnipotent being was also fireman and engineer, I disturbed him as little as possible.

Although the building was open from 8 in the morning until 10 o'clock at night, the men appeared to be free from academic engagements and ready for exercise at three different times, between 11 and 1 in the morning, between 4 and 6 in the afternoon, and between 8 and 10 at night. Now the physical and medical examinations which I had given in New York the winter before had become widely known. I offered this same examination, with individual prescriptions to the students at Harvard, and it became so popular that I had to employ a clerk to help me keep the statistics. From 10 to 12, from 2 to 4, and from 7 to 8, I examined, consulted and measured Harvard. The applicants for this test made appointments at the janitor's office, and the number, whose interest brought them to me, was exceedingly encouraging. Such prescriptions of individual exercise, where there is no competition or class enthusiasm to carry men along, call forth those who recognize the value of physical training and who are likely to be appreciative of results.

The examinations were as thorough as we could make them. First, each man filled out a history blank, on which he wrote his age, birth place, nativity of parents, occupation of father, resemblance to parents, natural heritage, general state of health, and a list of all the diseases that he had had during his life. All this information was necessary in order to interpret his condition and decide upon a future course. Following this historical outline, came various strength tests of the muscular force of the different parts of the body as measured by dynamometers, and tests to show the lung capacity. The next step was measurements. Every dimension of the body, apparently significant or insignificant, was given. The heart and lungs were examined carefully before and after exercising to show up defects, if any existed. Finally we made a careful record of the condition of the skin, of the spine, of the muscles, and of any other point which the tape measure failed to indicate. From this data, we prescribed an order of appropriate exercises, specifying the amount of work and the adjustment of the apparatus used. These directions, written on a card, included, besides a prescription of exercise, suggestions for diet, sleep, bathing, and clothing. None of the cards were printed formulae, but each one was made out according to the needs of the individual. Of course the prescribed exercises and advice were entirely suggestive, and we made no effort to force the man to carry them out. However, this gentle treatment accomplished exactly what I wished; it awakened a man's interest in himself and in his well-being. Just as boys learn most quickly when their interest is aroused, so the opportunity to help men physically is when they begin to attend to their bodily condition, wishing to remedy its defects, and to pride themselves on the purity of their skin, the firmness of their muscles, and their general carriage.

Whether the young man uses the gymnasium to accomplish these results or whether he chooses to develop himself by running, rowing, playing ball, shoveling snow, or sawing wood is of very little importance, provide that he achieves. The gymnasium, however, offers facilities for building up the body that no other one system can equal. Such was the purpose of its first designers, three thousand years ago. The introduction of the developing machines and the individual system offer advantages to a man who has previously found the feats of heavy gymnastics distasteful or discouraging. He does not have to compete with men whose superiority overawes him: he can compete with his own physical condition from week to week, and from month to month. Nor does he any longer have to worry about strain or injury. If he cannot lift his own weight, the machines can be adapted to the weight which he can lift. Moreover, they can be adjusted to develop the parts of his body that are weakest. He can work for an hour going from one piece of apparatus to another, keeping always within the limit of his strength, and adding slowly to his powers of endurance. Exercise can be prescribed for a man whose heart is weak, whose lung capacity is small, whose liver is sluggish, or whose circulation is feeble. And most especially, the man whose nerves are on edge can be restored to good condition.

At the end of every order of exercise, I prescribed gentle running, unless the man's condition would not allow it. This little spurt is the best conclusion of exercising; for it starts the perspiration, opens the pores, and makes the bath which follows more beneficial. The process of cleansing the skin after exercise, when it is in its most suitable state, is almost as valuable as the exercise itself.

Six months after the examination and prescription the men returned for a second examination, so that I might see what progress they had made, and amend the order and make new suggestions. Such was the system of individual exercise which we started at the Hemenway Gymnasium in 1880.

Athletics at Harvard did not stop with individual development. The numbers of men who voluntarily went in for heavy gymnastics and for the various teams made one feel that the gymnasium would never be deserted and that physical training was gathering enough prestige around itself to command its proper place in the college curriculum. Besides the regular' varsity crew, four class crews organized themselves, while innumerable baseball nines used the gymnasium daily. The boxing- and fencing-rooms were constantly in demand, and so many men, particularly freshman, used the bowling alleys, that we had long waiting lists. My following in the heavy gymnastics grew to such a number, that I had to teach two hours every day, from 4 to 6 o'clock. The enthusiasm and the skill of the boys called for the usual exhibitions. We worked on the horizontal and parallel bars, flying rings, trapezes, and at high-diving and tumbling. I derived the same pleasure from working with them that I had enjoyed at Yale and Bowdoin with the same class of men. Many of the prominent athletes of the college kept in form during the winter by working in the gymnasium, and these men practiced day after day, not to beat one another, but to perfect some particular stunt which they set out to do. They displayed so much talent that we decided to give a series of exhibitions at the end of the winter and to fit up the trophy-room in the front of the gymnasium.

These exhibitions, or meets, were much more varied than athletic meets today. In order to work up enthusiasm, I contented to take part myself in the first of these meets, given about the last of March. I worked with the students in the horizontal bars, high iron ladder, the double trapeze and the flying rings. Then I did a balancing stunt with a rocking chair which I had first performed professionally as a boy of eighteen, twelve years before. Although I had done this stunt at Yale and Bowdoin, and although from a physical point of view, I did not consider it the most difficult thing that I did, it created the greatest sensation at Harvard. This sensation did not arise entirely from the feat; Cambridge was shocked to see a college professor teetering in so unacademic a position. People did not approve of my appearing publicly as a performer in the work which I was supposed to be teaching. I think perhaps that the ground was well taken, although it did not occur to me in such a light at the time.

The exhibition was so successful, from a financial point of view, that we immediately started a series of three more under the auspices of the Harvard Athletic Association. The first was confined to gymnastic work, the second was a combination of athletics and gymnastics, and the third, to which only men were admitted, consisted of the finals of the earlier events and of deciding bouts in the middle and light weight sparring and wrestling matches. For years, until the Boston Athletic Association took them over, these meets were the greatest indoor athletic attractions which Harvard offered....

The records made at these early athletic meetings would not compare favorably with those made by the highly specialized performers of today, but at these meets one saw more all-round athletes, and a greater variety of stunts at Harvard in the early eighties than one sees now....

Harvard has never seen keener and more serious competition than developed in the pugilistic efforts at about this time. The art of wrestling had not been developed to anything like its present state, nor to the point which sparring had reached. Under the stimulus of club and class rivalry, it was almost impossible to keep the encounters within bounds. Things went so far that many of the students lured professional fighters to teach and train them, and some even insisted upon taking their masters into the ring with them as seconds and abettors. When I objected to this practice, I was roundly hissed by the spectators. At the time, there was nothing in the rules to prevent this practice, but I was resolved to stop it, and stop it I did. I slowly came to realize that young men, under the intense excitement of antagonistic contests, have to be restrained and hedged around with rules to protect them from themselves, and to save sports from deteriorating into an excuse for legitimately giving expression to bad feeling.

Tug of war was the other sport that the men entered into with zest of doubtful benefit. In the old fashioned tug-of-war, held out of doors, the men dug themselves into the dirt with their heels after the word "go." For the indoor contests, rosin and rubber sneakers were tried, but after a few trials, it was arranged to have the men start from fixed positions on planks bolted to the floor. Wooden cleats on this plank furnished a foothold. Four men were chosen for a team, and the last, the anchor, wore a big steel belt, lined with a padding of felt, and covered with leather. By actual test with a dynamometer, a strong man could stand a strain of over 2000 pounds. Under ordinary circumstances, the three rope men who used their bare hands to grasp the rope, could do themselves little harm because the strength of their grip would usually give way before they could injure themselves. But under the rabid competition, one thing after another was added to make the grip more secure, until leather jackets with leather armlets were adopted. When these jackets were smeared with fir balsam, nothing could pull the rope passed under the arms from the vice-like grip of the arms and hands. The last tug of war of this kind that I saw was in New York, when three of the Princeton teams lay on the floor in a dead faint after the pistol was fired. Although the men suffered no permanent injury, this event put an end to the tug of war as an intercollegiate contest.

We attracted all sorts of people to our meets. A group of Zuni Indians in their native costumes came to one of them. Dr. Cushing was studying their language and customs, and led them by way of diversion and enlightenment to the gymnasium. Strangely enough, the part of the program which excited them most, was the performance of Bachelder and Davis on the double trapeze. The Indians yelled with delight. They looked upon these two performers as spirit men, and treated them with a kind of religious veneration. Of all the enthusiasts in our audiences, they heaped the most flattering applause on our heads. Spiritual was one term which I had never before heard applied to gymnasts. But spiritual the Harvard athletes were in the eyes of these Americans.

Chapter 13

LACROSSE

During the 1860s and 1870s Canadians continued the process of modernizing lacrosse, which they had adapted from a traditional Indian ball game which the natives called baggataway. William George Beers of the Montreal Lacrosse Club had drawn up the first rules in 1860. He and his friends had pioneered the game in their city and the provinces of Quebec and Ontario. Their efforts resulted in growing excitement for the sport and the founding of the National Lacrosse Association (NLA) in 1867. Lacrosse even made inroads into the sporting culture of the United States, where a few amateur and collegiate clubs fielded teams during the late 1870s. But even as lacrosse gained in popularity, it experienced many of the growing pains and problems common among other sports of this period. These issues included the structure of the rules, championship competition, the conduct of players and spectators, professionalism, and interclub ethnic, religious, and social class tensions.

Throughout North America Indian tribes struggled to maintain their ancestral lands and customs as white settlers applied increasing pressure after 1860. In the United States after the Civil War the Union Army forced native peoples of the Great Plains to submit to their authority. The American soldiers rounded up remnants of once powerful nations and herded them onto reservations. Other smaller groups relocated in western cities and towns, where they tried to preserve their way of life, including their traditional rituals and pastimes. On a few occasions they played ball games for the amusement of white audiences. This chapter begins with newspaper accounts of two of these performances, held in 1868 in Cincinnati and St. Louis. The writers of these pieces praised the players' athletic skills, but they also added many negative comments about the Indians' personal characteristics.

While native North Americans kept their ball ritual alive either on their own territory or in front of white spectators, Canadians dreamed of transforming the natives' game into their country's national pastime. Montreal's sportsmen and clubs dominated Canadian lacrosse throughout this era, even as they coped with stiff challenges from men from Ontario in general and Toronto in particular. During the summer and fall of 1867 a new wave of enthusiasm resulted in the creation of nineteen new clubs and the formation of the NLA. This chapter includes the rules and constitution which that organization adopted in 1868, along with a revised code of 1879.

Over the next thirteen years Canadian lacrosse grew steadily, with the exception of a lull in interest between 1871 and 1876. In May and June of that year two teams chosen from the Montreal Lacrosse Club and the Caughnawaga Indians toured Great Britain. Beers was the captain of the Montreal contingent and the chief organizer of the trip. He and his companions realized that a hastily organized excursion to Britain in 1867 had failed to stir much interest there or at home, and they were determined to do better. The sportsmen viewed the latest journey as a missionary expedition, as they aimed to plant Canada's new national pastime on the soil of Great Britain. The players showcased their sport by staging spirited exhibition matches in Belfast and Dublin, Ireland, Glasgow and Edinburgh, Scotland, and Brighton and London in England. The grand finale for the visit was a command performance before Queen Victoria at Windsor. Thousands of Montrealers welcomed their heroes home in July with a gala celebration. The excerpts from newspaper accounts reprinted below suggest that the lacrosse contests stirred considerable excitement in Great Britain, partly because of interest in the new sport, but perhaps mostly because of curiosity about the Indians. Proof of the success of this enterprise appears in the founding of lacrosse clubs in such urban centers as Manchester, Leeds, London, and Bristol and the creation of the North of England Lacrosse Association in 1879 and the South of England Lacrosse Association in 1880.

By 1879 the total number of Canadian lacrosse clubs had reached 56, including 34 in Toronto and the rest of Ontario. But despite this preponderance of Ontario organizations, Montrealers maintained their dominance over the NLA through their control of key executive positions and the success of their teams in championship matches. This period also witnessed the intensification of a rivalry on and off the playing field among the Montreal Lacrosse Club, the Montreal Shamrocks, and the Toronto Lacrosse Club. A controversy over professionalism led to the renaming of the NLA as the National Amateur Lacrosse Association in 1880. But hard feelings over the power of the Montreal clubs and differences over rules, championship competition, and disorders on the field led to a split in 1886, when the Toronto Lacrosse Club persuaded the Ontario clubs to defect and establish a rival Canadian Lacrosse Association.

Canadian lacrosse faced a host of problems during its formative years, as did baseball, cricket, track and field, and other forms of athletics which were in transition from premodern to modern forms. The NLA had particular difficulty in coping with its trials because of the tensions among its three most powerful clubs. A vote of two-thirds of the delegates to a convention was required for approval of any new rule or by-law, but these rivalries made it almost impossible for any change to gain passage.

Differences over the structure of the sport concerned game length, the method of determining the winner, and the championship system. The first two were related: the rules of 1867 stipulated that a match was won when a team triumphed in three games out of five. (Each goal constituted a game.) But since some contests were over in as little as ten minutes, there was significant support for a time limit of up to two hours, with victory awarded to the side that scored the most goals in that period. The meeting of the NLA in 1877 defeated that suggestion. Long delays in starting matches also irritated many spectators, but this practice reflected a pre-industrial casual attitude toward time which proved difficult to change. Perhaps the most significant issue involved the traditional championship system, whereby the reigning team held the top spot until it was defeated by a challenger. Despite the objections of those who favored a series of matches or a formal league, the NLA retained the old way until 1885.

Championship contests were a major cause of the violence and other disorders among both players and spectators which plagued Canadian lacrosse during its early years. Urban rivalry between Montreal and Toronto fed these incidents, as did ethnic, religious, and social class tensions. The leading feud was between the Montreal Shamrocks (who were Irish, Catholic, and mostly working class) and the Montreal Lacrosse players (who were English, Protestant, and mostly upper-middle class). The Shamrocks presented a special challenge to the other leading teams because they appeared to put more importance on winning matches than on good sportsmanship. Their men employed a more physical style of play and were more willing to test the limits of the rules in championship contests. Compounding the problem was the unwillingness of the NLA's executives or council to establish a more effective judicial system or to grant more power to referees to curb objectionable behavior on the field.

The NLA did not act more aggressively on these issues because its executives assumed that the root of the trouble was the prevalence of professionalism. They blamed Indians who were paid to compete and especially those working class Shamrocks who were willing to play for prize money and who also received expense allowances and sometimes even jobs for their participation. The renaming of the organization as the National Amateur Lacrosse Association and the banning of Indian teams in 1880 was supposed to cure all of the sport's ills, but of course the troubles did not go away. The Shamrocks did drop a few of their players who were also professional runners, but they maintained their membership in the association. As before, their matches against their rivals from Montreal and Toronto generated both great excitement and strong ethnic, religious, and class feelings among both players and spectators. The letter from a Montreal lacrosse enthusiast and a newspaper account of a championship match reprinted below suggest both the popularity of lacrosse in Canada and the intensity of these rivalries.

Enthusiasm for the game of lacrosse also extended south of the border between Canada and the United States, especially in upstate New York and also in New York City. The first clubs were the Mohawk of Troy and the Maple Leaf of Buffalo. Forty members, mostly immigrant Canadian artisans, founded the New York Lacrosse Club in the great metropolis in 1865. In 1869 a prominent baseball figure imported two teams of Canadian Indians to the city to showcase the new game. Their exhibition led to the formation of the Knickerbocker Lacrosse Club, but the sport did not excite many New Yorkers over the next few years. November of 1877 witnessed a revival of interest as New York University defeated Manhattan College by a score of 2-0 in the first American intercollegiate lacrosse contest. During the following year a polo club in Newport, R.I. hosted the United States's first regular lacrosse tournament. The success of that event and the growing popularity of the sport contributed to the founding of the United States National Amateur Lacrosse Association. This chapter concludes with an account of the action at the Newport tournament, followed by the rules that governed the championship lacrosse cup offered by the Westchester Polo Club in 1879.

INDIAN CONTESTS, 1868

CINCINNATI

The following story describes ball play among a band of travelling Indians at Cincinnati in 1868. It includes some description of the religious rituals which were an integral part of their sport. These ceremonies were longer and more elaborate when the contests were held on Indian lands. This account is reprinted from the American Chronicle of Sports and Pastimes, 11 June 1868, p. 194.

THE GAME IN CINCINNATI.

Promptly at half-past three o'clock, between twenty and twenty-five Indians, mostly young men, strolled irregularly into the Union Grounds, west of Lincoln Park, and the hundreds of people there assembled greeted them with peals of laughter. They were barefooted, 'stripped to the buff,' which presented the bright tan color peculiar to the Indian epidermis, and wore dirty-looking cast-away pantaloons, turned up over the knees. There was observable a splotch of red on the faces of some, and some wore a girdle, or belt with a tuft of white horse-hair hanging behind. Each carried a pair of rackets, one in each hand. The racket—I don't know where the Indian advertiser got the word 'raquette;' perhaps it is the Choctaw for 'racket'—the racket, then is a 'bat,' with a loop-like ladle at the end, and the game of that name is best described in the language of an accommodating police officer on duty yesterday at the entrance. He said: "Racket is nothing but 'shinny' played overhead."

When the Indians reached the centre of the grounds, an obese redskin in pale-face toggery disposed them in a group, and producing a little red ball, held it up and commenced a chant, in which they all joined, composed of a discordant mixture of yelps, whoops, and grunts. This was accompanied by the whole party stooping down frequently, and suddenly rising up again, holding their rackets high over their heads all the while. Then the party separated into three squads, one going to either side of the ground and one remaining in the centre. The ceremony mentioned was, probably (for here my knowledge of 'Injun' fails me again), the decision which party should get possession of the ball. And then the game of 'shinny overhead' commenced, and was kept up for over an hour. In the meantime the obese redskin assumed the comfortable attitude of that traditional and venerable chief, who sat him down upon a rock, grasping his rifle with one hand, and meditating upon his long and brilliant career of aboriginal enjoyment and victory. Occasionally he scratched himself—but Cincinnati dust is irritating.

Sometimes the little red ball fell close to the spectators' stand, and a brace of contestants would follow, and use their ladles with wonderful dexterity to gain possession of it. It is 'foul' to handle the ball; it must be ladled out and thrown with the ladle. When they came near, the sun shone on their oozy bodies; their dark, sharp eyes sparkled with the excitement of the game, and their teeth glistened. Straight backbone, lithe form, and suppleness of limb are the most remarkable things in the appearance and movement of the party. On the grounds and animated by the play, the bearings and motions of the party presented a perfect picture of grace and strength. 'Distance,' however, 'lent enchantment to the view.' Propinquity satisfied the curious that there are worse odors than that of German soap.

The scramble to gain possession of the ball was the most entertaining feature of the game. It brought out the traits of the players. Some succeeded by sheer strength, others by sleight, others again by downright skill in handling the rackets, using one as a spoon to scoop up the ball and the other as a club to ward off the others. In the heat of the play three or four clouty 'squaws' made their appearance on the scene with buckets of water for the players to drink. From the careless manner in which the dipper was used and the reckless waste exhibited in throwing away what remained after each 'pull,' we infer that the admixture of 'fire water' was not as strong as the 'Deer-creek cocktail' of lasting memory.

A flat-headed rascal in a pair of black trowserloons, and nothing else, seemed to be the best player, for he marked his post two to one, and was more frequently applauded by his pale-face brothers.

During the game the players preserved an almost unbroken silence. We cannot say so much for their heads, for many a crack was dealt with sturdy arm and stubborn stick upon the black pates of the rival party. We saw one fellow tie up his shin, and wondered if that is not a more sensitive part than the head is said to be with other dark-skinned people.

ST. LOUIS

On June 29, 1868, teams composed of Choctaw and Chickasaw Indians played a ball game at St. Louis. Forty-one natives (including four or five women) had been temporarily located in that city under the command of Col. S.N. Folsom, who had led a Confederate regiment of warriors from those two tribes during the Civil War. The captains and most of the contestants in this match had also served on the side of the South. This account of the victory by the Choctaws first appeared in the American Chronicle of Sports and Pastimes, 9 July 1868, p. 242.

THE GAME IN ST. LOUIS.

Pursuant to advertised announcement, the Choctaws and Chickasaws played a match game of Indian ball play, or "raquette," at Base Ball Park, Monday, afternoon, June 29th. The crowd in attendance was not large, owing, doubtless, to the heat of the day, though there were many prominent citizens present. The base ball amateurs who witnessed the exhibition seemed to take great interest in it, and when a particularly good "hit" was made, applauded rapturously. General A.J. Smith, who has seen the "untutored" under other and less favorable auspices, and Colonel Taggett, of the Pay Department, were interested lookers-on.

Colonel Folsom being ill, Mr. Henderson was master of ceremonies. At about a quarter past four o'clock the "raquetters" appeared in the enclosure, attired like any other men who were quite illy dressed. Some were barefooted and some were not; all had some sort of covering on their heads; most of them wore no coats, and evidenced great carelessness in buttoning their shirts; their pantaloons were of every cut and texture, and the articles mentioned comprised their several wardrobes. Like other exhibitors, on the stage and in the modern gladiatorial "ring," they have to dress (or undress) for their respective parts, and on their *entre* repaired to the dressing room of the park. Small boys looked upon them with curious but not admiring glances as they disappeared.

In a few moments they were "dressed" and ready, but they did not appear "eager for the fray." As they emerged and formed in line, they gave utterance to yells and caterwaulings much more strange than pleasing. Proceeding to the flag post at the southwest angle of the grounds, they executed a war-dance, or something of the kind, and then marched to a point midway between the two posts, where another novel manoeuver was executed of a similar character.

Of the players, there were twenty-eight, including the captain of each party....

The uniform of the players was exceedingly primitive and simple, being a "breech clout" of blue or red flannel, and a cap, handkerchief, or ribbon on the head. Three or four of them, being destitute of the flannel, were compelled to wear pantaloons, and these, we were told, committed breeches of an established rule. It will be observed that this style of dress gave more freedom of action to the limbs, besides being decidedly cool. Although the sun was very hot, there was no danger of their "tanning."

The game commenced. The ball, a common base ball, was tossed into the air, and there was a scramble to catch it. One chap though he had it, but it was knocked out of his "racquette," and at length one of the "red" men succeeded in planting it against one of the posts. First count for Choctaws.

Then eight or ten of them rallied on the centre and again sent the ball up. Another tussle. The lookers-on began to enjoy the spectacle. After skirmishing and rallying, throwing and catching, "blue" sent a ball home. "Even Steven."

And so they "exhibited" for an hour and a half. The players showed their fleetness of foot and great expertness in throwing and catching the ball. It is not so easy to catch a ball between two sticks as it is with the hand, but there were three or four "fly catches" made, which would have excited the wonder and admiration of a champion in the business.

The last point was *chef d'ouvre*, and of course was in the programme. The ball was flying hither and thither—first one fellow would have it and then another—until secured by Jonas Nocknoley, a Choctaw. Taking a run towards the post, he three [sic] the ball, his sticks and a somersault, in "one time and one motion," the ball hitting the post fairly and squarely.

The game was remarkably well contested, and it was hard for the lookers-on to tell which was ahead when it ended, as one of the chaps who wore the breeches was counted with the blues when he belonged to the reds. He was one of the best players. The following is the score:

Choctaws, red	16
Chickasaws, blue	13

RULES OF LACROSSE, 1868

On 26 September 1867 forty-two delegates from twenty-seven clubs met in Kingston, Ontario to form the National Lacrosse Association. William G. Beers and his fellow Montrealers spearheaded this movement. They capitalized on the recent mania for their favorite game which had swept through Ontario that summer. The following code is the version that was revised and adopted on 25 and 26 September 1868, reprinted from William G. Beers, *Lacrosse, the National Game of Canada* (N.Y., 1869), pp. 251-256.

LAWS OF LACROSSE

RULE I—The Crosse.

Sec. 1.—The Crosse may be of any length to suit the player; woven with cat-gut, which must not be bagged. ("Cat-gut" is intended to mean raw hide, gut or clock strings, not cord or soft leather.) The netting must be flat when the ball is not on it. In its widest part the crosse shall not exceed one foot. No string must be brought through any hole at the side of the tip of the turn. A leading string, resting upon the top of the stick, may be used, but must not be fastened, so as to form a pocket, lower down the stick than to the end of the length strings. The length strings must be woven to within two inches of their termination, so that the ball cannot catch in the meshes.

Sec. 2.—Players may change their crosse during a match.

RULE II—The Ball.

The Ball must be India rubber sponge, not less than eight and not more than nine inches in circumference. In matches, it must be furnished by the challenged party.

RULE III.—The Goals.

The Goals may be placed at any distance from each other, and in any position agreeable to the captains of both sides. The top of the flag-poles must be six feet above the ground, including any top ornament, and six feet apart. In matches they must be furnished by the challenged party.

RULE IV.—The Goal-Crease.

There shall be a line or crease, to be called the Goal-Crease, drawn in front of each goal, six feet from the flag-poles, within which no opponent must stand unless the ball has passed cover-point.

RULE V.—Umpires.

Sec. 1.—There must be two umpires at each goal, one for each side, who must stand behind the flags when the ball is near or nearing the goal. Unless otherwise agreed upon by the captains, they must not be members of either club engaged in a match; nor shall they be changed during a match, except for reasons of illness or injury. They must be thoroughly acquainted with the game, and in every way competent to act. Before a match begins, they shall draw the players up in line, and see that the regulations respecting the crosse, spiked soles, &c., are complied with. They must also see that the regulations are adhered to respecting the ball, goal, goal-crease, &c., and, in deciding any of these points, shall take the opinion of the captains and the referee. They must know, before the commencement of a match, the number of games to be played. They shall have power to decide all disputes, subject to Rule VI, and to suspend, for any time during the match, any player infringing these laws; the game to go on during such suspension.

Sec. 2.—No umpire shall, either directly or indirectly, be interested in any bet upon the result of the match. No person shall be allowed to speak to the umpires, or in any way distract their attention, when the ball is near or nearing their goal.

Sec. 3.—When "foul" has been called, the umpires must leave their posts and cry "time," and from that time the ball must not be touched by either party, nor must the players move from the positions in which they happen to be at the moment, until the umpires have returned to their posts, and "play" is called. If a player should be in possession of the ball when the umpires leave their posts, he must drop it on the ground in front. If the ball enters the goal after the umpires have left their posts, it will not count. The jurisdiction of umpires shall not extend beyond the day of their appointment. They shall not decide in any manner involving the continuance of a match beyond the day on which it is played.

RULE VI.—Referee.

The umpires shall select a referee, to whom all disputed games and points, whereon they are a tie, may be left for decision, and who must be thoroughly acquainted with the game, and in every way competent to act. He shall take the evidence of the players particularly interested, the respective opinions of the differing umpires, and, if necessary, the opinions and offers of the captains, in cases where the discontinuance of the game is threatened. His decision shall be final. Any side rejecting his decision, by refusing to continue a match, shall be declared the losers. The referee must be on the ground at the commencement of and during the match, but during play he shall not be between the two goals.

RULE VII.—Captains.

Captains, to superintend the play, may be appointed by each side, previous to the commencement of a match. They shall be members of the club by whom they are appointed, and of no other. They may or may not be players in a match: if not, they shall not carry a crosse, nor shall they be dressed in Lacrosse uniform. They shall select umpires, and toss up for choice of goal. They shall report any infringement of the laws during a match to the nearest umpire.

RULE VIII.—Names of Players.

The players of each side shall be designated as follows: "Goal-Keeper," who defends the goal; "Point," first man out from goal; "Cover-point," in front of Point; "Centre," who faces; "Home," nearest opponent's goal. Others shall be termed "Fielders."

THE GAME

RULE IX—Miscellaneous

Sec. 1—Twelve players shall constitute a full field, and they must have been regular members of the club they represent, and no other, for a least thirty days prior to a match.

Sec. 2.—A match shall be decided by the winning of three games out of five, unless otherwise agreed upon.

Sec. 3.—Captains shall arrange, previous to a match, whether it is to be played out in one day, postponed at a stated hour, or in the event of rain, darkness, &c., or to be considered a draw under certain circumstances; and, if postponed, it is to be resumed where left off.

Sec. 4.—If postponed and resumed where left off, there shall be no change of players on either side.

Sec. 5.—Either side may claim at least five minutes' rest, and not more than ten, between each game.

Sec. 6.—No Indian must play in a match for a white club, unless previously agreed upon.

Sec. 7.—After each game, the players must change sides.

Sec. 8.—No change of players must be made after a match has commenced, except for reasons of accident or injury during the match. When a match has been agreed upon, and one side is deficient in the number of players, their opponents may either limit their own numbers or equalize the sides or compel the other side to fill up the compliment.

RULE X.—Spiked Soles.

No player must wear spiked soles.

RULE XI.—Touching the Ball with the Hand.

The ball must not be touched with the hand, save in case of Rules XII. and XIII.

RULE XII.—Goal-Keeper.

Goal-Keeper, while defending goal within the goal-crease, may pat away with his hand or block the ball in any manner.

RULE XIII.—Ball in an Inaccessible Place.

Should the ball lodge in any place inaccessible to the crosse, it may be taken out by the hand; and the party picking it up, must "face" with his nearest opponent.

RULE XIV.—Ball out of Bounds.

Balls thrown out of bounds must be picked up with the hand, and "faced" for at the nearest spot within the bounds.

RULE XV.—Throwing the Crosse.

No player shall throw his crosse at a player or at the ball under any circumstances.

RULE XVI.—Accidental Game.

Should the ball be accidentally put through a goal by one of the players defending it, it is game for the side attacking that goal. Should it be put through a goal by any one not actually a player, it shall not count.

RULE XVII.—Balls Catching in the Netting.

Should the ball catch in the netting, the crosse must immediately be struck on the ground so as to dislodge it.

RULE XVIII.—Rough Play, &c.

No player shall hold another with his crosse, nor shall he grasp an opponent's stick with his hands, under his arms, or between his legs; nor shall any player hold his opponent's crosse with his crosse in any way to keep him from the ball until another player reaches it. No player shall deliberately strike or trip another, push with the hand; nor must any player jump at to shoulder an opponent, nor wrestle with the legs entwined so as the throw his opponent.

RULE XIX.—Threatening to Strike.

Any player raising his fist to strike another, shall be immediately ruled out of the match.

RULE XX.—Foul Play.

Sec. 1.—Any player considering himself purposely injured during play, must report to his captain, who must report to the umpires, who shall warn the player complained of.

Sec. 2.—In the event of persistent fouling, after cautioning by the umpires, the latter may declare the match lost by the side thus offending, or may remove the offending player or players, and compel the side to finish the match shorthanded.

RULE XXI.—Interrupted Matches.

In the event of a match being interrupted by darkness or to any other cause considered right by the umpires, and one side having won two games—the other none—the side having won the two games shall be declared winners of the match. Should one side have won two games, and the other one, the match shall be considered drawn.

RULE XXII.—Amendments.

Any amendment or alteration proposed to be made in any part of these laws, shall be made only at the Annual Conventions of the National Association, and by a three-fourths vote of the members present.

CONSTITUTION OF THE NATIONAL LACROSSE ASSOCIATION, 1868

The convention which amended the rules of lacrosse in 1868 also ratified the following Constitution, which is taken from Henry Chadwick, *Chadwick's American Cricket Manual* (New York, 1873), pp. 115-120.

CONSTITUTION

Article I.

The name of this organization shall be "The National La Crosse Association of Canada."

Article II.

Its objects shall be to improve, foster, and perpetuate the game of La Crosse as the national game of Canada, and to promote the cultivation of kindly feelings among the members of La Crosse clubs.

Article III.

SEC. 1. Its officers shall be a President, four Vice-Presidents, a Secretary, and a Treasurer, and a Council of fifteen, to be elected annually by ballot; who shall be entitled to vote the same as delegates by virtue of their office. They shall hold office until their successors are elected.

SEC. 2. The Regular Secretary shall receive an annual salary of $100.

SEC. 3. A Minute Secretary may be appointed temporarily at each Convention.

SEC. 4. The Association may elect a permanent honorary President by unanimous vote, who shall have all the privileges of a member.

SEC. 5. Any vacancy occurring in either of the offices mentioned may be filled at any meeting of the Association regularly organized, or by a majority vote of the board of the board of officers.

SEC. 6. All officers shall be *ex-officio* members of the Council.

Article IV.

The President shall preside at all meetings of the Association and Council, with the usual privileges of the office. He shall have a vote in the election of officers and the admission of new clubs, and the casting vote in a tie. He shall call extra meetings whenever he shall deem it necessary, and special meetings whenever requested to do so by six clubs—three in Ontario and three in Quebec—no club to be from the same locality. The said clubs to state their reasons for wishing such a meeting.

SEC. 2. The Vice-Presidents shall perform the duties of the President during his absence or indisposition.

SEC. 3. The Secretary shall keep an accurate record of all the proceedings of the Association and the Council; a register of clubs in the Association, with their names, date of organization, number of members, days and places of playing, names of office-bearers, and address of the Secretary. He shall conduct all the correspondence of the Association and Council, keep a record of the decisions of the latter on points of appeal, complaint, etc. He shall notify all officers and clubs of their election, issue all notices of meetings, and annually report to the Association.

SEC. 4. The Treasurer shall receive and hold all the funds of the Association and disburse the same. He shall keep a correct account of moneys received and disbursed by him, and shall report at the annual meeting.

SEC. 5. The Council shall deliberate and decide upon all business submitted to them, and generally manage the Association. Shall meet previous to the annual meeting. Seven members shall form a quorum. The Secretary of the Association shall be Secretary of the Council. The Council may report through the Secretary.

Article V.

SEC. 1. The Association shall be composed of delegates from the several La Crosse clubs in Canada which have been duly admitted to representation, or which may be admitted in the manner hereafter provided. Each club shall be entitled to one delegate for every forty members; but no club can have more than three for any number. A club having less than forty, and not less than twenty, shall also be entitled to one representative. Fractions of a half or more than a half of a subsequent forty shall also be entitled to one delegate. Each delegate shall have one vote, and no voting by proxy will be allowed.

SEC. 2. Delegates may or may not be members of the club they represent. Proxies appointed by clubs must not appoint others as their proxies. No delegate shall represent more than one club.

SEC. 3. No delegates shall be admitted to the Convention unless he shall have filed with the Secretary a certificate of his election, signed by the President and Secretary of the club he represents.

Article VI.

SEC. 1. Any club desiring to be represented in this Association shall present to the Secretary, at least thirty days previous to the annual meeting of the Association, a written official application, signed by its President and Secretary, giving the name and date of organization of their club, number of members, days and places of playing, names of officers and delegates, and address of Secretary. The Secretary shall then record the name of the applying club on a temporary roll; and after the said club has paid its dues to the Treasurer, it shall be entitled to challenge and be challenged by clubs in the Association until the annual meeting. At the annual meeting the Secretary shall then submit the names, etc., of the applying clubs to the Committee on Nominations. Said Committee shall thereupon ascertain the condition, character, and standing of such club, and behavior at matches, and report the same with the said application, and their opinion thereon; and a ballot shall thereupon be had at such annual meeting, upon the admission of such club; when, if two-thirds of the delegates present vote in favor thereof, such club shall be declared duly entitled to representation in this Association, and may immediately sit and vote. Any informality or irregularity in the form or substance of the application may be waived by a two-thirds vote of the members present at the annual meeting.

Se. 2. No club shall be represented in this Association unless composed of at least twenty members, or by any delegate under eighteen years of age; nor shall any club be so represented until it has paid its assessments and signed the existing Constitution of the Association and Laws of La Crosse.

SEC. 3. No club, whose members average under sixteen years of age, shall be admitted.

Article VII.

The annual subscription shall be (10) ten cents per member of each club in the Association. The Council shall have the privilege of levying a special assessment to defray actual expenses if necessary.

Article VIII.

SEC. 1. At every Convention meeting one or more matches shall be played, the proceeds of which shall go to the treasury of the Association.

SEC. 2. All the expenses of advertising, hall, ground, etc., attendant on the Convention meeting, shall be defrayed by the Association.

Article IX.

SEC. 1. The Association shall have jurisdiction over all clubs on its roll. It shall see that the laws of La Crosse are strictly obeyed. Any one of its office bearers shall have power to report infractions of the rules to the Association.

SEC. 2. The Association shall form a central body, to which all questions as to points of play, club management, etc., may be referred.

Article X.

All matters of appeal, complaint, etc., shall be made to the Secretary in writing, with both sides of the question fully stated. The appellant shall send a copy of his appeal to the party against whose decision or opinion he appeals. The Secretary shall mail a copy of this to every member of the Council, who shall individually decide upon the case, and return his statement and decision. The Secretary shall then allow twenty-one days to elapse from the date of mailing, and shall then enter on the records a summary of the question, and the decision; specifying the names of the members and their decisions. The decision shall be published, and shall be a precedent from whence there is no appeal, except by a unanimous vote of the Council, or a four-fifth vote of the Convention.

Article XI.

No club in the Association shall play for a money challenge except with Indians. Any club playing for money (except with Indians) shall be suspended from membership in the Association.

Article XII.

SEC. 1. The Council may suspend or expel a club for notorious and continued foul play or unfair conduct, individually or collectively; negligence to pay assessments; or for any persistent infringement of the laws of the game or the rules of the Association.

SEC. 2. Any Club so suspended may be re-admitted by making an ample official apology and promising future compliance.

SEC. 3. Any club failing to pay its dues before the 1st of August, shall be fined 1 cent per member on their returns made, and no delegate shall be entitled to sit and vote until his club's dues are paid.

SEC. 4. Any club expelled can only be re-admitted by a special vote and resolution of the Council.

SEC. 5. Clubs outside of the Association shall not be recognized; nor must their challenges be accepted by clubs in the Association.

Article XIII.

Clubs must make their annual returns to the Secretary, and pay their dues to the Treasurer, after the 15th July, and not later than the 1st August in every year; and in the appointment of delegates shall abide by the numerical strength reported in the return, and for which dues have been paid.

Articles XIV.

No club shall admit or retain a person a member thereof who has been complained against to the Association for foul play or any other reprehensible conduct, and which the Association has censured or punished, shall be entitled to continue a member of this Association, or be admitted to membership thereof; and no new club shall be admitted a member therein which has among its members any one who has been convicted of such action; and no club in this Association shall play a match with any such club under penalty of forfeiture of membership of such Association. No club shall be admitted to membership in this Association unless it adopts in its club constitution the sentiments or words contained in this article.

Article XV.

SEC. 1. The Association shall hold its Convention annually, on the second Wednesday in August, alternately in the Provinces of Ontario and Quebec; the place of meeting to be decided by the Council.

SEC. 2. Clubs shall be notified of the time and place of meeting at least four weeks previously.

Article XVII.

SEC. 1. The Delegates from all clubs represented in this Association must annually sign the Constitution, or the resolution continuing it in force. Clubs neglecting to do so must send an official request to the Secretary.

SEC. 2. No alteration or amendments shall be made in any part of this Constitution, except by two months' notice, and by a three-fourths vote, at a Convention where two-thirds of the clubs on the Association rolls are represented.

SEC. 3. Twenty-seven delegates shall form a quorum at Annual Conventions.

TOUR OF GREAT BRITAIN, 1876

DUBLIN, IRELAND

The sporting party from the Dominion of Canada opened their excursion in the British Isles in mid-May with a game in Belfast, northern Ireland. Their next stop was Dublin. This report of their appearance in that city is from The Gazette (Montreal), 31 May 1876.

Dublin, May 15th, 1876.

Since our arrival here we have had glorious weather and nothing could exceed the kindness of our reception. The game which we represent has been as enthusiastically admired here as it was in Belfast, and that is saying a good deal. On Saturday afternoon we met on the grounds of the Irish Champion Athletic Club, Lansdowne Road. There was uninterrupted sunshine throughout the afternoon, and a light breese which swept over the ground had the effect of preventing the heat from being oppressively felt by those who were not under shelter from the sun's rays. About two o'clock the Indian team reached the ground in a brake and immediately proceeded to the tent provided for their use. They have attracted a large share of attention wherever they have made their appearance, their solemn manner and quaint costume being a constant subject of admiration. When later in the day they entered the theatre, to which we were all specially invited, in their war-paint and feathers, not a muscle betrayed the pride and delight which they experienced as the orchestra saluted them, but when I after-asked the chief how he liked it, he replied with a smile that it was "bully." Both they and we have been fully described in the daily papers and our build and training have received frequent compliments. But to return to Saturday's proceedings. As soon as we had reached the ground above mentioned, preparations were made to carry out the preliminary arrangements, and the goals were put up. In the meantime the ground had become thronged with visitors. On three sides of it there was a deep fringe of spectators, and on the fourth, though the people were somewhat more sparse, there was a goodly number also. The grand stand, the central portion of which was awned over, was filled to its utmost capacity. Indeed, I believe that seldom, if ever, has so large an assemblage been seen on the ground before....

...There is no necessity to describe the game to you. It was exciting enough, nevertheless, even to us, and was certainly interesting to the spectators. There was some splendid running, and the on-lookers were somewhat astonished at the rapidity with which a player carrying the ball on his *crosse*, closely pursued by an opponent, would, before his adversary could strike his *crosse* and dislodge the ball, hurl the ball to the opposite end of the ground. Then again, when the sides got into close quarters, "the scrimmages" for the ball were most exciting, and the well-know sharp crack of *crosse* on *crosse* was heard with much frequency. Neither of the captains played, Dr. Beers suffering from a cold, and Keraronwe being somewhat lame. The latter conduced to his own enjoyment throughout the greater part of the afternoon by smoking a large clay pipe, apparently of Irish manufacture. He never seemed ill at ease, and when later on in the day he was introduced to the Lord Lieutenant and the Duchess of Abercorn, he appeared quite comfortable, and immediately after shaking hands with her Grace he significantly touched his nose with the fore finger of his right hand. His conversation with the Viceroy and the Duchess was in French. He also addressed the multitude in his own tongue, his companions at intervals giving vent to their feelings, whether of assent to or dissent from their leader's remarks, by a low, funeral sort of groan. After the speech came an Indian dance, with a song, which, as may be expected, was a welcome novelty to the good people of Dublin. This exercise over, they all faced the Viceregal party, to whom they made an obeisance, and then turned towards the people on each side, and likewise salaamed them. The game was then resumed, the day's match being carried off by the redskins, who won three games out of five. In the evening...we all went to the theatre, where an ovation awaited us.

GLASGOW, SCOTLAND

When the lacrosse teams reached Scotland thousands turned out to see to see their performance. One of the newspapermen in attendance was a correspondent for the New York Herald who filed the following account and observations on the participants. His comments on the Indian chief are particularly interesting because he noted the differences between Karoniare's [Keraronwe's] public and private behavior and speech. The reporter also suggests that the British public's fascination with the natives from Canada stemmed largely from their reading of romantic novels. This piece was published in The Gazette (Montreal), 8 June 1876.

Glasgow, May 20, 1876.

The quiet, easy-going Scotch nature became thoroughly excited this afternoon. The game of lacrosse has taken the citizens of Glasgow by storm. To-day over 7,000 persons paid gate money to witness the game, and half as many more watched the sport from commanding positions outside. The result was one of the most spirited contests ever witnessed in the way of sport. The weather continued favorable, and the sun was not too warm for comfort.

Since my last night's letter I have had several interviews with the Iroquois, and, although they are in different costume from that in which they are described in "The Last of the Mohicans," I believe them to be thoroughly acquainted with the methods of scalp-raising employed to such startling effect by their ancestors of romance. There is ingenuity displayed in spelling and writing their names which shows them to be masters of phonography, which has found so many advocates since the days of "spelling bees."

THE GAME

was called at the appointed hour and a series of seven innings was played. The first goal was won for the Canadians within five minutes by one of those sudden and unexpected pieces of good fortune that win often times against the most expert playing. Nothing could have been finer than the passing of the Canadians, who, again and again, in the face of a foe not easily baffled, passed the ball from one end of the field to the other, and that without it once being missed by the player to whom it was thrown. The field was, therefore, divided off into a struggling mass at each end, with only two or three players in the centre, who, it may be remarked, had nothing to do.

THE SECOND INNINGS.

After about three minutes of rest the second innings began. In this the play of the Iroquois came out to greater advantage than had been previously seen in the preceding day. Evidently determined that their opponents should not get the same advantage over them that they had in the preceding struggle, the redskins played with unexampled determination. Their running, dodging and cat-like suppleness were simply admirable. The liveliest enthusiasm was manifested by the onlookers, who closely followed the movements of the game and gave frequent expression to their feelings of approval in cries of "Well played!" "Bravo!" "Big Indian!" This innings was one of the longest and best contested of the day, and resulted in a well-earned goal for the Iroquois.

THE THIRD AND FOURTH

innings were won by the same side. The captain of the dark side, Karoniare, displayed much excitement in both games. Throughout he envinced an energy in the direction of his team which betokened the fact that he had determined to win. Whenever his men made a play especially brilliant he would leap into the air half his own height, and utter a yell which started new and heretofore unknown echoes in the glen of classic Kelvin's stream. He smoked only occasionally, but made the same unmistakable signals with his tomahawk-pipe....

AFTER ROMANCE.

I asked him at his hotel, after his return from the game, what had excited him so during the day—whether it was the desire for success or not?

"No," he said, with a peculiar smile, "Canadians more goods as my boys. They (his players) young, weak, no breath. What make me happy, much people—much money I see our good father, Dr. Beers, have."

"REALITY."

To dispel the romance of this speech before it takes deep root in the minds of any of my young readers, fresh from the pastures green of the "hair-raising literature" of the weekly journals, I may say that the worthy captain of the Iroquois talks English quite well when he chooses, and that the slowness with which he speaks to strangers and those outside the lines (as I was) is ascribable to the difficulty which he finds in talking the Indian-English of "Ned Buntline." It is, of course, quite essential that he should talk badly, but he evidently finds it a bore.

THE LAST THREE GOALS

of the series of seven were won by the Canadians in rapid succession. Gradually it was noticed that the activity of Captain Karoniare relaxed, and finally he retired to a seat and allowed his men to finish as they pleased.

WINDSOR, ENGLAND

After leaving Glasgow the Canadian and Indian squads traveled to Edinburgh. They spent most of the month of June in England, sightseeing and entertaining curious spectators with displays of lacrosse at Newcastle-on-Tyne, Sheffield, Brighton, Hurlingham, and several sites in London. They had the privilege of competing on the grounds at Lords and on a field near Wimbledon Common. The following report of their appearance before Queen Victoria at Windsor Castle first appeared in an English newspaper and was published in The Gazette (Montreal), 12 July 1876.

Manchester, June 29, 1876

By one of those Royal commands which are interpreted as priceless favors, the Iroquois Indian team of "La Crosse" players and the representative team of Canadian gentlemen selected from the Dominion clubs had the honor of playing the game in which they are, one and all, remarkably skilled, before Her Majesty the Queen, yesterday afternoon, on the lawn below the slopes of Windsor Castle. This occasion was full of such incidents as will beyond a doubt be remembered by the Colonial subjects of Her Majesty to the end of their lives. The gracious and kindly reception which they experienced may by the outside world be taken for granted; but to the thirteen gentlemen of English blood, and the equal number of redskins belonging to a race partially reclaimed from a state of wild independence, the act of condescension was evidently a more than expected honor. Dr. William George Beers, captain of the team and his twelve companions, having been conducted by General Ponsonby to the ground, stood ready to be marshalled before the Queen, who, a little before half-past five o'clock, was driven on the path below the East terrace, in a chaise and a pair of greys, preceded by a single outrider. Accompanying Her Majesty in the carriage was the Princess Beatrice, and on foot were Prince Leopold and Prince Christian. The members of the Royal Household looked on from the terrace above, and there were several visitors, among whom were the Hon. E. Chapleau, Attorney-General of the Province of Quebec, and Mr. Dore, agent for the Dominion of Canada. The thirteen Iroquois first had the honor of being presented to the Queen by General Ponsonby, and the chief, who is familiarly called Big John, advanced respectfully to the side of the carriage and read from a curiously illuminated scroll of beech bark, mounted on blue silk, with a deep fringe and with rosettes of blue ribbon, a genuine Indian address. This document, with its translation, had some time ago been transmitted to Her Majesty, through Lord Carnarvon, and when the Queen desired to see the game of La Crosse played, she thoughtfully proposed that the address should be returned to the Indians, that they might have the gratification of presenting it in person.

The "pale-faces," as they are called in this loyal address of the Iroquois, were next presented, and then the game began. At either goal were stationed two umpires, those for the red-skins being Mr. William Waddell, of the London Athletic Club, and Mr. Byrne, agent for the Province of Ontario; while those for the Canadian gentlemen were Dr. Archer and Dr. Balkwell. Most readers are now familiar at least with the general nature of the game, and it is only necessary to say that a spirited goal was played and won by the whites, who have greatly improved by recent practice ever since their visit to the British Isles. In the excitement of the game the ball was tossed sometimes amid the long rye-grass on the opposite side of the path bounding the lawn on the north side, sometimes very near the royal carriage, and once under the legs of the outrider's horse, much to the amusement of the company. When the goal had been won, just as six o'clock was striking from St. George's Chapel, the Iroquois chief slowly advanced to the Queen with a beautiful basket of Indian grass, which her Majesty took very graciously from his hands. Then followed the most pleasing episode of little drama and all those who have read the appreciative description of Indian grace in the pages of Mrs. Jamieson and other truthful as well as graphic writers may credit the statement that these Iroquois carried themselves with a forest manliness very pleasing to behold, as each in turn, bowing at the side of the royal chaise, received from the Queen's hand a photographic portrait of Her Majesty, in what is generally known as cabinet size, the artists being Messrs. W.&D. Downey, of Newcastle-on-Tyne. After the red men had passed by, in true Indian file, their white antagonists in the friendly game likewise had the honor each of receiving from Her Majesty's hands the same gift; and it should be mentioned that the Queen had written her name on each portrait. If she could have known the emotion with which each recipient afterwards spoke of the gift, her own pleasure would have been almost as great. Before the carriage drove off, Dr. Beers, captain of the Canadian team, called for "Three cheers for Her Most Gracious Majesty, our beloved Sovereign;" and it is needless to say that the response was a hearty one.

After the Queen's departure all the players, the few visitors and the gentlemen who had given their service—a sinecure, as it happened—as umpires, were entertained at a *dejeuner* in the Orangery; and then, re-entering the carriages which had brought them to the Castle, they drove to the Eton playing fields, where Mr. Forbes, captain of the school eleven, assembled all the boys who had been practising—a goodly number. As the Canadian lacrosse players and their Indian opponents were going to Manchester that same night, and were therefore obliged to catch the train that was to start at twenty-five minutes past eight from Windsor for London, there was not time to finish a game; but, before it became necessary to draw the goals, some of the hottest play ever remembered by old lacrosse players was shown for the edification of the school, in the presence of Dr. Hornby, the head master. Boys are better critics of new games than men are. We have heard much against lacrosse from grave elders who will believe in nothing new; but the Eton boys, who play cricket and foot-ball, saw at once that here was a game with excellent points, and they quickly fell in with its characteristics. "What small goals they have!" said one observer. "There was a neat stoke," cried a second; and calls of "Well stopped," "Well run," "Well caught," were becoming loud and frequent when, in the midst of an exciting *melee*, the game was ended. Then the clapping of hands by all the boys betokened a genuine satisfaction; and a hearty cheer from the Canadians and Iroquois was taken up by the school, so that the departing players of lacrosse had nothing to regret in their visit to Windsor and Eton.

REVISED RULES OF LACROSSE, 1879

The National Lacrosse Association lapsed into a moribund state during the early 1870s, but a revival of interest in lacrosse led to the organization's resurrection in 1876. That year the sport also gained a boost from the tour of Great Britain described above. The Toronto Lacrosse Club took the initiative for the reorganization of the NLA. The timing was significant, for that year also marked the first successful challenge by the Toronto team for the championship. Control of the sport in Canada both on and off the field was beginning to tilt to Toronto and the province of Quebec. The following excerpts from the revised code reflect the delegates' increasing concern about roughness on the playing field. They also wished to define more clearly the regulations for championship competition. The amended rules were approved at several sessions held in Toronto in May, 1876, Montreal, August, 1877, Toronto, June, 1878, and Montreal, June, 1879. They are reprinted from W.K. McNaught, *Lacrosse, and How to Play It* (Toronto, 1880). pp. 156-168.

LAWS OF LACROSSE

...SEC. 2. No kind of metal, either in wire of sheet, nor screws or nails, to stretch strings, shall be allowed upon the crosse. Splices must be made either with string or gut....

RULE III.
THE GOALS.

The Goals must be placed at least 125 yards from each other, and in any position agreeable to the Captains of both sides. The top of the flag-poles must be six feet above the ground including any top ornament, and six feet apart. In matches they must be furnished by the challenged party....

RULE V.
UMPIRES.

SEC. 1. There must be two umpires at each goal who shall be disinterested parties, they shall stand behind the flags when the ball is near or nearing the goal. In the event of *"game"* being called, they shall decide whether or not the ball has fairly passed through the goal; and if there be difference of opinion between them, it shall be settled as provided for by Rule VI. They must not be members of either club engaged in a match; nor shall they be changed during a match without the consent of both Captains. They must see that the regulations are adhered to respecting the goal. They must know before the commencement of a match the number of games to be played....

RULE VI.
REFEREE.

SEC. 1. The Referee shall be selected by the Captains; and, in the case of *"Championship"* matches, must be appointed at least one day before the match. No person shall be chosen to fill the position who is not thoroughly acquainted with the game, and in every way competent to act. In the event of the Field Captains failing to agree upon a Referee the day previous to a match, it shall be the duty of the President of the National Lacrosse Association, or in his absence the Vice-President, upon being duly notified, to appoint a Referee to act during the match, such Referee, however, not to be one of the number proposed by either of the competing clubs.

SEC. 2. Before the match begins, he shall draw the players up in lines, and see that the regulations respecting the ball, crosses, spiked soles, &c., are complied with. Disputed points, whereon the Umpires or Captains disagree, shall be left to his decision. He shall have the power to suspend at any time during the match, any player infringing these laws, the game to go on during such suspension. In disputed games which are left to his decision, he shall take the evidence of the *players* particularly interested, the respective opinions of the differing *Umpires* and, if necessary, the opinions and proposals of the Captains in cases where the discontinuance of the game is threatened. He shall immediately call *"time,"* when *"foul"* has called by either Captain.

SEC. 3. The jurisdiction of the Referee shall not extend beyond the day for which he is appointed, and he shall not decide in any matter involving the continuance of a match beyond the day on which it is played. The Referee must be on the ground at the commencement of and during the match. At the commencement of each game, and after *"fouls," "disputed games,"* and *"balls out of bounds,"* he shall see that the ball is properly faced, and when both sides are ready shall call "play." He shall not express an opinion until he has taken the evidence on both sides. After taking the evidence, his decision in all cases must be final. Any side rejecting his decision by refusing to continue a match, shall be declared the losers.

SEC. 4. When game is claimed and disallowed, the Referee shall order the ball to be faced for from where it is picked up, but in no case must it be closer to the goals than ten (10) yards in any direction....

THE GAME

RULE IX.
MISCELLANEOUS

SEC.1- Twelve players shall constitute a full field. They must be regular members in good standing of the club they represent, and no other, for a least thirty days before becoming eligible to play in a match for their club. No member shall be allowed to change clubs more than once during the season, except in *bona fide* change of residence.

SEC. 2. The game must be started by the Referee facing the ball in the centre of the field between a player of each side; the ball shall be laid upon the ground between the sticks of the players facing, and when both sides are ready the Referee shall call play. The players facing shall have their left side toward the goal they are attacking....

SEC. 10. Should any player be injured during a match and compelled to leave the field, the opposite side shall drop a man to equalize the teams....

RULE XIV.
BALL OUT OF BOUNDS.

Balls thrown out of bounds must be "faced" for at the nearest spot within the bounds, and all the players shall remain in their places until the ball is faced. The Referee shall see that this is properly done, and when both sides are ready shall call play. The *"bounds"* must be distinctly settled by the Captains before the commencement of the match....

RULE XX.
DELIBERATE CHARGING.

No player shall charge into another after he has thrown the ball.

RULE XXI.
CROSSE CHECK.

The check commonly known as the "square" or "crosse" check, which consists of one player charging into another with both hands on the crosse, so as to make the stick meet the body of his opponent, is strictly forbidden.

RULE XXII.
INTERFERING.

No player shall interfere in any way with another who is in pursuit of an opponent in possession of the ball....

RULE XXV.
"CLAIMING GAMES."

When "*game*" is claimed by the side attacking a goal, the Referee or with Umpire shall immediately call "*time,*" and then proceed to give their decision. Until their decision has been given no game can be taken. The players shall keep their places, nor shall they leave them (unless the game be decided as won) until the game has again been started by the referee.

RULE XXVI.
SETTLEMENT OF DISPUTES.

In the settlement of any dispute, whether by the Umpires or Referee, it must be distinctly understood that the Captains, with one player selected by them, have the right to speak on behalf of their respective clubs; and any proposition or facts that any player may wish brought before the Referee must come through the Captains or the player selected by them.

RULE XXVII.
FLAG POLE DOWN.

In the event of a flag pole being knocked down during a match, and the ball put through what would be the goal if the flag pole were standing, it shall count game for the attacking side.

RULE XXVIII.
CHALLENGES.

SEC. 1. All challenges must be sent by post, registered, addressed to the secretary of the club intended to be challenges.

SEC. 2. Any club receiving a challenge from another club, shall, within one week after its receipt, notify the challenging club of the time and place at which they are prepared to play. The place named shall be at either of their places or residence, or some intermediate place; and the time mentioned shall be within three weeks from the reception of the challenge.

SEC. 3. On the day selected, if one club only put in an appearance, it shall be entitled to claim a victory by default. If its opponents refuse to fulfil their engagement, or do not appear upon the ground at the specified time, the club complying with the terms agreed upon shall be declared the winners of the match.

SEC. 4. If at the time of the reception of a challenge a club has on hand any other regular challenge undisposed of, the time for its acceptance shall be extended with a period not exceeding six weeks; and if it should have more than one regular challenge undisposed of, then within a period not exceeding an additional three weeks for every such challenge. Challenges shall not lapse with the end of the season, but shall continue in force until played off. Challenges so carried over shall date from the 10th of May of the new season into which they have been carried.

SEC. 5. A club must accept challenges in the order of their reception. Challenges can not be sent earlier than the tenth of May nor later than the ninth of October, inclusive, and no match shall be played earlier than the 24th of May, unless mutually agreed upon. The season shall be from the 24th May to the 31st October inclusive.

RULE XXIX.
CHAMPIONSHIP RULE.

Preamble. - In order to create a greater interest in our national game, the National Lacrosse Association of Canada invite all clubs to compete for the Championships, for which purposes the Association offer a Senior Championship Pennant, and a Junior Championship Pennant, the winning clubs to hold the same under the annexed rules, and also subject to the rules of the game. The holders of these pennants to be recognized as the Senior and Junior Champions of Canada.

SEC. 1. The club holding the "Championship" can not be compelled to play any club competing therefore, more than twice in any one year, and an intervening space of two months must elapse between such matches.

SEC. 2. In the event of the holders losing the "Championship," their secretary shall, within one week furnish to the secretary of the winning club, copies, certified by their President, of all challenges for the "Championship" at the time undisposed of, and at the same time give up the champion pennant to the winning club.

SEC. 3. The club winning the "Championship" shall take up these undisposed challenges, and treat them as their own, in accordance with and subject to Rule xxviii. (Challenges.)

SEC. 4. Should the Champion Club be challenged by a club belonging to another city or part of the Dominion, half of the net proceeds received from such match shall go towards defraying travelling and hotel expenses only of the visiting team and its captain.

SEC. 5. Should half the net proceeds amount to more than the actual expenses of the visiting team, they shall receive their expenses only - the balance belonging to the Champion Club.

SEC. 6. A statement, signed by the President and Secretary of the Champion Club, given to the competing club, shall be evidence of the amount of net proceeds taken at such match.

SEC. 7. Any club holding either of the Championships shall furnish security for the sum of $200, to the satisfaction of the President and Sec.-Treasurer of this Association, that the Champion Pennant will be given up to the winning club upon the adjudication of the game by the Referee, or as provided by Sec. 2 of this Rule.

SEC. 8. Upon the Pennant being surrendered to the winning club, the President and Secretary-Treasurer of this Association shall return or cancel the security given by the losing club.

SEC. 9. No club shall be entitled to hold both Championships, or play for the Senior Championship while holding the Junior Championship.

SEC. 10. City clubs competing for the Junior Championship, shall not have upon their teams any players over 21 years of age. Other than city or Indian clubs, shall be allowed to have players of any age upon their teams.

SEC. 11. Indian clubs shall be allowed to compete for these Championships, under the rules of this Association; but in that case they will be debarred from the privilege of playing for money, given them in Article xi. of the Constitution....

THE STATE OF CANADIAN LACROSSE, 1878

The New York Clipper, 1 June 1878, p. 75.

LETTER FROM A CORRESPONDENT IN MONTREAL

Our clubs have got fairly under way by this time, not so soon, however, as they imagined when the snow began "to steal away up the mountain." The Spring has been, perhaps, unusually damp this year, and the grounds of most of the clubs in this city have been partly above and partly under water, so that those members of clubs who were enthusiastic enough to already commence practice have to a great extent been doing some admirable floundering. However, that old veteran club in the game, the Montreal, has been making some extensive improvements on their field, or rather have continued improvements begun last year in the way of leveling their ground. Now, instead of a rather noticeable declivity and unevenness at the top of the field, there is a gradual and barely perceptible decline from the very excellent running track to the southeastern extremity of the field; and we opine that our Toronto friends will not have so much to grumble about, in the way of "that miserable field," as they have had heretofore. The Montreal Club is making a very pleasing departure, too, this year; they are admitting lady associate members, and are devoting afternoons and evenings on the grounds to the ladies for lawn tennis, badminton, croquet, etc. Already, I believe, several of Montreal's noted beauties have signified their desire to avail themselves of the pleasures of these gentle sports. I am glad to see this, as the fairer sex have, for some reason best known to themselves, been somewhat averse to their devotees taking any very active part in manly sports and exercises. Lately I have observed this aversion to be declining, and consequently hail with joy the inauguration of lady associate members to an active share of the club privileges. Keroniare the brave and the intrepid White Eagle of Caughnawaga have been for some time past "at daggers drawn," from some local quarrel, I believe, but have buried the hatchet, peacefully smoked the calumet, and once more appear on the field together. While the Indian veterans are coming forward, the white veterans are one by one dropping out of the field, and steadily devoting themselves to the commercial world. That old terror, Maltby, whose magnificent throws and steady play used to be a very rock to the club, has thrown up the stick—"too stiff in the joints." Bowie, after a brilliant tally of hard-fought fields, has retired from active life. "Stonewall" Becket, whose name was a bye-word of goal-minding, has also added his name to swell the list of retired members. In their places new and younger men are coming brilliantly forward. Aird, who served his apprenticeship in the Independents, is a new light, promising to be one of the brightest; Kay in goals promises well, while Summerhayes and Cairns are coming prominently to the front, and Griffin confidently assures me of his ability to *"feed the home."* The Shamrocks are on June 1 going to hold their own, they say, against their old opponents, the Torontos, for the championship, and a magnificent match is looked for. I have not yet learned anything regarding their team, but of course it will be good; shall endeavor to let you know something about them in my next. Tommy Farmer, Butler, "Old Steadfast" Hoobin and Hyland, of course, are "all there." I know nothing as yet of any changes. Among our younger friends, the Independents are arming and preparing themselves to give the Athletics "all they know how," for the honor of holding the junior championship flags, and a fine game is expected between these two spirited clubs. Their first teams played the longest match on record last year, which ended in a tie, 4h. 37m. Among our juniors the Sarfields are expecting to cross sticks with the winners of the flags. In that old castellated burgh, Quebec, the Thistles are prepared to hold their own, while cheering news comes from Lancaster and Lachine; Sherbrooke yet to be heard from. I have not heard from Ontario, but I am expecting news day by day. Altogether, we look out for a "live" season this year. Yours, etc.

Montreal, May 21, 1878 Cobra.

CANADIAN CHAMPIONSHIP, 1880

The New York Clipper, 18 September 1880, p. 205.

TORONTO VS. SHAMROCK

We in the States here know little of the excitement attendant upon the contests for the championship at lacrosse in Canada, and the deep interest taken in the meetings between those old-time rivals the Toronto Club and the Shamrock Club of Montreal. It would remind old cricketers of the rivalry of twenty-odd years ago between the New York and St. George cricket elevens; and old baseball players of the excitement attending the contests of the Atlantic and Excelsior clubs of 1860. *The Toronto Mail,* in referring to the contest of Sept. 4, says: "No better answer could be given to those who declare lacrosse is on the decline than the spectacle presented by the lacrosse field on Saturday afternoon, when the Toronto and the Shamrocks of Montreal, champions of the Dominion, met to cross sticks. In spite of the sweltering heat and the ominous clouds, three thousand people or more collected on the stand and the field, nearly a third of whom were ladies. It is gratifying to reflect that they were amply repaid for the discomfort to which they so cheerfully submitted by witnessing one of the finest games of lacrosse ever played in Toronto or anywhere else. Both teams had their very best men on the field, which of itself was a guarantee that the struggle was to be an earnest one. Among the Shamrocks were four—Giroux, Morton, Brennan, and McKeown—of the twelve who in 1875 lost the championship to their present opponents, while in the Toronto team there was only one left of those who took part in that memorable game which gave this city the lacrosse championship of the world for two years or so. Altogether the two twelves seemed as evenly matched physically as it could possibly be wished. ...Although beaten by three games to one, the Torontos distinguished themselves and retrieved much of their lost reputation. Another season, with plenty of practice, there is no reason why their present team should not prove themselves equal to travelling down to Montreal and returning with the lost championship. To do this, however, they must work hard and persistently, and their energetic captain, John Massey, will have his labors crowned with victory. The great strength of the Torontos was in their running and their general quickness. Their weakness was their throwing, which they require to work up, giving their attention not so much to long distance as to straight throwing. Of the individual play little need be said, for all worked well. Arthurs, Hughes, Gerry, Ross McKenzie, Garvin and Bonnell perhaps distinguished themselves the most for the Torontos, while Farmer, Morton, Giroux, Brennan, McKeown and Butler bore the brunt of the battle for the visitors."

THE FIRST LACROSSE TOURNAMENT IN THE UNITED STATES, 1878

On August 23, 1878, the Ravenswood, Union, and New York clubs entered the first lacrosse tournament held in the United States. The Polo Club of Newport provided the grounds, which suggests that the first American lacrosse players enjoyed the patronage of upper class gentlemen. This report is from The New York Clipper, 7 September 1878, p. 187.

THE LACROSSE TOURNAMENT

...The tournament was to have opened at 3 o'clock, but the usual delay occurred, and it was not until 3:45 that Macdonald and Slater faced the ball. Macdonald got it at the start, dodged a couple of men prettily, and then threw a beautifully judged ball right on the Ravenswood flags. Smith, at the latter's point, however, got it away for a moment, only to have it returned again by the Unions, who were attacking pretty vigorously. Their efforts were in vain, however, as the defense was too strong, and the ball was soon transferred to the Union flags, where Cluff, Goldsmith and Ritchie made it lively for the defense men. Away it went, now at centre, then at one goal, again at the other, the defense at each end of the field having all they could do to keep the ball out. The game had been under way about ten minutes when a long throw from the Union defense over the Ravenswood flags drew the latter's defense out. Williams, the Union's home man, got the ball, and, dodging the three opponents who attacked him, tipped it over from behind the flags to Macdonald, who struck at it to knock it through; but the ball went through the netting of his stick, and before he could pick it up again Smith swooped down on him and carried it off—a very narrow escape for the Ravenswood. Again another long throw lured out the Ravenswood defense, when Williams repeated his tactics, this time passing the ball to Lathrop, who was in front of the flags, with no one between to keep him from shoving it through. He lost his head, however, and instead of scoring a game for his side struck the ball wide of the goal, and so missed a splendid chance. After that very few opportunities were offered the Union home men, the ball being kept well in the field by the Ravenswoods until they got an opening, which they skillfully used, Ritchey winning the game in 19 minutes. The next two games were almost a repetition of the first, and deserve no especial mention, only lasting 7 and 5 minutes respectively, Cluff and Ritchie taking them after some very poor play on the part of the Union defense. The players on the Ravenswood side who especially distinguished themselves were Ritchey (goal), Smith (point), Wilson (even point), Nichols (field), and Cluff, Goldsmith and Ritchey (home). The Union players were in very bad form, and their team was very much weakened by the absence of three of their best men and the illness of Marquand and Flannery, which prevented those two players from doing much, Flannery especially playing very poorly, and being, apparently, through weakness, almost unable to use his stick. Their new goalkeeper, Morris, on whom they depended greatly, was a most remarkable failure, missing every ball that came in his way. The rest of the team it is best to say nothing about. Their defeat was totally unexpected to their friends, who had counted on an easy victory after their July 4 performance. The two teams will probably meet again in a few weeks, and doubtless the contest will be a much better one. After the Ravenswood vs. Union match was over, the winners took thirty minutes' rest, and then tackled the New York Club, who were to play the winners of the first match. There was a most remarkable difference in the appearance of the two teams as they took their places in the field, the Ravenswood men looking quite small in comparison with their opponents, whose magnificent physique showed to advantage in their striking costume of blue and yellow. The N.Y. team was captained by J.R. Flannery of the Unions. This match, from beginning to end, was splendidly played, and showed the stuff both clubs were made of, the Ravenswoods, although not so fresh as their opponents, playing with a determination and skill rarely shown on a lacrosse field. The New Yorkers excelled in running and throwing, while the Ravenswoods supported one another splendidly. It was touch-and-go for fifty-five minutes, until a mistake made by Inman in throwing the ball to Montant at centre, who muffed it instead of throwing it home, gave the Ravenswood fielders a chance to get it in on their opponents' flags before Inman could get back to save them; and so they won the first game, Cluff tipping it through. The second game was started after a few minutes' rest, and was as fiercely contested as the first, the New Yorkers seeming to be as fresh as at starting, while the Ravenswoods made up for their lack of it by putting extra steam into their playing. It was anybody's game from first to last; but luck was in favor of the Ravenswoods, and again Cluff credited a goal to his side. The third game was played in the twilight, and the majority of the players could only guess as to the whereabouts of the ball during the greater portion of it; but, like the preceding two, it was taken by the Ravenswoods, who, in this way, won the championship and the cup presented by Jas. Gordon Bennett. They certainly deserve great credit for their pluck and bottom, and earned their victory in a manner that showed well for their training, and promises much for their future. The New Yorkers, too, who had very little hopes of making more than a fair resistance to their opponents, surprised both themselves and their friends by the skill they exhibited in handling the crosse. They are probably the fastest team on the continent, and, properly coached, would, it is thought, capture at no distant day the championship of America, now in the hands of the Toronto Club. They owe considerable of their success in making such a good fight to the efforts of their captain, who handled them for all they were worth, and made them do wonders. Among the players most noticeable in this team, the Lamontagne brothers, Inman, Francis, and last, but not least, Muir, deserve especial praise. They handled their sticks like veterans, and never failed to be ready for duty when called upon by their captain. The weak point of the team is their home, not owing to the weakness of the players, but to the very bad style in which they attack goals. They had lots of chances, but did not take advantage of them as they should have done; still they are but beginners, and should only be treated to praise for their wonderful progress in learning the game. The tournament will give a vast impetus to lacrosse, and before the end of the next season we hope to see the game take firm hold here. A U.S. Nat. Lacrosse Association is to be formed this Fall. The first meeting of the delegates from the principal American clubs interested in the movement will take place in New York in a couple of weeks, when the necessary constitution, rules, etc., will be discussed and decided on. All the clubs who took part in the tournament speak in the highest terms of their treatment by the Polo Club, and express themselves well pleased at the result of their trip to Newport.

AMATEUR LACROSSE IN THE UNITED STATES, 1879

The United States National Amateur Lacrosse Association was founded on June 20, 1879. Its rules defined an amateur as "one who follows any regular business or occupation, who is not a paid player or attached as such to any club." It permitted clubs which employed a professional as a lacrosse teacher to play him in all matches, except those for the championship. The following championship rules are reprinted from the *Laws of Lacrosse, adopted by United States National Amateur Lacrosse Association* (Brooklyn, N.Y), 1879), pp. 31-33.

CHAMPIONSHIP RULES.

SEC. 1. The club holding the "Championship" cannot be compelled to play any club competing therefor, more than twice in any one season, and an intervening space of two months must elapse between such matches.

SEC. 2. Club holding "Championship" shall have the choice of grounds for all "Championship" matches.

SEC. 3. In the event of the holders losing the "Championship," their secretary shall, within one week furnish to the Secretary of the winning club, copies, certified by their President, of all challenges for the "Championship" at the time undisposed of.

SEC. 4. The club winning the "Championship" shall take up these undisposed challenges, and treat them as their own....

SEC. 5. Should the champion club be challenged by a club belonging to another city or part of the United States, two-thirds of the net proceeds received from such match shall go towards defraying travelling and hotel expenses only of the visiting team and its Captain.

SEC. 6. Should two-thirds the net proceeds amount to more than the actual expenses of the visiting team, they shall receive their expenses only—the balance belonging to the champion club.

SEC. 7. A statement, signed by the President and Secretary of the champion club, given to the competing club, shall be evidence of the amount of net proceeds taken at such match.

SEC. 8. In matches where the challenging club belongs to the same city or part of the United States as the champion club, the latter shall not be required to hand over to challengers any portion of net proceeds of such matches.

SEC. 9. Indian clubs shall not be allowed to compete for the Championship.

RULES GOVERNING CHAMPION LACROSSE CUP
WESTCHESTER POLO CLUB, 1879

FIRST.—This Cup shall be competed for annually, on the grounds of the Westchester Polo Club, Newport, R.I., by clubs belonging to the United States national Amateur Lacrosse Association, once each during the years 1879, 1880 and 1881, at such time as may be mutually agreed on by the Westchester and competing clubs. The first meeting to be held at Newport, on August 28th, 1879. The club winning the greatest number of matches to become the holders of Cup and United States Amateur Championship.

SECOND.—The Cup shall afterwards be subject to challenge from all clubs who are members of the United States National Amateur Lacrosse Association, and the holders thereof shall, in the interim that elapses between annual meetings at Newport, be obliged to defend it, and play all challenges for it in the order that they are received.

THIRD.—All matches for the Cup shall be played subject to Rules of the U.S.N.A.L.A., and regulations governing Championship.

FOURTH.—In the event of the holders of Cup being defeated, their Secretary shall, within one week, furnish winning club with copies of all challenges undisposed of, at the same time handing over the Cup to winning club. The club winning Cup shall take and treat such challenges as their own, playing them in the order they were received.

FIFTH.—The club holding cup shall be obliged to give security satisfaction to President and Secretary-Treasurer of the Association for the sum of $500, as a guarantee that they will surrender Cup to winning club as required by these rules.

SIXTH.—Upon Cup being surrendered to winning club, the President and Secretary-Treasurer of Association shall cancel or return security given by losing club.

SEVENTH.—Club holding Cup shall not be required to play matches for it before May first, nor later than November first, nor oftener than once in two (2) weeks; they shall not be obliged to play any club more than twice in same season, and may claim a delay of two (2) months between such matches.

EIGHTH.—This Cup shall not become the property of any club until November 1, 1881. The club winning it oftenest between August 28th, 1879, and November 1, 1881, to become its final owner.

NINTH.—In the event of the holders of Cup disbanding, or ceasing to exist as a club, the Cup shall be returned to the President of the Association, who shall hold it until a decision is arrived at by the officers of the Association in regard to its disposal.

TENTH.—All disputes, etc., in regard to Cup shall be left to and decided by the President and officers of the Association.

Chapter 14

PUB SPORTS

Between 1861 and 1880 billiards, bowling, and quoits experienced varying degrees of modernization in both the United States and Canada. During this period supporters of each pastime drew up rules and attempted to form governing bodies to promote their favorite game. But only billiards gained favor among a variety of classes, while bowling suffered a decline in public interest and quoits retained its position as a minor sport patronized by a small community of participants.

During these years billiards consisted of two different forms. The first involved upper class gentlemen who played in private homes or clubs. The second featured the masses who competed in poolrooms that were usually situated in saloons. The latter type predominated, and included a few skilled professionals who competed for prize money in front of sizable audiences. Increasingly billiards became a lower-middle class recreation patronized by gamblers and other elements of the "sporting fraternity." It apparently gained popularity at the expense of bowling because it was less expensive and more appealing to the members of the bachelor subculture who enjoyed frequenting gambling parlors and bars. The poolhall became the preferred place for men to congregate to enjoy each other's company and drink, wager, and play pool.

Critics of billiards objected to the vices associated with poolhalls, especially gambling, rowdiness, heavy drinking, and prostitution. Supporters responded by emphasizing the upper-class traditions of the game and its inherent wholesome qualities. "Billiards and the Family" points out the positive values of the sport for women and children. Editorialists declared that there was nothing inherently objectionable about the game, and that it was ideally suited for city dwellers and could be played in all seasons, day and night.

The Civil War did little to damage the popularity of billiards, and after the conflict it thrived in North American cities. In New York City proprietors of parlors charged players between ten and sixty cents per hour. In 1866 one report estimated that 12,000 people in the United States earned their livelihood through pool. While this number was probably too high, it still seems likely that the sport was a booming urban institution. It is certain that it was a favorite pastime of the African-American population. "Colored Amateur Tournament" suggests that black players were highly skilled and respected by their white counterparts.

These years witnessed the intensification of the rivalry between the two leading professional players of the era, Michael Phelan and Dudley Kavanaugh. Phelan retired from active competition in 1863, and Kavanaugh won the ensuing tournament for the championship of the United States. But Phelan remained the dominant force in professional pool, and in 1865 he was one of the founders of the new American Billiard Players Association. That year Kavanaugh was forced to forfeit his champion cue and was elected President of an anti-Phelan organization, the National American Billiards Association. The controversy heated up in 1870, when one sporting periodical accused Phelan of a conspiracy to dominate billiards and monopolize the right to manufacture and sell all the tables used in America.

Despite Phelan's efforts to standardize the rules of the game through his publications (including *Billiards Without Masters* and *The American Billiard Record*), various forms of the game were played across the continent during these years. "The Champion's Game of Billiards" presents the rules of a new version of the pastime which sportsmen hoped would become adopted across North America.

While billiards showed considerable growth and modernization during these years, bowling experienced a significant drop in popularity. The reasons for this trend are not clear, but a few commentators blamed the sport's troubles on the greed of proprietors of bowling alleys or the greater appeal of billiards. Some owners of lanes believed that the small pins commonly used made the sport too difficult, and they tried to experiment with larger bottle-shaped pins. But apparently that move did not increase interest among the public. Still, most cities had several bowling establishments, and some gymnasiums, private clubs, and saloons also had a few alleys on their premises. By the late 1870s enthusiasts had founded the National Bowling Association, the rules of which are reproduced in this chapter.

Finally, quoits retained a small following of players during this period, especially among Scottish immigrants. The game, which resembles horseshoe-pitching, was still primarily a country pastime, but there were also a few city clubs. The final documents in this chapter are a report of a championship match and the rules of the National Association of Quoit Players.

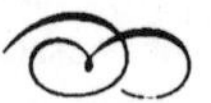

BILLIARDS

BILLIARDS AND THE FAMILY

Supporters of billiards believed that it was a refreshing and wholesome pastime that was well suited for family recreation. This editorial is reprinted from The New York Clipper, 4 June 1864, p. 58.

BILLIARDS AS AN EXERCISE FOR LADIES AND CHILDREN

It is a fact, and a pleasing one, that more attention is being paid to the physical culture of ladies and children than formerly. The idea that a lady must be thin, pale and delicate, to be beautiful, is far less generally entertained than it once was; and well rounded and developed limbs, full breast, rosy cheeks, and cherry lips are not deemed so forbidding as dandies and over-anxious mamas once thought them. Indeed, we are beginning to open our eyes to the truth, that women, like men, are of the earth earthy, and have duties to perform, which, without a proper amount of *physique,* it is impossible for them to accomplish. What is true of women in this regard, is also applicable to children; and, indeed, unless we have healthy women, we cannot have healthy children, and the race must necessarily degenerate. That extreme development of the mental faculties and the voluntary wasting away or training down of the physical to a mere nothingness, until our females and progeny look like etherial beings, or angels, as though they had no business on this sublunary sphere, is a delusion and a snare which it is neither desirable or profitable to cultivate. It is pleasing, we say, that more correct views are obtaining on this subject, and that the discovery has been made that women and children really have limbs to use, and are not intended as mere wax figures to be merely gazed upon. Our attention has been called to this subject by reading a brief paragraph recently, which stated that a billiard table had been introduced into some seminary for "the use of the young ladies." Ladies at billiards! Truly, this *is* a step in the right direction. And in a fashionable school at that. Verily, the world does move. This choice of exercise, too, is judiciously made, for, as an indoor exercise, we know of none better than an hour or two at the billiard table; because its effects are threefold. By it the mental faculties are exhilarated; the physical stimulated and developed; and the social fostered and cultivate. Incidentally, however we may state, that as an outdoor exercise, archery should find more countenance. Show us a female who takes exercise in her billiard room, with her arrows and quiver, on the back of her palfrey, or in winter on the skating pond, at proper intervals, and we will show you a happy, cheerful, graceful, beautiful woman, fit to be the partner of any lord of creation that ever wore small clothes. Let it not be supposed either, that any sacrifice of propriety need be made by such exercises. Horseback exercise, archery, and skating, are well known to have been patronised by ladies of high degree, and in Europe and elsewhere they have been considered accomplishments. In France and Germany, too, billiards has not been considered one whit behind them; and since the introduction of private billiard rooms into the mansions of our wealthier citizens, and the various tournaments played in presence of the ladies here, we are glad to be able to say that the stupid prejudice formerly entertained against the game among our females who should lead in all reforms, is fast dying away. As an example, we might state that one of the greatest and purest of women, Madame de Stael, was an advocate of billiards, and a brilliant player withal; and when exiled to Switzerland by Napoleon, she overstayed the limit of her time in Paris to superintend the removal of her billiard table. The late Duchess de Berri was also very fond of the game, and was a skillful wielder of the cue and mace; her example gave the tone to Parisian fashion; and today the billiard room is regarded as one of the chief and best attachments to a well ordered chateau in Europe; and it is fast growing to be so here. We might multiply examples endorsing the propriety and benefits that would accrue by the adoption of billiards as an exercise and pastime by females; but deem the foregoing enough to convince those of our land that they too may take the cue with profit. The above applies largely with regard to children and the home circle; for there is nothing more calculated to make them fond of home than the recollection of amusements shared in common. Our billiard tables and paraphernalia are the best in the world, without a doubt; but for family use, where children of short stature wish to play, there is something yet to be done; and if some enterprising manufacturer will take the hint here thrown out, and invent and patent a table that can be raised or depressed by screws, or springs, or some other contrivance best adapted thereto, we predict for him a large sale. We think the end might be best accomplished by resting the bed on screws, since less trouble would be experienced in getting and keeping the table "in true."

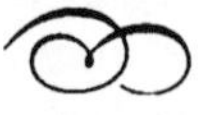

AFRICAN-AMERICAN COMPETITION

During this period African-Americans participated in a variety of sporting activities. These included baseball, boxing, wrestling, and billiards. This report of a black billiards match is reprinted from The Spirit of the Times, 18 February 1871, p. 5.

COLORED AMATEUR TOURNAMENT.

Let it be known that our colored citizens are not without ambition in a billiardistic way, and the balls, propelled by cues in ebony hands, are wont to echo muchly in the purlieus of the Eighth Ward of this city. Evening following evening the two tables in the room kept by Major Pool, at 149 Wooster Street, are nightly invested by a small brigade of negroes, and the balls are kept in lively agitation. Parties awaiting their turns, too, are numerous, and, with feet elevated before the fire, and reclining at an angle of about fifteen degrees, remind one forcibly of certain positions which were said to be assumed by certain Congressmen during parliamentary discussions. The room presents the appearance of a colored paradise, and the *habitues* seem perfectly at their ease, and undoubtedly regard their present *otium cum dignitate* as a faint reflex of the good time coming, and not far distant in the future. As we are of the humanitarian sort, we heartily wish them godspeed; but trust that their newly acquired importance may not be used as a means of inciting them to act of lawlessness and violence.

During the fall of 1870 considerable feeling was manifested between certain of the colored citizens who had acquired some knowledge of the game, and for the purpose of settling the point Major Pool procured a handsome cue which he offered as a prize to be contended for by the players who were so inclined, and which was to be symbolical of the Colored Championship. The cue is valued at $50. There were seven entries, consisting of J. Vaughn, C. Marsh, R. Huclus, William Miller, J. Joseph, W. Jackson, and the proprietor of the room, Major Pool. During the tournament, W.S. Widgeon of this city acted as referee, and J. Sands of Savannah and W.T. Jones of Philadelphia as scorers. The games were of 1,000 points each, at American four-ball caroms, each carom to count 3. The first game was between Vaughn and Marsh, the former winning by 244 points; highest run, 63. In the second game Huclus beat Miller by 196; highest run 54. Jackson and Joseph contended in the third game, and the former was vanquished by 199; highest run, 39. The fourth game produced a lively display between Pool and Joseph. Pool finally won by 135 points, his highest run being 39. The contestants in the fifth game were Huclus and Pool. Won by the former with a majority of 235, he having again scored 54 as his highest run. {Wouldn't that be a good number to play first in the lottery?} The struggles finally narrowed down to a contest between Huclus and Vaughn. After a long contest of one hundred and ninety-one innings, Huclus pulled out ahead, by a score of 1,000 to 963. His highest run was 36, as against 27 by his opponent. Huclus was then amid much excitement, proclaimed champion. But we are told that "uneasy lies the head that wears a crown," and it has been again verified in this instance; for on Tuesday last the Championship Committee were handed the appended document, which shows that Vaughn does not consider the result of the last game as a true index of the comparative abilities of himself and Huclus:

NEW YORK CITY, Feb. 14, 1871.

To Messrs. Wm. T. Widgeon, Wm. T. Jones, and S. Ellis, Committee for Colored Amateur Championship—*Gentlemen:* This is to notify Mr. Robert H. Huclus, Amateur Champion of New York City, that I hereby challenge him to play a match-game of billiards for the Championship and Champion Cue at the earliest possible time allowed by the regulations. As I desire to play the first game according to the conditions of the tournament, an early answer is solicited.

Yours respectfully, JOHN H. VAUGHN.

BILLIARDS.

THE CHAMPION'S GAME OF BILLIARDS.

THE RULES DECIDED UPON.

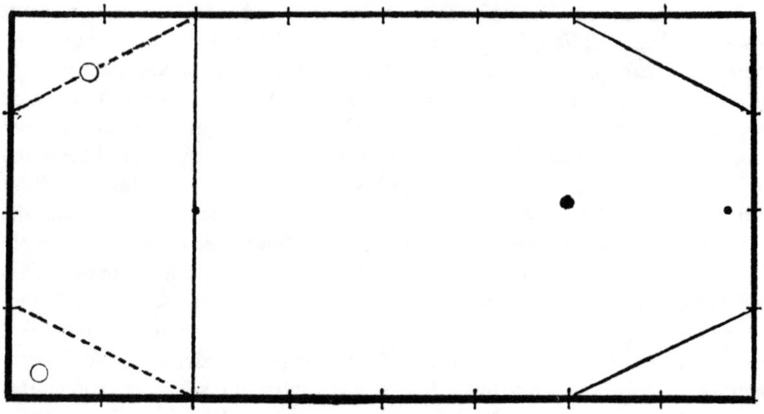

Arranging the Table.

REVISED RULES, 1879

The 1870s witnessed a lively debate on revising the rules of billiards. The outcome was the following new code, as described in The Spirit of the Times, 22 March 1879, p. 151.

THE CHAMPION'S GAME OF BILLIARDS.

The spots upon the table used in the champion's game are similar to those in the American or four-ball game, familiar to players as the light red spot, the dark red and pool or white ball spot at the foot of the table. The prominent improvement in the game is the introduction of four triangular spaces, one at each corner of the table, the object of which is to resist what is known as rail-nursing, without prohibiting it. A continuous line is drawn from the face of the end cushion, opposite the first "sight," (or diamond) from the corner, to the face of the side-cushion, opposite the second "sight," or diamond. Thus, on a 5x10 table, the line extends a distance of fourteen inches on the short rail, and a distance of twenty-eight inches on the side rail, and forms a triangular space, within which two balls can be played upon once only without sending at least one of them outside.

I. *Lead and Choice of Balls.*—Standing at the head of the table, and as far apart as practicable, the two contestants shall endeavor to simultaneously play the cue balls from within the string line against the lower cushion, the lead and the choice of balls to be won by him whose ball stops the nearer to the cushion at the head of the table.

II. *The Leading Stroke.*—1. He who has won in stringing may either require his antagonist's ball to be placed on the radius spot, and take the lead himself, or he may have his own ball spotted, and require his opponent to open the game. Whichever is to open the game may play from anywhere within a six-inch radius, of which the spot at the head of the table is the base, but can make no count unless his ball has hit the red before hitting the white. 2. After the opening stroke, the striker play at either ball from any position in which he may find his own, subject to certain rules as to foul stroke.

III. *Balls in Hand.*—In the opening shot, also, whenever by a counting stroke he has sent his ball off the table, or lodged it on the cushion rail, and likewise, whenever he elects to spot balls that are "fast," the striker is "in hand." The non striker's ball never becomes "in hand."

IV. *On the Count.*—One point shall be given the striker for every fair carom, and for every failure to hit an object ball he shall forfeit one point to his adversary.

V. *Balls in Balk.*—The object balls shall be in balk as soon as both have stopped within any one of the triangular spaces defined by the oblique lines. A ball *on* the line is a ball *within* it.

VI. *Foul Strokes.*—It is a foul, and no count can be made:

1. If a stroke is made except with the point of the cue.

2. If the cue is not withdrawn from the cue ball before the latter comes in contact with an object ball.

3. If when in hand the striker plays at a ball that is *inside* or *on* the string line, or if when in hand he plays from any position not within the six-inch radius.

4. If, in the act of striking, he has not at least one foot *touching* the floor.

5. If he strikes while a ball is in motion, unless it has come to a rest, as provided in Sec. 10 of Rule VI.

6. If he plays with the wrong ball, except as provided in note to this section.

7. If the player touches the cue ball more than once in any way, or hinders or accelerates it in any way than by legitimate stroke of the cue; or if, during a stroke or after it, he in any way touches, hinders, or accelerates an object ball except by the one stroke of the cue ball to which he is entitled.

8. As touching any ball *in any way* is a stroke, a second touch is foul.

9. It is a foul against the striker if any ball be disturbed, hastened, or hindered by an opponent or any one but himself, whether the ball or balls are at rest while he is aiming or striking, in motion after he has struck, or at rest again after he has struck, and pending his again taking aim; and he shall have the same option as is given his opponent in Sec. 8 of this rule.

10. Should a ball that has once come to a standstill move without apparent cause, while the player is preparing to strike, it shall be replaced. Should it move before he can check his stroke, it and all other balls set in motion by that stroke shall be replaced, and the player shall repeat his shot, inasmuch as but for the moving of the ball he might have counted where he missed, or missed where he counted.

11. It is a foul if the striker plays directly at any ball with which his own is in fixed contact.

12. It is a foul if more than two successive shots are made on balls both of which are within any one of the four interdicted spaces. The only way in which more than that

number can be made in succession within that space is by sending one or both balls out, and bringing them back and in again. Both balls being within the space, the striker can play once on them without sending either out; his next stroke must send at least one out; should it return, and both balls be again inside, he can play one shot, as before, without sending either out. This process may be repeated *ad libitum*. Should the second stroke fail to send a ball out, it does not count, the striker's hand is out, and the next striker play at the balls as he finds them.

13. It is a foul to place marks of any kind upon the cloth or cushions as a guide to play; also foul to practise the banking shot for the lead-off upon the plea of testing the balls, which, until the movement of banking, shall never be hit with a cue until the opening stroke is made; and it is also foul if the striker, in making a shot, is assisted by any other person in any way save by being handed the bridge, long cue, etc., by the marker, after he has requested the latter to do so.

14. It is a foul against the non-striker, and the striker cannot make a count on the ensuing shot, if a ball in play is lifted from the table, except it may be unavoidable in those cases in which it is provided that, because of foul or irregular strokes, the balls shall be transposed or replaced.

15. It is a foul if the striker, when he has the balls on the rail, attempts to remove obstruction from their path, though it is his privilege to demand their removal.

16. In order to restrict deliberate playing for safety, it shall be optional with the non-striker, if his opponent makes a miss in each one of three successive innings, to accept the third miss or reject it, and force his antagonist to hit at least one object ball, and for this purpose that antagonist's ball shall be replaced by the referee. Should two balls be hit by this stroke, there shall be no count.

Notes to Rule I.—Should the two balls come in contact, whether one only is in motion or both are, the player whose ball is clearly out of its true course—that is, on the opposite side of the table to that from which it was struck—shall be adjudged to have forfeited the lead and the choice. Should it happen that the balls come in contact midway while rolling to or from the upper cushion, thus implying that it is the fault of both players, they shall string again, as they must also in case the balls unobstructed have come to a rest at equal distances from the upper cushion. Should either cue ball come in contact with red ball, occupying its proper spot, its striker shall forfeit the lead, etc.

Note to Rule III.—When the non-striker's ball is forced off the table or lodges on the cushion, it is to be placed on the string-spot, if it is vacant; on the red spot, if that is vacant and the other is occupied; and on the pool-spot near the lower cushion, if both the other spots are occupied. This process is also to govern the cue ball forced off by a non-counting stroke; while the red ball, whenever forced off, shall be placed on the pool-spot if its own is occupied. When the striker forces his *own* ball off the table, etc., by a counting stroke, he can play from anywhere within the six-inch radius at any ball below it. If no ball is already below, the red must be taken up and placed on its proper spot. Should it happen that both white balls be sent off the table by a non-counting stroke, the ball of the incoming striker shall be placed on the radius spot, while the other shall be placed on the red ball's spot if it is unoccupied, or upon the pool-spot at the lower cushion, if that alone is vacant. Being never "in hand," the incoming striker whose ball is thus spotted may play upon any ball.

Note to Section 3 of Rule VI.—To simplify the duties of the referee, no claim of foul in either of these cases can be made *after* the stroke. The non-striker shall warn the striker beforehand. If the former fails to do so, the referee shall assume that the stroke was fair; if the latter, warned, refuses to alter his play, unless he has meanwhile appealed to the referee as to whether the ball is in or out, that official shall assume that a foul was contemplated, and presumptively perpetuated.

Note to Section 6 of Rule VI.—Should a foul not be claimed until the striker has made a second stroke, both strokes are valid, and he may continue with the wrong ball, or he may have the positions of the two whites reversed at once or at any other time during the run. The next striker, when it is his turn to play, shall have the same option, should he deem it hazardous to his interests to change the balls at once. Until he causes them to be changed, however, he must play with his opponent's ball, as that represents his own true position on the table. To play with his ball, without changing its position, is to make a foul. For the same reason, a player who has just used the wrong ball without detection is enjoined from claiming foul in case his opponent begins play with the *other* white ball. It is also a fair stroke if both white balls having been forced off the table, either is by mistake used in the next stroke. But the forfeiture of a miss incurred while playing the wrong ball, even when the striker is detected in so playing, must be paid the same as if he had used his own ball.

Note to Section 7 of Rule VI.—If it was a counting stroke, the striker who touches, hinders, or accelerates a ball, as above described, forfeits any count he may have made, and the next striker may either play at the balls as he finds them, or call upon the referee to place them in the relative positions they would have apparently occupied but for an interference that might have been designed. For the purpose of this rule, balls all at rest mark the line between a shot just made, and one that should have followed. For example, the cue ball touched before all the balls are at rest after a carom nullifies that stroke, and there shall be no count for it; touched except with the point of the cue, or prematurely with that instrument, after all the balls are at rest, the next stroke is affected, and no count can be made. The same process applies to object balls, as set forth in the succeeding rule prohibiting safety as an option.

Note to Section 8 of Rule VI.—There shall be no playing safety. Therefore, should a player in any way touch any ball before he is ready to strike, and afterwards touch his own ball or any other, his opponent shall have the option of playing at the balls as he finds them, or of having those replaced that may have been disturbed by the second stroke.

Note to Section 9 of Rule VI.—Should the disturbed ball be one on which the striker would seemingly have effected a count but for its being disturbed, hindered, or hastened, he shall have the option, provided he himself or representative did not disturb the ball or balls, of repeating the stroke on balls replaced, or of being credited with a carom, and allowed to play at the balls either as he finds them, or in the position they would have occupied, according to the judgment of the referee, had they not been disturbed.

Note to Section 11 of Rule VI.—The cue ball being "fast," the striker shall not have the option of playing directly upon the free object ball, or of playing at a cushion and returning upon either ball first, or of playing from within the "string" at balls spotted.

Note to Section 14 of Rule VI.—In case a singed fly or a speck of chalk attaches to a ball, the referee or the marker may remove it by means of a silk handkerchief or other light fabric. If it is on the ball where it can be seen, it can be removed without moving the ball more than slightly, if at all. If the striker alleges that it is at the base of the ball, or on the cloth, where it cannot be seen, the referee can only assume that it is not there; and then striker must play on, and so far uncover the obstruction that it may be got at without lifting the ball.

Note on Section 15 of Rule VI.—All obstructions shall be removed by the referee, or by the marker under the supervision of the referee.

BOWLING

Enthusiasts for the old game of bowling were determined to end the local variation of rules and establish a uniform code for the United States. This attempt at achieving a standard set of regulations is reprinted from ***Peck and Snyder's Latest Rules of Foot-ball*** (N.Y., 1879), pp. 25-27.

REVISED RULES OF THE NATIONAL BOWLING ASSOCIATION

RULE I. The game adopted to be played by clubs belonging to this Association shall be what is known as the American Ten Frame Game.

II. In the playing of match games there shall be a line drawn upon the alleys sixty feet from the head or front pin.

III. In the playing of match games, any wooden ball may be used including Wood's Patent Bush Ball, that does not exceed twenty-seven inches in circumference.

IV. The games shall consist of ten frames on each side, when, should the number of points be equal, the play shall be continued until a majority of points upon an equal number of frames shall be attained, which shall conclude the game. All strikes and spares made in tenth frame shall be completed before leaving the alley and on the same alley as made.

V. In playing all match games ten players from each club shall constitute a full team, and they must have been regular members of the club which they represent for thirty days immediately prior to the match; and they shall not play in a team representing any other club during the season.

VI. Players must play in the regular rotation, and after the first inning no change can be made except with the consent of the Captains.

VII. In match games, two alleys only are to be used; a player to roll but a frame at a time, and to change alleys every frame.

VIII. The Umpire shall take great care that the regulations respecting the balls, alleys, and all rules of the game, are strictly observed. He should be the judge of fair and unfair play, and shall determine all disputes and differences which may occur during the game. He shall take special care to declare all foul balls immediately upon their occurrence, unasked, in a distinct and audible voice. He shall in every instance, before leaving the alley, declare the winning club, and sign his name in the score book.

IX. In all matches the Umpire shall be selected by the Captains of the respective clubs, and he shall perform all the duties in Rule VIII, except recording the game, which shall be done by two scorers, one of whom shall be appointed by each of the contending clubs.

X. No person engaged in a match game, either as Umpire, Scorer or player, shall be directly or indirectly interested in any bet on the game. Neither Umpire, Scorer or player shall be changed during a match, except for reason of illness, or injury, or for a violation of these rules, and then the Umpire may dismiss any such transgressors.

XI. No person except the Captains shall be permitted to approach or speak with the Umpire, Scorers or players during the progress of the game, unless by special request of the Umpire.

XII. No person shall be permitted to act as Umpire, Scorer or Judge on setting up pins in any match unless he be member of a club governed by these rules.

XIII. Whenever a match game shall have been determined upon between two clubs, play shall be called at the exact hour appointed, and should either party fail to produce their players within thirty minutes thereafter, the club so failing shall admit a defeat, and the game shall be considered as won, and as such counted in the list of matches played; unless the delinquent club fail to play on account of the recent death of one of its members, or one of its members own family, and sufficient time has not elapsed to enable them to give their opponents due notice before arriving at the place to play.

XIV. A player must not step on or over the line in delivering the ball, nor after it has been delivered. Any ball so delivered shall be *deemed foul,* and the pins (if any made on such ball) shall be replaced in the same position as they were before the ball was rolled. It is also considered a foul ball if the hand is placed on any part of the alley beyond the line. All foul balls shall count as balls rolled.

XV. Should the first ball delivered on a full frame leave the alley before reaching the pins, the pins, if any made on such ball, shall not count but must be set up again, the ball to count as a ball rolled. After the first ball on each frame, all pins knocked down from the effect of the ball rolled by the player shall count to his credit; unless the ball should rebound from the back cushion, when the pins so knocked down shall be respotted and not counted.

XVI. No lofting or throwing balls upon the alley will be allowed. The ball must be rolled. Such balls will be considered foul at the discretion of the umpire.

XVII. In all match games two persons to act as Judges shall be chosen, one by each Captain, who shall take their positions at the head of the alleys, and see that the pins are properly set up and that no one interferes with them in any way until the player is through rolling. They will immediately report to the Captains any irregularities that they may notice during the progress of the game.

XVIII. Any club that shall be detected in tampering with the persons setting up the pins, or by any unfair means seeking to win a victory, shall, on proof of such conduct, be expelled from the Association.

XIX. To decide the championship hereafter, each club shall play one game with every other club in the Convention, said game to be played on a neutral alley. When a game is arranged between two clubs who occupy the same alley, said alley shall be considered as neutral, and the game may be played therein subject to mutual agreement. Any club having no engagement and receiving a challenge, must roll the game within fifteen days from the delivery of such challenge. Any other challenge received during said fifteen days must be acted upon and game played within ten days from date of completion of former game. The alley to be named immediately after the toss. The club failing to comply with the above forfeits the game. The club winning the greatest number of games on or before the September meeting of the Association in each year shall be declared the Champion.

XX. No person who has been expelled from any club, or who shall at any time receive compensation for his services as a player, shall be competent to play in match: any club giving compensation to a player, or having to its knowledge such a player in its team, shall be debarred from membership in the National Association, and they shall not be considered by any club belonging to this Association as a proper club to engage in a match game, and such club so playing with them shall forfeit its membership.

XXI. Any match games played by any club in contravention of the rules adopted by this Association shall be considered null and void, and shall not be counted in the list of match games won or lost.

XXII. Any club refusing to play any other club in the Association according to the rules, shall forfeit all claims to the championship, and all games played with such club shall be considered null and void, and shall not count in the list of games won or lost.

XXIII. A regulation pin must be used in match playing. Each pin, excepting the king pin to be from fifteen to sixteen inches in length and fifteen inches in circumference at the thickest part.

XXIV. Should the games played for the championship result in a tie between two or more clubs, a deciding game shall be played according to the rules of this Association.

XXV. Any club expelling a member shall immediately notify the Corresponding Secretary of the Association, and he shall notify the several clubs on the receipt of such information.

XXVI. No club shall issue or receive more than two challenges at a time.

QUOITS

CHAMPIONSHIP COMPETITION

After the Civil War Eastern quoit players engaged in a spirited competition for the honor of being recognized champion of the United States. The following report of a representative match first appeared in The New York Clipper, 8 December 1866, p. 274.

WILLIAM HODGSON VS. JAMES MCLAREN, 1866

The return at quoits between William Hodgson of Pottsville, Pa., and James McLaren, of Newark, N.J., for $300 and the championship of quoit pitching in America, came off on Thanksgiving Day, on the grounds of the Normal Quoit Club, corner of Broadway and Astor Place. This was the third occasion these two celebrated professors of this athletic and health-inspiring recreation have met together to test their relative superiority in skill in pitching. Hodgson has long been renowned as one of the best quoit players in the world, and for many years was the recognized champion of the game in England and Scotland, having successfully maintained his right to the title against all challengers. He is a coal miner by trade and about two years ago came to this country, where he found employment in the coal districts of Pennsylvania. His fame as a skilful player soon became extensively known and last year a match was arranged between him and James Gibson, who then was looked upon as the acknowledged champion quoit pitcher of America. The contest came off on the Caledonia quoit grounds at Newark, then as now kept by James McLaren, Hodgson's opponent in the present match. Gibson was defeated with seeming ease, and the ensuing day Hodgson and McLaren played a match for $100 a side on precisely the same condition, when McLaren came off the victor by 18 points in a game of 61 up. In justice to Hodgson it must be stated that both he and his friends attributed his defeat to his having celebrated too convivially the night previous his victory over Gibson, and subsequent events show that there was some foundation for this extenuating excuse. During the present summer, efforts were made to arrange another match between Hodgson and McLaren, which for a long time hung fire, owing to the backers of the former not being anxious to make another match except for a sufficiently large stake to compensate their man for neglecting his ordinary business. At last, owing to the spirited exertions of McLaren's principal backers, Messrs. J. Smith, of Paterson, and W. Lyons, of Jersey City, an agreement was entered into to play with Mr. Barnes of Philadelphia, Hodgson's principal backer, for $500 a side, and the match came off in Philadelphia, on the 29th and 30th of Oct., when Hodgson came off a very easy winner. Each man had now won a match, and the third and deciding game of the rubber was then arranged and came off on the above named day. The conditions were to play for $150 as side, 18 yards distance, stiff clay ends, 61 points up.

The day was far from favorable in the early part, necessitating a postponement, on account of the rain, of nearly two hours beyond the specified time, it being about 1 o'clock, P.M., when the game commenced. The fine quoit ground of the Normal Club was crowded with deeply interested patrons and admirers of this favorite pastime; the New York, St. Andrews, Normal, Newark, Paterson, Philadelphia and other quoit clubs being numerously represented. McLaren was attended by William Lyons, of Jersey City, as "director," and Hodgson by J. Dyott, of Pottsville; the ex-champion, James Gibson was referee, and Mr. Gleason, secretary of the Normal club, the score keeper. Hodgson was the favorite before the start, $50 to $40 being freely offered, and a good deal of money at these odds was invested. The play throughout was magnificent on both sides, and excited the admiration of the most experienced quoit pitchers. That of Hodgson was superb; his surprising ease and accuracy of delivery, coolness and judgment, being truly wonderful... Hodgson won by 17 points.

QUOIT CONVENTION, 1868

On March 23, 1868, a small number of quoit players representing six clubs from New York City and vicinity convened in Manhattan to organize the National Association of Quoit Players of the United States. The founders aimed to create a truly national organization, but the disappointing turnout at this meeting demonstrated the difficulties the sportsmen faced in gaining acceptance across the country. This gathering did manage to pass the following code of rules, which is reprinted from The American Chronicle of Sports and Pastimes, 26 March 1868, p. 98.

RULES AND REGULATIONS OF THE NATIONAL ASSOCIATION OF QUOIT PLAYERS.

RULE I. The distance for playing shall be eighteen yards.

RULE II. The mot shall not be more nor less than one inch above the clay.

RULE III. The measurement shall be from the centre of the top of the mot to the nearest iron in sight, without disturbing the clay.

RULE IV. In case of measurement, two opposing quoits being equal, it shall be declared a draw.

RULE V. In the case of two or four playing, twenty-two points shall constitute a game.

RULE VI. In the event of six playing, fifteen points shall constitute a game.

RULE VII. In the event of eight or more playing, eleven points shall constitute a game.

RULE VIII. In playing, the one getting the first shot shall lead off at the next end.

RULE IX. Each player shall have the privilege to select his own sized quoits.

RULE X. The mot shall be fixed in the clay at an angle of forty-five degrees.

Chapter 15

RACQUET SPORTS

The development of racquet sports in North America between 1860 and 1880 reflected the continuing influence of British sports on the upper classes in both Canada and the United States. The old game of rackets remained popular, and during the late 1870s a few athletically inclined gentlemen and ladies imported badminton and lawn tennis from the British Isles. The latter two pastimes proved to be especially appealing to women and were well suited for play at the new country clubs which were appearing near the major cities of the continent. Both badminton and lawn tennis were comparable to croquet in their adaptability to country and suburban living and their appeal to both sexes.

The modern sport of badminton evolved in England from an early form called battledore shuttlecock. The name was taken from the estate of the Duke of Beaufort, where a group of British army officers enjoyed this pastime in 1873. Several upper class American gentlemen who had traveled in India and England introduced the sport to New York City society in 1878, when they founded the Badminton Club of New York. Bayard Clarke, E. Langdon Wilks, and Norman R. Whitehouse organized this exclusive association, which met at the 71st Regiment Armory at the corner of 35th Street and Broadway. As many as 150 members played on weekends on nine courts. Men competed in tuxedos and Prince Albert coats and dancing shoes, while women wore long dresses. The first document in this chapter presents an early brief description of this game.

Lawn tennis was born in England in 1873, and the following year it was transplanted to both Canada and the United States. It appeared in Toronto in 1874, and two years later it took root in Ottawa and Montreal. Credit for first introducing lawn tennis into the United States goes to Miss Mary Ewing Outerbridge, whose relatives were active members of the Staten Island (N.Y.) Cricket and Baseball Club. While vacationing in Bermuda early in 1874 she observed British officers playing the new game. She brought back some racquets and a net to New York City. That spring her brother persuaded the club officials to grant her permission to set up her net and mark out a court on one corner of the grounds. Three years later she and several of her friends founded the Ladies Club, which was created under the jurisdiction of the Staten Island association. Wives and daughters of the male members took up the sport with enthusiasm and soon began arranging the first women's tournaments in the United States.

In 1875 and 1876 a few sportsmen also imported lawn tennis equipment and laid out courts in New England. Dr. James Dwight, sometimes called the "father of lawn tennis in America," first played the game during the late summer of 1875 on the estate of William Appleton at Nahant, Massachusetts, a seaside resort outside of Boston. In 1876 another gentleman brought lawn tennis to Newport, Rhode Island, and it soon joined polo as a fashionable recreation among the elite who summered there. All of these players also followed the rules which had been established in England earlier in the decade. The code reprinted below was adopted by several Philadelphia clubs and reflects some local modifications of the British regulations.

Rackets had long been a popular winter sport among the military garrisons and upper classes in Canada, with some following among the elite of the United States. It held its own during the 1860s, but it appears to have lost some ground during the following decade. In Canada that was due in part to the withdrawal of British troops. In 1861 Frederick W. Gates founded the Hamilton Racket Court in Ontario. Quebec City and Montreal also had clubs during these years, with the Montreal Racket Court Club using the St. George Street Court beginning in 1862. The Montreal association sponsored a ladies social group called the Sewing Club. For the gentlemen it staged occasional "stag" events such as boxing matches or ratting exhibitions.

During these decades New York City had several racket clubs, which occasionally hosted important regional and even international matches. In 1867 William Gray of England defeated Frederick Foulkes, another Englishman recruited as a member of the local Gymnasium Club. In 1875 William R. Travers, Rutherford Stuyvesant, A. Wright Sanford and a few of their friends from the New York City aristocracy founded the New York Racquet Court Club. Incorporated in 1876, its object was to promote "the social recreation and entertainment of its members and the practice and encouragement of an athletic game called Racquets and other gymnastic and athletic exercises." That spring it opened its new facility on Twenty-sixth street and Sixth Avenue, which included two courts (each 63 feet long, 31 1/2 feet wide, and 40 feet high), a gymnasium, running track, bowling alleys, billiard room, bachelor quarters, lounge, and reading room. Ladies were welcome on Thursdays. This chapter concludes with the rules and an editorial explaining the game and its beneficial effects for participants, especially baseball players.

BADMINTON

Both badminton and tennis were introduced into the United States in the late 1870s, and the first rules of both games were quite similar. In badminton the net varied from five feet six inches to six feet, and the court was sometimes shaped like an hourglass with dimensions of 28 feet by 20 feet. Shuttlecocks were often made of chicken feathers, and the rackets resembled those used for tennis. The following description of the game, which was one of the first to be published in the United States, is reprinted from Julian Marshall, *Lawn-Tennis and Badminton* (N.Y., 1879), pp. 31-32.

The chief difference between Lawn-tennis and Badminton is that the former is played with a ball, the latter with a shuttlecock. Badminton may be played in any room in a house, large enough for the game, or in the open air. It is played by two, three, four, six, or even more players, on opposite sides of a net, erected as for lawn-tennis, but higher. The net should be 5 feet 6 inches at the posts, and 4 feet 6 inches in the middle.

The Courts should be of the same sizes for the single and double games as specified for Lawn-tennis, but they may be made large or smaller in proportion to the skill of the players.

The rackets used in this game are lighter than those which are employed in Lawn-tennis, being 24 to 26 inches in length, and weighing from 8 to 12 ounces. The shuttlecocks are made after various patterns. For out-of-door play, especially in windy weather, a loaded shuttlecock, 1 1/2 to 2 ounces in weight and 2 1/2 inches in length, is the best. Lighter shuttlecocks, weighing about 1 ounce, may be used in the house. It is well, unless these be first rate in workmanship, to extract the feathers at first and re-fix them with strong glue, twining a thread or thin string in and out between the feathers, so as to contract their spread and make the shuttlecock fly faster.

THE GAME.

In general outline Badminton is played much as Lawn-tennis, with one great exception. The shuttlecock must always be returned on the volley, never on the half-volley nor after the bound. As soon as the shuttlecock touches the ground, the stroke is won by the Striker. The service is delivered under the same conditions as at Lawn-tennis, except that it may be given from any point between the base-line and service-line, and that it must drop, unless returned, between the service-line and base-line of the Court diagonally opposite to that from which it was served. If it drop out-of-Court, in the net, or short of the net, it is a fault.

If the shuttlecock, when served or returned, drop on any line, it should, as in Lawn-tennis, be deemed to have dropped within that line, on the side intended by the Striker. Some players count it against the Striker, or as a let; but the Lawn-tennis rule is the best.

If a let intervene between two faults, the faults are deemed to be consecutive. A shuttlecock which touches the net in passing should be deemed to have passed and to be in-play.

Badminton is generally scored as the game of Rachets, 15-up; and, when both sides arrive at 13, it is usual to set the game to 5 and to 3 at 14-all. The hand-out has the option of setting or not.

The Tennis-scoring method, however, introduced with perfect success in Lawn-tennis, will be found to work equally well in Badminton, and will materially strengthen the interest of the game.

LAWN TENNIS

During the late 1870s many cricket clubs in the vicinity of Boston, New York, and Philadelphia introduced the new game of lawn tennis. Before long that sport (along with golf) would undermine the popularity of cricket. Enthusiasts followed the rules of lawn tennis as established by the Tennis Committee of the Marylebone Cricket Club, but they also began the process of adapting the regulations to North American requirements. These laws are reproduced from ***Rules of Lawn Tennis, as adopted by The Cricket and Tennis Clubs of Philadelphia*** (Philadelphia, 1880), pp. 5-13.

THE LAWS OF LAWN TENNIS.

THE COURT.—The Court is laid out by lines forming a rectangular parallelogram, and is of two sizes, differing, however, only in width. The large or double-handed Court is 78 feet by 36 feet, ***inside measurement***, and the smaller or single-handed Court, 78 feet by 27 feet, ***inside measurement***.

Directly across the middle, and at right angle with its greatest length, is stretched a net so fastened to two posts standing 3 feet outside of the side lines, that the height of the net at each post, for the double-handed or *larger* Court, is 4 feet, and in the middle, over the Half-court line, 3 feet 6 inches; and for the single-handed or smaller Court, 4 feet 9 inches at the posts, and 3 feet in the middle, over the Half-court line.

The two Courts are divided by straight lines, thus,—one running the entire 78 feet of length equally distant from the side lines, so dividing the Court into halves, called the Half-court line, and two at right angles with this, at the distance of 22 feet from the net, and, therefore, 17 feet from the *base* lines, called the Service-lines.

BALLS AND RACKETS. {There is no restriction as to the shape or size of the rackets.}—The standard ball shall be hollow, made of india rubber, and covered with white cloth. It shall not be less than 2 3/8, or more than 2 1/2, inches in diameter, and not less than 1 7/8, or more than 2, ounces in weight.

Laws of the Game.

1. CHOICES OF SIDES AND FIRST SERVICE.—The choice of sides and the right of serving during the first game shall be decided by toss; provided that, if the winner of the toss choose the right to serve, the other player shall have the choice of sides, and *vice-versa*. The players shall stand on opposite sides of the net. The player who first delivers the ball shall be called the *Server,* and the other the *Striker-out*. At the end of the first game, the Striker-out shall become the Server, and the Server shall become Striker-out; and so alternatively in the subsequent games of the set.

2. SERVICE.—The Server shall stand with one foot outside the Base-line, and shall deliver the Service from any part of the Base-line of the Right and Left Courts alternately, beginning from the Right. The ball so served must drop within the Service-line, Half-court line, and Side-line of the Court, which is diagonally opposite to that from which it was served.

3. FAULTS.—It is a *fault,*

(a) if the ball served drops on or beyond the Service-line; or

(b) if it drops in the net; or

(c) if it drops out of the Court, or on any of the lines which bound it; or

(d) if it drops in the wrong Court; or

(e) if, in attempting to serve, the Server fails to strike the ball.

A fault can not be taken. After the first fault, the Server shall serve again from the same Court from which he served that fault.

4. SERVICE NOT TO BE VOLLEYED.—The service may not be volleyed.

5. SERVING BEFORE THE STRIKER-OUT IS READY.—The Server shall not serve until the Striker-out is ready. If the latter attempts to return the service, he shall be deemed to be ready.

6. BALL IN-PLAY.—A ball is *returned* or *in-play* when it is played back over the net, or between the posts, before it has touched the ground a second time.

7. BALL TOUCHING NET.—It is a good service or return, although the ball touch the net.

8. THE SERVER, WHEN HE WINS A STROKE.—The Server wins a *stroke,*

(a) if the Striker-out volleys the service; or

(b) if the Striker-out fails to return the service or the ball in-play; or

(c) if the Striker-out returns the serve or the ball in-play so that it drops, untouched by the Server, on or outside any of the lines which bound the Court; or

(d) if the Striker-out otherwise loses a stroke. (See Law 10.)

9. THE STRIKER-OUT, WHEN HE WINS A STROKE.—
The Striker-out wins a *stroke*,

(a) if the Server serves two consecutive faults; or
(b) if the Server fails to return the ball in-play; or
(c) if the Server returns the ball in-play so that it drops, untouched by the Striker-out, on or outside any of the lines which bound the Court; or
(d) if the Server otherwise loses a *stroke*. (See Law 10.)

10. EITHER PLAYER, WHEN HE LOSES A STROKE.—
Either player loses a *stroke*,

(a) if the service-ball or ball in-play touches him or anything that he wears or carries, except his racket, in the act of striking; or
(b) if he touches or strikes the service-ball or ball in-play with his racket more than once; or
(c) if, in returning the service-ball or ball in-play, he touches the net with any part of his body, or with his racket, or with anything that he wears or carries; or if the ball touch either of the posts; or
(d) if he strikes the ball before it has passed the net; or
(e) if the service-ball or ball in-play drops or falls upon a ball lying in either of his Courts.

11. STROKES, HOW SCORED.—On either player winning his first stroke, the score is called 15 for that player; on either player winning his second stroke, the score is called 30 for that player; on either player winning his third stroke, the score is called 40 for that player; and the fourth stroke won by either player is scored *game* for that player; except as below:

if both players have won three strokes, the score is called deuce; and the next stroke won by either player is scored advantage for that player. If the same player wins the next stroke, he wins the game; if he loses the next stroke, the score is again called deuce; and so on, until, at the score of deuce, either player wins two consecutive strokes, when the game is scored for that player.

12. GAMES HOW SCORED.—The player who first wins six games wins a *set*; except as below:

if both players win five games, the score is called *games-all;* and the next game won by either player is scored *advantage-game* for that player. If the same player wins the next game, he wins the *set;* if he loses the next game, the score is again called *games-all;* and so on, until, at the score of *gaems-all,* either player wins two consecutive games, when he wins the *set*. {It is often agreed not to play advantage-sets, but to decide the set by one game after arriving at the score of games-all.}

13. SIDES WHEN CHANGED, AND CONTINUATION OF SERVICE.—The players shall change sides at the end of every set. When a series of sets is played, the player who was Server in the last game of one set shall be Striker-out in the first game of the next.

Umpire.

14. (a) There shall be two Umpires, one on each side of the net. They shall call play at the beginning of the game; they shall *enforce* the rules of the game, and be the sole judges of fair and unfair play, each on his respective side of the net.

(b) No Umpire shall bet on the game he shall umpire.

(c) No Umpire shall be changed unless by the consent of both sides, except for violation of (b).

Three-handed and Four-handed Games.

15. ABOVE LAWS, HOW FAR APPLICABLE.—The above Laws shall apply to the three-handed and four-handed games, except as below:

(a) in the three-handed game, the single player shall serve in every alternate game;

(b) in the four-handed game, the pair who have the right to serve in the first game may decide which partner shall do so, and the opposing pair may decide similarly for the second game. The partner of the player who served in the first game shall serve in the third; and the partner of the player who served in the second game shall serve in the fourth; and so on, in the same order, in all the subsequent games of a set or series of sets;

(c) the players shall take the service alternately throughout each game; no player shall receive or return a service delivered to his partner; and the order of service and striking-out, once arranged, shall not be altered, nor shall the strikers-out change Courts to receive the service before the end of the set.

An Alternative Method of Scoring.

16. The above Laws shall apply to Lawn Tennis, played by the game, except as regards the method of scoring. The word *Hand-in* shall be substituted for *Server,* and *Hand-out* for *Striker-out.*

17, The Hand-in alone is able to score. If he loses a stroke, he becomes Hand-out, and his opponent becomes Hand-in, and serves in his turn.

18. The player who scores 15 points wins the game.

19. If both players have won 14 points, the game is *set to* 3. The score is called *Love-all.* The Hand-in continues to serve, and the player who first scores 3 points wins the game.

20. In the three-handed or four-handed game, only one partner of that side which is Hand-in shall serve at the beginning of each game. If he or his partner loses a stroke, the other side shall be Hand-in;

21. During the remainder of the game, when the first Hand-in has been put out, his partner shall serve, beginning from the Court from which the last service was not delivered; and, when both partners have been put out, then the other side shall be Hand-in.

22. The Hand-in shall deliver the service in accordance with Laws 2 and 3; and the opponents shall receive the service alternately, each keeping the Court which he originally occupied. In all subsequent strokes, the ball may be returned by either partner on each side.

23. One or more points may be given in a game.

24. The privilege of being Hand-in two or more successive times may be given.

25. Half Court: The players having agreed into which Court the giver of the odds shall play, the latter loses a stroke if the ball, returned by him, drops outside any of the lines which bound that Court.

Odds.

26. BISQUES.—A bisque is one stroke, which may be claimed by the receiver of the odds at any time during a set, except as below:

(a) a bisque may not be taken after the service has been delivered;

(b) the Server may not take a bisque after a fault; but the Striker-out may do so.

27. BISQUES GIVEN IN AUGMENTATION OR DIMINUTION.—One or more bisques may be given in augmentation or diminution of other odds.

28. HALF-FIFTEEN.—Half-fifteen is one stroke given at the beginning of the second and every subsequent alternative game of a set.

29. FIFTEEN.—Fifteen is one stroke given at the beginning of every game of a set.

30. HALF-THIRTY.—Half-thirty is one stroke given at the beginning of the first game, two strokes at the beginning of the second game; and so on, alternately, in all the subsequent games of a set.

31. THIRTY.—Thirty is two strokes given at the beginning of every game of a set.

32. HALF-FORTY.—Half-forty is two strokes given at the beginning of the first game; three strokes at the beginning of the second game; and so on, alternately, in all the subsequent games of a set.

33. FORTY.—Forty is three strokes given at the beginning of every game of a set.

34. HALF-COURT.—The players having agreed into which Court the giver of the odds of half-court shall play, the latter loses a stroke if the ball, returned by him, drops outside any of the lines which bound that Court.

RACKETS

The New York Club Court and the Gymnasium Club were two of the racket clubs of New York City during the 1860s. Both catered to gentlemen of the upper classes but neither survived the decade. These rules of the former association are reprinted from The Ball Players' Chronicle, 13 June 1867, p. 5.

RULES AND REGULATIONS OF THE NEW YORK CLUB COURT, 1867

1. Gentlemen wishing to play will enter their names on the slate, *(bona fide)* in their own handwriting, and shall be entitled to the Court, according to their numbers, *a tour de role*.

2. Exchanging numbers will be allowed only when it is done to equalize a match, and with the approbation of those next entitled to the Court.

3. The regular game will consist of a rubber of 15 aces for a single or double match.

4. On commencing a game, in a double match, whether odds are given or not, the side winning the toss shall have but one hand; but in a single match the party receiving the odds shall be entitled to them from the beginning.

5. The first service in each game of the rubber must be in the right Court from the left ring, and then in the left Court from the right ring, and so on alternately throughout the game, the out-hand going on in the same rotation.

6. The out-hand shall have the privilege of asking the service for the last ace of each game in either Court, and, in a double match, of placing either partner in that court, but must remain there until the end of the game.

7. The server must stand with at least one foot in the ring, and serve the ball first over the line on the front wall, and within the right or left Court, otherwise the ball will be foul. Serving two foul balls, missing the ball, or failing to strike the front wall, puts the hand out. No line ball is fair.

8. All balls served or played in the galleries, or out of the Court, although they may return to the floor, will count against the striker.

9. In serving or returning a ball, if it strikes the tell-tale, it is a hand-out or an ace.

10. When a ball is served fair, the player alone, in that court, is entitled to return it. If the ball be foul, either partner may return it.

11. A ball stopped by the striker or his partner, before either of the adversaries had struck at it, loses him either a hand or an ace.

12. If a ball going from the Racket strikes one of the opposing party above the knee, it is a let, and must be played over, unless the ball reached the front wall before touching the floor; if below or on the knee, the striker loses, unless the ball reaches the front wall as before. Should the ball strike his partner, it counts against the striker, though ball should go up.

13. A ball must be taken either before or on the first bound, and not touch the floor before reaching the front wall.

14. No ball will be dead until on or after its second hop. Using two hands to the Racket. "foul."

15. A ball returning from the front wall and striking a beam, or any part of the roof, or above the lower gallery, is foul.

16. As players must sometimes be involuntarily in each other's way, the marker will decide (when a "hinder" is claimed) if they are entitled to it. {There can be no hinder allowed when a ball has been struck at.}

17. One rubber only can be played by the same party; but should any of those going out be wanted to make up the next match, they must draw lots.

18. Only one set allowed.

19. On commencing the game, parties must toss for the first service, in making which they must cry "play," or time must be called. In other cases "time" can only be called before the server has struck.

20. A double match always to take precedence over a single match.

21. The marker's decision must be final, and without further appeal, in all cases when judgment is asked.

22. The out-player only can call for a new ball, except it be torn.

23. {Any person striking a ball unnecessarily, on or after the second hop, shall be liable to a fine of 25 cents.}

24. {No one will be allowed to play in the Court with nails in his shoes.}

{The Racket shoe should have an extra sole of buff leather.}

The paragraphs in brackets are those governing the game in this country.

EDITORIAL AND EXPLANATION OF AMERICAN RACKETS

Wintertime in northern climates of North America forced sportsmen indoors. While some sought refreshment through exercise in gymnasiums, others preferred the fun and competition of rackets. The following editorial extolls the virtues of that amusement. It is reprinted from The New York Clipper, 25 December 1875, p. 306.

THE PRACTICE GAME FOR BASEBALL PLAYERS

In the search for a Winter exercise for baseball players who desire to keep themselves in training, we found the old game of "fives"—called handball in this country—a capital exercise for active field movements, and for educating the sight in picking up low, swift balls. But experience has shown that it has one objectionable feature for a baseball player, and that is the soreness of the hands which it causes. Generally, the men who most excel in handball are large-handed ones, whose daily occupation makes their hands as hard and tough as a hide; but for the general class of people who practice ball-playing the sport is too severe in its injurious effects on the hands, and hence it fails to fully answer the purpose sought for in a Winter practice game for professional baseball players. One would suppose that a baseball player accustomed to catch balls from fielders while at first base, or to hold them from the pitcher while behind the bat, would be indifferent to using his hands for a bat, as in handball; but experience shows that the latter practice is as hard again on a player's hands as any work he is called upon to do in baseball, as either catcher or first-baseman. The large baseball is easier to hold and less painful to stop than the smaller one used in handball, the latter bearing very hard on the centre of the palms, so much so as to make them painful and sore in a short game, unless the player has a remarkable large and heavy hand and a tough, thick skin on the palms. In the place of handball, however, a very desirable substitute has been found in the game of American rackets, which differs only from the regular rackets—long in vogue in English sporting circles—in the smaller size of the bat and in its being made entirely of wood, and in the larger size of the ball. An advantage, too, possessed by rackets over handball, in its adaptability to the purpose of Winter practice and training for baseball players, is that, besides presenting an excellent school for fielding practice, it affords the very best training of the hand and eye for batting purposes. What with the great agility of movement in running forwards and backwards to reach the ball, and in jumping up and stooping low to get at it, a degree of sharp practice in fielding is arrived at which cannot fail to improve in every baseball player who plays rackets. Then too, the use of the small bat in training the eye to watch the comparatively little ball, and in practicing the arm to handle the bat in striking at it high and low and on each side, a degree of efficiency is arrived at which must naturally assist the baseball player in a more skillful use of the larger bat and ball in his own game. Besides these advantages, the exercise in rackets is such as to bring into active use every muscle of the body; and that, too, without any injurious strain on any particular portion of the muscular system, the game training him to endurance in fielding to a greater extent than any other exercise he can indulge in off the ball-field. To him it is far more recreative and beneficial than gymnastic exercise; though that, of course is necessary to a limited extent. As a recreation of itself, it possesses many features to recommend it to the young—and middle-age men, too—of sedentary habits. It does not take much time, it is very exciting, and is well calculated to drive away dyspepsia.

How the game is played.

The materials are simply a small wooden bat, in shape like a large spoon, only flat, and a small, elastic ball of about an inch and a half in diameter. Of course a racket court is essential, and these places are now springing up in all our large cities as fast as the game becomes popular. A good court is that of Barney McQuade, located in Madison street, near Grand. It is complete in nearly every respect, and a new and very handsome court is in progress of erection on Twenty-sixth street.

The game is played either by two or four contestants—the later is the livelier game. When played by two persons, one stands within the lines of the "inner court," and "serves" the ball for the player standing in the "outer court." "Serving" the ball consists of hitting it with the bat so that it rebounds from the end-wall of the court beyond the line which divides the inner from the outer portion. When this is done it becomes the object of the player in the outer court to bat the ball, on its *first* rebound, so as to return it to the end-wall of the court before it touches the floor—touching the side-walls of the court is immaterial, so that the ball first touches the end-wall before it reaches the floor. The effort to keep the ball in motion, rebounding from the end-wall, is then kept up by both players until one or the other fails to bat the ball—in returning it—to the end-wall, in which case, if it be the player "serving" the ball from the inner court, he "loses his hand," and thereby takes up his position in the outer court. If it be the player in the outer court who fails to return the ball to the end-wall, then his opponent scores an "ace," or one point in the game. This goes on until one party or the other scores 21 aces, which ends the game. A match at rackets consists of best two out of three games, best three out of five, or best four out of seven.

Chapter 16

TRACK AND FIELD

During the 1860s and 1870s several forms of walking, running, jumping, leaping, and field contests were popular in North America. In general these forms of athletics may be classified under two headings—pedestrianism and track and field. The first category included long distance walking and running races, along with the indoor six day "go-as-you-please" endurance tests which flourished during the late 1870s. The second type was the early track and field events first sponsored by Scottish Caledonian clubs. Urban amateur athletic clubs then adapted these games to suit their own purposes.

During this period patterns of modernization and issues of nationality, race, and social class strongly influenced the development of both pedestrianism and track and field. The proliferation of clubs, the founding of governing bodies, and the sponsorship of special races and meets are proof of increased bureaucratization. Specialization and rationalization were evident in the particular kinds of events and rules established by officials of national, regional, and local organizations. The fascination with statistics and the quest for records illustrate the trend of quantification. Democratization also made some progress, although here some qualifications are in order. On the one hand, participants from England, Canada, and the United States took part in many of the feature events, and in most cases Indians, blacks, and whites competed on an equal basis. However, social class concerns increasingly distinguished pedestrianism from track and field. In the former professionalism prevailed, as runners and walkers competed for prize money. In the latter the leading amateur clubs increasingly excluded professionals and all those who earned a living through athletics, thereby barring many lower class participants from their meets.

Long distance running and walking races continued to generate great interest in both Canada and the United States during these years. In 1861 Edward Payson Weston gained fame when he attempted to walk from Boston to Washington in ten days, with his arrival planned for the day before the inauguration of Abraham Lincoln on March 4th. Even though heavy snow delayed his arrival by one day, Weston's feat still attracted national attention. He became even more famous among the sporting fraternity in 1867, when he accepted a challenge to walk from Portland, Maine to Chicago, Illinois within twenty-six days. "The Great Weston Feat" recounts his successful completion of this marathon journey.

North American Indians prided themselves on their speed and stamina in running, and these years brought further proof of their reputation. Deerfoot, who was born on the Cattaraugus Reservation in upstate New York around 1830, was a celebrated pedestrian who competed in England during the early 1860s. Although the sporting press was convinced that some of his major matches were fixed, he did set several impressive records in long distance and one hour events. "Keraronwe vs. Deerfoot" is a report of a race in Montreal which matched two of the most celebrated Indian runners of that era.

Between 1878 and 1880 a mania for six-door indoor races swept across both England and the United States. Weston used his celebrity status to promote these contests, which gained greater public attention when an English nobleman, Lord Astley, offered a large silver and gold international belt to the champion. The first competition for this prize occurred in March 1878 at the Agricultural Hall in London. The event became known as a "go-as-you-please" race because the participants could either walk or run in their efforts to cover as much ground as possible within the allotted six days. The promoters laid out a track of loam and sawdust, and contestants were provided with tents for rest, sleeping, and refreshments. Weston withdrew from the inaugural contest because of illness, which was won by Daniel O'Leary of Chicago. The next few years brought a series of challenges for the Astley belt, which was complicated when O'Leary began promoting his own six day meets, offering the "O'Leary Belt" as a rival trophy to the Astley belt. This chapter includes the rules governing competition for both belts, and a narrative of the competition for the Astley belt held at Madison Square Garden in September 1879. The race for the O'Leary prize was also held at Madison Square Garden, a few weeks after the Astley contest. The craze for these marathon events also included females, as a few women competed in six day endurance trials for prize money. "The Women's Tourney" presents the results of yet another contest held at Madison Square Garden in 1879.

Two groups made major contributions to the formative years of track and field in North America. The first were the Canadian and American Caledonian clubs, which had been founded to preserve and promote Scottish culture and customs. These included the traditional Highland games of the old country. From the 1850s to the 1870s the Caledonian clubs' annual games drew thousands of spectators across North America. Feature events included footraces, tug of war, hurdling, jumping, pole vaulting, hammer throwing, and shot putting. The sponsoring clubs opened competition to all regardless of social class, ethnicity, or race, charged admission fees, and offered cash prizes to winners.

The second party instrumental in founding early track and field athletics included upper-middle class and affluent sportsmen who admired both the Caledonians and also the English athletic clubs founded during these years. Young gentlemen in many North American cities who sought exercise and good fellowship established associations to pursue their love of track and field games. Before long they decided to restrict their membership and their major meets to their own social class. They formulated a definition of amateurism which effectively excluded most black, Indian, or lower class athletes.

One of the pioneer athletic clubs and ultimately the most influential was the New York Athletic Club (NYAC). It originated with informal meetings of three young sportsmen in 1866, and was incorporated with fourteen members in 1868. That fall the NYAC held its first meet and began the process of formulating the rules for track and field competition that would become generally accepted by the late 1870s. This chapter includes an editorial on the creation of the NYAC and a summary of the rules it devised to govern athletic competition. The NYAC exerted its leadership role by constructing the first cinder track in the United States at its grounds at Mott Haven, by introducing the spiked shoe, and by sponsoring the first national amateur championships in track and field, swimming, boxing, and wrestling. During the 1870s many new clubs sprang into existence in emulation of the NYAC, including associations in Staten Island, Newark, Baltimore, Buffalo, Chicago, Detroit, St. Louis, San Francisco, and Montreal. In 1878 several organizations from the New York City vicinity founded the American Association of Amateur Athletes, which did not include the NYAC. One year later a resolution of differences between this organization and the NYAC led to its reorganization as the National Association of Amateur Athletes of America (N4A). This chapter concludes with its Constitution and By-laws.

Finally, this period also witnessed the rise of intercollegiate competition in cross-country running and track and field. Harvard, Yale, Princeton, and Columbia students introduced the sport of hare and hounds, or paper chasing, in which a group of "hares" dropped paper as a kind of scent for the "hounds" to follow. By the 1880s the sport became known as "cross country," but the runners continued to be called "harriers," and the term endures today. Intercollegiate track and field began at Springfield, Massachusetts in 1873, when James Gordon Bennett, Jr., publisher of the New York Herald, offered a prize trophy to the winner of a two-mile run. He scheduled this race to coincide with the college rowing regatta, and the tradition continued the following year at the intercollegiate rowing competition at Saratoga, New York. Bennett provided silver prizes for the winners of the five events: the 100 yard dash, one mile, three mile,

120 yard hurdles, and seven mile walk. About thirty students representing eight colleges participated in these races. At the 1875 regatta there were twice as many track events. The enthusiasm generated by these meets led directly to the founding of the Intercollegiate Association of Amateur Athletes of America (IC4A) in December 1875. The IC4A held its first games at Saratoga in conjunction with the 1876 intercollegiate regatta, but after the demise of the annual rowing meet it switched its site to the grounds of the NYAC at Mott Haven in upper Manhattan. Now divorced from rowing, intercollegiate track and field was free to develop on its own. By the 1880s students from the leading eastern universities were active participants in track and field.

PEDESTRIANISM

EDWARD PAYSON WESTON'S WALK FROM PORTLAND, MAINE TO CHICAGO, 1867

In 1867 George K. Goodwin of New York City bet $10,000 that Edward Payson Weston could walk from Portland, Maine to Chicago, Illinois within thirty days, exclusive of four Sundays, or twenty-six walking days. T.F. Wilcox put up an identical sum in wagering that Weston would be unable to compete his walk in the allotted time. The articles of agreement, signed August 7, 1867, are included in the following account of the great walk, reprinted from *Beadle's Dime Hand-book of Pedestrianism* (N.Y., 1867), pp. 26-32.

THE GREAT WESTON FEAT

The great pedestrian feat of walking from Portland to Chicago—1226 miles—by the post road, in twenty-six days, was successfully accomplished by Mr. Edward Payson Weston who arrived at his destination in Chicago on the morning of Nov. 28th, 1867—Thanksgiving Day—at 10 o'clock. The popular interest in this exploit, and the outpourings of the people which greeted him from point to point on his journey, have made this feat one of the athletic events of the age. Weston's undertaking was novel as it was great. He has demonstrated the physical endurance of an American, and done much to popularize an exercise which is alike pleasant and beneficial. Such a task as his would have killed the most powerful horse, while the man has thrived under the operation, Weston having gained two pounds since he left home. He has achieved what no man ever attempted before, and deserves honor for the pluck and persistency he has displayed in the undertaking.

We give below the terms of the wager made on the occasion.

"I, George K. Goodwin, of New York City, do wager and bet the sum of ten thousand dollars (10,000) in United States currency with T.F. Wilcox, of New York City, that Edward Payson Weston, late a resident of Boston, Massachusetts, and aged but 28 years, can and will make a fair and honest walk, to the distance of 1,200 statute miles, of 1,728 yards each in length, in thirty consecutive days, and without walking between the hours of 12 P.M. on Saturday and 12 P.M. on Sunday, making a deduction of four entire days, and leaving but twenty-six secular days in which to walk the distance, the said T. F. Wilcox wagering $10,000 that the said Weston can not perform the feat according to the following conditions: 1st. That Weston shall walk by the old post road. 2d. That he shall walk one hundred miles in twenty-four continuous hours, as part and parcel of the journey. 3d. If he fails in making the one hundred miles in twenty-four hours, after five trials, he is to forfeit six-tenths of the wager. 4th. Should Weston fail in reaching Chicago, then Goodwin forfeits the entire $20,000, the amount wagered. 5th. Weston to be accompanied by two sworn witnesses for each side, who are to make statements, under oath, of the progress of the pedestrian. 6th. Weston to start at 12 P.M. on Sundays from the precise place where he stops at 12 P.M. on Saturday. 7th. If Weston walks to make time between 12 P.M. on Saturdays and 12 P.M. on Sundays, then he forfeits the wager. 8th. If Weston accomplishes his feat, Goodwin is to have paid over to him, upon his arrival in Chicago the sum of $20,000."

The time of the starting was subsequently changed to October 29th, on which day he commenced walking at Portland, Maine, at 12 o'clock, meridian.

Mr. Weston received a perfect ovation on his arrival in Chicago, the streets through which he walked to the Sherman House being thronged to an extent unprecedented in the history of the city. One of the editors of the Chicago Republican who visited him at the hotel at Hyde Park, thus describes the interview.

"Feeling some desire to have a personal interview with the great 'walkist,' my wish was happily anticipated by a brother member of the Chicago press, who sent in my card, to which Mr. Weston courteously responded. Entering the room I was cordially met by the pedestrian, with whom I had the pleasure of entering into an interesting conversation. In the room were Weston's wife and three or four gentlemen. Weston's face bore very distinct marks of acute nervous anxiety. The strain had affected his visage until he had the appearance of a man turned thirty years of age. He had on his walking costume. Round his waist he wore a colored belt, four or five inches broad, on the clasp of which were the letters "E.P.W." Mr. Weston commenced by telling me that he purposes soon visiting Detroit, where he doubted not that he would receive better treatment than in Toledo, where he said he could not obtain even a cup of tea. He expressed himself in better health and condition than when he started from Portland, being two pounds heavier. His feet which are quite small he said were in perfect condition, not being at all sore or swelled. Speaking about the one hundred mile feat, he affirmed that he had honestly and earnestly striven to accomplish it each time. The last attempt he had to abandon on account of the frightful condition of the roads. He also contended that he had walked 1,316 miles instead of 1,226, as mentioned in the terms of the agreement. He bitterly complained of the treatment received in parts of Ohio. At Norwalk he was knocked down and returned the blow for the first time during his journey. Two attempts were made to poison him. One was averted by an attendant, who first tasted the food, and, it operating upon him, Weston took warning. This hostility, he thinks, came from men who, having bet against him, were anxious to prevent his winning the wager."

The evening of the day of Weston's arrival in Chicago, he addressed a crowded assembly at the Crosby Opera House, by whom he was most enthusiastically greeted, and before whom he delivered the following interesting address, containing a brief account of this trip.

LADIES AND GENTLEMEN: I feel very thankful to you for the kind manner in which I have been received in Chicago today. I am not quite so vain to take it all as a compliment to myself alone, or to my action during the past thirty days; but as a compliment to an American who, I think, has, in the art of walking, if I may so term it, eclipsed any act of a similar nature across the water. The fatigue and trouble through which I have passed is entirely forgotten when I think of the kind manner in which my exertions have been rewarded. I have received a great deal of censure from various parties for not accomplishing one portion of the feat—that of walking one hundred miles inside of twenty-four consecutive hours, during this walk, which was originally understood to be one thousand two hundred and twenty-six miles. I can only say, if the assertion of this amounts to anything, and in my heart I know I speak candidly and honestly when I say that I used every exertion to accomplish this feat. I tried, but in vain. I had every obstacle to contend with. I agreed to walk one hundred miles inside of twenty-four consecutive hours, but I agreed that those miles should be at a measurement of one thousand seven hundred and twenty-eight yards each; and when I say that I don't contend that I can do more than any other American citizen; but the miles, or many of them, that I was obliged to travel, were Indiana miles. (Laughter.) I will merely state one anecdote which though I was very sleepy this afternoon, I tried to tell as well as I could. I started from Calumet, Ind., to come to Illinois, and we engaged a pilot there. I asked the pilot before we started—"Pilot, how far do you call it from here to Chicago?" "Well," says he, by the road we take—let me see—nine and two are twelve, and three is eighteen, "says he; "just forty-four miles from here to Chicago by road, and forty-one by railroad. The road is very good," says he; "there is some sand." I found "some sand." (Laughter.) I started and I had glorious company, and we pulled over that road at the rate of four miles an hour for four hours. When we stopped for tea we were just seventeen miles from Calumet, or, in other words, seventeen of the forty-four miles that this guide had kindly informed me was the distance form Calumet to Chicago. On leaving here we got another guide—another Hoosier. (Laughter.) "My friend," I said, "will you be kind enough to tell me how far it is from here to Chicago?" "Well," says he, "it's just forty-five miles by the wagon road." (Great applause and laughter.) So I had been four hours getting one mile backward! I though I had done well, but that was not Chicago, and if Chicago had been one hundred miles off I felt bound to get there before twelve o'clock to-day because I had an invitation to dine here, and I have a peculiar faculty for keeping my appointments, especially on Thanksgiving Day. In this manner I have been thwarted when I have tried to perform this feat of walking one hundred miles inside of twenty-four hours. I had no opportunity to look over my route and time-table to make any estimate in regard to that, but now I contemplate having an opportunity of doing so—to-morrow evening. I want to state here that I have been for the past week under a fearful state of excitement from the fact that I have received an innumerable number of letters, a great many of them anonymous, threatening me with use of a coffin to get into Chicago with, from the limits; that is, I was promised to die just outside of Chicago, but I feel that I don't look like a dead man. (Applause.) I have been requested to make some few remarks to-night on athletic sports. I don't profess to be a lecturer, and I do not know that I ever made a speech in my life until to-day. But I will do the best I can. During the past forty-eight hours I have had a great deal of road to travel over, nice road; Indiana road. I have a peculiar love for that road, and I have not had any opportunity to prepare any proper remarks. What remarks I make I must apologize for, because they may be somewhat disconnected. There are many sports termed athletic sports, such as gymnastics, rowing, yachting, base-ball playing, horse-racing, and pedestrianism. I do not think that prize-fighting comes under the same head. There are other sports termed brutal sports, such as dog-fighting, cock-fighting, and prize-fighting. I have been associated, or rather people have tried to associate me with the latter class of people—prize-fighters. I say it here, as I have always said it, if it were for no other reason, if I had not better principle guide me than the respect that I have for my family, and the respect that I have for my mother, I would not allow myself to be associated with men who stand up and hammer each others faces to pieces for a few thousand dollars. Why pedestrianism should be classed as a crime, or why a person, because he can walk a few miles, more or less, should be called a prize-fighter, or because he bets on that race should he be called a gambler, I "can't see it." Athletic sports tend to strengthen the youth of any country—tend to strengthen not only their bodies, but immediately through their bodies, their minds. A sound mind will be all the sounder for dwelling in a sound body; and that is a combination we all want. Such sports—if you can term them such—as prize-fighting, not only tend to ruin the morals, but go to the length of brutalizing men—to forget that they are images of the Great Creator. I have not contended, and I don't wish to, that in performing this feat of walking which my friends, the reporters, have been pleased to term a great and unequaled pedestrian performance, I have done any more than any American citizen can do. In walking thirteen hundred and sixteen miles in twenty-six days, while it is a very fair walk for this season of the year, when you come through Indiana-[laughter]-yet, at the same time, I don't contend that I have done any more than any American young man can do. But I must contend—and it is with pride I do say it—that I think it would puzzle an Englishmen to do it. He might find some fault with the miles; but then they call them "English miles." As I remarked this afternoon, I don't propose to join the sporting fraternity; but I do propose, so long as I can stand on two feet, if any Englishman gets up and walks from Portland, Me., to Chicago, Ill., the distance I have walked, better than I have, I shall think it my bounden duty, out of respect to the plaudits that I have received from the American people, to get up and beat him. (Tremendous applause.) I will have to do it, and I think that I can. (Renewed applause.) There are many of you, probably, who have some curiosity to know in what manner this race has affected me bodily. As you have probably seen, as I have, for my friends the reporters here, have given it to me right and left through the press, Biblical allusions, etc., I have been under a great state of excitement during the whole time. One reason is it has been a bad season of the year for walking, although my Creator has been exceedingly kind to me in giving me as little bad weather as one could possibly expect at this season of the year. Still, I have been obliged to strain my nervous system to the utmost in order to accomplish this task, and have hardly known what I have been about some of the time. I was laboring under great disadvantages throughout the entire journey, and, as I remarked before, I do not wish to take the flattering receptions I have received in the cities through which I have passed as a compliment to myself entirely, (I hope I am not so vain as that,) but as a compliment to the energy of an American citizen; and I think any one will say the same, that any American young man that will try it will do as well as I have. I hope he will do better, and, be assured I would not be jealous, and would not try to walk further or do better than he has; but I would simply suggest that if any one is ambitious to do any thing of the kind, that he should avoid Indiana (applause), unless he takes the Michigan Central railroad. The bed of the road is splendid, and I propose to take it on my way home, but I propose to take a car along with me. As I told my guide last night—I would keep asking him how far we were—when I win this race I am going out in Indiana and buy land by the mile and will make a fortune in a few days, for if I buy five miles I have got the whole State. (Laughter.) In conclusion, let me once more ask you to pardon the manner in which I have made these few remarks to-night. I have had no opportunity to prepare them; I am not a public speaker, and never made a speech before until this afternoon, and then I confess I was sleepy, and, to use a common expression, I didn't know whether I was afoot or horseback. I hope before I leave Chicago to have a chance to meet many of your citizens, and let me take this opportunity to thank you most sincerely for your cordial and hearty welcome. (Great applause.)

At the conclusion of the above address, which was listened to with great attention, the assemblage dispersed and the great pedestrian returned to the Sherman House escorted by a large crowd.

The notoriety attendant upon Weston's famous exploit has led to quite a pedestrian *furore,* and a walking fever has set in which, we trust, will draw public attention from the brutal exhibitions of the prize ring.

KERARONWE VS. DEERFOOT, CANADA, 1870

Montreal sportsmen sponsored both interracial and segregated athletic events in such sports as running, snowshoeing, and lacrosse. The contest between Deerfoot from New York State and the local favorite Keraronwe drew much attention in Canada. Keraronwe was already reknown as a champion snowshoer and expert lacrosse player. This report is reproduced from The New York Clipper, 10 September 1870, p. 181.

THE GREAT THREE MILE RACE: KERARONWE DEFEATS DEERFOOT

The match hitherto announced in our columns between these celebrated Indians, Deerfoot and Keraronwe, for $400, three miles, came off on the Montreal Lacrosse grounds, Montreal, C. E., on Saturday, Aug. 27th, and terminated in the defeat of the veteran Deerfoot by his more youthful opponent. He belongs to the Seneca tribe of Indians, and lived for a long time in England, where he won many matches and gave a number of exhibitions of his fleetness of foot which were considered truly marvellous and earned for him the name he bears. In these matches he has beaten the most celebrated pedestrians in England, making 11 miles and 790 yards in an hour, Jan. 12, 1863, a feat never accomplished by any other. A few years ago he returned to America, residing most of the time in Buffalo. He is now about forty-five years of age. Keraronwe, an Iroquois Indian, is a native of Caughnawaga and is well known to the people of Montreal. He holds the title of Champion Snow-Shoe Runner of Canada, and is considered the swiftest man in that part of the country. On one side was youth and muscle—on the other, age, prestige and experience. The weather was beautifully cool and fine and the ground in splendid condition. Some of the little hollows and irregularities on the course were levelled over, so that the track, which, however, is not one of the best for the purpose, was in very fair running order. The course was measured off a quarter mile around the field, and was marked with small colored flags. At the starting point the Red, White and Blue was hoisted, around which stood the starter, the judge, the representatives of the press, &c. The course was kept free from intrusion by a number of policemen, and a fair and uninterrupted contest was the result. The judges were Mr. Hughes and a member of the Lachine Boating Club. Jas. Taylor, of the Tyne crew, was starter. By half-past five, the time at which the men made their appearance on the ground, the grand stand and the ground in front were filled with spectators, a large proportion of whom were from the primitive precincts of Caughnawaga. Indians of all shades of complexion, squaws dressed in all the colors of the rainbow and more, and papooses of all sizes and ages; the whole population of Caughnawaga, in fact, turned out to witness the triumph or defeat of their champion.

Previous to the match two other races were announced to take place, namely, a mile race, open to all, for prizes of $4 and $2; and a half mile race, Indians barred, for prizes of the same amount. For the first there was only one entry, that one being Daillebout, whose known abilities were, no doubt, the cause of his having the course all to himself. He was allowed to run around alone, and did the quarters in the remarkably good time of 1 min., 1:12, 1:15 and 1:13 respectively. For the second race there were two entries:—G. Anderson and J. Logan, the former winning in 2:16.

In a few minutes the two dusky rivals were seen slowly approaching the starting point, accompanied by their respective backers; the younger bare legged, with light pumps on his feet, and the older arrayed in light colored tights. The physique of the two men presented a marked contrast; Deerfoot being nearly a head taller than his opponent, and of rather an engaging build; while the other looked the very perfection of a running man, the muscles of his legs standing out with marked prominence at every step he took, and his deep chest bespeaking almost unlimited power of lungs. Deerfoot walked slowly around the course for the purpose of becoming acquainted with the ground, and then took his place beside his rival. The men shook hands, a few seconds' pause took place, the starter gave the word "go" and the men darted off, Keraronwe leading amid the cheers of his friends; the other, by the time the first corner was reached, a couple of yards behind. Keraronwe made the first lap in a minute (exactly the same time made by Daillebout a half an hour previous), Deerfoot in 1:08. After this the men settled down steadily to their work, Keraronwe running down the incline at the west end of the field at a frightful rate of speed, and Deerfoot gaining on him coming up the east end; passing the starting point from five to eight seconds behind him each time. This order of things was kept up until the eleventh round was reached, when Deerfoot began rapidly to reduce the distance between him and his rival; making the eleventh lap only one second behind him. His backers now commenced to look up, many believing that the old man had been holding himself back for the last round. Even bets were now freely offered on him, whereas hitherto, 5 to 4 found very few takers. But those who staked their money on him were doomed to be deceived. On the last round it was found that Keraronwe had also more work in him, and was able to defy the utmost efforts of his rival. After the eleventh lap had been made the excitement grew intense, and a great portion of the crowd, ignoring both ropes and police, burst across the course and gained the centre of the field whence they could follow the fortunes of the men as they tore along for the winning post. Up the incline at the last corner Deerfoot gained close on his opponent, but it was only for a moment. As the tape appeared in view, the other went ahead again, and won amid the most tremendous enthusiasm. Deerfoot, finding the match lost, slacked off on the last side, and when Keraronwe touched the tape was some twenty-five yards behind. The victor was immediately hoisted on the shoulders of two burly Indians, and carried in triumph to the dressing booth, where he received the congratulations of the many braves, squaws, and papooses above alluded to, with the modesty which belongs to a hero. Time: 15:38.

THE ASTLEY BELT RACE, 1879

In 1879 a series of races for the Astley belt heightened public interest in six day races in both England and the United States. In March Charles Rowell of England challenged Daniel O'Leary for the title. He won easily when O'Leary withdrew after only three days. Rowell agreed to defend his championship against Edward Payson Weston in June. After a sprained ankle forced Rowell to withdraw, Weston defeated three rivals and claimed the belt. That set the stage for the next challenge, scheduled for September at Madison Square Garden in New York City. This report on that event is reprinted from The New York Clipper, 27 September, 4 October 1879, pp. 210, 218, 220.

THE OPENING DAY AT MADISON-SQUARE GARDEN

As we write the contestants in the fifth race for the belt presented by Sir John Astley are hard at work in Madison-square Garden, this city, having started at 1 A.M. on Monday, Sept. 22. Notwithstanding that the price of admission was placed at a dollar, the crowd present at the start was fully as great as upon the occasion of the previous contest for the same trophy at this place, the throng fully testing the capacity of the Garden. By dint of hard work, day and night, from Saturday morning, a pretty good track, composed of sifted loan and tanbark, with a light top dressing of sawdust, had been prepared. It was not as wide by three feet as before, but still it afforded plenty of room for the thirteen competitors, each one of whom had a tent to himself, furnished with everything necessary. The appearance of the Garden was much the same as during the tournaments held last Spring, and the scene just previous to the start strongly reminded one of the sweepstakes race in which Rowell, Ennis, Harriman and O'Leary started on March 10 last. The most intense excitement prevailed among the spectators, and it was with great difficulty that they could be prevented from encroaching upon the track; but there was a strong force of police present, and, considering the immense crowd, comparatively good order was maintained. The pedestrians were started promptly at one o'clock A.M. Monday, Sep. 22, and nearly all commenced the long journey at a walk, notable exceptions being Hazael and Rowell, the former going off with an easy lope and the latter again setting to work with the dog-trot so familiar to New-Yorkers. Rowell was the favorite with the betting fraternity, the bookmakers offering 1 1/2 to 1 against him, 2 1/2 to 1 against Weston, 3 to 1 against Hazael, 10 to 1 against Guyon, 30 to 1 against Panehot or Ennis, 20 to 1 against Krohne or Hart, 35 to 1 against Merritt, and as much as 50 to 1 against the others. The bookmakers had their stands erected in the centre of the main floor, and drove quite a thriving business, Rowell, Weston, Guyon and Krohne being in most demand, the opinion being general that Hazael would not hold out till the end of the week. The latter took the lead at once, completing his first mile in 6 min. 10 sec., while Rowell was on his seventh lap and Weston on his fifth. Taylor struck into a steady run, from which he never varied, and he was ere long second man—a position which he held for hours. The only man who kept to a walk for any length of time after starting was Federmeyer, whose long hair and beard and odd attire caused him to present a strange appearance. He walked steadily for several hours, and then, finding that he was getting further and further behind, he changed his gait to a jog, which did not carry him along much faster, and he retained the last place. A great deal of interest was manifested in the colored boy Hart, who walks much better than he runs, and whose style is very much like that made familiar to New Yorkers by O'Leary. He is a tough-looking lad, and seems likely to make an excellent record during the week....

While we are writing, those of the competitors who by their performance have proved themselves worthy of participating in the fifth contest for the trophy offered by Sir John Astley, and emblematic of the championship of the world in long-distance, go-as-you-please pedestrianism, are still contending for the supremacy, and nearing the end of a race which, from a sporting point of view as well as financial, has been decidedly more successful than any other similar six-day tournament ever held here or in England. In no other contest of like duration have the chances appeared so even as in this, nor the public interest been excited and sustained from first to last by the spectacle of the four or five leading men separated from one another by so short a distance, and all doing so well that the foremost man is forced to continually crowd the fastest previous record, and occasionally excel it. It had been expected by nearly everybody except Manager Hess that the placing of the price of admission at one dollar to all parts of the house was a mistake which would have the effect of limiting the attendance during the middle of the week. Had the competition proved a one-sided affair, no doubt these anticipations would have been realized; but the character of the contest increased to such an extent the interest already felt in the result that the public extended a more than liberal patronage throughout the six days. Taken as a whole, the class of people who have visited the Garden during the week have been superior to the general character of the supporters of like events, and, while we hold that the privilege of gratifying their desires should not be placed beyond the reach of the masses of the people, there can be no doubt that to this fact is attributable the excellent order which has been maintained. The arrangements for keeping the people informed of the state of the contest were about on a par with previous tournaments, the positions of the six leading competitors being indicated on a huge blackboard placed at the east end of the building, upon which the miles made by each man were placed opposite his name. The lap-scoring was done by means of dials painted on a long board fence erected at the outer edge of the inner circle and facing the north, opposite to which was the scorers' and press-stand, built up against the wall in front of the ladies gallery. The fence alluded to might have been made a little lower, as it was just high enough to prevent the spectators on the main floor and on the south side of the house from obtaining a view of the finish. The scoring was attended to by members of different athletic clubs, some of whom were experienced in the business and attentive, while others were inexperienced and seemingly careless as well, which was no recommendation to persons appointed to discharge duties of so important a nature. The track is not so wide by about three feet as before, and, being made in a hurry, was rather soft at first, but has been well looked after, and the pedestrians have had little reason to complain of it since the first day. As we had from previous experience been led to anticipate, the attempt to prevent smoking even on the floor of the house (except along the edge of the track) was a pronounced failure, as it always must be on such occasions, and where the lessees are anxious to sell all the poor cigars they can at high prices. The miserable performance of Weston (as compared with the great record given him in London) has shaken public confidence in the honesty of his alleged English performance. Just why he has not done better we cannot say, for he is a man whose recuperative powers are remarkable, and we had cause to expect better things of him. Perhaps his poor showing has been in part due to the time wasted in exhibitions while on the track that were not appreciated by the spectators, instead of attending strictly to the business of getting as far ahead as possible, and he might have done better had it been certain that he was not to be the recipient of any money other than that which he won by the activity of his legs. At all events, he cannot rightly ascribe his failure to the fact that people were permitted to smoke, and it is foolish for him to do so. In view of the fact that when he accomplished 550 miles in London, as reported, the spectators were not prevented from blowing a cloud and indulged extensively in the habit, while pipes of all sorts and all degrees of color and rankness were much oftener to be seen than fragrant Havanas; so that the excuse made by himself and friends on that score falls to the ground....

THE LAST DAY, SEPT. 27,

A greater number of persons remained within the building over night than on any previous night since Monday, and very many did not vacate their seats after daylight streamed in through the windows, evidently intending to remain until the close of the contest. Our account of the proceedings of the fifth day left Rowell, Merritt, Hazael, Hart, Ennis and Krohne at work, and about half-past one they were joined by Guyon, who was soon followed by Weston, the former having had about four hours' repose and being very lame. After running his total up to 440 miles, even, Hazael retired to his tent, where he indulged in a sleep of two hours' duration and refreshing soundness. Krohne had preceded him, but not to spend even that much time off the track, knowing that if he was to get up to 450 miles he could not afford to remain idle long at a time. After completing his 412th mile, still within a lap of being twenty-five miles ahead of Ennis, Weston again took a recess, remaining away nearly three hours, despite the remonstrances of those who were interested in him, and saw that he was able to "go right along." The others kept company until break of day, save an occasional visit, at long intervals and only for a few minutes at a time, to their tents, so that the crowd of people who were looking on found the time not to hang so heavily upon their hands as usual early in the morning; and the show was sufficiently interesting not only to keep them awake, but also to at times awaken their enthusiasm, to which they gave vent in cheers and loud applause, at times sounding strangely. At four o'clock the score stood: Rowell, 464 miles 7 laps; Merritt, 454 miles 7 laps; Hazael, 440 miles; Hart, 426 miles; Ennis, 387 miles 1 lap; Krohne, 386 miles 1 lap. Federmeyer did not return after he left the track before nine o'clock the preceding evening, and shortly after two o'clock the scorers received notification that he had withdrawn, much to the disgust of Bob Smith, who on the morning of the fifth day had hopes of making the Frenchman do 450 miles, and get a pull at the pot; but Federmeyer found walking here under proper supervision and well attended decidedly different from trundling a wheelbarrow, as he did at the Rink, where he was alleged to have done 407 miles when thus weighted. It will be seen that the colored pedestrian had at last succeeded in passing Guyon—or "Handsome George," as he was styled by the ladies—who took great interest in him, and thought it a shame that so good looking a fellow should be thus left in the lurch. He struggled hard against his physical infirmities in the effort to regain fourth place, but unavailingly, Hart being too fresh and sound for him to successfully tackle, no matter what he might be able to do under different circumstances; and, although they remained but a short distance apart for hours, the position was plainly Hart's, and, barring accident, must remain so till the end. Hazael rejoined the travellers a few minutes past four o'clock, and lap after lap and mile after mile was worked off a four-mile an hour gait, Rowell, Merritt, Hazael and Hart walking close together in Indian fashion, with the big limbed little Britisher walking erect and treading firmly at the head of the quartet, his carriage contrasting strongly with that of Hazael, who, notwithstanding the peculiarity of his mode of progression, is a dangerous man for anybody to tackle. In the meantime Hart and Guyon were having a sharp contest, George having limbered up a bit and trying how his sore feet and swollen limbs would bear a run. Round and round they went, while the spectators cheered like mad. Ennis and Krohne were walking steadily, and shortly before seven o'clock Weston came onto the track again, daylight finding all the contestants at work, and feeling better, now that they were well into the closing day of the tiresome contest. At seven o'clock the dials told the following tale: Rowell, 476 miles 5 laps; Merritt, 466 miles 4 laps; Hazael, 453 miles 3 laps; Hart, 436 miles 3 laps; Guyon, 434 miles 2 laps; Weston 413 miles 4 laps; Ennis, 399 miles 1 lap; Krohne, 397 miles 4 laps. Before eight o'clock Norman

Taylor, who had been enjoying a nine hours' sleep, came out and remained on the track long enough to raise his score from 213 up to 220 miles 1 lap, when he concluded that it was time to take breakfast and a rest, which he proceeded to do, remaining in his tent for nearly two hours, when he returned, ran six miles more, and went off again for a couple of hours. Fresh delegations now commenced to arrive at the Garden, some dropping in on their way to business, and others coming to make a day of it and bent upon securing a good seat from which to view the exciting scenes of the evening. A halt by Hazael about 10:30 enabled Merritt to gain a couple of miles upon him, and these he never afterwards lost, while Rowell had gained a little upon Samuel. The positions of the men at one o'clock were: Rowell, 499 miles 6 laps; Merritt, 488 miles 3 laps; Hazael, 473 miles 5 laps; Hart, 453 miles 2 laps; Guyon, 452 miles; Weston, 434 miles 2 laps; Ennis, 418 miles 3 laps; Krohn, 417 miles 5 laps; Taylor, 226 miles 4 laps. The competitors maintained the same relative positions throughout the afternoon and evening. Rowell drawing away a couple of miles farther from Merritt by running while the latter adhered to a walk, and, although Hazael ran with Rowell, Merritt gained ground when George slackened up and managed to widen the distance between them. Every seat in the building was taken possession of early in the afternoon, and late comers had to content themselves with standing positions. The crowd in the evening was large, and hundreds of those present could obtain glimpses of the men only semi-occasionally; but yet they entered fully into the spirit of the occasion, and good naturedly joined in the plaudits started by those who had an opportunity to witness the struggle. For hours before the time set for ending the contest had arrived the result had been a foregone conclusion; but the excited spectators urged them forward just the same as if there had been a prospect of any one of the contestants bettering his position. Bouquets, baskets of choice flowers, horse-shoes and other fanciful floral designs were presented in profusion, Rowell, of course, being honored with the greatest number and variety of such gifts, the principal offering at the shrine of British grit, brawn and stamina being a huge shield of flowers and pampas grass, presented by the members of the Albion Society, whose monogram was formed of flowers. This was so large that two men had to carry it around the track before the champion, who was cheered at every step. Before half-past eight o'clock Merritt ran in his ungraceful way around the track, waving above his head a large English Union Jack, and was vociferously applauded for the act; but the cheering was not so deafening as it was when, just afterwards, Rowell followed suit, carrying an American flag. This fairly set the spectators crazy. Some expected to see Hart come around waving aloft the black flag, but he didn't. The first man to quit the track for good was Weston, who went off quietly, upon completing his 455th mile, at 6h. 15m. 37s., although he held himself in readiness to return in case there was any chance for Ennis to overhaul him. The next departure was Hazael, who completed 500 miles at 8h 3m 5s., and after making one more circuit stopped, at 8h. 4m. 50s. Rowell finished 530 miles at 8h 28m. 45s., and, after walking hand-in-hand with Merritt and Hazael to the judges' stand, and announcing that they had quit, went to his tent, and as soon as possible donned his street-costume and was taken in a carriage to the Ashland House. Hart scored 482 miles at 9h 15m. 20s., and after doing four laps more he stopped, his total time being 140h. 24 min. 40s. Guyon had finished his task at 9h. 12m. 30s., when he competed 471 miles. Merritt reached the end of his 515th mile at 8h. 32m. 25s., when he declared his labors ended.

Krohne had placed 450 miles to his credit at 9h. 48m. 25s., and after making another lap for good measure stopped. Ennis had completed his 450th mile at 9h. 24m. 25s., concluding with a run, and after tacking on one more circuit he went into his tent, but, upon hearing that Krohne had tied his score, came out again and covered an additional lap, finally retiring at 9h. 51m. 32s., the last man to leave the track. Taylor's 250th mile was finished at 9h. 20m. 50s., and he quit after doing another lap. The pedestrians lost no time in putting on their street-apparel, and leaving the building upon giving notice of their final retirement, and with the early departure of the leading division all interest for the majority of the spectators was lost; and, with throats raw from continual cheering and palms sore from vigorous applauding, they began to leave the building, which was pretty well emptied by the time the last man left the track, although it still lacked over an hour of eleven o'clock. The principal performers found it a difficult task to reach their carriages in waiting outside the Garden, so great was the crush of cheering humanity. As stated, Rowell was taken to the Ashland House, a short distance down Fourth avenue, while Merritt was taken first to a Turkish-bathing establishment, and thence to the Glenhan Hotel, on Third avenue. Hazael was conveyed to Harry Marten's Williamsburg, L.I., while Hart went to the St. Omer Hotel, Weston to the Rossmore Hotel, Guyon to the Putnam House, Ennis and Krohne to their uptown residences, and Talyor to Scott & Earl's. Thus ended the greatest and most exciting six-day pedestrian contest ever held anywhere, and the only one in which three men traveled five hundred miles.

RULES FOR THE O'LEARY AND ASTLEY BELTS, 1879

The first six day race for the championship belt offered by Daniel O'Leary was held at Madison Square Garden, 6-11 October 1879. Nicholas Murphy of Haverstraw, N.Y. won the prize and $5,000 by covering 505 1/8 miles in 139h. 51m 30s. The following rules for both the O'Leary and Astley competitions are reprinted from The Spirit of the Times, 18 October 1879, p. 271.

Rules Governing Future Competitions for the O'Leary Belt.

1. All matches for the Belt shall be for $500 a side.
2. The Belt shall be subject to challenges from any man in the world.
3. Challenges must be sent to the stakeholder, accompanied by $100, and the remaining $400 must be made good when articles are signed.
4. Challenges shall date from the day of their receipt by the stakeholder, and the holder must arrange a race with the first challenger.
5. The holder of the Belt must name date and place, sign articles, and deposit his $500 stake-money four weeks from the date of challenge.

6. The holder must name a day not less than three months, nor more than six months, from date of challenge.

7. The holder must name either New York City or Chicago, Ill., as the place for the race, provided that, by unanimous consent of the stakeholder and all the contestants, it may be agreed to hold the race in some other American city where a suitable building can be procured.

8. After a match is made, any person may join in the race by signing the articles and depositing $500 stake-money with the stakeholder four weeks before the date set for the commencement of the race.

9. The winner shall receive all the stake-money, and must give to the stakeholder satisfactory security for the safekeeping of the Belt, and its prompt return when called for.

10. No share of the gate-money shall be given to any competitor who does not travel 450 miles.

11. All necessary and reasonable expenses shall be paid from the gate-money, and the remainder shall be divided among those competitors who go 450 miles or further, in accordance with the following rules: if only one man finishes 450 miles he shall take all. If two men, the division shall be two-thirds and one-third. If three men, four-sevenths, two-sevenths, and one-seventh, and for all other numbers the division shall be on the same principle, each man receiving twice as much as the next behind him.

12. The holder must deliver the Belt to the stakeholder ten days before the date of the race.

13. The Belt shall become the personal property of any man who wins it in three successive races, or holds it for eighteen consecutive months, provided that if, at the expiration of the eighteen months, he shall be under challenge, that match must be contested and won by him.

14. The Editor of THE SPIRIT OF THE TIMES, New York City, shall be the official stakeholder in all contests for the Belt, shall appoint all officials, and decide all questions not expressly provided for in these rules.

Rules Governing Competitions for the Astley Belt.

1. The winner will have to defend his claim to the Belt for eighteen months, and, should he wish to have it in his possession, he must give security to the appointed trustees, and undertake to restore it, when called upon, in good condition.

2. In case of the Belt being won by any person resident out of the United Kingdom, the trustees shall, if they think fit, demand the deposit of security to the value of $500 before permitting the trophy to be taken out of the country.

3. The holder of the Belt shall not be called upon to compete in more than two matches within each current year, and in case of his winning it in three consecutive matches or sweepstakes it shall become his absolute property, providing that the whole of the said matches or sweepstakes have been *bona fide* in every respect.

4. The holder of the Belt must accept all challenges (subject to the above conditions), for not less than $500 a side, and be prepared to defend his right to the same within three months from the issue of any challenge.

5. In the event of a match being made, anybody may join in by depositing $500 with the appointed stakeholder within four weeks previous to the day fixed for the commencement of the race; the winner to take the Belt and the whole of the stakes; the gate receipts (after all expenses have been paid) to be distributed among the competitors as may be agreed upon beforehand, with the approval of the trustees.

6. The Committee of the A.A.C. are the appointed trustees. The editor of the *Sporting Life* is nominated stakeholder for any matches that may arise for the Belt.

7. All appeals upon questions not provided for by these conditions shall be made to the trustees of the Belt, whose decision shall in all cases be final, and subject to no appeal in a court of law or otherwise.

FEMALE PEDESTRIANS

1879 was also a banner year for female contestants in long distance events. Madame Anderson covered 2,700 quarter miles in the same number of hours on a track in Brooklyn, while Madame Exilde La Chapelle walked 3,000 quarter miles in 3,000 hours in Chicago. New York City and San Francisco were the sites of six day races for women, in which the winners covered between 306 and 372 miles. The year's grand final took place in late December at Madison Square Garden. This report on the results is reprinted from The New York Clipper, 27 December 1879, p. 314.

THE WOMEN'S TOURNEY

The six days' competition, go-as-you-please, between women, for prizes of $1,000 and a belt to first, $750 to second, $500 to third, and $250 to fourth, with a gold medal to the contestant who should make the neatest and best appearance on the track, commenced at Madison-square Garden, this city, at 12.01 A.M. December 15, and was concluded shortly before 11 P.M. on Saturday, 20, the elapsed time being nearly 143 hours. The score-sheets show that of the twenty-five who started the leading six at the close of each day's tramping were as follows, only the mile scores being given: [first five days omitted]...Sixth day—Howard, 393 1/2 miles; Tobias, 387 3/4; Massicott, 384 1/2; Rowell, 378 1/2; Kilbury, 354; Mme. Anderson, 351 3/4; Cameron, 339 1/2; C. Anderson, 336 1/4; Cushing, 295 3/4; Edwards, 288.... There were about eight hundred people present at the start, and upon each of the following evenings this number was augmented, while at the time of closing a large number of spectators were in the building. Paper was plentiful, however, and it is scarcely probable that the promoter, D.E. Rose, made money out of the affair. To his credit, it must be said, the promises he made were faithfully kept, and the prizes paid to the contestants immediately upon the conclusion of the contest. It was stipulated in the contract that Mr. Rose should deduct $25 from each of the money prizes as an entrance-fee, and accordingly Amy Howard received $975 and the belt, Mme. Tobias $725, May Massicott

$475, and Maggie Rowell $225. Fanny Edwards was awarded the gold medal. It is stated that there were irregularities in the scoring during the first few hours of the contest, but it was not the result of any intention to commit fraud; and as the contestants probably lost as much as they gained by the alleged failure to promptly call the hour-time (the weights had been surreptitiously removed from the big regulator, and no chronometers were provided by which to keep the mile-time), this did not, we think, have any material effect upon the final score. We think it probable that the competitors covered the full distance with which they were severally credited, but so long as cause for doubt exists there is an obstacle to the acceptance of the record. Frank Whittaker was referee.

TRACK AND FIELD

THE FOUNDING OF THE NEW YORK ATHLETIC CLUB

On 17 June 1866 three young gentlemen of New York City, John C. Babcock, Henry E. Buermeyer, and William B. Curtis met in a private house on Sixth Avenue to plan an American athletic club. They selected that residence for their weekly meetings and exercise sessions whenever inclement weather prevented them from engaging in outdoor workouts on local tracks. On 8 September 1868 fourteen men gathered to formally organize the New York Athletic Club by signing a muster roll, electing officers, and appointing committees. They decided to hold their first meet on November 11th of that year. On that occasion about twenty-five hundred spectators (including many women) were entertained by Harvey Dodsworth's band and the athletic events. Those included footraces at seventy-five yards, two hundred and twenty yards, four hundred and forty yards, and a one mile walk. The field events were the standing broad jump, standing high jump, running broad jump, running high jump, standing three jumps, and putting the shot. A novel race between two French velocipedes also amused the crowd. The following editorial on the NYAC and its prospects is reprinted from The Spirit of the Times, 10 October 1868, p. 121.

We have very great satisfaction in announcing that the first semi-annual games of the New York Athletic Club will take place upon November 11th. It is a gratifying fact that healthy and strengthening pastimes are daily growing into greater favor with the community, which the vitality and the increasing prosperity of the athletic organizations in this city amply testify. We believe that the benefit of such institutions as that to whose exhibition we have alluded can not be too highly appreciated by any class of the people; but we would more especially urge their value on the youth of our cities and colleges, whose business pursuits and recreations are unexceptionally of a sedentary character. To those young men who are for many hours of the day excluded from air and exercise, the cultivation of their physical power becomes a necessity if they would escape the doom of early senility; and it must necessarily be through their exertion and combined support if these organizations are to become permanent and flourishing.

Of late years we have noticed a commendable change in the recreations of Young America in large cities. A quarter of a century ago, although outdoor sports found favor in many, they did not enjoy that general popularity which today very happily has become their own exclusively, to the detriment of other less wholesome amusements. Base-ball, cricket, yachting, skating, and rowing have now one score of devotees where a quarter of a century back they numbered but one. The people have learnt the inestimable worth of such relaxations, and throw themselves into them with a vigor and delight that is the real secret of their success.

The New York Athletic Club, although but in its infancy, shows remarkable promise of becoming the leading institution of its kind in this country, and will, doubtlessly, in course of time, fill the same position in this country occupied by the London Athletic Club in England. The club was founded some few months ago by a number of gentlemen who were fully aware of the benefits to be derived from such an organization, and foresaw the probable advantage to be subsequently gained from it by the young men of New York. The prospects are undoubtedly encouraging, and give considerable assurances of success; but we would suggest that, in order to complete the organization and render it perfect, those designing to become members (who hesitate, thinking the club insufficiently formed) should at once join and put their shoulder to the wheel, and in a very short time every obstacle will be no more. It cannot be expected that a club like the present can become an accomplished fact without some little difficulties have been wrestled with and successfully overcome. It is the intention of the members of the club to extend its patronage to all species of gymnastics, rowing, swimming, and skating; but at present the funds of the organization being unequal to the fulfillment of these designs, it has been determined to institute a series of semi-annual games, in which pedestrianism is to take the prominent position. The first of these will take place, as we before said, on the 11th prox. In the spring of 1869 the procural of grounds for the club is designed by its members, on which a running track will be constructed and the necessary buildings erected. In its efforts to acquire stability and strength, the New York Athletic Club has our hearty support and cordial approval, believing as we do, that in such recreations becoming dear to the young men of the nation, we have an additional safeguard against the truth of the dismal doctrine of the degeneration of the human species.

In the approaching games the various Caledonian clubs of this city have been invited to contest, so that a very interesting exhibition may be looked for with confidence. The exercises comprise jumping, leaping, racing, putting the shot, and throwing the hammer. Naturally enough, the Caledonian Club, which has for so long occupied the most prominent position as an athletic club in this city, will strain every nerve to keep ahead of its friendly but vigorous rival. After this year the games will take place in May and October. For its approaching exhibition the club has secured the Empire City Skating Rink, an enormous structure with a ground-floor and raised seats, having a capacity to accommodate an audience of at least ten thousand persons. As the display will take place by gaslight, a very large attendance may be anticipated.

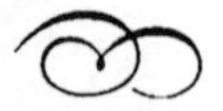

RULES FOR ATHLETIC MEETINGS

The following rules were adopted by the New York Athletic Club and were generally followed in early American track and field meets. They are reprinted from Capt. Fred. Whittaker, ed., *Handbook of Summer Athletic Sports* (New York, 1880), pp. 49-55.

AMERICAN ATHLETIC RULES.
MEETINGS.

Officers.—The officers of an athletic meeting shall be: One clerk of the course, with assistants, if necessary; one starter; one judge of walking, with assistants, if necessary; one scorer, with assistants, if necessary; three timekeepers; three judges at the finish; three measurers; one referee.

Clerk of the Course.—He shall record the name of each competitor who shall report to him; shall give him his number for each game in which he is entered, and notify him, five minutes before the start, of every event in which he is engaged. The assistants shall do such portions of his work as he may assign to them.

Starter.—He shall have entire control of competitors at their marks; shall strictly enforce Law 3, and shall be the sole judge of fact as to whether or no any man has gone over his mark. His decision in such cases shall be final and without appeal.

Judge of Walking.—He shall have entire control of competitors during the race; shall strictly enforce Law 8, and his decision as to unfair walking shall be final and without appeal. The assistants shall do such portion of his work as he may assign to them.

Scorer.—He shall record the laps made by each competitor, and call them aloud when tallied, for the information of the contestants. He shall record the order of finishing and the times of the competitors in walking and running races. The assistants shall do such portions of his work as he may assign to them.

Timekeepers.—Each of the three timekeepers shall time every event, and in case of disagreement the average of the three shall be the official time. Time to be taken from the flash of the pistol.

Judges at the Finish.—Two shall stand at one end of the tape, and the third at the other. One shall take the winner, another the second man, and the other the third man; they shall also note the distances between the first three as they finish. In case of disagreement the majority shall decide. Their decisions as to the order in which the men finish shall be final and without appeal.

Measurers.—They shall measure and record each trial of each competitor in all games whose record is one of distance or height. Their decision as to the performance of each man shall be final and without appeal.

Referee.—He shall, when appealed to, decide all questions whose settlement is not provided for in these rules, and his decision shall be final and without appeal.

Competitors.—Immediately on arriving at the grounds each competitor shall report to the clerk of the course, and receive his number for the game in which he is entered. He shall inform himself of the times at which he must compete, and will report promptly at the start, without waiting to be notified. No competitor allowed to start without his proper number.

Inner Grounds.—No person whatsoever allowed inside the track except the officials and properly accredited representatives of the press. The authorized persons will wear a badge, and intruders will be promptly ejected. Competitors not engaged in the game actually taking place will not be allowed inside or upon the track.

LAWS.

1. *Attendants.*—No attendants shall accompany a competitor on the scratch or in the race.

2. *Starting Signals.*—All races (except time handicaps) shall be started by report of pistol fired behind the competitors. A miss fire shall be no start. There shall be no recall after the pistol is fired. Time handicaps shall be started by the word "Go."

3. *Starting.*—When the starter receives a signal from the judges at the finish that everything is in readiness he shall direct the competitors to get on their marks. Any competitor starting before the signal shall be put back one yard, for the second offense two yards, and for the third shall be disqualified. He shall be held to have started when any portion of his body touches the ground in front of his mark. Stations count from the inside.

4. *Keeping Proper Course.*—In all races on a straight track, each competitor shall keep his own position on the course from start to finish.

5. *Change of Course.*—In all races on other than a straight track, a competitor may change toward the inside whenever he is two steps ahead of the man whose path he crosses.

6. *Fouling.*—Any competitor shall be disqualified for willfully jostling, running across, or in any way impeding another.

7. *Finish.*—A thread shall be stretched across the track at the finish, four feet above the ground. It shall not be held by the judges, but be fastened to the finish posts on either side, so that it may always be at right angles to the course and parallel to the ground. The finish line is not this thread, but the line of the ground drawn across the track from post to post and the thread is intended merely to assist the judges in their decision. The men shall be placed in the order in which they cross the finish line.

8. *Walking.*—The judge shall caution for any unfair walking, and the third caution shall disqualify the offender. On the last lap an unfair walker shall be disqualified without previous caution.

9. *Hurdles.*—The regular hurdle race shall be 120 yards, over 10 hurdles, each 8ft. 6in. high. The first hurdle shall be placed 15 yards from the scratch, and there shall be 10 yards between each hurdle. There may be (by special announcement) hurdle races of different distances and with different number and length of hurdles.

10. *Jumping.*—No weights or artificial aid will be allowed in any jumping contest except by special agreement or announcement. When weights are allowed there shall be no restriction as to size, shape, or material.

11. *Running High Jump.*—The height of the bar at starting and at each successive elevation shall be determined by a majority of the qualified competitors. In case of tie the referee shall decide. Three tries allowed at each height. Each competitor shall make one attempt in the order of his name on the programme; then those that have failed, if any, shall have a second trial in regular order, and those failing on the trial shall then

take their final trial. Displacing the bar and nothing else, counts as a "try." A competitor may omit his trials at any height, but if he fails at the next height he shall not be allowed to go back and try the height which he omitted.

12. *Pole-Leaping*.—The rules for this game shall be the same as those of the running high jump.

13. *Hitch-and-Kick*.—The competitors are allowed unlimited run, but must spring, kick, alight, and hop twice with the same foot. The height of the object at starting and at each successive elevation, shall be determined by a majority of the qualified competitors. In case of a tie the referee shall decide. Three tries allowed at each height. Each competitor shall make one attempt in the order of his name of the programme; then those who have failed, if any, shall have a second trial in regular order, and those failing on this trial shall then take their final trial. Hitting the object, and nothing else, counts as a kick, and kicking higher than the object without hitting it is not a kick. Springing from the ground counts as a try. A competitor may omit his trials at any height, but if he fail at the next height he shall not be allowed to go back and try the height which he omitted.

14. *Standing High Jump*.—The competitors may stand as they please, but must jump from the first spring. The height of the bar at starting and at each successive elevation, shall be determined by a majority of the qualified competitors. In case of a tie the referee shall decide. Three tries allowed at each height. Each competitor shall make one attempt in the order of his name on the programme; then those who have failed, if any, shall have a second trial in regular order, and those failing on this trial shall then take their final trial. Displacing the bar and nothing else, counts as a "try." A competitor may omit his trials at any height, but if he fail at the next height he shall not be allowed to go back and try the height which he omitted.

15. *Running Wide Jump*.—The competitors shall have unlimited run, but must take off behind the scratch. Stepping any part of the foot over the scratch in an attempt shall be "no jump," but shall count as a "try." Each competitor allowed three trials, and the best three men have three more trials each. Each competitor shall be credited with the best of all his jumps. The measurement shall be from the scratch line in front of the jumper's feet to the nearest break of the ground made by any part of his person. The same rules govern running hop step and jump, and all similar games.

16. *Standing Wide Jump*.—Competitors must jump from the first spring. Stepping any part of the foot over the scratch in an attempt shall be "no jump," but shall count as a "try." Each competitor shall be credited with the best of all his jumps. The measurement shall be from the scratch line in front of the jumper's feet to the nearest break of the ground made by any part of his person. The same rules govern standing three jumps, standing hop, step and jump, and all similar games.

17. *Putting the Shot*.—The shot shall be a solid iron sphere weighing 16 lbs. It shall be put from the shoulder with one hand, from between two parallel lines, 7 ft. apart. Touching the ground outside either line with any part of person, before the shot alights, shall make the attempt "no put," which counts as a "try." Each competitor allowed three trials, and the best three men have three more trials each. Each competitor shall be credited with the best of all his puts. The measurement shall be from the nearest break of the ground made by the ball, perpendicularly to the scratch line, extended, if necessary, to meet this perpendicular.

18. *Throwing the Hammer.*—The hammer-head shall be a solid iron sphere, weighing 16 lbs., the handle shall be of hickory wood, and the length of hammer and handle, over all, shall be 3 ft. 6in. The competitor shall stand at and behind the scratch, facing as he pleases, and throw with either or both hands. Touching the ground in front of the scratch with any portion of the person, before the hammer alights, shall make the attempt "no throw," which counts as a "try." Letting go of the hammer in an attempt counts as a "try." Each competitor allowed three trials, and the best three men have three more trials each. Each competitor shall be credited with the best of all his throws. If the head strike first the measurement shall be from the nearest break of the ground made by it. If the handle strikes first, one length of the hammer shall be allowed from the mark made by the end of the handle toward the mark made by the head of the hammer, and the measurement shall be from this point. The measurement shall be to the scratch line half-way between the thrower's feet.

19. *Throwing the Hammer with a Run.*—The hammer-head shall be a solid iron sphere, weighing 16lbs., the handle shall be of hickory wood, and the length of hammer and handle over all shall be 3 ft. 6in. Unlimited run is allowed, and the competitor may deliver the hammer as he pleases. Letting go of the hammer in an attempt counts as "a try." Each competitor allowed three trials, and the best three men have three more trials each. Each competitor shall be credited with the best of all his throws. If the head strikes first, the measurement shall be from the nearest break of the ground made by it. If the handle strikes first, one length of the hammer shall be allowed from the mark made by the end of the handle, toward the mark made by the head of the hammer, and the measurement shall be from this point. The measurement shall be to the nearest footprint at the delivery. The footprints of the competitors shall be effaced after each throw.

20. *Throwing Fifty-six Pound Weight.*—This shall be of solid iron, and any shape of weight and handle is allowed, provided the whole weighs 56 lbs. The competitor will stand at and behind the scratch, facing as he pleases, grasping the weight by the handle, and shall throw it with one hand. Touching the ground in front of the scratch with any portion of the person, before the weight alights, shall make the attempt "no throw," which counts as "a try." Letting go of the weight in an attempt shall count as "a try." Each competitor allowed three trials, and the best three men have three more trials each. Each competitor shall be credited with the best of all his throws. The measurement shall be from the scratch line (in front of the throwers's left foot), to the nearest break of the ground made by the weight, exclusive of handle.

21. *Tossing the Caber.*—The length of the caber to be 16ft., the diameter at the thick end not more than 8 in., and at the small end not more than 4 in. The caber must be held by the small end, and tossed over so that the small end shall fall and remain beyond the butt. The competitors shall have unlimited run, but must take off behind the scratch. Stepping any part of the foot over the scratch in an attempt shall be "no toss," but shall count as "a try." Each competitor allowed three trials, and the best three men have three more trials each. Each competitor shall be credited with the best of all his tosses. The measurement shall be from the small end of the caber perpendicularly to the scratch line, extended, if necessary, to meet this perpendicular.

22. *Throwing the Ball (Lacrosse, Cricket, or Base-ball).*—The lacrosse ball shall be thrown from the lacrosse, the cricket and base-ball from the hand. The competitors shall have unlimited run, but must take off behind the scratch. Touching the ground in front of the scratch-line with any part of the person before the ball alights, shall make the attempt "no throw," which shall count as "a try." Each competitor allowed three trials, and the best three men have three more trials each. Each competitor shall be credited with the best of all his throws. To facilitate the measurement, a line shall be drawn parallel to and 300 ft. in front of the scratch-line. The measurement shall be from the nearest break of the ground made by the ball, perpendicularly to the measuring line, extended, if necessary, to meet this perpendicular.

23. *Tug-of-War.*—In tug-of-war the following rules will be observed: (1.) the side creases to be 12 ft. from the center crease. (2.) The mark on the rope to be over the center crease when the word "heave" is given, and the team hauling that mark over the crease on its own side to be the winners. (3.) No footing holes to be made before the start. (4.) The contestants to wear socks, slippers, boots or shoes without spikes. (5.) The rope to be 1 1-2 in. in diameter. (6.) Immediately before the contest the captains of all the contesting teams shall draw their numbers. (7.) Not less that five minutes shall be allowed each team between heats. (8.) Captains shall toss for choice of sides before each pull. But if the same two teams pull more than once during the day, they shall change ends at each successive pull. (9.) With two teams, they shall pull best 2 in 3. With three teams, one and two shall pull, then two and three, and three and one. With four teams, one and two shall pull, then three and four, and the winners pull the final. With five teams, first round, one and two, three and four, five has a bye; second round winner of first heat pulls with five, and winner of this heat pulls the final with the winner of second heat of first round. With six teams, first round, one and two, three and four, five and six; second round winner of first and second heats. Winner of this heat pulls the final with winner of third heat, first round. Where more than six teams are entered, the arrangement of trials shall be on the same principle as in the above examples.

24 *Bicycling.*—When ordered into position for a start the men shall mount their machines, and one assistant for each competitor will hold his machine with its front wheel at the mark; at the starting signal the attendants are allowed to push the machine forward but not to follow it up. Riders must pass each other on the outside, and be a clear length of the bicycle in front before taking the inside; the inside man must allow room on the outside for other competitors to pass. Any competitor infringing this rule will be disqualified. In a race without using the handles, competitors must ride with the arms folded, or the hands and arms otherwise kept quite off the machine. Any competitor touching any part of his machine with his hands or arms will be disqualified. The Laws of Athletes govern all points not above specified.

NATIONAL ASSOCIATION OF AMATEUR ATHLETES OF AMERICA, 1879

On 22 April 1879 representatives of seven athletic associations met in New York City and created a new governing body for track and field. The founding clubs were the New York, Scottish-American, Manhattan, Staten Island, American, Plainfield, and Union of Boston, Massachusetts. The convention adopted the rules for the government of Athletic Meetings and the Laws of Athletics of the New York Athletic Club. The following constitution and by-laws are reprinted from The Spirit of the Times, 3 May 1879, p. 299.

CONSTITUTION

Article I.

Name.—This Association shall be known as the National Association of Amateur Athletes of America.

Article II.

Object.—The object of this Association shall be the protection of the mutual interests of its members and the advancement and improvement of amateur athletic sports.

Article III.

Membership.—The membership of this Association shall be limited to amateur athletic clubs, and any associate club not giving at least one public out-door athletic meeting each year, to consist of not less than five games, open to all amateurs, will thereby forfeit its membership.

Article IV.

Definition.—An amateur is any person who has never competed in an open competition or for a stake; or for public money; or for gate-money; or under a false name; or with a professional for a prize, public money, gate-money, or where gate-money is charged; nor has ever, at any period of his life, taught or pursued athletic exercises as a means of livelihood.

Article V.

Management.—The management of this Association shall be intrusted to an Executive Committee, consisting of nine members, who shall be elected for a term of three years, except that, of the first Committee elected, three shall be chosen by lot to go out of office at the first annual meeting, three at the second, and three at the third, in order that three members of this committee shall be elected at each annual meeting of the Association. No club shall have more than one representative in the executive Committee. Vacancies in the membership of the executive Committee, arising from any cause whatever, shall be filled by the Executive Committee until the next meeting of the Association. They shall, from among their number, elect a President, Vice-President, Secretary, and Treasurer, who shall serve until the next annual meeting, and perform their several duties as prescribed in the By-Laws, and generally such duties as pertain to their office.

Article VI.

Application for Membership.—Any amateur athletic club desiring to join the Association shall send to the Secretary an application for membership, a copy of its constitution and By-Laws, and a list of its officers and members. The Secretary shall submit this application to each member of the Executive Committee in turn, and these members shall endorse their decision. The approval of seven members of the Executive Committee shall be necessary to constitute an election.

Article VII.

Annual Meeting.—The annual meeting of this Association shall be held at 8P.M. on the evening of the yearly championship games.

Article VIII.

Special Meeting.—A special meeting may be called at the written request of not less than one-third of the clubs comprising this Association, of which fifteen days notice shall be given by the Executive Committee.

Article IX.

Representation.—At all meetings each club may be represented by not more than three delegates, each of whom can take part in all discussions, but in the decision of any matter each club shall be entitled to only one vote.

Article X.

Duties of Members.—Each associate club agrees to adopt the definition of an amateur as found in Article IV. of the Constitution, and to enforce said definition at all athletic meetings given under its auspices; and further agrees to conform to all the laws, rules, and regulations of the Association, and to abide by the rulings of the Executive committee.

Article XI.

Dues.—The dues shall be $10, payable upon admission to the Association, and at each annual meeting thereafter. No club, whose dues remain unpaid, shall be entitled to vote at the annual election.

Article XII.

Discipline.—Any violation of the rules of the Association shall render a club liable to suspension by the Executive Committee until the next meeting of the Association, and expulsion, by a two-thirds vote of the clubs represented at such meeting.

Article XIII.

Amendments.—No addition, alteration, or amendment shall be made to this Constitution at any meeting, except by a two-thirds vote of the clubs represented. At least thirty days' notice of any such proposed change must be given to the Executive Committee, of which due notice shall at once be sent to the clubs belonging to this Association.

BY-LAWS

Article V.

Championship Games.—The championship games shall include:

Running—100 yards; 220 yards; quarter mile; half mile; one mile; three miles.

Hurdle racing—120 yards, 10 hurdles, 3 ft. 6 in. high.

Walking—One mile; three miles; seven miles.

Running high jump; running broad jump; pole leaping.

Putting the shot, 16 lbs; throwing the hammer, 16 lbs.; throwing the 56 lb. weight.

Bicycle race, two miles.

Individual tug-of-war; tug-of war, teams of five men.

The Executive Committee may omit any of the above competitions, or add such games as in their judgment may seem proper....

Article VII.

Mode of Deciding Upon Status of Any Athlete.—Sec. 1.—In the event of any application for the decision of the Executive Committee upon the applicant's status as an amateur athlete, it shall be the duty of the President to appoint a sub-committee of three to investigate the case. This committee shall report to the Executive Committee, at their next meeting, who shall thereupon take such action as they deem proper and just in the premises.

Sec. 2—Upon application from any club, a member of this Association, asking for a decision of the committee upon the status of any individual, a committee shall be appointed, and report, as specified in Sec. 1. and the decision of the Executive Committee be duly transmitted to the enquiring club.

Sec. 3.—Each person whose amateur standing is being investigated, shall receive twenty days notice of the meeting at which his case will be decided, shall be permitted to be present in person, to examine the witnesses, read all written testimony, and submit his own sworn statement. He must also answer all questions asked him by the Committee.

Sec. 4.—The unavoidable expenses attending such investigation shall be borne by the club or individual making the application.

Sec. 5.—It shall be the duty of this committee, if they deem an entry at the championship meeting a proper subject for investigation, to entertain the question, irrespective of any protest being entered.

Chapter 17

WINTER SPORTS

Between 1860 and 1880 winter sports flourished throughout North America, as men and women braved the frigid temperatures, ice, and snow to enjoy their favorite recreations. Curling, hockey, skating, and snowshoeing shared the common feature of being cold weather pastimes, but they differed markedly in their respective origins and social characteristics. Curling was a popular game among Scottish immigrants across the continent, while early forms of hockey and competitive skating were popular among a variety of groups in both Canada and the United States. Like lacrosse, snowshoeing was an indigenous Indian athletic activity which was adapted by Canadians to suit their sporting purposes. All four sports exhibited characteristics of modernization during this era, as each produced clubs, rules, governing bodies, and special matches.

North American curling was introduced and promoted by Scottish immigrants, and throughout the nineteenth century the "roarin' game" was closely associated with "Auld Scotia" and the frozen lochs of the old country. The sport was also connected with the ideal of democratic participation of all ranks of society. It thrived among the urban middle classes and in some rural villages, but it was also patronized by elements of the elite. In Canada the sport enjoyed a large following in Quebec and especially Ontario, and by the 1870s the opening of the railways facilitated its expansion into the Prairies. During these years the game was generally played on outdoor rinks, but the introduction of covered sheds increased its popularity. The Canadian branch of the Royal Caledonian Curling Club and the Quebec Curling Club both sponsored competition for special medals and cups. This chapter begins with the rules governing those events during the late 1870s.

In the United States every major Scottish community had at least one curling club, and a few had many more. The northeastern states produced many associations, with the New York City region numbering at least a dozen by 1869. Other American cities which sent curling teams to international matches against Canadian clubs during these years were Albany, Cleveland, Paterson (N.J.), Buffalo, Jersey City (N.J.), Milwaukee, and Detroit.

The origins of hockey are shrouded in mystery, and in some ways the controversy over the birthplace of this sport resembles the debate over the true site of the first modern baseball game. The sport evolved from early versions of field hockey, sometimes called "shinney" or "hurley" in Europe. In these forms players used sticks to try to knock a ball through a goal. In Canada partisans from three cities—Kingston, Ontario, Halifax, Nova Scotia, and Montreal, Quebec—have argued that sportsmen from their respective towns invented the game. Proponents of the Kingston claim maintain that a British garrison created ice hockey when they used field hockey sticks and a lacrosse ball on their town's frozen harbor in 1855. But Nova Scotia historians counter with evidence of much earlier contests of "hurley" on the ice on Long Pond near Windsor in their province, as well as in Halifax.

As is the case with the baseball dispute, the key issue concerns the precise definition of the modern sport of hockey, which in turn hinges on the formation of the first clubs and rules. Probably the strongest case belongs to the advocates from Montreal, who state that a group of students from McGill University invented the modern game and revised its rules during the 1870s. On 4 March 1875 The Gazette (Montreal) reported on a hockey match played the previous day between two sides which included several McGill students. It stated that the game was "much in vogue on the ice in New England and other parts of the United States." It also noted that it was usually played with a ball, but that the contestants substituted "a flat block of wood" which would slide along the ice and thus would not strike any spectators. The writer concluded that the sport resembled lacrosse in the use of goals, but "in the main the old country game of shinty gives the best idea of hockey." One of the players, Henry Joseph, later gave the major credit for the invention of ice hockey to his teammate and captain of the victorious side, James George Aylwin Creighton. According to Joseph, Creighton conceived of the game after a lacrosse exhibition on ice failed. A few McGill scholars formed a hockey club in late January 1877, and they played a series of three matches at the Victoria Skating Rink against a squad called the "Victorias"—which included members of the Montreal Lacrosse Club and the Montreal Football Club. Two years later W.F. Robertson, Richard F. Smith, and W.L. (Chick) Murray revised the rules of the game. Their version featured a square puck cut from a rubber ball, nine players on a side, and an onsides restriction which was borrowed from a current football pass rule. The hockey selections presented here include two accounts of games played in 1875 and 1876, along with the first published regulations of 1877.

Skating had long been a favorite recreational winter pastime in North America, and during the late 1860s and 1870s it entered a new phase in its development into a competitive sport. These years witnessed the founding of skating clubs in numerous cities and the creation of the American Skating Congress between 1868 and 1871. Although female participation in skating was commonplace, many girls and women were still shy about appearing in public programs. This chapter includes documents describing events and rules for the American Skating Congress, along with accounts of a ladies' contest and a tournament in Montreal.

Snowshoe racing was one of the premier winter sports in Canada during the 1860s and 1870s, especially in Montreal. Through the leadership of the Montreal Snow Shoe Club, this demanding pastime experienced a golden age between 1867 and 1880. The patronage provided by many of the elite sportsmen and the attraction of gambling partly explain its popularity. Snowshoeing also experienced a considerable degree of modernization prior to 1880, but during the following decades it lost considerable ground to other cold weather recreations.

Although the American Civil War retarded the growth of snowshoe racing among the general population in Canada, that conflict did increase interest in the sport among military garrisons. Participation among private citizens declined because of their concern over a possible annexation attempt by the United States. Many gentlemen shifted their allegiance from sporting clubs to rifle companies or other volunteer organizations.

On the other hand, some officers patronized the sport or attended races because they believed that it promoted fitness and discipline. A more significant factor which inhibited the development of the sport was the skating mania that swept though Canadian cities during the 1860s.

1867 marked the beginning of the Confederation era of Canadian history, and it also brought renewed enthusiasm for snowshoeing in its three forms of recreational tramping, track racing, and cross country steeplechase competition. Clubs recruited many new members and attendance increased substantially at annual races. The two major factors behind this explosion of interest were the patronage provided by the most prestigious lacrosse clubs and the widespread practice of gambling. William George Beers and other founders of lacrosse were also enthusiastic about snowshoeing, and there was extensive cross membership between the Montreal Lacrosse Club and the Montreal Snow Shoe Club. Newspaper reports of feature events suggest that the public was eager to wager on the sport. This chapter includes an account of the Montreal Snow Shoe Club's annual meeting for 1875.

Snowshoeing experienced considerable modernization during these years, although not to the same degree as many other North American sports. By the early 1870s the racing program set by the Montreal Snow Shoe Club had become standard for major competitions. The order of events included a two mile Indian race, an open one mile, a hurdle race, a half-mile boy's race, a 100 yard dash, a garrison or open half mile race, a premier two mile club race, and a final half-mile dash. The shorter hurdle and dash races were contested in heats, with victory going to the man who first won two races. In 1871 a convention of snowshoers from several Montreal clubs set the weight and size of the shoe at one and a half pounds with no less than ten inches of gut at the widest part. Seven years later the Montreal Snow Shoe Club promulgated the "Laws of Snow Shoe Racing," which listed nineteen sections of regulations on equipment, competition, wagering, and procedures for decisions and appeals. As a result of all of these efforts, snowshoeing flourished in Montreal, Quebec City, Ottawa, Toronto, and smaller cities throughout the Dominion. Yet the failure of the sport's adherents to form a nationwide governing body curtailed its long-term prospects.

Like lacrosse, snowshoeing originated as a native Indian recreation which was adapted by Canadians for their sporting purposes. Indians were usually more skilled and faster than their Canadian counterparts, but generally they were not permitted to join athletic clubs or to compete on equal terms with white snowshoers. Major meets normally began with an "Indian race," which was a feature attraction for audiences. The remaining events were closed to Indians, although there were a few exceptions. Although spectators admired the skill and stamina of the native contestants, they also frequently ridiculed them with racist treatment and remarks. Novelty events such as potato-picking contests or exhausting tests of endurance degraded Indian participants. "Iroquois Club Races" presents an example of a meet held by the Caughnauwaga Snowshoe Club in 1876.

At its peak, Canadian snowshoeing was an upper-middle class recreation with a distinctive social ethic. It was associated with strong character values of manliness, discipline, morality, and proper conduct. All forms of liquor, wine, and beer were prohibited at club functions, even at their fancy annual dinners. Women were barred from all recreational tramps and competitive races, but were permitted "romantic strolls" during the 1870s. However, female spectators were welcome at major races, presumably because of their beauty and the inspiration they provided for the men and boys. Club sponsorship of concerts and winter carnivals during the 1870s and 1880s further highlighted the social aspects of snowshoeing.

The demise of snowshoeing in the late nineteenth century was due to a variety of cultural factors as well as the nature of the sport itself. As a recreational activity it ultimately lost ground to its long-time rival, ice skating. As a competitive individual sport it was not as appealing to the public as team sports—especially hockey. Like pedestrianism, its summer counterpart, it was a physically demanding activity which was ill-suited to a rapidly urbanizing and industrializing society. Because of the requirements of snow and suitable terrain, it could not become a profitable commercialized sport. Basically a premodern pastime, it was not easily adaptable to changing social conditions. The lack of a national governing organization and the merger of the Montreal Snow Shoe Club into the Montreal Amateur Athletic Association in 1881 severely limited the sport's chances for new rounds of growth.

CURLING

CANADIAN BRANCH OF THE ROYAL CALEDONIAN CURLING CLUB

Championship competition in curling was keen in the late 1870s, as is evident from the following rules for a gold medal tournament. These regulations are reprinted from The Gazette (Montreal), 3 January 1876.

RULES FOR GOLD MEDAL COMPETITION, 1876

All the regularly organized curling clubs of Canada who may wish to compete, to do so during the week beginning Sunday, the 16th and ending Saturday, the 22nd of January, according to the following rules, and the two clubs which make the highest scores to play against each other two rinks, according to the rules for district medals of R.C.C.C...., on some covered or open rink, which may be fixed upon on as nearly as possible equi-distant from the competing clubs. The match will be played during the first fortnight of February.

Returns of the score with the following information: state of the ice, whether played with "granite" or "iron" "stones," whether played on open air ice or in a covered rink, to be sent on or before the 30th of January, to

CAPT. FREDK. WARD, A.D.C.,

Government House,

Ottawa.

The members of the Canadian Branch of the R.C.C.C. who may happen to be in Montreal, have kindly consented to adjudicate on any dispute that may arise between competing clubs.

Rules to be observed in the primary competition for the gold medal presented by His Excellency the Earl of Dufferin.

1. Eight players to be selected to compete for the club at the points.

2. Lots shall be drawn for the order of playing; each competitor shall change position one place each end, viz: No. 1 to play last, second end; No. 2 to play first, second end, and last third, and so on; he shall use two stones, and play them the one immediately after the other.

3. The length of the rink from hack to Tee not to exceed 42, nor be less than 32 yards, the change of length to be determined by the umpire.

4. Two circles 8 feet in diameter shall be drawn around the Tee at each end of the rink, and a central line or score between the tees to the hog score.

5. Every competitor to play four shots, two from each end, at each of the eight following points of the game, viz: Striking, Inwicking, Drawing, Guarding, Chap and Lie, Wick and Curl in, Raising and Chipping the winner, according to the following definitions:—

a Striking.—A stone placed upon the Tee to be struck out of the 8 feet circle. The Tee to be considered the central point of circle.

b Inwicking.—One stone is placed upon the Tee, and another with its inner edge two feet distant from the Tee, and its fore edge on a line drawn from the Tee at an angle of 45 degrees with the central line (in two of the changes to be on the opposite side of the central line from what it is in the other two), the stones played to hit against the latter and perceptibly move the former.

c Drawing.—The stone played to be within the 8 feet circle.

d Guarding.—A stone to be placed behind the Tee, touching the central point. The stone played to rest, however little, on the central line and completely to clear the Hog score, but must not move the stone placed as described above.

e Chap and Lie.—A stone placed on the Tee to be struck out of the 8 feet circle, but the stone played to be within it.

f Wick and Curl in.—A stone is placed with its inner edge, 7 feet distant from the Tee, and its fore edge on a line making an angle of 45 degrees with the central line (in two chances on the left, in the other two on the right hand), the stone played to hit this stone and rest within the 8 feet circle.

g Raising.—A stone placed with its centre on the central line and its inner edge 7 feet distant from the Tee, to be struck into the 8 feet circle.

h Chipping the Winner.—One stone is placed on the tee, and another with its inner edge 10 feet distant, just touching the central line and half guarding the one of the Tee; the stone played to pass the guard and perceptibly move the other.

6. Each successful shot shall count one, whatever be the point played. In a and c the stone played at must be struck entirely without the 8 feet circle and clear of the line forming the circle, to be determined by the square. In c, e and f the stone played, and in g the stone played at to rest entirely within the 8 feet circle and clear of the line forming that circle, to be determined by the square. In d the stone played must rest not entirely clear of the central line, to be determined by the square.

7. The competition to be presided over by and the score kept under the supervision of a member of some other club than the one competing, and not connected in any way with the competing club. This Umpire will see that these rules are strictly adhered to, and will sign his name to the return of the score, stating the club to which he belongs.

8. The Umpire will see that no one stands on the ice in such a way as to interfere with the playing. Advice may be given to the player, but no one but the player himself may sweep his stone.

The Silver Medal to be played for in accordance with the foregoing rules by all the members of the winning club, and a return to be sent to Capt. Fredk. Ward, A.D.C., as soon as circumstances will permit.

(Signed)

R. FREDK. WARD, A.D.C.

QUEBEC CURLING CLUB CHALLENGE CUP, 1877

These rules are reprinted from the records of the Montreal Caledonia Curling Club, Vol. 1, Minute Book, 1875-1885, National Archives of Canada, with permission of the Montreal Amateur Athletic Association.

REVISED RULES AND REGULATIONS

Resolved, That it is desirable, in the interest of Keen Curling, and with a view to develop, foster and encourage the "roaring game," in this, perhaps of all other countries, the best adapted for its successful prosecution, that a Challenge Cup should be purchased, and be open for competition to all Curling Clubs in the Dominion, who agree to the following conditions, viz:

1st. The Cup to be called the Quebec Curling Club Challenge Cup.

2nd. The Cup to be a perpetual Challenge Cup.

3rd. The Cup to be played for on the Ice of the Club having it in possession, unless it should waive its right, in which case the match may be played on such other Ice as may be agreed on, but no match to take place with less than 5 degree frost registered in the shade outside the rink building, except by mutual consent.

4th. The Winning Club, at the beginning of any season, shall, unless sooner defeated, play at least six matches therein should as many clubs have sent in challenges, but shall not be obliged to play more, and shall hold itself in readiness to play the first match within 15 days after the formation of the first sheet of playing ice, and at intervals of 15 days thereafter while continuing to hold the Cup, till the aforesaid number of matches has been completed; and if, during such season, any other club wins the Cup, the same rule as to the interval of 15 days must be followed, and such club, as well as any subsequent Winning Club during that season, must play as many matches as, added to those already played, will complete the number of six matches during said season.

5th. Challenges must be accepted in rotation and registered in the club minutes, and all Challenges must follow the Cup.

6th. The receipt of any Challenge must be acknowledged within 5 days thereafter, and in the event of its being received out of curling season, its acceptance or otherwise must be notified to the Challenging Club immediately after the formation of the first sheet of playing Ice.

7th. Should the club holding the cup use metal, and the Challenging Club use stone, or *vice versa*, the match must be played with an equal portion of metal and stone, unless by mutual consent, each club respectively providing the metal or stone for the other.

8th. The number of Rinks in all matches must not exceed four, nor be less than two, at the option of the challenging Club, the number to be mentioned in the challenge.

9th. The time of each match to be not less than four hours, but more if agreed upon.

10th. In the event of the club holding the Cup being unwilling or unable to play the challenging club or clubs in their rotation, the one first entitled to a match is also entitled to the Cup, subject to the foregoing conditions.

11th. All matches must be governed by the rules of play adopted by the Royal Caledonian Curling Club, and in the event of any dispute arising with respect to the rules of play, or the interpretation of these conditions, the branch here is to be considered the exponent and judge, subject to appeal to the parent society.

12th. The Quebec Curling Club reserves the right, at the beginning of every season, to amend or add to these conditions, should the changing circumstances of Curling seem, in their opinion, to warrant its exercise.

C.F. SMITH,
President.
GEO. ROLT WHITE,
Secretary.

Quebec Curling Club,
1st December, 1877.

HOCKEY

AN EARLY NEWSPAPER REPORT, 1875

The following is one of the first newspaper accounts of an ice hockey match in Canada. The contest matched nine men from a Montreal football club against a team of nine skaters. This story is reprinted from The Gazette (Montreal), 17 March 1875.

VICTORIA SKATING RINK.

The hockey match which was played at the Victoria Skating Rink yesterday afternoon was a great success. There was a very large attendance of spectators, who seemed to take a lively interest in the game.

The only drawback to the thorough enjoyment of the match was the state of the ice, which had just enough water on its surface to render a tumble anything but a dry and uninteresting proceeding. And it was not alone the players whom this condition of the ground affected. Every other minute the little circle of wood, which did duty for the ball, would get knocked close up to the spectators, and in the frequent scrimmages to draw the game more toward the centre the spectators would get very liberally drenched. Such little mishaps, however, were taken with great good nature, a hearty laugh and merry smile being the only token that some fair lady had been victimised....

The Foot Ball team wore their uniform of red and black stripes, which looked, if somewhat odd, certainly picturesque, and very easily separated the two sets of players; the other nine were chiefly distinguishable by the sign of the white shirt. As far as appearances gave any indication, the Foot Ball men were by far the stronger crew, and this seemed likely to be confirmed in the outset, the first game being won by them in 8 minutes, with some first-rate play. The next game was taken by the whites, and with an even score the third game was started, both sides laying themselves out to their work with an evident determination to be the victors. After three quarters of an hour's play, the game finally resulted in favor of the reds.

And here the tide of victory turned, and the whites took game after game, till the score stood in their favor at 5 to 2. Captain Creighton, whose individual play deserves a special encomium, did all he could to get his men well together and make them play into each other's hands, but to no purpose. They seemed to have lost that organized system which distinguished their play at the beginning of the afternoon, and the result was a well deserved victory for their opponents, who certainly did play exceedingly well and with remarkable science. On this side, Messrs. Barnston, Torrance, Gough and Baylis are deserving of special commendation for their smart and plucky play; and of the foot ball nine Captain Creighton, Mr. Clouston, the two Campbells and Messrs. Joseph and Henshaw may fairly be singled out as having shown themselves exceedingly proficient in this somewhat rough and ready game, the last mentioned gentleman (Mr. Henshaw), notwithstanding the success of the other side, being a most wary and valuable goal keeper, and but for whom the score would have shown up still worse for the red stripes.

The band played a number of lively airs during the afternoon, and what with the music and the laughter, the place seemed quite gay, players and spectators evidently enjoying the fun immensely, though it must have been aggravating to some of the hockey men, as occasionally happened, to find themselves on their backs in the water and to hear the peals of merry, good-natured laughter that sprang from white throats warmly nestling among their furry wrappings.

MONTREAL FOOT BALL CLUB VS. VICTORIA SKATING CLUB, 1876

This report suggests the social appeal of the new sport. It is reprinted from The Gazette (Montreal), 7 February 1876.

HOCKEY ON THE ICE.

The absence of their Excellencies Lord and Lady Dufferin, and the low temperature of the atmosphere account in great measure without doubt for the diminished attendance, yet despite these two circumstances the spectators, both ladies and gentlemen, towards four o'clock were quite numerous. The Foot Ball Team played in their uniform—red and black striped jerseys, &c., the Victoria Club in their shirt sleeves, with red sashes round their waists, and many of the ladies wore the colors of their favorite side. The band of the Victoria Rifles played throughout the afternoon. The game was conducted under the "Hockey Association" rules, Messrs. W. Hutton, President of the Rink, and Philip Cross acting as umpires. The game was extremely lively and interesting, and while the cold was kept at back by wrappers and overcoats, was watched with the greatest interest. It opened at 2.45, the ball having been placed in the centre of the Rink, and in a moment there was abundance of entertainment provided. Skaters darted hither and thither in the most vigorous confusion; several coming with alarming rapidity to a point—a shock—and two measured their length on the ice. A scramble, the puck is away and glides to the feet of two young ladies, who smilingly watch the sport; a rush for the coveted object and a youth of lengthy proportions stumbles, with the greatest possible awkwardness, into one of the young ladies' laps—shock No. 2—but no casualties to record. She blushes, he reddens, the spectators laugh, and he is away to fresh fields and pastures new. A couple of the players are noticed as having a *penchant* for losing momentary command of their legs, and surveying the scene from a seated position. Each assault upon the ice, which has long been white with the cuttings flying from the glistening and swift-moving steel, leaves a perceptible mark, and the number of falls may be counted almost as easily as the rings of a tree. An unexpected collapse has a natural tendency to make people laugh, and such occasions were of frequent occurrence. Collisions were, however, inevitable, and they were taken by the players with the greatest possible good humor, though, as may be readily imagined, bruises as a consequence were far from being exceptions.

The differences of style in the play of the two teams was at once apparent, the Foot Ball nine following the peculiarities of their own game, the "forwards" keeping "on the ball" as much as possible, and the "half-backs" watching every chance for a "run in," while the "backs" took care of the ball when played past their own men. The Victoria Team, on the other hand, not having any definite arrangement of their men, appeared to trust to their individual skill to be in the right place at the right time. Their defence and organization—the strong points of the Foot Ball Team—gave them a great advantage over their opponents, as far as the play went, though the Victorias, whose nine comprised many of the best skaters in the Rink, and consequently showed to more advantage on the ice than the Foot Ball men (who have a very limited choice), made up in skating and quickness much of what they lost in organization. The Foot Ball Team were, moreover, unable to secure the aid of some of their best players, and showed great pluck, under the circumstances, in challenging such a notable skating club as the Victorias.

The Foot Ball Team had the best of the first half hour's play, and a goal was, after a short struggle, very prettily scored for them by Gough. Ends were then changed, but with no definite result until "time" was called. After some ten minutes' play of the second half-hour, the ball went off Esdaile's foot just through the posts, having been incautiously played in front of goal by a Foot Ball man. Great cheering followed this victory, and, encouraged by their success, the Victorias made a desperate attack on their opponents' goal, playing all they knew. The ball was dangerously near the Foot Ball goal line—in spite of the efforts of their "forwards"—nearly the whole time, and the utmost caution of their "backs" and goal-keeper was needed to save their flags. In this emergency the skill and coolness of the Foot Ball goal-keeper were admirably displayed. Shot after shot, straight at the goal, was made by Taylor, Barnston and Torrance, and was played off with equal precision. The play of the Victorias was excellent, and the Foot Ball "backs" had all they could do to keep off their adversaries, whose clever skating and greater quickness were too much for the "forwards," but here all the coolness and decision won in many a hard fought match came to their aid, and the second half hour ended with no further advantage to the Victorias.

Through the third and final half-hour, the contest was keenly disputed, each side being anxious to score the game and win the victory. The Foot Ball men having got their "second wind," showed again the doggedness and persistency so characteristic of their play, and in spite of the best endeavors of both sides, no "goal" was won, and when—soon after four o'clock—"time" was called, the match ended in a draw....

EARLY RULES, 1877

This story describes a match for a dinner between eight gentlemen of the St. James' Club and eight of the Metropolitan Club at the Victoria Skating Rink in Montreal. St. James' colors were blue and white; the Metropolitan's were red and black. The Metropolitans won easily, despite playing one man short. The officials included umpires for each side and one referee for the match. The rules reprinted here very closely resemble field hockey rules written in England in 1875. This piece first appeared in The Gazette (Montreal), 27 February 1877.

THE RULES OF THE GAME

1. The game shall be commenced and renewed by a Bully in the centre of the ground. Goals shall be changed after each game.

2. When a player hits the ball, any one of the same side who at such a moment of hitting is nearer to the opponents' goal line is out of play, and may not touch the ball himself, or in any way whatever prevent any other player from doing so until the ball has been played. A player must always be on his own side of the ball.

3. The ball may be stopped, but not carried or knocked on by any part of the body. No player shall raise his stick above his shoulder. Charging from behind, tripping, collaring, kicking or shinning shall not be allowed.

4. When the ball is hit behind the goal line by the attacking side, it shall be brought out straight 15 yards, and started again by a Bully; but, if hit behind by any of the side whose goal line it is, a player of the opposite side shall it [sic] out from within one yard

of the nearest corner, no player of the attacking side at that time shall be within 20 yards of the goal line, and the defenders, with the exception of the goal-keeper, must be behind their goal line.

5. When the ball goes off at the side, a player of the opposite side to that which hit it out shall roll it out from the point on the boundary line at which it went off at right angles with the boundary line, and it shall not be in play until it has touched the ice, and the player rolling it in shall not play it until it has been played by another player, every player being then behind the ball.

6. On the infringement of any of the above rules, the ball shall be brought back and a Bully shall take place.

7. All disputes shall be settled by the Umpires, or in the event of their disagreement, by the Referee.

THE PLAY

commenced at 4:30 and continued for three-quarters of an hour at a stretch, the total result of the games to be called at the termination of the second three-quarters of an hour. The ice was soft and the general condition of the rink was not favorable for good play. Probably in no game is there to be seen so much "bullying" as in this. Indeed, the "bully" is indispensable, for without, hockey is a thing of naught. However, the term although not euphonious, is merely a technical one, with which every hockey player is familiar.

The St. James' men soon distinguished themselves through their captain, who turned a complete somersault, which, doubtless, under other circumstances, he would never have thought it possible he could achieve. Even a professional acrobat would have envied that well-formed body describing a circle through space and alighting with an ominous thump on the wet and soft ice. Galt, on the same side, was the next to fall, and he fell nobly, while his stick got between another man's legs in the most extraordinary manner. And then came the fun. To an outsider the falls seemed to be an important part of the game. It was soon seen that the St. James' men were not sound on their legs, although the sound on their sticks could be heard all over the building. It was a good moral sight to see the disappointment which several shaky gentlemen experienced in failing to get at the ball. The interest soon became concentrated at the west end goals (the St. James') and fruitless efforts were made to get the ball through, but thanks to the energy of the St. James' goal-keeper, and the length of his body, he kept it at a safe distance from the flags. Here Joseph made some fine play, and Whitehead distinguished himself by knocking the ball, and were about to add a player too, almost out of time. Geddes soon came to the rescue, and toying with the ball in his peculiar and graceful way, succeeded in putting it through the goal and scoring the first game for the Metropolitans. Time, 15 minutes.

THE SECOND GAME.

The St. James' men looked disappointed but hopeful, and went to work with a will. But their legs were "unreliable" and went under, leaving them deposited on the ice while the ball was—somewhere else. During several of these *melees,* Hart saved the game by this elongated stopping, but unfortunately for the St. James' men, Creighton made some admirable play into Geddes' hands, who put the ball through in a twinkling, thus scoring the second game for the Metropolitans. Time, 3 minutes.

THE THIRD GAME.

Whitehead now changed places with Hart, and kept goal, the former playing forward. Gordon, of the St. James', here showed some good play, but [illegible] for the frailty of the human understanding! down he went, and remained there for a minute. He got up and looked regretfully at the ball at the other end of the rink, and bided his time. David and Whitehead next got hold of it, but it again slipped through their fingers. Hart saved the goal several times and the contest became hot and keen, the St. James' men showing that they were on their metal, but the Metropolitans were too many for them, and Geddes again took the ball from their men and sent it through the goal for the third time, making the third game for his side. Time, 7 minutes.

THE FOURTH GAME

was long and earnest. The goals were changed, and the St. James' men resolved either "to do or die." Hart proved to be the saviour of his side on half a dozen occasions, when by really clever playing he saved the ball passing the flag by purely physical exertion. "We haven't had a single chance of a goal yet," he remarked mournfully, and by way of reviving the energies of his side he issued stentorian instructions, but the energy of the St. James' men had become a thing of the past. Falls were frequent, and several unavoidable blows were exchanged instead of cards, with no other unpleasant results than a few bruises and much wet clothing. But fate seemed against the St. James' men and "time" was called at 6 o'clock when the Referee decided that the St. James' men had lost the match. In point of superiority the Metropolitans had decidedly the advantage as they were more active, better skaters, and played with some show of science. However, the next interesting point will be the dinner, which no doubt will be a good one and about which we presume there will not be two opinions.

SKATING

PROGRAMME OF THE SKATING CONGRESS, 1868

The following description of skating movements was prepared by Mr. Eugene B. Cook, an enthusiastic supporter of the sport, who aimed to establish a permanent code for contestants. These regulations are reprinted from Henry Chadwick, *Handbook of Winter Sports, Embracing Skating, Rink-Ball, Curling, Ice-Boating and American Football* (New York, 1879), pp. 23-24.

No. 1. Plain Forward and Backward Movement.—This is simply the plainest form of skating, and the step taken is a short one in comparison to that of the outside roll.

No. 2. Lap Foot—As in the Field Step and in Cutting a Circle.—This is the movement preliminary to the acquirement of the outside edge roll. It consists of a series of forward [steps?] as in which one foot laps over the other, thereby obliging the skater to form a circle.

No. 3. Outside Edge Roll Forward.—By this the skater makes almost half a circle, while leaning alternately to the right and left on the outer edge of his skate. It is one of the easiest and most graceful of the programme figures.

No. 4. Outside Edge Roll Backward.—This is the same style of movement made while going backward. In doing both of these rolls the skater, at the finish of each roll, changes the edges slightly so as to obtain the necessary impetus for the roll on the other side.

No. 5. Inside Edge Roll Forward.—This is the same form of roll as the outer edge, as regards the extent of the circle, only it is made on the inside edge. It is in fact an extension of the plain forward movement, substituting half-circles on the inside instead of a short and nearly straight cut.

No 6. Inside Edge Roll Backward.—This is the same movement done backward. It is more difficult to accomplish than the outer edge backward, the loss of balance being easier.

No. 7. The Cross Roll Forward.—This is simply an extension of the lap foot movement—a sort of reserve of the outside edge roll, in one respect. It is the primary movement in learning most of the difficult figures which follow it.

No. 8. The Cross Roll Backward.—The same movement, only in a more difficult form, being done backward.

No. 9. Change Of Edge Roll, Forward—Beginning Either On Outside Or Inside Edge.—This enables the skater to make a double curved line, the one following the outside edge roll half-circle being made on the other side by a dextrous turn of the foot from one edge to the other. The two lines thus made form the outside lines of an oblong figure of eight.

No. 10.-Change Of Edge Roll, Backward.—This is the same except in its being a backward movement and more difficult in balancing on the change.

The above are the essential rules to becoming a good skater.

The remainder of the movements of the programmes are as follows:

No. 11. —(a)—"On To Richmond."—This is, cross one foot in front of the other, and with back stroke the outside edge go backward or forward.

(b)—Reverse "On To Richmond."—That is going forward by forward outside edge. Stroke given alternately by each leg.

No. 12. "Locomotives"—Forward, backward, sideways—single and double.

No. 13.—Waltz-step.

No. 14.—Spread Eagles. Inside and outside edges.

No. 15.—Figure Threes (a)—Beginning inside or outside edge. On field and in eight. Including "flying threes."

(b) Double three, beginning inside or outside edge.

No. 16.—Grape-Vines.—Including "Philadelphia Twist Vine," etc.

No. 17.—Toe and Heel Movements.—Embracing pivot-circles, toe spins (*pirouelles*), and movements on both toes, etc.

No. 18.—Single Flat Foot Spins, and double foot whirls.

No. 19.—Serpentines. (a)—Single foot forward and backward; right and left.

(b)—Following feet—forward and backward; right and left. In "two foot eight."

No. 20.—Figure Eight.—On one foot, forward.

No. 21.—Figure Eight.—On one foot, backward.

No. 22.—Changes of Edge.—Single and double.

No. 23.—One Foot Loops.—Inside and outside edges. Simple and combination.

No. 24.—One Foot Ringlets.—Inside and outside edges. Simple and in combination.

No. 25.—Specialties.—Embracing original and peculiar movements.

No. 26.—General Display of Combined Movements, at the option of the contestants.

WOMEN'S SKATING

Skating was one of the few sports in which females participated in North America during the 1860s and 1870s. But the following newspaper report suggests that many girls and young women were reluctant to compete in public in front of large audiences and members of the press. This story first appeared in The American Chronicle of Sports and Pastimes, 16 January 1868, p. 18.

THE LADIES' PRIZE CONTEST

was another interesting feature of the skating occurrences of the week. The affair took place on Major Oatman's cozy skating pond, on the corner of Fifth avenue and Fifty-ninth street, on Saturday the 11th instant. The Major had made every preparation calculated to lead to a very successful and attractive display of fancy skating by most of the lady experts of the city who are ambitious of skating fame; but though he had a glittering field of ice, a fine day—sunshiny, though the air was keen—a large crowd of outside spectators, which is a very important feature to contestants in skating for prizes, and a very fashionable attendance of visitors on the pond, the affair did not prove to be as successful as anticipated, the display on the occasion being decidedly mediocre in comparison to what could have been done had our most skilled lady skaters entered the list as competitors. As it was, but two ladies entered their names as contestants, and though this limited number did not warrant the tender of the valuable prize, Mr. Oatman very liberally allowed it to be competed for rather than disappoint the assemblage present. The prize was valued at $50, and was a very handsome one indeed. It consisted of a gold wreath, with a star in the centre, to which was attached a golden skate of the New York Club pattern. This was suspended, by a blue silk ribbon, from a scroll on which was inscribed the words, "The ball is up," a gold ball being on the face of the scroll. It was 4 P.M. before preparations were made for the contest, the delay being occasioned by the absence of some of the best lady skaters, who were expected to take part in the match. At that hour a portion of the pond was roped in, and judges were selected from among leading members of the New York Skating Club present, those chosen being Mrs. E.F. Miller and Messrs. H.P. Sears and A.P. Baudoine. An immense crowd of spectators surrounded the outside of the pond on all sides, while on the ice the largest assemblage seen on this Fifth avenue pond this season were gathered, considerable interest being taken in the proceedings. The only contestants who entered were Mrs. Whitney, one of the fair skaters of Boston, and Mrs. Jackson, a lady skater well known on the Brooklyn ponds. The former was very modestly attired in black silk, and not *en costume* for the occasion; while Mrs. Jackson was dressed in a very handsome skating sacque and cap, trimmed with white fur, and she presented quite an attractive appearance. The trial of skill commenced with the outside roll backwards and forwards, the New York Club programme being used for the occasion.

In the first series of movements, including the forward, backward, cross-foot, and other variations of the outside edge movements, Mrs. Whitney, of Boston, took the lead, her skating being very graceful and easy. But when the more complicated movements of the club programme were tried, Mrs. Jackson, of Brooklyn, excelled, the Boston lady not having practised them. As Mrs. Jackson scored the greatest number of points, she took the prize medal, the score standing 29 to 20 in her favor. Mrs. Miller, one of the most finished of our lady skaters, one of the judges on the occasion, before and after the contest was the most observed of the fair ones on the pond, from her grace of movement and skillful execution of the intricate figures now in vogue among the fancy skaters at the park ponds. We noticed, also, a very pretty girl in a brown dress, accompanied by a good skater, and also two young Misses, who are promising performers....

The principal objection on the part of the lady skaters to these contests is, that they are so publicly advertised that it places them in the light of professionals, and though we do not know of any reasonable objection on this account, still our lady amateurs do not seek such notoriety by any means. Anything of the kind of a private character, would, no doubt, be participated in by many who do not care to see their names in print as professionals. But there are some independent enough to enter the lists without regard to the notoriety attached to a contest of the kind, while others take part in these affairs just for the frolic of them.

AMERICAN SKATING CONGRESS, 1871

The first efforts to found a national skating organization in the United States began in Pittsburgh in February, 1868, when a small group of enthusiasts issued a call to clubs around the country for support for the new American Skating Congress. But the response was disappointing both at that meeting and also the session of 1869, held in March in Rochester. The next appeal met a more favorable reception, as delegates from eleven clubs gathered in New York City and Brooklyn in February, 1871. Most of the clubs represented were from the New York City vicinity, but there were a few gentlemen present from New England, upstate New York, and Canada. The meeting approved a new constitution and championship code. Its revised programme of movements closely resembled the regulations established a few years earlier by the New York Skating Club. The following rules for the championship are reprinted from The New York Clipper, 18 February 1871, p. 364.

RULES GOVERNING CONTESTS FOR THE CHAMPIONSHIP

1. The emblem of the Championship of America shall be held for two years, subject to the challenge of all comers; the holder, however, shall not be compelled to accept any challenge for a less sum than $100 a side, which is to accompany any challenger, to make it binding, unless the challenge is accompanied by a consent of both champion and challenger to the forfeit being waived. All challenges to be through the President of the Congress, who is to be stakeholder.

2. The holder of the champion emblem shall be compelled to skate at any match within two weeks from the time he is challenged (if there is good ice, of which the stakeholder, or such person or persons as he may appoint, are to be judges), or forfeit the emblem, the time to date from the time the stakeholder notifies the champion (which he shall lose no time in doing, and the delivery of a telegram or letter at the usual place of residence of the champion shall be deemed notification) that he is challenged, the champion to have the naming of the day for the match, giving the President of the Congress seven days notice thereof.

3. The champion and challenger may mutually agree when to skate a pending match, provided that the place agreed upon shall be either a rink or park represented in the Congress, and that the President of the Congress shall be notified of such agreement, within one week from the time that the champion is notified that he is challenged. In the event of the President not being notified of such agreement within said time he shall be at liberty to fix the time and place for the contest, giving both champion and challenger three days' notice thereof. In the selection of the place, the President shall choose (as far as consistent with the hereinafter mentioned considerations) the rink or park, represented in the Congress, nearest to, equidistant by ordinary mode of travel from the residences of the champion and challenger, if they reside in different places, but he shall take into consideration the probable amount of entrance money to be obtained at different places and the general interests of the champion and challenger, or he may ignore the question of equidistance entirely if he obtains the consent of both contestants.

4. The person who shall first challenge the winner of a match about to come off is entitled to priority, but the party who has once contended unsuccessfully with the champion during his championship is prohibited from re-challenging until ten days have elapsed after his defeat, so as to give other skaters a chance to contest.

5. All matches for the championship shall be *bona fide,* and any party guilty of disreputable conduct in regard to the matches for the championship shall be deemed

in disgrace, and will not be recognized at our future meetings or in our social gatherings.

6. In all contests for the championship there shall be three judges, who shall be selected by the President of the Congress. They shall be men of known integrity and ability, and, as far as practicable, acceptable to the contestants. The President shall as soon as possible notify the contestants who the judges that he has selected are. If the contestants and president all consent, with a view to saving of expense, that there shall be but one judge, that shall suffice; but such judge shall be appointed by the President, and the decision of that judge shall be final; if there are three judges, the decision of any two shall be final. In the selection of a judge or judges the President may consult with the executive committee, or as many of them as practicable.

7. If the champion fails to comply with any of the conditions prescribed in these rules he shall forfeit the emblem of championship to the challenge, but no money stake; if the challenger fails to comply with any of the said conditions he shall forfeit to the champion the money stake (if any) in the hands of the stakeholder, and shall also forfeit all right to proceed with the then pending match.

8. Any person winning the championship is bound by the above and any future laws that may be adopted by the American Skating Congress, and the President may require him (if he shall deem it necessary) to give security for the safe keeping of the emblem while in his possession, and the surrender of it to him, or such persons as he may appoint, before the commencement of a contest; therefore, in order that it may be presented to the winner after the decision of the contest, or if he shall fail to comply with the laws of the Congress, but should he hold it successfully for two years, it shall then become his absolute property, and he may retire as ex-champion.

9. Although it is heretofore provided that the champion shall hold the emblem subject to challenge for two years, yet it is hereby declared that if, seven days previous to the expiration of the two years, there shall be no match pending or challenge in the hands of the President, none can be received except by consent of the champion, whose time shall be virtually considered to have expired; any match, however, pending seven days previous to the expiration of two years must be skated, and the two years shall not be considered to have expired until the match is decided, unless there shall be no ice in that season to skate it, in which case the match shall be off and the champion shall retain the emblem permanently.

SKATING IN MONTREAL, 1876

Canadians also organized intercity skating tournaments. The following account of a competition at the Victoria Skating Rink in Montreal suggests that the judges weighed both technical skill and artistic elegance in choosing the champions. It is reprinted from The Gazette (Montreal), 5 and 9 February 1876.

SKATING TOURNAMENT.

The announcement that the tournament would commence at the Rink yesterday afternoon attracted a very large number of visitors to the scene, and as early as one o'clock desirable seats were occupied by parties of ladies and gentlemen interested either directly in the young gentlemen and lady competitors for honors in the skating art, or in witnessing what must of necessity be the best skating of the season. The boys under fifteen years of age were to commence at two o'clock, the Misses under fifteen shortly afterwards, while the ladies' match was to take place just before the close, at half-past four o'clock. About half-past two o'clock the Governor-General, Lady Dufferin and party arrived and were soon in the place of honor on the dais. His Excellency, however, donned his skates and was soon skimming over the clear ice, taking great interest in the competition. As one after another of the young gentlemen essayed his task, Lord Dufferin gave proof of his own powers, quietly cutting a few figures—threes, eights, rolls and other intricate movements—in a style that showed plainly he was no novice in the art. Dressed in an overcoat of sealskin, trimmed with otter, that came well down over pantaloons of grey that in turn adjusted themselves nattily over the dashing pair of club skates that fitted neatly the Balmoral boot, His Excellency showed the vigor of a young man, and the causal observer viewed with some surprise the curly iron-grey locks that fell below the otter band of his sealskin cap, drawn down well upon his ears.

As we have said, it was expected that some of the best skating of the season would be witnessed, and the expectation was more than realized. The writer has witnessed tournaments in New York, Chicago and Boston, and must accord to Montreal the palm for skaters; in fact it is matter of notoriety that St. Lawrence skaters are the finest in the world. To the ladies especially do these remarks apply, for the grace and elegance of their skating was delightful in the extreme. The programme for the gentlemen numbers the following movements from which it will be observed that the test is an extremely trying one. 1. Plain forward and backward; 2. Roll do do do; 3. Outside edge, forward and backward; 4. Inside do do do do; 5. Single and double threes, on each foot, alternately, on inside and outside edges; 6. Plain eights, forward and backward; 7. Double do do do do; 8. Bracket do; 9. Loop do; 10. Slip do; 11. Endless do; 12. Front and back roll with loops and threes; 13. Grape vines; 14. Philadelphias; 15. Endless bracket; 16. Locomotives; 17. Shamrocks; 18. Pyramids; 19. Serpentine roll, once round rink, forward and backward; 20. Specialties.

E. Reinhardt, P. Besserer and Philip Mussen were the competitors, and the prize fell to the first named.

The competition for the Misses' prize did not take place, there being only one entry made, while the rules of the rink allow no prize to be given unless three competitors enter. This occasioned some surprise to His Excellency, and he expressed himself somewhat disappointed at it. Nothing is so pretty a sight as to see a group of young Misses, and it was matter for regret to all that there was no competition.

Next came the ladies competition, and Miss C. Fairbairn, Miss Bethune, Miss Clare and Miss Rhynas were the competitors. The first-named won the Governor-General's medal, and Miss Bethune the Rink prize, though the skating was so well together nearly all through as to make it impossible to the uninitiated to observe the difference.

The following programme, however, gave the judges the opportunity of discriminating:—Plain forward, plain backward, roll forward, roll backward, outside edge, forward; outside edge, backward; plain three, both feet, each alternately; double three, both feet, each alternately; plain eight, two feet forward; plain eight, two feet backward; double eight, plain outside edge; eight, with loops; back and front roll, with loops and threes; back grape vine; specialties.

This closed the afternoon skating, and His Excellency and party left the Rink about half-past five.

The attendance in the evening was very large, the ladies being well represented; Her Excellency, Countess Dufferin, was present, but Lord Dufferin was absent in consequence of a slight indisposition.

Three graceful little misses—Miss Barlow, Miss Craig, and Miss Jones, all of this city, the two latter merely entering to fill up the required number,—skated for a club prize, which was won of course by Miss Barlow, who won the highest encomiums and the hearty plaudits of the spectators for her extreme gracefulness, proficiency, and dexterity.

W.W. Hart, of St. John, New Brunswick, Curran Morrison, of Toronto, B.A. Taylor, E.H. Goff, and T.L. Barlow, entered for the Governor-General's Medal; and F. Jarvis and W. Barnston, Montreal, W.W. Hart, St. John, N.B., B.A. Taylor, Montreal, Curran Morrison, Toronto, E.H. Goff, T. L. Barlow and A. Torrance, of Montreal, for a special prize—a medal offered for competition by Messers. Barney & Berry, skate manufacturers, of Springfield, Massachusetts. The competitions were not finished at eleven o'clock, when they were adjourned until this afternoon. Her Excellency, on leaving her seat, was conducted down ice and to the entrance of the Rink, by Mr. Hutton. The Judges, however, decided that Governor-General's medal lay between Messers. Barlow and Taylor; and the Barney and Berry prize between Messrs. Barnston and Jarvis, previous winners of the Governor-General's medal, and consequently debarred from the present competition. The gentlemen mentioned were frequently applauded; also Mr. Morrison, a very fine skater; he is a son of Mayor Morrison, of Toronto....

The close of the competition for the champion medals took place at the Victoria Skating Rink last night, the competitors for the Barney & Berry medal being Messrs. Barnston and Jarvis, and for the Governor-General's medal Messrs. Morrison, Taylor and Barlow.

Skating commenced soon after eight o'clock, each competitor in turn taking the ice. There was a very large attendance of spectators, who applauded most enthusiastically all through the performance. For the Barney & Berry medal, the judgment of the spectators all through seemed to be in favor of Mr. Barnston, and we should imagine the judges would have little difficulty in making a decision in this competition. They themselves say that such skating as Mr. Barnston's never was before seen in Canada, and, indeed, it would be hard to find anyone in the world, we should think, to exhibit a more perfect picture of grace and elegance than was shown in his movements last night. His programme of specialties comprised forty-eight different figures, which he skated without a single hitch, finishing off with cutting his initials—*W.S.B.*— on the ice in the most perfect manner imaginable. We most heartily congratulate Mr. Barnston on the acquisition of his well deserved honors, as every one must do who watched him skate—some with envious if admiring eyes, for there is a sort of *nascitur non fit* style in his graceful movements that makes one despair of ever coming anywhere near the champion.

The competition for the Governor-General's medal was a much closer contest, and though probably each spectator had his or her favorite among the three contestants, the result was still really in the balance until the marks were added up and the total came out in favor of Mr. Barlow. The ice was in beautiful condition, just soft enough to prevent the skate from slipping, and everything that could be desired for specialties. Mr. Morrison, who represented the Toronto Skating Club, seemed really more at home on the ice than either of his two adversaries. Some of his figures were, to all appearances, perfectly unique, the rapidity of his movements being something extraordinary, and the "locomotives" and figures on the point of the skate being especially wonderful. Mr. Morrison was loudly applauded as he went through each figure, and while we cannot help feeling a certain amount of pleasure in the fact that the medal has not gone from Montreal, we may assure the Toronto Skating Club that they have every reason to feel exceedingly proud of the prowess of their chosen representative, who gave undeniable proof that he required no one down here to give him lessons in skating, as a city sheet, in a recent issue, hinted in a most gratuitously insulting manner.

Mr. Taylor skated very nicely, but seemed rather nervous, and chose some not very pretty looking figures to commence with. We trust that this defeat, which, in view of the winner's excellent skating, is no dishonor, will not dishearten him from competing again, as there was really so little difference in the two performers that the judges must have had no small difficulty in deciding between them.

Mr. Barlow, the remaining competitor, and the winner, came nearer Mr. Barnston in the style and figures on the list of his specialties than any of the others. He received unlimited encouragement from the spectators, with whom he seemed to be a great favorite, and we think no one will venture to dispute the judges' decision in his favor, for he is, next to Mr. Barnston—the ladies, of course, excepted—the prettiest skater on the Rink.

The Tournament finished about half past ten, as soon as possible after which the result was announced by the judges. These gentlemen are also to be greatly congratulated upon the result, their post being, if honorable, an arduous and not very enviable one; but we think that there can be no two opinions as to the perfect judgment and fairness exercised in their selection of the victorious competitors. The Tournament was, taken all in all, a very excellent display of skating, and, especially last night's portion of it, perhaps the finest exhibition that has ever been witnessed in Canada.

SNOWSHOE RACING

The premier snowshoe organization in Canada was the Montreal Snow Shoe Club, which was reorganized at "Dolly's chop house" in 1850. Its activities, which were widely adopted by other associations, included "musters" twice weekly. At its regular "tramps," the ranking officer took the lead and no one could pass him without his permission. The "whipper-in" was an experienced snowshoer who brought up the rear and kept everyone together. The club also sponsored races and long-distance cross country steeplechase events. The following is a description of a typical annual competition, reprinted from The Gazette (Montreal), 15 February 1875.

MONTREAL SNOW SHOE CLUB — GRAND ANNUAL MEETING.

The first meeting of the season came off Saturday afternoon on the Montreal Lacrosse Grounds. The day was rather cold for watching the sport, but notwithstanding this several hundreds of our citizens assembled, the Grand Stand being well crowded. The large number of fashionably dressed ladies whose presence graced the occasion seemed to enjoy the sport, and their sparkling eyes and smiling faces, with an occasional peal of merry laughter at a luckless tumble, added an additional charm to the fascination of Saturday afternoon's races, and made tumbles frequent.... The Committee of Observation in the trees and on the fences did not turn out in large numbers, but made up any deficiency of that kind by the attention and earnestness with which they viewed the sport and applauded their favorites.

THE TRACK

was unusually heavy from the large quantity of snow which had fallen during the week, and the time was accordingly much slower than it would have been with a harder track. The back stretch was the best spot for a "brush," and here it was that any attempts in that line were made. A short turn at the end of the back stretch and a slight slope just before turning into the "home" made it disagreeable work for runners. That part of the track opposite the Grand Stand was the scene of the dash and hurdle races, and was much cut up, the runner having the choice of place, gaining considerable advantage thereby. However, all things considered, there have been worse tracks, and better time made on them in the old days when Maltby, Harper, Armstrong, Robinson, Rose, James, Frank Wood and other "cracks" made warm work for the winners of a race or were to the fore themselves. The

INDIAN RACE

brought out Kerarонwe, Daillebout, Thomas and three or four other redskins. Keraronwe took the lead and kept it to the finish, followed by Lefebvre, Daillebout and Thomas, the rest being nowhere. Indian races as a general thing are stereotyped affairs, Keraronwe being sure to win on all occasions.

THE HUNDRED YARDS

was in heats; best two in three, and R. Stewart, C. McIvor and R. Summerhayes started. In the first heat Summerhayes was victorious in 13 1/2 seconds, with Stewart second and McIvor third. In the second heat Summerhayes came to grief in the deep snow, and fell, Stewart winning the heat in 14 1/2 seconds, with McIvor second, Summerhayes finishing his distance. The third heat and race was won by Summerhayes in 12 1/2 seconds, Stewart second and McIvor third. The

TWO MILE CLUB RACE

for the club cup was contested by six competitors, T. Hodgson, George Roy, W.W. McLarin, H. Downs, McNabb, McKenzie and Summerhayes. At the word "go" Roy went off at a warm pace, followed by Summerhayes, Hodgson, Downs, and McKenzie. On the "back stretch" Hodgson challenged the leader, and after a slight brush took first place, closely waited on by Roy, McLaren about twenty yards behind, the rest coming on slowly. The first quarter was reached by Hodgson in 1 34. On commencing the second quarter all dropped off except Hodgson, Roy and McLaren, who finished the half mile in this order in 3 14—Hodgson and Roy close together, with McLaren thirty yards behind. The third lap in 5 08 was much the same as the second, except that McLaren dropped out, leaving the race between Hodgson and Roy, and in this order the mile was arrived at in 7 02 and the 5th quarter in 8 53. On entering the 6th lap, Hodgson looked rather weary, while young Roy seemed to be taking things coolly, and some thought he would be good for the race—10 48. The 7th round was very like the 6th, and 12 44 was the time. The 8th and last quarter was now looked for with much interest, many thinking Roy sure of the prize, but on turning into the "home stretch" Hodgson put on a spurt and won the race at a gallop in 14 21; Roy second, about 30 yards behind.

HALF MILE, OPEN.

W. Roy and McKensie of the Montreal club, and McKenna of the Canada, entered for this race. McKensie went off at a hot pace, closely followed by Roy, with McKenna in company. The quarter was made in 1 24, and the pace was so hot that McKensie ran into the dressing room, which example was followed by McKenna, leaving the race to Roy, who cantered over the course, and won the race in 3 12 1/2.

BOYS UNDER 4 FEET.

Whether from the difficulty of finding boys of the required shortness who are able to run a quarter on snow-shoes or not we do not know, but only two youngsters entered—T McNulty and Dowd. Dowd got a toss in the snow, and McNulty won the race. The next race was the

HALF-MILE DASH

in uniform, for members of the club who were not winners of a race previously. The race brought out six members in full uniform, looking very pretty in their white blanket coats, red sashes and blue tuques, as they dashed off at the word. The runners kept dropping off one by one until Kearns had the track to himself, and this young gentleman won the race in 3 11. "The race of the day" was now next on the programme and was looked forward to with great interest. It was the

OPEN QUARTER MILE.

Davy, of the Caledonian Club, and Summerhayes, of the Montreal, were the only competitors. Notwithstanding this, it was the most closely contested of all the races. At the word both started together, and there was a race for the lead, which was taken by Davy, Summerhayes being close behind. On the back stretch, however, Summerhayes went for his man and the pair raced together for more than a hundred yards neck and neck, amid the cheers of the excited spectators. At the end of the back stretch Davy had to give way and Summerhayes took the lead. It looked as though Davy would try for the lead again on the home stretch, but the speed of the leader was too much for him and he was shaken off by Summerhayes, who won by a dozen yards. Time 1 19 1/2.

THE OPEN MILE.

William Roy, Hodgson, of the Montreal and Laing of the Caledonia were the starters. Hodgson went off at a tremendous pace, evidently intending to "mark the time" for the others, Roy and Laing keeping well together. In this order the quarter in 1 25 was made, and Hodgson and Laing visited the dressing room leaving the race a rather tame affair, and a walk over for Roy, who finished the mile in 6 44 1/2.

THE LAST RACE

was a hurdle race over four hurdles, distance 100 yards; heats—best two in three, and was won by Hodgson in two straight heats beating Summerhayes, who was somewhat cramped by his exertions in the other races. The race brought the meeting to a close at about half past four o'clock. The Montreal Club have reason to feel proud of keeping all the open prizes in the Club; although the fact that there was very little competition may be urged there are clubs enough in the city to put competition in the field, and if any of them have the mettle they should have been on the track on Saturday afternoon to make the running more lively.

The system of starting was the old way by the word "Go," which is well enough when there are few competitors. The start by pistol shot, however, is much better, when there is a large field. The time was kept by Mr. George Robinson and Mr. Grant.

THE DINNER

of the Club came off Saturday night in the Terrapin Restaurant, and was attended by a very large number of the club members. In the absence of the President, Mr. Grant occupied the chair, supported on the right by the Honorary President, Mr. N. Hughes,

Dr. Hingston, Col. Bond and Maj. Whitehead. On the left of the chair were Alex McGibbon, Esq. and a large number of invited guests. Much regret was felt that Cols. Stevenson and Oglivie and other guests were unable to be present. The table was served in the Terrapin's best style, and the bill-of-fare was in keeping with the reputation of mine host, who evidently knows what snowshoers most do admire in the culinary art. The chair was taken at 8 o'clock, and after ample justice had been done to the good things provided, Mr. Hughes gave "The Queen," which was responded to by the National Anthem; in the course of his remarks, Mr. Hughes mentioned that loyalty was one of the features of the club and that he himself had once the honor of shouldering a musket in H.M.'s service. Then followed "The Royal Family," and "The Governor-General," both of which were received with loud cheers. A song "God Bless Our New Dominion," by D.E. Cameron, with a chorus by the club, was then given, after which a telegram was read from President Davidson, announcing the probability that he would be in time for "God Save the Queen," as the "express was on snowshoes." A song was given by D. Mills; "The Army and Navy," was then given, and responded to by Col. Bond and Major Whitehead, the former of whom advised the club to assist the volunteer force by joining the regiment of the latter in a body, the Major saying he would be very proud to command them if such should happen to be their wish....

AN INDIAN MEET

Snowshoe racing, an indigenous sport among Canadian Indians, was especially popular among the native peoples who inhabited the environs of Montreal. Some of the most skilled native lacrosse players (such as Keraronwe) were also expert snowshoers. As the following report suggests, whites were amused by these Indian displays of talent, but on certain occasions some of the spectators misbehaved. This piece first appeared in The Gazette (Montreal), 3 April 1876.

IROQUOIS CLUB RACES.

The races of the Caughnauwaga Snowshoe Club came off on Saturday afternoon. The mildness of the weather had the effect of attracting many spectators, a number of ladies also being present. The snow was soft and the track consequently heavy. The first race was for old-time champions and among the competitors were Thomas (old Thomas, as he is known) Francois Delorimier, Louis Lefebvre and Francis Albert. Old Thomas ran one of his waiting races, sticking at Albert's heels until the finish when he made a brush to pass him. Albert would not have this, however, and put out his hand to keep back the old man—the pair coming home with a rush together and abreast. Thomas entered a protest, claiming the race on a foul, which was allowed, and Albert went to second place. Time for the half-mile, 4.47. In the five-mile race, in which

Keraronwe was to take a fresh runner up each mile, and on the last two was to compete with Daillebout, Keraronwe was doomed to be the second man. He beat one after another of the first three Indians, but Daillebout was too much for him, and after running a stern chase for a mile and a half, he gave up and Daillebout cantered on, winning at his ease. Keraronwe was unlucky and lost time by his shoes coming off. The remaining races were uninteresting. A 40 yards race on all fours caused some merriment. The sight was original and funny, the men tripping and going head first into the snow several times, snowshoes on hands and feet being too much even for Indians. The Indian who won the heats is named in English Fly-away-all-to-nothing, his Indian cognomen being unpronounceable. In the boys' race for Indians and Whites, young White Eagle showed some splendid style, and beating McNeice a hundred yards in the half mile. This closed the sports, no entries being made for the white men's two-mile race. The races were badly conducted, all the loafers who generally crowd the fence when policemen are about, crowded—in the absence of these officials—into the field, walked over the track, pelted snow-balls first at each other, and afterwards at the ladies and gentlemen who passed out of the gate when the races closed. It was a disgraceful scene, and worthy the blackguardism for which Montreal roughs are becoming famous. Several exhibitions of fisticuffs occurred between persons who resented the snowball-throwing, but the odds were in favor of the loafers, and no policemen being present, arrests were not made. It is really too bad that this sort of thing should be tolerated in a city of this kind, and should it not be put an end to in some way, our sports of lacrosse and snowshoe are likely to be henceforth unattended by the fair sex—whose presence at athletic gatherings goes so far to popularize the games and pedestrianism.

THE LAWS OF SNOW SHOE RACING, 1878

By the late 1870s snowshoe racing in Canada had evolved from an indigenous Indian activity into a modern sport. The Montreal Snow Shoe Club took the lead in developing and promulgating rules to govern competition. The following code was revised, amended, and approved by that organization on December 11, 1878. It is reprinted from the papers of the Montreal Amateur Athletic Association, National Archives of Canada, with the permission of the Montreal Amateur Athletic Association.

I—OF THE SHOE.

1. The snowshoes shall be made of wood, and hide or gut.

2. The shoes, including strings shall not be less than 1 1/2 lbs. in weight, at start and finish of competitions and shall measure not less than 10 inches gut, in width.

3. In Boy's races, snowshoes of any width and weight may be used.

4. Objections to a Competitor's shoes must be made before the start.

II—OF STARTING.

1. All starting shall be by report of pistol after a preliminary caution.

2. A snap cap is a start.

3. There is no recall.

4. If any Competitor starts before the signal, he shall be put back one yard for each of the first two offences and disqualified upon a third repetition.

III—OF POSITION AT STARTING.

1. Competitors shall draw lots for choice of position at starting.

2. In races of heats, the Competitors' positions at the end of each heat shall decide their choice of positions at starting for the next heat.

IV.—OF HEAT RACES.

1. In races run in heats, competitors must race out their distance in order to qualify themselves for starting in the remaining heats.

2. Only the winners of heats shall be allowed to start for a fourth and deciding heat.

3. When a dead heat is run, the two making the dead heat are entitled to start as if each had won a heat.

4. The positions of Competitors in a race of heats shall be decided by their positions in the final heat. But the winner of a heat takes precedence of a non-winner, even though the latter shall beat him for place in the final heat.

V.—OF BRUSHING.

1. No Competitor shall cross the track of another Competitor to take it, until he shall be six feet in advance of that Competitor.

2. In races round a course, a Competitor must pass on the outside. But if a Competitor in advance deliberately draws out of his track and leaves his successor room to pass him on the inside, that successor may do so.

VI.—OF DISQUALIFICATIONS.

1. The judges may disqualify a Competitor for persistent false starts, for disobedience to their orders or to those of the starter, or for deliberately jostling or impeding any other Competitor.

VII.—OF WINNING.

1. That Competitor is winner, whose breast first reaches the tape.

VIII.—OF HURDLE RACES.

1. In hurdle races a runner who leaps on a hurdle, runs through or around it, vaults it, or passes it in any other way than by fairly leaping over it, commits a foul and shall be disqualified.

IX. OF RUNNING FRAUDULENTLY.

1. Whenever a competitor shall not run to win, he shall be disqualified for twelve months from starting for any race governed by these rules.

X.—OF LOSING A SHOE.

1. So long as both snowshoes remain attached to the feet or ankles a runner may continue his race.

2. A runner cannot, however carry his shoe in his hand in event of its slipping from his feet.

XI.—OF ASSISTANCE.

1. It shall be considered foul for any Competitor to be assisted by any one during a race whomsoever, when such assistance necessitates touching that Competitor.

XII.—OF ACCIDENTS AND INTERFERENCES.

1. In cases where a Competitor meets with an accident in ordinary course the judges may not interfere.

2. If an accident be caused by the friends of another Competitor in assisting him, then that other Competitor shall be disqualified.

3. If there be sufficient proof *or a reasonable belief* in the minds of the judges, that the accident was caused by collusion between a Competitor and other persons to defeat another Competitor, then the Competitor causing the accident directly or indirectly, shall be for twelve months disqualified from starting for any race governed by these rules, and the judges shall order the race to be run over again.

XIII.—OF TIME BETWEEN HEATS.

1. In all races of heats, where the distance shall be 200 yards or less, the time allowed between heats shall be not less than two minutes, nor more than five minutes. In all races of heats, where the distance exceeds [missing] yards and does not exceed half a mile, the time allowed between heats shall be not less than four minutes, nor more than ten minutes.

XIV.—OF HOUR OF STARTING.

1. The judges shall decide all matters of time connected with starting.

2. No delay after the appointed time for starting shall be permitted for the convenience of any competitor.

XV.—OF OBJECTIONS.

1. Any objection to a Competitor for fouling must be made within five minutes after the conclusion of the race.

2. *Objections as to qualifications, entries, &c., must be made before the start,* unless the fact on which the objection is based was not known to the objector at the time. In this later case, objections may be made within twenty-four hours after the race.

3. This does not apply to sec. 4 of Rule I.

XVI.—OF POST ENTRIES.

1. Post entries, except for consolation races shall not be allowed.

XVII.—OF JUDGES BETTING.

1. Judges must not bet upon a race over which they preside.

XVIII.—OF DECISIONS AND APPEALS.

1. The decision of the judges on matters of fact is final.

2. A club shall be considered the best judge of its own By-Laws, qualifications of membership, &c.

3. From the decision of the judges on any question of interpretation of law, an appeal shall lie to three experts, the appellant selecting one, the Judges another, and these two, deciding on a third. Such appeal must be declared at once.

XIX.—OF DISTANCES.

1. In races of heats there shall be no distance when the course is less than 440 yards.

2. Where the course is of 440 yards, the distance post shall be 50 yards from the finish. Where the course is of 880 yards, the distance post shall be 80 yards from the finish.

3. If a Competitor shall not have reached the distance post by the time the winner shall have reached the winning post, such Competitor shall be distanced and must not start for any succeeding heat of such race.

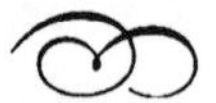

SELECTED BIBLIOGRAPHY

PRIMARY SOURCES

MANUSCRIPT COLLECTIONS

New York Knickerbocker Base Ball Club, Correspondence books, Game books, and Score books, New York Public Library.

Philadelphia Cricket Club, Minute Books and Scrapbooks, Historical Society of Pennsylvania.

Pythian Base Ball Club, Philadelphia, Correspondence and Minutes, American Negro Historical Society Papers, Leon Gardner Collection, Historical Society of Pennsylvania.

Spalding Collection, New York Public Library.

Tecumseh Baseball Club of London, Minute Book, 1868-72, D.B. Weldon Library, University of Western Ontario.

Walter Camp Papers, Yale University Archives.

NEWSPAPERS AND MAGAZINES

The American Chronicle of Sports and Pastimes (1868)

The American Cricketer (1877-80)

The Ball Players' Chronicle (1867)

Chicago Tribune (1875-76)

The Gazette (Montreal) (1865-80)

The New York Clipper (1860-80)

The New York Herald (1860-80)

The New York Times (1860-80)

Turf, Field, and Farm, (1873-1880)

Wilkes' Spirit of the Times (1860-80)

ARTICLES, BOOKS AND PAMPHLETS

GENERAL WORKS

George Beers, "Canadian Sports," *The Century Magazine* 14 (1877), 506-27.

Henry Chadwick, *Beadle's Dime Book of Cricket and Football. Being a Complete Guide to Players, and Containing All the Rules Laws of the Ground and Games* (New York, 1866), and by the same author, *Beadle's Dime Guide to Skating and Curling* (New York, 1867); *Handbook of Winter Sports. Embracing Skating, Rink-ball, Curling, Ice-boating, and American Football* (New York, 1879).

Charles Peverelly, *The Book of American Pastimes* (New York, 1866).

B.W. Dwight, "Intercollegiate Regattas, Hurdle Races and Prize Contests," *New Englander* 25 (1876), 256.

A.K. McClure, *Three Thousand Miles Through the Rocky Mountains* (Philadelphia, 1869).

Moses Coit Tyler, *The Brawnville Papers. Being Memorials of the Brawnville Athletic Club* (Boston, 1869).

F.O. Vaille and H.A. Clark, eds., *The Harvard Book*, Vol. II (Cambridge, Mass., 1875).

Capt. Fred Whittaker, ed., *Handbook of Summer Athletic Sports* (New York, 1880).

AQUATICS

William Blaikie, "The International Rowing Match, 1869," *Harper's Monthly* 40 (1869), 50-67, and by the same author, "Ten Years Among Rowing Men," *Harper's Monthly* 47 (1873), 408.

Beadle's Dime Guide to Swimming (New York, 1869).

"The College Regatta," *Yale Literary Magazine* 30 (1864), 11.

Commodore Ashbury's Reply to the Report of the New York Yacht Club in Relation to the Races With 'Livonia' for the America's Cup, In October, 1871 (London, 1872).

Letters Addressed By The New York Yacht Club to the Royal Yacht Squadron of England, In Reply to Commodore Ashbury's Pamphlet in Reference To the Races of 'Livonia' For the America's Cup (New York, 1872).

Report of the Committee Appointed by H.G. Stebbins, Esq., Commodore of the New York Yacht Club, To Take Action in the Matter of the Challenge of Mr. James Ashbury, Owner of the Yacht Cambria for the Possession of the Challenge Cup, Won by the "America" in 1851 (New York, 1870).

Report of the Committee of Arrangements, and Correspondence with Commodore Ashbury in Relation to Races With the 'Livonia' For the America's Cup (New York, 1872).

A.G. Sedwick, "The Harvard and Oxford Boat Race," *Nation* 8 (1869), 432.

James M. Whiton, *A History of American College Regattas* (Boston, 1875).

BASEBALL

Bryce's Canadian Baseball Guide (London, Canada, 1876).

Henry Chadwick, *Chadwick's Convention Base Ball Manual* (Boston, 1870-71).

James W. Haynie, ed., *Baseball Rules and Regulations* (Chicago, 1871).

Constitution and Playing Rules of the National League of Professional Base Ball Clubs (Philadelphia, 1876).

Proceedings of Convention of the National Association of Professional Base Ball Players, Held in New York City, March 17, 1871 (New York, 1871).

BICYCLING

Charles E. Pratt, *The American Bicycler. A Manual for the Observer, the Learner, and the Expert* (Boston, 1880), 175-181.

BLOOD (ANIMAL) SPORTS

George P. Burnham, *The Game Fowl* (Melrose, Mass., 1877).

J.W. Cooper, M.D., *Game Fowls. Their Origins and History* (West Chester, Pa., 1869).

F. H. Gray, *Cocker's Manual* (No place of publication, 1878).

BOXING

American Fistiana (New York, 1873).

William Edgar Harding, *Champions of the American Prize Ring* (New York, 1880).

Edwin James, *The Life and Battles of John Morrissey* (New York, 1879), and by the same author, *The Life and Battles of Tom Hyer* (New York, 1879).

CRICKET

Henry Chadwick, *Chadwick's American Cricket Manual* (New York, 1873).

Robert A. Fitzgerald, *Wickets in the West. Or the Twelve in America* (London, 1873).

The Halifax Cricket Tournament. An Account of the Visit of the American Twelve of Philadelphia to Halifax in August, 1874 (Philadelphia, 1874).

Official Hand-book. Containing the Programme of Arrangements During the Visit of the English Gentlemen Eleven to Philadelphia (Philadelphia, 1872).

Official Report on the International Cricket Fetes at Philadelphia in 1868 and 1872 (Philadelphia, 1873).

"Wickets in the West," *The Canadian Monthly and National Review* 4 (1873), 38-42.

CROQUET

Captain Mayne Reid, *Croquet. A Treatise with Notes and Commentary* (New York, 1869).

"Croquet: Its Implements and Laws," *Godey's Lady's Magazine* 74 (1867), 141-43.

"The Game of Croquet," *Harper's Weekly* 10 (1866), 566; *Harper's Monthly* 34 (1867), 528.

EQUESTRIANISM

John B. Irving, *The American Jockey Club* (New York, 1866), and by the same author, *Official Summary of Races at Jerome Park* (New York, 1866).

Rules and Regulations For The Government of Racing, Trotting, and Betting. As Adopted By The Principal Turf Associations Throughout The United States And Canada (New York, 1866).

Rules and Regulations to Govern All Trials of Speed Over The Various Courses Associated Under The Name of the National Association for the Promotion of the Interest of the American Trotting Turf (Providence, R.I., 1870).

Rules and Regulations for the Government of Racing, Trotting, and Betting (New York, 1866)

Hiram Woodruff, *The Trotting Horse of America. How to Train and Drive Him. With Reminiscences of the Trotting Turf* (Philadelphia, 1874).

FIELD SPORTS

Horsman dolls, inc., *Book of Instruction in Archery* (New York, 1879).

"The International Rifle Match," *Harper's Weekly* 26 (1874), 838.

Arthur B. Leech, *Irish Riflemen in America* (London, 1875).

GYMNASTICS

Constitution and By-laws of the Philadelphia Gymnastic Club (Philadelphia, 1872).

"Gymnastics," *The Canadian Illustrated News*, 11 December, 1875, 379.

Thomas Wentworth Higginson, "Gymnastics," *Atlantic Monthly* 7 (1861), 283-302, and by the same author, "The Gymnasium, and Gymnastics in Harvard College," in F.O. Vaille and H.A. Clark, *The Harvard Book* (Cambridge, Mass., 1875), II, 186-190.

Ledyard S. Sargent, ed., *Dudley Allen Sargent. An Autobiography* (Philadelphia, 1927).

LACROSSE

William G. Beers, *Lacrosse. The National Game of Canada* (New York, 1869).

William K. McNaught, *Lacrosse, and How to Play It* (Toronto, 1880).

PUB SPORTS

Dudley Kavanaugh, *The Billiard World. Containing the Rules of the Games of Billiards as Played in the United States and Europe.* (New York, 1869).

Michael Phelan, *The American Billiard Record. A Compendium of Important Matches Since 1854* (New York, 1870).

RACQUET SPORTS

Rules of Lawn Tennis As Adopted By The Cricket and Tennis Clubs of Philadelphia (Philadelphia, 1880).

TRACK AND FIELD

Beadle's Dime Hand-book of Pedestrianism (N.Y., 1867).

WINTER SPORTS

Edward W. Bullinger, *Guide to Skating* (New York, 1862).

Henry Chadwick, *Beadle's Dime Guide to Skating and Curling* (New York, 1867).

Constitution and By-Laws of the Brooklyn Skating Club of the City of Brooklyn (New York, 1869).

Edward Gill, *The Skater's Manual* (New York, 1867).

SECONDARY SOURCES

GENERAL WORKS

Melvin L. Adelman, *A Sporting Time. New York City and the Rise of Modern Athletics, 1820-70* (Urbana, Illinois, 1986).

John R. Betts, *America's Sporting Heritage, 1850-1950* (Reading, Massachusetts, 1974), and by the same author, "Sporting Journalism in Nineteenth Century America," *American Quarterly*, 5 (1953), 39-56; "The Technological Revolution and the Rise of Sports, 1850-1900," *Mississippi Valley Historical Review*, 40 (1953), 231-256; "Home Front, Battle Field, and Sport during the Civil War," *Research Quarterly* 42 (1971), 113-32.

John A. Blanchard, '91, *The H Book of Harvard Athletics, 1852-1922* (Cambridge, Mass., 1923).

David Brown, "Canadian Imperialism and Sporting Exchanges: The Nineteenth Century Cultural Experience of Cricket and Lacrosse," *Canadian Journal of History of Sport* 18 (1987), 55-66, and by the same author, "Prevailing Attitudes Towards Sports, Physical Exercise and Society in the 1870s: Impressions from Canadian Periodicals," *Canadian Journal of History of Sport* 17 (1986), 58-70.

Arthur C. Cole, "Our Sporting Grandfathers: The Cult of Athletics at Its Source," *Atlantic Monthly* 110 (1932), 88-96.

"College Beginnings," *The American College* I (December 1909), 36, 221-224.

David S. Crockett, "Sports and Recreational Practices of Union and Confederate Soldiers," *Research Quarterly* 32 (1961), 335-47.

Samuel Crowther and Arthur Ruhl, *Rowing and Track Athletics* (New York, 1905).

Paul R. Dauphinais, "A Class Act: French-Canadians in Organized Sport, 1840-1910," *International Journal of the History of Sport* 7 (1992), 432-442.

Robert D. Day, *The British Army and Sport in Canada. Case Studies of the Garrisons at Halifax, Montreal, and Kingston to 1871* (Edmonton, Alberta, 1981).

John Dizikes, *Sportsmen and Gamesmen* (Boston, 1981).

Foster Rhea Dulles, *A History of Recreation. America Learns to Play*, rev. ed. (New York, 1965).

Lawrence W. Fielding, "Sport and the Terrible Swift Sword," *Research Quarterly* 48 (1977), 1-11, and by the same author, "War and the Trifles: Sport in the Shadows of Civil War Army Life," *Journal of Sport History* 4 (1977), 151-68, and by the same author with William T. Weinberg, Brenda G. Pitts, and Richard A. Fee, "The Demise of Officer Involvement in Soldiers' Sport During the American Civil War," *Canadian Journal of History of Sport* 16 (1985), 72-86.

Paul H. Fudge, "The North West Mounted Police and Their Influence on Sport in Western Canada, 1873-1905," *Journal of the West* 22 (1983), 30-36.

Harvey Green, *Fit For America. Health, Fitness, Sport, and American Society* (New York, 1986).

Allen Guttmann, *From Ritual to Record. The Nature of Modern Sports* (New York, 1978), and by the same author, *Sports Spectators* (New York, 1986).

Stephen Hardy, *How Boston Played: Sport, Recreation, and Community, 1865-1915* (Boston, 1982), and by the same author, "The City and the Rise of American Sport, 1820-1920," *Exercise and Sport Science Review* 9 (1981), 183-219.

Robert Henderson, *Ball, Bat, and Bishop* (New York, 1947) and by the same author, *Early American Sport. A Chronological Checklist of Books Published Prior to 1860 Based on an Exhibition Held at the Grolier Club* (New York, 1937).

Nancy Howell and Maxwell Howell, *Sports and Games in Canadian Life, 1700 to the Present* (Toronto, 1969).

Richard M. Hurd, *A History of Yale Athletics. 1840-1888* (New Haven, Conn., 1888).

Frederick W. Janssen, *History of American Amateur Athletics* (New York, 1885), and by the same author, *A History of American Athletics and Aquatics, 1829-1886* (New York, 1888).

George B. Kirsch, "New Jersey and the Rise of Modern Sports, 1820-1870," *Journal of Regional Cultures,* 4 & 5, (1984-85), 41-57.

John A. Krout, *Annals of American Sport* (New Haven, Conn., 1929).

Guy Lewis, "The Muscular Christianity Movement," *Journal of Health, Physical Education and Recreation,* 37 (May 1966), 27-42.

Peter Lindsay, "A History of Sport in Canada, 1807-1867," (Unpublished Ph.D. dissertation, University of Alberta, 1969), and by the same author, "The Impact of the Military Garrisons on the Development of Sport in British North America," *Canadian Journal of History of Sport and Physical Education,* 1 (1970), 33-44.

James d'Wolf Lovett, *Old Boston Boys and the Games They Played* (Boston, 1907).

John A. Lucas and Ronald A. Smith, *Saga of American Sport* (Philadelphia, 1978).

John A. Lucas, "Thomas Wentworth Higginson. Early Apostle of Health and Fitness," *Journal of Health, Physical Education and Recreation* 42 (1971), 30-33.

Herbert Manchester, *Four Centuries of American Sport, 1490-1890* (New York, 1931).

Alan Metcalfe, *Canada Learns to Play. The Emergence of Organized Sport, 1807-1914* (Toronto, 1987), and by the same author, "Tentative Hypotheses Related to the Form and Function of Physical Activity in Canada During the Nineteenth Century," in *Proceedings of the First Canadian Symposium on the History of Sport and Physical Education* (Ottawa, Ontario, 1971), 153-69; "Organized Sport and Social Stratification in Montreal. 1840-1902," in Richard S. Gruneau and John G. Albinson, eds., *Canadian*

Sport. Sociological Perspectives (Don Mills, Ontario, 1976), 77-101; "The Evolution of Organized Physical Recreation in Montreal, 1840-1895," *Historie Sociale—Social History*, 11 (1978), 144-166.

Morris Mott, "Ball Games in the Canadian West: An Historical Outline," *Journal of the West* 23 (1984), 19-25, and by the same author, "The British Protestant Pioneers and the Establishment of Manly Sports in Manitoba, 1870-1886," *Journal of Sport History* 7 (1980), 25-36.

Roberta Park, "'Embodied Selves': The Rise and Development of Concern for Physical Education, Active Games and Recreation among American Women, 1776-1865," *Journal of Sport History*, 5 (1978), 5-41, and by the same author, "British Sports and Pastimes in San Francisco, 1848-1900," *British Journal of Sports History* 1 (1984), 304.

Frederick L. Paxson, "The Rise of Sport," *Mississippi Valley Historical Review*, 4 (1917), 143-168.

Charles A. Peverelly, *The Book of American Pastimes* (New York, 1866).

Frank Presbrey, *Athletics at Princeton. A History* (New York, 1901).

Benjamin G. Rader, *American Sports*, second edition (Englewood Cliffs, N.J., 1990), and by the same author, "The Quest for Subcommunities and the Rise of American Sport," *American Quarterly*, 29 (1977), 355-369.

Gerald Redmond, "Imperial Viceregal Patronage: The Governors-General of Canada and Sport in the Dominion, 1867-1909," *International Journal of the History of Sport* 6 (1989), 193-217, and by the same author, *The Sporting Scots of Nineteenth Century Canada* (Rutherford, N.J., 1982).

Steven A. Riess, *City Games. The Evolution of American Urban Society and the Rise of Sports* (Urbana, Illinois, 1989).

Henry Roxborough, *One Hundred—Not Out—The Story of Nineteenth Century Canadian Sport* (Toronto, 1966).

Michael A. Salter, "Play in Ritual: An Ethnohistorical Overview of Native North America," *Stadion* 3 (1977), 230-243.

Barbara Schrodt, "Changes in the Governance of Amateur Sport in Canada," *Canadian Journal of History of Sport* 14 (1983), 1-20, and by the same author, "Problems of Periodization in Canadian Sport History," *Canadian Journal of History of Sport* 21 (1990), 65-76.

Ronald A. Smith, *Sports and Freedom. The Rise of Big-Time College Athletics* (New York, 1988).

Dale A. Somers, *The Rise of Sports in New Orleans, 1850-1900* (Baton Rouge, La., 1972), and by the same author, "The Leisure Revolution. Recreation in the American City, 1820-1920," *Journal of Popular Culture* 5 (Summer 1971), 125-147.

Richard A. Swanson, "The Acceptance and Influence of Play in American Protestantism," *Quest* 11 (1968), 58-70.

Robert B. Weaver, *Amusements and Sports in American Life* (Chicago, 1939).

Paula Welch, "The Relationship of the Women's Rights Movement to Women's Sport and Physical Education in the United States, 1848-1920," *Proteus* 3 (1986), 34-40.

Luke White, *Henry William Herbert and the American Publishing Scene, 1831-1858* (Newark, N.J., 1943).

James C. Whorton, *Crusaders for Fitness. The History of American Health Reformers* (Princeton, N.J., 1982).

Mary Ann Wingfield, *Sport and the Artist*, Vol 1: Ball Games (Woodbridge, Suffolk, England, 1988).

S.F. Wise, "Sport and Class Values in Old Ontario and Quebec," in W. Heick and R. Graham, eds., *His Own Man. Essays in Honour of A.R.M. Lower* (Montreal, 1974).

Norris W. Yates, *William T. Porter and the Spirit of the Times. A Study of the Big Bear School of Humor* (Baton Rouge, La., 1957).

AQUATICS

Charles Boswell, *The America. The Story of the World's Most Famous Yacht* (New York, 1967).

Jerome E. Brooks, *The $30,000,000 Cup. The Stormy History of the Defense of the America's Cup* (New York, 1958).

Andrea Brown, "Edward Hanlan, The World Sculling Champion Visits Australia," *Canadian Journal of History of Sport and Physical Education* 11 (1980), 1-44.

Roland F. Coffin, *The America's Cup. How It Was Won by the Yacht America in 1851 and Has Been since Defended* (New York, 1885).

"The College Regatta," *Yale Literary Magazine* XXX (1864), 11.

E. Merton Coulter, "Boating as a Sport in the Old South," *Georgia Historical Society*, 27 (1943), 231-247.

William G. Durick, "The Gentlemen's Race: An Examination of the 1869 Harvard-Oxford Boat Race," *Journal of Sport History* 15 (1988), 41-63.

Richard A. and Richard J. Glendon, *Rowing* (Philadelphia, 1923).

Geoffrey F. Hammond, *Showdown at Newport: the Races for the America's Cup* (London, 1974).

Robert F. Kelley, *American Rowing. Its Background and Traditions* (New York, 1932).

Guy M. Lewis, "America's First Intercollegiate Sport. The Regattas from 1852 to 1875," *Research Quarterly*, 38 (1967), 637-648.

Charles F. Livermore, "The First Harvard-Yale Boat Race," *Harvard Graduates' Magazine* II (Dec. 1893), 226.

Alfred F. Loomis, *Ocean Racing. The Great Blue-Water Yacht Races, 1866-1935* ((New York, 1936).

Joseph J. Mathews, "The First Harvard-Oxford Boatrace," *New England Quarterly* 33 (1960), 74-82.

New York Yacht Club, *Centennial, 1844-1944* (New York, 1944).

Irene W. Norsen, *Ward Brothers. Champions of the World* (New York, 1958).

John Parkinson, Jr., *The History of the New York Yacht Club from Its Founding Through 1973* (New York, 1975).

Douglas Phillips-Birt, *The History of Yachting* (New York, 1974).

Herbert L. Stone and William H. Taylor, *The America's Cup Races* (Princeton, N.J., 1958).

W. S. Quigley, *The America's Cup* (New York, 1903).

William P. Stephens, *American Yachting* (New York, 1904).

James Wellman and W.B. Peet, *The Story of the Harvard-Yale Race, 1852-1912* (New York, 1912).

James M. Whiton, "The First Harvard-Yale Regatta (1852)," *Outing* LXVII (June 1901), 286-289 and by the same author, *A History of American College Regattas* (Boston, 1875).

BASEBALL

Melvin L. Adelman, "The First Baseball Game, the First Newspaper References to Baseball, and the New York Club. A Note on the Early History of Baseball," *Journal of Sport History*, 7 (Winter 1980), 132-135, and by the same author, "Baseball, Business and the Work Place: Gelber's Thesis Reexamined," *Journal of Social History* 22 (1989), 285-301.

Thomas L. Altherr, "'The Most Summery, Bold, Free, & Spacious Game': Charles King Newcomb and Philadelphia Baseball, 1866-1871," *Pennsylvania History* 52 (1985), 69-85.

Robert Knight Barney, "Of Rails and Red Stockings: Episodes in the Expansion of the 'National Pastime' in the American West," *Journal of the West* 17 (1978), 61-70, and by the same author, "Diamond Rituals. Baseball in Canadian Culture," *Baseball History* 2 (1989), 1-18.

"Baseball! The Story of Iowa's Early Innings," *Annals of Iowa*, 22 (January 1941), 625-654.

Greg Lee Carter, "Baseball in Saint Louis, 1867-1875: An Historical Case Study in Civic Pride," *Missouri Historical Society Bulletin* 21 (1875), 253-63.

W. Harrison Daniel, "'The Rage' in Hill City: The Beginnings of Baseball in Lynchburg," *Virginia Cavalcade* 28 (1979), 186-91.

Harry Ellard, *Baseball in Cincinnati* (Cincinnati, Ohio, 1907).

Strephen Freedman, "The Baseball Fad in Chicago, 1865-1870: An Exploration of the Role of Sport in the Nineteenth-Century City," *Journal of Sport History* 5 (1978), 42-64.

Steven M. Gelber, "Working at Playing: The Culture of the Worplace and the Rise of Baseball," *Journal of Social History* 16 (1893), 3-22, and by the same author, "'Their

Hands Are All Out Playing': Business and Amateur Baseball, 1845-1917," *Journal of Sport History* 11 (1984), 5-27.

Warren Goldstein, *Playing for Keeps. A History of Early Baseball* (Ithaca, N.Y., 1989).

Colin D. Howell, "Baseball, Class and Community in the Maritime Provinces, 1870-1910," *Social History* 22 (1989), 265-286.

George B. Kirsch, *The Creation of American Team Sports. Baseball and Cricket, 1838-72* (Urbana, Illinois, 1989), and by the same author, "Baseball Spectators, 1855-1870," *Baseball History, 1 (1987), 4-20.*

David Lamoreaux, "Baseball in the Late Nineteenth Century: The Source of Its Appeal," *Journal of Popular Culture* 11 (1977), 597-613.

Fred W. Lange, *History of Baseball in California and the Pacific Coast Leagues, 1847-1938* (Oakland, California, 1938).

Brian McGinty, "The Old Ball Game," *Pacific Historian* 25 (1981), 13-25.

Cecil O. Monroe, "The Rise of Baseball in Minnesota," *Minnesota History,* 19 (1938), 62-81.

Harold Peterson, *The Man Who Invented Baseball* (New York, 1969).

Francis C. Richter, *The History and Records of Base Ball* (Philadelphia, 1914).

Harold Seymour, *Baseball. The Early Years* (New York, 1960).

Albert Spalding, *America's National Game,* (New York, 1911).

Joseph S. Stern, Jr., "The Team That Couldn't Be Beat: The Red Stockings of 1869," *Queen City Heritage* 46 (1988), 50-58.

Ronald Story, "The Country of the Young. The Meaning of Baseball in Early American Culture," in Alvin L. Hall, ed., *Cooperstown: Baseball and American Culture* (Westport, Conn., 1991), 324-342.

Ian Tyrrell, "The Emergence of Modern American Baseball c. 1850-1880," in Richard Cashman and Michael McKernan, eds., *Sport in History. The Making of Modern Sport History* (Queensland, Australia, 1979), 205-226.

David Q. Voigt, American Baseball, 1 (Norman, Oklahoma, 1966), and by the same author, "The Boston Red Stockings: the Birth of Major League Baseball," *The New England Quarterly* 43 (1970), 531-549.

Carl Wittke, "Baseball in its Adolescence," *The Ohio State Archeological and Historical Quarterly,* 61 (April 1952), 111-127.

BICYCLING

Tommy W. Rogers, "The Bicycle in American Culture," *Contemporary Review* 221 (1972), 200-203.

BLOOD (ANIMAL) SPORTS

Gerald Carson, *Men, Beast, and Gods. A History of Cruelty and Kindness to Animals* (New York, 1972).

Martin and Herbert J. Kaufman, "Henry Bergh, Kit Burns and the Sportsmen of New York," *New York Folklore* 28 (1972), 15-19.

BOXING

Nat Fleischer, *Heavyweight Championship. An Informal History of Heavyweight Boxing from 1719 to the Present Day* (New York, 1961).

Elliot J. Gorn, *The Manly Art. Bare-Knuckle Prize Fighting in America* (Ithaca, N.Y., 1986)

William Edgar Harding, *John C. Heenan* (New York, 1881).

Alexander Johnston, *Ten and Out! The Complete Story of the Prize Ring in America* (New York, 1927).

Alan Lloyd, *The Great Prize Fight* (New York, 1978).

Frederick Locker-Lampson, *My Confidences* (London, 1896).

Andrew S. Young, *John C. Heenan, Of Troy, N.Y.. Champion Pugilist of America* (New York, 1882).

CRICKET

J. Thomas Jable, "Latter-day Cultural Imperialists: The British Influence on the establishment of Cricket in Philadelphia, 1842-72," in J.A. Mangan, ed., *Pleasure, Profit, Proselytism. British Culture and Sport at Home and Abroad* (London, 1988), 73-98.

George B. Kirsch, "American Cricket. Players and Clubs Before the Civil War," *Journal of Sport History*, 11 (1984), 28-50, and by the same author, "The Rise of Modern Sports. New Jersey Cricketers, Baseball Players, and Clubs, 1845-60," in *New Jersey History*, 101 (1983), 53-84.

John A. Lester, ed., *A Century of Philadelphia Cricket* (Philadelphia, 1951).

John I. Marder, *The International Series. The Story of the United States versus Canada at Cricket* (London, 1968).

The Merion Cricket Club, 1865-1965 (no place of publication, 1965).

George M. Newhall, "The Cricket Grounds of Germantown and a Plea for the Game," *Site and Relic Society of Germantown Historical Addresses* (Germantown, Pa., 1910), 184-90.

Jones Wister, *A 'Bawl' for American Cricket, Dedicated to American Youth* (Philadelphia, 1893), and by the same author, *Jones Wister's Reminiscences* (Philadelphia, 1920).

William R. Wister, *Some Reminiscences of Cricket in Philadelphia Before 1861* (Philadelphia, 1904).

CROQUET

Robert M. Lewis, "American Croquet in the 1860s: Playing the Game and Winning," *Journal of Sport History* 18 (1991), 365-386.

EQUESTRIANISM

Dwight Akers, *Drivers Up. The Story of American Harness Racing* (New York, 1938).

Newell Bent, *American Polo* (New York, 1929).

Dan M. Bowmar III, *Giants of the Turf. The Alexanders, The Belmonts, James R. Keene, the Whitneys* (Lexington, Ky., 1960).

Peter Chew, *The Kentucky Derby. First Hundred Years* (Boston, 1974).

Jim Henry, *Galloping Ghosts. The Story of the Kentucky Derby, 1875-1933* (Louisville, Ky., 1934).

John Hervey, *Racing in America, 1666-1866*, 2 vols. (New York, 1944), and by the same author, *Lady Suffolk, The Old Grey Mare of Long Island* (New York, 1936); *The American Trotter* (New York, 1947).

Kentucky Jockey Club, *Golden Anniversary of the Kentucky Derby and Churchill Downs* (Louisville, Ky., 1924).

Bernard Livingston, *Their Turf. America's Horsey Set and Its Princely Dynasties* (New York, 1936).

Charles B. Parmer, *For Gold and Glory. The Story of Thoroughbred Racing In America* (New York, 1939).

William H.P. Robertson, *The History of Thoroughbred Racing in America* (Englewood Cliffs, N.J., 1964).

Charles E. Trevathan, *The American Thoroughbred* (New York, 1905).

W.S. Vosburgh, *Racing in America, 1866-1921* (New York, 1922).

John H. Wallace, *The Horse of America, in His Derivation, History and Development* (New York, 1897).

Peter G. Welsh, *Track and Road. The American Trotting Horse. A Visual Record 1820 to 1900 from Harry T. Peters "American on Stone" Lithography Collection* (Washington, D.C., 1967).

Hiram Woodruff, *The Trotting Horse of America* (New York, 1868).

Frank A. Wrench, *Harness Horse Racing in the United States and Canada* (New York, 1948).

FIELD SPORTS

Robert Davidson, *History of the United Bowmen of Philadelphia* (Philadelphia, 1888).

Robert P. Elmer, *Target Archery. With a History of the Sport in America* (New York, 1946) and by the same author, *Archery* (Philadelphia, 1933).

Russell S. Gilmore, "Another Branch of Manly Sport: American Rifle Games, 1840-1900," in Kathryn Grover, ed., *Hard at Play. Leisure in America, 1840-1940* (Amherst, Mass., 1992).

FOOTBALL

Parke Hill Davis, *Football. The Intercollegiate Game* (New York, 1911).

David Riesman and Reuel Denney, "Football in America. A Study in Cultural Diffusion," *American Quarterly* 3 (1951), 309-25.

Wintrop Saltonstall Scudder, "An Historical Sketch of the Oneida Football Club of Boston, 1862-65," (Typescript, 1926) in library of Racquet and Tennis Club, New York City.

GYMNASTICS

Erich Geldbach, "The Beginnings of German Gymnastics in America," *Journal of Sport History* 3 (1976), 237-272.

Mary Lou LeCompte, "German-American Turnvereins in Frontier Texas, 1851-1880," *Journal of the West* 26 (1987), 18-25.

Henry Metzner, *A Brief History of the American Turnerbund, rev. ed., (Pittsburgh, 1924).*

Claire E. Nolte, "Our Brothers Across the Ocean: The Czech Sokol in America to 1914," *Czechoslovak and Central European Journal* 11 (1993), 15-37.

LACROSSE

Alan Metcalfe, "Sport and Athletics. A Case Study of Lacrosse in Canada," 1840-1889," *Journal of Sport History,* 3 (1976), 1-19.

PUB SPORTS

Robert Craven, ed., *Billiards, Bowling, Table Tennis, Pinball, and Video Games: A Bibliographic Guide* (Westport, Conn., 1983).

Ned Polsky, *Hustlers, Beats, and Others* (Garden City, N.Y., 1969).

RACQUET SPORTS

Park Cummings, *American Tennis* (Boston, 1957).

Diane Moore Hales, "A History of Badminton in the United States from 1878 to 1939," (Unpublished Masters thesis, California State Polytechnic University, Pomona, California, 1979).

Robert Henderson, *The History of Racquets in New York City* (New York, 1939).

Christopher G. Marks, *Rackets in Canada and the Montreal Racket Club* (Montreal, 1990).

Malcolm D. Whitman, *Tennis. Origins and Mysteries* (New York, 1932).

TRACK AND FIELD

John Cumming, *Runners and Walkers* (Chicago, 1981).

Edward Lamb, "'Weston the Walker' Made Pedestrianism a Way of Life," *Smithsonian* 10 (1979), 89-98.

Don Morrow, "The Powerhouse of Canadian Sport. The Montreal Amateur Athletic Association, Inception to 1909," *Journal of Sport History*, 8 (Winter 1981), 20-39.

George Moss, "The Long Distance Runners in Ante-Bellum America," *Journal of Popular Culture*, 8 (1974), 370-382.

Gerald Redmond, *The Caledonian Games in Nineteenth-Century America* (Rutherford, N.J., 1971).

WINTER SPORTS

Hugh W. Becket, *The Montreal Snow Shoe Club. Its History and Record* (Montreal, 1882).

Sylvie Dufresne, "The Winter Carnival of Montreal, 1803-1889," *Urban History Review*, 11 (1983), 25-45.

Donald Guay, "Les Origines du Hockey," *Canadian Journal of History of Sport* 20 (1989), 32-46.

Brian McFarlane, *One Hundred Years of Hockey* (Toronto, Canada, 1989).

Don Morrow, "The Knights of the Snowshoe. A Study of the Evolution of Sport in Nineteenth Century Montreal," *Journal of Sport History*, 15 (1988), 5-40.

Morris Mott and John Allardyce, "Curling Capital: How Winnipeg Became the Roaring Game's Leading City, 1876-1903," *Canadian Journal of History of Sport* 19 (1988), 1-14, and by the same authors, *Curling Capital: Winnipeg and the Roarin' Game, 1876 to 1988* (Winnipeg, Manitoba, 1989).

W.L. Murray, "Ice Hockey. The Fastest Game in the World," *McGill News* 18 (1936), 26-29.

E.M. Orlick, "McGill Contributions to the Origin of Ice Hockey," *McGill News* 25 (1943), 13-17.

Michael Vigneaux, "Tentative De Response sur les Origines du Hockey Moderne (The Origins of Hockey)," *Canadian Journal of History of Sport* 20 (1989), 15-26.

INDEXES

INDEX OF NAMES

INDEX OF SUBJECTS

INDEX OF INSTITUTIONS

INDEX OF GEOGRAPHIC AND PLACE NAMES

FROM ACADEMIC INTERNATIONAL PRESS*

THE RUSSIAN SERIES

1 S.F. Platonov **History of Russia** (OP)**
2 **The Nicky-Sunny Letters, Correspondence of Nicholas and Alexandra, 1914-1917**
3 Ken Shen Weigh **Russo-Chinese Diplomacy, 1689-1924** (OP)
4 Gaston Cahen **Relations of Russia with China...1689-1730** (OP)
5 M.N. Pokrovsky **Brief History of Russia** (OP)
6 M.N. Pokrovsky **History of Russia from Earliest Times** (OP)
7 Robert J. Kerner **Bohemia in the Eighteenth Century**
8 **Memoirs of Prince Adam Czartoryski and His Correspondence with Alexander I** (OP)
9 S.F. Platonov **Moscow and the West.** (OP)
10 S.F. Platonov **Boris Godunov** (OP)
11 Boris Nikolajewsky **Aseff the Spy**
12 Francis Dvornik **Les Legendes de Constantin et de Methode vues de Byzance** (OP)
13 Francis Dvornik **Les Slaves, Byzance et Rome au XI[e] Siecle** (OP)
14 A. Leroy-Beaulieu **Un Homme d'Etat Russe (Nicholas Miliutine)...**
15 Nicolas Berdyaev **Leontiev** (In English)
16 V.O. Kliuchevskii **Istoriia soslovii v Rossii** (OP)
17 **Tehran Yalta Potsdam. The Soviet Protocols**
18 **The Chronicle of Novgorod**
19 Paul N. Miliukov **Outlines of Russian Culture Vol. III** Pt. 1. The Origins of Ideology
20 P.A. Zaionchkovskii **The Abolition of Serfdom in Russia**
21 V.V. Vinogradov **Russkii iazyk. Grammaticheskoe uchenie o slove**
22 P.A. Zaionchkovsky **The Russian Autocracy under Alexander III**
23 A.E. Presniakov **Emperor Nicholas I of Russia. The Apogee of Autocracy**
24 V.I. Semevskii **Krestianskii vopros v Rossii v XVIII i pervoi polovine XIX veka** (OP)
25 S.S. Oldenburg **Last Tsar! Nicholas II, His Reign and His Russia** (OP)
26 Carl von Clausewitz **The Campaign of 1812 in Russia** (OP)
27 M.K. Liubavskii **Obrazovanie osnovnoi gosudarstvennoi territorii velikorusskoi narodnosti. Zaselenie i obedinenie tsentra** (OP)
28 S.F. Platonov **Ivan the Terrible** Paper
29 Paul N. Miliukov **Iz istorii russkoi intelligentsii. Sbornik statei i etiudov** (OP)
30 A.E. Presniakov **The Tsardom of Muscovy**
31 M. Gorky, J. Stalin et al., **History of the Civil War in Russia** (Revolution) (OP)
32 R.G. Skrynnikov **Ivan the Terrible**
33 P.A. Zaionchkovsky **The Russian Autocracy in Crisis, 1878-1882**
34 Joseph T. Fuhrmann **Tsar Alexis. His Reign and His Russia**
35 R.G. Skrynnikov **Boris Godunov (OP)**
36 R.G. Skrynnikov **The Time of Troubles. Russia in Crisis, 1604–1618**
38 V.V. Shulgin **Days of the Russian Revolutions. Memoirs From the Right, 1905–1907.** Cloth and Paper
40 J.L. Black **"Into the Dustbin of History"! The USSR From August Coup to Commonwealth, 1991. A Documentary Narrative**
43 Nicholas Zernov **Three Russian Prophets. Khomiakov, Dostoevsky, Soloviev** (OP)
44 Paul N. Miliukov **The Russian Revolution** 3 vols.
45 Anton I. Denikin **The White Army** (OP)
55 M.V. Rodzianko **The Reign of Rasputin—An Empire's Collapse. Memoirs** (OP)
56 **The Memoirs of Alexander Iswolsky** (OP)

THE CENTRAL AND EAST EUROPEAN SERIES

1 Louis Eisenmann **Le Compromis Austro-Hongrois de 1867**
3 Francis Dvornik **The Making of Central and Eastern Europe** 2nd edition (OP)
4 Feodor F. Zigel **Lectures on Slavonic Law**
10 Doros Alastos **Venizelos—Patriot, Statesman, Revolutionary** (OP)
20 Paul Teleki **The Evolution of Hungary and its Place in European History** (OP)

FORUM ASIATICA

1 M.I. Sladkovsky **China and Japan—Past and Present** (OP)

THE ACADEMIC INTERNATIONAL REFERENCE SERIES

The Modern Encyclopedia of Russian and Soviet History 55 vols.
The Modern Encyclopedia of Russian and Soviet Literatures 50 vols.
The Modern Encyclopedia of Religions in Russia and the Soviet Union 30 vols
Soviet Armed Forces Review Annual
Russia and Eurasia Facts & Figures Annual
USSR Documents Annual
USSR Calendar of Events (1987-1991) 5 vol. set
USSR Congress of Peoples's Deputies 1989. The Stenographic Record
Documents of Soviet History 12 vols.
Documents of Soviet-American Relations
Gorbachev's Reforms. An Annotated Bibliography of Soviet Writings. Part 1 1985–1987
Military-Naval Encyclopedia of Russia and the Soviet Union 50 vols.
China Facts & Figures Annual
China Documents Annual
Sino-Soviet Documents Annual
Encyclopedia USA. The Encyclopedia of the United States of America Past & Present 50 vols.
Sports Encyclopedia North America 50 vols.
Sports in North America. A Documentary History
Religious Documents North America Annual
The International Military Encyclopedia 50 vols.

SPECIAL WORKS

S.M. Soloviev **History of Russia** 50 vols.
SAFRA Papers 1985-

*Request catalogs **OP–out of print